The
PROMISE
and the
BLESSING

The PROMISE and the BLESSING

A HISTORICAL SURVEY OF THE OLD AND NEW TESTAMENTS

MICHAEL A. HARBIN

ZONDERVAN ACADEMIC

ZONDERVAN ACADEMIC

The Promise and the Blessing
Copyright © 2005, 2022 by Michael Harbin

Requests for information should be addressed to:
Zondervan, *Sparks Dr. SE, Grand Rapids, Michigan 49546*

Zondervan titles may be purchased in bulk for educational, business, fundraising, or sales promotional use. For information, please email SpecialMarkets@Zondervan.com.

ISBN 978-0-310-10905-1 (softcover)

ISBN 978-0-310-10906-8 (ebook)

ISBN 978-0-310-14493-9 (audio

Contents in Brief

PART ONE: THE PROMISE

PART TWO: THE BLESSING

Contents

QUMRAN SCRIPTORIUM
See Introduction.

HAMMURABI'S CODE
See chapter 7.

PHILISTINE TEMPLE.
See chapter 10.

TEMPLE AT HEIROPOLIS
See Chapter 22.

HITTITE CHARIOT
See chapter 13.

PART TWO: THE BLESSING

STONE MANGER
See chapter 18.

CANAANITE IDOL
See chapter 9.

CITY GATES OF PERGA
See chapter 21.

ARCH OF TITUS
See chapter 27.

BUST OF NERO
See chapter 26.

ABSALOM'S PILLAR.
See chapter 12.

List of Maps and Charts

MAPS

CHARTS

וְהִתְבָּרֲכוּ בְזַרְעֲךָ כֹּל גּוֹיֵי הָאָרֶץ
(GEN. 22:18)

Και εν τω σπερματι σου ενευλογηθησονται πασαι αι πατριαι της γης.
(ACTS 3:25)

And in your seed all the families of the earth shall be blessed.
(AUTHOR'S TRANSLATION)

Preface

The Bible is a unique book. It has been a worldwide bestseller for decades. In whole or in part, it has been translated into almost two thousand languages or dialects. It claims more than forty authors who wrote over a period of fifteen hundred years and in three different original languages. Yet it has a striking unity that captivates and mystifies. While many do not accept the key claims of the Bible on issues such as prophecy and salvation, even they generally admit that it is superb literature and deserves study on that account alone.

Unfortunately, many of us are not as familiar with the Bible as we would like to be. We have heard a number of individual stories many times. We may even have heard many sermons on key passages. But we are not really sure how the Bible all fits together. Intuitively, we feel that it has a structure and unity, that it has major themes that can be traced throughout as well as historical continuity. I cannot count the number of times that my students have said something like, "I thought I knew the Old [or New] Testament because I have heard the stories so many times. But now I'm beginning to understand how it all fits together. Suddenly it all makes sense." It is that experience that has led to this work.

Even scholars tend to specialize on particular aspects of the Bible. Consequently, while countless surveys of the individual testaments and works on individual books have been written, very few works survey the whole Bible as a unit. That is the purpose of this book. It is not designed to take the place of the Bible but to provide a general framework showing how the pieces fit together. This framework is derived directly from the Bible itself and developed through a historical perspective. After all, the Bible claims to report historical events. Once that general framework is established, the various books and stories become more significant and more highly cherished.

The most difficult part of this book has been the question of what to include. I did not want to lose sight of the big picture by getting bogged down in details, but the details give the flavor and flow of the overall work. Consequently, I have designed this book to be read on two different levels. The text is written so that the reader may read straight through to follow the flow of the general argument. Then I amplify the material in sidebars and in notes at the back of the book so that they do not interfere with the basic presentation. Some of those explain certain points in more detail. Others evaluate alternative views. Many direct the reader to other sources for further information. These are designed for the reader who wants to verify the data or wishes to investigate a given point in more depth.

At Taylor University we teach the Bible in two courses, a survey of the Old Testament followed by a survey of the New Testament. Many other schools do the same. My goal was to have a textbook that would present a unified theme for these two courses. Some schools have a single Bible survey course. My desire as I developed this work was that it would be adequate for those courses too. Necessarily, in the process, a lot is condensed or covered somewhat lightly. For this reason, I have included appropriate Bible readings as part of the chapters so that the student might both read the entire work and verify that what is being presented in this book is indeed accurate. My prayer is that the reader will come away from this book with a greater appreciation of how God has worked in history and what that means to each of us.

I would like to express my appreciation to my wife, Esther, and to Bill Heth, Ron Duddleston, and Lee Kinser. They strongly encouraged me in this project and read the manuscript, providing helpful insights. I also thank Taylor University, which provided sabbatical time that allowed the bulk of this project to be done, and my Biblical Literature students for the summer and fall of 2001, who worked with me through the first draft. And I would like to thank Moisés Silva for his careful review and helpful suggestions.

Abbreviations

ANE	Ancient Near East
ANET	*Ancient Near Eastern Texts Relating to the Old Testament*, ed. James B. Pritchard. 3rd ed. Princeton, N.J.: Princeton University Press, 1969.
ANF	*The Ante-Nicene Fathers*, ed. Alexander Roberts and James Donaldson. Grand Rapids: Eerdmans, 1971 reprint ed.
BDAG	Walter Bauer, *A Greek-English Lexicon of the New Testament and Other Early Christian Literature*. 3rd ed., rev. and ed. by F. W. Danker. Chicago: University of Chicago Press, 2000.
BAR	*Biblical Archaeology Review*
BAReader1	*Biblical Archaeologist Reader*, vol. 1, ed. David Noel Freeman and Edward F. Campbell Jr. Cambridge: American Schools of Oriental Research, 1975.
BAReader2	*Biblical Archaeologist Reader*, vol. 2, ed. David Noel Freeman and Edward F. Campbell Jr. Cambridge: American Schools of Oriental Research, 1978.
BCE	Before the Common (or Christian) Era; analogous to B.C., or "before Christ."
BDB	Francis Brown, S. R. Driver, and Charles Briggs, *A Hebrew and English Lexicon of the Old Testament*. 1907, reprint Oxford: Clarendon Press, 1977.
BKC	*Bible Knowledge Commentary*, ed. John F. Walvoord and Roy B. Zuck. Wheaton: SP Publications, 1985.
CAA	*Chronology of the Apostolic Age*, Harold Hoehner, Th.D. diss., Dallas Theological Seminary, 1965.
CE	Common (or Christian) Era; analogous to AD, or Anno Domini, "in the year of our Lord."
DSS	Dead Sea Scrolls
HBC	Jack Finegan, *Handbook of Biblical Chronology*, rev. ed. Peabody, Mass.: Hendrickson, 1998.
KJV	King James Version of the Bible
LXX	Septuagint (Greek translation of the OT)
NASB	New American Standard Bible
NIV	New International Version of the Bible
NPNF	*The Nicene and Post-Nicene Fathers of the Christian Church*, Series 1 and 2, ed. Philip Schaff. Grand Rapids: Eerdmans, 1974 reprint ed.

NRSV	New Revised Standard Version of the Bible
NT	New Testament
OT	Old Testament
RSV	Revised Standard Version of the Bible
TDOT	*Theological Dictionary of the Old Testament,* ed. G. Johannes Botterweck and Helmer Ringgren. 12 vols. Grand Rapids: Eerdmans, 1974–2003.
ZPEB	*Zondervan Pictorial Encyclopedia of the Bible,* gen. ed. Merrill C. Tenney. 5 vols. Grand Rapids: Zondervan, 1976.

Introduction

OVERVIEW

This introductory chapter describes the two basic schools of biblical interpretation. We then examine what our approach should be and address the role of archaeology in our understanding of biblical history.

There are a number of ways to study the Bible. We could work our way through it book by book. We could take a thematic approach by following key themes, such as prophecy or salvation or love, through both the OT and the NT. We could look at major sections, such as the Pentateuch or the prophetic literature or the Gospels. Each of these approaches is profitable.

In this book, which presents an overview, we will take a historical approach. That is, we will follow the sequence of historical events portrayed in the Bible, looking at the various biblical books within that context. In the process, we will try to understand each book as it may have been understood by its original audience. We use this method for several reasons. The Bible was certainly written within a historical context as God dealt with individuals and groups. Some books are records of events written shortly after the events occurred; Joshua and Philemon, for example, seem to fit into this category. Other books, such as 1–2 Chronicles, cover longer periods of time, even drawing on a number of sources. Still others are not historical at all, such as Psalms and Proverbs; however, even though these works are collections of material written at various stages, we can find convenient slots in our survey to pause and note how that material fits in the historical sequence.

GLENDALOUGH MONASTERY. A typical Irish monastery, active from the sixth to twelfth centuries. Here Scripture was copied, preserving it during the Middle Ages and helping to preserve Western civilization.

HOW SHOULD I INTERPRET THE BIBLE?

There are two basic approaches to understanding the Bible that divide the entire field. Because these approaches differ drastically, we need to describe them briefly before beginning our study. The major distinction between the two is how they view the origin and nature of the biblical text.

The Traditional View

The first school of thought in biblical interpretation may be labeled the *traditional* view, often known as the *conservative* view. This has been the dominant position held throughout the history of the church, at least up to the last century or so. *Basically, this school accepts the biblical documents at face value.*[1] Since the biblical documents claim to record history, this view begins by accepting that claim as a working hypothesis. It assumes that the documents are indeed historical, even while carefully assessing that claim. It then tries to correlate

THE BASIC ISSUE IN BIBLICAL INTERPRETATION

When we speak of the two major approaches to biblical interpretation, we are talking about the very basic issue of understanding what the Bible *is*. This fundamental question regarding the nature of the Bible builds on the role of what I call *supernormal* (in preference to the standard term, *supernatural*).[2] Is there supernormal intervention into space-time history or not? As we get into the actual study of the Bible, we find that there are also a number of specific ways of interpreting the text. We call the process of interpretation *hermeneutics*. However, particular methods of interpretation are subordinate to the more basic issue we are addressing here.

how the various historical materials (biblical and extrabiblical) fit together, recognizing that there are gaps in our understanding. In the process, the biblical documents are weighed and evaluated, keeping in mind that they have been critically appraised continually since their composition. Aware that there are problems in the text we presently have, this view asserts that when we look at various periods of history, we must include *all* the evidence before we come to a conclusion. If there are conflicts in evidence (and our biggest problem is lack of evidence, not conflicting evidence), we must weigh it and gauge the alternatives as in any other area of history. Moreover, if there are records of divine intervention in human history, these are viewed soberly as plausible, true accounts.

The Modern View

In distinction, the second school of interpretation is often called the *modern* view, also known as the *liberal* or *critical* view (the latter term is unhelpful because it could imply that the traditional view does not analyze issues critically).[3] *The modern view approaches the biblical documents as suspect at best.* While these documents claim to be history, they are assumed to be late forgeries until conclusively proven otherwise. This view gained dominance in scholarly circles during the latter part of the nineteenth century. Its supporters continue to label the bulk of the Bible as "myth,"[4] though their position on certain matters has often changed as a result of corroborating evidence. The real issue underlying the thinking of these scholars is a set of philosophical assumptions rather than conflicting evidence. In general, these conjectures reflect a spirit of naturalism, which can be simplistically reduced to the idea that miracles cannot happen. The miraculous accounts that appear in the Bible must therefore be regarded as, at best, "embellishments" of the text.

These two views actually represent a rather wide spectrum of interpretive thought. There is also a problem in using labels not only because doing so immediately seems to attach emotional nuances to the discussion, but also because individuals will differ on particular issues while agreeing on broader principles. Therefore, I will use these labels merely for convenience' sake, recognizing the risk of oversimplification. They should be understood as reflecting general trends.

SHATTERED MYTHS

Three examples of historical realities once thought mythical by liberal scholars:

- *Nineveh:* Nineveh is mentioned a number of times in the OT, and its destruction and loss are foretold. After the city was destroyed, its location was forgotten. Consequently, its existence was questioned by modern scholars until archaeologists uncovered it in the 1840s. (See Arnold C. Brackman, *The Luck of Nineveh* [New York: Van Nostrand, Reinhold, 1981], 11–14.)
- *Belshazzar and his position:* Daniel 5 tells of a Babylonian ruler named Belshazzar. When excavation of Babylon began, it was determined that the last king of Babylon was Nabonidus, with no place for Belshazzar. Scholars asserted that Daniel was in error, but later discoveries showed that Nabonidus had a son (named Belshazzar), who shared the throne with his father but apparently died with the overthrow of Babylon before he could exercise sole kingship (Alfred Hoerth, *Archaeology and the Old Testament* [Grand Rapids: Baker, 1998], 378–82).
- *The Hittites:* Although they are mentioned in eleven books of the OT (notably Genesis, Exodus, and Joshua), the Hittites were long viewed as a nonexistent people. Then the excavation of an ancient site in Turkey called Bogaskoy in 1906–7 proved the existence of the Hittites. Suddenly an entire civilization was opened to archaeology (C. W. Ceram, *The Secret of the Hittites* [New York: Schocken Books, 1973], 3–45). See also *ZPEB*, 3:166.

THE DEVELOPMENT OF THE MODERN VIEW

While there have always been people who questioned the authority of the Bible and the authorship of individual biblical books, the modern view gained dominance in the 1800s after several scholars developed new theories about how the OT was composed.[5] These theories were brought together by Julius Wellhausen in his foundational work, *Prolegomena to the History of Ancient Israel* (1878).[6] Very quickly, certain influential scholars adopted Wellhausen's theory for the OT and then subsequently applied his principles to find multiple sources in the NT.

The process began with the Pentateuch. Scholars have long struggled with certain problematic issues in these books. The relationship of Genesis 1 and 2 (which we will look at later) is a key example. Looking at issues of style, vocabulary, and subject matter, Wellhausen and others concluded that despite the claims of the Bible and other evidence to the contrary, the five books we have today are a product of several writers over centuries. Because of archaeological discoveries that have challenged Wellhausen's assumptions (such as when writing was invented), this premise more recently has been modified to include underlying oral traditions put together centuries after the books claim to have been written. Wellhausen's theory is also called the Documentary Hypothesis, or the JEDP theory (named after the four basic hypothetical documents or sources seen in the text).[7] The theory argues that these different sources were gathered into the collection we have today between the times of King Josiah and Ezra (i.e., somewhere around 650–450 BCE). After Wellhausen's argument about the origins of the Pentateuch won general acceptance, the same principles of multiple sources were applied to the rest of the OT and the NT.

Even before Wellhausen published his work, archaeology had begun challenging many of his assumptions, most of which have been abandoned even by a majority of modern scholars (except for a couple of basic philosophical presuppositions). However, the Documentary Hypothesis, with some modifications, is still widely accepted despite the fact that there is no concrete evidence of the sources proposed and that the process creates more problems than it solves. The key operating principle that Wellhausen used was that God is either limited or restricted, and miracles are impossible. Thus, Wellhausen and his school of thought began with deistic ideas. Deism taught that God could not (or at least most emphatically *would* not) intervene in space-time history. This is at best an unprovable assumption. However, the entire theory rests on it.

THE JEDP THEORY. A graphic representation of a modern assumption of how the OT developed, in contrast to the traditional view.

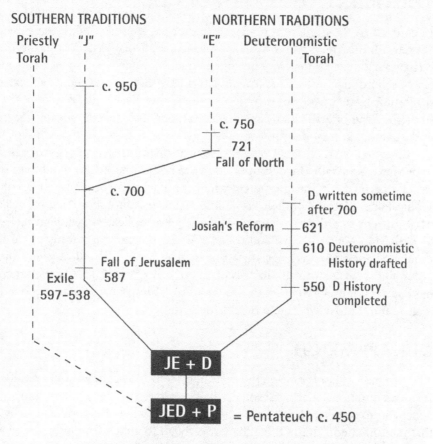

A MODERN CRITICAL VIEW OF THE ORIGIN OF THE OLD TESTAMENT

SOUTHERN TRADITIONS

Priestly Torah   "J"

NORTHERN TRADITIONS

"E"   Deuteronomistic Torah

c. 950

c. 750

721 Fall of North

c. 700

D written sometime after 700

Josiah's Reform — 621

610 Deuteronomistic History drafted

Fall of Jerusalem 587

Exile 597–538

550 D History completed

JE + D

JED + P = Pentateuch c. 450

Under this scenario, the other books were either composed or written down from oral traditions sometime after this.

WELLHAUSEN'S ASSUMPTIONS ABOUT THE PENTATEUCH

- Since Moses lived before writing began, he could not have written the Pentateuch (but archaeology has shown that writing had existed for about two thousand years before Moses).
- The use of different names for God in the text indicates different authors or sources (but several studies have refuted this idea).
- Repetition or duplication of similar accounts shows separate sources (but repetition is generally common, including in Hebrew literature).
- Religion has evolved from polytheism to monotheism (but a process of degeneration of religion from monotheism to polytheism is discernible throughout the world; see Michael A. Harbin, *To Serve Other Gods: An Evangelical History of Religion* [Lanham, Md.: University Press of America, 1994]).

(For further discussion of these concepts, see Harrison, *Introduction to the Old Testament*, 505–31.)

THE TRADITIONAL VIEW OF GOD

In contrast to the modern school, the traditional approach takes the view that God, by His nature, *may* intervene in space-time history on occasion, and in fact is recorded as having done so. Further, the traditional view maintains that a number of subordinate or lesser spiritual beings have also intervened or appeared in space-time history. Some of these lesser beings are fallen angels who oppose God (thus the issue of evil), a concept the liberal school in general does not seem to understand or at least does not accept.[8]

Likewise, the traditional view argues that supernormal events or miracles are to be viewed critically (by definition, they are not normal). As a number of writers have pointed out, the question of whether miracles can occur or not is a philosophical one.[9] Because of their very nature, science cannot *prove* that miracles do not exist—or that they do. The basis of science is replication, while miracles are by definition nonreplicative and thus fall under the category of historical-legal proof.[10] Science demonstrates what *normality* is. That is, it tells us what should occur, not what historically has occurred. In other words, just as the scientific method cannot prove whether the infamous O. J. Simpson was innocent or guilty, it also cannot prove whether a miracle occurred.

OUR APPROACH

The two basic schools of thought regarding the Bible begin with drastically different assumptions. The traditional school assumes that the Bible is a historical document to be taken at face value. Scholars who follow this approach recognize that there are items in the Bible that are difficult to understand or believe. However, because the Bible has been shown correct so often, these scholars prefer to take a "wait-and-see" attitude regarding controversial areas. The modern school, on the other hand, assumes that the Bible is essentially pious fiction to be accepted only when supported by modern science, despite the fact that this assumption is constantly being shattered by archaeology.[11]

In this book, we will follow the first view, because I consider that in scholarly work it is more honest to allow the text to have its say until *proven* wrong, especially when it has been proven correct so often. As we go along, I will illustrate the historicity of the Bible in a variety of ways, although I will also point out areas where questions still remain. For example, I will show how the OT and NT characters fit within their historical time frames. I will provide key anchors to other events in the ANE and the Mediterranean area, including some we can calculate down to the very day. Also, we will show how the biblical records fit closely with the written evidence from other areas of the region. As a result, I will be able to demonstrate that the Bible is a unified document portraying actual historical events.

THE VALUE AND LIMITATIONS OF ARCHAEOLOGY

As we have noted, one of Wellhausen's weaknesses was that he did not take archaeology into account as he developed his theories. Archaeology as a science developed in the last half of the 1800s. Since then it has made many contributions to our understanding of the Bible. The key contributions have come from various ancient libraries that have been found. As a result of these discoveries, we are better able to place biblical studies within cultural contexts. We have come to realize that biblical history fits within an overall ANE historical context, although there is some debate on how the pieces fit in.

However, archaeology has both strengths and weaknesses. On the one hand, we cannot ignore it, but on the other hand, we must be careful not to expect too much from it. For example, archaeology does not *prove* the Bible.[12] As part of our groundwork, we need to look at some of the limitations of this discipline.

Archaeology does not prove the Bible.

ARCHAEOLOGICAL TRENCH. A view of excavations at Bethshean showing how archaeologists dig a trench but avoid digging out key structural features such as walls. It also shows the stratigraphy (the various layers) of the site.

The Problem of Historical Losses

To put the problem in perspective, we need to think through the process that produces what we now call an archaeological site. Most of the sites we see in the Middle East are the buried ruins of cities that were abandoned after being

A TYPICAL TEL. An artificial hill, or tel, like this one at Lachish, that is formed over centuries as new cities rise on the ruins of older ones.

destroyed by either natural disaster or human conquest. The survivors would take whatever they could with them, and in the case of conquest, the looters would first plunder the city and then usually burn it, destroying everything that was flammable. For the most part, what was left behind was the trash and debris no one wanted; anything valuable had been taken.

Over the years, this residue deteriorated. Even stone is subject to erosion. Limestone and marble, two of the most desirable building materials because they are easily worked and give very pleasing results, are quickly eaten away by acidic water. This is a very real problem in modern cities, even where the material is less than a century old. The problem is compounded in ancient cities, even in areas with dry climates.

For historical purposes, the most desirable discoveries are writing materials, but these (aside from engraved stone monuments) are also the ones most prone to destruction: papyrus, parchment, and wood. One exception is found in Mesopotamia. At an early date, the people of Mesopotamia used clay to write on because it was cheap and easy to work with. The most important tablets were baked in kilns; the others were allowed to dry slowly. A fortuitous result of the burning of cities in this area is that many of the clay tablets were hardened in the fire, producing a crude type of ceramic. However, even this process was generally incomplete, and many of these tablets have broken and crumbled over the centuries.

THE BEGINNINGS OF ARCHAEOLOGY

The first serious archaeological expedition was the excavation of Nineveh in 1845–54 by A. H. Layard, only thirty years before Wellhausen's work was published. While this discovery was important and started a trend, in some respects, archaeology did not begin gaining consideration until after the famous excavation of Troy by Heinrich Schliemann between 1870 and 1890, about the same time Wellhausen was writing.

HOW MUCH HAS BEEN EXCAVATED?

One noted scholar estimates that what archaeologists have recovered is but a fraction of a percent of what is there—which in turn is a minute fraction of what was produced (Edwin Yamauchi, *The Stones and the Scriptures* [Grand Rapids: Baker, 1972], 146–57). In some respects, archaeological work is as if we arrive on the scene of a town hall or library that has burned and are able to pick up a few scraps here and there that survived the destruction. Now, based on this material, we try to reconstruct the entire history of the town. As Yamauchi states, "Far more than our need of these [archaeological] materials for an understanding of the Bible is our need of the Bible for an understanding of the materials" (p. 21).

The Problem of Limited Excavation

Very often after a city was destroyed, a new one would be built on the ruins. Without bulldozers to remove the debris, the people merely leveled the old site and built new buildings. Sometimes they used the stone from the previous city. Sometimes they dug through the foundations. After a period of years, the cycle would repeat itself, and gradually an artificial hill or mound would rise up.

Today there are thousands of these mounds (called *tels* or *tells*) waiting to be excavated. It is estimated that there are over 450 in modern Israel alone. Politics, weather, funding, and restrictions on the number of people involved serve to limit the number of sites to work on. Then the question arises, Which of these tels are really important? Archaeologists often do not know until they start the work.

Archaeologists most often use trench or square methods that effectively reveal only part of the site. Usually, even after years of digging, less than 10 percent of a city has been excavated. While this method is the most practical, archaeologists do risk missing valuable data in the part that is still buried. Thus, the data that they have been able to recover is but a small part of what is there.

TEL STRATIGRAPHY.
An example of typical stratigraphy observed as a tel is excavated.

The Problem of Nonwritten Sources

Most of the material we recover through excavation is ambiguous. Archaeology provides two types of data: some of the material is in written form, but the vast majority is nonwritten. Interpreting the various artifacts included in the latter category can be quite puzzling. Recently, my family went to Spring Mill State Park in southern Indiana, which contains a restored American frontier village. Within the museum is one exhibit that shows a number of tools used by the pioneers who lived there. Viewers are asked to try to guess what these isolated tools were used for. Some were relatively easy to identify, but we found it impossible to guess the use of others that have been replaced by more sophisticated mechanisms in our more technological society. Many of the tasks that these pioneers performed on a daily basis are now obsolete and forgotten. The disparity is even greater when we are looking at another culture. And while we might recognize a particular item, such as a ceramic pot, deciding how it was used is another question and often opens intense debate.[13]

Even when we can determine what the use of an item was, it tells us little about the person who used it. We can deduce a certain level of technology. We might be able to infer a certain socioeconomic status (e.g., a comb made out of ivory suggests a rich person). But beyond this, we know little.

The Problem of Dating

In the same way, nonwritten material is very difficult to date. In fact, archaeological dating is often publicly proclaimed with far greater confidence than it deserves. Dates are changed regularly when new information comes to light or when new theories are developed. Some years ago, for example, an archaeologist modified by five thousand years the suggested date of a woman's skeleton found in Texas, and the change resulted simply from challenging and adjusting a single assumption in the interpretation of the original data.[14]

Usually nonhistorical items are dated by comparison with other material of a similar sort or by various dating methods. Both have limitations. The most famous method used in archaeology is called Carbon−14 (^{14}C) dating. This method works on organic materials because all living organisms absorb the element until they die, after which the ^{14}C decays. Scientists measure the amount of ^{14}C still present to determine an approximate date of death. This dating is based on several assumptions, and its accuracy depends on many factors. Generally speaking, the older the item is, the greater the likelihood of error obtained through this process.[15]

Some dates can be established with great accuracy, but these are based on written documents. For example, we have written references to solar eclipses, which provide very solid chronological anchors. From about 2500 BCE on, we have varying bodies of writing giving us bits and pieces of history. Historical material too can be problematic, however, and so the challenge is putting all these pieces together into a coherent whole.

The Problem of History

Even when we have historical documents, we encounter a number of problems. One of the biggest is that what the contemporaries thought was important does not always correlate to what *we* think is important, for we have knowledge of subsequent events. As a result, the lives of many persons who turned out to have been significant are poorly documented. And for the most part, the figures we read about in the Bible were not the movers and shakers of their day. For example, while Abraham was rich, he was not in charge of a nation nor did he lead large armies. Likewise, Jesus really had a small following and a limited ministry in his lifetime. It was not until after His death that the true significance of His life began to be felt.

I have stated that I intend to take a historical approach. Thus, I need to explain what is meant by *history*. For a working definition, history is *the recording*

WHAT'S THIS? An antique device—not easily recognized—that points up the problem facing archaeologists as they find items from unfamiliar cultures that existed thousands of years ago. These happen to be wine-strainers from the 5th century BCE.

of eyewitness accounts of events in written form. History begins with writing, and so any culture that does not record its events in written language is by definition prehistorical, regardless of when the people lived. Thus, we have prehistoric people even today in some of the more remote places of the world.

> History is the recording of eyewitness accounts of events in written form.

This principle also gives us our basis for defining civilization. Usually the concept of civilization is predicated on the knowledge of writing. As such, we find that civilization (and history) began no earlier than 3200–3100 BCE in Sumer, at the mouth of the Tigris-Euphrates Rivers. Virtually all scholars agree on this point.

The Development of Writing

All writing began as pictograms, in which the writer used pictures to convey concepts. As different cultures used different media, these pictures became more abstract. In Mesopotamia, where they used clay as a primary writing material, the pictures became a collection of wedge marks called *cuneiform*. In Egypt, where they mainly used papyrus, the pictures became stylized drawings that we know as *hieroglyphs*.

CUNEIFORM TABLET. A clay tablet, now in the Hittite Museum in Ankara, Turkey, that survived when its city of origin was burned.

The earliest documents were primarily economic. However, by the middle of the third millennium BCE (2700–2400), a few tablets appear containing parts of some of the myths and legends of the time. Some of these are earlier versions of accounts that we have in later form from Babylon and Assyria.

HISTORY AND WRITING

Egyptian history is normally thought to have begun a couple of centuries after it did in Sumer (I. J. Gelb, *A Study of Writing* [Chicago: University of Chicago Press, 1963]). Recently, new discoveries of early writing in Egypt have been made. Some have suggested that this pushes the date of Egyptian writing prior to that of Mesopotamia, but the figures are still subject to review and revision. After writing began in Sumer and Egypt, a new form of writing was developed in Elam (in the Zagros Mountains of what is now Iran) a century or so later. Another new form developed in the Indus Valley region (modern Pakistan) a couple of centuries after that, followed by yet another new form in China, the last "cradle of civilization," approximately fifteen hundred years after Sumer. Each of these new forms apparently started with some type of pictograph that later became more abstract so that the symbols represented sounds. In Mesopotamia and Egypt, the symbols generally represented syllables. The early Elamite and Indus Valley scripts have yet to be deciphered. In China the symbols represented words (which in Chinese essentially consist of one syllable). The transition to an alphabet did not occur until about 1800 BCE, when writing developed in the region of what is now Israel and Lebanon. Hebrew writing developed out of that. Later this "alphabet" was adopted by the Greeks and subsequently by the Romans, from whom we received it.

By the time of Sargon II (c. 2300 BCE), who built a large empire around the city of Akkad,[16] we find a number of documents that relate history and mythology as well as mundane affairs of everyday life. Over the past 150 years, several archives have been discovered in a variety of cities. The most recent major find was in the mid-1970s in modern Syria. The site, Tell Mardikh, contains the remains of an ancient city called Ebla. The library there appears to date from the time of Abraham, covering the period from just before Sargon to a few centuries afterward (c. 1500 BCE).[17]

What does this mean for biblical studies? It suggests two very important things. First, the patriarchs would not only have been familiar with writing, but they also could have been literate. If our dating of Abraham is correct, he lived in approximately 2000 BCE. By his time, writing was very common. Moses lived about five hundred years later and most likely was able to read and write. In fact, Moses may well have used three different languages—Egyptian, Akkadian (the lingua franca of the day), and Hebrew.

Second, the early use of writing lends credence to the position that the OT documents are indeed what they claim to be: eyewitness accounts written down by people who observed the events. That does not require that the writer of each book saw all of the events he wrote about. The Bible contains a number of citations of other books—books we no longer have today—that were used as source documents. But this is the same way we write history today.

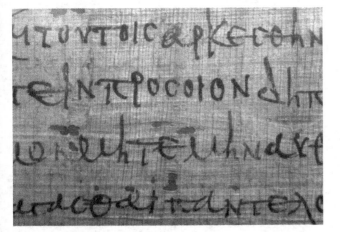

PAPYRUS. Writing material made from the stalk of a reed that grows in Egypt.

LOOKING AHEAD

The points just surveyed constitute part of what is often called *biblical introduction*. They lay out some of the issues we deal with as we study the Bible and work with the multitudes of critics. Each of those points could be substantiated in great detail, and I would refer the interested reader to other works that develop them.[18] For our purposes, we must content ourselves with this brief survey, which is a necessary background for our overview of the Bible. Admittedly, this introduction has addressed issues of the OT more than the NT. However, the time covered in the OT is much greater and much further removed from us. It is also the foundation for the NT, and we will build on that foundation as we proceed.

We will work with the developing canon as we follow the historical events, bringing in data from extrabiblical sources when they touch on the issues at hand. And as we look at the contents of the biblical books, we will evaluate them as historical documents that demand our critical attention.

MISSING SOURCES

There are approximately twenty-one books that OT writers cite as sources but that no longer exist. We do not find quite the same use of other accounts in the NT for several reasons: (1) many of the NT "books" were originally letters; (2) most of the NT citations are from the OT; (3) the writers of those books were essentially contemporaneous with the events they recorded; (4) the gospel writers claimed to be eyewitnesses. While Luke, for example, writes as a historian, his sources appear to be verbal accounts from the actual witnesses (although there is some indication that he also may have used other written gospel accounts).

REVIEW QUESTIONS

1. What are the key characteristics of the traditional view of biblical interpretation?

2. What are the key characteristics of the modern view of biblical interpretation?

3. How did the modern view develop? What are some of the assumptions that led to that process?

4. How are the traditional and the modern views of God different?

5. What is the value of archaeology to biblical studies?

6. What are some of the limitations of archaeology?

7. What is history, and why is it important?

THE MIDDLE EAST. A view from a NASA satellite of the region that shows where most biblical history took place.

THE PROMISE

1

CHAPTER

The Origin of the Bible

OVERVIEW

The writing and preservation of the biblical text are interesting and exciting stories, though we have only part of the picture. As we look at how and where the Bible was written, we also will note how it has been accurately preserved over the centuries.

STUDY GOALS

▶ Give an overview of how the Bible probably came to be written.

▶ Explain what *canon* means and its significance.

▶ Show the accuracy of the modern Bible.

THE RECORDING OF GOD'S WORD

Read Exodus 19–20.

God's written Word began to come together on a sun-soaked plain in the Sinai peninsula. After God had brought the descendants of Abraham, Isaac, and Jacob out of Egypt, He led them to the foot of Mount Sinai, where Moses had been commissioned more than a year earlier. There God started the process of making this motley throng of Israelites, Egyptians, and others into a nation. Moses went up on the mountain and received most of the material included in the books of Genesis, Exodus, and Leviticus. That was the foundation of God's written Word.

God could have done it differently. He could have given His revelation to the nation as a whole. When we look at the account in Exodus 19, we find that God had the people prepare themselves so that He might speak to them directly. They cleansed themselves for two days. The anticipation must have been intense as they recollected all that had happened during the past year.

Moses had come out of the desert in a spectacular manner, proclaiming that God, after more than four hundred years of silence, had spoken to him. He presented signs to the elders of Israel, then went to meet Pharaoh, asking for his people's deliverance. Word quickly spread among all the Israelites in Egypt that there was a major power struggle going on between Moses and Pharaoh. Clearly, the evidence Moses was presenting to show that God was working was hard to hide from both Egyptians and Israelites. After the introductory signs, such as turning his staff into a snake and then back into a staff, he turned the Nile River to blood.

Then things got serious. Over the following months, one plague after another struck at the heart of the Egyptian economy and its pantheon of gods. Even the most jaded Israelites (and many Egyptians) were starting to believe that it was indeed possible that the God of Abraham existed—and that He meant what He said. Then, in the following spring, just three months before the people arrived at Sinai, the cries of mourning pierced the Egyptian night as family after family discovered their firstborn dead.

Pharaoh finally relented and sent the Israelites away, although he later changed his mind and chased after them. Then there came the awesome experience at the Red Sea.

SINAI MOUNTAINS. Rugged peaks surrounding the location where the nation of Israel camped while Moses went up Mount Sinai.

After several days of camping and waiting, Israel watched Pharaoh's army appear over the horizon. That was when God told Moses to stretch out his arm. A strong wind came up out of the northeast. It seemed to bring the aroma of the Promised Land with it, if anyone had the peace of mind to consider it. The next day the nation passed through parted waters, then watched the sea close over the pursuing Egyptian army.

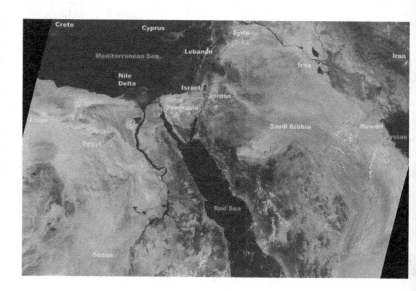

Only three days later, the water supplies were desperately low, and the people cried in bewilderment because the springs at Marah were too bitter to drink. God sweetened the water

SINAI PENINSULA. A view from a NASA satellite. The traditional location of Mount Sinai is near the southern tip of the triangle known as the Sinai peninsula, although other sites have been proposed.

for them. After a month, the food supplies began to dwindle. Again they grumbled and complained, and God sent—well, something. "What [Heb. *man*] is it?" they asked, and the name stuck—*manna* (Ex. 16:15, 31).[1] God would provide it on a daily basis (except on the Sabbath) for the rest of the desert period, all the way up to the time they crossed the Jordan River and entered the land. Following the giving of the manna and several other challenges, the people arrived at Sinai, just three months after the last of the plagues on Egypt.

Now, with all of these acts that God had performed still fresh in their minds, He was going to speak directly to them. What an awesome day! The morning came, and the people had purified themselves sufficiently. They waited anxiously behind the roped-off area, and Moses stood there with them. Then they heard God's voice. It was like thunder. "I am the LORD your God, who brought you out of Egypt, out of the land of slavery. You shall have no other gods before me" (Ex. 20:2–3). This was followed by the rest of the Ten Com-

When God's voice proved too scary, the people asked Moses to bring God's word to them.

mandments. The people backed away in terror from the awesome scene. When the voice stopped, they asked Moses himself to speak God's word—it was too scary for them to hear it directly from the Lord.

So that was what Moses did. Over the next several months, he wrote down, at God's direction, the books we call Genesis, Exodus, and Leviticus.[2] Genesis gave the background to the overall situation, explaining why humankind was in trouble and what steps God had already taken to resolve it. After recounting God's creation, Genesis cited seven key failures of humankind, followed by God's call of Abraham. The rest of the book traced the line of Abraham to the point where it became an embryonic nation—which was taken to Egypt to incubate.

In Exodus the account quickly jumped four hundred years to the current generation. It focused on the birth of Moses because he was the next individual God spoke to. The people recalled vividly the following events: the plagues and the Exodus. They certainly would have raised an uproar if Moses had gotten it wrong. Exodus ends with an account of how the Israelites built the various items God had commanded in order to provide a focus for their religious ritual. The book of Leviticus describes the ritual processes and the implementation of what we might call early Israelite religion, the precursor to Judaism.[3]

The whole purpose of these three books (or this three-part book) was to explain to the nation why God had intervened so mightily on their behalf and what He expected from them in response. As we will see, the purpose of God's intervention was to set into motion a process that would profoundly affect world history by setting the stage for the coming Messiah. But that would be hundreds of years later. In the interim, God had a purpose for this group of people camped on the plains of Sinai.

THE IDEA OF CANON

Those three books became the first "canon." This concept is crucial. The word *canon* (referring to a group of writings regarded as authentic) is used to describe the body of literature we call the Bible or Scripture. This English term is a transliteration from the Latin, which borrowed it from the Greek, which in turn had taken it (in the form *kanna*) from a Semitic language, probably from Hebrew *qaneh*, meaning "reed" or "measuring stick" (cf. Ezekiel 40–44, where the prophet has a vision in which a man uses a *qaneh* to measure the temple).

As we look over the following fifteen hundred years of biblical history, we see that the canon *as we have it today* developed gradually. What we mean is that various books were added to the three given at Sinai as God deemed necessary. Most of the material was written in Hebrew. The Hebrew text of the original three books was very close to (but not exactly) what we have today. At times editorial comments were added (e.g., Gen. 26:33 states that the city of Beersheba was called by that name "to this day," and Josh. 7:26 notes that a great heap of stones stands "to this day").[4] Moreover, at times some elements of the Hebrew language were apparently updated, as is done with modern translations, though very often the community retained even archaic linguistic features. Such revisions, however, were apparently no longer being made by NT times.[5]

> The Bible as we have it today developed gradually over the span of fifteen hundred years.

If the book of Job was composed at an early date (see ch. 5, below), it was likely included in the first canon, along with Genesis, Exodus, and Leviticus. The first actual new book added to this initial canon would have been Numbers, a travelogue that records how the fledgling nation journeyed from Sinai to the Transjordan. Numbers was followed by Deuteronomy, which records the renewal of the covenant (the treaty between God and the nation) across the Jordan River from Jericho just before Moses died. The rest of the books of the OT were added over the next thousand years, as we shall trace in the following chapters.

Near the end of the process, parts of some books were written in Aramaic. This language, which is closely related to Hebrew, became the lingua franca (the international trade language) of the ANE as early as the eighth century BCE (cf. 2 Kings 18:26), and it was adopted by the Jews at the time of the Exile. The Aramaic segments of the OT are confined to three passages that apparently deal with issues of primary relevance to the Gentiles (Ezra 4:8–6:18; 7:12–26; Dan. 2:4–7:28; note also two words in Gen. 31:47 and a sentence in Jer. 10:11).

After the time of Ezra and Nehemiah and the Israelites' return from the Exile, the OT canon was completed. This does not mean that the Jews stopped writing books. The community of God-fearers,[6] however, did not consider the books written after this time as measuring up to the original standard. Some of these later writings constitute what we today call the Apocrypha and Pseudepigrapha.

When the Jews were scattered throughout the world in the Diaspora (after the Babylonian exile), they began translating the OT into their everyday languages. The most important translation of the OT is the Greek, often called the

THE TRADITIONAL VIEW OF THE GROWTH OF THE OT. An alternative to the modern model shown in the Introduction. Everyone agrees that the OT grew over a thousand-year period, but not all agree on when the books were written and in what order.

A CONSERVATIVE VIEW OF THE ORIGIN OF THE OLD TESTAMENT

1446	Moses wrote Genesis–Leveticus	721	Isaiah, Micah
	Moses wrote Numbers/Deuteronomy (1–33)		Psalms, Proverbs completed
	Job (?)		Nahum, Habakkuk, Zephaniah
1400	Joshua written	587	Jeremiah, Lamentations, 1 & 2 Kings
1100	Judges/Ruth added		Ezekiel
1000	First sections of Psalms written	539	Daniel
	First sections of Proverbs written		Haggai, Zechariah
	Song of Solomon/Ecclesiastes		Esther
	1 & 2 Samuel		1 & 2 Chronicles, Ezra, Nehemiah
800	Joel, Obadiah, Jonah	c. 400	Malachi
	Amos, Hosea		

APOCRYPHA AND PSEUDEPIGRAPHA

The term *apocryphon* (plural *apocrypha*), which means "hidden," originally was used to refer to books that were considered inappropriate for public reading as part of the worship service. The writings included in what we call the Apocrypha (also called Deuterocanonical books because they were officially acknowledged as part of a second canon by the Roman Catholic Church in the sixteenth century) are not accepted as canonical by Jews and Protestants, but they have been popular and considered worth reading on a personal level. The term *Pseudepigrapha* refers primarily to books that falsely attribute their authorship to a noted biblical figure, but it is also applied more generally to other noncanonical Jewish works (in addition to those that are part of the Apocrypha). These books will be examined in more detail in chapter 17.

ST. GEORGE'S MONASTERY. Located in the Wadi Qelt between Jerusalem and Jericho, one of the many monasteries that helped preserve and copy biblical manuscripts in the centuries after the Romans destroyed Jerusalem.

Septuagint.[7] The Septuagint is a product of the Exile. Although Ezra and Nehemiah consolidated the nation after the return, a number of Jews remained scattered throughout the Middle East. After Alexander the Great (d. 323 BCE), Greek displaced Aramaic as the lingua franca. Aramaic was close enough to Hebrew that a literate Aramaic speaker, with some effort and help, could read the Hebrew. That was not the case with Greek. Within a few generations, many Greek-speaking Jews were no longer able to understand their Bible. To compensate, the Jews in Alexandria commissioned a translation of the Hebrew-Aramaic text into Greek. This translation became the text of choice of many Jews outside of Palestine and served as a background to most of the NT citations of the OT.

After a hiatus of about four hundred years, the NT writings began to be added to the canon, following the same procedures: God guiding men to write books as He deemed necessary. The early NT books fell into two basic categories: eyewitness accounts of the Messiah (the Gospels), and letters from key witnesses written to various groups of believers (the Epistles). The book of Acts, which recounts part of the history of the early church, and the book of Revelation, which gives the church hope of the second coming of the Messiah, finish it off. The question of whether this later collection should be considered Scripture was one factor leading to the division between Judaism and Christianity (although the key issue was whether Jesus was the Messiah).

Clearly the first books of the OT were accepted readily by God's people because they were witnesses to much of what the books recorded. They had seen Moses go up the mountain, and they had heard God speak. Other books were added through the years as they were accepted by the community of believers. This addition process started soon after the initial canon. Moses wrote Numbers and Deuteronomy, and they were added within about forty years of the initial canon. But the fact that Moses wrote them was not the deciding factor. He also may have written the "Book of the Wars of the Lord" (Num. 21:14) and the "Book of Jashar" (Josh. 10:13; 2 Sam. 1:18). We no longer have those; they were never canonical.

Joshua followed in the footsteps of Moses and wrote the book of Joshua, which was included in the canon. Evidence suggests that these later canonical books were, *from the time they were written, accepted by the community as inspired* because they measured up to the original standards. We see this point illustrated in Daniel 9:2, where the author identifies the writings of Jeremiah, a contemporary of Daniel, as Scripture.

Today we really don't understand how the early Jews distinguished between the canonical and noncanonical, although in many cases the qualitative differences are very clear. For example, the apocryphal book Bel and the Dragon reads more like a Hardy boys mystery than a scriptural account in the life of Daniel. We do know that the canon involves the concept of inspiration. As such, however, it must include two roles of the Holy Spirit: first in inspiring the writer, and then in verifying this inspiration through the community as a whole. It appears that very soon after the Exile, the books we find in our OT had been widely accepted within the Jewish community as canonical.[8]

As the canon gradually took shape, it became the standard and authority for the community and for individuals. Thus, from the time Moses brought the Law down from the mountain, the nation of Israel, then Judaism, and finally Christianity had a *written body of law and standards* by which behavior was measured. It was also the standard by which future writings were measured.

It is important to realize that Christianity began with the assumption that the Jewish canon was authoritative. This point is often overlooked, but it is crucial. First, the concept of Messiah (or Christ) comes from the Jewish canon. Jews who

THE AUTHORSHIP OF DEUTERONOMY AND JOSHUA

Modern scholars have objected for several reasons to the claim that Moses wrote Deuteronomy. One of the most significant is that chapter 34 records Moses' death, but Joshua, as the next administrator of the covenant, probably added that section to complete the account of the transition in the nation's leadership. As for the book of Joshua, its authorship is debated as well (as is that of most other OT books). There is, however, strong evidence to support the traditional view that Joshua himself wrote it. The author appears to be an eyewitness to the events, as shown by the "we" references in certain sections. Rahab is stated to still be alive (Josh. 6:25), and a number of historical and geographical references suggest an early date. Finally, Joshua is recorded as adding to the Book of the Law (Josh. 24:26), which would logically be the book that was included in the canon.

knew Jesus measured His life against that standard. A number of Jews rejected Him, but that was because of preconceived notions of what the Messiah was to do. Many looked at the data and agreed that Jesus met the standards of the OT. Those who accepted Him became the first church—a significant community of Jews. Second, early followers of the Messiah (or the Christ) measured NT writers against the OT standard and used the same process of guidance by the Holy Spirit to validate the new writings.

At its beginning, Christianity used the Jewish Bible.

So the NT was written and accepted in a manner similar to the OT, but with several key distinctions. First, while the OT was primarily written to God's people when they were concentrated in the land of Israel, the NT was primarily written to groups of God's people throughout the Roman Empire where they had scattered. For this reason, the NT books were written in Greek instead of Hebrew. These NT books also took somewhat longer to be accepted by the overall community of God's people, for it was more widely dispersed.[9] Second, while the OT focused on God's work of deliverance of the nation from Egypt and the implications of that event in terms of a future Messiah, the NT was written to demonstrate that the Messiah had already appeared as a historical figure and to explain the significance of His coming. The focus of the NT is therefore on the resurrection and the implications of that event for the relationship of humanity to God.

JOHN RYLANDS PAPYRUS. A fragment of the gospel of John that has been dated to about CE 125. This would place it within thirty to forty years of the probable time of the book's composition.

As mentioned above, the church accepted the OT canon from the beginning. After all, the Christian community was totally Jewish for at least eight years and predominantly Jewish for another decade or so. Individual NT books were clearly accepted at a very early stage. By approximately 64 CE, Peter was referring to Paul's letters, written mainly during the previous decade, as Scripture (2 Peter 3:16). This important detail is reminiscent of Daniel's similar reference to Jeremiah (Dan. 9:2).

The Epistles primarily deal with the implications of the gospel that was being proclaimed. Many of them predate the written Gospels, probably for two reasons. The early church was convinced that the return of Jesus was right around the corner and thus, at first, a written argument that He was the Messiah did not seem to be needed. Moreover, evaluating the implications of the gospel was the first need of the church. The Gospels, in the form they have come to us, were written down as the church gradually realized that the second coming of Christ was not going to be as soon as anticipated, and the eyewitnesses of Jesus' resurrection began to be martyred and otherwise die off.

The focus of the Gospels is on Jesus and His claim to be the Messiah. As such, they omit much of what we would like to know about the life of Jesus. What was He like as a child? How did He play with other children? What kind of student was He? How did His parents treat Him? How did He relate to His brothers and sisters? He is termed a carpenter, but we know nothing about His work. He is called a Nazarene, but we know nothing of His hometown. Thus, as biographies, the Gospels leave a lot to be desired. However, the way they are structured gives us a hint that their purpose is something else. For example, the bulk of each gospel (from about 27 percent of Luke to almost 40 percent of John) covers the last week of the life of Jesus (less than one-tenth of one percent of His life).

John's gospel gives a hint as to what that purpose is. He writes that he only included a few of the miracles that Jesus had performed in order that the reader "may believe that Jesus is the Christ, the Son of God" (John 20:30–31). The key is the word *Christ*, the Greek equivalent of *Messiah* (they both mean "Anointed One"). Thus, a good definition of a gospel might be "a book that proclaims that Jesus is the Messiah and gives evidence to demonstrate that fact." The primary evidence that Jesus is the Messiah was His crucifixion and resurrection, which is why the Gospels spend so much time on the last week of Jesus' life. He presented Himself as Messiah and was crucified for making the claim; however, the resurrection vindicated Him (see, e.g., Rom. 1:4; 1 Cor. 15).

> Peter referred to Paul's letters as Scripture.

Because most of the NT books are letters to various churches throughout the Mediterranean region, it took some time for *all* of the churches in various cities to amass a complete (or nearly complete) collection. For example, Paul wrote his letter to the Christians in Colosse with instructions for them to pass it on to the church in Laodicea (and likewise for the Colossians to read the letter written to the Laodiceans, see Col. 4:16). Similarly, the letter we call 2 Corinthians was also addressed to all of central Greece (2 Cor. 1:1). Each individual church that received a letter would either hand-copy it and then forward the copy or have the other church send a scribe to make a copy to take back. In this manner, copies of

WHEN WERE THE GOSPELS WRITTEN?

There are two basic schools of thought regarding the date and relationship of the four gospels. The traditional approach accepts the statements of the early church fathers, who place the composition of the gospels from about the middle to the end of the first century. The modern approach maintains that they were written well after the year 70, and in the past some have argued that the gospel of John was not written until the middle of the second century. Currently, however, the two schools are only a few decades apart on their suggested dates of composition, which creates problems for the assumption that the "mythical" elements developed gradually. (See further below, ch. 18.)

HOW WERE THE NT BOOKS BROUGHT TOGETHER?

The history of the NT canon is a complicated process. One issue involved was the need to fight heresies, which began even during the lives of the apostles. One heretic, Marcion, developed his own canonical list by about 150 CE, but this seems to have been primarily an effort to exclude certain books with which he disagreed. Shortly after, we begin to find more orthodox writers specifying which books they felt belonged in the canon. Even so, because of geographical differences, the topic was debated until 397. During that process, some local churches had other books, such as the *Shepherd of Hermas*, which they felt also had a claim to canonicity. In the end, the church as a whole agreed that some of these were good books but, as in the case of the OT Apocrypha, decided to leave them out.

CODEX SINAITICUS. A Greek manuscript discovered by Count Constantin Tischendorff at St. Catherine's Monastery during the mid-1800s. Now housed in the British Museum, it is dated to the early fourth century and contains much of the Bible.

the individual letters gradually spread throughout the early church. By 70 CE there apparently were local churches all the way from Spain to India and from England to Ethiopia (see ch. 26, below).

As can be imagined, hand-copying these letters would be a slow process. Still, indications are that by early in the second century, most of the local churches within the Roman world were largely in agreement as to which writings should be included in the NT canon. This agreement was not formalized, however, until the third council of Carthage in 397.

The authors of the OT canon are often considered *prophets*, that is, God's spokesmen (prophets performed other roles besides giving predictions about the future, so books written by them were not necessarily "prophetic," that is, predictive in character). This concept also applies to the NT authors, although for them we generally use the term *apostle* ("sent one"), which usually refers to the original twelve disciples of Jesus. Paul was not part of this circle but was marked out as an apostle in his calling. Not all of the NT books were written by apostles, however. Mark and Luke were two key authors who do not appear to meet any criteria of apostleship, although they are often considered spokesmen for the apostles Peter and Paul respectively.

THE ACCURACY OF OUR MODERN BIBLE

One concern often expressed is, How do we know that the Bible available to us has been preserved accurately? Modern critics have noted that because the Bible was copied by hand so many times, differences arose in the manuscripts. Therefore, they have concluded, the Bible cannot be trusted. However, careful study and evaluation shows just the opposite. While there are textual differences, for the most part they are spelling or grammatical variations, easily explained. Further,

GREAT SCROLL OF ISAIAH. One of the most significant of the Dead Sea Scrolls, dating to between 200 and 150 BCE. It demonstrates that the Masoretic text has been stable since that time and thus shows the reliability of modern English translations.

when we examine the text carefully, we find that the foundational beliefs of Christianity are based on solid textual evidence; moreover, doctrines usually arise from a wide variety of passages.

Let us consider first the OT text. Until just after World War II, the earliest Hebrew manuscripts we had for the OT dated from about 900 CE. We did have several copies from this general time period, including the Leningrad Codex (named after its location in a museum in Leningrad) and the Aleppo Codex (from the city in Syria where it was found). These followed what is called the Masoretic text, named after the scribes who meticulously transcribed copy after copy.

The OT books, of course, were written from about the fifteenth to the fifth century BCE. Because more than thirteen hundred years had passed between the completion of these writings and the oldest manuscripts available to us, the common accusation by modern scholars was that the text had changed substantially

LOST BOOKS

Interestingly, the canon (both OT and NT) does not include everything written by the biblical authors. A number of other books composed by prophets and apostles, though used by God's people for a time, were ultimately lost because they were not considered canonical. Some examples in the OT include "the Book of the Wars of the Lord" (Num. 21:14), "the Book of Nathan the Prophet" (1 Chron. 29:29), "the Book of Gad the Seer" (1 Chron. 29:29), "the Book of Shemaiah the Prophet" (2 Chron. 12:15), and "The Book of Iddo the Seer" (2 Chron. 12:15). Examples in the NT include two more letters to the Corinthians by Paul (cf. 1 Cor. 5:9 and 2 Cor. 2:4), and the letter to the Laodiceans (Col. 4:16).

THE MASORETES

During the first millennium of our era, the Hebrew text was copied by a school of scribes known as the Masoretes ("transmitters"). They used a very meticulous process that included even counting words and letters to ensure a correct copy. An interesting feature of their work is the distinction between *Ketib* ("what is written") and *Qere* ("what should be read"). In passages where the scribes believed from their oral tradition that the written text was inaccurate, they were unwilling to change even such copyist mistakes. Rather, they made notes in the margin that reflected both what they had received in the written text and what they understood the original text to be.

over the centuries. In 1948, however, the academic world was astounded by the discovery of the Dead Sea Scrolls.

Since then, many other manuscripts have been discovered in the Judean desert. Among these, every book of the OT has been identified except Esther. One of the most significant is the Great Scroll of Isaiah, which was found to include the entire book of Isaiah. This scroll has been dated to about 150–100 BCE Its text is "almost identical" to the text in the Hebrew Bibles.[10]

Turning to the Greek NT, an astounding point from an archaeological perspective is the number of manuscripts available. More than five thousand have been catalogued, some of which have been dated to within a century of the claimed or traditional date of composition.[11] While this material would lead us to assume that we have an accurate picture of who Jesus was and what He did, there are still people today who deny the NT accounts. Typically, such people begin with the assumption that Jesus was solely human and then try to manipulate the data to fit that theory.

MANUSCRIPTS

A *manuscript*, by definition, is a document written by hand. Thus, prior to the invention of the printing press in the fifteenth century, all copies of the Bible were manuscripts. In ancient times, the pages were put together in the form of a *scroll* (or roll). The term *codex*, on the other hand, indicates that the manuscript was produced in a form similar to that of modern books; this method was first popularized by the early Christians.

LOOKING AHEAD

Even this brief survey shows that the Bible is a unique book, in terms of both origin and preservation. As we look at its content, we will find that this uniqueness is even more remarkable than we have presented to this point.

REVIEW QUESTIONS

1. What is the traditional view of how the Bible was written?

2. How does the traditional view of the origin of the Bible differ from the modern view presented in the introduction?

3. What is the concept of canon, and why is it important?

4. In the NT, why were many of the Epistles written before the Gospels?

5. Why did it take time for the NT canon to be agreed upon?

6. What is the significance of the Dead Sea Scrolls?

2
CHAPTER

This Is the Way the World Was

OVERVIEW

The first question the Bible addresses is, Where did everything come from? To understand the answer, we need to appreciate the careful craftsmanship that has produced the book of Genesis. We also need to know that the world as originally created was somewhat different from the world in which we live today.

It would seem that when God gave the Israelites their first canon at Mount Sinai, it was designed to answer several questions. One of the key concerns in their minds probably was, What does God now expect from us? God's answer is evidenced by various lifestyle issues set forth in what we call the "Law," which we will cover later. But there must have been other questions. Two that readily come to mind are, Why us? and Why is God doing this? Both of these are answered in the book of Genesis. But before they are addressed, a prior issue is dealt with—one of the key questions about life: Where did it begin? As we will see, this topic is foundational to all the others.

The Bible begins with a basic answer to that question, although it does not give us anywhere near the detail we would like, and even

> The world we live in is not in the same shape as when God designed it.

the information we have is debatable. Rather, it records just enough data to demonstrate two key points: (1) the universe in which we live was entirely created by God, and (2) the world in which we live is not the way God created it. But to understand these ideas, we need to appreciate how Genesis is organized.

EAGLE NEBULA. A computer-enhanced photo taken by the Hubble space telescope that reveals some of the awesomeness of deep space. Modern astronomy has pointed to a creation event, although the nature of that event is debated. The current model is called the Big Bang.

THE STRUCTURE OF GENESIS

From a literary perspective, Genesis is a well-structured book. The author uses a stylistic marker to break the book into sections. This structural indicator, which clarifies the author's intentions, is the Hebrew word *toledot*, often translated "generations." For example, if we look up Genesis 5:1 in most English translations, we find a phrase like "Now these are the generations of Adam"; a list of some of Adam's descendants (a genealogy) follows.

However, the word must mean more than a list of descendants. For example, in the *toledot* of Noah in Genesis 6:9, we find not a genealogy, but the account of the Flood. Likewise, in Genesis 2:4, a reference to the *toledot* of the heavens and the earth is followed by a recap of the Creation. Here, modern translations read something like "This is the account of the heavens and the earth ..." (NIV/NASB). Therefore, a better translation of the phrase "these are the *toledot* of ..." might be "this is what became of...."

As shown in the chart, the term *toledot* appears ten times in Genesis. It normally seems to serve as a marker introducing each section. The key exception is the opening creation account in Genesis 1:1–2:4. Given the overall pattern and the subject matter of each section, the opening account would then be an introduction to the whole book. This understanding will prove important when we look at the relationship between the first two chapters, a key factor leading to the modern liberal interpretation of the Bible.

In terms of the overall structure of the book, we might also group these various *toledot* segments together into three major sections based on their general focus. The first major section, 1:1–11:26, sets the stage by explaining where life, the universe, and everything in it came from. It also explains how the perfect world God created became the mess we struggle with today. The second major section, 11:27–37:1, tells of God selecting from humankind a single man who was to be an instrument of God. The author's purpose seems to be to show how God began to fix the mess the world is in. The process begins by establishing a line of individuals who had a special relationship with God. The final segment, 37:2–50:26, shows the purpose of that relationship as it began to transform an individual into a nation that was to mediate between God and humanity. In other words, these three sections answer the three questions we noted above.

THE TOLEDOT SECTIONS OF GENESIS

Section	Subject
1:1-2:3	No Toledot—Preface
2:4-4:26	Heavens and Earth
5:1-6:8	Adam
6:9-9:29	Noah
10:1-11:9	Ham/Shem/Japheth
11:10-11:26	Shem
11:27-25:11	Terah
25:12-25:18	Ishmael
25:19-35:29	Isaac
36:1-37:1	Esau
37:2-50:26	Jacob

The first question is, Where (or How) did it all begin? As we look at the issues involved in how we got the world in which we live, Genesis 1–11 focuses on three lessons: Where did the world come from? Why is the world in such a mess? and What happens when you ignore God? This section of Genesis only gives broad answers to all three questions, leaving many more questions in our minds. Still, there is enough information to point us in the right direction as long as we keep the issues in perspective.

THE TWO CREATION ACCOUNTS

The first two chapters of Genesis contain some of the most controversial material in the Bible. Until the mid-1800s, most scholars viewed these two chapters as a straightforward *cosmology,* that is, a description of the origin and structure of the universe. Since then, many scholars have abandoned that view. Today most people in our culture look to geology or astronomy textbooks to find an explanation of how the world came into existence and how, over time, today's world came to be.

In terms of biblical studies, the primary cause for this change was the work of the German scholar Julius Wellhausen, who published his *Prolegomena to the History of Israel* in 1878. In this book, Wellhausen picked up on the ideas of another German scholar, Karl Graf, regarding how Genesis 1 and 2 fit together. Wellhausen was able to develop Graf's ideas into a coherent theory and make it

Read Genesis 1–4.

ILLUSTRATION OF THE ULTRASTRUCTURE OF A TYPICAL CELL. The anatomical components of this cell are seen in three-dimensions and color-coded. The outer cell membrane (brown) is furrowed, with the inner cytoplasm colored white. A central nucleus with nucleolus (green) houses the genetic material and has a membrane with pores. Continuous with the nucleus is the endoplasmic reticulum (ER, yellow), a membrane system in the cytoplasm studded with ribosomes (blue dots). A golgi body (blue membrane structure) receives glycoproteins from the ER. Four mitochondria (colored magenta) store energy for the cell and engage in aerobic respiration.

popular. In the process, he made a number of assumptions, which we discussed in the introduction. The heart of this theory (often called the Graf-Wellhausen hypothesis) was that Moses could not have written the Pentateuch (especially Genesis); therefore, what we call the Pentateuch today was a compilation of various documents from a variety of sources. Graf and Wellhausen identified four sources: J (from *Jahwe*, German for *Yahweh*), E (from the Hebrew word for God, *Elohim*), D (from Deuteronomy, which was viewed as a separate work added at the end), and P (a source written by priests to justify their existence). Because of these four sources, the Graf-Wellhausen hypothesis is also sometimes called the JEDP theory. This way of looking at the Bible is also called "source criticism" (i.e., critically examining the text to find its literary origins).

It had earlier been observed that in Genesis 1 the word *Elohim* is used consistently to refer to God. Beginning with Genesis 2:4, in contrast, we find the phrase *YHWH-Elohim* (translated as "the LORD God"). Some scholars concluded that the two sections were written by two different authors, which would explain the various differences in the way the creation process is described. More recent scholarship, however, has shown that these assumptions are not valid. Moreover, when we look at the terms used for God, we find an interesting distinction.

Elohim. This name, which is used in Genesis 1:1–2:3, is the plural of *El*.[1] It is usually viewed as a "plural of majesty."[2] As used throughout the OT, the term reflects the *transcendence* of God, that is, His separation from and superiority over creation.[3] As used in Genesis 1:1–2:3, which discusses the order and structure of creation, it points out the power and majesty of the transcendent Creator God.

YHWH (Yahweh). This name is apparently derived from the Hebrew verb *hayah*, "to be," and thus related to the phrase translated "I AM" (see Ex. 3:14). As such, it denotes the eternally existing quality of God and emphasizes the personal, eternal, and all-sufficient aspects of God's nature and character. But as used throughout the rest of the OT, this term also shows the *relational* aspect of God. When we note how it is used in Genesis 2:4–4:26, we see a section that emphasizes the relationships of creation, especially between God and man. Here the name *YHWH* points toward the covenant God who is *immanent* (that is, within creation). Interestingly, in the part of Genesis 2 known as the "second creation account," it is used as a compound term, *YHWH-Elohim*, pointing to a God who is both transcendent and relational.

Once we realize how these names are used for different purposes to reflect different roles of God, we begin to have a better feel for the structure of Genesis 1 and 2. In chapter 1, where the title *Elohim* is used consistently, we are given an overview of God as the Great Creator who is outside of creation. The description of the act of creation here is straightforward and matter-of-fact. In chapter 2, where the name *YHWH* is used, we see in contrast a focus on man and his relationship to the rest of creation as well as to his Creator. This distinction is even more evident when we observe that this second account is arranged topically rather than chronologically.

THE ORDER AND STRUCTURE OF CREATION

I have suggested, on the basis of the *toledot* structure, that Genesis 1 is an introduction. As such, its function is to briefly answer the question, Where did the world come from? It does so in thirty-four verses, and virtually every reader comes away from that section wanting to know more. However, it is clear that the writer does not intend to give us the detail we would like to have. His purpose is merely to show that the entire cosmos is created, and that it is God who is the source. The brevity of the material has led to tremendous controversy even among those who claim to take the Bible as a document inspired by God. There is not enough time to sort out all of the issues; therefore, we will merely make several observations.

As we look at Genesis 1, we see a carefully laid out process of creation, though it is expressed in very broad brush strokes. This process consists of seven stages, the last stage being completion, the Sabbath rest of God.

These stages are portrayed as seven days, a description that has created much controversy. On the one hand, we have a text that seems to give a very explicit time frame. On the other hand, we have scientific data that seems to show that the universe is much older than a literal seven-day creation would allow. A variety of approaches have been taken in an attempt to resolve this disparity.

One group dismisses the Genesis account as purely mythological, or perhaps, at best, poetry. According to those who hold this view, the account is to be viewed as a "prescientific" attempt to explain the origin of the world. If one follows this view, the entire account can be dismissed as a poetic way of saying that God created the universe, and the "days" are mere literary devices used by the writer to give structure.[4]

YHWH TO *ADONAI* TO JEHOVAH

The name *YHWH* is often translated "Lord." The Jews would not pronounce God's name, and the actual pronunciation has been lost (though many think it may have been Yahweh or the like). As a substitute, they used the term *Adonai*, which means "my Lord" or "my Master." When the Masoretes added vowels to the Hebrew text during the several centuries after Christ, they used the vowels of *Adonai* for *YHWH*. It was this composite "word" (the consonants of God's name with the vowels of *Adonai*) that was transliterated as Jehovah in the King James Bible.

Another view notes that the Hebrew word for "day" can also mean an extended period of time. Those who hold this view look at the various physical phenomena used to date the universe, such as its vastness and the amount of time it would take for the light from distant galaxies to reach us. Taking these and other factors into account, they propose a long period of development that would allow God to use various tools, such as evolution, to produce the world we have today.

A third group argues that we should take the account as a straightforward presentation. Those who hold this view observe that the word *day* with a number as used elsewhere in the OT refers only to a literal day. They argue that all of the methods used to measure the age of the universe are based on various assumptions, which may or may not be valid. Moreover, the Bible suggests that the universe was fully functioning from the beginning of its creation, which implies that it already had an appearance of age, just as Adam had the appearance of a mature man the moment he was created. Another argument used is the statement that God rested on the seventh day (Gen. 2:2), which is difficult to fit into a long chronology.[5]

The problem we have to address is that God is beyond space-time and thus not limited by our criteria.[6] Would God be dishonest to create a fully functioning finished product if in doing so there was an "appearance of age"? On the other hand, when we look at the heavens and see how great the cosmos is, must we limit its history to a few thousand years? Then again, must God be restricted to using "natural" physical cause-and-effect processes such as evolution in the creation process? Unfortunately, even in Christian circles, there has been much name-calling as we have tried to evaluate these complex issues. While these questions are very relevant to the study of this book, they are not issues that can be resolved here.

HOW LONG IS A "DAY"?

Those who believe that the Hebrew word for "day" in Genesis 1 means a long period of time use several arguments based on the text itself. For example, a literal twenty-four-hour day that includes a period of daylight and darkness (i.e., a complete rotation of the earth) assumes that the sun is illuminating the earth, but the sun was not created until the fourth day. Moreover, in Genesis 2:4 we read a summary statement about the entire creation that uses the expression, "in the day that YHWH God made the earth and the heavens" (literal translation). We need to keep in mind that context does determine the nuance, and even in English we often find words used with different meanings within a single document.

APPARENT AGE

Some have argued that "apparent age" is deceit on God's part. However, two points must be kept clearly in mind. First, there is no tag on the universe giving a date of creation. Rather, our dating is based on certain assumptions and interpretations of the data. The most critical aspect is the assumptions, which are usually unexamined. Second, we see numerous cases of supernormal intervention where it is clear that "apparent age" is a necessary result of the process. One very simple example is the case of the turning of the water into wine at the wedding in Cana. Based on the reaction of the partygoers, the finished product would necessarily be chemically identical with a wine produced from grapes that flowered, fruited, ripened, and were squeezed, fermented, and aged. All these time-consuming steps were circumvented in the supernormal transformation. Thus, *deceit* does not seem to be an appropriate term to use when dealing with supernormal intervention.

If we consider the perspective of the Israelites at Sinai, we can see that the writer's purpose was to show how God created the various *aspects* of creation, beginning with the concept of light and ultimately ending in the creation of man, described as both male and female. The order presented seems to be chronological, although there are still serious questions of how the specific details of these aspects fit together (e.g., the nature of the "expanse" in Gen. 1:6–7 or the creation of light prior to the creation of light sources). These questions remain, regardless of what view one takes on the subject.

> Would it be deceitful for God to create instantaneously a fully functioning, finished product instead of making it grow?

Consequently, we will merely note that there are two key truths that we should derive from this section. The most important truth is that God created the universe and that He did so in an orderly process, and the result was very good. As such, this says much about the awesomeness of God; He is greater than anything we can imagine. His greatness is evident in the macrocosm as we look through powerful telescopes and see stars and galaxies. It is also evident in the microcosm, as we delve into living cells and discover how intricately they are put together. As I look at the creation and the wide variety of living creatures, I am also struck by the wisdom of God and even by His sense of humor. Perhaps the most important aspect of this whole process, however, is the fact that humankind is also a creation of God.

The second truth is that from the outset humankind has been given a key position of responsibility within the created universe. This position is one of world management or stewardship. Included in the command to take care of the world are both genders (male and female) and the anticipated numerous offspring of the first couple. The summary statement in Genesis 1:27 that humankind is created male and female is amplified in Genesis 2. Moreover, this created couple is commanded to multiply and fill the earth—and given the authority to manage it.

With the creation of humankind, God declared that the creation was "very good," and the text states that He rested. God's rest was based on the completion

THE HEAVENLY EXPANSE

All the different views regarding Genesis 1 have problems with the "expanse" (KJV, "firmament") that is called "heaven" or "sky" and that is said to separate two bodies of water (vv. 6–7). For example, many who hold to a short-term creation have suggested that the waters above the expanse were in the form of a water-vapor canopy, which later caused the Flood; but they must explain how the stars, sun, and moon could have been placed in the expanse (1:14–16). The long-term evolutionist view has no solution but to say that the writer wrote from scientific ignorance and that we can dismiss the passage as a poetic description; but the material appears to be written as a historical narrative (as even some critical scholars agree), and so this view conflicts with the doctrine of inspiration.

of the creation process, and in turn it became the foundation for a Sabbath rest for humankind.

THE RELATIONSHIPS OF CREATION

As we enter chapter 2 of Genesis, we find what appears to be a "second creation account." A careful analysis, however, reveals that this passage is actually a restatement of certain aspects of the original account with amplifying details of certain points. The flow of this section is *topical* rather than *chronological*, and the emphasis is on certain relationships within the creation. One reason many people have misunderstood this point is that they have missed the literary indicators: the *toledot* statement in 2:4 shows that this so-called creation account is part of a section that also includes Genesis 3 and 4. As such, it describes key relationships of the original creation story, shows how those relationships were broken, and then specifies some of the early consequences of the breaking of those relationships.

We have already observed that humankind had a unique position in the original structure of creation: world management. But clearly one person, or even one couple, could not manage an entire globe. So God established an initial territory where the original man (called Adam, or "the man") was given responsibility. This management zone was called Eden. The text seems to indicate that in this zone, God provided animal help for Adam (domesticated animals, or the "beasts of the field"). But these animal helpers were inadequate; as the text states, there was no helper suitable for him. At this point, God made Eve, the special helper who seems to have been in the design plan all along (as indicated by Gen. 1:27).

We are not given any information on how the management process worked out in this original world economy. We are not even told how long it lasted. Rather, the writer quickly rushes on to the next critical event, one that has affected the rest of world history. It is important to remember that as we come to the end of Genesis 2, we do not come to the end of the "second creation account." Rather, we move toward a climax that tells us what happened to God's creation.[7] What little understanding we have of the original world is primarily derived by inference from the changes that came about as a result of the fall of man.

Based on the data we have, we can make these observations about the world as it was originally made:

1. *It had a temperate climate.* We base this inference on several bits of data. First, as is commonly known, Adam and Eve were naked prior to the Fall. If we assume that physically they were similar to modern man and woman (although without any of the physical weaknesses to which we are prone), this detail suggests a moderate climate. In addition, we note that there was no rain before the Flood: a mist was adequate to provide water (Gen. 2:5–6). Finally, we observe that seasons were originally noted by the stars (1:14), and we do not see cold and heat associated with the seasons until after the Flood (8:22).

ADAM AND EVE IN THE GARDEN. A painting by Ooster that portrays the striking condition of the world before the Fall—an environment where, according to Genesis, all things worked well.

2. *Adam and Eve had a vegetarian diet.* At the outset, they were told they could eat from "every seed-bearing plant on the face of the whole earth and every tree that has fruit with seed in it" (Gen. 1:29). It was not until after the Flood that Noah and his descendants were told that they should eat meat.[8]

3. *Adam and Eve did not fight weeds, thorns, and thistles.* These items are a result of the Fall (Gen. 3:18). The lack of weeds suggests a garden where every plant grew in its place, and that place was determined by Adam. The lack of thorns and thistles suggests a lack of what we call defense mechanisms.

4. *Adam and Eve had a close relationship with God.* Apparently every evening they walked through the garden with God (cf. Gen. 3:8). I sometimes try to imagine what these walks would have been like, and the best I can come up with is Adam and Eve telling God what they had seen and learned that day. In my imagination, their times together had the freshness and excitement of a five-year-old telling her daddy what she learned in school.

5. *Adam and Eve had a close relationship with one another.* Eve was designed to complement her husband perfectly. Their strengths meshed and supported one another—and they knew it. As a result, there was no jealousy or competition as they worked together to do the job God had given them.

6. *Adam and Eve managed only a small portion of the globe.* How big was the garden? That is a question for which I have no answer. The text clearly indicates that it was a section of the world that had been specially planted in preparation for Adam. The implication was that the management zone would increase as the world population increased. The text also suggests that there were special animals in the garden that Adam named, but again we are not sure what this means. Clearly the garden was finite and relatively small, because after the Fall, they were

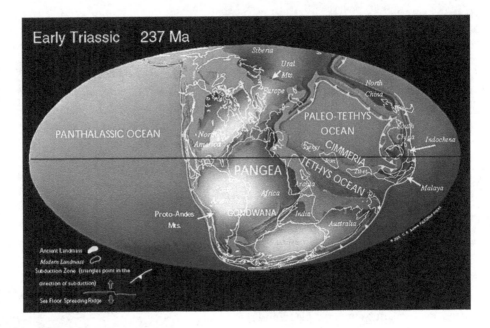

expelled and the gates were guarded by cherubim. Given the extensive global remodeling implied by the Flood, I suspect the location of the garden is now a moot point.

LOOKING AHEAD

When we look at the Fall in the next chapter, we will find that it points to four key areas of relationship that were broken. These broken relationships have left the world in the miserable shape we find it today. Our attempt to understand what the world was like before those relationships were broken is somewhat analogous to our efforts to appreciate the beauty of classical Athens based on piecing together in our minds the ruined remnants. They will be unsatisfactory at best.

REVIEW QUESTIONS

1. What is the term *toledot*, and why is it important?

2. What is the significance of the two creation accounts? How are they similar, and how are they different?

3. What is the significance of the use of the different names of God in Genesis 1 and 2?

4. What are the different views on the seven days of creation in Genesis 1:1–2:3? What are the strengths and weaknesses of each?

5. How are relationships key to the creation account?

6. What do we know about the world in which Adam first appeared?

3
CHAPTER

Why the World Is Such a Mess

OVERVIEW

If a good God made the world, why is it such a mess? The Fall explains not only the breakdown in relationships, but also many of the other problems we encounter. Then the narrative of the Flood amplifies some of the details.

STUDY GOALS

▶ Note the significance of the fall of man and its effects on the world.

▶ Review the nature of relationships broken as a result of the Fall.

▶ Show how God demonstrated mercy after Adam and Eve fell.

▶ Trace the pattern of failure of the first generations of humankind.

▶ Evaluate the nature and significance of Noah's flood.

Because of its consequences, the Fall may be regarded as the most significant event in the history of the world. First, as we will explore in this chapter, the Fall hurt every relationship in which every person in history has been involved. This includes relationships with God, fellow humans, their environment, and even themselves. Second, as a result of the Fall, there have been several judgments on humankind. The most significant was the Flood, which drastically rearranged our entire environment, producing a new climate and affecting the geological record. Third, because of the Fall, God provided a means of reconciliation that involved the incarnation of Jesus the Messiah and His crucifixion and resurrection. These three consequences intertwine to provide the theme for the entire Bible.

HUMANITY'S RELATIONSHIP WITH GOD

Read Genesis 3–4.

The first and most important relationship broken was that between humankind and God. We recall from our overview of Genesis 1 three key aspects of the original relationship. First, man was a created being and was finite—made specially by the same God who made the rest of the universe. We think of humankind as the pinnacle of creation, so it is very humbling to realize that we are made of the same physical material as the universe in which we dwell. Still, when humankind was created, God declared that the result was "very good."

Second, humankind was a unique creation, specifically described as being in the *image of God*. What this term means is somewhat uncertain, but there are aspects that we can pick up through studying various descriptions of God and humankind (that is, through theology). First, Scripture distinctly states that this phrase applies to both male and female. Beyond this, we might note that humans are spiritual beings, which distinguishes them from animals. A number of other traits might be observed, including rational and abstract thinking ability, a will, creativity, verbal communication, and a sense of humor. While other aspects can be suggested, these suffice to point out that humankind is unique.

THORNS AND THISTLES. One effect of the Fall announced by God. These may be either "thorns" (modified branches) or "spines" (modified leaves). God's declaration suggests that prior to the Fall, plants did not require them as a defense mechanism.

Third, man had a special relationship with God that involved cognitive communication. God put Adam in charge of the garden and gave him commands to carry out. Adam was presented with the animals and gave them names that reflected their character. The narrative suggests that, on a daily basis, Adam had communion with God as he walked through the garden. Many theologians

IS GOD MALE?

The distinction between gender (a grammatical category) and sexuality (a physical feature) is an area of much confusion. God is always spoken of in the masculine gender, which is not the same thing as saying that He has male sexuality. Of course, God is also spoken of as Father, which is suggestive of a specific relationship. However, in recent years there seems to be a tendency to reverse the imagery. Biblically, it is not accurate to say that God is viewed as Father because society was patriarchal; rather, society was patriarchal because it was an image of God as Father. Since God is the Designer and Creator, it is likely that human procreation was deliberately designed to illustrate something about God. Thus, the earthly father relationship is a very imperfect reflection of a greater, one might say *real*, father relationship.

believe that when God appeared during OT times in human form (a "theophany"), it was a manifestation of the second person of the Trinity, the Son, who would become incarnate as Jesus the Messiah thousands of years later in history.

Humankind's special relationship with God is key to the brokenness of the Fall.

This special relationship with God is key to the brokenness of the Fall. After Adam and Eve ate of the fruit of the tree of the knowledge of good and evil (which was not an apple, whatever it was), their first reaction was to make fig-leaf coverings because they were naked. It would seem that at least part of what is addressed is their new feeling of guilt and shame, which resulted from their disobedience. Then, when God appeared in the garden, they hid. When God asked them why, they admitted that they now feared God. Not only was the relationship broken, but fear had replaced the earlier openness and trust.

Later we learn that this broken relationship was what is known as "spiritual death." Figure 3A is an abstract representation of humanity as originally created. Here we have tried to show the key feature that distinguishes humans from animals. Both have physical bodies. Both also have an immaterial part, *nephesh* in Hebrew, that is often translated "soul." The *nephesh* seems to be the nonphysical part of both humans and animals that makes them living beings. Passages such as Leviticus 17:11 associate this *nephesh* with the blood. This feature puts both humans and animals in distinction to plants, which have a different type of life, one without blood and thus without a *nephesh*. Associated with this soul are such common features as mind, emotions, and will.

Unlike the animals, however, humans have another nonphysical aspect, which is called *ruach* or "spirit." This term is more difficult to define. If animals have mind, emotions, and will, then the distinctiveness of

Figure 3A.
HUMANKIND BEFORE THE FALL. A simple model showing the relationship between the body, the soul, and the spirit for all human beings.

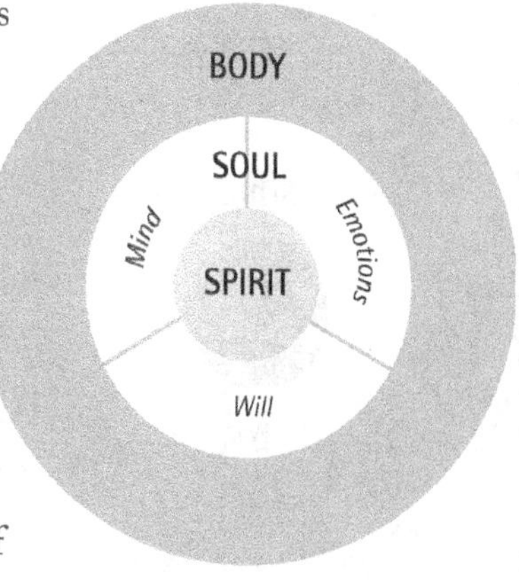

SPIRITUAL DEATH

Theologians use the term *spiritual death* to describe the state of fallen humankind. While a number of passages allude to the concept of being separated from God, perhaps the clearest is Ephesians 2:1–2, "As for you, you were dead in your transgressions and sins, in which you used to live when you followed the ways of this world." In this passage, a tension is reflected in that the readers are described as being both dead and alive (specifically, practicing a lifestyle of sin). Their experience of death was prior to their new birth in Jesus, so the point is that sinners are dead in their spiritual relationship with God.

humans does not lie there. It *is* clear that there are qualitative differences between the mind, emotions, and will of humans as opposed to animals. For example, only humans have abstract reasoning ability. However, these qualitative differences alone do not explain how humans differ from animals. The distinction lies in the contact with the spiritual realm. Only humans have a spiritual dimension, which places them in a category with other spiritual beings, including angels and God.

But humans are not clearly cognizant of those other spiritual beings for two reasons. First, we are also physical; and second, we have died spiritually. Figure 3B portrays how this spirit of man died as he was separated and alienated from God in the

> Just as a black hole in outer space sucks in light so that the view of its entire neighborhood is distorted, so each person is born with what may be termed an egocentric reality—a view of life distorted by self.

Fall. Although Adam and Eve died spiritually, they did not lose their *ruach*. Rather, the spirit may be viewed as having collapsed in upon itself so that it no longer is a channel of communication with God, but rather is a self-focused center. This notion correlates with what Pascal described as a "God-shaped vacuum."

As such, it now distorts each person's view of life. The effect may be similar to how a black hole in outer space sucks in light so that the view of its entire neighborhood is distorted. Each person is born with what may be termed an egocentric reality—a view of life distorted by self.

Humans now fear God, although their fear is often disguised as disdain. At the same time, they intuitively recognize the reality of God and their need for Him. So, as Paul discusses in Romans 1:18–32, humans still have a religion, but it is one in which they worship the creature rather than the Creator. Consequently, even today, people try to hide from God, although their methods are more sophisticated than those of Adam and Eve.

Figure 3B.
HUMANKIND AFTER THE FALL. A simple model showing the relationship between the body, the soul, and the spirit while the person is spiritually dead.

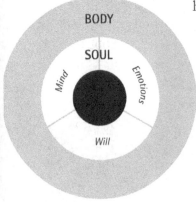

The OT, however, also anticipates the coming of the Messiah. Figure 3C models a person who has received Jesus Christ. Here, the Holy Spirit becomes the medium of communication with God and thus effectively replaces the dead human spirit, filling that God-shaped vacuum.

HUMANITY'S RELATIONSHIP WITH HUMANKIND

The second relationship that was broken at the Fall is that of individual human beings with one another. Again, we can only infer bits and pieces regarding the original relationship of the members of the human race. We are not given much information about the period between the creation of the first couple and the Fall. Moreover, although God had commanded Adam and Eve to procreate, the Fall occurred before any children had been born. As a result, the pre-Fall discussion that we have in the Bible concerns only Adam and Eve.

What we can infer is that there was a complementary hierarchy of the members of the human race that was to expand as the race expanded. Adam named Eve, and Eve was to help him. Eve complemented Adam in that she was a helper totally appropriate for him (as the KJV translates it, "an help meet for him"). This suggests that even as they were created in their finiteness, both Adam and Eve had certain strengths (and thus, conversely, what we might now call weaknesses, which in the original couple would perhaps be better termed "finite limitations") that complemented each other.

Based on the relationship between Adam and Eve, we might draw the inference that as humankind was to expand into a world-ruling hierarchy, each person would have a position of authority within it that would be in perfect accordance with his or her abilities. As the population grew in this scenario, the size of the "garden" would also grow. Furthermore, it would appear that in such a world each person's desires and goals would be in accordance with his or her abilities.

All this changed after the Fall. We see it first as Adam and Eve try to pass the blame on to each other. God asked Adam whether he had eaten from the tree, and Adam blamed the *woman* whom *God* made. When God asked Eve, she in turn pointed the finger at the *serpent*. The consequences of the Fall are announced in the curse when God addressed Eve: "I will greatly increase your pains in childbearing; with pain you will give birth to children. Your desire will be for your husband, and he will rule over you." (Gen. 3:16). Two relationships are addressed here, that of mother and child and that of husband and wife.

While the text speaks of childbirth, more than the physical pain of the actual birth seems to be involved. First, generally where the Hebrew word here translated "pain" is used, it means "vexation, grief, anguish," or some type of emotional pain. Second, the phrase "your pains in childbearing" renders a difficult expression—

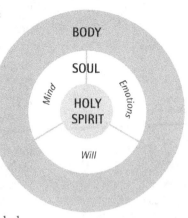

Figure 3C.

HUMANKIND AFTER RE-GENERATION. A simple model that, anticipating the coming of the Holy Spirit after the resurrection of Jesus, shows the relationship between the body, the soul, and the spirit for a person who has been restored to God through Jesus' atonement.

literally, "your pain and your conception." While scholars have usually taken the phrase to mean physical pain in the process of giving birth, other possibilities include an accelerated birthrate or, coupled with the next phrase, other types of pain experienced later in the parenting process. This latter is borne out by historical evidence when we evaluate the struggles between parents (mothers especially) and their children. Part of the pain a parent experiences "in childbearing" is the emotional pain as a child grows and does not live up to the expectations of the mother or father.

> Rather than a smoothly running hierarchy, we now have competition, with each person seeking to advance the self rather than the world.

The second relationship noted in Genesis 3:16 is that of husband and wife. The observation is addressed to the woman, but the object of the relationship is the man. The expression "your desire will be for" is used only one other time in the OT, and that is in the next chapter, where Cain is told by God, "sin is crouching at your door; it desires to have you" (4:7; lit., "its desire is for you"). This phrase seems to suggest a seeking of dominance. In the next clause of 3:16 ("and he will rule over you"), the Hebrew word for "and" may just as likely be translated "but," so what we seem to see here is conflict between the previously perfectly complementary couple. Thus, rather than a smoothly running hierarchy, we now have competition, with each person seeking to advance the self rather than the world.

This passage then sets the pattern we see in human relationships. Although specifically addressed only to the original couple, the results have clearly spread throughout the human race. It is a pattern of self-seeking and personal advancement at the expense of others; it is a picture of grief and sorrow as a result of failed relationships.

WAR. One of the interpersonal conflicts that is a consequence of the breakdown of human relationships. This in turn has led to today's weapons of mass destruction.

HUMANITY'S RELATIONSHIP WITH SELF

The third area of relationship affected by the Fall is internal, or psychological. It is logical to suggest that before the Fall, both Adam and Eve were in perfect mental health. At this point of our text, we see only hints of the internal problems that develop, two of which we will look at here.

The first evidence of psychological problems is manifested when Adam and Eve realize they are naked, which suggests guilt and shame. This is why they try to cover themselves with fig leaves.

The second evidence is reflected in Adam's response to God when God asks him whether he has eaten of the tree. Adam exhibits self-deceit when he tries to pass the blame on to the woman ("she gave me") and back to God ("the woman you put here with me"). In other words, Adam is saying, "God, it's not my fault. I was doing fine until the woman came along, and after all, *You* gave her to me."

> Most psychological problems are grounded in two issues: guilt and self-deceit.

It has been suggested that most psychological problems are grounded in these two issues: guilt and self-deceit. Of course, other factors that affect our mental well-being include the defective relationships already discussed, not to mention physiological problems as a result of a now defective world.

HUMANITY'S RELATIONSHIP WITH THE WORLD

The uniqueness of man's stewardship position is amplified in the Genesis 2 account of the Creation. Adam is placed in a specific location, the garden of Eden, with guidelines given to manage it. The location of this garden has been debated, but if the Flood was as extensive as indicated later in Genesis, the garden was obviously destroyed in the rearrangement of the earth's surface. As noted at the end of the previous chapter, the purpose of the garden would seem to be an initial geographical limitation to the work that Adam was to do personally. Obviously, one person (or couple) could not directly oversee an entire globe. This was the reason behind the command in Genesis 1 for humankind to multiply and as a whole to manage the world.

Adam's position of world manager was illustrated by the fact that he named the animals. In Israelite culture, the giving of a name was viewed as a demonstration of a superior position. One of the problems of this section is its relationship with Genesis 1:24–25, which places the creation of the animals prior to the creation of man (cf. Gen. 2:19 NRSV, "So out of the ground the LORD God formed every animal of the field"). The text suggests two possible solutions. First, the Hebrew grammar leaves open the possibility that the animals had been created earlier and brought to Adam at this point (cf. NIV, "Now the LORD God *had formed* out of the ground all the beasts of the field" [italics added]). Second, the terminology ("beasts of the field") raises the possibility that the animals named at this point were only those we call domesticated animals, that is, those with which man was to have a special working relationship.

The world over which man had responsibility was not the same as the world in which we live. The environment was perfect. We read that there was no rain, but only a daily overnight mist to water. One theory that has been inferred from the changes created by the Flood is that originally the earth was covered by a water-vapor canopy that protected it from harmful radiation and maintained a uniform climate both around the globe and throughout the year. The surface area of the land regions was probably much greater than today, including all of the land above the continental shelves. In addition, there apparently was one continent that was more spread out, for presumably the high mountain ranges had not yet been squeezed up. These factors all changed as a result of the Fall and the Flood.

As we look at God's admonitions to Adam, we note two aspects of His judgment, both of which address man's relationship with the world. The first aspect is that the ground is cursed because of man. What this means is not completely clear. On the one hand, it seems to set up the next aspect of judgment, which involves exhausting labor on the part of man to grow his crops. On the other hand, it seems to be a separate aspect of judgment.

This cursing of the ground may be what Paul addresses in Romans 8:20–21 (NASB), where he notes that all of creation was subjected to "futility" and "slavery to corruption." If so, then what we see here may be God announcing His temporary acceptance of Satan's usurpation of man's position of authority over the world. We do see later that even Jesus accepted the fact that Satan had become "the ruler of this world" (John 12:31 NRSV). At the same time, Jesus anticipated Satan's future demise. This concept, however, takes us into a realm totally separate from ours, the spiritual. It also implies a warfare between fallen angels and God. This warfare is mentioned a number of times throughout the Bible and seems to lay a foundation for many of the struggles we face today—but that is an entirely different subject and must be dealt with elsewhere.

The second aspect of judgment is that difficult labor would be necessary for human sustenance. In a general sense, this means that agriculture would become a very laborious occupation: the ground would now produce thorns and thistles instead of the products desired. Consequently, man would have to labor "by the sweat of [his] brow" for his food. There are two factors involved in this judgment (Gen. 3:19): weeds and thistles.

THE SERPENT

In our discussions about the Fall, we have to this point neglected the serpent. Any way we look at it, this is a difficult issue. Exactly what creature is involved? Why did Eve not express surprise when it spoke? How is Satan related to it? With regard to these and other questions, the biblical writer has not seen fit to give us the information. At the end of the Bible, however, we are given some insight when Revelation 12:9 identifies Satan as the serpent who deceives.

Our concern at this point is that the serpent is also cursed, but there is an interesting detail here that we must note and keep in mind. God gives an anticipation of a later judgment on the serpent in the form of the first prophecy of a coming redeemer or messiah. In Genesis 3:15, God tells the serpent, "I will put enmity between you and the woman, and between your offspring and hers; he will crush your head, and you will strike his heel." This prophecy is known as the *protevangelium*, meaning, "the first [announcement of the] gospel." The immediate

THE PROTEVANGELIUM

There are several interesting insights in Genesis 3:15. First, the conflict involves the seed of woman, not of man, and this language anticipates the virgin birth. Second, the bruise on the heel suggests a wound that is not fatal. Normally, serpent bites were considered deadly, but here it clearly is not. As we look to the NT fulfillment, this detail may be viewed as an anticipation of the resurrection. Finally, this seed of woman will give a head wound to the serpent, usually viewed as a victorious declaration. Thus, in the conflict between the two, the serpent gets in the first blow, but the final and ultimate blow is by the seed of woman on the serpent.

manifestation of this prediction is a perpetual battle between good and evil in this world. However, it is anticipated that the ultimate outcome will be the victory of the Messiah.

GOD'S MERCY

While the picture is largely negative as we read these curses, we also find at least four demonstrations of God's mercy in this passage.

First, physical death did not occur immediately. Part of the warning to Adam was that if he ate of the fruit, he would die. Satan told Eve that she wouldn't die. Actually, the way the phrase is worded in Hebrew, it could also be translated, "It's not absolutely sure that you'll die." In either case, it was a half-truth. Adam and Eve died spiritually at the point of disobedience. Physical death came later, allowing an opportunity for repentance and the beginning of the process of redemption.[1]

Second, we see the beginning of this process of redemption. God made "garments of skin" to cover Adam and Eve (Gen. 3:21), which means that some animals had to die. Since we do not read about a climate change until after the Flood, these coverings must have been designed to hide the nakedness and shame of Adam and Eve.

> Humankind was exiled from the garden, not specifically as punishment, but to prevent the now disobedient humans from eating from the tree of life and thus living forever in their sinful state.

Third, humankind was exiled from the garden, not specifically as punishment, but to prevent the now disobedient humans from eating from the tree of life and thus living forever in their sinful state. It also indicates that physical death would be a vital aspect of the process of redemption.

Fourth, as already mentioned, there was a promise of a redeemer. It is this promise that sets the stage for Genesis 4, humankind's next failure.

FAILURE UPON FAILURE

Read Genesis 4–11.

We noted earlier that the book of Genesis seems to be divided into three major sections, the first of which runs up to Genesis 11:27 (a verse that introduces the *toledot* of Terah, the father of Abraham). My suggestion was that this section sets the stage for the original audience at Sinai by showing how the world became the mess we see today. We have seen the first failure of humankind in the Fall. The rest of this section traces at least six other major failures.

As we pick up the account in Genesis 4, we note that Eve bears her first son, Cain. She declares, "With the help of the LORD I have brought forth a man," a statement that can also be translated, "I have acquired a man, the LORD." Apparently Eve feels that he is the one promised in Genesis 3:15 (who by the time He comes will be given the title Messiah). Soon, Cain is followed by his brother Abel, although no particular importance is attached to his birth.

Fratricide

We are told very little about the two boys. It is clear that Genesis 4:2 covers a lot of time—from Abel's birth to the point where both were occupied with their careers. We are told nothing about the rest of the family, although it is apparent from later comments that Adam and Eve had more children. In fact, it would appear that Cain, if not Abel, was married by the time of the incident (cf. Gen. 4:17). The important point is how the family demonstrates the pattern of failure we have already noted.

The two brothers were very different, one choosing to grow crops and the other to tend flocks. This observation makes a very interesting statement about the economic situation. When Adam was driven from the garden, it was to "cultivate the ground" (Gen. 3:23 NASB). At this stage, humankind was still on a veg-

WHERE DID CAIN GET HIS WIFE?

We read that Cain, after he "went out from the LORD's presence ... lay with his wife, and she became pregnant" (Gen. 4:16–17). Because there is no indication of his getting married in exile, the text suggests that this was the wife he took with him. The question that naturally arises (very often as a challenge to the biblical record) is where Cain got his wife. Actually, we could ask the same question about Seth and all of his brothers. If indeed Adam and Eve were the first man and woman and there were no others, then clearly their children would have to intermarry to provide a subsequent generation. While we find this idea somewhat abhorrent, there have been a number of cultures in which brothers and sisters of certain families married. One of the most notable was ancient Egypt, where sometimes a pharaoh would marry his sister to preserve the purity of the family heritage. From a biological perspective, the problem is that inbreeding enhances the chances that recessive genes would dominate and thus introduce harmful characteristics. In the case of Cain and his contemporaries, the gene pool would have been at a very early stage, when the genetic structure was at its purest. It is entirely likely that many of those recessive genes had not even developed yet.

etarian diet (which apparently did not change until after the Flood; cf. 9:2–3). The only use of animals mentioned to this point was when God made garments of skin for Adam and Eve to take the place of the fig leaves. This information suggests that the primary purpose of keeping the flocks was to provide animals that could be slain for garments; thus animal sacrifice was meant to remind humans of the seriousness of the event that made clothes a necessity. Other subsidiary purposes might include milk and other dairy products, although we have no information on that point.

But the text jumps over all of that and takes us to a point where the two brothers bring sacrifices to God. We are not even told whether these were the first sacrifices they had brought, although I am inclined to believe they were not. One reason is that it would seem unlikely that Adam and his family did not sacrifice during the period from the expulsion from the garden to this event. It is probably not even the first sacrifices that the boys had brought on their own. Key to the situation, the text seems to suggest that Cain and Abel had different attitudes regarding their sacrifices. Abel brought the firstlings, that is, the best he had. Cain merely brought an offering.

Apparently it was for this reason that God rejected Cain's sacrifice, because later God told Cain that if he did well, he would be accepted. Instead of following God, Cain murdered his brother Abel.[2] As a result, he was driven from the expanding family and developing civilization, although apparently taking his wife along with him. In the process, he was given a sign of God's protection so that anyone finding him (other descendants of Adam and Eve who might recall Abel) would not take vengeance into their own hands but would leave retribution to the Lord.

False Pride

After dealing with Cain, the writer discusses highlights of the development of the pre-Flood civilization, although at this point he only addresses the line of Cain[3] and some of the advances associated with it. Within seven generations of Adam, we see the development of animal herding, metallurgy, cities, and musical instruments.

Cain's line is covered in a perfunctory manner until we reach Lamech, who is the sixth generation after Adam (some mention is made of Lamech's sons, but here the line appears to end). Lamech is interesting for two reasons. One is the fact that he had two wives: his is the first recorded case of bigamy. The second is that he seems to take pride in having killed a young man: when we read his "song" (Gen. 4:23–24), we sense a note of arrogance that seems to exalt how "bad" he is compared with Cain.

What Happened to Adam?

We might note that it is only here, at the end of Genesis 4, that we reach the end of our first *toledot* passage, which relates what happened to the heavens and the

IS POLYGAMY ALLOWED?

A question often raised is, Why does God permit polygamy? As I read the Bible, my impression is that this is one of various practices that God tolerated in OT times but did not authorize. There is no place where God specifically says that it is acceptable for any man to marry more than one woman (although there are some guidelines in the law that protect the rights of the second wife of those who do). Rather, as Jesus notes in Matthew 19:3–9 and Mark 10:2–9, the ideal is for one man and one woman to become one.

earth (see Gen. 2:4). While this section only covers three chapters of text, much has happened, and the world is in poor shape. It is at this point that the writer begins a new *toledot* section to tell us what happened to Adam. In the process, he gives us the line of Seth.

As we look at these genealogies, there is some question regarding how exhaustive they are. For example, by comparing Luke 3 with Genesis 11, we note that Luke includes a Cainan between Arphaxad and Shelah in the line of Shem. This gap in Genesis is no real problem, for the Hebrew terminology ("father," "son," "beget") can include distant ancestors and descendants. Moreover, we usually assume that the son mentioned is the oldest and thus the heir, but there is strong evidence that this is not always the case. For example, we know that Abraham was not the oldest of the three sons of Terah, yet he became the continuation of the line; the same is true of Abraham's grandson, Jacob. Now Cain and Abel were certainly grown up (and at least Cain was married) before the murder of Abel. It is thus very likely that there were a number of other brothers and sisters between Abel and Seth who are not mentioned. Consequently, the people listed (with some exceptional additions) are those who provide the lineage of the Messiah (and in the short term for Abraham, the father of the nation of Israel).

THE RAINBOW. The sign of God's promise not to destroy the world again through a flood. Some have proposed that prior to the flood, the earth was covered with a water-vapor canopy. If that is correct, this would have been the first time physiological conditions had permitted a rainbow.

The Flood

After telling us what became of Adam, the writer opens a new *toledot* section, spending some time on the Flood. Here there are two complex issues that need to be addressed, both of which are very controversial. The first is the cause of judgment. The second is the nature of the Flood itself.

The cause of judgment. The text of Genesis 6 tells us that the cause of the Flood was the intermarriage of "the sons of God" and

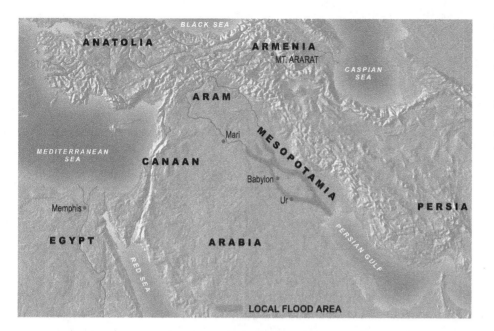

"the daughters of men." The meaning of this statement has been debated, and there are three dominant proposals. Some argue that the sons of God are human judges or rulers; others argue that they are the godly line of Seth and that the daughters of men are the offspring of Cain (or the rest of Adam's children). Still others argue that the sons of God are fallen angels, and the daughters of men are human women. Most likely the latter view is correct, especially since at this time, according to Genesis 6:4, the Nephilim (which probably means "the fallen ones") were on the earth.[4] In any case, the cause of judgment is increasing evil on the earth. While the nature of this evil is not specified, the most likely reference is to an increasing pattern of false worship.

The nature of the judgment. The judgment God sent was a flood that destroyed most of life on the earth. From a remnant, God started again. While there are several issues involved in this event, three key questions stand out.

Perhaps the most critical is the question of historicity: Was there such a flood? The factuality of this event was generally accepted up to the eighteenth century, when many aspects of the Genesis record began to be questioned. As a more critical spirit enveloped biblical scholarship, the Flood came to be regarded as a mythical event. Today, those who view it as mythical are inclined to treat the biblical account as an embellishment of an actual event in history, although there is tremendous debate as to what event that might have been. After archaeology began to develop and the ruins of cities in Mesopotamia began to be excavated, several cities were found to have mud layers pointing to floods. Initially, some archaeologists made a connection with the flood of Noah, which some still accept today.[5] More recently, evidence of a major flood in the region of what is now called the Black Sea has been proposed as the explanation.[6] In both cases, proponents see these floods as the historical event that lay behind the deluge described in the Bible.

This brings us to the second key question: Was the Flood local or global? Both of the suggestions given above are based on the premise that the Flood was local, that it covered a limited geographical region of the earth and no more. The biblical text asserts that the Flood was global; it enveloped the entire earth. A number of specific points must be addressed as one evaluates the question.

1. God gave a 120-year warning that the Flood was coming (Gen. 6:3). With this much warning, Noah and his family could have moved to higher ground rather than build an ark if they had known that the Flood was to be local.[7]
2. The ark was huge (Gen. 6:14–16). What Noah built was not a lifeboat, but a major barge-like vessel. If the description is accurate, it was clearly designed to hold more than local domestic livestock.[8]
3. The outcome was devastating (Gen. 6:17; 7:23). God declared that one of the victims of the destruction would be birds. In the event of a local flood, birds would be able to fly away from the spreading flood waters.
4. The Flood lasted a year (Gen. 7:12, 24; 8:5,13). The period of rain was forty days and nights. More important, the duration of the flood state was a year.[9]
5. The Flood covered mountains (Gen. 7:20). According to the text, the water was fifteen cubits above the highest mountains.[10] Even if the tops of the mountains were lower than today, this information implies more than the notion of a valley being filled. Tied to this point is the final resting place of the ark—"on the mountains of Ararat" (Gen. 8:4). This place is understood to be a region in the northeast portion of what is now

GRAND CANYON. Possibly caused by rapid erosion when a large lake covering half of Utah drained relatively suddenly. Some scientists suggest that the lake was left after the flood of Noah.

Turkey. It is a mountainous plateau several thousand feet above sea level. The specific mountain that is traditionally identified as Ararat is listed as being 16,804 feet above sea level.[11]

6. God promised never to destroy all flesh by flood again (Gen. 9:11). While there have been many local floods throughout history, the promise was that there would never be another flood like this one, which destroyed all flesh.[12] If the Flood had been only local, this declaration of God is negated, for there have subsequently been many floods. In the NT, Peter uses the Flood as an analogy of God's final judgment, which will be a judgment of fire (2 Peter 3:3–7).

If the Flood was indeed a global flood, what are the implications? At a minimum, it would seem to indicate that many of those who are looking for evidence are looking in the wrong places. A global flood would leave its traces in the geological record rather than the archaeological. That is, the deposits would be sweeping landscapes rather than mud layers in cities. Several organizations are beginning to evaluate and organize possible evidence of the Flood, but much work still needs to be done.

The third question relates to the significance of this event to the original audience that stood at Mount Sinai. Two areas of significance are noted. First, the Israelites would have understood that the Lord was a God of both judgment and mercy. In the case of Noah, God judged the world but had mercy on a remnant. This element likely brought to mind to the nation of Israel that they too were a remnant. For us, it brings to mind Peter's warning about a coming judgment. Second, the Flood highlighted for them the pattern of failure that we have been seeing. Because of the failure of humankind, God purified the world. But as we will soon see, even this purification process was inadequate. The problem is the human heart. For this reason, the biblical writer will soon start showing God's process for heart renewal. But before he does that, there are several loose ends to tie up regarding the structure of the world.

> A global flood would leave its traces in the geological record rather than the archaeological.

ARID ENVIRONMENT. A result of the Flood (and thus indirectly of the Fall). The drying-out process in the earth's environment has been documented for the past five thousand to seven thousand years, although its cause has been debated.

Noah Falls off the Wagon, Followed by Ham's Faux Pas

After the Flood, three more failures are cited. First, Noah got drunk. We are given no explanation or excuses—the event is just noted. While he was drunk, his son Ham "saw his father's nakedness, and told his two brothers outside" (Gen. 9:22). They carefully backed into the tent with a blanket and covered their father. After sobering up, Noah cursed Canaan, the son of Ham. While we do not really understand what was involved or why Canaan was cursed instead of Ham, the

METEOR CRATER. In northern Arizona, one example of the kind of major disaster that scientists believe may have occurred centuries ago. Such a disaster may have precipitated the flood of Noah.

significance to the Israelite audience would have been clearer. They were about to go into the land of Canaan. This episode would serve to encourage them regarding the outcome of that invasion.

The Befuddlement of Language

The seventh failure of humankind came some time later. One family had survived the Flood—Noah and his three sons and their wives. After the Flood, God told the remnant of humankind to multiply and disperse. The people multiplied but did not disperse. Rather, they gathered in the land of Shinar (Mesopotamia), where they began building cities and a tower, by which means they sought to reach up to the heavens.

While we know today that a physical tower could not actually reach to heaven, we really don't understand what they were trying to achieve. Did they really think that it could? Or was this to be a unifying symbol? Whatever the purpose, it was their motivation that brought the next judgment on humankind. Their desire was to keep from being scattered abroad. The judgment was a breakdown of languages.

With the resultant loss of communication between groups, God's desire was carried out. Humankind was dispersed. The result of the dispersion was actually anticipated in the previous chapter (Gen. 10), which is called the Table of the Nations. While more work needs to be done, not enough recognition has been given to the accuracy of this table.[13]

A PROBLEMATIC PASSAGE

The meaning of "saw his father's nakedness" (Gen. 9:22) is unclear, and a wide variety of theories have been proposed. The most dominant include: (1) Ham saw his father without any clothes; (2) Ham had a homosexual relationship with his father; (3) Ham had sexual relations with his mother while his father was drunk. Several other passages in the OT use a similar phrase to refer to improper sexual relationships (see Lev. 18:8–19; Deut. 22:30; Hab. 2:15). While the first interpretation is the most likely, Noah's subsequent curse seems unduly harsh for the deed.

But why was the curse placed on Ham's son, Canaan? The most reasonable explanation is that just as Ham showed disrespect to his father, the end result would be Canaan's showing disrespect to his father. Even so, this does not explain the nature of the revelation that seems to elevate Shem over both of his brothers. One very clear point is that it is totally erroneous to argue (as has been done) that since the black races are descended from Ham, they are cursed and are to be slaves. First, this is not a curse on all the progeny of Ham, just on Canaan (whose descendants were not black). Second, if one were to follow that logic, the descendants of Japheth (that is, the Indo-Europeans) would also have a subservient role to the Semites.

LOOKING AHEAD

It is in this section (Gen. 10:1–11:9) that we begin to see the narrowing in focus that will dominate the rest of Genesis. We have seen the *toledot* of Noah's three sons, which is not a genealogy but an explanation that shows how they became the various nations, many of which the people at Mount Sinai had probably never heard of. Then we were given the explanation for language diversity and separation. Now (11:10–26) the writer gives us the *toledot* of Shem. This takes us down to Terah, the father of Abraham. As we read through the book, it becomes clear that the shift is to explain to the people at Mount Sinai their own ethnic history, and more important, why God had intervened to bring them out of Egypt. But those are the subjects of subsequent chapters.

PETRIFIED WOOD. Another indicator of disaster: the petrification of large trees in northern Arizona. The indications are that an entire forest was buried rather quickly. The process of petrification has been demonstrated in historical archaeological sites.

REVIEW QUESTIONS

1. What does it mean to say that humankind was created in the image of God?

2. What is the difference between soul and spirit? Why is that important?

3. What are some implications of humanity's broken relationship with God?

4. What are some implications of humanity's broken relationship with humankind?

5. What are some implications of humanity's broken relationship with self?

6. What are some implications of humanity's broken relationship with the physical world?

7. How did God show mercy after the Fall?

8. Why did Cain's sacrifice get rejected?

9. How did Lamech show false pride?

10. What are some key arguments for a global flood as opposed to local?

11. Why did God confuse the language of humankind?

4

CHAPTER

Abraham and Son(s)

OVERVIEW

Having presented a brief overview of global history, the biblical writer now turns to the origin of the nation of Israel. The story begins with the call of Abraham and God's covenant with him. It continues as God shows the uniqueness of the promised son, Isaac.

STUDY GOALS

▶ Show the importance and background of Abraham.

▶ Evaluate the significance and nature of the Abrahamic covenant.

▶ Trace Abraham's spiritual journey.

▶ Contrast Abraham's two sons, Ishmael and Isaac.

▶ Show Isaac as the heir of the covenant.

In Genesis 1–11, the writer has quickly whisked through centuries, if not millennia, of history. Unexpectedly, at the end of chapter 11, he slows down and begins to focus on one person: Abram (later called Abraham). In addition, he devotes more space to that person than he has given to the entire history of the cosmos to this point. From a literary perspective, these are signals that Abraham is very important. When we recall that he was to be the founding ancestor of the special nation formed at Mount Sinai, his importance becomes clear. We will soon learn, however, that he is important for other reasons as well—reasons that carry over into the NT.

THE *TOLEDOT* OF TERAH

Read Genesis 11.

Given the importance of Abraham and the structure of Genesis, it is very surprising that we do not find a *toledot* section dedicated to him. Instead, we read about the *toledot* of Terah, his father (Gen. 11:27; the next *toledot* statement, in Gen. 25:12, relates to Ishmael, Abraham's son). Moreover, we are not told much about Terah. He lived in Ur of the Chaldeans (the KJV uses also the form "Chaldees").

> Given the importance of Abraham and the structure of Genesis, it is very surprising that we do not find a *toledot* section dedicated to him.

ZIGGURAT AT UR. A Chaldean temple in Ur, the city where Abram lived—an edifice now in ruins but once apparently associated with worship of the moon god Sin.

He had three sons—Abram, Nahor, and Haran—the last of whom died in Ur. Terah left Ur with Abram and his wife, Sarai, and Haran's son, Lot, and headed for the land of Canaan. He died on the way.

Why is this extensive section the *toledot* of Terah rather than of Abram? I suspect the answer is given somewhat subtly. The writer tells us that Terah left Ur to go to the land of Canaan but did not get there; rather, he stopped and settled in Haran, where he died (Gen. 11:31–32). God then told Abram to leave Haran and go on to Canaan.[1] The text states that when he and Sarai arrived there, Canaanites were living in the land (note the words "At that time" in Gen. 12:6). At this point, God told Abram that Canaan would be given to his *descendants*, which seems inconsistent, since the original call was for *Abram* and company to go to the land. The answer to this puzzle does not show up until Genesis 15:13–16, when Abram is told that his descendants would not occupy Canaan for a long period because "the sin of the Amorites has not yet reached its full measure."

These somewhat cryptic comments are supplemented by an interesting sequence through these chapters. In Genesis 12, as we saw, the Canaanites are said to be in the land. In 13:7, it is the Canaanites and the Perizzites. By the time we get to chapter 15, the list has expanded to "Kenites, Kenizzites, Kadmonites, Hittites, Perizzites, Rephaites, Amorites, Canaanites, Girgashites and Jebusites" (vv. 19–21). All these different tribes were probably somewhat related. Late in the third millennium BCE (around the year 2000), the land of Canaan was apparently uninhabited for a period, perhaps because of a drought.[2] Near the end of that time, there is evidence of unrest and of people movements, sometimes called the Amorite invasions.[3]

Our suggestion, then, is that Terah and Abram were called to a specific place at a specific time—a time when they would be able to move into an empty land. Terah's delay in Haran put them outside the window of opportunity as others settled the territory.[4] So when Abram moved in, the land was partially occupied by others, and God honored that occupancy—for a while. One reason God allowed these intruders to stay is that some of them were worshipers of Him (e.g., Melchizedek, who was a Jebusite). More than this, because Terah demonstrated disbelief and disobedience by settling in Haran, he forfeited his part of the upcoming covenant. Thus, although the section is described as the *toledot* of Terah, the subsequent covenant is with Abraham.

UR OF THE CHALDEANS

Ur of the Chaldeans (or Babylonians) was a city-state in the southern region of Mesopotamia. At the time Terah's family lived there, Ur was under the dominion of the Gutians, who would soon be forcibly removed. Soon afterward the city would enjoy a period of prosperity that today we call Ur III, or the Third Dynasty of Ur. The site was excavated by C. L. Woolley in the 1930s. See P. R. S. Moorey, *Ur "of the Chaldeans"* (Ithaca, N.Y.: Cornell University Press, 1982).

ABRAHAM

Read Genesis 12.

We know him as Abraham, but his original name was Abram.[5] He was born in Ur, probably in the year 2166 BCE Ur was a pagan city, a focal point of worship of the moon god Sin. Did Abram worship this god? Genesis 31:53 states that Abram, his brother Nahor, and their father, Terah, all worshiped the true God. Yet Joshua 24:2 implies that they worshiped other gods. Perhaps this family was beginning to compromise and incorporate elements of pagan worship into their belief system.[6] If so, this could have been one reason Abram and Terah were told to leave Ur—they were being corrupted. Another reason is that God was ready to take the next step in preparing the way for the Messiah. This purpose would require a demonstration of faith that ran directly counter to the increasing paganism of the culture. It would also require possession of a piece of land.

As they traveled from Ur, Terah decided to settle in Haran,[7] and Abram stayed with his father. After Terah died, however, the Lord commanded Abram to move on to Canaan (Gen. 12:1), and he obeyed.

The Abrahamic Covenant

The story of Abram's journey (Gen. 12) was critical for the original audience at Mount Sinai because it explained why they had been brought out of Egypt and why they were going to the land of Canaan. They learned that Canaan was the land God had promised to give to His servant Abram and, more specifically, to his descendants—that is, the people gathered at Sinai. They also learned that the promise would be fulfilled if they, like Abram, were obedient.

> At times Abram exhibited the most amazing faith; at other times he committed the most grievous mistakes.

As we read the biblical narrative, we soon discover that Abram was a complex person who had his ups and downs. At times, he exhibited the most amazing faith, as when he left his relatives to go to the land God promised. At other times he committed the most grievous mistakes, as when he impregnated his wife's servant in order to produce an heir as God had been promising but had not yet granted. A careful study of this section should serve to convince the reader of the historicity of the events being described. Abram was one of the key heroes of the nation of Israel, and the

A HISTORIC BIRTH

The birth of Abram is the first event we can date historically, working back from anchor points that show up later in the historical texts. The reason we can go no further is that we do not know the age of Terah when Abram was born. As such, the earliest person we can place into ANE chronology with any confidence is Abram. If our understanding of the date of the Exodus is correct (see ch. 6, below), Abram was born in 2166 BCE, which places his arrival in Canaan about 2091. The Ur III dynasty ran from about 2100 to about 2000 BCE.

GILGAMESH

The literature of the ANE usually minimizes the faults of its heroes and highlights their virtues. A prime example is Gilgamesh, who was the king of Uruk in Mesopotamia not quite a thousand years before the time of Abram. The *Epic of Gilgamesh* consists of a number of his adventures. He has weaknesses: he is told he can obtain immortality by remaining awake for seven days, but he falls asleep. Yet the narrative says nothing about his committing sins such as Genesis reports concerning Abram. The point that sets the gods against Gilgamesh is that he becomes too good and prideful. (See Alexander Heidel, *The Gilgamesh Epic and Old Testament Parallels* [Chicago: University of Chicago Press, 1963], 5–7.)

tendency in the ANE (like human nature everywhere) was to play down the mistakes of heroes and play up their strengths. Most heroes become larger than life over the passage of time.

In the narratives of the biblical patriarchs, however, we see mortal men committing momentous errors. If these had been "cleverly invented stories" (cf. 2 Peter 1:16), the Israelites could have done a much better job of disguising the failures of their heroes. But the purpose of this section is to show that it was not through any special effort on Abram's part that God made him the ancestor of the great nation that was now gathered at Sinai. In fact, Abram was an ordinary man with whom most people could identify.

Abram must have wondered why Canaán was chosen as the land of promise. We now realize that the nation of Israel was to represent the living God to the other nations of the world. For this purpose God chose a very central location. If you look at a map of the area, you will see that the land of Canaan straddles the land bridge between Africa (Egypt) and Asia (Mesopotamia), the regions with the most significant civilizations of the day. Because of its location, Canaan also controlled sea travel between the East and the West.

But Abram had no way of knowing these details. He was simply given a command and some promises. The command was to leave Haran and move to Canaan. If he did that, God would fulfill three promises. These promises are the heart of what we call the *Abrahamic covenant*.

1. *Abram will have a special territory.* The land is significant, and Abram was given claim to it. We will see, however, that he personally was not to possess the land. The actual possession was deferred four hundred years (Gen. 15:13), after the sin of the current inhabitants had reached a point that required judgment.

2. *Abram is going to become a nation.* Earlier the narrative had noted that his wife Sarai was

ABRAM'S JOURNEYS. The likely route Abram took from Ur in Chaldea north to Haran and then southwest to Shechem in the land of Canaan and subsequently to Egypt.

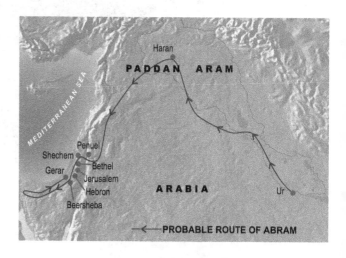

BLESS YOU!

The term *blessing* is somewhat vague. While we assume that the word represents good things, Scripture shows that some of God's "blessings" are somewhat mixed. Although Abraham's descendants are blessed, they end up in slavery in Egypt or in captivity in Babylon or in a diaspora throughout the world. Furthermore, while there is a broad aspect to this blessing in all of Abraham's descendants, there is also a narrow aspect in one of his descendants—the Messiah. The term seems to focus more on success of mission than on economic prosperity. In other words, those blessed by God are given a guarantee that they will achieve the desired objective. In the case of Abraham and the nation of Israel, the blessing meant that they would be the channel for the coming of the Messiah and the establishment of God's kingdom.

barren (Gen. 11:30). This may have been the case so that God could show His power in producing the offspring.[8]

3. *Abram will be a blessing.* There are two aspects to this promise. One is the positive concept of a blessing for Abram and his offspring: those who bless him and his descendants (the Israelites or Jews) will be blessed. But second, anyone who treats them contemptibly[9] will be put under a curse by God. The reason for this promise is suggested in the last line, which hints at the coming Messiah: "In you all the families of the earth will be blessed" (Gen. 12:3 NASB).

Abram's Ups and Downs

Read Genesis 12–16.

As we look through the next few chapters, it becomes very obvious that Abram was a finite, fallible human being. He no sooner got to Canaan than he went off to Egypt because of a famine.[10] Times got hard, so he looked for an easier way.

RUINS OF MARI. A city-state near Haran, where Abram spent a number of years. Tablets from Mari have revealed several customs that reflect issues in Abram's life.

(Ironically, this incident is recorded in the same chapter that relates God's promises, highlighting the contrast.) Once he got to Egypt, he compounded his failure by asking Sarai to lie. Abram realized that his wife was still a good-looking woman, and he feared that someone might kill him in order to marry her. So he concocted the half-lie that she was his sister (Sarai was in fact his half sister, Gen. 20:12). Sure enough, she caught the eye of the Egyptian officials and ended up in Pharaoh's palace.

This sequence of events shows that Abram had a long way to go in learning to trust God. First, in spite of God's rich promises concerning the land, he left it to get food. Second, he did not trust God to protect him in a foreign land, so he resorted to falsehood. Third, he placed his personal well-being above that of his wife, allowing Pharaoh to take her for his harem (and receiving great riches in appreciation). In the end, God protected Sarai and restored her to Abram, but they were expelled from Egypt.

The next events (Gen. 13) show Abram's good side. He and his nephew Lot, now both wealthy, had so much livestock that they were getting in each other's way and so needed to divide the territory.[11] Although Abram was the patriarch and should have had first priority, he gave Lot first choice on property.

Today the region where Lot settled, in the valley of the Dead Sea, is one of the most barren places on earth. Climatological studies, however, indicate that this region has been drying out for the last four thousand years or so. Apparently, at the time of Abram, there was much rainfall, which made this protected valley a lush agricultural region. After Lot chose the lush valley, God reiterated His promise to Abram, assuring him that the outcome of this decision would be beneficial. Abram then moved to Hebron.

CAMELS. Previously believed to be domesticated much later than the time of Abram, but now evident as having been domesticated by that time.

Subsequently, we see another high side of Abram's character. In chapter 14, we are told of his daring rescue of Lot, who had been abducted by King Kedorlaomer and his allies. However, the writer's purpose for including this account goes beyond the great military drama. Rather, the focus is on the aftermath, where we are introduced to a fascinating though somewhat enigmatic character, Melchizedek.

Melchizedek, whose name means "king of righteousness" (cf. Heb. 7:2), was king of Salem (an earlier name for the city now called Jerusalem). He was a Jebusite, that is, from one of the tribes that had moved into the land. He was also a priest of *El Elyon*, the Most High God, another title for the same God that

Abram worshiped.[12] Abram had sworn not to keep for himself any of the goods that he recovered, a reward he was certainly entitled to; however, he was more than willing to give a tithe (one-tenth) of the entire bounty to Melchizedek as God's representative. This act shows that Abram had a high regard for Melchizedek's role as priest and his spiritual state. It also gives us a little insight into the relationship between Abram and the inhabitants of the Promised Land.

After the heady victory, Abram evidently felt somewhat depressed (cf. Gen. 15:1). Perhaps he was starting to have second thoughts regarding Lot's spiritual state. He certainly was struggling with the fact that he had no children (15:2). He then received a second promise, and this promise relates specifically to the children, although the issue of the land is also involved. At the end of chapter 15, we see a ceremony where God validated His promise. This ceremony correlates with what we see in other documents from this period regarding treaties. Normally the two parties to the treaty would walk between the split animals, indicating their willingness to be destroyed if they should violate the agreement. In this case, God alone passed through to show the promise to be unilateral.

> **Abram had a high regard for Melchizedek's role as priest and his spiritual state.**

The next event recorded after this tremendous promise is another failure on Abram's part. Sarai got frustrated in her childlessness and offered her maid Hagar as a surrogate mother. We have legal documents from Mari (an ancient city in the Euphrates Valley) that reflect a similar situation, for they contain the provision that the child of a maid belonging to a barren wife would become the legal heir of the husband fathering the child. Despite the apparent legality and social accept-

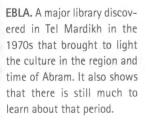

EBLA. A major library discovered in Tel Mardikh in the 1970s that brought to light the culture in the region and time of Abram. It also shows that there is still much to learn about that period.

A MAN OR A THEOPHANY?

The letter to the Hebrews, in comparing Melchizedek's priesthood with that of Jesus (Heb. 7:1–17), describes Melchizedek as follows: "Without father or mother, without genealogy, without beginning of days or end of life, like the Son of God he remains a priest forever" (v. 3). These words have suggested to some that Melchizedek was not a real human but a theophany. Since the writer is drawing an analogy between the two, however, it is more likely that he regards both as historical figures. Theophanies are generally understood to be preincarnate appearances of the second person of the Trinity, the Son. Thus, if Melchizedek was a theophany, we would have the writer of Hebrews comparing the Son with the Son, which would not really be an analogy.

ability of the act, however, it clearly represents another slip in Abram's faith. Key to our understanding of the incident is the fact that we have no record of his asking God about the matter—he merely took action.

Reiteration of the Abrahamic Covenant

Thirteen years after the birth of Ishmael, God reiterated the promises He had made to Abram. Genesis 17 contains what is often called the Abrahamic covenant. In reality, this passage is merely the fullest expression of that covenant. The distinctive element of this reiteration is that not only does it involve *land, blessing,* and *seed,* but there is also an emphasis that the seed is to be from Sarai. The word *seed* is later seen to be ambiguous, for it can have either a singular or a plural reference. In the context of Abram, the focus is immediately upon a multitude. However, Paul picks up on the ambiguity in Galatians 3:16, where he applies the promise to Jesus as the Messiah, the singular seed who will fulfill the promise.

Read Genesis 17.

Abram had at this time reached the point of totally giving up. It was then that God changed his name from Abram (meaning "exalted father") to Abraham ("father of a multitude"). God reiterated the promise of land and gave Abraham the sign of circumcision. God also verified that the offspring would come from barren Sarai, whose name was now changed to Sarah ("princess").[13]

The Demise of Sodom and Gomorrah

The beautiful, fertile land that Lot had chosen (Gen. 13) had turned rotten and was ready for judgment. God appeared to Abraham beforehand and told him what would happen to Sodom and Gomorrah (Gen. 18:20–21). In the account, however, this announcement seems secondary. The first order of business was for God to assure Abraham and Sarah that they would have a child. By this time, the

Read Genesis 18–20.

idea had apparently become a joke to the elderly couple, for Sarah laughed (18:12).

After this interchange, as God was about to leave, He informed Abraham that Sodom and Gomorrah would be destroyed. There seem to be two reasons for this announcement. First, it assured Abraham that he was correct in allowing Lot to choose what, on the surface at least, seemed to be the choicer location. Second, it allowed Abraham the opportunity to intercede for his nephew. Abraham virtually bartered with God, as with a local merchant, until finally they agreed that if there were ten righteous people in the city, Sodom would not be destroyed.[14] For the audience at Mount Sinai, hearing the announcement regarding Sodom's destruction together with this promise of mercy would have helped solidify that the God who graciously gave gifts was also the same God who judged vile behavior. It would also explain features of the land they were getting ready to possess.

When the angels arrived in Sodom, it was soon evident even to Lot that things were much worse than he had expected. In spite of that, the angels had to practically drag him out to safety. The effect of the city on his family was even more evident; Lot's wife looked back and was lost (transformed into a pillar of salt). Then, Lot's two daughters got him drunk on consecutive nights and slept with him so that they could become pregnant. The offspring of the sons who were born, the Ammonites and the Moabites, would become obstacles that the Israelites at Mount Sinai would ultimately encounter. Meanwhile, Abraham, off in the distance, saw the smoke of the destruction of the cities.[15] There is no record that Abraham ever saw his nephew again.

Not long after this event, Abraham moved to a different region of the land. While in Gerar, he lied about his relationship with Sarah again. This time, God directly intervened before the king of Gerar had an opportunity to become intimate with her. Thus, God ensured that there would be no question regarding the parentage of the coming son.[16]

PYRAMID. One of the pyramids built, as part of humanity's quest for immortality, about five hundred years before Abraham traveled to Egypt.

Read Genesis 21.

The Birth of Isaac

Finally, after decades of waiting, the heir was born. Because God had told Sarah that despite her laughter at His promises she would bear a son, she said, "God has brought me laughter, and everyone who hears about this will laugh with me" (Gen. 21:6). Thus, the son was named Isaac ("he [God] laughs").

With the change in Sarah's maternal status, relations between her and Hagar deteriorated. The antagonism came to a climax when Ishmael began to ridicule his little brother on the day Isaac was weaned. Sarah was livid and demanded that

Hagar and Ishmael be driven out into the desert. This time Abraham did pray about it. God told him to listen to his wife, so Hagar and Ishmael were sent out the next day. While God accommodated Sarah, however, He did not abandon Abraham's mistress and son. They were protected by an angel, and Ishmael became a patriarch in his own right. This status is shown to us by the inclusion of a *toledot* section ("this is what became of . . .") devoted to Ishmael tucked between the lives of Abraham and Isaac (Gen. 25:12–18).

Abraham's Test

From here we jump to the supreme test given to Abraham when he was well over a hundred years old (the exact age is not given). God told him to sacrifice his son Isaac as a burnt offering.[17] The point of the sacrifice was to bring out whether Abraham really trusted God. Earlier he had attempted to find substitutes for God's promises—first, Eliezer, his lifelong servant; then Ishmael, his illegitimate son. Twice over the years, Abraham had argued with God that Ishmael should be the heir. Now it is clear that Isaac is to be the heir, and in Abraham's mind, at this point there does not seem to be any consideration of an alternative. But how could that be possible if he killed the lad? The writer to the Hebrews

Read Genesis 22.

ISHMAEL AND THE ARABS

It is generally accepted that the Arabs are descendants of Ishmael. The names of his sons (Gen. 25:13–15) are reflected in the names of various Arabian tribes and regions. Islamic tradition claims that the well where Hagar and Ishmael were revived was located in what is now Mecca, but this city is more than 700 miles (as the crow flies) from Beersheba, where Abraham lived when the incident took place.

states that Abraham figured that God could resurrect the boy after the sacrifice (Heb. 11:19). Of course, we learn that after Abraham showed faith and obedience, God provided a substitute.

Final Events in the Life of Abraham

Read Genesis 23 and 25.

After Sarah died, Abraham bought a cave near Hebron in which to bury her. Today, if you go to Hebron, you may still visit the site where Abraham, Sarah, Isaac, Rebekah, Leah, and Jacob were buried. It is a Muslim mosque situated over a cave that was last entered by the Crusaders in 1119.[18] Since then (after the city was retaken by the Arabs), entrance has been forbidden to all.

Sometime after Isaac grew up, Abraham arranged a marriage for him, which we will discuss later. Abraham then took another wife, whose name was Keturah. Through her, he had six more sons, and he also had other sons through concubines. These sons too became the ancestors of nations, but Isaac was the line of the blessing.

Summary

In summary, what do we know about Abraham? He was an ordinary man with a very human nature. He was called of God, and he struggled in his faith. More important, God finally did give him the son He had promised, who was the next link in the family line. At a minimum, this narrative showed the Israelites at Mount Sinai that God had long had an interest in them.

ISAAC

Read Genesis 24.

Given all of the issues leading up to his birth, we expect to find Isaac a very special person. Instead, we get the impression that his only importance was as the son of Abraham and the father of Jacob. In fact, we are told only three things about him.

DEAD SEA BRINE. A brine pool along the shore of the Dead Sea. When the water evaporates, it leaves a heavy deposit of salt. Today these salts are valuable mineral sources.

Servant Sent to Haran to Get a Wife for Isaac

The first thing we are told about Isaac is how Abraham procured a wife for him. He sent his servant back to Haran to arrange a marriage with a relative. Why go all this way for a wife? This decision may be a sign of the downward spiral of the local inhabitants. Approximately sixty years had passed since the rescue of Lot, and Melchizedek may well have been dead. As is often the case after the death of a great spiritual leader, the Jebusite community may have begun moving away from God.[19]

The account of Abraham's servant finding Rebekah is remarkable. He asked for a sign from Abraham's God to show him the woman He had chosen for Isaac. The sign was to be that the right woman would volunteer to water his ten camels (Gen. 24:14).[20] Rebekah, the granddaughter of Nahor,[21] Abraham's brother, showed up, and the servant asked her for a drink. After Rebekah volunteered and had watered the camels, the servant learned that she was a relative of Abraham—just the people he had been sent to find. When he arrived at their house, he quickly related his quest and the sign that had been given to him. Rebekah's father and brother, recognizing that YHWH was in control, agreed that she should marry Isaac (Gen. 24:50–51). Rebekah not only agreed to go but left the next day without a prolonged farewell. When they arrived in Canaan, she and Isaac were married.

below left to right
MACHPELAH. A mosque in Hebron marking the location of the cave where Abraham, Isaac, and Jacob and their wives are buried.

MACHPELAH'S CAVE. The entrance to the cave, thought to be the burial tomb of the patriarchs, which has been sealed since the time of the Crusades.

Isaac Passes His Wife Off as His Sister

Read Genesis 26:1–11.

As Yogi Berra is supposed to have remarked, it was "déjà vu all over again." Or, we could say, like father, like son. In his dealings with Abimelech, the Philistine king, Isaac attempted the same deception that Abraham had twice used with Sarah. The results were similar. Although Abimelech accepted Isaac's word that Rebekah was his sister, Isaac was discovered behaving toward his wife in a manner appropriate only for married couples. Abimelech was irate, but he recognized that God was with Isaac, so he invited him to stay in the land under his protection.

Isaac and Rebekah Have Twins

Read Genesis 25:21–26.

There are several signs that Rebekah's twins were significant. First, we learn that the mother was initially barren, a sign that almost always serves to emphasize the importance of the subsequent birth. Second, the pregnancy was an answer to Isaac's prayer on behalf of his wife; after twenty years of marriage, she conceived. Third, the two fetuses struggled within the womb. What Rebekah felt was evidently far in excess of the normal movement of a fetus, for she specifically asked God what was happening. Notice the way her question was worded: "Why is this happening to me?" (Gen. 25:22); that is, if this pregnancy was of God, then why was it so hard? The answer was important and twofold: Rebekah was to have twins, and they would both father a nation; more significantly, the older would serve the younger. Fourth, this event seems to be reported out of chronological sequence. It is likely that the birth of the twins occurred after Isaac passed his wife off as his sister (the latter incident is recorded in ch. 26). As we read on, it soon becomes clear that most of the *toledot* section under the name of Isaac is really about his son Jacob.

PARALLEL ACCOUNTS

The three incidents of deception involving the wives of Abraham and Isaac have striking similarities, and some scholars argue that they all are variations of one story. The settings are dissimilar, however, and the resolution differs drastically in each.

Figure	Location	How Discovered	Consequences
Abraham	Egypt	Response to plagues	Sent away
Abraham	Gerar	Response to dream	Bought off
Isaac	Gerar	Observed	Remained and prospered

We might make a correlation to Henry VIII and five of his six wives: Catherine of Aragon, Anne Boleyn, Anne of Cleves, Catherine Howard, and Catherine Parr. A quick glance shows several parallels. These wives had only two names among them (Anne and Catherine). The first two wives were rejected because they did not produce sons. Catherine of Aragon and Anne of Cleves were divorced. Catherine Howard and Anne Boleyn were executed. All these similarities might suggest that Henry's escapades really are different versions of the same story from different sources. Of course, we know from historical records that these events all happened and that Henry's problem was even more complex than this summary suggests.

REVIEW QUESTIONS

1. Why is this section of Scripture called the *toledot* of Terah even though he dies almost at the beginning?

2. What is the significance of the Abrahamic covenant, first for the nation of Israel and then for the Bible as a whole?

3. Describe Abraham's spiritual odyssey.

4. Why was Lot wrong in choosing to live in Sodom and Gomorrah?

5. Why did God destroy Sodom and Gomorrah?

6. What was Abraham's greatest test?

7. Why is Isaac disappointing to us?

5
CHAPTER

Jacob and His Tribes

OVERVIEW

Abraham's grandson, Jacob, proved to be the transition figure from a family line to a nation. While Jacob's character and methods left much to be desired, God worked with him. It was his son Joseph, however, who had the faith and character that preserved the nation. Job, a follower of God who was not from Abraham's family, possibly lived during this time.

STUDY GOALS

▶ Contrast Isaac's twin sons, Esau and Jacob.

▶ Evaluate Jacob as the next heir of the covenant.

▶ Show the expansion of the covenant from an individual line to a family line.

▶ Trace Joseph's role in preserving the family from famine and apostasy.

▶ Evaluate Job as a contemporary of the patriarchs.

▶ Discuss the significance of Job's trials and restoration.

Although we are still in the section designated as the *toledot* of Isaac, the focus is beginning to shift. We have already noted that Isaac is a somewhat disappointing figure after the tremendous buildup in earlier chapters. Now we find that he is soon displaced by his son Jacob. In fact, after Abraham, Jacob is the most dominant figure in the book of Genesis, and in many respects, the rest of the book is about him. Like his grandfather, Abraham, Jacob is noted for God's promises to him, although he himself does not appear to deserve them. Jacob is essentially the beginning of God's fulfillment of His word to Abraham.

> Like his grandfather, Abraham, Jacob is noted for God's promises to him, although he himself does not appear to deserve them.

The story begins with the troublesome pregnancy of Rebekah, who gave birth to twins, Esau and Jacob. The boys were fraternal twins and were physically very different. The oldest had a ruddy complexion and lots of hair, so they called him Esau ("hairy").[1] Jacob, on the other hand, was smooth-skinned. As they came out of the womb, Jacob was grabbing the heel of his brother, so he was called "heel grabber."[2]

As they grew older, their differences showed up in a variety of ways. Esau liked to hunt and loved the outdoors; Jacob tended to stay home. Esau seemed to live for the moment; Jacob was always planning ways to get ahead. It is likely for this reason that the parents began to show favoritism. Isaac liked Esau, but Rebekah favored Jacob.[3] This would certainly lead to trouble.

OASIS OF ISMAILIA. Date palms growing in Egypt in what appears to be barren sand, indicating that there is moisture underneath.

THE CASE OF THE BIRTHRIGHT

Read Genesis 25:27–34.

After the boys had reached maturity, we are told of a time when Esau had a bad day (perhaps several bad days) hunting. So he trudged back to the settlement with both his hands and his stomach empty. When he got there, he found that Jacob had made a lentil stew, the aroma of which seemed to fill the entire camp. The smell accentuated his hunger, and Esau asked for a bowl. Jacob made a bargain that in exchange Esau would give him the birthright. Starved, Esau agreed, ate the stew and bread, and then wandered off. The text states that Esau "despised" his birthright. Some have suggested that he did not take the agreement seriously. However, we soon learn (Gen. 27:36) that Esau was very aware that the birthright was no longer his.

THE CASE OF THE BLESSING

Sometime later, Isaac, getting on in years, realized that he was nearing death. The text does not indicate how old he was at this point; however, by carefully piecing together other chronological data, we estimate his age to have been about 136. (According to Gen. 35:28, then he would live another forty-four years.) But the text also notes that he was blind, which may have contributed to his foreboding. He therefore planned to bless his favorite son, Esau. Before he did so, however, he asked Esau to go hunt for some wild game to make a savory dish. As the account unfolds, we find Rebekah scheming with Jacob to prepare similar food

Read Genesis 27.

from a kid. She disguised Jacob as his older brother, using Esau's clothes; she also used the hair from the kid to emulate Esau's hairy skin. The charade succeeded, and Jacob received the blessing that was intended for Esau.

The relationship of the meal to the blessing is unclear. There is only one other instance of an aged father blessing his son before he dies, and that is the same Jacob later in this same book. In that case, there is no mention of a meal. In fact, Isaac's blessing itself raises questions. Clearly, it is distinguished from the birthright. The issue is especially confusing when we see the content of the blessing. For the most part, what Isaac said to Jacob indicated a life of prosperity, a "blessing" that easily could have been

> ## BIRTHRIGHTS AND BLESSINGS
>
> Genesis seems to distinguish between a child's birthright and a father's blessing. The birthright was the special privilege of the firstborn whereby he inherited a double portion of the estate (cf. Deut. 21:17). If so, one son would have received two-thirds of Isaac's wealth and the other, one-third. The blessing, by contrast, had to do with a divine objective—in this case, to guarantee that there would be a male heir in each generation who would continue the line that would eventually produce a Messiah.

BEDOUINS IN CAMP. A nomadic people, sometimes portrayed as retaining the culture and traditions prevalent during the times of the patriarchs.

given to Esau as well (with the caveat that he would, indeed, serve his brother). So why did Isaac assert to Esau that the blessing was gone?

We find a key in the final phrase of the blessing: "May those who curse you be cursed and those who bless you be blessed" (Gen. 27:29). The relationship of this phrase to the promise God gave Abraham in Genesis 12 suggests that perhaps what we are seeing is the insertion of this son into the line of the Abrahamic covenant. That would explain the distinction between blessing and birthright. It would also help explain why, after the death of Jacob, no blessings are recorded. After that time, all descendants of Jacob were included in the line of blessing, that is, the line of the Abrahamic covenant.

Jacob had no more than left his father's tent after receiving the blessing when Esau showed up with a savory dish made from the game he had brought back. At that point, Isaac realized what had happened and acknowledged that Jacob had indeed been given the blessing. After tremendous protest, Esau talked his father into giving him a "blessing" also. This, like the blessing given to his brother, was really a prophetic declaration regarding his descendants. It had its positive aspects, but it pales in comparison to the promise that had been given to Jacob.

Esau was furious. Suspecting that his father was on his deathbed (and certainly Jacob's fraud would seem to hasten the event along), Esau let it be known that once Isaac was gone, Jacob would also be history. At that point, Rebekah intervened again.

HARAN. The city where Abram stopped and where Jacob fled to escape Esau and to obtain a wife.

JACOB MEETS HIS MATCH

Read Genesis 28–31.

Using the undesirable character of Esau's wives (who were both Hittites) as an excuse, Rebekah persuaded her husband to send Jacob to Haran to get a wife from among their relatives. Thus, Jacob fled the wrath of Esau, but he really left home with nothing and did not know when he would return. While en route, Jacob had an interesting encounter with God at Bethel. There he received from God the promise that Abraham and Isaac had also been given—the land, many descendants, and a future worldwide blessing (Gen. 28:14). His response to this revelation suggests that his spiritual state was very open to question. After the vision, he promised that if God were to be with him during the journey, and bring him back safely, *then* he would make Him his God.

Without further ado, Jacob arrived in Haran, where he began looking for his relatives. In some ways, the narrative that follows is one of the most humorous and ironic portions of the Bible. Jacob, "the supplanter," met Rachel, the younger daughter of his uncle Laban, at a well. He then rolled away the stone from the mouth of the well, even though it normally took several shepherds together to move such a large stone.

Apparently Jacob was smitten at first sight, and Laban was aware of it. After a month, Laban offered to pay him for the work he was doing. Jacob then proposed to work seven years for Rachel. Laban agreed. The text tells us that the time "seemed like only a few days to him because of his love for her" (Gen. 29:20). But Jacob must also have been counting the days, for once his time was completed, he asked Laban to set up the marriage. The ceremony was planned, and there was a great party. But to Jacob's chagrin, the next morning he found that he had married the *older* sister—the one who was not quite so attractive.[4] Irately, he approached his father-in-law, who calmly told him that the custom was that the oldest daughter must be married first.[5] However, Laban quickly offered a *new* deal—another seven years for the younger daughter as a second wife. Jacob reluctantly agreed, and a week later he married Rachel.

HARAN ARCHITECTURE. Beehive-type houses in the Haran region, the architecture of which provides cooling in a warm climate.

LABAN'S PLOT

Although the text does not mention it, Jacob must have told his uncle why he was in Haran—after all, the whole purpose of the trip was to get a wife (Gen. 29:13 does say that "Jacob told him all these things"). Laban was the brother of Rebekah and had been present when she went off with Abraham's servant to marry Isaac. Those arrangements had included no long waiting period, no chicanery, just a pure arranged marriage (with the usual dowry). Surely Isaac had provided the wherewithal for his son to get a wife. We also are not told what work Jacob was doing, but we may have been given a hint when he watered Rachel's flocks. Thus, it would appear that Laban is plotting against his nephew from the start, anticipating the projected marriage and getting as much out of it as possible.

The next two chapters relate how God supplied the riches that He had promised to Jacob. We are told of how the two wives connived to outdo each other for producing sons, and when Rachel found she was barren, she gave Jacob her servant Bilhah as a surrogate mother. Leah followed suit with Zilpah, her own servant. As a result, in a relatively short time, Jacob acquired eleven sons and at least one daughter.[6] His final son, Benjamin, would not be born to Rachel until they returned to Canaan.

Having fulfilled his contract, Jacob wanted to leave, but his father-in-law offered to let him continue to work for livestock. Jacob agreed and spent the next six years working to acquire sheep and goats.[7] After this period, he sneaked off, tired of Laban's changing the conditions (ten times according to Gen. 31:41).

The narrative records another case of dishonesty. This time it was Rachel, Jacob's favorite wife, who pulled a fast one on her father by stealing the household *teraphim* (probably meaning "idols"). Laban caught up with Jacob and his family, but he could not find the *teraphim*, because Rachel deceived him. Laban then reluctantly let Jacob go.

JACOB RETURNS HOME

Read Genesis 32–35.

Even after twenty years, Jacob feared returning to meet his brother. He divided his property to make it less of a target and sent bribes on ahead to placate Esau, only to find that his brother had mellowed and become prosperous in his own right.[8] En route, Jacob wrestled with God and was given the new name Israel, "One who strives with God." It would seem that it was only after this event that Jacob really became a man of faith, albeit a faith that wavered (perhaps up to the point when he learned that Joseph was alive in Egypt).

We then learn that Jacob's fears of his brother were unfounded—or perhaps, God interceded so that whatever Esau had planned with the four hundred men was thwarted (cf. Laban's words in

BEDOUIN GIRL. A Bedouin wearing her veil when in the presence of strangers so as to reflect a tradition of modesty. She is churning goat's milk.

TERAPHIM

The reference to the *teraphim* (a plural form) is problematic. They are generally thought to be household idols, but this is not certain. Laban does assert in Genesis 31:30 that Jacob has stolen his gods. We also learn from 35:2 that Jacob's wives had some idols. So, overall, that may be a valid conjecture. It has also been suggested that the *teraphim* were associated with inheritance claims—which would be extremely ironic in this story, for Laban's sons resented Jacob's wealth, saying, "Jacob has taken away all that was our father's" (Gen. 31:1 NASB).

Gen. 31:29). When the two met, Esau was gracious, warmly welcoming his brother back.

As Jacob moved back into the land, he still didn't trust his brother, and the two went their separate ways. We read no more about Rebekah, and the narrative says nothing about Jacob returning to his father until after the time he spent in Shechem and Bethel. Although he had vowed to return to Bethel if God watched over him during his journey, he settled in Shechem, where he bought land. Shechem was only about 15 miles north of Bethel, but God's direction at the beginning of chapter 35 shows that Jacob was in the wrong place at this time.

It was at Shechem that the tragic episode of the rape of Dinah took place. While she was visiting the women of the town, a prince by the name of Shechem saw her and raped her. He then decided that he wanted to marry her and had his father, Hamor, start the negotiations. Jacob was silent about the rape, but when Dinah's brothers heard about it, they planned revenge. They used circumcision as a ploy and asserted that Dinah could marry Shechem only if all the men of the city underwent the procedure. Shechem and Hamor persuaded the rest of the men to submit to circumcision by arguing that they could then absorb the riches of Jacob's family. Simeon and Levi waited until the men were incapacitated; then they attacked the

> Having broken his promise to God to return to Bethel, Jacob was in the wrong place at this time.

WRESTLING WITH GOD

The event related in Genesis 32:24–32 is very strange, to say the least. Some have suggested that this passage was originally a tale of a struggle with a river spirit or demon for the right to cross the river. But a quick glance at the text shows that Jacob had already crossed the river back and forth several times. Even when we take the text at face value, however, we see problems: Why did God come to him? Why was God in the form of a man? Why did they wrestle? Was Jacob merely struggling with his conscience? Why did the match last all night? Why did the coming of daylight force an end to the match? We are not given answers to these questions, but it would appear that God had an important lesson to teach Jacob about trust. As a result, Jacob got a new name—but he also limped for the rest of his life as a reminder of the encounter.

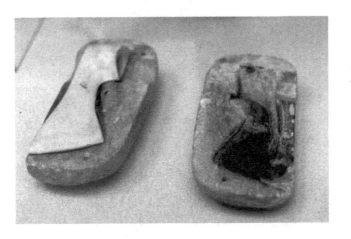

BRONZE AGE WEAPONS AND TOOLS. High-quality, molded bronze implements that show fairly high technical know-how. The Bronze Age began between 4000 and 3000 BCE and ended with the advent of the Iron Age sometime before 1000 BCE.

city, killed every male, and seized all their possessions. Jacob rebuked his sons, however, for he feared what message this act would send to the region. This story is one of two episodes that seem to be setting the stage for the movement of the family to Egypt. The second is the relationship between Judah and Tamar (Gen. 38).

God next told Jacob to move to Bethel. In preparation for the move, the family finally cleaned out all of the idols they had acquired. At Bethel, God appeared to Jacob and reiterated the Abrahamic covenant and promises. It was subsequent to this promise that Rachel died while giving birth to Benjamin. She was buried along the way to Bethlehem.[9] Isaac then died, and the mention of this event completes the *toledot* of Isaac. But as we have seen, the focus has been on his son Jacob.

WHAT HAPPENED TO ESAU?

Read Genesis 36.

After giving the account of Isaac's death, the author turns to Jacob's brother. Esau had a number of sons who became leaders of the Edomites. For the Israelites at Mount Sinai, this information would be important for several reasons. Edom would eventually be a neighbor, one they would dominate (as indicated in the "blessing" Isaac gave Jacob). There would be animosity between the two nations, and the *toledot* sections of Isaac and Esau explain why. Moreover, although the Israelites did not yet know it, those under the age of twenty and their children would have to go around Edom to get into the Promised Land, and they would not be allowed to interact with the Edomites during the journey (Deut. 2:4–8).

Read Genesis 37.

JOSEPH AND HIS BROTHERS

The last *toledot* section ("This is what became of . . .") in the book of Genesis is that of Jacob, even though we have been told about him for a number of chapters. Further, as soon as we read in 37:2, "This is the account [lit., these are the *toledot*] of Jacob," the text focuses attention on his son Joseph. Clearly, Joseph was critical to what happened to Jacob.

The stage is set for us immediately when we note that Joseph was his father's favorite. This favoritism was evident to all the brothers. Jacob gave him a special coat that provoked their jealousy. They also hated Joseph because he related dreams that seemed to foretell a position of dominion and authority over his brothers and parents. More important, from the perspective of the brothers, he was a tattletale, for he brought home a bad report on their behavior in the fields. We can only conjecture what the brothers may have done that precipitated this report. They certainly were not saints, as a number of incidents recorded in the text indicate.[10] However, as is often the case, when they were caught, they blamed the one who turned them in rather than admit their fault.

As a result of all of this, when the opportunity arose, the brothers plotted to kill Joseph. It was Reuben who stopped the talk of murder possibly because he hoped to use this opportunity to get back into his father's good graces. Instead, they threw Joseph into an empty pit or cistern.[11] Judah came up with the idea of selling him into slavery when he saw a caravan traveling down the "coastal highway" (a major trade route between Egypt and Mesopotamia). So when the caravan came along, Joseph went with it.

THE STRANGE CASE OF JUDAH

Read Genesis 38.

The writer interrupts the story of Joseph to relate an event in the life of Judah. He has moved away from his brothers, so this incident apparently takes place sometime after the events of chapter 37. In his new setting, Judah married a Canaanite woman and had three sons. His wife subsequently died.

After the boys matured, Judah arranged a marriage between his oldest son, Er, and a Canaanite woman, Tamar. Before they had any children, however, Er was struck dead by God because he "was wicked in the sight of the LORD" (38:7 KJV). Based on the use of a similar phrase elsewhere, apparently he was going into idolatry.[12] After Er died, Judah instructed his second son, Onan, to take Tamar as a wife to raise a son to inherit Er's estate. Onan, however, refused to get his brother's widow pregnant, and he too was struck dead by God.[13] At this point, Judah sent Tamar home, supposedly to wait for his youngest son to come of age. Years later, Tamar figured out that Judah was lying to her, so she disguised herself as a temple prostitute and seduced him. She became pregnant and had twins.

As we read this somewhat sordid account, we are perplexed about why it is included in the OT. I would suggest two reasons: first, one of the twins that Tamar bore, Perez, was an ancestor of David (Ruth 4:18–22; 1 Chron. 2:5–15; cf. also Matt. 1:3–16; Luke 3:23–33).[14] Second, as we look at the overall pattern of events, we gain an understanding of why God moved Jacob and his family to Egypt—to remove them from the increasing spiritual degradation of the country.

JOSEPH IN EGYPT

Read Genesis 39–41. Now the author returns to Joseph in Egypt. There are three phases of his life there. The first phase was his time as a slave in the house of Potiphar, the captain of Pharaoh's guard. God caused Joseph to prosper while he was working in this household, so Potiphar gave everything into his hands, worrying only about what he would have for his next meal. After some time, Potiphar's wife tried to seduce the young lad, who resisted her advances. Rejected, she accused him of attacking her, and Potiphar had Joseph put into prison.[15]

The second phase of Joseph's life in Egypt was the period he spent in prison. Even there he prospered and was put in charge of other prisoners. When Pharaoh's chief butler and baker were cast into prison, they had dreams, which Joseph interpreted for them as prophetic. The interpretations were correct, and as Joseph predicted, the butler was returned to his office but the baker was executed. The butler promptly forgot his helper.

Two years later, Pharaoh[16] had two dreams that paralleled each other. Pharaoh's dream interpreters were totally baffled, and he was frustrated. However, the butler finally remembered Joseph, who was cleaned up and brought out of the prison. Through God's guidance, Joseph interpreted the dreams as foretelling seven years of abundance followed by seven years of famine. He also gave advice on how to prepare the nation for these two events, and his advice was so sound that Pharaoh put him in charge of carrying out the preparations.

INTERPRETING DREAMS

Archaeologists have discovered Egyptian dream catalogs that show the process by which dream interpreters in the ANE normally worked. A person would tell the interpreter the contents of his dream. The interpreter would then look up the salient elements in the standard catalog (e.g., see *ANET*, 495). For the cases related in Genesis 40 and 41, apparently no catalog information was available; the people involved knew the dreams were significant, but they had no data to help them figure out the meaning.

JOSEPH MEETS HIS BROTHERS

The famine that hit Egypt also hit Canaan. Because of Joseph's work, Egypt had food, which led Jacob to send his sons to Egypt to buy grain. Benjamin, Jacob's youngest son, was kept at home. In his position as the Egyptian minister of agriculture, Joseph met and recognized his brothers. After twenty years of separation and in his Egyptian regalia, they did not recognize him. Recalling his dreams,

Read Genesis 42–45.

Joseph accused his brothers of being spies and set them up for a test. After they had been in prison for three days, he told them that he would send them home but would retain a hostage. If they were honest men, he said, they should go back and bring Benjamin to Egypt with them. Simeon was kept as the hostage, and the brothers returned home.[17] When they got home, they found their money in the grain bags with the grain, adding to their puzzlement and fear. Jacob refused to allow Benjamin to go, blaming the brothers for the loss of both Joseph and Simeon.

HITTITE DEER. A golden deer, showing the degree of technical metallurgical skill of the Hittites during the time of the patriarchs. This indicates that while the Hittites were centered in Anatolia (Turkey), they were not confined there, for deer like this have never resided there.

However, the famine was just as bad the following year, and the family had little choice but to return to Egypt. Judah now began to show positive leadership and offered himself as surety for his young half brother. With great misgivings, Jacob allowed Benjamin to go with his older brothers.[18] When they arrived, Joseph gave them red-carpet treatment, entertaining them in his house. They tried to return the money from the first trip, but Joseph assured them that he had the purchase money, and so the silver they found in the bags must have been from their God. During the festivities, Joseph showed overt favoritism to Benjamin, to the astonishment of the others. Then, when he sent them on their way, it was again with the money in their bags—as well as his personal cup in Benjamin's bag. Joseph allowed them to proceed some distance on their way home before he sent his steward after them. When the cup was found in Benjamin's bag, the brothers returned to Joseph fearing the worst.

Judah interceded on behalf of his brothers and offered himself in Benjamin's place. With this, Joseph was no longer able to maintain the charade. Sending his servants out of the room, he revealed himself to his brothers. He also revealed that there would

> When Judah offered himself in Benjamin's place, Joseph was no longer able to maintain the charade.

be five more years of famine, and he urged the family to move to Egypt. Pharaoh echoed this request, and a train of wagons took the brothers back to bring their father and the rest of their families to Egypt.

THE FAMINE

The fact that both Egypt and Canaan suffered famine suggests that it was divinely caused. Egyptian agricultural success is dependent on the flooding of the Nile River, which is a result of monsoon rainfall in central Africa. Agricultural success in Canaan, on the other hand, is dependent on rain that normally comes in from Europe via the Mediterranean Sea. The experience of Joseph stands in contrast to that of Abraham in Genesis 12, who went to Egypt because of a famine in Canaan.

INCUBATING A NATION

Read Genesis 46–50.

While the reunion of the estranged brothers is the obvious climax to the story, the writer of Genesis has a few loose ends to tie up, showing that there is much more to the account. We need to recall that this section relates "what became of" Jacob. In this sense, there are two key aspects: first, what became of Jacob personally, and second, what became of the line of Jacob, the descendants of Israel.

Jacob, personally, was finishing his spiritual pilgrimage. Once more he was about to leave the land, but the circumstances were much different from those related in chapter 28, when he was fleeing Esau. Now it was under God's direction, and God appeared to him before he left the land to give him an assurance that what he was doing was correct. So Jacob and his family, seventy strong, arrived in Egypt. Jacob and five of the brothers were introduced to Pharaoh and then moved to the land of Goshen.[19]

Chapters 48 and 49 present two scenes of blessing. The first is that of Joseph's sons, Ephraim and Manasseh. In the process, Jacob deliberately crossed his arms to bless the youngest, Ephraim, with his right hand. He also named Ephraim first. Joseph was upset, but Jacob assured him that what he had done was intentional. Both sons would be counted as heirs of Jacob, which apparently means that Joseph was receiving the birthright, that is, the double measure of the inheritance.

The second scene of blessing has Jacob calling all of his sons. When we look at the account, we note that all twelve sons are blessed (and here Joseph is addressed, not Ephraim and Manasseh). We also see that some of the "blessings" are far from positive. For example, Reuben was told he would lose his position of preeminence. Simeon and Levi were told that they would be dispersed throughout Israel. Since Jacob was telling each of his sons what would happen to them "in days to come" (Gen. 49:1), by the time we finish this section, we have a broad picture of tribal destinies as part of the nation.

For the audience at Mount Sinai, Jacob's blessing would have been climactic as they reached the end of this book that told of the nation's origins. The Israelites would understand that all the descendants of Jacob, regardless of which wife they were descended from, had a part of the national inheritance. They would also have anticipated that there would be different tribal futures, although there would have been a lot of discussion regarding what that all meant. Some points were obvious, such as the prediction that the Joseph tribes would grow tremendously (Gen. 49:22) or that the Messiah would come from Judah (v. 10). Others would be much more obscure and open to question—and in fact, in some respects are still obscure to us today.

After giving some final instructions, Jacob died, was embalmed, and was buried in the cave of Machpelah at Hebron, where Abraham and Isaac were buried (along with their wives). Joseph himself lived a long life, seeing his great-grandchildren. Before he died, he requested that his bones be carried with his people when they finally left Egypt sometime in the future. Apparently Joseph recognized how all of this fit together into God's promise to Abraham in Genesis 15 that after four hundred years his descendants would return to Canaan. Perhaps that was why Joseph could be so forgiving of his brothers, both when they came to buy grain and after Jacob's death. With this, the writer closes the book, and when the account picks up in Exodus, it is four centuries later.

INTERLUDE: JOB

Another carefully crafted book from an early period is the book of Job. Where to include it in our survey is problematic. First, Job was not an Israelite, so he really does not fit into our overall historical structure. Second, the dating of the book is debated. A number of its characteristics, including the archaic language, suggest that the book was written at an early date[20] and that Job himself lived at about the same time or shortly after the time of Abraham. We see described in the book a similar culture that counts wealth in terms of animals, and Job himself seems to have been seminomadic like Abraham. Furthermore, Job personally offered sacrifices on behalf of his family, serving as a patriarchal priest. With these details in

SEVENTY OR SEVENTY-FIVE?

Genesis 46:27 records that the members of Jacob's family, including the family of Joseph, totaled seventy, and this number is repeated in Exodus 1:5. In the NT, however, Stephen gives the number as "seventy-five in all" (Acts 7:14). Two solutions have been proposed. Because seventy-five is also the number that the Septuagint (LXX) has in both of the OT accounts, some have suggested that Stephen is merely quoting that Greek translation. There is still the question, however, of why the LXX has a different number in both places. The most common explanation is that the LXX omits Jacob and Joseph but includes Joseph's seven grandchildren (who are cited in 1 Chron. 7:14–15 and 20–25). It is argued that this reckoning parallels the Hebrew in Genesis 46:8–26, which omits Jacob, Joseph, and his two sons. Another possible explanation comes from Genesis 48:5–6. There Jacob tells Joseph that Ephraim and Manasseh would be listed as his sons, but "your offspring that have been born after them shall be yours; they shall be called by the names of their brothers in their inheritance" (NASB). We are not told how many other sons Joseph had, but it is not unreasonable to suggest that he may have had five more, bringing the total of the three generations (Jacob, his sons, and his grandsons) to seventy-five.

mind, we will view Job as a contemporary of Abraham's son or grandson and place his account here. If this setting is correct, it may suggest that the book of Job was part of the original canon that the nation of Israel took with it from Mount Sinai.[21]

Why was this account included in the canon? There seem to be three key reasons. First, the book of Job addresses a crucial question we all ask: Why do bad things happen to good people? As we follow the patriarchs, we find that while they are viewed as very human, they are also portrayed as "good people." So the question lurking in the back of the minds of the people listening to what Moses had to say about Abraham and his descendants would have been, If God chose our ancestors, why did they end up in slavery in Egypt? This question would have arisen especially in connection with the story of Joseph. The premise of Job is that much of what happens in this world involves issues far beyond moral cause and effect.[22]

These comments lead to the second reason. As the book of Job explores the question of why bad things happen to good people, it points out that there is a spiritual realm in which moral agents are involved in a struggle. We are introduced to a character there called Satan, who is presented as the one who attacked Job. Thus, we see that there is a personal source of evil in the world who is in rebellion against God.[23]

A third reason to include the book of Job in the canon would have been to show some of the traits of God. In Job the Israelites would see that God was not limited to the descendants of Abraham to find people who served Him. This truth would indicate that the mixed multitude that came out

IBEX. Probably the animal called a mountain goat in Job 39:1.

THE AUTHOR AND STRUCTURE OF THE BOOK OF JOB

The identity of the author of the book of Job has been lost in history. Based on the material we have, it seems likely that it was written by an observer of the discussion between Job and his friends and then was handed down through the generations. The author structured the material in an interesting way. As we have noted, Genesis uses a key term, *toledot,* as an outlining feature. Job uses what is called a frame story structure, which contains a poetic core framed by a prose setting. Beyond this, it seems to follow a pattern called *chiasmus,* in which the book works up to a midpoint, then reverses direction, addressing topics previously discussed in a somewhat mirror-imaging fashion. This is very clear in the narrative's introduction and conclusion. The chiastic structure of the poetic section is less clear but is demonstrated by Francis I. Andersen in *Job: An Introduction and Commentary* (Downers Grove, Ill.: InterVarsity, 1976), 20.

SATAN

Satan seems to be a title rather than a proper name. The Hebrew word is used in Job (also in Zech. 3:1–2) with the definite article, meaning "the adversary" (other names, such as Elohim, "God," can also occur with the definite article). The term here seems to point to a key spiritual being who is described in more detail later in the prophets (Isa. 14; Ezek. 28).[24] There we find that he is a fallen angel and seems at one time to have been the head of the angelic hierarchy but chose to rebel against God. As such, the title Adversary would be appropriate, and this title apparently assumed the qualities of a proper name. (This development should not be surprising, because most names in the OT are descriptive terms; e.g., Abraham means "father of a multitude.")

of Egypt could all be accepted, and it may well point to the acceptance of individuals and groups within the Promised Land, such as Rahab and the Gibeonites. It also demonstrated God's graciousness.

Why Job?

The book opens by introducing Job. The narrator sets the stage by showing Job's character and how he had been prospered by God. The scene then switches to the spiritual realm, where we read of a confrontation between God and Satan. Satan asserts that the only reason Job serves God is that he views God as his sugar daddy who protects him. In response, God allows Satan the opportunity to show that to be the case, and Job has to experience Satan's touch without knowing the reason why. At the end of this section, Job has lost everything except his wife (and she seems to have turned against him). His health has been taken from him, and he is in physical pain, sitting on a pile of ashes in mourning when his "friends" show up.

Read Job 1–2.

Debating Pain

The heart of the book of Job is this extended section of speeches. It is presented as a discussion, but for the most part the speakers are talking past each other. Job is in severe depression because he does not understand why he has such a sudden reversal of fortunes—and God does not seem to be listening. His "friends" assure him that there is a very simple reason. Since bad things happen as punishment for bad deeds, Job must have done something bad. If he will only confess his sin, God will forgive him and restore him. Job, of course, is willing to do so if he can only figure out what to confess.

Read Job 3–37.

God Intervenes

When the two sides have finally depleted their arguments, God appears and gives them a pop quiz. Its purpose is to show that humans really know very little about the physical realm. The conclusion is that they know even less about the spiritual realm, where the real answers to these issues lie. Job confesses his presumption, and God vindicates him before his friends. After this, Job receives back "twice as much as he had before" (42:10).

Read Job 38–42.

Evaluation

As a patriarchal figure, Job would have spoken clearly to the Israelites, which is probably why the book was included in the canon. The stories of Job and Joseph are parallel in that both suffered tremendously for no fault of their own, even though both would have admitted that they were not perfect. At a deeper level, this book would have served to warn the people that as God's chosen, they, like Job, would be subjected to tests as God continued to address the problems of sin and Satan. This brings us to our next chapter, where we see what happened to the descendants of Jacob in Egypt.

REVIEW QUESTIONS

1. How did Esau lose his birthright? How did he lose the blessing?

2. What is the difference between a birthright and a blessing?

3. Why did Jacob go to Haran (both the real and cover-up reasons)?

4. What happened to Jacob in Haran, and why did he stay there twenty years?

5. What is the significance of Dinah?

6. Why did Joseph not get along with his brothers?

7. What are the implications of the incident between Judah and Tamar?

8. What is the significance of Joseph in the biblical record?

9. Describe Joseph's reunion with his family.

6

CHAPTER

Let My People Go!

OVERVIEW

The Exodus is the key event of the OT. The writer skips over the four-hundred-year period when Jacob's descendants were in Egypt and picks up the story with the birth of Moses. He describes how God used Moses to deliver this mob of people out of bondage. This part of the story ends with the Israelites at Mount Sinai, where God establishes them as a full-fledged nation.

As we finished the book of Genesis, we noted that the nation of Israel had descended to Egypt in embryonic form and was left there to incubate for four hundred years. The twelve sons of Jacob had become the nucleus around which the nation would be developed (the twelve tribes). Now we will look at the hatching process, so to speak, which is described in the book of Exodus. These are now times that the original audience would have been personally familiar with—they had been there. And from our perspective, these are times for which we have firmer historical knowledge. The Exodus is the anchor point of the OT, both historically and theologically.

THE BACKGROUND TO THE EXODUS

Read Exodus 1.

To understand the context of the Exodus, we have to begin with Joseph. If our proposed dating is correct, Jacob moved to Egypt in approximately 1876 BCE, when Joseph was thirty-nine. Joseph died in about 1805 BCE under the reign of Amenemhet III (reigned 1840–1792 BCE), who is viewed as the last significant pharaoh of the Twelfth Dynasty and the Middle Kingdom.[1] Shortly after Joseph's death, Egypt entered a time of turmoil called the Second Intermediate Period, which lasted from about 1800 to about 1550 BCE. During this period, there were five dynasties, Thirteen through Seventeen, which did not reign successively (two or more dynasties claimed authority over different portions of the land at the same time). One of these, the Sixteenth (perhaps the Fifteenth also), was actually a dynasty of foreigners, a group of Semites called the Hyksos.

Records indicate that the Hyksos were especially disliked by the Egyptians over whom they reigned. Beginning about 1570, an Egyptian general named

SHEPHERDESS IN THE WILDERNESS. A scene perhaps similar to what Moses saw after he fled from Egypt to Midian, where he met his wife.

Kamose (or Kamoses)[2] began the process of driving out the Hyksos. This job was completed by his brother, Ahmoses I, who founded the Eighteenth Dynasty and the New Kingdom. He likely is the pharaoh who "did not know about Joseph" (Ex. 1:8), and his fear or hatred of the Hyksos led to the persecution of the Israelites, for they too were Semitic.

Ahmoses was followed by Amenhotep I and then Thutmoses (or Thutmose) I, Thutmoses II, and Thutmoses III. It is Thutmoses III who is of interest for our purposes, for he reigned for fifty-four years during the fifteenth century BCE. The length of his reign accommodates the forty years that Moses spent in exile. According to the Egyptian data, however, there is more to the story. Thutmoses III was not the legitimate son of his father, Thutmoses II, but was the son of a concubine. The wife of Thutmoses II was a woman named Hatshepsut, herself a daughter of Pharaoh (thus she married her brother, not an unusual occurrence).[3] She had no children herself but became the foster mother of Thutmoses III. She was also a very dominating woman who desired to be the pharaoh (and attempted to pass herself off as pharaoh c.1504–c. 1483). The Egyptian data indicate that she served as regent for Thutmoses III for the first seventeen years of his reign, after which there was a fairly sudden shift in power marked by noted changes in Egyptian policy and politics.

If my understanding is correct, she was just the type of woman who would defy the pharaoh and adopt a boy from an ethnic group from which he had decreed that all male children be put to death. The timing would also indicate that Amenhotep I (her grandfather) may have been the pharaoh who made that

> Hatshepsut was just the type of woman who would defy the pharaoh and adopt a boy from an ethnic group from which he had decreed that all male children be put to death.

HATSHEPSUT. The probable daughter of Pharaoh, who wanted to become the pharaoh herself. This statue shows her wearing a male goatee—propaganda to win her acceptance as the ruler of the land.

THUTMOSES III. Nephew and stepson of Hatshepsut, and probably the pharaoh during Moses' exile in Midian.

decree a year or two before his death in 1525 BCE.[4] It would then be especially ironic that she called the boy Moses, which means "son" in Egyptian. It is also likely that Hatshepsut later played the two boys (Moses and Thutmoses) against each other to maintain her position of strength.[5]

At the age of forty, Moses killed an Egyptian overseer and then fled the countryside. Throughout history, one of the sad realities has been that members of the aristocracy have had virtually unlimited privileges, especially when it has come to the lives of commoners. One would expect no repercussions to this act. However, Moses was an outsider—a Semite. Given that, one wonders if this event provided Thutmoses III with the leverage he needed to ensure that he got the throne. By this time, Hatshepsut would be getting older and perhaps was no longer able to maintain the balance she needed to keep her power. Indications are that by this time Thutmoses had also consolidated his leadership of the military.

As we continue our examination of the Egyptian data, we find that Thutmoses III died about 1450 BCE. His death would have led to God's calling of Moses, Moses' return, the year of the "plagues," and the Exodus in March–April of 1446 BCE under the reign of Amenhotep II. Here the data become even more interesting. Amenhotep II was not followed by his oldest son, but there is no record to explain what happened to him.[6] Even more interesting is the "Dream Stele" found at the base of the Sphinx. Erected by a younger son, Thutmoses IV, who *did* succeed Amenhotep, it relates how he apparently had not expected to be pharaoh but had a dream that told him he would be. Thus, we have a situation in which a pharaoh ruled long enough to account for the forty-year exile of Moses and whose son meets the criteria we would expect in the pharaoh of the Exodus, including having his oldest son die mysteriously. More than this, we also have a "daughter of Pharaoh" who would match the biblical record.[7] All of this suggests a match in terms of the dating of the Exodus.

THE CALL OF MOSES

Read Exodus 2–4.

The OT covers the four-hundred-year period in Egypt in a single chapter, Exodus 1. From the perspective of the biblical writer, not much significant happened

THE DREAM STELE

According to the text on the Sphinx (or Dream) Stele, Thutmoses IV had a dream in which the god embodied in the monument told him that, although he was not slated to sit on the throne, he would be made pharaoh if he cleaned the sand from around the paws of the Great Sphinx (*ANET*, 449). Presumably, Thutmoses did so. Soon his older brother died, and Thutmoses subsequently became pharaoh.

THE SPHINX. An image that predated Abraham and was partially buried in sand in the time of Moses. Thutmoses IV placed a stele between its paws stating that in response to a dream he cleaned away the sand and was made pharaoh.

during that period. There was a dynastic change, and the status of the Israelites slipped from guests to slaves. Meanwhile, their population grew, prompting an Egyptian backlash. This sets the stage for the birth of Moses.

Most of us are familiar with the account of the birth of Moses and how his mother managed to hide his existence. When we read the text carefully, we realize that she was aware of the daily routine of the daughter of Pharaoh and of her personality. The infant was placed in a basket amid the "bullrushes" or reeds, a shallow place away from the current. Miriam, Moses' older sister, stood watching, wondering what would happen. The daughter of Pharaoh chose to defy her father's decree and took the child to the palace. We have no idea about her moti-

MULTILINGUAL MOSES

Acts 7:22 (NASB) states that Moses was educated "in all the learning of the Egyptians." This means he would have learned to read Egyptian. He also would have learned Akkadian: we have uncovered a number of tablets from the ruins of Amarna, a city built by Akhenaton (Amenhotep IV), showing that during this time Egyptians used Akkadian, the international language of trade. Moses would not have learned to write Hebrew while in the palace; however, of the three languages, Hebrew would have been the easiest to learn (the other two used numerous symbols for syllables and words).

Evidence indicates that Hebrew or a related dialect may already have been a written language at this point. A number of graffiti-type inscriptions have been discovered in the Sinai and eastern Egypt in a script called "Proto-Sinaitic," which some scholars have identified as an early Semitic alphabet. (See William F. Albright, *Proto-Sinaitic Inscriptions and Their Decipherment* [Cambridge: Harvard University Press, 1969].) These inscriptions were apparently made by miners working turquoise and copper mines. They date from the time of Hatshepsut and Thutmoses III. So what we have here are writings from the time of Moses apparently inscribed by "commoners," if not slaves.

JETHRO OR REUEL?

It was not unusual for people in the ANE to have more than one name. The name Jethro means "abundance," while Reuel means "friend of God." The former may have been his original name, and the latter may have been given to him as an adult (compare Abram/Abraham).

vation, but if the woman was Hatshepsut, this act would seem to go along with her personality. Perhaps this was her way of getting back at her husband for fathering a son by a concubine.

The boy Moses grew up in the palace and in that situation undoubtedly received a fine education. Most likely he learned to read and write Egyptian, Akkadian, and Hebrew. Sometime after reaching adulthood, he began to think for himself, and he tried to intervene on behalf of his people. This resulted in the death of an Egyptian overseer, and Moses fled to the desert. There he met Jethro, also named Reuel.

Jethro was a priest of God—apparently the same God the Israelites served.[8] He was also a herder of sheep, and it was through his daughters and his flocks that he met Moses when the latter intervened on behalf of the daughters at the watering trough. Moses accepted an invitation to stay with Jethro and eventually married one of his seven daughters, Zipporah. Apparently Moses was now content in this second career and seemingly had no further thoughts about Egypt or his people.

But God had not forgotten them, as the text points out (Ex. 2:23–25). After the death of the pharaoh from whom Moses had fled (probably Thutmoses III), God met with Moses. This meeting did not occur immediately after the pharaoh's death. It would have to take place in a specific location, the mountain called either

BURNING BUSH. A bush at St. Catherine's monastery in the Sinai desert that tradition claims as the burning bush of Moses. This appears unlikely although it may be the same variety of plant.

Horeb or Sinai, and God waited until Moses was tending his flocks in that region. At that time, Moses noted a bush that was burning but was not being consumed. Deciding to investigate, he was confronted by a voice telling him to remove his sandals because he was on holy ground.

During the ensuing discussion, Moses learned that God intended to use him to get the Israelites out of Egypt. After the fiasco of his previous attempt to help the Israelites, Moses wanted no part of this, and he used every excuse he could think of to beg off. But God would not let him off the hook, and eventually Moses reluctantly agreed to go. In the process, however, we learn that his brother, Aaron, was provided as a mouthpiece for Moses.[9]

God also provided a sign to show that Moses was acting under divine authority: when the people had been delivered, they would worship at the same mountain. This sign would be an important lesson for the original audience that was at Mount Sinai receiving God's revelation. They would see that God was in control and intended them to be there. They would also see Moses in all of his humanity, a man who was in his current position, not because he wanted to be there, but because he was challenged by God.[10]

THE CONFRONTATIONS WITH PHARAOH

In addition to the sign of the return to Mount Sinai, God gave Moses several other signs to establish his position before both the people and Pharaoh. He was able to stick his hand inside his robe and have it come out leprous and then reverse the process. He was able also to cast down his staff and have it convert to a large snake and then revert back when he picked it up. With this, Moses began a series of confrontations with Pharaoh. We know them as the ten plagues.

Read Exodus 5–10.

The plague sequence struck a serious blow to the entire agricultural cycle of Egypt, which we have seen began with the rise of Sothis (Sirius) in June, signaling the coming flood of the Nile, and culminated the following spring at the time of the first Passover. As such, the plagues were also directed at the gods of Egypt, whose role was to ensure the agricultural prosperity of the country. However, matching specific plagues with specific gods is very difficult. Many of the gods were local in nature; thus multiple gods had multiple functions, and several merged over the centuries. The chart below is an attempt to show the pattern. It is interesting to note that the first four plagues harassed rather than produced serious long-term consequences. It was only after Pharaoh continued to resist that the plagues progressed from being a show of force to having serious consequences.

There seem to have been several purposes for these plagues. First and most obvious, they were signs to show the power of God so that Pharaoh would listen. However, the plagues were also chosen as direct challenges to the spiritual hierarchy of Egypt. As the chart indicates, each plague struck at a particular strength or venue of a key Egyptian god, pointing out that the gods of Egypt were unable to protect themselves, let alone the Egyptian people. Furthermore, the plagues were designed to promote an attitude of fear within the Egyptians so that when the Israelites left, they would not go empty-handed (Ex. 3:21–22). The Israelites' plundering of Egypt would be a form of recompense for the years of slavery.

THE PLAGUES AND THE GODS OF EGYPT

Plague	Purpose	Polemic
1. Nile turned to Blood (Ex. 7:14-25)	To show God's sovereignty over the Nile river, the source of Egypt's life and prosperity.	Osiris-(the Nile was his bloodstream). Khnum-guardian of the Nile.
2. Frogs (Ex. 8:1-15)	To show God's ability to produce life.	Heqt-fertility goddes, pictured as frog.
3. Gnats (Ex. 8:16-19)	To show God's control over all aspects of life. (Here the magicians could not copy.)	Geb-an earth god. Seth-god of cultivated plain.
4. Flies (Ex. 8:20-32)	To show God's control over the pests of life.	Sekhmet-bringer of plagues.
5. Cattle died (Ex. 9:1-7)	To show God's control over life and the agricultural realm.	Apis-bull of creator god, Ptah.
6. Boils (Ex. 9:8-12)	To show God's control over health.	Khonsu-healing god. Isis-goddess of healing.
7. Hail (Ex. 9:13-35)	To show God's control over the elements of nature.	Napri-goddess of grain.
8. Locusts (Ex. 10:1-20)	To show God's control over the agricultural realm.	Seth-god of cultivated plain.
9. Darkness (Ex. 10:21-29)	To show God's control over light, and thus over the entire cosmos.	Re, Amun, Aten, Horus, Amun-Re—any of several sun gods.
10. Death of firstborn (Ex. 11:1-12:36)	To show God's control over life and the house of Pharaoh.	Osiris-god of resurrection and deity of Pharaoh.

When we look at the nature of the plagues, it is clear that they took about a year to run their course. This shows that the Egyptians were dealing with a God who was patient and had staying power. Then, in connection with the last plague, the original audience was given a concrete reminder so that over the centuries their descendants would recall this event, which would become a focal point to their national and ethnic identity—the Passover. More than this, the Passover event would become the model for the ultimate sacrifice of the Messiah that God would send centuries later.

An additional difficult issue comes up in this confrontation: the hardening of Pharaoh's heart. The significance of this point has been debated by scholars for centuries, and we cannot resolve it here. We should note, however, that up through plague five, the text says either that Pharaoh "hardened his heart" (e.g., Ex. 8:15) or that his "heart was hardened" (e.g., 7:13 NASB). It is only in the description of plague six, the boils (Ex. 9:8–12), that we read that the Lord hardened Pharaoh's heart, although God anticipated that action (Ex. 4:21; 7:3). My suggestion would be that up to this point, Pharaoh was making his own decisions, which God foreknew. But then God took matters into His own hands to ensure that the sequence ran to the end, for one of the purposes of this sequence was to set up a model for the process of redemption in the tenth plague.

THE PASSOVER EVENT

The last "plague" is given special attention because it was so much more than just a plague. Rather, it was the foundation for a ritual that would become the religious *Read Exodus 11–13.*

foundation of Israel to this day. God told Moses that after this event, Pharaoh would let the people go. In preparation of this freedom, the people were to perform a ritual, which was then to be repeated annually as a reminder of God's work on behalf of His people.

The first Passover event began with the selection of a lamb. It was to be chosen on the tenth of the month of Nisan, the lunar month that begins the religious year for Israel. This lamb was to have no defects and might be either a sheep or a goat. Each family was to select a lamb unless the family was too

PASSOVER CELEBRATION. An event that remains a central focus of Jewish life and religion and is commemorated every year by Jews around the world. The celebration begins by recounting why that night is so important to their history.

LUNAR CALENDARS

Ancient Israel used two calendars, both of which were lunar. The religious calendar began with the spring equinox (when the length of day and night are almost equal). The first new moon after that day began the month of Nisan, also called Abib. Since the spring equinox falls around March 21, we usually equate Nisan with March–April. The political year began in the fall with the Feast of Ingathering or Tabernacles in the month of Tishri (September–October), the seventh month in the religious calendar. Today this civil new year is called Rosh Hashanah. Both new years are referred to in Exodus (12:2; 34:22).

These texts suggest that from the beginning of the nation there was a dual calendar, which we find confusing today. However, we do the same thing in a variety of ways in our own culture. We follow a calendar year that begins on January 1. We also follow a school year that begins around September 1. Different levels of government and many companies use a fiscal year that begins at various times; for the U.S. government, it is currently October 1. Some churches also observe a liturgical year, which does not have a "new year," but it begins either with Easter in Eastern churches, or with the first Sunday of Advent (near the end of November) in Western churches.

The spring festivals find typological fulfillment in the crucifixion of Jesus as the Messiah and in the founding of the church (this topic will be covered below, in chs. 19 and 20). Consequently, many scholars argue that there will be a yet-future typological fulfillment of the fall festivals in the second coming of Jesus, when his kingdom will be established on earth. These two roles of the Messiah may then provide some explanation for the two calendars.

small, in which case several neighbors were to share one. The reason is that there were to be no leftovers after it was cooked. The lamb was to be kept until the fourteenth day of the month of Nisan (the night of the full moon). At twilight the head of the family was to kill the lamb and save its blood. Some of the blood was to be painted on the door posts and lintel of the house. The lamb was then to be roasted whole (insuring that no bones were broken). With the lamb, the people were to eat bitter herbs. As God laid out this ritual, He made clear that it was to be performed annually to remind the people of their deliverance from Egypt.

> Any household that had blood on the doorposts was "passed over," and from that we get the name of the event.

Each member of the family was to be fully dressed and prepared for a journey as he or she ate. Previously, the Israelites had been told to request gold, silver, and jewelry from the Egyptians. Through God's intervention, the Egyptians acceded to the request. While we are not told specifically, we can safely assume that the Israelites were also all packed and ready for a rapid flight from Egypt.

After the Passover lamb had been eaten and the remnants burned, God passed through the land. He visited each household and "struck down" the firstborn of both man and beast (Ex. 12:29). However, any household that had blood on the doorposts was "passed over" (v. 27), and from that we get the name of the event. In these families there was no death—just the anticipation of an upcoming journey out of slavery.

Pharaoh lost his son, and with this loss, he finally broke. Nevertheless, it was God who told Moses and the people to leave.

PASSAGE OUT

It would take some time for a large number of people to gather out of their houses to join with their leader and to begin heading east. They camped at Etham, a spot otherwise unknown. Then they moved out, changing direction so that they arrived on the shores of the Red Sea, where they again camped. These events likely took about a week (the time of the period of unleavened bread). It gave time for Pharaoh's spies to observe that the people were "wandering around the land in confusion" (Ex. 14:3) and for him to gather his troops to pursue them.

Read Exodus 13–15.

One of the points of controversy concerning the Exodus relates to the path the newly released nation followed. Traditionally it has been thought that the nation traveled southeast to the shores of the Red Sea, where they camped until Pharaoh's army approached. As we read the text, we note that at that point Moses raised his staff, a strong wind arose out of the east, dividing the waters, and the people passed through. After the people had crossed, Moses stretched his staff over the sea again, the wind stopped, and the sea drowned the army. Clearly, this calls for a major dose of the "miraculous"—something that has been disputed.[11]

ARE THE NUMBERS TOO LARGE?

The question of the size of the Israelite population is difficult. The text states that there were 600,000 men. When we include the women and children, the number jumps to an estimate of between one and two million—a mind-boggling number. For this reason, a number of scholars reject it. Some of them simply blow it off. For example, John Bright says that the figure "is out of the question" and, without any justification, states: "The number that participated in the exodus was hardly more than a very few thousand" (*A History of Israel*, 4th ed. [Philadelphia: Westminster, 2000], 134).

Others argue that the Hebrew word *'eleph*, which is normally translated "thousand," does not really mean "thousand" but refers to some type of family or military grouping. According to this argument, for example, when Numbers 1:21 states that the tribe of Reuben numbered "forty-six thousand and five hundred," the meaning is that the tribe consisted of forty-six units, totaling five hundred men. Because there are several times that the word does seem to denote such a family or fighting unit (e.g., Judg. 6:15), this argument seems plausible on the surface.

However, there are three problems. First, the way the figures are written leads the reader to expect a numerical term. In the case of the tribe of Gad, for example, the text reads literally, "five and forty *'eleph* and six hundred and fifty" (Num. 1:25).

Second, when one adds up the tribal figures and compares them with the total for the nation, they add up only if the word is taken to mean "thousand." Adding the individual tribal totals in Numbers 1 gives 598 *'eleph* and 5,550, but the national total in verse 46 is given as 603 *'eleph* and 550 (on the other hand, if the word means "thousand," both figures come to 603,550).

Third, the reason the issue comes up to begin with is the problems that a large population group would face in the desert; for example, how were they able to eat? The Bible specifically states that this *was* a problem. In fact, it was only through direct intervention by God that the people were able to survive. This may be a case where our human rationality presents a hurdle in understanding how God operates. As such, it is best to accept the numbers as presented, even though we do not grasp how those figures can be accurate.

The key question is the location of the Red Sea episode. The Hebrew name translated "Red Sea" is *Yam Suph*. Because the word *suph* means "reed," it has been argued that this body of water could not have been what we call the Red Sea today. The argument is that reeds necessarily indicate a shallow body of water, probably fresh water. Many scholars have then moved the location of the crossing further north, either to the region of the Bitter Lakes, or even to a sand bar ridge along the Mediterranean Ocean. However, the term *Yam Suph* is used in a number of places in the OT, many of which clearly reflect what we today call the Red Sea. For example, in 1 Kings 9:26, Solomon is credited with building a fleet of "ships at Ezion Geber, which is near Elath in Edom, on the shore of the Red Sea" (Elath is modern Elat on the coast of the Gulf of Aqaba, and Edom corresponds to modern Jordan). In addition, a shallow body of water does not adequately account for the destruction of Pharaoh's chariots. Finally, the term *Yam Suph* can also mean "Sea of Ending."[12]

Several indications point to a crossing of the Gulf of Suez branch of the Red Sea at a location approximately 10 kilometers south-southwest of the modern city of Suez (see map). On the west side of the gulf, a point of land (called Ras el-'Adabiya) juts out into the bay. To the west and south of this point, a mountain

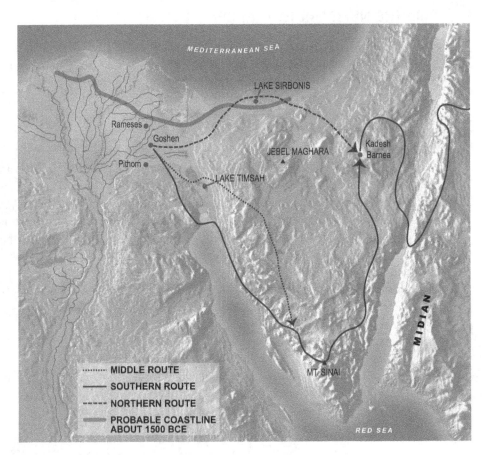

ROUTES OF THE EXODUS. Three possible routes for the Israelites' departure from Egypt. The Northern Route goes along the coastal highway, which God told them to avoid. (And the sandbars around "Lake Sirbonis" may not have existed at that time.) The Middle Route as proposed includes Lake Timsah, one of the Bitter Lakes, and ignores the text of passages such as Numbers 21:4; it is based on the interpretation of *Yam Suph* as "Reed Sea," which is understood to require a shallow, freshwater location. The traditional, most likely route is the Southern Route across the northern tip of the Red Sea.

ridge (Jebel 'Ataqa) comes close to the sea, blocking travel to the south. There are also ruins of a fortress (Heb. *migdol*) on this mountain ridge.[13] Thus, if the Israelites were camped in this region and an army approached from the north, they would have been trapped between the sea on the east, mountains to the south and west, and the army to the north.

Beneath the water of the gulf at this point is an underwater reef or ridge about 7 kilometers long that crosses the entire gulf (or did before the Suez Canal was dug). The average depth of this ridge is about 7 meters. Recent oceanographic studies indicate that under a moderate easterly wind that blew for several hours, the water would be driven back from this ridge, exposing it to the surface.[14] Moses lifted his staff and the wind blew all night (while the column of cloud stayed between the nation and the Egyptian pursuers).

Finally, on the east side of this ridge (about 3 kilometers from the coast) are springs which to this day are called the springs of Moses ('Ayum Musa). The text tells us that three days after the crossing, the people were upset because the water at Marah was bitter. So God sweetened the water for them. While it is unlikely that 'Ayum Musa is Marah (which according to the text was three days into the desert), we do see an ancient tradition that associated Moses with these springs.

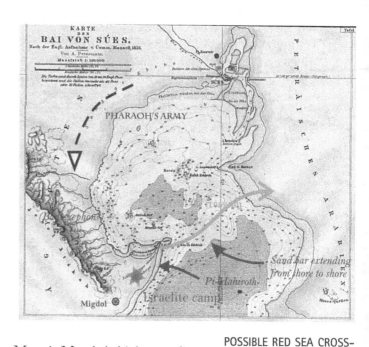

POSSIBLE RED SEA CROSS-ING. An 1856 map that shows the location of the underwater ridge over which the Israelites may have traveled, with the east wind God provided pushing the waters away. Possible locations for the landmarks given in the Exodus text have been super-imposed on this map.

That all of this correlates with the description in Exodus is strongly suggestive that Ras el-'Adabiya may be the location of the Red Sea crossing. Thus, my conclusion is that the Exodus is an actual historical event that took place the way the text tells us (see map).

LOOKING AHEAD

After the people of Israel crossed the sea, God told Moses to extend his staff again. This time the wind stopped and the waters returned rapidly to their normal state. With this, the people celebrated on the eastern shore. Moses wrote a song, and his sister Miriam and the women danced. But this was only the beginning of the journey. The goal for the mob that Moses brought out of Egypt was Sinai. There this mob would be converted to a nation.

REVIEW QUESTIONS

1. Why is the dating of the Exodus important?

2. How did we arrive at the date of the Exodus proposed in this chapter?

3. How were the birth and childhood of Moses unique, and how did they prepare him for the special task God had in mind?

4. Describe the confrontations between Moses and Pharaoh.

5. What is the significance of the Passover event?

6. Describe the first Passover.

7. Describe what happened at Yam Suph.

The Date of the Exodus

Even for those who affirm that there was a historical Exodus event, there is still debate regarding *when* it occurred.[15] Various dates have been suggested by researchers, but only two have been widely accepted: an early date in the middle of the fifteenth century BCE (the year 1446 is frequently offered) and a late date in the thirteenth century BCE (c. 1260). Perhaps the best way to understand these different views is to trace how the two proposed dates were derived. Traditionally scholars understood the Exodus event to have occurred during the fifteenth century, based on the OT genealogies and the lengths of kings' reigns. For example, Bishop James Ussher (1581–1656 CE) developed a chronology that put the Exodus at 1491 BCE. For these scholars, however, there was very little information linking the OT data to secular history.

Two events changed that. A French scholar named Jean François Champollion deciphered the Rosetta Stone in 1822 CE, allowing us to read Egyptian hieroglyphics. Then in 1835 the British scholar Henry Greswich Rawlinson set out to decipher the Behistun Inscription, leading eventually to a knowledge of Akkadian, and thus the ability to read the clay tablets that appeared through the excavations of Nineveh by Austin Layard beginning in 1847. With these two languages—hieroglyphics and Akkadian—scholars were able to develop historical ties with both Egyptian and Mesopotamian civilizations (and later with other civilizations through them).

STUDY 1: DECIPHERING LANGUAGES

The process of learning an unknown language is quite involved. The task is made easier if we have access to a text written in both the unknown language and one that is already understood. The Rosetta Stone was actually written in three languages: ancient Egyptian (hieroglyphs), later Egyptian (Coptic), and Greek. In the case of Akkadian, written in cuneiform script, the situation was more difficult. The key discovery was an inscription by Darius the Great found near Behistun, Persia, and carved in three different languages: Old Persian, Akkadian, and Elamite. All three languages used cuneiform, but the number and values of the individual signs were quite different for each. Henry Greswich Rawlinson had to lower himself by ropes to copy the text from the face of a high cliff. But to get to Akkadian (which was not deciphered until 1855), Rawlinson first had to decipher Old Persian and use parallel sources written in Greek. The stories of how some of the early archaeologists and linguists found the texts and cracked the languages rival the adventures of Indiana Jones. C. W. Ceram has written a good survey, *Gods, Graves, and Scholars,* rev. ed. (Toronto: Bantam Books, 1967).

For chronological information, we depend largely on the work of an Egyptian writer named Manetho, who produced a history of Egypt for Pharaoh Ptolemy II (reigned 285–246 BCE). This history, written in Greek and preserved fragmentarily in citations by other ancient writers, included a listing of all the pharaohs of Egypt, divided into thirty-one dynasties, before Alexander the Great's conquest.[16]

From Manetho's data, in 1849 Karl Richard Lepsius reached some conclusions regarding the date of the Exodus. According to Acts 7:23 and 30, Moses was about forty when he killed the Egyptian and fled into the desert. He was there about another forty years.[17] Since God appeared to Moses at the end of that forty-year exile and stated that the men who had sought his life were now dead (see Ex. 2:23; 4:19), it is generally concluded that the pharaoh from whom Moses fled must have reigned more than forty years. Two people from the general time frame (what we call the New Kingdom) fit this criterion: Thutmose(s) III and Rameses II, who were about 150 years apart. Lepsius also observed that the Israelites are said to have built the city of Rameses (Ex. 1:11).[18] As already noted, the traditional understanding of the OT chronology suggested a date in the fifteenth century BCE for the Exodus. Information from the newly deciphered hieroglyphic records placed Rameses' rule somewhere between 1600 and 1100 BCE, but probably around 1400 BCE. Based on those items, Lepsius concluded that the pharaoh from whom Moses fled was Rameses II. That would make Merneptah (Rameses' son and successor) the pharaoh of the Exodus. At the time of Lepsius, the data all fit together.

Over the past century and a half, however, further data have refined the dates of the Egyptian dynasties. It is now generally agreed that Rameses II ruled about 1290–1224 BCE, and Thutmose III about 1504–1450 BCE. After the Egyptian dates were adjusted, scholars had to make a choice—either change the pharaoh from whom Moses fled, or change the date of the Exodus. For a variety of reasons, many scholars agreed that Rameses II was the pharaoh Moses fled. Thus, his son Merneptah (reigned 1224–1214 BCE) must have been the pharaoh of the Exodus despite the fact that the data no longer fit.

STUDY 2: MERNEPTAH'S STELE

In fact, this conclusion has created problems. One of the most serious difficulties was the discovery of an inscription called the Merneptah stele. On this stone document, Merneptah (the son of Rameses) claims a victory over Israel in the land of Canaan, showing that during his reign Israel was already in the land of Canaan: "Israel is laid waste, his seed is not" (*ANET,* 378). Thus, Merneptah could not have been the pharaoh of the Exodus, for that identification does not leave room for the Exodus, the forty years in the desert, and the five to ten years of conquest during his reign. For this reason, many scholars have suggested that the pharaoh Moses met on his return to Egypt was Rameses, the same one from whom he had fled about forty years earlier. The text, however, specifically says that the men who wanted to kill Moses (including pharaoh, according to Ex. 2:15) had died (Ex. 4:19). Disregarding that contradiction, there is still not enough time for all the events. Even if Moses had fled during the first year of Rameses' reign (1290 BCE), the Exodus would have taken place about 1250 BCE; and after the forty years of wandering, the conquest would have begun about 1210 BCE—ten or more years *after* Merneptah claims the Israelites were already settled in the land.

The question then is, does this fit the rest of the data? The answer lies in a correlation between the biblical record and Akkadian records.

The key historical anchor for the OT record is the Assyrian Eponym Lists, which record the years of the Assyrian kings, each year denoted by the name of a key official.[19] In addition, important events occurring during the year are recorded. One of these events was a solar eclipse that can be dated to June 15, 763 BCE. Another event was the battle of Qarqar, involving King Ahab of Israel and Shalmaneser III of Assyria (see ch. 13, below). Assyrian records indicate that it occurred exactly ninety years before the eclipse, thus in 853 BCE. A third event involving an Israelite king is shown on a basalt monument called the Black Obelisk, which shows King Jehu of Israel giving tribute to Shalmaneser III in the eighteenth year of the latter's reign, that is, 841 BCE.[20]

STUDY 3: THE HEBREW CALENDAR

Two factors affect the dating of OT events. Israel, which used a different calendar than we do, had both a religious new year in the spring (marked by the Passover) and a civil new year in the fall (marked by Rosh Hashanah). In addition, the way the kings counted the time between their coronation and the next new year varied. Sometimes the coronation counted as the first year; at other times, the first full year counted as the first year. (See Edwin R. Thiele, *The Mysterious Numbers of the Hebrew Kings*, 3rd ed. [Grand Rapids: Zondervan, 1983].)

Putting these three items together and working through the biblical chronologies, we have a solid chain back to the division of the nation of Israel into the northern and southern kingdoms in 931 BCE. This means that Solomon took the throne in 971 BCE. When we turn to 1 Kings 6:1, we find that Solomon began to build the temple in the fourth year of his reign—*480 years after the Exodus*. The fourth year of Solomon's reign would be 967 or 966 BCE, probably the latter. If the temple was begun in 966, then the Exodus took place in 1446 BCE.[21]

MERNEPTAH STELE. A stone inscription that shows that during the reign of Merneptah of Egypt (c. 1230 BCE), Israel was already well established in the land of Canaan.

STUDY 4: FORTY YEARS

According to 1 Kings 6:1, Solomon began to build the temple in the 480th year after the Exodus. Since the construction of the temple can be dated firmly to the middle of the tenth century BCE, the Exodus must have taken place in the fifteenth century. Some scholars, however, argue that "forty years" was a conventional way of expressing the length of a generation (or more generally, a long period of time). So it is maintained that 1 Kings 6:1 refers to a period of twelve generations, and since a generation was really only about twenty-five years long, the time between the Exodus and the building of the temple was about three hundred years. This calculation would put the Exodus at about 1260 BCE and the conquest at about 1230 BCE, which in turn would place Israel in the land about ten years prior to Merneptah.

There are three problems with this view. The text does not talk about generations, but about years. The OT views a generation as a period of forty years, as shown by the desert experience, where God told the people they would wander for forty years until that generation died. (Even today we tend to think of a generation as consisting of forty years; e.g., the media marked the transition from the Second World War generation to the Baby Boom generation during the 1990s.) And in the book of Judges, we run into further complications if we try to squeeze all the events recorded in that book into a period of about 150 years.

When we compare these facts with archaeological data from Palestine,[22] we can be fairly confident about the date of the Exodus. While 1446 BCE may not be the exact date, it is likely within a couple of years of the event. In some respects, this is one of the most solidly dated events we have from the ANE.

CHAPTER

Making a Nation Out of a Mob

OVERVIEW

At Mount Sinai, God gave the Israelites an organizational structure through Moses. Commonly called "the law," this was in reality a socioeconomic-judicial-political-religious system that covered all areas of relationship within the nation. In addition, God provided an organized religion for the first time, giving the nation a tabernacle, a sacrificial system, a priesthood, and a religious calendar.

STUDY GOALS

▶ Evaluate the Old Testament law as a covenant.

▶ Evaluate the Old Testament law as a legal system.

▶ Evaluate the Old Testament law as a socioeconomic-judicial-political-religious system.

▶ Trace the events of the year at Sinai.

▶ Review the sacrificial system.

▶ Review the national festivals.

The book of Exodus tells us that the group that came up out of Egypt was a mixed multitude (Ex. 12:38). This description suggests that a number of Egyptians came up with them, an inference supported by reports of later events (see Lev. 24:10). It is likely that other non-Egyptians who had also been enslaved took advantage of this opportunity to leave. This mixture of ethnic, cultural, and religious backgrounds would prove to be problematic over the next several centuries. But first, the original audience had to understand what God expected of them.

When the Israelites left Egypt, they had no real national structure. The reason was simple. When they had gone to Egypt, they had been merely a large extended family. While in that country, they had lived under Egyptian law and had been part of the Egyptian economy and social structure. Although they had their own cultural and religious practices, it is likely they had also absorbed ideas and practices from those around them. When they left, they were joined by non-Israelites. That mixed multitude took their different ideas and practices with them.

At Sinai, that mixed multitude needed to be molded into a national entity in preparation for the time when God would plant them in the land promised to Abraham. The rest of Exodus and the whole of Leviticus describe this process, which consisted in giving the people a socioeconomic-judicial-political-religious system. The material in these books is sizable and somewhat obscure, but an overview of Israel's initial organization is critical for our understanding of what happens later.

MARAH. The oasis today called Marah, which may likely be where the bitter waters were made sweet.

GOD VISITS THE NATION AT SINAI

Read Exodus 16–19.

At the end of Exodus 15, we left the Israelites engaged in a celebration that culminated in a victory song from Moses and a dance led by Miriam. From the shore of Yam Suph, and led by the cloud of God's glory, they began the march to Mount Sinai, where God had told Moses to bring the people. We are given only a few incidents from the trip. We are told of how God gave the people manna, quail, and water. We also read of the attack by the Amalekites and how Joshua led the quickly formed Israelite army to pursue them.[1] After three months of journeying, the nation arrived at Sinai just as God had instructed Moses two years earlier.

THE MENU: ALWAYS MANNA, SOMETIMES QUAIL

We have already noted (ch. 1) that the word *manna* derives from the Israelites' question "What is it?" This manna had special characteristics often overlooked in discussions. A basic description of the material is given in Exodus 16:31. Beyond this, we are told that it appeared early in the morning as a residue left by the dew. However, it appeared only Sunday through Friday; on Saturday (the Sabbath) there was no manna. The manna lasted only one day and could not be stored for future use—except on Friday, when the people received a double amount that lasted through Saturday. This process continued throughout the entire time the people were in the desert (forty years) and stopped only after they crossed the Jordan River and entered the Promised Land (Josh. 5:12). All of this serves to remind us that the manna was a special provision of God, just as the people were reminded daily of their need to trust in Him.

The nature of the quail provision is not clear to us. According to Exodus 16:13, quail was given at the same time as the manna. In Numbers 11:31–34, however, this event appears to have taken place after the Israelites left Kadesh Barnea, more than a year later. Many commentators seem to suggest that the manna was constant throughout the time of journeying while the quail was intermittent, but this is not evident from the text. Most of the later references to God's provision focus on the manna.

Once there, God had Moses tell the people to cleanse themselves in preparation for a visit from God. As we noted in chapter 1, when the big day arrived, the people were frightened out of their wits (Ex. 20:18). As a result, they asked Moses to act as an intermediary for the rest of God's revelation. Moses agreed to do so, and the content of that revelation is the threefold book we call Genesis, Exodus, and Leviticus.

GOD'S COVENANT

Beginning with Exodus 20, we find many different commands given to the people of Israel. Collectively, they are often called "the Law." These commands have created much discussion among Christians, who ask whether they are obligated to "keep the Law."[2] Several issues must be made clear if we wish to understand this material. First, what we are looking at here is a covenant, that is, a "treaty." Second, the word that is most commonly used to describe this section of the OT is *Torah*, which means "teaching." And third, this entire section is predicated on something God has already done.

Read Exodus 20:1–21; 24:1–18.

The Law as Covenant

In a number of passages, we see what Moses was writing described as a *covenant* (e.g., Ex. 24:7–8; 31:16; Lev. 24:8; the point is emphasized again in Deut. 5:2, where Moses reiterates the covenant). So what is a covenant? Basically, it is a formal agreement between two parties, either nations or individuals. Thus, it would be similar to what we know today as a treaty. On a personal level, a marriage is a covenant. Because of its formal nature, in Bible times there was normally a ceremony signifying the ratification of the covenant. An animal sacrifice, and thus the shedding of blood, was often part of the ritual, showing the seriousness of the relationship (see again Ex. 24:8).

Several scholars have analyzed international treaties from the third millennium to the middle of the first millennium BCE and have observed that there were two standard types: parity treaties and suzerain-vassal treaties. Both of these had standard formal structures that differed for different periods of history.[3] Based on this knowledge, it is commonly accepted that what we are looking at here is a suzerain-vassal covenant or treaty. God is setting Himself up as the suzerain or sovereign exercising political control over the nation, the vassal. In this light, the Law expresses a national relationship between Israel and its political leader.

The last part of this section tells how the nation ratified the covenant (Ex. 24:3) as Moses and seventy-three other leaders of the nation went up on the mountain with God. They had a celebratory dinner and offered sacrifices. After the sacrifices, Moses told the people, "This is the blood of the covenant that the LORD has made with you in accordance with all these words" (24:8).

HAMMURABI'S CODE. A code of law established by King Hammurabi of Babylon prior to 2000 BCE, predating Moses by several centuries. It was almost entirely case studies in contrast to the apodictic law of the Ten Commandments, and it did not show the treaty structure.

The Law as Teaching

The Hebrew word translated "law" is *torah*, which comes from a verb meaning "to teach, instruct." This would suggest that the section we call "the Law" is not really a law as we think of it, but a teaching (although there are certainly legal aspects to it). The heart of the Torah is a list of ten items that we call the Ten Commandments (literally, "the ten words"). When we look more carefully at the treaty structure, we find that they are essentially ten general subject areas that are then amplified with examples or case studies. The purpose of these was to teach the nation how to live within the structure of the covenant.

> The section we call "the Law" is not really a law as we usually think of it, but a teaching.

Another way of expressing this concept would be to say that the commandments showed the people how to have proper relationships. When we looked at the Fall, we noted the focus on broken relationships and the subsequent failures in life as a result. Now the nation was being given instructions, showing the people how to live in a right relationship not only with God but also with one another. These two areas of relationship became the two major categories encompassing the entire teaching. Four of the commandments address the people's relationship with God, and six address their relationship with others within the covenant community.

We should also note that scholars divide ANE law into two categories—*apodictic* and *casuistic*. The ten words fall into the apodictic category; that is, they are declarations of God based on His authority as the suzerain. They are not philosophically reasoned responses. For example, God does not expound on murder by saying something like this: "Because the willful, unlawful taking of another person's life shows a devaluation of human life and is harmful to the community, therefore, such an act is subject to punishment by the state." Rather, God declares, "You shall not murder." The reason is simply that God said so.

After the ten general instructions are listed, God gives Moses a long series of case studies (casuistic laws), that is, examples of how each basic principle or teaching might apply to daily life. According to the rabbis, there are more than six hundred of these. One of our mistakes is that we get hung up on the case studies, the illustrations of basic principles, when we should focus on understanding the basic principles and applying them to our current culture and situation.

The Law Based on What God Had Done

The third key point that must be kept in mind is that the Law did not establish a relationship between God and the people. We have already observed how the original audience had been given the entire prehistory of the nation, which made clear that the relationship had been established initially with Abraham. It had been reinforced through the blessing line and amplified to the entire people when Jacob blessed *all* of his sons. It was verified by the Exodus. Now God was giving the people instructions on how to live *within* the relationship.

> Keeping the law did not *establish* a relationship between God and His people; it provided instructions on how to live *within* the relationship.

This point is demonstrated when we look at the overall passage. The Ten Commandments begin with the declaration, "I am the LORD your God, who brought you out of Egypt, out of the land of slavery" (Ex. 20:2). Thus, there is an implied cause-and-effect relationship between this declaration and the ten words. Because God delivered the nation from Egypt, the people were to respond by heeding the commandments.

The principle is further demonstrated when we note that there is no provision for revoking the covenant. The people may be obedient within the covenant and prosper. Or they may be disobedient within the covenant and suffer. At this point, God merely indicates the good things that will come if they are obedient. Later we will find warnings of the consequences of disobedience. However, these never include being cast away. There is also a note of caution in that God warns the people that the upcoming conquest will not be a one-time event. It will take several generations to drive out the inhabitants of the land so that the land will not become fallow until they have increased enough to fully occupy it. Implied in this caution would seem to be a challenge to win the inhabitants of the land to YHWH.

THE LAW AS A SOCIOECONOMIC-JUDICIAL-POLITICAL-RELIGIOUS SYSTEM

Read Exodus 20:22–23:33; 25:1–31:18; Leviticus 25–27.

To bring out the all-encompassing nature of the OT law, we can say that it is a socioeconomic-judicial-political-religious system. When we start looking at the specifics—that is, the casuistic (or case study) laws—we see how they covered all aspects of the Israelite culture. Reading through the material, we find many things that seem strange to us because we are looking across a wide cultural gap between a simple agrarian society and our postindustrial society that spans approximately 3,500 years. We also find that the bulk of the material focuses on the religious aspects.

But as we think about it, this makes sense. For the most part, the culture of the Israelite nation was that of its ancestors, ultimately dating back to the earliest history of humankind. However, up to this point they had never had a God-directed religious system. More than this, the nation was being formed to serve a special function—it was to be the national intermediary between humankind and God: a kingdom of priests (Ex. 19:6). As such, the people were to demonstrate both proper worship and special social functions and mores. To this end, God gave them new standards designed to raise the people's sensitivities to both God and others. The following are but a few highlights of that system.

The Law as a Socioeconomic System

As a socioeconomic system, the Law served both to put restrictions on greed and to provide a safety net for the disadvantaged. Israel would be an agricultural society, and the land God was giving them would be *the* source of wealth. As such, the land could not be sold (Lev. 25:8–55). Rather, it could be leased, with the lease lasting up to forty-nine years. At that point, the Jubilee year, the land reverted to the family that had originally received it from God after the conquest. In addition to retaining the source of wealth within the family, this practice served to remind the people from whom they had received the land in the first place.

Everyone was to depend on God. To encourage such dependence, every seventh year the people were to refrain from sowing crops, a custom that obliged the people to trust God to meet their needs. This seventh or Sabbath year was also a

---

GENOCIDE AS JUDGMENT

One of the tension points we find in the biblical narrative is the question of the destruction of all the inhabitants of Canaan. From our perspective, this amounts to genocide, and we find it reprehensible. When we step back from the situation, however, we find that the issue is not so black-and-white. We see that there is a principle of divine judgment in which Israel is to be the instrument of a just and righteous God. We also find cases in which Canaanites, who in general were condemned to death, were not only spared execution but absorbed into the nation. Later in Scripture we encounter three specific cases: the Gibeonites, Rahab and her family, and Ruth (see chs. 9 and 10, below).

time when the poor (usually understood as the widow, orphan, or stranger) would be able to harvest from whatever grew "voluntarily," whether in the field or in the orchard (Lev. 25:1–7).

Ancient Israel was not a leveraged society like ours. Usually people borrowed money only in extremely adverse circumstances. As such, it was the poor who had to do so. Consequently, money was to be loaned to poor people generously and without interest (Ex. 22:25).

Later these laws would be amplified to give further specifics. For example, farmers were told to allow for gleaners to go through their fields after the harvest to gather produce that had been missed (Deut. 24:19–22). Also there was provision for destitute people to "sell" themselves into indentured servitude for a period of six years (Ex. 21:1–11).

All in all, the system God laid out for the nation represented an advance over the nations around them.[4] There was allowance for the skilled and ambitious to get ahead, but there was also a safety net for those who met adversity. While there was an understanding that those who failed to work could anticipate poverty (a point stressed later in the book of Proverbs), the primary function of this part of the Law was to ensure that everyone had a fair chance.

The Law as a Judicial-Political System

The original political organization of the nation of Israel is not clear. On the way to Sinai, Moses appointed leaders of tens, fifties, hundreds, and thousands (Ex. 18:21). Once they were settled in the land, it appears that leadership was local, organized around the town or community. The elders of the city and town were the primary leadership there, but we are never told what constituted an "elder."

At Mount Sinai we find evidence of some type of *national* leadership as shown by the seventy elders who met with Moses, Aaron, Nadab, and Abihu on Mount Sinai for the ratification of the covenant.[5] After the nation settled in the land, we find little evidence regarding the political situation. It is clear there was no king until Saul, and the book of Judges observes that, as a result, everyone did what he or she wished. The judges, as we will see, were mostly regional, but they usually worked with the leaders of several tribes at once.

PUNISHMENT TO FIT THE CRIME

The OT carefully distinguishes between manslaughter (involuntary killing) and murder. The punishment in the former case is that the guilty party had to remain at the city of refuge until the high priest died. In many respects, this provision was also meant to protect him from the avenger (or kinsman redeemer). The punishment for murder was execution by stoning. In the case of murder, there was no sanctuary, whether in the city of refuge or even, later on, in the temple.

Overall, the men of the nation were directed to meet three times a year. While the primary focus of these meetings was worship, it would seem likely these meetings also served to promote national unity. In this context, I would suggest that they were political. Statutes that tie the high priest into legal issues hint at this. For example, in the case of manslaughter, the person involved would flee to a city of refuge (Num. 35:6–32). There he would be examined by the leadership, and if found to be truly guilty of only manslaughter, he would remain there until the high priest died.

The legal system was concerned with justice. A number of the case studies address how the people were to exercise justice. Interestingly, the Law also warned against partiality, whether in favor of the poor or of the rich (see Ex. 23:3; Lev. 19:15). As we look at the legal system, we find that the Law set limits to what punishment might be inflicted for a given crime. Here again, what God gave Israel was a step above the cultures around it.[6] These limits are the thrust of the notorious "eye for eye" passage in its context (Ex. 21:24). The subject is personal injury, and the limits of the punishments are dictated by the extent of the injury. However, these do not seem to be mandated punishments. Lesser penalties could be decreed, apparently at the discretion (and mercy) of the victim.[7]

> The Law warned against partiality, whether in favor of the poor or of the rich.

The Law as a Religious System

The bulk of the last half of Exodus and the book of Leviticus set forth instructions for worship. In the process, several changes were made to the Israelite culture. Before this time, sacrifices were performed by the family leader. There were no priests and no central place of worship, which suggests that worship was individual, perhaps sporadic, and certainly unguided. To change this, Moses was given instructions for a tabernacle, a priesthood, a sacrificial system, and a liturgical calendar. Before these directions were implemented, however, trouble arose in the camp.

THE PEOPLE GROW IMPATIENT

While Moses was on the mountain receiving instructions from God, the people grew restless. He had gone up the mountain several times, and the people had already ratified the covenant (Ex. 24). After this ratification, Moses started getting the more detailed directions relating to the tabernacle. However, this time Moses was gone too long for the people. They went to Aaron and asked for "gods"[8] to lead them because they didn't know what had happened to Moses (Ex. 32:1).

Aaron accommodated the people by molding a calf from the gold they contributed. When it was completed (highlighting how long Moses was up on the mountain), the people held a celebration that turned into an orgy. After Moses interceded on their behalf, God sent him back down. When Moses saw what the people were doing, however, he smashed the tablets on which the commands were written;[9] he then ordered the golden calf burned and ground up, and the metallic powder spread on their drinking water.

The people repented after this chastisement, but the incident illustrates how the nation was not united in its understanding and worship of God. These divisions would be passed on to future generations and would crop up again and again. In fact, this pattern would be one of the distinguishing characteristics of the people of Israel for at least a thousand years.

CALF AND SHRINE. A calf image and shrine excavated in Ashkelon that illustrates the type of image Aaron made when Moses stayed on the mountain a long time. This seems to have been a common image in the Palestine-Egypt region.

Read Exodus 32–34.

GOD'S TABERNACLE

The first of these two Scripture passages lays out the guidelines for the tabernacle. The second describes the construction process and tells us that it was built according to plan. Essentially the tabernacle was a tent within a curtained courtyard. The entire structure was designed to be portable so that the people could take it along with them. There is also the possibility that the structure was designed to be moved to different locations within the land.[10]

The tabernacle had three sections. First was the courtyard, approximately 150 by 75 feet, which was defined by the curtains that hung on wooden frames. Oriented with the long axis pointing east-west, it had an entrance gateway on the east side. In addition to the inner tent, the courtyard contained a bronze (or bronze-

Read Exodus 25–31; 35–40.

ACACIA TREE. The kind of tree, which grows in the Negev desert and the Sinai peninsula, that provided sturdy wood for the tabernacle and ark of the covenant. (Date palms, shown in the background have wood that is too fibrous to use for durable construction.)

covered wood) altar for the animal sacrifices (Ex. 27:1–8) and a bronze basin for washing the hands and feet of the priests (30:17–21).

Beyond the altar and basin was the actual tent of the tabernacle, which was approximately 15 by 30 feet.[11] It too was made of wooden frames and curtains woven from linen, covered with goat hair cloth and animal skins. This structure was divided into two sections. The outer (or front) section was called the Holy Place. Here the Israelites had three items: a table that held the bread of the Presence, an incense altar, and the lampstand. The first two symbolized the nation before God. The twelve loaves of the bread of the Presence represented the Israelites' presence before God (Ex. 25:30), and the incense offered in the morning and evening symbolized their prayers. The lampstand seems to have served a practical purpose of providing light within the closed tent.

The final portion of the tabernacle was the Holy of Holies. This room held only the ark of the covenant. The ark was basically a gold-covered wooden box with rings on the sides to allow it to be carried. It was approximately 3-3/4 by 2-1/4 by 2-1/4 feet in size. On top of the ark was a lid called the "atonement cover" (Ex. 25:17–22; KJV, "mercy seat"). Here were two cherubim with their wings stretched across the top, meeting in the middle. This was the place where God met with the nation, and thus it would have been the focal point of the *Shekinah*, the manifestation of God's glory.[12] No one was allowed into the Holy of Holies except the high priest on the Day of Atonement—and then only after extensive ritual cleansing.

THE SACRIFICIAL SYSTEM

Read Leviticus 1–7.

Most of us, when we think of the sacrificial system, think of offerings to atone for sin. While these offerings were part of it, in reality the system was much more complex.[13] Sacrifices were performed also to show consecration or to give thanks to God. While the fundamental concept of the sacrificial system in its entirety was "atonement," this notion seemed to carry several nuances in the general context of the OT law. The basic idea of atonement is a harmonious relationship brought about by bridging a gap between two parties.[14] There seem to have been three general categories of offerings. We will look at them in the order they are presented in the text.[15]

Consecratory Offerings

Consecratory offerings served the function of dedicating a person or a thing to God. While the text states that such an offering will "make atonement for him" (Lev. 1:4), the emphasis seems to be on the fact that the burnt offering will provide "an aroma pleasing to the LORD" (1:9, 13, 17). This is key when we see the pattern of usage for these sacrifices. They were performed at the time of the coronation of a king, the anointing of a high priest, and the dedication of the tabernacle and temple. They were also used before an army went into battle or at the birth of a child.

The basic consecratory sacrifice was the burnt offering, when the entire sacrificial animal was burned on the altar. The animal used for a burnt offering depended on the wealth of the person. It could range from a bull or an ox for a rich person to a dove for a very poor person. A burnt offering was sacrificed daily for the nation as a daily reminder of its consecration to God. In this case, the offering was a male lamb.

In addition to the burnt offering, two optional gifts could be made as part of the consecratory offering. The first was the cereal offering (Lev. 2; 6:14–23), which could accompany burnt offerings, peace offerings, and others. It consisted of a mixture of flour and oil (and in some cases frankincense). Some of the cereal offerings went to the priests. The second was the drink offering (Ex. 29:40–41; Lev. 23:13; et al.). This was an offering of wine that accompanied both burnt offerings and peace offerings. The amount prescribed was approximately a liter. It was poured out on the fire and burnt.

Expiatory Offerings

Expiation deals with sin. There are three basic offenses: violation of the rights of others where restitution is possible, sin where restitution is not possible, and high-handed sin. For the latter category, there was no sacrifice (see Num. 15:30–31); in such a case, the normal consequence was execution. For the other two, there were similar but distinct expiatory offerings.

For high-handed sin, there was no sacrifice.

Guilt offerings (Lev. 5:14–6:7; 7:1–7). This sacrifice involved a situation in which someone had been denied his rightful due and restitution was possible. In essence, then, it addressed issues of property. It was a reparation as well as an acknowledgment that the offerer had defrauded his countryman. He admitted his guilt by repaying (with a "fine" amounting to 20 percent or more of the value of the stolen item) and then brought the guilt offering. The guilt offering had to be a ram.

Sin offerings (Lev. 4:1–35; 6:24–30). Like a guilt offering, a sin offering addressed a situation in which the rights of others had been denied (e.g., manslaughter or seducing an unmarried woman). In such cases, no restitution was possible. As in the case of the burnt offering, the required animal varied with the offender's socioeconomic status. Again, it ranged from a bullock (or ox) down to

MODEL OF THE TABERNACLE. A model built by Alac Garrard, based on the description in the book of Exodus.

a turtledove. On the Day of Atonement (Yom Kippur), the high priest offered a bull on behalf of the entire nation (after he offered a bull for himself).

In the case of the consecratory and expiatory offerings, the person bringing the sacrifice placed his hand on the animal to identify with it as he slew it. The priest collected the blood, sprinkled some around the altar and, on the Day of Atonement, took some into the Holy of Holies. The remainder of the blood was drained out at the base of the altar. The fatty portions (e.g., the kidneys and their fat) were burned. In the case of the bull for the nation or priest, the rest of the carcass was disposed of outside of the camp. The normal procedure, however, was to give the main portion of the body to the priests for food.

Communal Offerings

The third category of sacrifices involved a variety of offerings that apparently did not necessarily have to be done in the central sanctuary (see Deut. 12:10–32, esp. vv. 21–27). In general, they were celebrations expressing gratitude to God. They are called communal sacrifices because they were eaten by the community as a whole (or at least by close friends and family). In the process, the fatty portion was offered to God, but the rest was eaten by the offerer and friends. The three differ solely in what they celebrated.

> Communal offerings were celebrations expressing gratitude to God.

Peace offerings (Lev. 3; 7:11–36). The term comes from the Hebrew word *shalom* ("peace, welfare"). It was usually an offering that reflected a state of celebration because things were going well. For example, at the end of a good harvest, a person might decide to have a celebration to give thanks to God. Or he might decide to give a celebration to thank God for a new child or for a wedding.

THE SACRIFICIAL SYSTEM

We can recognize two purposes for the sacrificial system. The first was to show that sin was a serious business that required the shedding of blood. From our perspective today, we recognize that the sacrificial system also pointed to Jesus Christ as the perfect sacrifice. We see this at His baptism, when John the Baptist declares, "Look, the Lamb of God, who takes away the sin of the world!" (John 1:29). The writer to the Hebrews draws a very strong analogy (typology) between the OT sacrifices and the work of Christ (Heb. 9–10). In 9:12 he states that Jesus "did not enter by means of the blood of goats and calves; but he entered the Most Holy Place once for all by his own blood." He also notes in 10:4 that "it is impossible for the blood of bulls and goats to take away sins."

The second purpose was to unite the community in worship of God. In this respect, the time of sacrifice would almost be "party time." However, these "parties" would be celebrations of God. He would be seen as the God of grace and mercy who forgives (expiatory) or who deserves our devotion (consecratory) or who intervenes on our behalf (communal).

Votive offerings (Lev. 7:16–17; 22:17–20). This term denotes the aftermath of a vow or promise. The offerer has been through a hard time, and during this experience he or she has made a promise to God that is to be carried out after experiencing deliverance.[16] After God had intervened, one had to do several things. First, the person had to carry out the promise. Then, the community was called together for a celebration that included a votive offering and a declaration of what God had done. Often this celebration would include a special song written for the occasion. These are known as "declarative praise psalms."

Freewill offerings (Lev. 7:16 et al.). The last category seems to be a catchall, an offering that was apparently given on no special occasion but whenever the person felt like giving praise to God. Thus, it is called a "freewill" offering.

Overall, then, as we look at the sacrificial system, we see a ritual structure designed to promote a harmonious relationship. Some of the sacrifices focused on the sin that broke the relationships. Others were of a positive nature, drawing the people together to praise and worship God. When we come to the NT, we will find that it is the former that were abolished in the sacrifice of Jesus Christ, but that is a later part of our story.

GUIDELINES FOR PRIESTHOOD

The nation of Israel was to be "a kingdom of priests" (Ex. 19:6). That is, they were to be God's representatives on earth and to represent the people of the world to God. As such, they were to have a distinct lifestyle. In some respects, we clearly see that their lifestyle was held to higher standards. In other respects, we can say only that it was distinct. In a similar way, the tribe of Levi had a special position within the nation, for it was the priestly line. The priests represented God to the people of Israel, and also represented the

Read Leviticus 8–22.

> The nation of Israel was to be a kingdom of priests; as such, the people were to have a distinct lifestyle.

people of Israel before God. As such, they were to have an even more distinctive lifestyle. This section gives aspects of both groups, and they are somewhat intertwined.

The priesthood was inaugurated with the consecration of Aaron. A key word that shows up in this process is *anoint*. Beginning in Leviticus 8:10, we see that the tabernacle was anointed. The altar and all the items of the sacrificial system were anointed. Aaron was anointed. The Hebrew verb used is the one from which we get the word *Messiah*, the Anointed One.[17] The idea is that through this dedication ceremony, the priesthood and tabernacle system were established as working entities.

This entire process was serious business. That fact was pointed out sharply in the tragic incident of Nadab and Abihu, Aaron's sons. We are told only that they "offered strange fire before the LORD" (Num. 3:4 KJV). Apparently this means that they took coals from an unconsecrated fire, not the brazen altar. From our perspective, this irregularity seems somewhat trivial, but from God's perspective, it was an act demeaning to His position as God and as suzerain. To illustrate the seriousness of the situation, the two died, consumed by fire from God. Moses then warned Aaron that he needed to continue with the dedication process—worshiping God was more important than mourning two sons who had disobeyed.[18]

HYSSOP. Probably the plant referred to frequently in the instructions for cleansing ceremonies in Leviticus and Numbers and elsewhere in the Bible. If this is that hyssop, several sprigs would be gathered to serve as a rough brush.

While the priests were assigned many tasks (e.g., Lev. 13–14, where the priest determined whether a skin blemish was leprosy), their primary function was to serve as intermediaries between the people and God. As such, once the priesthood was established, only priests could perform sacrifices, including communal sacrifices. This restriction seems to be the reason the Levites were scattered throughout the nation so that people could give praise to God through peace and freewill offerings among their friends and neighbors. A second key function of the priesthood seemed to be to communicate God's word to the people. Specifically, priests gave God's blessing and were responsible for guarding God's word and reading it to the people (Deut. 10:8; 31:9–13).

OFFERINGS THROUGHOUT THE LAND

This topic raises some difficult questions. Originally, when the entire nation was in one camp, all offerings were performed at the same altar—the one in the tabernacle that was not far from anyone's tent. As the covenant was reiterated in the book of Deuteronomy, when the nation was getting ready to go into the land, some aspects of worship seem to have been modified so that peace and freewill offerings were allowed in the hometowns. Deuteronomy 12:21 suggests that the people were permitted to perform some sacrifices and eat them within their own towns if the distance to the central sanctuary was too great. However, even this passage does not fully clarify the problem.

But just as the priests were to be distinct, so were the people. They were to avoid the pagan religious practices of the nations around them. They were to adopt lifestyles that reflected a higher calling. Specific examples are given in this portion of the text. Some of these are understandable because they reflect high standards of hygiene, such as the laws regarding bodily discharges or prohibitions against eating scavengers. Others we find a bit more perplexing, such as the prohibition against eating lobster or rabbit. However, God does not choose to give reasons but merely states that these are the instructions for people's conduct.

TIME TO CELEBRATE

Our tendency, as we read through this material, is to be overwhelmed by all of the negatives. However, there are some exciting positives. One of the most exciting is the holidays. God set forth seven national holidays, then directed the nation to gather for three of them. These three mandatory festivals were to be times when the people stopped their work and gathered together for sacrifice that involved a communal meal. Thus, it was a time of national celebration. There were other festivals throughout the year as well as a mandatory day of rest each week—the Sabbath. Each was to remind the original audience of specific things God had done for them. By extension, then, they were to remind future generations of the acts God had done in the past.

Read Leviticus 23–27.

SABBATH. One of the unique institutions of Israel's religion. The Sabbath as a day of rest for people served several functions, including restoring physical strength and reminding people that they are created beings. The celebration of this day is taken seriously in Judaism to the present day.

The Sabbath

The Sabbath, or seventh day, was to be a day of rest, which within this context meant that work did not go on as usual. Some necessary activity was allowed. But the Sabbath was to be a day when everyone in the nation got a break. After the Exile, the religious leaders began trying to quantify what should be regarded as work, but that issue will concern us later (see ch. 17). The purpose of the Sabbath was to remind the people that God was their Creator (a direct reference to the creation account in Genesis) and that they were but human.

The Passover

The first festival where everyone was to assemble was the Passover, which was to commemorate the Exodus. By reenacting the dinner that their ancestors ate the night God brought

TWO MORE FEASTS

Associated with the Passover feast were two celebrations that are less familiar. The first was the Feast of Unleavened Bread, which began on the day after Passover and lasted seven days. This week-long period was a time when the people cleaned out all yeast from their houses and ate nothing that was leavened. We have noted that this week probably corresponds to the period from the original Passover to the first encampment. The second celebration was the Festival of Firstfruits. Here the people were to bring the first of the harvest to the high priest in thanksgiving for the full reaping they anticipated God would provide. This feast was apparently celebrated on the day after the Sabbath after Passover (Lev. 23:15), that is, the first Sunday after Passover.

them out of Egypt, the people were reminded that God was their Redeemer. We will see later that there is also a representation of God's ultimate redemption that would be reenacted in the ministry of Jesus (see ch. 17).

HIGH PRIEST. An artist's rendering of a high priest offering incense in the tabernacle on Yom Kippur.

Pentecost

The second festival that all the people were to attend was the Feast of Ingathering, celebrated on the fiftieth day after the offering of the sheaf at Passover (Lev. 23:15). It is also known by other names, such as the Feast of Weeks and Pentecost (a later term derived from the Greek word for "fifty"). This feast took place when the harvest began, and the people brought symbolic loaves of bread (made with leaven) to present to God as a thanksgiving for the harvest. Later this festival was associated with the founding of the church.

Tabernacles

The third festival at which the people were to gather was called Tabernacles or Booths (Heb., Sukkoth). This festival was to remind the people of the period they spent in the desert. They were to live in a booth for one week. It was to be a period of no work, so it would be a great social time. Associated with the Feast of Tabernacles were two holy days. The first was the Feast of Trumpets, which was to be merely a day of rest; it was also the civil new year (known today as Rosh Hashanah). The other was the Day of Atonement, or Yom Kippur.

While Yom Kippur was the most significant day in the liturgical calendar, the focus of its celebration was inside the tabernacle rather than among the people (see Lev. 16). It was on this day (and this day only) that the high priest entered the Holy of Holies with incense after performing sin offerings for both himself and the nation. The most significant aspect of this

SUKKOTH. Also called the Feast of Tabernacles or Feast of Booths, a celebration that reminded the Israelites of their time of wandering and God's provision. Today it is often celebrated by building a makeshift "booth" or "tabernacle" in which the family lives during the holiday period.

observance was the selection of two goats, one of which was sacrificed as a sin offering for the nation. The other was presented before the Lord alive: the high priest confessed the sins of the nation "and put them on the goat's head" (6:21) after which the goat was sent off into the wilderness bearing the sins of the people. While there is no direct correlation between this holy day and what we see fulfilled in the NT, clearly there is a parallel with the process of Jesus bearing the sins of the people.

LOOKING AHEAD

The book of Leviticus ends with guidelines regarding the Sabbath year, the year of Jubilee, vows, and tithes. With these instructions, the basic structure of the complex socioeconomic-judicial-political-religious system that was to become the foundation of Israelite society was in place. The tabernacle had been built. The tablets of the Law were in the ark of the covenant. The priesthood had been established. The nation was organized around the tribal structure. The nation had its first canon, which we have identified as the first three books of our Bible. This entire process took about a year. Now it was time for the people to move to the land God had promised.

REVIEW QUESTIONS

1. What does it mean to say the Law is a covenant?

2. What does it mean to describe the Law as teaching?

3. How is the Law based on what God had done?

4. How is the Law a socioeconomic-judicial-political-religious system?

5. What happened when the people got tired of waiting for Moses?

6. Describe the tabernacle.

7. What were the three main categories of sacrifice, and what were they used for?

8. What was the purpose of the priesthood?

9. What were the key holidays of the nation, and what was their significance?

8

CHAPTER

Just a-Lookin' for a Home

OVERVIEW

As the Israelites approached the land God had promised, an advance reconnaissance party was sent out. When the party returned, the people decided they could not take the land. As punishment, God told them they would wander for forty years. This part of the story ends with the nation across the river from Jericho, rededicating itself and ready to possess the land.

After organizing the nation for a year, God told Moses to count the people in preparation for the move to the land He had promised. This event opens the book of Numbers, and this is often about as far as we get into the book. The numbers get tedious, and there seems to be little purpose to them. For the original audience, however, these lists served as an organizing structure. The figures given are supposed to be the number of men who were able to go to war, and they reflect major military fighting units. The census would also provide a basis on which to divide the land. The nation was organized around the twelve tribes. We have already observed how this was a mixed company. Apparently, then, those who had been outsiders were now "adopted" into specific tribes, and their families would be counted as part of those tribes from here on out.[1]

The census also helped impress the original audience with the great work of God's sustenance. While it is possible that some of the people planted gardens during the long stay at Sinai, the text clearly points out that the primary source of food for the entire people was from God's provision of the manna. At this point, they were not aware that they would be eating it for almost forty years, but the fact that God had been faithful for the previous year would have been encouraging. Another purpose of the census would be to validate God's sustaining for the entire forty-year period of wandering, but that would not be seen until after the period was over and a second census showed how the nation had maintained its strength. This final purpose, however, would be one of the key points for later generations, including ours.

However, as we delve into this book, we find that there is much more. The book of Numbers is really a travelogue. Beginning with the first census, it tells of the travels of the nation of Israel over the next forty years. Interspersed are pas-

MORE LARGE NUMBERS

The large census numbers presented early in the book of Numbers raise many questions. It is difficult to imagine this many people moving through the desert under any circumstances. As noted earlier (see above, ch. 6), some have suggested that the word 'eleph, usually translated "thousand," can mean a military unit, yet the numbers add up accurately only if the value is a thousand. Moreover, we note a parallel between the civilian and military structures. The former consisted of officials over tens, fifties, hundreds, and 'alaphim (plural of 'eleph, Ex. 18:21, 25); in such a sequence, the logical conclusion is that the word refers to thousands. The next larger unit was the tribe. The military organization, similarly, consisted of commanders of hundreds and commanders of 'alaphim (Num. 31:14, 48, 52, 54; cf. Deut. 1:15). Here again, the next larger unit was the tribe. While the large numbers may be difficult to accept, the best explanation still seems to be to take them at face value.

sages that amplify specific aspects of the law, showing how the people adjusted to the new national guidelines. The book ends with a second census, as the nation is poised to go into the land God promised. Overall, Numbers is a monument to God's faithfulness.

TAKING STOCK OF THE PEOPLE

The first census, at the beginning of Numbers, was directed by God. It served not only to count the people but also to organize them (Num. 1:3–4; 2:34). The census went one step further when it numbered the tribe of Levi, which was not given an inheritance among the twelve tribes but was to be a tribe of priests. Actually, as the text points out, the tribe of Levi was also the substitute for the firstborn of the rest of the nation (Num. 3:11–13). This description refers back to the first Passover, when the firstborn of the Israelites were spared as the death angel passed through the land of Egypt. Now God asked for a reckoning by the substitution of the Levites for the firstborn. Thus, the men of Levi who were one month old and older were numbered. This number fell short of all the firstborn of Israel by 273, who were then "ransomed" by the payment of five shekels each (3:44–51). The Levites were also divided into family groups for purposes of assigning the jobs of ministry.

Read Numbers 1:1–10:10.

> The first census served not only to count the people but also to organize them.

Beyond this, the sacred nature of the national mission was emphasized by further explication of the high standards God expected. This section seems to be preparing the nation for the first celebration of the Passover after the Exodus, commemorating one year of freedom from Egypt.

In this light, God had the people send out of the camp those who were unclean (Num. 5:1–4). The issue of "cleanness" and "uncleanness" is problematic for us today. A number of factors were involved. First, and perhaps most important, being unclean was not an issue of sin. Clearly sin separated human beings from God and thus required repentance and sacrifice. But someone who was unclean was not viewed as a person in sin. Second, being unclean was sometimes an issue of hygiene. We see this aspect in cases where physical problems, such as a discharge of bodily fluids (see Lev. 15), rendered a person unclean.[2] We also see it in cases where uncleanness required short-term isolation and bathing. However,

Being "unclean" was not necessarily a result of sin.

uncleanness went beyond simple matters of hygiene. For example, a woman who had a baby was unclean, but her period of uncleanness lasted one week if the child was a boy and two weeks if the child was a girl (Lev. 12).[3] In some respects, uncleanness merely served to remind the people of their humanness in the presence of a pure and holy God.

Strangely, we now find two texts that address faithfulness. The first passage deals with unfaithfulness to the marriage vow (Num. 5:11–31).[4] The second passage addresses the important issue of the Nazirite vow (Num. 6). A Nazirite was a person who consecrated himself or herself for a particular purpose, that is, a special period of faithfulness. Normally this was for a short period of time and was accompanied by a vow or promise to God. Associated with this promise were three obligations. The Nazirite could not cut his hair for the period of the vow, had to refrain from drinking wine (or other alcoholic drinks) and from eating anything made from grapes, and was to avoid becoming unclean through touching dead bodies.

The nation then dedicated the altar as a leader from each of the tribes brought special offerings before the Lord (Num. 7). This was followed by the dedication of the Levites (ch. 8). Finally, they celebrated the second Passover on the first anniversary of the Exodus (ch. 9).

The last verses of this section discuss the process that would be followed for the entire period of wandering. It harks back to the completion of the tabernacle, which we saw in Exodus 40, and notes how the *Shekinah* glory of God would direct the travels of the people. This pillar of cloud (at night a pillar of fire) would settle on the tabernacle during the period of camping and lift up when the nation was to move out.

THE NAZIRITE VOW

The term *Nazirite* comes from a Hebrew verb meaning "to consecrate" or "to separate." The Nazirite normally made a vow or promise associated with a request from God. There is no reason given for the specific requirements on the part of the Nazirite. An example of this type of vow is the case of Hannah, mother of Samuel. While most vows lasted for a limited period of time, some Nazirites were under lifetime vows, including Samson, Samuel, and John the Baptist. A noted NT example of a person taking short-term vows is the apostle Paul (Acts 18:18; 21:23–26).

A DIFFICULT TEXT

Numbers 11:4–35 is one of those difficult texts in the OT. We have seen that there were seventy elders at Mount Sinai where the people initially ratified the covenant. Now Moses again picked seventy elders. However, it is likely that this is the same group, and it is only now that we see them developing into something more than an ad hoc gathering. This text also seems to repeat the provision of quail in Exodus 16, in both cases in response to the grumbling of the people. The nature of this event has been debated. Is it a normal migration or a special provision? Also, is this the same event, or a different one? It has been noted that quail do migrate across this region, heading south in the fall into Africa and north in the spring. However, this incident would seem to be out of season for that migration, and the numbers seem unusually high, suggesting God's special provision. Likewise, it is best to see this as a separate event but analogous to what happened a year earlier.

MOVE 'EM OUT

God now directed Moses to begin the march to the land that had been promised. It had been more than four hundred years since the ancestors of the people had gone down to Egypt, and they were finally fulfilling the promise made to Abraham in Genesis 15.[5] The direction of the march seems to have been almost due north—the most direct route into the land.

We might think that the people, after a year of sitting at Sinai, would have been excited to advance under the promises of God. Not everyone was enthusiastic, however. Very quickly many, if not most, of the people began to murmur and complain about the manna.[6] Moses became despondent about the whole situation and took his complaints to God. God provided help in leadership and quail for the people. But because of their greed, God also sent a plague on the people, killing an unknown number.

Following this incident, a second complaint arose against Moses, this time from his own brother and sister. While the ostensible reason was that he had married a Cushite woman, the real reason was a concern for power. Moses was not willing to address this issue, but God was. He directed the three to the tent of meeting, where He spoke to them verbally and then struck Miriam with leprosy. When Moses interceded on her behalf, God cured her—after a week of isolation.

As the people moved on north, Moses sent out an advance reconnaissance party consisting of twelve men—one from each tribe. The twelve passed through the land, observed its inhabitants and returned with samples of grapes, figs, and pomegranates. The cluster of grapes was so large that two men carried it between them. The land was everything God had promised and more. The men reported, "It does flow with milk and honey" (Num. 13:27). Nevertheless, they also saw a

Read Numbers 10:11–20:13

FRUIT OF THE LAND. A bunch of grapes, a common sight in Palestine. When the advanced reconnaissance party went into the land of Canaan, they found it was fruitful. They brought back a bunch of grapes so large that it took two men to carry it. Even today Israel is noted for producing good grapes.

SIBLING RIVALRY

God's response at the tent of meeting in Numbers 12 suggests that Miriam was the instigator of the complaints against Moses. She alone was struck with the leprosy (v. 10). Miriam was the oldest of the three siblings. Aaron was three years older than Moses (Ex. 7:7), while Miriam had been old enough at the birth of Moses to watch over him when he was placed in the Nile as an infant (Ex. 2:4). Thus, we probably see here some resentment from sibling rivalry.

The issue for Aaron and Miriam does not seem to have been racial, for the term *Cushite* is somewhat ambiguous with respect to ethnic identity. While this may refer to a second marriage, there is no other evidence to suggest that Moses had married a second woman. Their complaint, then, seems to have been against Zipporah, but that's a surface issue. The real concern, as seen in their question, is that they feel they too have received religious revelation and should be equal authorities with their brother.

problem: the land was already occupied with strong people, and the cities were large and well fortified. At this point the twelve divided. The majority saw no way to go up against the inhabitants of the land. But two of them, Joshua and Caleb, realized that it did not matter what the odds were against them because God was with the Israelites and had promised to give them the land.

The people listened to the majority report and began to lament their terrible situation. In their minds, they had been brought out into the desert to die (although the God who had brought them out had preserved them for over a year under adverse circumstances). Abandoning all hope, they cried to elect a new leader who would take them back to Egypt.

The land was everything God had promised and more.

MORE FRUIT OF THE LAND. Pomegranates, a fruit used as a design element for the tabernacle and, later on, the temple.

Moses, Aaron, Joshua, and Caleb expressed sorrow at this state of affairs and tried to sway the people back to seeing God at work. But the people refused to listen and attempted to stone their leaders. At this point, God intervened, showing forth His glory from the tent of meeting. In front of the people, He told Moses to stand back so that He could destroy them, but Moses interceded on their behalf, pointing out that the issue was God's honor. I am sure it was humiliating for the people to hear directly from God that the only reason He was not destroying them was that the leader they had just rejected had put in a good word for them. But the next words were even more sobering. Every adult in the camp who had observed God's works and had refused to believe God's words would *indeed* die in the desert. The only exceptions would be Joshua and Caleb.

With this judgment, the nation was to turn south and begin wandering. The people had not yet understood the seriousness of their continued disobedience. The next morning they decided that they would go on up and begin the now forbidden conquest—without God. While Moses warned them not to disobey once more, they were resolved to try to rectify the situation. Instead, they ran into the Amalekites and the Canaanites and were beaten soundly, being driven back to Hormah. So they began their period of wandering.

Sometime after this, there was another rebellion. This time it was headed by Korah, one of the Levites, along with several members of the tribe of Reuben and 250 others. As is often the case, there was a degree of truth in their case as well as a personal agenda. The truthful part was their statement to Moses, "The whole community is holy, every one of them, and the LORD is with them" (Num. 16:3). Indeed, everyone in the congregation was holy, but that did not mean everyone had the same level of authority or the same responsibilities. The personal agenda was that Korah wanted power and privileges beyond the responsibilities his family had been given in setting up and taking down the tabernacle (see 4:4–20).

God told Moses to have the claimants for the priestly position bring their censers to the tent of meeting the next day. Korah and most of the group appeared, but Dathan and Abiram refused, castigating Moses in the process. At the presentation of incense, God opened up the earth to swallow the pretenders—Korah and his group at the tent of meeting, and Dathan and Abiram at their own tents.[7]

> Everyone in the congregation was holy, but that did not mean everyone had the same level of authority.

Although it was clearly God's judgment that took these rebels, by the next day the people were blaming Moses and Aaron for their deaths. God then judged the obstinate people with a plague. What is surprising is that Moses and Aaron once again interceded for the people before God. Even so, another 14,700 died. To emphasize the choice of Aaron as high priest, Moses took staffs from leaders of each of the twelve tribes, including Aaron for the tribe of Levi. He wrote their names on their staffs and deposited them before the tent of the meeting. The next

JUDGMENT AND MERCY

The Israelites who were above twenty years of age were condemned to die in the desert. Those who were nineteen and younger would be able to go into the land, but they would be relatively old by then. There was also a special punishment on the ten spies who brought a bad report. They died of a plague soon afterward. The time of the wandering was set at forty years to correspond to the forty days the party had searched out the land. This forty-year delay should also be seen as an act of mercy to the people in the camp, for it would allow them to have a fairly normal life span (the youngest of those who would not be permitted to enter would be sixty if they died just before the end of the wandering).

day Aaron's staff had grown, producing buds, blossoms, and ripe almonds. Once again, God made His point.

Interspersed with the accounts of these events are several other passages giving further specifications regarding the duties of the community in their covenant with God as their suzerain. There are specifics regarding offerings, the Sabbath, the duties of the Levites, the red heifer, and aspects of uncleanness. The structure of this material gives the appearance of its being added as events occurred or as truths were revealed. This feature supports our observation that Numbers is basically a travelogue that was being added to the canon as the people journeyed on.

Near the end of this period, Miriam died and was buried. This event occurred at Kadesh, but it seems to have been a different place than Kadesh Barnea.[8]

The final incident in this section is Moses' major sin. After the people grumbled because of a lack of water, Moses was told to speak to the rock in order to bring forth water. Instead, Moses said, "Listen, you rebels, must we bring you water out of this rock?" (Num. 20:10). He then struck the rock twice with his staff. As a result of this act, Moses was told that he would not be able to enter the land.

These events served to remind the original audience (as well as all future generations) that God was serious in His claims. There was no room for pretenders or false claims of authority. It did not matter whether the one making the claim was the established high priest (Aaron) or just a member of the "masses" (Korah); God did not tolerate false pride. Neither was there any favoritism with him. Despite all that Moses had done (or perhaps even because of it), pretension on his part was dealt with directly and somewhat harshly. At the same time, God did not hold grudges. Aaron, despite his having joined Miriam in rebellion, was still the anointed high priest—and God defended that position by causing his staff to bloom. Moses, despite his failure in striking the rock, was still the designated leader—and would take the people on to the land (even though he was restricted from entering). This information would serve to encourage future generations who found themselves straying from God's ways. They knew that God would not arbitrarily reject them for making mistakes. Of course, the other side of the coin was that they could be sure that God would judge them for failing to obey.

> God did not tolerate false pride. Neither was there any favoritism with him.

A HARSH PUNISHMENT

The punishment Moses was given seems to be out of proportion to the transgression; however, we are not privy to the tone of his declaration nor to what was going through his mind. His behavior seems to indicate an attitude of superiority, and his use of the word *we* seems to suggest that he was beginning to identify too closely with God against the people. Regardless, we do not see Moses protesting the punishment, and he continued to lead the people toward their destination.

ELIM. The second stopping place for the Israelites after they crossed the Red Sea. It was an oasis with twelve springs of water, but the people were eager to move on and put more distance between them and the Egyptians.

MOVING TO THE TRANSJORDAN

At this point we find the nation near the end of the forty-year period of "wandering." As we look at the list of way stations, we realize that this was a time during which the nation did not really wander, but rather functioned as a mobile city. They mostly camped, moving from point to point without really getting closer to their objective. Over the forty-year period, they stayed in twenty-some different locations. The exact path the nation followed is not clear for two reasons. First, most of the places mentioned in the summary list of Numbers 33 are not known today. Second, it does not seem to be a complete list (e.g., Kadesh Barnea is not included).[9] Giving such information, however, is not the purpose of this section. Rather, the point is that God preserved the people despite their rebellious spirit, and at the right time He brought them to the land He had promised. Several incidents that occurred in the interim are mentioned in this section to highlight that truth.

Read Numbers 20:14– 25:18, 31:1–54; 33:1–49.

Bypassing Edom
After the nation had crossed east of the Jordan Valley extension (through Ezion Geber on the Gulf of Aqaba), they came to the borders of Edom. A strong kingdom at this time, Edom was inhabited by the descendants of Esau, the brother of Jacob. At this point, the path Israel took intersected a major thoroughfare called "the king's highway" (Num. 20:17). Moses sent messengers to the king of Edom asking for permission to use this thoroughfare to pass through his land. He

NOT FIT FOR A KING

From our perspective, "highway" is far too generous a term for the route called "the king's highway." It might correspond better to the Chisholm Trail, which in the late nineteenth century was the route for cattle drives from Texas to the railheads in Kansas. Basically, it was a route where herds and caravans had worn away the grass and trampled down the soil. However, it was also one of the two major north-south thoroughfares by which trade went from Egypt to Mesopotamia. The other was the coastal highway, which ran along part of the Mediterranean coast of Israel.

promised the king that they would not leave the main route during the journey.[10] Moreover, they promised to pay for any provisions they might use (including water). The king of Edom not only refused but also threatened armed conflict. God, however, did not desire conflict for His people with the descendants of Jacob's brother, so He directed the Israelites to circle around Edom.

The Death of Aaron

This circle brought them to Mount Hor, another site whose location is uncertain today.[11] Here God told Moses that it was time for Aaron to "be gathered to his people" (Num. 20:24). Before his death, the high priesthood was to pass to Eleazar, his son. So Moses, Eleazar, and Aaron went up on Mount Hor, where they removed the vestments of the high priest from Aaron and put them on Eleazar. There Aaron died at the age of 123.

The Bronze Serpent

Leaving Mount Hor, the people had to travel south along the coast of Yam Suph (the section known today as the Gulf of Aqaba) to circle Edom. As they continued down through the desert, the people began to grumble again. This time, God sent fiery (poisonous) serpents among them. Many were bitten and a number died. The people realized their failure and asked Moses to intercede with God on their behalf. At God's direction, Moses made a bronze replica of the serpents, which was to be put up on a pole. When the people looked to the bronze serpent, they lived. This bronze serpent would later become a stumbling block for the people as they began to offer incense to it. Consequently, Hezekiah destroyed it approximately seven hundred years later. Interestingly, this incident in the wilderness was used by Jesus to illustrate how His death on the cross would provide life for all humankind: "Just as Moses lifted up the snake in the desert, so the Son of Man must be lifted up, that everyone who believes in him may have eternal life" (John 3:14–15).[12]

Sihon and Og

As the people of Israel worked their way up the east side of the Dead Sea, they soon encountered other nations. The first was a kingdom of Amorites.[13] As he had done with Edom, Moses sent messengers to King Sihon in Heshbon, the Amorites' capital city, asking permission to pass through the land. Like the Edomites,

Sihon not only refused but also gathered troops to block the route. Sihon, however, took matters further and attacked the Israelite camp. This action proved suicidal: Sihon was not only defeated, but his people were wiped out and the Israelites took his land.[14]

During the mop-up campaign, Joshua and his troops encountered another king in the Transjordan region, Og, king of Bashan. The name Bashan refers to the high plains east of Galilee and thus seems to have been much farther north from the Israelites' route of travel. Given the location of Bashan, it is not clear why this war was waged. The text notes that Og came out to Edrei to do battle, but even Edrei is north of the area where the Israelites were apparently located at this time.[15] Still, Israel defeated him and his people and took his land.

Balak and Balaam

Israel was now camped on the plains of Moab, directly across the Jordan River from Jericho. This development appears to have put Balak, a Moabite king, in a precarious situation. Israel had conquered and eradicated two powerful city-states (or nations) on his northern flank. Although the Israelites had no intention of moving south, Balak did not know that, and he feared for his own security. He took two steps to resolve the issue. The first was to establish a military alliance with the Midianites, who lived further east. The second was to secure spiritual help. He and his allies sent messengers north to a town named Pethor, near the Euphrates River; they were to summon Balaam, a man who had a reputation for being able to curse or bless and who seemed to have some type of relationship with YHWH. Although God did not desire Balaam to go, Balaam kept arguing. So God allowed him to do what he wanted (instead of making him do what he knew he should). To reinforce His warning message, God spoke to Balaam through his donkey en route.

When Balaam arrived in the Transjordan, Balak took him up on a mountain to look over the plains. He explained the situation and asked for Balaam's curse on these people he feared. After going through the mandated ritual, Balaam gave his prophetic declaration—an announcement that Israel was blessed by God and

BALAAM

The exact nature of Balaam's relationship with YHWH is debated. Joshua 13:22 describes him as a diviner. Yet in Numbers we see him giving a prophetic declaration that apparently comes directly from YHWH. Furthermore, when he was invited down to Moab, Balaam's first response was to tell the messengers that he needed to inquire of YHWH (and this name is used rather than the more generic "God"). Then, when he finally persuaded God to allow him to go, God sent an angel (the angel of YHWH) to meet him and his donkey. This all seems to suggest that Balaam had a special relationship with God, but he abused his position, which led to his death.

could not be cursed. After hearing four such declarations, Balak fired his prophet, and the text here suggests that Balaam went on his way. This, however, was not the end of the matter. Apparently Balaam gave his former employer some advice before he left: you cannot fight them, but you can seduce them.

With this, the Moabites invited the Israelites to partake in their worship of Baal (a fertility god).[16] Their rituals involved meals and sacred prostitution. Some of the Israelites succumbed. One Israelite even brought a Midianite woman to his tent in front of the people who were weeping before the tent of meeting. In response to this brazen act, Phinehas, the son of Eleazar the high priest, took a spear, followed them, and ran it through the embraced pair within the tent. God judged the people for their disobedience by sending a plague. Overall, about 24,000 people died.[17]

God then told Moses that the Israelites were to attack the deceitful Moabites. Later, as he recounted this part of the conquest, Joshua observed that one of the casualties of this conflict was Balaam the son of Beor. Following this battle, the nation of Israel began to focus on entering the land God had promised.

This entire section would serve to remind the generation entering Canaan how God had both taken care of their predecessors and tried to purify them. As later observers, we note how the people continually failed to live up to God's standards, yet He faithfully worked with them to take them one step further. We also notice that some claimed God's name yet worked for their own agendas and selfish ambitions. Interestingly, God used them as well to advance His own goals, which would be for the good of all humankind—all the families of the earth.

> The people continually failed to live up to God's standards, yet He faithfully worked with them to take them one step further.

KING'S HIGHWAY. The major route of travel in the Transjordan region, called the King's Highway, even though it was more of a trail across the plateau. Today the route is a paved, major highway.

REDEDICATION BEFORE CONQUEST

Encamped on the eastern shores of the Jordan River, the people began to concentrate on preparing to go into the land. However, several matters had to be completed before they could do so.

Read Numbers 26–30; 32; 34–36.

First, Moses conducted a second census of the new generation. A quick glance at these figures shows that the overall size of the nation was about the same as it had been at the start of the

> The second census reminded the original audience of God's faithfulness through hard times.

Exodus. This detail reminded the original audience of God's faithfulness through hard times. Interestingly, several tribes had drastically decreased in numbers (e.g., Simeon, which was now only about a third of its original size), while others had had significant growth (e.g., Manasseh, which was more than 60 percent larger).[18]

Second, Joshua was commissioned to succeed Moses as the leader of the nation. His new position seems to have been mediator of the covenant. As such,

CAMPSITES OF THE NATION OF ISRAEL

The book of Numbers is a travelogue covering the journey of the nation of Israel from Egypt to the plains of Moab, on the Jordan River just across from the land God promised. The people camped at a number of locations, including the following.

Rameses (the starting point)	Kibroth Hattaavah	Hor Haggidgad	*Beer
Succoth	Hazeroth	Jotbathah	*Mattanah
Etham	*Wilderness of Paran	Abronah	*Nahaliel
Pi Hahiroth	*Kadesh Barnea	Ezion Geber	*Bamoth
(Crossing the Red Sea)	Rithmah	(At tip of the Red Sea)	(Mount Pisgah, battle with Sihon)
Marah	Rimmon Perez	Wilderness of Zin/Kadesh	*Heshbon
Elim	Libnah	(Miriam died)	*Edrei
Coast of the Red Sea	Rissah	*Waters of Meribah	(Battle with Og)
Wilderness of Sin	Kehelathah	Mount Hor	Dibon Gad
Dophkah	Mount Shepher	(Aaron died)	Almon Diblathaim
Alush	Haradah	*Hormah	Abarim
Rephidim	Makheloth	Zalmonah	Plains of Moab
(Wilderness of Sinai, giving of the Law)	Tahath	Punon	(Campsite stretched from Beth Jeshimoth to Abel Shittim)
	Terah	(Fiery serpents)	
*Wilderness of Paran	Mithcah	Oboth	
*Taberah	Hashmonah	Iye Abarim	
	Moseroth	*Wadi Zered	
	Bene Jaakan	*Wadi Arnon	

*These sites are not listed in the summary itinerary of Numbers 33.

he represented the people before God, and God before the people. Moses was told at this point that he would soon leave the people and go up to a mountain where he would die. Analysis shows that some of this material is arranged topically rather than in a strictly chronological order. That seems to be the case from here to the end of the Pentateuch. For example, it is after this appointment that we read of the revenge against the Midianites in Numbers 31, which chronologically would seem to fit better with 25:17.

Third, we learn that several of the tribes have been eyeing the land on the eastern side of the Jordan River (an event that seems to have occurred chronologically before the Balaam incident). This region was good grazing land, and the tribes of Reuben and Gad and half of the tribe of Manasseh asked for permission to settle in this region. Initially, Moses was upset, comparing this request with the unbelief that had occurred a generation earlier at Kadesh Barnea. The tribes demurred, however, asserting that they were willing to participate in the conquest, but that this land seemed to fit their every desire. They argued that they would settle their families into the villages and cities, build sheepfolds, and then go with the rest of the nation through the conquest.[19] Moses agreed, and this region became part of Israel but a part noted for its grazing (somewhat like the west Texas of ancient Israel).

Fourth, Moses described the land in the region west of the Jordan (modern Israel), which would become theirs. He laid out borders and told them to allocate the land by lots when they finished the conquest. He also set apart two groups of cities. The larger group was cities for the Levites, who would not receive a tribal inheritance but would be dispersed throughout the nation. As we have already observed, part of the reason for this decision seemed to be that they could represent God to the people in terms of teaching and offer certain sacrifices. Included in these Levitical towns were six that were called cities of refuge: three were on the west side of the Jordan and three on the east side.[20] These were sanctuaries for people who had committed manslaughter.

The final act of Moses was to reiterate the covenant. This rededication is set forth in the book of Deuteronomy.

TREATY RENEWAL

Read Deuteronomy 1–34.

Earlier we observed that the relationship between the nation of Israel and God was that of a covenant, specifically a treaty between a suzerain and His vassal. This relationship is evident in the terminology used throughout Exodus, Leviticus, and Numbers. It is also evident within their literary structure, although that feature is most apparent in the case of the book of Deuteronomy. The chart on the next page shows Deuteronomy laid out within that structure.

The relationship being discussed in Deuteronomy is a reiteration of that which we saw established at Mount Sinai. Deuteronomy 29:1 indicates the connection when it states that the covenant made while the Israelites were in Moab

TREATY STRUCTURE OF DEUTERONOMY

Title/Preamble: Introduction (1:1-4)

"First address" by Moses
    Historical Prologue (1:5-4:49)

"Second address" by Moses
    Covenant Stipulations (5:1-26:19)
        General Stipulations: The so-called Ten Commandments (5:1-33)
        Specific Stipulations: Amplification of the general stipulations
        (6:1-26:19)

    1. God's authority as Sovereign (6:1-12:32)
    2. God's uniqueness as focus of worship (13:1-18)
    3. The unique value of God's name (14:1-14:27)
    4. God's position as the Creator (15:1-16:17)
    5. Basic guidelines on social structure (16:18-18:22)
    6. Basic guidelines on human life (19:1-21:23)
    7. Basic guidelines on relationships (22:1-23:18)
    8. Basic guidelines on the value of personhood (23:19-24:7)
    9. Basic guidelines on the value of personal dignity (24:8-25:4)
    10. Basic recognition of the rights of others (25:5-26:15)

    Summary (26:16-19)

"Third address" by Moses
    Witness Section (or Covenant renewal) (27:1-26)
    Blessings and Cursings (28:1-68)
    Establishment of a perpetual trust (29:1-31:13)
    The Succession of the mediator (31:14-34:12)

is "in addition to" the covenant at Mount Sinai (Horeb).[21] In terms of content, the book of Deuteronomy is really a reiteration of much of what we have already seen. The historical prologue is a summary of the historical events that transpired during the forty years between Mount Sinai and the occasion when the nation was across the Jordan River from Jericho. The major stipulations are virtually identical. The minor ones have a number of differences but are similar in that they bring out nuances of the same major stipulations. This observation emphasizes the point we noted earlier that these minor stipulations really serve as illustrations of how the key principles were to work in everyday life.

More significant for our purposes are the last four sections, under the general category of the "third address" by Moses. Here we see clear guidelines for future generations. Two items stand out. The first is the establishment of a perpetual trust; the second is the succession of the mediator.

A Perpetual Trust

The idea of a perpetual trust is a legal concept that takes the stipulations beyond the present generation. There are several indications of this concern through this section of the text, most specifically Deuteronomy 29:15, which states that in addition to the people standing there, the covenant covered "those who are not here today." The context suggests that the reference was to their descendants.[22]

Incorporated with this section are guidelines for a ceremony in which the people of the nation would renew the covenant on a regular basis. As laid out in Deuteronomy 27, this ceremony was to take place at Mount Ebal and Mount Gerizim, a pair of peaks located in the central highlands. Here large stones were to be set up and whitewashed. On these stones the words of the Law (the covenant between God and the people) were to be written for public observation. Following this, the people were to gather on the two mountains—six tribes on Ebal and six tribes on Gerizim. The tribes on Mount Ebal (today characterized as a barren peak) were to proclaim the curses that would result if the people did not obey the covenant. The tribes on Mount Gerizim (in contrast, a well-forested peak) were to proclaim the blessings that would result as long as the people obeyed the covenant stipulations. If the difference in the mountains was this significant, this ceremony must have provided a dramatic visual image.

AMNON GORGE. A major obstacle on the east side of the Dead Sea. After passing through it, the Israelites began to encounter opposition from Moabites and Ammonites.

We are not told specifically when these renewal ceremonies were to take place, but Deuteronomy 31:10–13 suggests that it would be associated with the Sabbath year celebrations. At that time, the people were to gather at a specific location (unnamed in this context), where they would have the entire Law read to them so that they would be familiar with and follow its precepts.[23] As we read the blessings and curses, we note that there is a heavy emphasis on the curses as a warning. Furthermore, there is a progression to them. This aspect would be significant later when Josiah rediscovered the Law and noted that the people were at the next-to-the-last step (see 2 Kings 22 and the discussion in ch. 14, below). Joshua 8:30 shows that the Israelites observed this ceremony during the conquest as commanded. We have no record of follow-up celebrations, but it is likely that they took place during periods when the people tried to obey the entire Law. However, the failure to observe this ceremony was part of the reason the nation eventually suffered exile.[24]

The Succession of the Mediator

Although Moses had been the mediator between God and the people for nearly forty years, he would not be allowed to go into the land. Therefore, before the nation could proceed, the torch of leadership would have to be passed. We have already seen that Joshua was Moses' designated replacement. He had been mentored by Moses for most of the past forty years (Ex. 24:13) and had already experienced leadership as the general of the armies (Ex. 17:9). He had shown his faithfulness by believing God at Kadesh Barnea (Josh. 14:8). He had also spent many hours at the tent of meeting with his mentor (Ex. 33:11). Just so that there would be no mistake, however, Joshua was commissioned publicly before the people (Deut. 31:14–23).

EBAL AND GERIZIM. Twin mountains in what would later be called Samaria. The valley between the peaks had a prominent trade route and was the site of the covenant renewal ceremony that was conducted regularly generation after generation in keeping with Deuteronomy 27.

EBAL AND GERIZIM

How did Moses know of these two peaks? Of course, the directions were being given by God, whom we may presume to have been well acquainted with the geography of the land. In addition, two of the spies who had been part of the original reconnaissance party, Joshua and Caleb, would be leading the nation into the land. Another interesting point is that these peaks were located in the section of the country that would become part of the Northern Kingdom. If the book of Deuteronomy was written as late as critical scholars suppose, we need to ask why the priesthood at Jerusalem (especially after the exile of the Northern Kingdom) would incorporate a directive for covenant renewal in that location.

With this, Moses had wrapped up his work. Still, he had a few final words for the people—and they were not very complimentary. He told them that he fully expected that after his death they would act corruptly and turn from God's ways. Nevertheless, he taught them one final song (Deut. 32) and gave them a final blessing (Deut. 33).[25]

The text then records the death of Moses, which raises a question. The traditional understanding is that Moses wrote Deuteronomy, but if so, how could he write of his own death? Most likely Joshua appended this section. He was now the mediator. The book of Joshua tells us that he was given the responsibility to add to the Book of the Law, a task he faithfully carried out.

LOOKING AHEAD

As we wrap up our discussion of the Pentateuch, we find the nation finally ready to go into the land. Forty years have passed since the original group left Egypt, making the date approximately 1406 BCE. This generation has just renewed the covenant with God that the previous generation had made at Mount Sinai. We note a more positive spirit within the people but still see evidence that many of them had not really understood who God was or accepted His authority. The people carried this book of the covenant with them so that they had a history of how God worked with their parents and earlier generations. This book would serve to remind them of God's faithfulness.

One interesting point, however, is that the location of entry has been changed from Kadesh Barnea. Instead of the most direct route from Sinai up a gentle slope to the central plateau, they will be entering the land through Jericho—one of the strongest cities in the land. To get in, then, they will need God to work just as mightily as He had in the past.

REVIEW QUESTIONS

1. Why does the book of Numbers begin with a census?

2. What is a Nazirite?

3. Why did the people refuse to go into the land after they reached Kadesh Barnea?

4. What was Korah's revolt?

5. Why was Moses not allowed to enter the Promised Land?

6. Who were Sihon and Og?

7. Who were Balak and Balaam?

8. Why and how did the nation renew its covenant with God across the river from Jericho?

CHAPTER

9

Joshua Fit the Battle of Jericho— and Hazor Too

OVERVIEW

After crossing the Jordan River in a miraculous way, the people spent the next five years or so conquering the land that had been promised. This conquest, which consisted of three major campaigns, raises some questions, especially regarding God's instruction to destroy the inhabitants of Canaan. The Israelites were able to take control of the land but did not fully conquer it.

The book of Joshua tells of the conquest of the land of Canaan. As we read through this account, we find an interesting mixture of expressions. In some cases, we read that God fought the battles. In other cases, we read that the people fought the battles. What we see is that whatever the military strategies the Israelites pursued in waging their victorious battles, God was behind them all. (See, e.g., Josh. 10:6–15; 23:3; 24:8–13.) This conquest took several years, probably about five. Unfortunately, we are not given a chronology. The fighting included three major campaigns and ended with the people of Israel in control of the land but not having completely conquered it. As we will see later, God designed the process this way to allow several generations to experience His work. The overall goal seems to have been to strengthen the nation's confidence in God. Instead, the people stumbled because they failed to trust God and obey Him.

As we look at the account of the conquest, we are left with some questions. The key issue concerns God's instructions to the Israelites to destroy the people who currently occupied the land. We see this as harsh—in fact, as a form of genocide. So before we look at the conquest narrative, we need to examine this problem.

WHAT IS A "BAN"?

God's order to destroy the Canaanites is usually expressed by the use of the Hebrew word *ḥerem*.[1] This term can be translated in a variety of ways. For example, in Joshua 6:17 the KJV says that Jericho will be "accursed." The NASB uses the expression "under the ban." The NRSV renders, "devoted . . . for destruction."

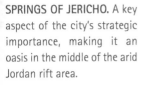

SPRINGS OF JERICHO. A key aspect of the city's strategic importance, making it an oasis in the middle of the arid Jordan rift area.

The NIV says only that it will be "devoted." So what does the word mean, and why is this important?

The primary reason it is important involves the historicity of the conquest. Beginning with the assumption that this "ban" meant total destruction (indicating a burning to the ground) of all the cities on which this edict was given, archaeologists have looked for burn layers in these cities to establish a correlation. Since they have not been able to find them, some have argued that the conquest did not occur. However, a closer look suggests that this argument is based on false assumptions.

To understand what the word meant for the audience involved in the conquest, we need to look at how the term was used. When cities were placed under *herem,* specific guidelines were usually given, stating what was to be done. Normally the instructions did not include burning the city. In fact, in the entire conquest, only three cities are said to have been burned.[2] Rather, the directions specified what to do with the people and the spoils. In the case of Jericho (Josh. 6:17–21), Joshua was told that all human life was to be destroyed along with all animal life, including oxen, sheep, and donkeys—with the exception of Rahab and her family. Furthermore, the people were specifically warned against taking any of the loot. Earlier, in the case of Heshbon, the city of Sihon, human life was exterminated, but all the animals and spoil were retained and given to the people (Deut. 2:34–35). This latter example appears to be more the norm.[3]

> The conquest of Canaan was not undertaken for the sake of conquest, but to prepare for a Messiah whose mission was to redeem the world.

Even this kind of punishment, however, gives us problems because of the high value we place on human life. Here we have a second reason why understanding the term *herem* is important. God has a different perspective, which is sometimes puzzling. In God's view, the right to physical life is not an absolute, and individual humans may forfeit that right by the decisions they make. Certainly, human life is not limited to the temporal (or physical) realm, and God is more interested in the spiritual than the physical.[4] In this light, we need to remember that the conquest of Canaan was not undertaken for the sake of conquest, but to prepare for a Messiah whose mission was to redeem the world. Within this context, the picture is one of judgment. Therefore, the bottom line seems to be whether God has the right to judge individuals and people

A HIGH VIEW OF HUMAN LIFE

The order to destroy the Canaanites does not indicate that God places a low value on human life. The Bible elsewhere makes clear that He attaches great importance to it. One piece of evidence is the divine institution of capital punishment. Human life is so valuable that God demands the highest repayment possible: since the life taken cannot be restored, the criminal must forfeit his life (Gen. 9:5–6). Related to this principle is the distinction made in the law between murder and manslaughter (discussed previously). A third piece of evidence comes from the NT, which tells us that God sacrificed His Son to reconcile humanity to Himself.

UGARIT

Most of our information on Canaanite religion comes from a place called Ugarit (modern Ras Shamra), a city located north of Israel in what is now Syria. Although the city was outside Canaan proper, its culture is often described as Canaanite and had many similarities with the kinds of societies that existed in Palestine. Ugarit was excavated primarily in the 1930s, and the ruins have been dated from the fifteenth to twelfth centuries BCE (the period from about the time of Moses to that of the judges). The documents we have recovered, dated from about 1360 BCE or later, include several epics—long poems that tell the stories of the gods.

groups. If so, then we need to look at the lifestyles of those Canaanites who were declared to be *ḥerem*. Was their destruction arbitrary, or were there reasons for a holy God to judge them?

CANAANITE IDOL. An idol thought to represent *chemosh*, one of the many Canaanite idols in a pantheon that grew larger over time.

CANAANITE RELIGION

Why were the Canaanites judged? To answer this question, we need to look at two aspects. The first involves the gods of the Canaanites, and the second involves their mode of worship. As we look at the available documentation, we find that by the time of the conquest the Canaanites had developed an extended hierarchy of gods. This system demonstrated a degraded view of God and religious ideals.

The data suggest that early in their culture the Canaanites had very few gods (most likely only one), although the evidence is not as solid as it is for some of the other ANE cultures. The indications are that the early Canaanites served only El, the Semitic term for god/God. However, by the time of the conquest, the number of gods within their pantheon had increased tremendously. El was a "shadowy figure"[5] who held an apparent place of honor but didn't really figure into the worship. In early Canaanite texts, he was characterized as the "father of years." His dwelling place was called "the source of the two deeps" or "two floods." He was a particularly remote god and sent his instructions by messengers. By the time of the inscriptions found in Ugarit, which was around Moses' day, he was viewed as the father of seventy other gods. In the written material that has been excavated in the land of Israel, we have found references to El, but we have not found any Canaanite sites of worship that were dedicated to him.

Rather, the focus was on Baal. The term *ba'al* is a general Semitic word for "lord" or "master." By the time of our historical documents (including those from Ugarit), Baal had become the de facto head of the pantheon. He was a fertility god, and thus his worship served an important function for the pagans in a land that depended so much on rain. He appeared to be a carryover from the Amorites, who settled in Canaan around the time of Abraham. Baal was described as the son of Dagon, another fertility god (who figured prominently in the Philistine pantheon). He was often called Baal-Zebul, which probably means "prince Baal."

While Baal was a specific god, the term seems also to have been used in the sense of lord or master to refer to other gods. For example, in the OT there is reference to Baal-Zebub, "lord of the flies" (2 Kings 1:2–3, 6, 16; some believe that Hebrew scribes introduced this name as a deliberate distortion of Baal-Zebul). In addition, the term is used for many other local gods or for gods of a particular shrine/location (that is, high place) in the OT and in other ANE literature. For example, among the Phoenicians, we read of Baal-Shaman, Baal-Melech, and Baal-Zaphon. All of these were gods of the fishing fleets.

The third key figure was Asherah. In Canaanite texts, she was viewed as the wife of El, but she assumed the role of goddess of fertility. As such, she was associated with Baal. The Hebrew word 'asherah is often translated "grove" in the OT because it was associated with the trees that were planted around an altar of Baal. Little more is known of this goddess.

I have already mentioned the fourth key figure, Dagon, who was an early fertility god. In some documents, he was viewed as the father of Baal. The evidence is that Dagon was adopted by the Philistines (a people who had come from the Aegean area) *after* they settled in Canaan along the coast.

While these four were the key figures, the Canaanites had a pantheon of at least seventy gods and goddesses.[6] It appears that the pantheon was also growing, although it was by no means as large as the pantheon of Egypt. Overall, the picture of the gods and goddesses of Canaanite religion had degenerated into a soap opera, with incestuous relationships and other abominations set forth in the pantheon. Of course, these were supposed to represent the "higher ideals" that guided the people.

The abominations showed up in the methods of worship, which were probably the most significant cause of judgment.[7] From the OT data, we see that several reprehensible practices dominated their religious rituals. We do not have much written material from other sources that show how the Canaanites

CANAANITE MONOTHEISM?

The Canaanite evidence points to a prehistoric worship of El, apparently as sole god. *El* is the same word the Hebrews used for God (although the Hebrews more commonly used *Elohim*, the plural form of *El*). This is not too surprising, for Canaanite and Hebrew are related languages. While many scholars see the worship of El as evidence for a developing (evolving) monotheism, the overall evidence seems to show a culture that was turning from the worship of God (that is, El) to an increasing polytheism. This development correlates with the biblical evidence we saw earlier: Melchizedek, a Canaanite, served El Elyon, God Most High, but apparently later generations pushed El aside and began to serve a multitude of other gods. This concept is developed further in Michael A. Harbin, *To Serve Other Gods: An Evangelical History of Religion* (Lanham, Md.: University Press of America, 1994), 25–43.

One form of Canaanite sacrifice involved taking the milk of a ewe, bringing it to a boil, and then cooking the ewe's lamb in the milk. This ritual clarifies the commandment in Deuteronomy 14:21 that forbids "boiling a kid in its mother's milk." Later generations forgot the reason for the command, but it became the foundation for the kosher practice of not cooking meat and dairy products together.

performed their rituals, but some of the archaeological data from Palestine corroborates the existence of these practices.

One of these practices was *self-mutilation*. The idea behind this ritual was that a worshiper showed sincerity by cutting or otherwise mutilating the body. It appears in the OT during the contest between Elijah and the priests of Baal, when the latter "slashed themselves with swords and spears, as was their custom" (1 Kings 18:28).

Religious prostitution was another abominable practice mentioned in various passages (e.g., Judg. 2:17; Jer. 7:9; Amos 2:7). Sexual relations in the sanctuary were connected with the fertility rites, demonstrating a concept sometimes called sympathetic magic.[8] Practitioners believed that through the practice of ritual prostitution in the temple, the god or goddess would have pity on the people and send rain to cause the crops to grow. It was an overt attempt to manipulate the deities.

> The Canaanite spiritual abominations showed up in the methods of worship, which were probably the most significant cause of judgment.

A third Canaanite ritual was the *sacrifice of infants*. This custom is talked about in Leviticus 18:21 and is also mentioned in 2 Kings 23:10. The prophet Jeremiah condemned the people of Israel for adopting this reprehensible practice (Jer. 19:4–5, 15). Kleitarchos, a Greek writer from about 300 BCE, wrote that the ritual involved taking a hollow metal idol dedicated to one of the Canaanite gods—such as Molech, the god of fire (also known as Baal-Melech)—filling it with flaming coals until it was red hot, then laying the infant on the sizzling outstretched arms of the idol as a demonstration of piety. This practice of infant sacrifice seems to have brought on the final judgment. The conquest of the land of Canaan must be viewed within that context.

JOSHUA ASSUMES COMMAND

Read Joshua 1–2.

The first chapter of Joshua shows a major transition. For the fledgling nation of Israel, this was the first time since leaving Egypt that they had been without Moses. Now God told the new leader, Joshua, to take charge. It was time for him to lead the people into the land. This transition must have been very intimidating for Joshua and the people, and God recognized it. Three times in His short address, God told Joshua, "Be strong and courageous." Joshua said the same thing to the people.

God also told Joshua, "Do not let this Book of the Law depart from your mouth" (Josh. 1:8). These words remind us that the material we have read to this point was recorded in a book that Joshua and the people had before them. We also

INFANT SACRIFICE

Some scholars claim there was no such god as Molech, but that what is being described in the biblical texts is a *type* of sacrifice. Others have pointed out that the OT texts clearly refer to a person who was the focus of this worship. In some respects, the issue is a moot point, for the practice of infant sacrifice is just as reprehensible whether performed to a variety of gods or to only one. Although none of the hollow idols described by the Greek writer Kleitarchos have yet been discovered, the results of the practice are very evident in ruins of various cities, including Carthage, a colony of Tyre and Sidon, as well as the original Phoenician cities (see David Soron, Aicha ben Abed ben Khader, and Hedi Slim, *Carthage* [New York: Simon & Schuster, 1990]). There is now some evidence from one of the key Canaanite cities, Ashkelon (although this is still debated; see Rick Gore, "Ancient Ashkelon," *National Geographic*, January 2001, 66–93).

note how God expected the people to live out the contents of that book in their daily lives. These instructions would be important in the days and years ahead. Joshua passed the same word to the people and told them to get ready because they would cross the Jordan in three days.

At about the same time, Joshua sent two "spies" across the Jordan River for reconnaissance. It seems somewhat strange that Joshua would send out spies after the fiasco from forty years earlier; however, he must have sensed a need for further information, and there is no indication that God objected (although it does not seem that God suggested it either). The two spies arrived at the house of Rahab the prostitute ("harlot," NASB). Her residence was located along the walls of the city and was probably an inn. As such, it was a place where people came and went, and thus a good place to gather information. Likely hoping to remain inconspicuous, the two men were nevertheless observed going in and recognized as Israelites.

The king of Jericho sent messengers to Rahab asking her to hand over the two strangers, presumed to be spies, but she lied to protect the men.[9] Instead of turning them in, Rahab hid them on the roof of the inn. After the messengers had left, hurrying to cut off the fords across the Jordan River, she talked with the Israelites. She told them that the people of Jericho were terrified of what was going to happen—the reputation of Israel's God had swept through the land. She then asked the Israelites to spare her and her family when they conquered the land.

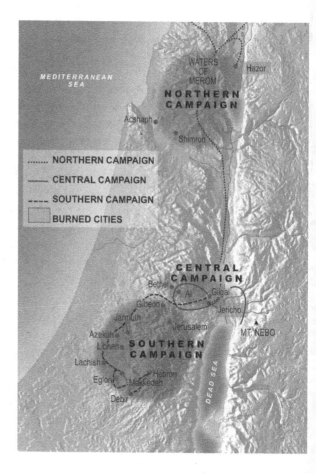

THE CONQUEST OF CANAAN. Significant landmarks in the Israelites' struggle to gain control of the land of Canaan.

The two Israelites quickly agreed. They told Rahab to put a scarlet rope in the window of her house when the Israelites came. Otherwise they would not be responsible for what happened to her. She agreed and then lowered the men over the wall. They slipped out to the west, the opposite direction from the Israelite camp. After hiding out for three days, they returned to Joshua. Their report to him was very positive. The fear of the people was seen as a clear indicator that God had given them the land.

ENTERING THE LAND

Read Joshua 3:1 – 5:12.

Joshua told the people to get ready and to consecrate themselves, since God was going to do something great the next day. As we look at this account, we realize that the special nature of their crossing of the Jordan River served a multiple purpose. First, it helped solidify Joshua as the new leader of the people. Second, it reminded the people of the earlier crossing of the Red Sea, thus unifying the nation. The older people, those who had been under twenty at Kadesh Barnea, would recall that event and relate it to the younger generations. Third, the crossing of the Jordan served to remind the nation of God's power. We are told that the time picked for the crossing was when the Jordan was at flood stage (Josh. 3:15). The Israelites had been camped across the river for several months and could have crossed earlier, so this timing made the supernormal nature of the upcoming event even more dramatic. Not only would it remind the nation of the power of God, it would also serve to warn the nations in the land.

The process was very ordered and dramatic. The priests with the ark went first. As they stepped into the river, it stopped flowing and backed up several miles upstream. The priests moved to the middle of the river channel and then stood there, holding the ark. At this point, the people crossed over. Before the priests were allowed to move out of the riverbed, Joshua had twelve men (a man from each tribe) take twelve large stones from the riverbank and build a cairn in the middle of the riverbed. They also took twelve large stones from the middle of the river and built a cairn on the west bank.[10] After these monuments had been built, the priests were allowed to join their brothers on the west bank of the Jordan River in the land God had promised. After all this, the river began to flow once again.

AN EARTHQUAKE?

Historically, earthquakes have blocked the Jordan River, backing up the flow of the water. Some have argued that some such natural event allowed the Israelites to cross. Even if an earthquake occurred, however, the timing was amazing. Joshua announced to the people three days in advance that they were going to cross over. Then, just as the priests reached the water, the flow stopped and remained stopped until the people had crossed and the monuments were erected. Then, as the priests left the riverbed, the flow began again.

The spectacular crossing of the Jordan served one other function. It frightened the inhabitants of the land so that they did not dare to attack Israel at their camp on the west bank. This was important, because after the crossing, God required the men who had not been circumcised to undergo that ritual. While this was an important act to show their inclusion within the Abrahamic covenant, it also served to incapacitate the army for several days. This vulnerable condition reminded the original audience of how God was indeed their suzerain. As such, God would take care of His own when they were obedient.

> Only God would take His entire army and in effect incapacitate them just after they crossed over into the territory they were to conquer.

As the men healed, Passover time arrived, and they celebrated the festival that reminded them of their deliverance from Egypt. As we noted in chapter 7, associated with Passover is the Feast of Firstfruits—the time when the first of the harvest is brought to God. On this occasion, the nation enjoyed the firstfruits of their new land, and with that the manna stopped.

It must have been a very exciting holiday, given that the people had now reached the objective for which they had been working for forty years. At the same time, it was probably a very sobering moment as they now confronted the idea of the actual conquest. But God had given them reasons for encouragement. The constant provision of manna for forty years (as well as clothes that had not worn out; see Deut. 8:3–4) showed that their suzerain was indeed taking care of them. They had conquered the regions on the other side of the Jordan, so their troops had already been exposed to battle—and had seen victory. Furthermore, they had the reports from the spies in Jericho. God was working in the hearts of the inhabitants of the land, and victory seemed certain.

JERICHO. The first city conquered after the Israelites crossed the Jordan. Its strategic location and strong walls made it a solid defense of the entire central highlands. Today the mound of the central part of the city is being surrounded by the expansion of modern Jericho.

JERICHO. Ruins that give evidence that Jericho was destroyed in a way similar to the OT description. Some scholars, based on their view of Scripture, have debated whether it was the Israelites who destroyed the city.

DIGGING UP JERICHO

Jericho illustrates the problems involved in archaeology. This city has been excavated twice, with different conclusions. John Garstang, who excavated part of the city in the 1930s, concluded that the evidence corroborated the biblical account. He dated the destruction of the uppermost major layer, called City IV (showing evidence of a Late Bronze Age culture), to about 1400 BCE (primarily based on pottery, Egyptian scarabs found in graves, and the absence of imported pottery from Mycenea). The walls had fallen outward, indicating destruction of the type associated with an earthquake. Grain that had burned but not been looted was found stored (John Garstang and J. B. E. Garstang, *The Story of Jericho* [London: Hodder and Stoughton, 1940]).

In the 1950s, Kathleen Kenyon excavated another part of the city. She never overturned Garstang's evidence and agreed that City IV had been destroyed violently. But she argued that he had interpreted the data incorrectly. She ignored the Egyptian scarabs, dated the fallen walls to the Early Bronze Age, and argued that there was no evidence of Late Bronze ruins for Joshua to attack (Kathleen M. Kenyon, *The Bible and Recent Archaeology* [Atlanta, Ga.: John Knox, 1978]).

More recently, other archaeologists have raised serious questions regarding Kenyon's work. For example, John J. Bimson (*Redating the Exodus and Conquest* [Sheffield: Almond, 1981]) carefully evaluated a number of her assumptions and concluded that the pottery evidence pointed to a destruction in the fifteenth century. Bryant Wood came to similar conclusions based on four lines of evidence. One of the most telling is a quotation from Kenyon's report that shows how the bricks from the wall fell outward and down the slope. Another is a radiocarbon dating of the destruction layer to 1410 BCE ± 40 years ("Did the Israelites Conquer Jericho?" *BAR* 16, no. 2 [March/April 1990]: 44–59). The crux of the matter is that the ruins in Jericho show the characteristics that would be expected if the biblical account is accurate.

The Battle of Jericho

The first objective was Jericho, one of the strongest cities in the region. It guarded the entire lower region of the Jordan Valley and access to the central plateau. Once this city was taken, the entire land was opened up. But Jericho was a tough one. So despite what the song says, Joshua did not fight this battle. Rather, God Himself fought Jericho.

Read Joshua 5:13–6:27.

As we follow the text, we read that Joshua apparently was out surveying the city. In the process, he encountered a man holding a drawn sword. Joshua challenged this person, asking which side he was on: "Are you for us or for our enemies?" The stranger's response is surprising. He was on neither side but had come as "commander of the army of the LORD." This reply served to remind Joshua that the question was not whether God was on his side, but whether he was on God's side. Joshua understood the point and prostrated himself.[11]

Now God told Joshua how the battle would be fought. He and the people were to march around the city once a day for six days. On the seventh day, they were to march around it seven times, and then the priests were to blow trumpets and the people were to shout. They did so, and the walls collapsed. The army rushed in to mop up, wiping out every living creature except Rahab and her family.

There were several lessons here for the Israelites. First, God was fighting for the nation because they were part of His program. As such, He did not really need the military might of the people, although He let them participate in the cleanup. Second, Jericho was the firstfruits of the land and therefore belonged to God. Third, and often overlooked, God was willing to accept anyone who had the faith to seek Him. In this case, it was Rahab and her family. She was a Canaanite, and her occupation was undesirable. Nevertheless, she was accepted into the nation of God's people and in fact married into the tribe of Judah and became an ancestress of David (and thus ultimately of Jesus; see Matt. 1:5).

The Battles of Ai

After Jericho, the next objective was Ai, a town located on the central plateau. After reconnaissance, Joshua decided that the town did not need the entire army, so he sent three thousand men. To his dismay, his troops were routed, and thirty-six men were killed. Joshua immediately went to God to ask what was wrong.

Read Joshua 7:1–8:29.

God told Joshua that the problem was that someone in the camp had stolen from Jericho. Joshua gathered the nation and explained the situation. At this point, they began a process of selection by using lots.[12] It would seem that the purpose of this process was to give the guilty party a chance to confess and ask for mercy. Since that never happened, the process worked down to Achan ben Carmi (Josh. 7:18). When Joshua confronted him, he finally confessed, and he and his family were stoned.[13] Their bodies were covered with a mound of rocks as a warning to future generations.

Following this, Joshua turned his attention again to the town of Ai. He picked a larger group (30,000) and followed God's strategy of setting an ambush.

WHERE WAS AI?

The identification of this city is one of the more controversial archaeological questions. For the past several decades, the site of Khirbet et-Tell has been identified as Ai. Recent excavations, however, have not supported this identification (Bryant G. Wood, "Kh. El Maqatir, 1999 Dig Report," *Bible and Spade* 12, no. 4 [Fall 1999]: 109–14). The group that has excavated Khirbet el-Maqatir reports that they reached a major burn layer showing that the city had been burned at about 1400 BCE (Bryant G. Wood, Presentation at the Near Eastern Archaeological Society, Nashville, Tenn., November 2000). Another difficulty is that the ruins at et-Tell seem too small for the population listed. Joshua 8:25 says that 12,000 were killed; however, this number likely includes people who lived outside the city walls.

Ai? Tel el Maqatir, which may be the site of the city of Ai.

While the people were permitted to take spoil from Ai after it was conquered, the town itself was burned. It is likely that any spoils taken included harvesting the crops of the fields left behind. With this victory, Joshua and his army had a major foothold on the central plateau and had in essence divided Canaan (see map on page 183).

Following the victory over Ai, Joshua moved the people north to Mount Ebal and Mount Gerizim. There they built an altar to God and wrote the law on stones as Moses had directed (Deut. 27:2–3). They also had a covenant renewal ceremony at which the people heard the leaders read the Law, and they pronounced the blessings and curses antiphonally from the two mounts. We are not told when this ceremony took place, but from the guidelines in Deuteronomy 31, it was likely during the autumn at the Feast of Booths. This would put it about six months after they had crossed the Jordan River.

The Southern Campaign

Read Joshua 9–10.

During this period, word of Israel's successes was spreading. The Canaanites responded in two different ways. The majority of the states gathered their forces to form an alliance against the invaders. But the people of Gibeon, a major city-state about 10 kilometers northwest of Jerusalem, chose to respond differently. They decided that they would not wait to be annihilated. Instead, they would try to join Joshua and his group. If Joshua was not willing to make alliances, they would try to trick him. They selected envoys to dress in their oldest, most worn clothing and to carry stale, dried-out provisions. These men were to present themselves as having come from a far distance. Most likely they circled around to enter the Israelite camp from the other side.

> In dealing with Gibeon, the one thing Joshua did not do was ask God.

When they arrived, they asserted that they were from a foreign country and desired to form an alliance. Joshua and the leaders examined these envoys, trying to find holes in their story. The one thing they did not do was ask God. So they formed a mutual defense treaty (probably of the type in the ANE known as a parity treaty). Three days later, as the Gibeonites prepared to return home, the truth came out—they were from just over the plateau.[14] The people complained about the situation, but Joshua and the leaders said that they could not wipe them out because of the oath. Rather, they would make them woodcutters and water bearers for the entire community and for the altar of God (Josh. 9:27).

Upon hearing of the alliance between the Gibeon group and the Israelites, King Adoni-Zedek of Jerusalem panicked. He called upon the kings of Hebron, Jarmuth, Lachish, and Eglon to join him in a campaign against Gibeon as punishment for what they had done. The five kings attacked Gibeon, and the Gibeonites sent messengers to Joshua asking for help. This time Joshua asked God, who confirmed that they should keep their word, regardless of how it had been coerced.

Joshua and his troops marched all night and surprised the attacking soldiers, who then fled before the superior numbers. What follows is one of the most controversial and least understood passages in the Bible. Taken at face value, the text states that the sun stood still, allowing the nation to finish the battle as they chased the enemy down the valley of Aijalon. This seems impossible in any modern understanding of how the universe works,[15] but regardless of the details, the overall conclusion was that God assisted Joshua and his troops, first by hailstones and then by some celestial effects. At the end, the southern alliance was defeated, and the kings were trapped in a cave at Makkedah. After destroying the armies, Joshua executed the five kings. He then attacked and took the cities of Makkedah, Libnah, Lachish, Gezer, Eglon, Hebron, and Debir. The mop-up operations brought the entire Negev as far as Kadesh Barnea under their control. With this, Joshua and his troops returned to Gilgal, having control of approximately two-thirds of the land.

The Northern Campaign
Following these victories, Jabin, the king of Hazor, decided it was time to act and developed an alliance among the remaining forces in the region (Josh. 11:1–3). *Read Joshua 11–12.*

These forces gathered at a location called the waters of Merom. The exact location of this site is not known, but given the use of chariots, the Jezreel Valley is very likely.[16] This area would also make sense in terms of tactics, since the goal was to destroy the Israelite camp at Gilgal in the Jordan River valley. However, the Israelites were able to attack the Canaanites first, and they scored a decisive victory. Joshua's troops then pursued fleeing Canaanites as far as the Sidon area (about 70 to 100 kilometers, depending on the location of Merom). Hazor, the major city, was burned, and the rest of the cities captured.

With the conclusion of this campaign, the Israelites now had control of the land God had promised, as described in Joshua 12. The entire campaign appears to have taken about five years, for according to Joshua 14:10, Caleb observed that it had been forty-five years since he had performed his reconnaissance at Kadesh Barnea. Even after these successes, however, many Canaanites were still living in the land. When we get into the period of the judges, we will see that God had several reasons for allowing this situation. First, the population of the Israelites was not large enough to completely resettle the land from the tribes they were displacing. Second, the delay would be a test of the faith and faithfulness of subsequent generations. A third reason was to allow the people who had participated in the conquest to this point the opportunity to enjoy the land they had conquered. Another possibility, although it is never overtly expressed, may have been to allow the Canaanites an opportunity to turn to Israel's God and to become part of that people (like the Gibeonites).

> Even after the Israelite successes, many Canaanites were still living in the land.

HAZOR. A major center in the North, and the third and last city that Joshua burned.

DIVISION OF THE LAND

The next ten chapters give a detailed description of the division of the land, which was done by lot with God directing the outcome. While it might be a good exercise to find the boundary indicators on a map, many of the sites are uncertain. However, any good Bible atlas shows the basic outline of the various territories.

Read Joshua 12–22.

The Levites were not given a territory but were given specific cities throughout the entire region. Likewise, when the tribe of Simeon received its share, it was within a broader territory given to Judah. By the time of the united kingdom, the tribe of Simeon had been essentially absorbed by Judah. This fulfilled the prophecy given by Jacob in Genesis 49.

Two special allocations were made. The first was that of Caleb, one of the two spies who had expressed trust that God would give them the land. We find him now, forty-five years later, still exhibiting the same trust. As Judah was given its share, he asked for the city of Hebron as his portion of the inheritance because it was strong and fortified.

The other special allocation was given to the family of Zelophehad of the tribe of Manasseh, who had five daughters and no sons. When his daughters came and asked for an equal portion of the inheritance on behalf of their father, it was granted to them.[17]

At this point, Joshua also designated the cities of refuge. These were Levitical towns set aside so that someone who had inadvertently committed a capital crime (e.g., manslaughter) could escape there and be protected until a trial had been conducted. If the crime was demonstrated to be inadvertent, the person could remain in the city of refuge until the high priest died.

With the division of the land, Joshua dismissed the Transjordanian tribes (Reuben, Gad, and half of Manasseh) about 1400 BCE.[18] Their departure almost caused a civil war. When they got to the Jordan River, they decided to erect a monument in the form of a large altar. The rest of the tribes heard of it and understood it to be an altar that would take away from the tabernacle. The Transjordanian tribes protested that they had not intended it for worship but as a memorial to remind their descendants of their loyalties to the people across the river. This response satisfied the rest of the tribes, and they departed in peace.

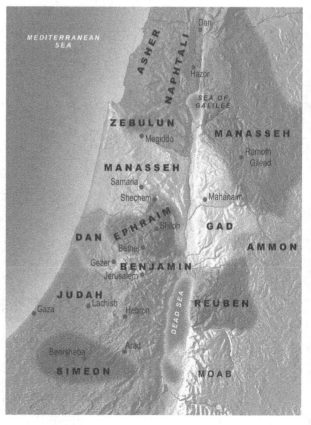

TRIBAL BOUNDARIES. The distribution of the various Israelite tribes in the land of Palestine.

JOSHUA'S FAREWELL

Read Joshua 23–24.

Sometime after this, Joshua called together the people to give a final farewell. Chapters 23 and 24 contain two speeches—one to the leaders and one to the people. In them, Joshua reminded the people of several things. First, he pointed out that God was the one who had brought them to the land and had given it to them. As part of the process, Joshua reminded them, they were living in houses they had not built and enjoying the produce from vineyards and olive trees they had not planted. Second, he made clear that they were not finished with the conquest, that there were many peoples yet to be driven out. Moreover, God would assist them in this process. Third, he reminded them that they had the law of God in the book of Moses to serve as a guide. The key guideline was that they were not to serve the gods of the people who had occupied the land before them. He noted that some of the Israelites were already serving those gods or were still clinging to the gods they had brought from Egypt. Joshua challenged the people to put away those foreign gods and to serve YHWH, the true God. However, as we will see, the people failed to do so. This behavior was to become a pattern that would plague the nation for the next thousand years.

After this final challenge, Joshua died at the age of 110. We are not given Joshua's age throughout his career, so we are unable to determine the date of his death. He was likely at least as old as Caleb, who at the end of the conquest was 85. If so, that means Joshua died no later than 1375 BCE. However, based on the picture we see in the book of the Judges, which suggests that he was older than Caleb, it is likely that he died a few years earlier than that.

THE SHEPHELAH. The transition zone between the central highlands occupied by Israel and the coastal plains. This rugged terrain provided a natural barrier that separated Israel from international affairs for centuries.

DISTINGUISHING CULTURES

Identifying a clear line of demarcation between the Israelite and Canaanite cultures is a difficult archaeological task. Sometimes this expected distinction is labeled the difference between the Bronze Age and the Iron Age or between the Middle Bronze and the Late Bronze cultures. However, it is clear from Judges that the early Israelites did not possess iron and thus were also part of the Bronze Age culture. They may also have been on the same technological level as the Canaanites they displaced. Careful archaeology suggests that what we should be looking for is a subtle distinction between two similar cultures, such as the difference between the Late Bronze IIA and the Late Bronze IIB levels (Randall Price, *The Stones Cry Out* [Eugene, Ore.: Harvest House, 1997], 158).

A significant point is that Joshua did not appoint a successor as mediator for the covenant. This set the stage for a period where the nation kept floundering—the subject of the next chapter.

REVIEW QUESTIONS

1. What does the Hebrew word *herem* mean? Why did God place the Canaanites under this ban?

2. Describe the Canaanite religion. Biblically speaking, what was wrong with it?

3. Who was Rahab, and why is she important?

4. What was unique about the way the Israelites entered the land? Why might God have done it that way?

5. Describe the "battle" of Jericho.

6. What went wrong at Ai? How was the dilemma resolved?

7. Describe the southern campaign.

8. Describe the northern campaign.

9. Which cities were burned? What did the people do with the rest of them?

10. Describe the allocation of the land to the various tribes.

11. How did Joshua challenge the people of Israel in his farewell speech?

10

CHAPTER

The Best of Times, the Worst of Times

OVERVIEW

Soon after occupying the land, many Israelites began adopting Canaanite practices. When they got into trouble and asked God for help, He sent judges to deliver them. The biblical writer mentions a number of them but covers three in some depth. The last section of the book of Judges relates two episodes that show how bad things had become. The story of Ruth, however, provides a positive contrast.

STUDY GOALS

▶ Show how the Israelites adapted idolatry after Joshua died.

▶ Describe the office of judge.

▶ Trace the three major and several minor judges.

▶ Discuss the two appendixes to Judges that show the depravity of the nation.

▶ Present Ruth as a reflection of how the system was supposed to work.

The book of Joshua ends with the nation finally settled in the land that had been promised. The time was about fifty years after leaving Egypt (including forty years in the desert, five years for the conquest, and then five years or so before Joshua gave his farewell). The book of Judges covers the period between the conquest and the decision on the part of the people to have a king (that is, approximately from 1400 to 1070 BCE).

The book of Ruth takes place at the end of that period and serves as a bright counterpoint to the dark picture painted in Judges. In some ways, it shows how the system should have worked, while Judges shows what actually happened.

A NEW GENERATION

Read Judges 1:1 – 3:6

The book of Judges makes it clear that we are now looking at the next generation. The arrangement of the narrative is both topical and chronological. The individual judges seem to be generally listed in sequential order, though with some overlap. However, the introductory section provides an overview of the entire period, and the final section relates two events that could have occurred at any time during that period.

Most of the material in the introductory overview reflects the difficulties of the nation rather than its successes. As such, it gives us just a few highlights. We are told of how Judah and Simeon did well in their conquests but could not take control of several areas because the inhabitants had iron chariots.[1] The same was true of the other tribes, and specific unconquered cities throughout the nation are listed.

Then rather abruptly we are told of how the angel of the Lord appeared and condemned the people for failing to keep their part of the covenant. The key to this condemnation is Judges 2:2, "You shall not make a covenant with the people

RAMPARTS OF TROY. Typical of the Bronze Age, a major city surrounded by stone walls with gateways approached by ramps. The Philistines, having come out of the Aegean Sea area during this period, built their cities similar to Troy in Asia Minor. The gates were made of wood and have generally not survived. When Samson stormed out of Gaza, he yanked the wooden gate out of the stone wall.

of this land, but you shall break down their altars." The concept of a covenant with the Canaanites involved tolerating and eventually adopting their pagan religions. As a consequence, the inhabitants of the land would become a snare to the Israelites.

This entire section seems hard to follow because we don't arrive at the cause of these problems until Joshua 2:6. The crucial verse is 2:10, which notes that the people served God only as long as Joshua's generation was alive. As the new generation matured and took leadership, the people went after the false gods of the people of the land. However, we must recall that this was an overall condemnation not only of that generation, but of the generations to follow. The passage makes clear that each time God sent a judge, the people would return to God only for that judge's lifetime. After the judge died, the people returned to their evil ways until God again sent hard times. The entire process was a downward spiral, with each generation worse than the previous one.

We also need to understand what the book means by "judges." We tend to interpret the word in terms of judicial procedure: a judge is one who arbitrates legal issues. Some of the "judges" in this period (e.g., Deborah) did handle legal matters, but that was not their function within the context of this book. Rather, the focus was on their national service to bring the people back to God by intervening in times of foreign oppression. The judges themselves were people chosen by God for specific circumstances. They tended to work regionally (as opposed to nationally). Because of this, there seems to have been overlap, as shown in the chart on page 198. Each judge also seems to have been given specific gifts from God to accomplish his or her task. These differed with every judge, and only some of them were spectacular gifts, such as the ones we associate with Samson.

TERRITORY OF THE JUDGES. The spheres of influence of three major judges of Israel— Deborah, Gideon, and Samson.

THE PROCESS BEGINS

The process began early. Because of the apostasy of the people, God allowed Cushan-Rishathaim from Mesopotamia to move in and oppress the people. After

Read Judges 3:7–31.

eight years, the people began to cry out to God. In response God raised up for them the first judge, Othniel, the nephew of Caleb who had won Caleb's daughter by conquering the city of Debir, formerly called Kiriath Sepher (Judg. 1:11–13). Through God's Spirit, Othniel led the uprising, and the Israelites were able to win deliverance. As a result, there was peace for forty years.

Then the cycle began again. The Israelites again "did evil." This time God's instrument was King Eglon of Moab, who was allied with the Ammonites and the

CHRONOLOGY OF THE JUDGES *

Oppressor	Yrs. of Oppression	Judge	Yrs. of Peace	Tribe	Est. Dates (BCE)
Mesopotamia (Cushan-Rishathaim)	8	Othniel	40	Judah	1385-1377 1377-1337
Moab (Eglon)	18	Ehud	80	Benjamin	1337-1319
Philistines	?	Shamgur	?	?	1319-1239
Canaanites (Jabin/Sisera)	20	Deborah	40	Ephraim	? - 1239 1239-1219 1219-1179
Midianites (Oreb, Zeeb, Zebah, Zalmunna)	7	Gideon	40	Manasseh	1179-1172 1172-1132
Civil War (Abimelech)	3	Tola	23	Issachar	1132-1129
Ammonites	18	Jair	22	Manasseh**	1129-1106 1129-1107
Philistines	40	Jephthah	6	Gad	1124-1106
		Ibzan	8	Judah	1106-1100
		Elon	10	Zebulun	1100-1092
		Abdon	7	Ephraim	1092-1082
		Eli			1082-1075 1105-1065
		Samson		Dan	1085-1045
		Samuel		Ephraim	1075-1055 1065-1045

* The chronology of the Judges necessarily incorporates some overlap. This chart was developed with three arbitrary anchors. Othniel was put 15 years after the completion of the conquest, which is assumed to be 1400 BCE. Samuel overlapped Saul, who apparently began his reign in 1050. BCE. Jephthah was placed 300 years after the conquest of Sihon, which was about 1406 BCE. The rest of the figures are derived from the text of Judges and 1 Samuel, with a few arbitrary overlaps so that they fit within that outline.

**Jair's tribe is not given. He is identified as from Gilead, the Transjordan region of Reuben, Gad, and Manasseh. His burial place at Kamon was probably in the Manasseh region.

Amalekites. Interestingly, we find that he occupied Jericho ("the City of Palms," Judg. 3:13).[2] After eighteen years, the people cried out to God, and He raised up Ehud to be judge. Using his left-handedness, Ehud was able to smuggle a sword into a meeting with Eglon and kill him. Ehud then escaped and sounded the alarm to gather the Israelite troops. Taking advantage of the loss of the Moabite king, the Israelites drove out their oppressors. Here we find the longest period of peace during the time of the judges.

At the end of this section, we read of one more judge who served at the end of this period, Shamgar.[3] All we are told about him is that he attacked the Philistines (which would put him on the southwest side of the country). We are not even told how long he served as judge.

DEBORAH

The heart of the book of Judges focuses on three people. They are sometimes called major judges because of the amount of material devoted to them.[4] They illustrate the pattern we have already noted. The first major judge was a woman, which I find very interesting—indeed, she held a position of leadership even before she assumed the role of deliverer.

Read Judges 4–5.

As the account begins, we see the same pattern: the Israelites did evil and as punishment were subjugated. This time the oppression came from the north, specifically from Hazor, which had been rebuilt from the time of Joshua's conquest. If our dating of the judges is correct and Deborah began her work around 1239 BCE, then it had been about 160 years since Joshua had destroyed the city at the end of the conquest. The leaders of Hazor were Jabin, the king, and Sisera, the commanding general. Deborah lived farther south in the region of

MOUNT TABOR. The mountain whose steep slopes Barak and Deborah used to put the Canaanite chariots at a disadvantage. God then provided rain that allowed the Israelites to finish off the victory.

DEBORAH'S SONG

In the battle against Sisera's army, according to the Song of Deborah, "the clouds poured down water" and the "river Kishon swept them away" (Judg. 5:4, 21). This sudden rain seems to have turned the soil into mire, bogging down the chariots and making them easy targets for the Israelites who were on the slopes above. Judges 5 is ancient poetry and somewhat difficult to understand, but there are interesting expressions within it. For example, verse 20 talks of how the stars fought from heaven. This language seems to suggest involvement of angelic beings, but that allusion is not clear. Another interesting point is how Deborah condemned the other tribes for not participating in the conflict. These words may indicate that all the tribes (or at least the northern ones) were asked to participate but that God had known in advance that only two would do so.

Ephraim, where she had acquired a degree of fame as a prophetess[5] and a judge (in a legal sense). As prophetess, she sent for a leader of the tribe of Naphtali named Barak. The word she had for him from God was that he was to take ten thousand militia from Naphtali and Zebulun and go to Mount Tabor. There, he was told, God would bring the Canaanites, and he was to defeat them.

Barak accepted her word, but he put up one qualification: "If you go with me, I will go; but if you don't go with me, I won't go" (Judg. 4:8). Deborah agreed but told him that there would be a cost. If she went along, he would not get honor for the victory; rather, it would go to a woman. It is to Barak's credit that he was unconcerned about who got the honor, and he agreed to the condition.

> If Deborah went along, the honor for the victory would go to a woman.

In the narrative account of the battle, we are told only that Sisera and his army (including nine hundred chariots) were routed. In Deborah's victory song, however, we learn that God intervened in the form of sending sudden rain on the battlefield. With the battle clearly lost, Sisera fled on foot, ending up in front of the tent of Jael, the wife of Heber, a Kenite. She invited Sisera in, because at the time, the Canaanites and the Kenites were on friendly terms. When Sisera asked for some water to assuage his thirst, she gave him milk (which would have been warm, for there was no refrigeration) and covered him with a rug.[6] After he had fallen into a deep sleep from exhaustion, she took a tent peg and drove it through his skull, killing him. When Barak, who was pursuing Sisera, showed up, Jael showed him the dead general. Thus, when Deborah wrote her victory song, it was

PALM TREE. A date palm, probably the kind of tree under which Deborah held court when she was called to be a judge in Israel.

WHO WERE THE KENITES?

Jael's husband, Heber, is identified as a Kenite. The Kenites were the relatives of Moses' father-in-law. A number of them joined the Israelites as they came into the land. Judges 1:16 tells of how they settled in the land, although the area they chose was in the south, near Arad. Jael's heroic deed occurred about 160 years later.

Jael who received the credit for killing the Canaanite general (Judg. 5:24–27).

Following this battle, the Israelites were able to overthrow the rest of the Canaanite forces. Apparently Hazor was burned again and this time remained unsettled for several hundred years, probably until the time of Solomon.

CARPET WEAVING. A handcraft developed thousands of years ago and still prized today. Originally rugs were used as coverings with the shag side down—which is the way Jael would have covered Sisera.

GIDEON

The second major judge is to me the most intriguing. The scene has shifted to the middle of the land, in the region of Manasseh. This episode begins with those same words, "The Israelites did evil in the eyes of the LORD." The oppression came from the east: the Midianites and their allies. When Israel asked God for help, He sent a prophet to tell them that the reason for the oppression was that they were worshiping the gods of the people in the land rather than maintaining spiritual integrity.

Read Judges 6–9.

Then the angel of the Lord showed up at Gideon's place, where he was threshing wheat in the winepress as he was hiding from the Midianites. While we are not sure what was going through his mind, we are given a hint in the conversation that is recorded. First, the messenger greeted him saying, "The LORD is with you, mighty warrior" (Judg. 6:12; remember, this is a man who was hiding). Gideon's response was to ask why the Lord no longer performed special deeds as he had done for their ancestors. To this, the Lord told Gideon to go in "this your strength and deliver Israel" (v. 14, my translation).

Two questions arise out of this exchange: What was Gideon's strength? And how was Gideon a "mighty warrior"? His strength seemed to be the faith he had just expressed in his response to God, a faith that accepted the historical accounts of God's works and expected them to be repeated. Thus, he was viewed as a "mighty warrior" because he was willing to obey God despite his natural fear. However, he always made sure that he understood the message correctly.

Gideon's strength seemed to be his faith.

We see that concern as the account develops. To verify that the one who appeared to him was God, Gideon asked permission to offer a sacrifice. This request was granted, and when the sacrifice was brought, the "angel" touched it with his staff, and the entire sacrifice was consumed. That night, following God's directions, Gideon took another bull from the herd of Joash, his father, and tore down his own father's altar to Baal.[7] He then built instead an altar to the Lord and offered his sacrifice on it (using the wood of the Asherah pole to burn the sacrifice).

THE ANGEL AT THE THRESHING FLOOR

The appearance of the angel of the Lord to Gideon is viewed by many scholars as another case of a theophany, that is, a manifestation of God himself. We see strong indications of this in verse 14, where we are told that the Lord spoke to Gideon, and again when the figure is said to accept Gideon's sacrifice (a kind of homage God's messengers would refuse). Most likely this "angel" was the second person of the Trinity, the Son. As for the location where this incident took place, it should be noted that threshing floors were normally on hilltops in order to take advantage of breezes to blow away the chaff. This blowing chaff, however, also would have served as an easy identifier for the Midianite raiders. Winepresses tended to be in lower regions, usually under trees that provided shade.

WINEPRESS. A structure, kept under trees for cooling shade, where grapes were placed on the upper tier and squeezed to allow the juice to run into the lower tub. Gideon threshed wheat at a winepress to avoid discovery by the Midianites.

right
THRESHING FLOOR. Usually located atop a hill to allow breezes to blow away the chaff, a structure with a flat surface so that oxen or donkeys could easily pull the sledges that broke the chaff from the grain kernels.

The next day the people of the town found the altar broken. They concluded that Gideon had done it and demanded that Joash hand over his son. Joash argued that if Baal was truly a god, he could defend himself. Not only did he refuse to hand over his son—he also asserted that anyone who fought for Baal would be put to death.

With this, Gideon was almost ready to lead the troops into battle against the Midianites. After calling them together, he verified that he had understood God correctly. Two nights running he put a sheep fleece out on the ground (ironically, on the threshing floor he had avoided earlier while threshing wheat) and asked for God's verification. The first night he asked God that the fleece be wet with dew while the ground was dry, and the second night he asked that those be reversed.[8] Both requests were granted, and Gideon led his troops toward the Midianites.

Because Gideon was a man of great faith, God was going to ask more of him. After sounding the alarm by blowing the trumpet[9] and sending messengers throughout the region, Gideon had gathered 32,000 troops—more than three times the number Deborah and Barak had used. Now God told him the number was too large. God wanted to be sure that the people would not think the upcoming victory was a result of their own strength. After all, the primary purpose was to remind the Israelites who their suzerain was and to show them that they had erred. So God had Gideon announce that anyone who had any fears was free to return home with no questions asked. As a result, 22,000 troops left, so that Gideon had an army the same size as Barak's.

But even this was too many. God told Gideon to survey the troops as they drank water from the local watering hole. Most of the troops knelt down and put their faces in the water. A small minority knelt down and used their hands to bring the water to their mouths. These were kept, and the rest were sent home. Now Gideon had but three hundred troops to face a large multitude of Midianites and their allies (apparently in the range of 135,000; cf. Judg. 8:10). Here he really had to trust God. To increase his confidence, God sent him into the enemy camp the next night to listen to the conversation. There he heard one of the Midianites relating a dream. His friends were interpreting it as showing that God was going to defeat them by the hand of Gideon.[10]

That night Gideon arranged his "army" around the Midianite camp just after they had changed the mid-watch. Each of his soldiers had a trumpet, a torch under a pitcher, and a sword. At Gideon's command, they all broke their pitchers, whipped their torches into flame, sounded the trumpets, and shouted. This racket awoke the camp of the Midianites and their allies. In the darkness, these disparate armies began fighting each other—while Gideon and his army observed. Soon Gideon and his handful of troops were pursuing the remnant. They also sent messengers to nearby tribes and asked for help. Several tribes, including Ephraim, sent help. After they had finished mopping up, the Ephraimites complained that they had not been in on the original battle. But Gideon was able to mollify them by pointing out that they had captured two of the key Midianite leaders.

However, not everyone was willing to help. As Gideon and his troops crossed over into the region of Transjordan, he asked for provisions from the Israelite towns of Succoth and Peniel. He was refused this aid, and he promised retribution on his return. After routing the last of the Midianite army and capturing its leaders, he returned and exacted retribution as promised.

At this point, the Israelites asked Gideon to be king, but he refused. He desired to focus the worship of Israel on God and decided to set up an ephod with

ANCIENT DIPLOMACY

Gideon's response to the Ephraimites is somewhat of a riddle: "What have I accomplished compared to you? Aren't the gleanings of Ephraim's grapes better than the full grape harvest of Abiezer?" (Judg. 8:2). What he does is downplay his own role as compared to the significance of destroying the Midianite leaders. Abiezer was the family from the tribe of Manasseh to which Gideon belonged, and thus his riddle suggests that while Ephraim felt that all they had were the leftovers (the gleanings), these were actually better than the first victory he had accomplished (the full grape harvest).

GIDEON'S EPHOD

An ephod was a vestlike garment worn by a priest. Exodus 28 describes the ephod that was designed especially for the high priest. It was attached to a breastpiece containing precious stones on which were engraved the names of the tribes. It also had a pouch in which were kept the Urim and Thummim, objects used for special inquiries of God. Gideon's ephod seems to have been designed to focus the attention of the people on God. Unfortunately, it became an object of worship itself. The total weight of the contributions from the spoil was about 350 ounces of gold, which would have produced a product weighing about 30 pounds (troy weight).

contributions from each of the Israelite leaders. Even these good intentions went wrong, however, and the ephod became a religious snare for the Israelites.

Gideon then retired. He had many wives who produced seventy sons, as well as at least one concubine who had a son named Abimelech. After Gideon died, the people again went after false gods (this time the text says they "prostituted themselves," Judg. 8:33). Law and order also broke down, and Abimelech persuaded the people of Shechem to make him king. They gave him silver from their temple, which was dedicated to Baal-Berith, and with this money he hired a gang of ruffians. Abimelech then took this gang to his father's house at Ophrah and executed all but one of his brothers. The youngest brother, Jotham, escaped, but before he fled, he gave a parable to the people of Shechem and pronounced a curse on them for their dishonorable deeds.

Three years later there was a falling out between the men of Shechem and Abimelech (their "king"). Abimelech led his forces against the town and destroyed it. He then advanced on the nearby town of Thebez, which had apparently joined Shechem in the revolt. As they assaulted the town, a woman dropped a millstone from the tower on his head, mortally wounding him. At this he requested that his armor-bearer finish him off so that it could not be said that a woman had killed him.

SEVERAL MINOR JUDGES

Read Judges 10–12.

After the civil war of Abimelech's day, the text tells of six minor judges, leaders who generally receive just a note in passing. As was the case with Shamgar, we have little information about Tola and Jair. We are told more regarding Jephthah.

The situation is familiar. The people did evil in the eyes of God, and God sent the Ammonites to oppress them.[11] The people cried out to the Lord, but He responded by stressing their continual rebellion and told them to cry out to the gods they had chosen. The point hit home, and the Israelites put away the foreign gods. They also met at Mizpah to discuss the situation. They decided to ask for help from Jephthah. Because he was the son of a prostitute, Jephthah had been ostracized and had left home. He had also accumulated a large following of

God told the Israelites to cry out to the gods they had chosen; the people got the point.

adventurers. It was this demonstrated leadership that attracted the Israelite leaders, and they agreed to make Jephthah their head so that he might deliver them.

Jephthah is most noted for the promise he made to God before he went to war: "If you give the Ammonites into my hands, whatever comes out of the door of my house to meet me when I return in triumph from the Ammonites will be the LORD's, and I will sacrifice it as a burnt offering" (Judg. 11:30–31). He won the battle, but when he returned, the first thing that came out to meet him was his daughter, his only child. The usual translation of the vow implies that he then performed a human sacrifice. The word translated "and," however, could also be rendered "or,"[12] and in this case, it seems to indicate that Jephthah anticipates two possible outcomes.

This interpretation is supported, first, by the response of the daughter, who asks for time to lament that she will not be able to marry—not that she is going to die (11:37). Second, the text never uses the words "sacrifice" or "burnt offering" in this section, but rather that "he did to her as he had vowed" (v. 39). Third, human sacrifice was an abomination among pious Israelites. While it was sometimes practiced in the land, it took place always in the context of service to false gods. In this light, I would suggest that Hannah's dedication of Samuel to God (1 Sam. 1:11) is the model for what we see here.

The extended narrative on Jephthah is followed by a short section that lists three more judges. Ibzan, Elon, and Abdon are cited as people who judged Israel for short periods of time. The significant point of these final three leaders is that each served in different regions. Moreover, we are not told that the whole nation of Israel enjoyed the periods of peace pointed out under the earlier judges. This overall pattern will come to a climax with the last major judge, Samson.

SAMSON

Perhaps the most famous figure in the book of Judges is Samson. His great strength is legendary, and everyone knows that it was connected with his hair. The fact that he was a tragic character whose fate was entwined with a woman adds to the mystique. However, there is a lot more to the story.

Read Judges 13–16.

Like all the other episodes in this book, it begins with the observation that Israel did what was evil in the eyes of the Lord. This time the oppressors were the Philistines. It is interesting to note that the people suffered for forty years—yet they did not ask God for help. Rather, they feared irritating their oppressors. The story picks up with Manoah, a man from the tribe of Dan, whose wife was barren. We are told that the angel of the Lord appeared to her and told her that she was going to become pregnant. However, specific guidelines were given for her pregnancy and for the soon-to-be-born boy, for he would be a lifelong Nazirite.[13] Manoah

> The people suffered for forty years—yet they did not ask God for help.

asked for verification, and the angel appeared to him and verified the message. In due time, Samson was born.

As a young man, Samson became intrigued by Philistine women. His first act was to insist that his parents arrange a marriage with a woman from Timnah.[14] Reluctantly they did so, and as they made the trip to Timnah, they ran into a lion. When Samson faced this beast, he was specially empowered by the Spirit of the Lord, and he killed the lion with his bare hands. On a later trip, he noticed that the lion's carcass had dried up and bees had taken up residence in it. He then took the honey from the dead body and ate it, violating part of his Nazirite restrictions.

As the marriage arrangement continued, they arrived at the weeklong celebration, normally a time when alcoholic beverages flowed freely. It seems as if Samson was also imbibing, given that he made a wager with thirty Philistines over a riddle. Obviously the riddle he proposed was not something that could be reasoned out. The Philistines came to that conclusion and threatened Samson's bride and her family. She used every trick she could to get the answer from Samson, and finally succeeded. She told the Philistines, who promptly gave their answer to Samson. He was furious because he knew where they got the answer. He went down to Ashkelon, killed thirty other Philistines, and took their clothes to pay off his wager. Because Samson then abandoned his wife, she married another man.

Sometime later Samson cooled down and decided to go to his wife. When he found out that she was now someone else's wife, he became angry again. This time he trapped three hundred foxes and tied their tails together in pairs. He attached flaming torches to them and released them into the grain fields. The result was tremendous destruction of the ripened grain as well as olive orchards and vineyards. The Philistines soon figured out who did it, and they burned Samson's wife and father-in-law to death. Thus began open conflict between the Philistines and the Israelites.

The men of Judah became upset with Samson for disturbing the Philistines who ruled over them, so they turned him over. But Samson broke free when the Spirit of the Lord came on him, and he killed a thousand Philistines with a donkey's jawbone. Although he was a reluctant leader, Samson kept the fight going for twenty years.

Then he met Delilah, a Philistine woman who lived in the valley of Sorek. When they figured out that Samson was enamored with Delilah, the Philistine leaders bought her off to try to get the secret of his strength. Like his former wife, she used every trick in the book, but for a while he put her off by giving false answers. Finally, he told her the truth: he was a Nazirite and his hair had never been cut. Samson was aware that cutting his hair would violate his Nazirite restrictions. Unfortunately, as soon as Delilah found out his secret, she waited until he was asleep and then cut his hair. One of the most tragic statements in the Bible comes next. When Samson awoke, hearing that the

> Samson did not know that the Lord had left him.

PHILISTINE TEMPLE. Excavations at Tel Qasile showing the two central pillars of the Philistine temple there. These would have been similar to the two pillars Samson used to destroy the temple to the god Dagon.

Philistines were there, he planned to leave, "but he did not know that the LORD had left him."

Samson was captured, and the Philistines gouged out his eyes and put him to work at a grain mill in Gaza. Sometime later, the Philistine leaders planned a big feast at the temple of Dagon, their god, to celebrate the capture of their enemy. Samson was brought in to be a laughingstock. He was placed by the central pillars of the building, which held an overflow crowd of about three thousand. By this time, his hair had begun to grow again, perhaps symbolizing a new Nazirite dedication. Samson prayed, asking God for one last surge of strength. With this, he pushed down the central pillars, killing more Philistines as he died than he did during his life.

TWO APPENDIXES

The last five chapters of Judges give two accounts that illustrate how depraved the nation had become.[15] Both incidents involve Levites, who were supposed to be the spiritual leaders of the nation. And both are characterized by the phrase, "Each man did what was right in his own eyes."

Read Judges 17–21.

The first account involves a man named Micah who lived in Ephraim. Micah had stolen a large amount of silver from his mother. When she pronounced a curse on the thief, he admitted his guilt and returned the money. She then gave it back to him to make an idol, which he did. After he had set up this idol in a shrine, an out-of-work Levite named Jonathan ben Gershom[16] from Bethlehem came by. Micah hired him to be a priest to him and to tend his shrine.

Some time later, men from the tribe of Dan came through looking for new territory for their people because they were being pressured by the Philistines from the west. They found Micah's shrine and asked if they would have success in their mission. Jonathan assured them that they would, and they went on their way. Later they found a Canaanite city named Laish far to the north. It was isolated enough that they felt confident in attacking it, and then they returned for their families and friends. As they migrated north, they stopped at Micah's place again. This time they took the shrine (and idol). When Jonathan tried to stop them, they gave him a chance to go with them and serve the same idol for a larger audience. They also threatened him with death if he tried to stop them. Jonathan went with them, and they soon reached Laish. After conquering the city, they called it Dan.

The second episode involved a Levite who lived in Ephraim and who had a concubine from Bethlehem. She ran away, and he went after her. His father-in-law detained him, and after several false starts, the Levite and his concubine headed back late in the day. He refused to stop at the Canaanite city of Jerusalem and instead made it as far as the city of Gibeah in Benjamin. They were going to camp in the city square, but an old man invited them to his home instead. That night some wicked men assaulted the house demanding that the *man* be sent out to them. The Levite kicked his concubine outside, and she was then assaulted by the men all night. Finally, she crawled to the door, where she died. When the Levite came out the next morning, she did not respond, so he put her body on the donkey and returned home.

The Levite then cut the woman's body into twelve pieces and sent them to all the areas of Israel, no doubt with an explanation of what had happened. In response, the people of Israel gathered together and demanded that the leaders of Benjamin give up the men of Gibeah for punishment. They refused, and the result was a civil war. The people inquired of God regarding how the war should be

HIGH PLACE OF DAN. Ruins of the altar in the city of Dan, which became a center of idolatry early in the history of the nation of Israel.

WHAT WERE THE MEN OF GIBEAH AFTER?

The text says literally, "Bring out the man who came to your house so we can know him" (Judg. 19:22; NIV, "so we can have sex with him"). Some have tried to argue that the men were violating rules of hospitality. The Hebrew verb for "know," however, is often used to indicate sexual relations (e.g., Gen. 4:1, literally, "Adam knew his wife and she conceived"). In other words, what the men of Gibeah were after was homosexual rape.

fought and were somewhat frustrated when they followed God's directions and lost on the first two days.[17] On the third day, they were able to win, however, and in the process, they almost wiped out the tribe of Benjamin. Only six hundred men survived. They realized that the tribe was in danger of extinction, but they were also in an awkward situation, for they had made a vow that they would not allow the men of Benjamin to take wives from any other tribe.

They found two loopholes. First, the men of Jabesh Gilead had not come up to the battle. So they went there, killed off all the men and married women, and brought four hundred virgin women to Benjamin. This was not enough, so they set up a ruse whereby the remaining men would be able to kidnap wives during an annual festival at Shiloh.

The book culminates with the most tragic observation. "In those days Israel had no king; everyone did as he saw fit" (Judg. 21:25).

INTERLUDE: RUTH

Although the events recorded in the book of Ruth took place during the same period, this narrative is like a breath of fresh air after the book of Judges. It demonstrates how some of the socioeconomic measures given by God, such as gleaning and the kinsman-redeemer, were to function. It demonstrates how non-Israelites were to be accepted into the nation. It demonstrates the importance of faithfulness within the covenant. And it also tells of the not-so-blue-blood ancestry of the nation's greatest king.

Read Ruth 1–4.

The story begins with a picture similar to what we have seen in the book of Judges. There was famine in the land, likely as a result of God's punishing the nation during one of the periods of its disobedience. As a result, a man from Bethlehem named Elimelech took his family to Moab. While there, he died. Subsequently, his two sons married Moabite women. Then they too died, leaving three widows.

> The narrative of Ruth is like a breath of fresh air after the book of Judges.

The mother, Naomi, decided to go back to Bethlehem, because she had heard that there was food there. This move made sense, for Bethlehem was where her relatives were. Her two daughters-in-law started out with her, but she urged them to return to their homes. Orpah did so, but Ruth adamantly refused, making a beautiful speech showing that she had adopted Naomi's God.

Once back in Bethlehem, Ruth went out to glean in the fields, taking advantage of the provision in the law for widows and orphans. She found herself in a field belonging to one of her father-in-law's relatives, Boaz. The text shows that Boaz had a good relationship with his workers. He also quickly noted Ruth and asked about her. His manager had positive things to say, and Boaz invited her to join his workers for lunch and encouraged her to stay in his fields.[18] He also directed his workers to make sure there would be plenty for Ruth to glean.

BETHLEHEM FIELDS. Workers in fields "white" for harvest in the eastern outskirts of Bethlehem. Women still harvest grain in the same fields Ruth once worked.

Ruth gleaned in Boaz's fields throughout the different harvests, beginning with the barley harvest in May and continuing through the wheat harvest in late June. At the time of threshing, probably in July, Naomi instructed Ruth to dress in her best clothing and visit Boaz at the threshing floor when there would be celebration (and he would be somewhat inebriated). Ruth followed her directions and lay down at his feet after everyone was asleep. Boaz awoke and recognized that someone was at his feet. When he asked who was there, Ruth proclaimed that she was asking for her rights since he was their kinsman-redeemer. He responded that there was actually another relative who was closer and had the first rights but that he would ensure that the issue was resolved the next day. He gave her a large amount of grain to take to her mother-in-law and sent her home before daylight so that no one would start rumors.

That morning Boaz went to the city gate where legal transactions were conducted. He selected ten witnesses and, when the other relative came by, announced that he had some business. He began by pointing out the need to redeem the land owned by Elimelech. At this point, the relative was eager. Then he found out that marriage to Ruth was involved, at which point he backed out.[19] Boaz agreed to take his place, and the transaction was completed by the other relative's passing his sandal to Boaz.

A RISKY MOVE

The Moabites were distantly related to the Israelites, for they were descendants of Lot through his oldest daughter (Gen. 19:37). However, because of their lack of hospitality during the Exodus, they were forbidden to "enter the assembly of the LORD" even to the tenth generation (Deut. 23:3). Thus, Moab was not the best place for Elimelech to move to, and it definitely would not be a place in which a good Israelite man would normally look for wives for his sons.

THE KINSMAN-REDEEMER

In Israelite society, the kinsman-redeemer (Heb. *go'el*) had several responsibilities under the law. In case of murder, he ensured justice (e.g., Num. 35:19). He was also responsible for redeeming land that had been leased if it was to be returned prior to the year of Jubilee. Finally, he was responsible for marrying the widow of the deceased relative if there were no male heirs. Ruth was asking Boaz to fulfill these last two responsibilities.

So Boaz and Ruth married and soon had a son. The genealogy at the end of the book shows that they were the great-grandparents of David.

LOOKING AHEAD

As we wrap up this chapter, we need to step back a bit and evaluate what we have seen. The nation is now in the Promised Land, but it has not been faithful to the covenant. Instead of doing what God had ordained, the Israelites did evil in God's eyes. As the last verse of Judges puts it, "Everyone did as he saw fit." In other words, "relativism," as we call it today, was the standard of the day.

Still, God has been faithful to His people, preserving them while at the same time judging them. This demonstration of faithfulness should have served as a reminder of the covenant, which was unconditional. God was their suzerain, and they could obey and be blessed or disobey and suffer.

Judges and Ruth were probably written early in the period of the monarchy, likely by Samuel. They represented a warning to the subsequent generations regarding what would happen to them should they continue on the way they had been going. But they also showed hope, demonstrating that God was both faithful and compassionate. Furthermore, the book of Ruth represented a testimony of how outsiders could be accepted within the covenant community by putting their faith in the God of the covenant. Both books were added to the increasing canon.

We now come to a point of transition where the nation would decide to make drastic changes in their leadership. Would that help them to be more faithful? That is the subject of the next chapter.

REVIEW QUESTIONS

1. What happened between the generation of the conquest and the next generation?

2. Describe the Israelites' sin cycle.

3. Why was Deborah significant?

4. What were Gideon's weaknesses and strengths?

5. What are minor judges, and what role did they play?

6. Evaluate Samson's character and career.

7. What is the function of the two appendixes at the end of the book of Judges? How well do they fulfill this function?

8. What is the point of the book of Ruth?

11
CHAPTER

Give Us a King Like the Rest of the Nations

OVERVIEW

After a prolonged period of foreign oppression, the Israelites concluded that they needed a king to resolve their national security problems. Samuel, the last judge, anointed Saul as the first king. Because of Saul's disobedience, God had Samuel anoint David, who remained loyal to Saul despite the latter's attempts to kill him. As this chapter of the story ends, Israel's king lies dead from suicide on the battlefield, and the nation is ready to turn to David.

STUDY GOALS

▶ Show how Samuel was a transition figure from the judges to the monarchy.

▶ Explain why the people of Israel decided they wanted a king.

▶ Show how God gave the people the king they wanted.

▶ Describe the character flaws that make Saul a tragic figure.

▶ Show the contrast between Saul and David.

▶ Trace Saul's life to his tragic death.

We have now arrived at a crucial point of transition for the nation. From our perspective, the transition seems sudden, but a closer look shows that it was lengthy. In fact, we could say that it took a couple of generations. In the process, the nation went from a divided people who focused on their tribal and local identities to the semblance of a unified state. The two books of Samuel were written at the end of this transition process. Their purpose was to show future generations the reason for having a king and how the people had rejected God in the process. As we will see over the next several chapters, however, the transition to a national unity was never completed because the nation was not unified in its worship of God.

THE LAST OF THE JUDGES

Read 1 Samuel 1–7.

Up to this point, the nation had been led by judges and priests. Theologians call the type of government exercised during this period a *theocracy*, that is, one in which God was the ruler.[1] The priests were God's intermediaries in internal affairs. As we saw earlier, their responsibilities included worship and sacrifice but also should have included socioeconomic issues. Politically, each town or village ran its own affairs. When national issues arose, God raised up the judges—and less obviously, prophets—who gave guidance and leadership for specific issues.

Because the nation was never united spiritually, it was not really united politically either. From the time of Othniel on, the only time there was any semblance

SHIP FRESCO. A fresco from Santorini, an Aegean island, that illustrates ships used during the middle of the second millennium BCE. Ships like these probably carried the "Sea Peoples"—of whom the Philistines were a part.

of unity was when outsiders oppressed various regions. Even then, the usual response was regional.

We have also seen that the priesthood, the spiritual leadership, left much to be desired. As we begin the book of Samuel, we find that the priestly system was actually corrupt (or had corrupt elements). It was into this situation that God intervened.

Samuel begins with the account of a priest named Elkanah who had two wives, Hannah and Peninnah; he had apparently married the latter because Hannah was unable to have children.[2] Elkanah is noted for being faithful in his worship at the tabernacle, which was now situated in Shiloh. Annually he would take his family to worship there, and it is in connection with one such journey that we are introduced to Hannah's predicament. She had become very distraught from the irritation created by the other wife, the one who had children. As a result, she had forgone the festivities and had gone into the tabernacle to pray.[3]

Hannah prayed fervently, and Eli the priest mistook that fervency for being drunk (which says a lot about the people he saw in the tabernacle). Hannah protested that she was not drunk but just miserable, and she had poured out her soul before God. In the process, she made a promise (or vow): if God would give her a son, she would dedicate him to God (that is, make him a Nazirite) for life. God soon answered her prayer, and she faithfully fulfilled her promise. Samuel was brought to the tabernacle to serve God.

Things were not going well in the tabernacle. Eli had apparently been a faithful follower of God, but his sons were not. In fact, the text states that they did not

WHO WROTE 1 AND 2 SAMUEL?

Our English Bibles, following the Hebrew, name these books after Samuel, who likely began the work of writing the narrative. Samuel's death, however, is recorded in 1 Samuel 25, while the narrative continues on to cover the reign of David. Therefore, the final author must have lived at the time of Solomon or later, and the prophet Nathan is a likely candidate. The Septuagint calls these two books 1 and 2 Kingdoms (or Reigns), making the next two 3 and 4 Kingdoms.

MYCENAEAN CITY. Remains from the Mycenaean culture, which was located in Crete and Greece but spread throughout the Mediterranean region. It entered Canaan with the Philistines, predominantly after the fall of Troy.

know the Lord. They saw their position as an opportunity for self-satisfaction. As such, they robbed the people's sacrifices (not following the legal guidelines regarding their portions) and slept with the women who served in the tabernacle.[4] God first brought a prophet to condemn Eli for honoring his sons above God, because, although he knew they were in the wrong, he acquiesced to their behavior. God then spoke through young Samuel in a scene that would be amusing if it were not so serious. After mistaking God's call at night for Eli's voice, Samuel finally listened to God's message. This word was the same as that of the earlier prophet: God was going to remove Eli's family from the priesthood.

The occasion arose as a result of increasing Philistine incursions. We noted in the previous chapter that when Samson began antagonizing the Philistines, the Israelites criticized him because they viewed these oppressors as their rulers. Now they were apparently expanding their territory (moving further northward and inland), and the situation had reached the point at which the Israelites could not tolerate it anymore. There seems to have been a breakdown of the pattern we saw in the book of Judges, because we do not see that the people cried out to God. Rather, Samuel was regarded as a prophet who had revelation from God. But God would not be able to work within the nation until the corrupt leadership was removed.

TABERNACLE OR TEMPLE?

When referring to the sanctuary in Shiloh, the text uses the terms "temple" (1 Sam. 1:9; 3:3) and "house of the LORD" (1:24), both of which suggest a more permanent facility than "tabernacle" or "tent." However, 2 Samuel 7:6 quotes God as telling Nathan that He had been dwelling in a tent the entire period before David. A closer examination of the terms "temple" and "house" suggests that each could be used in a broader sense denoting the tabernacle.

In this situation, the Israelites gathered their forces at Ebenezer, near Aphek, to fight the Philistines. The latter went out to squash this uprising and quickly inflicted heavy casualties on the Israelites. The Israelite leadership decided that the reason they had lost was that they did not have the ark and so needed to bring it to battle.[5] Here we see a complete misunderstanding of what the ark was. It was supposed to be the place where God met the nation, and as such, it was holy, not because of what it was, but because of who was there. The Israelites were viewing it as a holy relic through which they could manipulate God. They soon found out they were wrong.

The priests brought the ark up from Shiloh (and I am sure both Samuel and Eli watched it go with misgivings). The battle was engaged, the Israelites lost soundly, and the ark was captured. In the process, the priests carrying the ark, including Eli's sons Hophni and Phinehas, were killed. When Eli got the news, he fell backward off his seat and broke his neck. As soon as Phinehas's pregnant wife heard the news, she went into labor. She gave birth to a baby boy whom she called Ichabod (a Hebrew name that apparently means "there is no glory") because "the glory has departed from Israel" (1 Sam. 4:22). She too then died.

SEA PEOPLES IN CYPRUS.
Site of the city called Kittim in the OT, on the island of Cyprus. After the fall of Troy, there was a general emigration of the Sea Peoples out of the Aegean region.

Before telling us about Samuel, the writer relates what happened to the ark. The Philistines took this prize of war to Ashdod, one of their major cities, where they presented it as a trophy before their patron god, Dagon. The next day, however, they found the image of Dagon facedown before the ark. They reset their idol so that it would be above the ark, and the next day, they again found the image of Dagon facedown, but now with the head and hands broken off. Moreover, the people were struck by a plague of some type.

Intimidated by this obvious demonstration of the superiority of Israel's God, the Philistines in Ashdod decided that their best course of action was to send the ark to another city, Gath. The people of Gath too were afflicted with the plague, and they quickly decided they needed to get rid of the ark, so they sent it to Ekron. However, by this time the word was out, and Ekron didn't want the ark. The Philistine leaders then got together and decided to send it back to Israel.

To make sure that it was Israel's God who had caused this episode, they put the ark on an oxcart with two mother cows, which had never been harnessed,

ELI'S LEADERSHIP

The conduct of Eli presents an interesting situation. He is portrayed as being an old man who told his grown sons that they were in the wrong (although they did not listen to him). Apparently, however, he was unwilling to follow through and take the prescribed legal actions—which is why God indicated that He would put them to death (1 Sam. 3:13). Eli was also condemned for getting fat on the wrongly taken sacrifices (2:29). Still, young Samuel was entrusted to his care, and when Eli died at the age of ninety-eight, we are told that he had "judged" the nation for forty years.

yoked to the cart. They penned their calves in the opposite direction from Israel and let the cows go. The fact that they headed straight toward Israel was seen as verification that the God of Israel was involved. In addition, they included with the ark on the cart a wooden chest that contained five gold replicas of the tumors caused by the plague and five gold rats (one for each of the five Philistine cities) as a guilt offering to Israel's God. After a seven-month absence, the ark returned to Israel. It first arrived at Beth Shemesh, a Levitical city in the territory of Judah. The men of Beth Shemesh sacrificed the two cows as a burnt offering (which indicated a consecration of the item) and had a feast celebrating the return of the ark. Then seventy men looked into the ark, for which reason they were struck down by God. Because of this tragedy, the Levites of Beth Shemesh became terrified—rumors of the events in Philistia had likely preceded the ark—and decided to move the ark to Kiriath Jearim. This is ironic,

> Both the Philistines and the Israelites were terrified because of the consequences of mishandling the ark of the covenant.

because Kiriath Jearim was one of the Canaanite cities of the Gibeonite alliance.[6] The ark remained there until David took it to Jerusalem some twenty years later.

Apparently while this was going on, Samuel began promoting revival. He told the people to put away the false gods they had been serving and return to YHWH with their entire hearts. A good portion of them did so. Based on the obvious effort of the people, Samuel called a gathering at Mizpah, where they fasted and confessed their sin. The Philistines heard of the gathering, however, and interpreted it as a precursor for war. The idea that the Israelites would gather solely for confession and repentance never entered their minds.

Word of the advancing Philistine army frightened the Israelites, and they did the smartest thing they could do: they cried to Samuel to intercede with God on

REPRESENTATION OF THE ARK OF THE COVENANT. One concept of the ark of the covenant, the decorative aspects of which are not well described in the book of Exodus. During this period the ark seemed to be the focus of Israelite worship rather than the tabernacle or temple in which it was located. Later on, that focal point would shift to Jerusalem and the temple.

TUMORS

The Hebrew word for "tumors" ('ophel, 1 Sam. 5:6, 9, 12) is not clearly understood. It basically means "swelling" and has been interpreted to refer to boils, tumors, hemorrhoids, or buboes (a swelling associated with bubonic plague). Because the Philistines included gold replicas of both the "tumors" and rats in their offerings to appease God at the end of this incident, this whole situation is often viewed as an outbreak of bubonic plague. This is not to say that the outbreak was a natural event. The judgment must be related to what had happened within the temple in Ashdod. Moreover, we must keep in mind that there had been no problems before the ark entered Philistine territory and that later the ark stayed at Abinadab's place in Kiriath Jearim for many years without incident.

their behalf. Samuel did so, making a burnt (consecratory) offering. God intervened by sending a great thunderstorm. The Israelites followed and drove the Philistines down from the central plateau. With this victory, Israel apparently broke free of Philistine rule; however, it would not be until the time of David that these enemies stopped being a concern for the Israelite military. Samuel raised a stone he called "Ebenezer," which means literally "stone of help," as a reminder of how God had once again helped Israel.[7]

THE FIRST KING

Following the raising of Ebenezer, Israel was in a state of peace, such as we find mentioned a number of times in the book of Judges. Samuel was the judge now, and he made a yearly circuit from Bethel to Gilgal to Mizpah, although he moved back to the family home in Ramah.[8] Things were fine for a number of years until Samuel grew older. He appointed his sons as judges, but as was often the case, the sons did not have the same faith and integrity as their father. Interestingly, they are recorded as serving in the south at Beersheba. Perhaps because they were that far away from home, they thought they could get away with corrupt activities.

Read 1 Samuel 8–11.

Now, however, the people were no longer willing to put up with such corruption, and they asked Samuel to give them a king like the rest of the nations. Two issues were involved: the failure of Samuel's sons to serve God and national security. The Israelites seem to have grown tired of the foreign oppression. Unfortunately, they identified the lack of a strong human leader as the cause and did not realize that the reason for the oppression was a spiritual one—their failure to serve God.

Samuel took the request personally, as if *he* were being rejected. When he took the request to God, he was told that *God* was the one they were rejecting, not Samuel.[9] The Lord also told Samuel to warn the people of what a king would do, but they were adamant. So God gave them what they wanted. As is often the case, what they wanted really wasn't the best thing for them. More than that, the first king He gave them fit *their* idea of what a king should be. (As we shall see later, the second king would be the kind God desired.)

The selection of the king was a twofold process: first the private announcement to Saul and then the public selection. The private announcement came when

THE CHRONOLOGY OF 1 SAMUEL

First Samuel 7:2 states that the ark remained in Kiriath Jearim twenty years. However, David took it from this town to Jerusalem after he had united the country following the death of Saul's son Ish-Bosheth (2 Sam. 6), and Saul's reign is usually thought to have lasted *forty* years. The figure forty comes primarily from Jewish tradition as recorded in Josephus (*Antiquities of the Jews* 6.14.9, but in 10.8.4 he records twenty years). It also shows up in our English translations of Acts 13:21, which says literally, "And they asked for a king, and God gave them Saul, son of Kish, a man of the tribe of Benjamin, forty years." Some scholars, however, understand forty to be his age when he became king (which would correlate with the fact that his son Jonathan was old enough to be married). The only verse in the OT that addresses the length of Saul's reign, 1 Samuel 13:1, is problematic. The Masoretic text says: "Saul was years old when he began to reign, and he reigned two years over Israel" (note that there is no number before "years old"). The NIV emends the text, reading "thirty years old" and "reigned over Israel forty-two years," but possibly verse 1 serves to give a time reference for verse 2 (cf. KJV, "and when he had reigned two years over Israel, Saul chose him three thousand men of Israel"). (See Eugene Merrill's excellent discussion of this passage in *BKC*, 1:443–45.)

Saul and his servant were looking for Saul's father's donkeys that had wandered off. Unable to find them, Saul and his servant ended up in Zuph, the district where Samuel's hometown was located (the name of the town was Ramah or Ramathaim Zuphim; see 1 Sam. 1:1, 19). There they met Samuel, who was about to perform a sacrifice.[10] God had told Samuel the day before to expect Saul, whom he was to anoint as king. Samuel took Saul to the place of sacrifice, where a special portion of the sacrifice had been set aside for him, and he joined the people in the meal.

The next day, as Saul was getting ready to leave, Samuel anointed him and told him that he would be the first king of Israel. To ensure that Saul did not think this madness, Samuel gave him three signs or short-term prophecies to verify his message. On his way home, he would meet a party announcing that the donkeys had been found; a second party would give him a gift; and then he would meet a third party consisting of prophets, as a result of which he would be filled with God's Spirit and would prophesy. All three came true as Samuel had related them. Saul returned home but did not tell his relatives about Samuel's anointing.

After this, Samuel once again called the people to Mizpah, the place where they had asked for the king. Here he announced that the king would be selected, but he also reminded them that in the process they were rejecting God. The selection was made by lots, similar to what we saw when Achan was identified as the thief after the first battle of Ai. The process narrowed the choice down to Saul, but Saul was not there. God told the people that he was hidden among the baggage.[11] And indeed, that is where they found him—hiding out of insecurity or perhaps a sense of fear. When he was brought forth and presented to the people, he stood a full head taller than anyone else. Clearly, this was the man who could lead the people into battle—a man who met their expectations of what a king should be. Or that was the way it seemed at the time, although to be sure there were some naysayers.

The people returned home, and Saul went back to his farm. The first kingly action required of Saul had to do with Jabesh Gilead, a city across the Jordan River that was besieged by the Ammonites under Nahash. The men of Jabesh Gilead sued for peace but were told that the price would be that each man had to have his right eye gouged out. They asked for a week to seek help. Feeling secure in his situation, Nahash granted their request. Messengers arrived in the region of Benjamin, where the untested "King" Saul was plowing a field (Israel really didn't know what to do with a king yet). Filled with God's Spirit—analogous to the case of the judges—Saul killed the oxen he was using to plow and cut them into pieces, which were sent to the twelve tribes (a national signal to rally, similar to what we saw earlier in Judg. 19:29).

Saul made a daring night attack on the Ammonites, using excellent strategy and tactics. He divided his troops into three columns and hit the Ammonite camp from three directions. The rout was complete. After such a victory, there was some discussion of retribution against those who had expressed doubt about Saul. But he refused to take revenge, instead expressing thanks for the victory that YHWH had given Israel. At this point, Saul seemed to have been a good choice.

MIZPAH. The hilltop to which the prophet Samuel called the people of Israel for the anointing of Saul as their first king.

SAUL'S CHARACTER FLAWS

Read 1 Samuel 12–15.

This section of 1 Samuel seems to be arranged more topically than chronologically. The point is to show that Saul had a fatal character flaw that soon became evident. He tended to act impetuously. Had Saul trusted in God, he would have been able to overcome that flaw. After all, as the anointed king, he had God's Spirit working within him. However, Saul never seemed to differentiate clearly between YHWH and the gods of the Canaanites. As a result, he ended up a tragic figure with an ignominious end.

The first incident occurred at Micmash. Saul was camped with his troops in war with the Philistines. The latter had gathered on the other side of the ravine east of Beth Aven. Their numbers were staggering, and the Israelites were losing heart. Each night more Israelites deserted and hid in the hills or in caves. But Saul had been told by Samuel to wait for seven days. On the seventh day, Samuel would arrive and perform the consecratory offering so the army could go to war. When the seventh day came, Samuel had not arrived, so Saul decided to present the offerings himself. He had no more than finished the burnt offering when Samuel arrived.

Samuel was obviously upset and asked Saul what he thought he was doing. Saul argued that it was Samuel's fault: the prophet had not arrived when expected

THE SINS OF THE FATHERS

One of the tragedies of Saul's failure was that it affected his family. Jonathan was a man of faith and integrity, and it seems that he would have been a better king than his father, perhaps as great as David turned out to be. But because of Saul's failure, he did not get a chance. This calamity would serve to warn readers of the story that their actions affect those around them.

(although he was right on time), therefore Saul felt compelled to offer the sacrifices himself.[12] Samuel told him that it had been a foolish act and that he had disobeyed God's command. Consequently, there would be no dynasty for him—the next king would be from another family. The key was that this other king would be "a man after [God's] own heart" (1 Sam. 13:14).

The next incident took place a short time after the first in basically the same location. Jonathan, Saul's son and the one who would have been the next king, was out in the ravine between the two camps. As he surveyed the situation, he suggested to his armor-bearer that they climb the cliff to the Philistine outpost to see whether God would work through them.

In this event, Jonathan showed great faith. He recognized that God worked with just a few to win great victories (as evidenced by the account of Gideon). He also showed great spiritual wisdom. While he was willing to walk into the Philistine camp in faith, he also wanted to make sure that when he did so, God was indeed with him. Rather than presume upon God, he suggested to his armor-bearer a sign by which they could be sure that God would be with them in this action. They would reveal themselves to the Philistine

Saul did not seem to understand the spiritual dimension.

sentry and then base their actions on the response. The initial reaction was ridicule: "The Hebrews are crawling out of the holes they were hiding in." This was followed by the challenge Jonathan was hoping for: "Come up to us and we'll teach you a lesson." Jonathan and his armor-bearer climbed the steep cliff and soon were engaged in a fight. They killed twenty men in a short time. This abrupt action frightened the Philistines, and they began to run.

Saul was still sitting in his command tent when the news of the flight came to him. He quickly mustered his troops and determined that Jonathan was miss-

WEAPONS AND ARMIES

Inserted in the narrative is the editorial comment that smiths could not be found in Israel to sharpen tools or weapons, and as a result, most of the army did not have swords (1 Sam. 13:19–22). The reference seems to be to a lack of iron weaponry because of a Philistine monopoly on the ironworking guild. Another observation is that many of the "soldiers" were conscripts: unskilled fighters who depended primarily on numbers to win. A skilled warrior under the right circumstances could put a larger force to rout.

ing and thus was presumed to be the source of the rout. Saul had the high priest Ahijah, son of Eli, check with God using the Urim and Thummim. Based on that revelation, he sent his men into the battle. However, Saul had also placed the men under an oath to fast until evening, when *he* had avenged *himself* on *his* enemies. Clearly Saul viewed this war as a personal fight and not a fight for God. Like so many others, Saul did not seem to understand the spiritual dimension.

In the course of the pursuit, Jonathan saw a honeycomb in the woods and used the butt of his spear to get some of the honey, which helped revive him. By now, some of the other soldiers had caught up and told him about his father's oath. Hearing that, he apparently refrained from taking further honey, but he observed that Saul's oath had been an unwise one.

At the end of the day, after having pursued the Philistines across the central plateau and down the valley of Aijalon, the starving soldiers fell on the plunder and began eating the meat raw (a violation of the OT law). Saul chastised the soldiers and then had an altar set up where they slaughtered the animals properly.[13] After everyone had eaten, Saul asked the priest to inquire of God whether they should continue to pursue the Philistines. The priest got no response. Saul concluded that it was because of a sin among the people, specifically a violation of the oath he had exacted on them. This time the indicators pointed to Jonathan. He admitted that he had eaten some honey out of ignorance. Saul then demonstrated another impetuous action when he decided that Jonathan would have to die as a result. But his army stopped him.

Saul broke off the pursuit of the Philistines, and the Israelite army returned home, apparently in control of the situation. That was not the case, however. We are told that later Saul fought the Moabites, the Ammonites, the Edomites, the kings of Zobah, as well as the Philistines. But the author glosses over these struggles (and Saul's family) in his concern to relate to the reader the key demonstration of Saul's character flaw, the one that got him ejected from the throne. It is not clear how long after the events at Micmash the next event occurred. We do know that Samuel was still alive, for Samuel served once again as God's messenger.

Saul was given a mission. His job was to attack the Amalekites, who had assaulted the Israelites on their way out of Egypt (see ch. 7, above). At that time God had told Joshua not to continue his pursuit of these marauders, for they would be taken care of later. It was now later.[14] Saul was told that these enemies were under *ḥerem*. When we discussed this word in chapter 9, we noted that each time God gave this directive, He spelled out the details (see p. 178). Here they were the following: "Do not spare them; put to death men and women, children and infants, cattle and sheep, camels and donkeys" (1 Sam. 15:3). With these specifics in mind, Saul took his army out, had a great victory, and brought

PHILISTINE COFFIN. An anthropoid coffin (that is, presenting a human image), distinctive of the Philistine culture in Canaan.

back "Agag and the best of the sheep and cattle, the fat calves and lambs—everything that was good" (v. 9).

God now had a follow-up message for Samuel to carry, a message that unsettled the prophet and kept him from sleep. When Samuel met up with the army, he found that Saul had set up a memorial to himself in celebration of the victory. He also found Saul exuberant, proclaiming that he had carried out God's directions. At this point, Samuel sarcastically asked Saul the cause of the bleating of sheep and lowing of cattle he heard. Saul dismissed it as something the people had brought back for Samuel's God.

Samuel reminded Saul how God had brought him up from obscurity and that all he asked was obedience. Saul still did not get the picture, but proclaimed that he had done what God had asked. Samuel explained to him that while it might seem good to offer sacrifices, God wanted obedience, not an act that had the appearance of honoring God but was in fact no more than rationalized disobedience. For this act, Saul had now been rejected from the throne. In response to Samuel's sharp declaration, Saul finally admitted guilt, but it was too late.

Samuel performed one last sacrifice with Saul at his passionate request. He also made sure that Agag, the Amalekite king, was executed. After this Samuel returned home, and he didn't want anything more to do with Saul.

PREPARING A NEW KING

Read 1 Samuel 16:1–18:4.
With the rejection of Saul as king, God now took steps to prepare the new king. He told Samuel to go to Bethlehem because the man was there. The trip was made under the guise of a sacrifice (Samuel's route went through Benjamin and Saul's hometown of Gibeah). In Bethlehem, Jesse, a descendant of Boaz and Ruth, was invited to the sacrifice. Jesse presented seven of his sons to Samuel, and they were all fine, strapping young men. But God told him that none of them was the one. When asked, Jesse admitted there was another son, the youngest, who was out taking care of the sheep. Apparently he was not considered old enough yet for the "adult" business of sacrifice to God. When David appeared before Samuel, God told him, "He is the one." So before his entire family, David was anointed as the next king of Israel. At the time of the anointing, the Spirit of the Lord came upon David.[15]

The text then notes that the Spirit of the Lord left Saul and he began to be harassed by an evil spirit. The sequence suggests that this happened at the same time David received the Spirit. However, it appears that the arrangement is topical and does not follow a strict chronology—the topical arrangement highlighting even more the contrast between the two. In any case, Saul's servants suggested that David be sent for, to provide music that would soothe the anguished king. Thus David began to live with the current king in a somewhat strange mentoring situation.

WHICH CAME FIRST?

Because some parts of the narrative are arranged topically, it is not certain that all of the events recorded in chapter 16 happened before the battle with Goliath. It might seem more likely that the battle occurred first, followed by the anointing, followed by the visit of the evil spirit. In support of this view is the observation of Saul's servants that David was a brave man and a warrior (1 Sam. 16:18). Moreover, at the time of the Goliath incident, David's brothers show no awareness that he had been chosen as the next king by God. The problem with this view is the indication that David was sent to serve with Saul immediately after defeating Goliath (18:2). Consequently, Eugene Merrill suggests that the events did occur as written, with a period of time between chapters 16 and 17 during which David returned home. He suggests that the question by Saul about David's father (17:55–58), rather than indicating ignorance, represented a note of admiration for a father who could bring forth such a son (Eugene H. Merrill, *An Historical Survey of the Old Testament* [Grand Rapids: Baker, 1991], 195).

This section is followed in the text by the account of the battle with Goliath. The author shows us that David was apparently exhibiting one of the attributes of a king: fighting in single combat on behalf of the entire nation.[16] Thus, the sequence seems to be that we are shown Saul's failure and then, in contrast, David's success. As might be expected, these circumstances led to jealousy.

Just about everyone has heard the story of David and Goliath. Goliath was the Philistine with the pituitary gland problem: he was considered a giant. While the actual height of the man is debated, it is clear that he intimidated everyone, even Saul, who was a head taller than any other Israelites. The Philistines knew this, so as they brought out their forces again and camped in the Elah Valley, Goliath engaged in psychological warfare. With the Israelite army lined up on the other side, each day Goliath would go out and issue a challenge for one-on-one combat. The idea was that the representative of each side would go at it, and the individual combat would decide the outcome of the battle. But Saul, the one probably viewed by the people as the logical choice, was afraid. So the armies sat in their camps for forty days.

> In his encounter with Goliath, David was apparently exhibiting one of the attributes of a king: fighting in single combat on behalf of the entire nation.

It was into this situation that David came. His three oldest brothers had answered Saul's call for troops, and Jesse had sent David to the bivouac with provisions. When David heard Goliath's taunt, he became angry. David, a young man full of faith, demanded to know how the Israelites could stand not taking up that challenge. In his mind, an insult against God's armies was an insult against God Himself. David's brothers were aghast at the brazenness of their little brother, but others took him seriously and sent word to Saul.

When David was presented to Saul, he told the king that if no one else was willing to go up against the giant, he would. Saul suggested that David, as an untrained shepherd, had no chance against a trained fighter. But David noted that

HOW TALL WAS GOLIATH?

The Hebrew text states that Goliath was six cubits and a span in height. According to the usual equivalence of 18 inches for a cubit and 6 inches for a span, he would have been about 9 feet 6 inches tall, which seems unreasonable to many. Historically, however, a cubit was the length of a forearm from the elbow to the fingertips, and a span was the width of a spread hand (similar to the method of calculating the length of the English "foot," which historically has ranged from 9-1/2 inches to 13-1/2 inches). In many cases, people used the appropriate body part to measure the object, and David may have used his arm and hand to measure Goliath after killing him. Scholars suggest that David was probably average height for his day, about 5 feet 2 inches to 5 feet 4 inches, so his "cubit" would probably have been closer to 14 to 15 inches. On that basis, Goliath would have been 7 feet 6 inches more or less—not too much taller than some NBA basketball players. It should also be noted that the LXX and at least one copy of the Dead Sea Scrolls express his height as four cubits, which even under the standard measurement would make him a measly 6 feet 4 inches. Again, it is best to go with the original text even though we find it difficult. The point is that Goliath was of unusual height, which intimidated even the best in Israel.

he had already killed both a bear and a lion as he watched his father's sheep. More than this, he was confident in YHWH, who would protect him because the battle was His. Here for the first time we see the difference between David and Saul. David understood the spiritual dimension and had a high regard for YHWH even if he did not always do what he should.

After trying on Saul's armor (which must have been somewhat humorous because Saul was so big), David decided to face Goliath in his normal shepherd's garb and use the sling he was familiar with. In the valley between the two army lines, he picked up five smooth stones. When Goliath saw that David was just an adolescent, he was furious and insulted. Cursing this young man, Goliath tried to get close so that he could quickly dispatch the young upstart. David used his speed to avoid Goliath and with the first stone hit him in the forehead. The giant collapsed, apparently unconscious. David rushed up, drew Goliath's sword, and finished him off before anyone knew what was happening. When the Philistines saw this, they fled, and the Israelites pursued them.

Saul wanted to know more about this amazing young man, so he sent Abner, his general, to bring him forward. After talking to Saul, David became great friends with Jonathan. From what we saw earlier about Jonathan's faith, it is clear that the two men were kindred spirits both in their faith in God and in their approach to life.

ROYAL RIVALRY

Read 1 Samuel 18:5–24:22.

The remainder of 1 Samuel presents the conflict between David and Saul. We see David becoming more king-like, while Saul slips both in character and popularity. The focus of this section of the book is more on David than on his predecessor, but we will divide our discussion somewhat topically and save portions of this material for the next chapter (although it will become clear that this division is somewhat arbitrary).

While the relationship of the two began in a positive light, we soon see that in addition to his other character flaws, Saul had a spirit of jealousy. It may have stemmed from the same insecurity that caused him to hide in the baggage when he was originally selected to be king. It was certainly enhanced when David took Saul's place on the battlefield against Goliath. But it came to a head as David was appointed general in Saul's army. As the triumphant Israelite army returned from battle, they were greeted by the women singing, "Saul has slain his thousands, and David his tens of thousands" (1 Sam. 18:7). This higher accolade for David grated on Saul's soul, and he began to suspect David of kingly ambitions, although there was no evidence to demonstrate that.

HORNED ALTAR. A full-scale reproduction of a horned altar discovered in the excavation of Beersheba.

Over these next chapters, we see Saul turning into a madman obsessed with killing one of his greatest supporters. In the process, he personally made at least two direct attacks on David's life with a spear (1 Sam. 18:10–11; 19:10).[17] He plotted twice to get rid of him in battle by promising his daughters to David in marriage. Saul had first pledged his oldest daughter, Merab, to David after the defeat of Goliath. Later he changed the requirement (18:17), adding more victories as the price, but ended up giving the girl to another man. Saul then turned around and offered his second daughter, Michal, but again on condition of greater victories. This time the price was one hundred Philistine foreskins.[18] David not only provided them but doubled the figure. This time Saul had no choice but to give his daughter as he had promised. However, as we will see later, Michal became a stumbling block to David and never did bear any children.

DAVID'S WEAPON

David was not using what we call a "slingshot"—a Y-shaped stick with elastic cords that shoots a marble-sized stone. The ancient sling was a weapon of war that could be deadly. It consisted of two leather thongs about 30 inches long with a leather patch tied in between. The rock that was used would be somewhere between a golf ball and a baseball in size. A skilled baseball pitcher can throw a fastball at approximately 100 miles per hour. The extension that the sling provided would almost double that speed. For a classroom exercise at the U.S. Naval Academy, we calculated the impact force of a stone from a sling and found that it would have been greater than that of a bullet from a small bore rifle. Skilled slingers were very accurate. Thus, a stone from a sling hitting even a man in full armor in the forehead could very easily knock him unconscious.

ISRAELITE GENERALS?

Throughout this book we will use the term *general* to refer to senior military commanders. The Israelite army apparently did not have a formal rank structure, although as we have already seen, the text talks about leaders of different sized groups having a rough equation to a modern army's units from squads or platoons (tens) through battalions (thousands).

David was appointed "general" by Saul (1 Sam. 18:5 NIV, "Saul gave him a high rank in the army"). While we find it surprising that a man as young as David would be selected for such a position, this would not have been so unusual in the ANE. Leadership was based on demonstrated skill on the battlefield, which may not have anything to do with age. A case in point is Alexander the Great, who was only sixteen when he was appointed general. Based on his proven battle skills, he became king of Macedonia at the age of twenty after his father died.

As the account goes on, we read of at least seven times when Saul sent or led troops against David, but David always escaped, usually with the help of other Israelites.[19] The first was when David was at home (1 Sam. 19:11), and Michal helped him escape. Then they pursued him to Samuel's home in Ramah (19:18), and Samuel helped him escape. He fled to Nob, where the priest Ahimelech helped him escape. (Subsequently Saul, in a paranoid moment, killed Ahimelech and eighty-five priests, accusing them of conspiracy.) David went from there to Gath, where he was helped by Achish, the Philistine leader. He had to flee Gath by feigning insanity when Achish's advisors questioned his presence in their city. Later he went to Keilah, where he delivered the people from attack. Pursued by Saul, he fled when he understood that the people of Keilah would turn him over to his enemy (23:11).[20] Saul pursued him to Maon (23:25) but had to break off the pursuit because of a Philistine attack. After that it was on to En Gedi (24:1) and finally to the desert of Ziph (26:1–2).

BRONZE CALVES. Images used by the Philistines, probably similar to the images used by the Israelites when they turned away from worship of the true God at different times in their history.

On the last two occasions, David had opportunity to kill Saul without fanfare and thus simply solve the problem. In both cases, however, he refused to take the life of his enemy because God had anointed Saul. Since it was God who had told Saul that he would be removed from the throne, David apparently trusted that God would handle the issue even though he understood that his own life was in jeopardy.

SAUL'S FINAL FAILURE

As we near the end of Saul's life, we find a man who was at his wits' end. He was preparing for another battle with the Philistines, and he was afraid. Samuel was dead. His best general and many of his troops had been driven away by his own actions. God was not answering his pleas.

Read 1 Samuel 28:3–25; 31:1–13.

Desperate, Saul decided to consult a medium. His servants told him of a woman at Endor. Since Saul himself had removed mediums from the land, he had to go in disguise. When he arrived, the woman was reluctant because of Saul's directives, but after he swore that she would not be punished for her actions, she agreed. Saul's request was for Samuel to be consulted, and when Samuel actually appeared, the woman realized the situation and was angry at Saul for his deceit. Samuel, in turn, chastised Saul for what he was doing. He informed Saul that this was exactly what he had predicted earlier regarding how the throne would be taken from him. The next day, both Saul and his sons would die on the battlefield.

Disheartened, Saul ate and then left Endor. The next day, the battle did not go well and the Philistines were prevailing. Saul's sons, Jonathan, Abinadab, and Malki-Shua, were killed. Saul himself was mortally wounded by archers, and he asked his armor-bearer to finish him off so that the Philistines would not capture him and abuse him (as had happened to Samson). The armor-bearer refused, so Saul fell on his own sword and committed suicide on the battlefield. It was a tragic end to a tragic figure.

> The people had been given the king they had asked for, but he was not what they had hoped for.

The people had been given the king they had asked for, but he was not what they had hoped for. Although Saul had fought many wars during his entire reign, things were not any better. And surely at this point, the people were asking, "Now what?" But God's man was already prepared and waiting to step into place.

SPIRITISM

The term *medium* apparently refers to a person who consulted a familiar spirit, representing it as a consultation with the dead. It was a practice forbidden in the OT, but it had clearly managed to survive because of the lack of spiritual integrity of the people. It is surprising that Saul, who vacillated so much spiritually, had actually outlawed the practice, although this order may have been a political ploy to unite the various elements of the fledgling country. In this situation, when Samuel actually appeared, the medium was shocked.

REVIEW QUESTIONS

1. Why did God reject Eli's family from the priesthood?

2. What was significant about the birth and childhood of Samuel?

3. Why did the Israelites decide they needed a king?

4. What were the good features that made Saul appear to be the right choice at first?

5. What were Saul's fatal character flaws, and how did he demonstrate them?

6. What did God look for in a king?

7. How did David show that he had kingly qualities?

8. Contrast David and Saul during the years after David was anointed.

9. What was tragic about Saul's death?

12

CHAPTER

A Kingdom United

OVERVIEW

For two generations, the nation flourished. First David united and expanded the kingdom, though he also showed his human frailties. Solomon was wise and successful in the ways of the world, but he failed spiritually. The glory of these two kings is also demonstrated in the field of literature: David's poetry shines in the Psalms, while Solomon's wisdom is shown especially by Proverbs but also by Ecclesiastes and the Song of Songs. At the end of Solomon's reign, however, the kingdom was about to split.

STUDY GOALS

▶ Describe David's kingly qualities in contrast to Saul.

▶ Introduce Hebrew poetry.

▶ Trace David's consolidation of the country as the new king.

▶ Show how David failed, even as a man "after God's own heart."

▶ Describe Solomon as David's heir through God's grace.

▶ Introduce Hebrew wisdom literature.

▶ Evaluate Solomon's failure.

We have already met David as the king God chose because he was a man after God's own heart. Although he had been anointed by Samuel while still a youth, David continued to regard Saul as the rightful king. Thus, for a number of years until Saul's death, David was the "king elect," so to speak, waiting for his throne. Throughout that period, he continued to fight against Israel's enemies and kept on the run to avoid battles with the Israelites who followed Saul. After Saul died, David had the difficult task of uniting a country that had a long history of tribal allegiances and spiritual instability. His success provided the Israelite people with their first real sign of hope since Abraham. His failures hinted that the problems were much deeper and would require a more radical solution.

DAVID'S LONG MARCH TO THE THRONE

Read 1 Samuel 25:1–28:2; 29:1–30:31.

As we saw in chapter 11, above, David was driven out from the presence of Saul, who tried to kill him numerous times. God protected him in every instance, and David demonstrated his faith and integrity when he twice had the opportunity to kill the king but refused. While fleeing from Saul, David spent most of his time in the southern region of Judah. This made sense because David was a shepherd from the tribe of Judah and thus was familiar with the lay of the land. Unfortunately, the strategy proved to be troublesome once Saul died, because the northern tribes did not know or trust him. Out of this time in Judah, we are given several incidents that illustrate David's character.

The first incident is recorded in 1 Samuel 25. Sometime after Samuel died, David and his troops were in the region of Maon. The text implies that he had made an agreement with at least one of the local sheepherders: David would provide defense against marauders in exchange for provisions. In this type of situation, payday would be at sheep-shearing time, when the landholder could evaluate his profits. Having heard that the flocks were being sheared, David sent a party of ten men to collect their wages from Nabal.

These men reminded Nabal of their good work and asked him to check with his own employees to validate their claim. Nabal, however, tried to pretend that he didn't know David, and he sent the men away empty-handed. Furious, David

A CONTRACT BETWEEN DAVID AND NABAL?

There is no specific record of such an agreement, but several points in the narrative of 1 Samuel 25 suggest it, especially verses 15–17, where Nabal's own employees act as if they owe David something and observe that David and his men never took anything that did not belong to them. Moreover, David fumed that his watching the man's property was for nothing (v. 21). Finally, David sent only ten men, a sufficient number to carry back what would have been a fair wage; if this had just been a shakedown, he more likely would have sent a larger party as a show of force.

took an oath that he would kill every male in Nabal's family. Then Abigail, Nabal's wife, intervened. As soon as she heard what had happened, she gathered up provisions to deliver to David and his men.[1] Abigail met David and company as they were descending from the hills ready to attack the homestead. She leapt from her donkey, prostrated herself before David, and asked forgiveness for her husband. His name was Nabal ("fool"), she blurted, and he had acted accordingly.

David praised Abigail for her wisdom and praised God for sending her. He also canceled his oath (in sharp contrast to Saul when he made his oath at Micmash). Thus, Abigail saved her husband, who did not appreciate it, however. When she returned, he was drunk, so she waited until the next morning to let him know what had happened. Upon hearing the report, he had a stroke or a heart attack and died ten days later. After the death of Nabal, David asked this wise woman to marry him, and she accepted. She became David's third wife.[2]

David's willingness to kill a fool who cheated him is sandwiched between, and contrasted with, two occasions when he had opportunity to kill Saul. The first was at En Gedi, where David was hiding in a cave. When Saul came in to use the cave for a restroom, David cut off the edge of his coat. After Saul had left, David stood in the opening of the cave and announced what he had done to show the king that he was not out to get him. The second event was in the Desert of Ziph. Saul and three thousand troops were chasing David. While they were asleep, David and

EN GEDI. A lush garden spot deep in the Judean desert, with a waterfall and a cave—a cave such as the one David hid in when fleeing from King Saul.

two other men slipped into Saul's camp and stole his spear and water jug from beside his head. Once again, from a distance, David announced himself to Saul, pointing out that he had no desire to kill his king.

Harassed, David finally decided to leave the land and went to Philistia, where he made an arrangement with the king of Gath. Achish allowed David and his men to settle in Ziklag. From there they practiced guerrilla warfare over the next year, attacking towns belonging to Canaanite tribes. He told Achish that he was raiding several regions in Judah, and the king, believing that David was alienating himself from his people, actually trusted him. Consequently, when the Philistines gathered for the big campaign against Saul, Achish was sure that David would be delighted to join, and he brought him along. Fortunately for David, the other Philistine leaders were not as trusting, and they demanded that he be sent away from the battle. Thus, when the Philistines killed Saul, David was nowhere near and was actually fighting another battle.

As David returned home, he discovered that the Amalekites (the group Saul was supposed to have destroyed) had attacked Ziklag and taken the women and children hostage. Following God's guidance, David and his men caught up with the Amalekites and rescued their families. In the meantime, Saul was dying on the battlefield in the battle against the Philistines.

DAVID AS POET

Read 2 Samuel 1.

As 2 Samuel opens, we find David receiving the news of Saul's death. Three days after the two battles recorded at the end of 1 Samuel, a man arrived at Ziklag from the Israelite camp. In response to David's inquiries, he gave an accurate report with a couple of embellishments—and those embellishments cost him his life. The man reported accurately how Saul had been mortally wounded and requested his fellow soldier to finish him off. But he presented himself as the one who was asked to do it, and who actually killed Saul. He thought that David would appreciate his claim to have eliminated his enemy and would reward him. That showed that this man—who happened to be an Amalekite—did not know David. In fact, David and his men mourned the death of the king even though they had been fleeing him for some time. David then had the Amalekite executed for presuming to kill God's anointed.

> David and his men mourned at the death of the king even though they had been fleeing him for some time.

David then composed a psalm to commemorate Saul, his king, and Jonathan, his best friend. This is not surprising, for we have already seen that David was an accomplished musician who had served Saul in his madness. He is also reputed to be Israel's greatest poet. In that light, let's pause to take a brief look at Hebrew poetry.

WHAT IS HEBREW POETRY?

Poetry is difficult to define. Even in English, we sometimes see prose that we feel is poetic in quality. Then there are "poems" that we would not recognize as such had the writer not told us they were poetry. It is even more difficult when looking at translations of poems originally written in other languages. A working definition of poetry that I developed while teaching English literature is *a piece of literature that uses the sounds of the language to enhance its meaning*. As such, a key feature of poetry is that it appeals as much to the emotions as to the intellect.[3] This should tell us up front that much of the power of poetry will be lost in translation, and that is the case with Hebrew poetry.

One aspect of Hebrew poetry that translators work hard to carry over is *parallelism*, which has been observed by scholars for the past two hundred years or so to be the primary indicator of Hebrew poetry. Parallelism might be defined as

PLAYING THE HARP. A man who walks through the Old City in present-day Jerusalem, dressed like King David and playing a replica of a harp such as David might have used.

the balancing of ideas.[4] In our English Bibles, a verse in a poem such as a psalm is usually a poetic line. Although each verse seems actually to contain two lines (and sometimes three), these are really half lines, each of which contains an idea. Study of these shows structured relationships between the two halves, such as repeating the idea or saying the opposite. We call this structured relationship "balance."[5]

When we look at poetry in the Bible, we find that it serves a central function, which is to assist the reader in the worship of God. Given that poetry appeals to the emotions, we could say that it helps focus both the mind and the emotions on God. Within that context, poetry served the people of God as they dealt with many issues of life. Thus, different types of psalms serve different functions.

Laments

A large number of psalms are categorized as *laments*. A lament is an expression of grief or sorrow. In other words, something was going wrong in the poet's life, and he wrote to complain expressing his hurt. In the Bible, these complaints are addressed to God in the expectation that God is the only one who can do something about it. The psalms listed in the reading are a small sample of these.[6]

Read Psalms 3, 4, 22, 35, 44, 51, and 80.

The song David wrote after the deaths of Saul and Jonathan was a lament written after the fact (and in this instance, as if we couldn't tell from the structure, the author tells us specifically that was the case). However, most laments are written during the trauma of the event and actually reflect a cry for help. Psalm 3 ends with David crying out to God with the impassioned plea for him to hit his enemies in the jaw and knock out all their teeth.

Two other types of psalms are similar to laments: songs of trust and songs of confession. A song of trust focuses more on the confidence

ANGLICAN BISHOP ROBERT LOWTH, a professor of poetry at Oxford, coined the term *parallelism* and defined its meaning in his *Lectures on the Sacred Poetry of the Hebrews*, which was published in 1753. He called parallelism "that phenomenon whereby two or more successive poetic lines strengthen, reinforce, and develop each other's thought.... the follow-up lines further define, specify, expand, intensify, or contrast the first."

HARSH PSALMS

We are sometimes shocked by the harsh nature of the retribution the psalmists ask from God. One thing we need to remember is that these are cries for help uttered in the emotions of a traumatic situation. Very often the writer is using hyperbole to convey his point. Beyond this, the psalmist is giving the situation over to God to handle, while at the same time making a few hopeful suggestions as to how God might act.

the writer has in God than on the situation (e.g., Ps. 4). A song of confession focuses on the cause of the troublesome situation. The author recognizes that he has sin in his life and is addressing that problem. We see this feature in Psalm 51, where David is confessing his sin to God and asking for forgiveness.

One interesting feature of laments is that they often contain promises. For example, in Psalm 35, David wrote that he would sing God's praises after the help had come (v. 18). As part of the worship system, this promise would be fulfilled in conjunction with a votive offering in which the writer would gather the people for a sacrifice, a dinner—and another psalm.

Praise Psalms

Read Psalms 2, 8, 19, 30, 32, 110, 118, and 124.

The other major category of psalms is *praise psalms*. By definition, praise psalms are very positive; they talk about God's goodness and power. Praise psalms in the Bible fall into two subcategories. The first consists of poems that speak of God's character and are very general in content. They are called *descriptive praise psalms* because they depict and extol God's greatness. For example, in Psalm 8, David talks about God as the great Creator. That psalm speaks of such attributes as God's tremendous power and wisdom and, at the same time, God's concern with the lowly. But no specific acts are mentioned that God has performed.

SHEEP DRINKING FROM STILL WATERS. A scene such as might have inspired part of the cherished Psalm 23.

A KING LIKE MELCHIZEDEK

In the royal psalms, the line between the human and the divine king sometimes seems to blur. For example, Psalm 110:4 refers to the king as "a priest forever, in the order of Melchizedek." The priest was an intermediary between God and human beings, and according to the law of Moses, all priests had to be Israelites from the tribe of Levi. As we have already seen, Melchizedek was neither. Theoretically, a priest could be king, but after the promise that the kingly line and the Messiah would come from David, who was of the tribe of Judah, no king from that nation ever could have been a priest. Moreover, Jesus made reference to this psalm when he asked the Jewish leaders whose descendant the Messiah would be (Matt. 22:42). He then posed the question, "How could David call him Lord?"

One type of descriptive praise psalms describes God in His role as the great suzerain, or king, over the nation. Called *royal psalms*, they also address the human king as God's representative. It is sometimes difficult to see where the man stops and God begins, and thus these psalms are often viewed as prophetic anticipations of David's heir, the ideal king with divine attributes. This person was often called the Messiah.[7]

In contrast, other praise psalms focus on specific deeds God has done. Interestingly, this is the one type of Hebrew poetry for which nothing comparable has been found in the rest of the ANE. That is, there are no known records in other cultures of that region of songs written to declare the things their gods had actually done in space-time history.[8] We have already seen some of these in the Israelite culture. In Exodus 15 we saw the psalm Moses wrote when God sealed the deliverance of the sons of Israel by destroying Pharaoh's army in the Red Sea. Likewise, in Judges 5 we saw the psalm Deborah wrote when God destroyed the forces of Jabin of Hazor. On a smaller scale, David seems to have written Psalm 30 when he successfully brought the ark to Jerusalem and dedicated the temple site.

> There are no records in other cultures of the Middle East of songs written to declare the things their gods had actually done in space-time history.

Many of these praise psalms apparently were the result of promises made to God when things were not going so well. That was the case with Hannah's praise in 1 Samuel 2. Since these praise psalms were sung at a gathering around a votive offering, one would expect that there were a number of lament-praise combinations—that is, praise psalms that follow on the heels of a lament after the prayer has been answered. While that is likely, many of the songs in the book of Psalms do not record the occasion on which they were written. Psalm 18 was composed after God delivered David from Saul. However, David wrote laments about Saul and his men in Psalms 54, 57, and 59, so it could have been after any of those—and given the situation with Saul, on many other occasions as well. Since this

THE TEACHING STRUCTURE OF PSALMS

The nation may well have used the psalms topically, as follows:

1. Introduction (1–2)
2. Worshiping God in Times of Trouble (3–41)
3. Teaching Worship to the Next Generation (42–72)
4. Consequences of Wrong Worship (73–89)
5. Worship and Repentance (90–106)
6. Worship and Hope (107–150)

This outline corresponds to the five-book division in the Hebrew text itself. At the end of book 2 is a very interesting verse: "This concludes the prayers of David son of Jesse" (Ps. 72:20). This comment suggests that the original Psalter consisted of those psalms and that others were added later. If that is the case, I propose that book 3 was added at the time of the temple dedication under Solomon, and books 4 and 5 were added at the time of Hezekiah, when the nation was undergoing a religious revival. During the early stages, there would have been some flexibility in order and possibly even some movement of psalms among the books. By the time of the Dead Sea Scrolls, however, the Psalter as we know it was considered to have reached final form.

psalm is also recorded in 2 Samuel 22, it could have been a psalm written after the fact to reflect all of those occasions generically.

Psalms as a Guide to Worship

Read Psalm 1.

While we have already seen several psalms recorded in the historical narrative, most of them are in the book of Psalms. As we have it today, this book is a collection of 150 psalms that lacks any chronological order (e.g., Psalm 2 was written by David, while Psalm 90 was written by Moses). When we look more closely, we notice that the book is broken up into five smaller books in what I would suggest is a topical arrangement.[9] The purpose seems to have been to guide the nation to worship. We earlier noted that individual psalms could be used in specific worship situations. Thus, the overall pattern would provide the Israelites worship themes or patterns (somewhat similar to how our hymn books are arranged by topic, usually beginning with God).

KING OF JUDAH

Read 2 Samuel 2–4.

Having lamented the death of his friend Jonathan and King Saul, David turned to the business of providing leadership to the nation in his role as king.[10] This was no easy task, for there was no established pattern for providing a transition of power. Furthermore, although God had distinguished through Samuel's anointing who the next king was to be, many in Israel did not care what God wanted. They decided to go with the dynastic approach. Although Saul had lost three sons in the same battle in which he died, one of his sons, Ish-Bosheth, was still alive. While not a strong leader himself, Ish-Bosheth did have the support of Saul's army and the key general, Abner. So Saul's tribe of Benjamin and the northern tribes crowned him king.

After inquiring of God, David moved from Ziklag back into the land of Judah. He settled in Hebron, Caleb's city, and the people of Judah proceeded to crown him king. As a result, the young nation was now divided and involved in a civil war that lasted about two years. Only three incidents are related about that war, and they all tie together to show how David won the kingdom. Overall, it was a process in which the forces of Ish-Bosheth were getting weaker while those of David were getting stronger.

Early on, there was an incident involving the key generals of the two sides: Abner led the forces of Ish-Bosheth, and Joab led David's. They met at a pool near Gibeon and decided to have a "contest."[11] This incident resulted in the death of the twenty-four men involved and a general battle. In the course of the hostilities, Abner killed Asahel, the brother of Joab, defending his own life. Joab held a grudge thereafter.

Sometime later, Ish-Bosheth accused Abner of sleeping with one of Saul's concubines. Furious, and perhaps disillusioned with the quality of leader Ish-Bosheth was, Abner decided to go over to David's side. He sent David a message proposing an agreement, and David in turn asked him to demonstrate his seriousness by bringing back Michal, David's first wife and Saul's daughter (David sent the same request to Ish-Bosheth, who complied). Subsequently, Abner met with David, but when Joab found out about the meeting, he managed to kill Abner through treachery.[12]

With Abner dead, Ish-Bosheth really did not have the assets to hold out long, and the people knew it. Consequently, two of his generals, Baanah and Rechab, killed him and took his head to David. Again David showed how he viewed such actions by having the two men executed. He accused them of being "wicked

HOW LONG WAS THE CIVIL WAR?

According to 2 Samuel 2:10, Ish-Bosheth was king for two years, which suggests that the civil war lasted two years as well. However, the next verse says that David ruled from Hebron for seven and a half years. This difference can be understood two ways. Either Ish-Bosheth was not crowned for five years, meaning the civil war occurred later, or there was a period of five years after David defeated his enemy before he moved the capital to Jerusalem. The latter seems more likely. Second Samuel 5:5 implies that he ruled over Judah only while in Hebron, but after the men of Israel accepted him as king over their part of the nation while he was established in Hebron, it is unlikely that he immediately conquered Jerusalem and moved his capital there. A five-year transition would not be unreasonable.

MY KINGDOM FOR A WIFE

Apparently one of the ways of claiming the throne in the ANE was to take over the harem (or concubines) of the previous king (Roland de Vaux, *Ancient Israel* [New York: McGraw-Hill, 1965], 1:115–17). As such, Ish-Bosheth's accusation of Abner amounted to a charge of treason. In view of this practice, having married the king's daughter also gave David a political claim to the throne, which was weakened because she was living with someone else. Having her back reinforced David's authority. One of the ironies of this text is that David sent his messengers to Ish-Bosheth, who complied with the request.

men" who "killed an innocent man in his own house and on his own bed" (2 Sam. 4:11; the word translated "innocent" usually means "righteous").

KING OF ISRAEL

Read 2 Samuel 5–10.

The elders of the northern tribes then came to David and asked him to be king over the entire nation (see 1 Chron. 11:1–3). David agreed and set out to unify the tribes.

First he selected a new capital. The choice of Jerusalem was brilliant. It was a city that had never really been occupied by Israel and was held by Jebusites.

> The choice of Jerusalem as the new capital was brilliant.

Thus, it technically belonged to no tribe. Furthermore, it was located on the border between Benjamin (Saul's tribe) and Judah (David's tribe). Indeed, the tribal boundary between the two passed down the ridge of Mount Zion (Josh. 15:8–9), so later both David's palace and Solomon's temple would straddle the line. Jerusalem therefore transcended tribal allegiances and held a central location for most of the tribes. Finally, the city was located on the main north-south highway that traversed the central plateau, making it easily accessible.

The only problem was that Jerusalem was a well-defended city. In fact, the Jebusites boasted that the blind and lame would be adequate to defend the city against David. The text indicates that David's forces used the "water shaft" to breach the walls (2 Sam. 5:8; see 1 Chron. 11:4–9).[13] After the city was taken, David began to transform it into a national capital. Hiram, the king of Tyre, assisted him in building a new palace. In this process of national unification, David took new wives and concubines.[14] He also fought more wars and began subduing the enemies around him.

Most significantly, David brought the ark to Jerusalem to integrate the religious and political capitals. The ark had been in Kiriath Jearim for twenty years. David involved the entire nation in its return, consulting the leaders and bringing 30,000 troops. The mood was very festive as they went to the house of Abinadab. They set the ark on a brand-new oxcart, and with instruments playing and people dancing, they set out for Jerusalem, about a fifteen-kilometer trip uphill. Suddenly, tragedy struck. The cart hit a bump, the ark teetered, and when Uzzah reached up to steady it, he was struck dead.

David had not followed proper procedures—the ark was to be carried by the priests on the poles (1 Chron. 15:13). Angry and afraid, he stopped the advance. They moved the ark to the house of Obed-Edom, a Gittite (that is, from Gath), while David tried to figure out what to do. Three months later, the text relates, God had been blessing Obed-Edom. Confident that this showed God was not angry, and having learned how to handle the ark, David and the priests went to retrieve the ark properly (1 Chron. 15:15).

> ### JEBUSITE JERUSALEM
>
> Jerusalem had been captured and burned by the tribe of Judah sometime after Joshua (Judg. 1:8). By the time of the unnamed Levite and his concubine (Judg. 19), however, the Jebusites had reoccupied and rebuilt it. Jerusalem remained a Jebusite city until the time of David.

Celebration broke out as the ark returned to Jerusalem. David was so exuberant that he danced in the streets, to the embarrassment of his wife Michal. Apparently the other wives had no problem with this celebration, and this may tell us more about Michal's spirit than anything else. The two argued over the issue (2 Sam. 6:20–22), and David made it clear that he put God before her.[15]

WARREN'S SHAFT. A shaft that ties into the springs of Gihon and Hezekiah's tunnel complex, which is very likely the "water shaft" Joab used to capture Jerusalem from the Jebusites.

Sometime afterward, David began to plan how next to honor God. He decided that the best thing he could do would be to provide a permanent temple in place of the tabernacle. We are given very little information regarding the state of repair of the tabernacle, but if our chronology is correct, it was approximately 450 years old.[16] David took his plans to his prophet advisor, Nathan, who told him it was a great idea.

That night God instructed Nathan to convey to David that while building a temple was a good idea, it was not his to carry out. Near the end of his life, David told the people that God had informed him that he was not to build the temple because he was a warrior and had shed blood (1 Chron. 28:3). One of the lessons from this decision would be that God had different missions in store for different people. Even though He would not let David build the temple, God did promise him that the coming Messiah would be from his line (2 Sam. 7:13–16). This promise is known as the Davidic covenant, which placed David

THE MILLO. Meaning "filled-in area," the area where David built what the NIV calls the "supporting terrraces" after capturing Jerusalem. Recent excavations suggest that the Millo was behind this sloped retaining wall.

in a special place within the Abrahamic covenant we saw earlier.

Furthermore, David became the standard of faith for subsequent kings. That this was the height of David's career is evidenced by the next three chapters, which relate his accomplishments. There we read of further compassion on his part toward the house of King Saul and more military victories. In a period in which there was a power vacuum in the ANE, Israel was poised to become the dominant power.

A HERO WITH FEET OF CLAY

Read 2 Samuel 11–24.

While David had a heart that instinctively turned to God, he also failed at times. Early on in our study, we looked at the fall of man and saw the breakdown in relationships as a result. Thus far, we have seen the implications of those breakdowns in the life of David solely as failures on the part of others. Now we see them in David himself. The writer wants us to understand that David, who was as good as men get and was the standard by which all other kings were measured, was also flawed.

It all began when David started sloughing off from his duties. He was a warrior, and his place was with his armies on the battlefield. But that spring he stayed home. One evening as he was walking along the roof of his new palace looking over the city,[17] he saw a young woman bathing in the courtyard of her house. Liking what he saw, he sent messengers to "invite" Bathsheba to the palace. She spent the night, and in due time, she sent word to David that she was pregnant.

HITTITE FRIEZE. A frieze depicting Hittite troops, of whom Uriah was one of the most noted. Apparently Uriah, the husband of Bathsheba, had converted to Israel's religion, since he served in David's army.

David's first response was a cover-up. Bathsheba's husband was Uriah the Hittite. David sent a message to Joab, his general, asking that he send Uriah back to Jerusalem on some pretext or another. When Uriah arrived, David listened to his report and then suggested that he spend a day or two at home before returning to the battlefield. His purpose was to get Uriah to sleep with his wife so that he would think the baby was his. It didn't work. After two attempts failed, David sent Uriah back to the front lines with a sealed message that condemned him to death. Joab followed the king's directions so that Uriah ended up as a casualty on the battlefield; then he sent word back to David that the deed was done.[18] As soon as Bathsheba had performed the requisite mourning, David married her, thinking he had solved his problem.

But David had overlooked God. After the child was born, God sent Nathan, the prophet advisor, who gave a hypothetical situation hinting at the current case. David

> David pronounced a judgment by which he condemned himself.

pronounced a judgment by which he condemned himself. What is important, however, is his reaction as soon as the sin was pointed out to him. Earlier, King Saul, when confronted by Samuel, had rationalized his behavior. David, on the other hand, said, "I have sinned against the LORD." Nathan assured him that he would live (both the adultery and the murder were capital offenses) but that the child would die. David fasted and prayed when the child became ill, but after he died, David stopped mourning.[19] Soon Bathsheba had another child, whom they called Solomon.

URIAH THE HITTITE

Here is another case of a foreigner who had a position of trust within David's kingdom. It is not clear, however, what Bathsheba's nationality was. That Uriah had a very high sense of loyalty and integrity might suggest that he had become a follower of YHWH, but we are never told that (and it does not affect the significance of the story).

ABSALOM'S PILLAR. A tower, at the edge of the Kidron Valley, named for David's son Absalom, though there does not seem to be a historical connection. Absalom was buried in a pit and was probably not reburied. Many kings of Israel are thought to be buried farther downstream in the Kidron Valley.

David's judgment when Nathan had come to him earlier was that the man who had stolen the lamb must pay four times over. Nathan told him that the sword would not depart from his house, and throughout the rest of the book we read of how David paid four times over. The first punishment was the death of the child born from the illicit affair. The next came when his son Amnon raped Tamar, Amnon's half sister. David was furious but did nothing, most likely still feeling guilt about his own failings. However, her full brother Absalom plotted to avenge her, which led to the third stage: two years later, he arranged the murder of Amnon in a clever plot, and David mourned the loss of his son.[20] Absalom fled and remained in exile for three years, until Joab intervened. When Absalom returned to Jerusalem, however, David still refused to meet with him. Two years later, Absalom coerced Joab to arrange a "reconciliation."

Step four resulted from Absalom's plotting a coup d'état. He would sit in the city gate and greet strangers, listen to their stories, lament that the king wouldn't do anything, and then proclaim what great things *he* would do if he were king. After a while, having won over the people, he staged a revolt. David quickly fled Jerusalem, and Israel was once again in the midst of a civil war. Psalm 3, a lament, was written at this time.

David crossed the Jordan and in the process learned that there were many, such as the priests Zadok and Abiathar and his general Joab, who were still loyal to him. Others took advantage of the situation to advance themselves, such as Ziba, the steward of Mephibosheth,[21] and Shimei, a distant relative of Saul's who felt David was getting his just deserts. Then there were those who sold out, such as the wise counselor, Ahithophel.

Ahithophel advised Absalom to sleep with his father's concubines on the roof of the palace to show that he had taken over. A tent was set up for this purpose, and Nathan's prophecy (2 Sam. 12:11) was fulfilled. He also advised Absalom to pursue David immediately. This advice was undercut by Hushai, a counselor loyal to David but who pretended to

A CONFUSED KING

David's behavior after the death of Absalom is somewhat confusing, probably because David himself was confused. He fired his successful general, Joab (probably for killing Absalom against orders), and put Amasa, who had been Absalom's general (2 Sam. 17:5), in his place (19:13). Then David mourned for his son—the defeated enemy—instead of congratulating his troops, who had risked their lives for him.

throw in with Absalom. Hushai recommended waiting until he could gather his forces. Absalom decided to follow Hushai's advice, and Ahithophel committed suicide, sensing that the revolt would fail.

With the extra time, David was able to collect his wits and his forces.

The battle took place in Ephraim, which was still largely forested. As Absalom rode out to battle, his long, flowing hair got caught in an oak tree, leaving him hanging. When Joab heard this, he immediately killed the usurper and *then* sent to tell David. It is notable that David was more concerned with the loss of his son than with the successful quelling of the revolt.

David returned to Jerusalem, but his effectiveness had been lost. Dissension between the northern tribes and Judah increased. Even as he tried to restore order, another revolt occurred. This time it was led by Sheba, a man from Benjamin. David's new general, Amasa, was slow in organizing the troops, and Joab was sent to help. He killed Amasa, took over command, and successfully put down Sheba's revolt.

The books of Samuel end with a few incidents needed to tie up loose ends. For the original audience, several things would stand out. The nation had now had two kings, and neither had been what was expected. Both had begun well. Saul, the focus of the first volume, proved to be a spiritual failure. David, the focus of the second volume, was much stronger spiritually but also had times of failure, and the nation was still fractured. In terms of the amount of material devoted to David, we see that it concentrates on two periods: one covers the time when he was the "king-elect" running from Saul, and the other deals with the phase following his sin with Bathsheba, with a special emphasis on the Absalom revolt. These both highlighted the divided nature of the nation, and thus at this point, the future of the nation was problematic.

SOLOMON AS KING

We have just surveyed two books dedicated to the interrelationship of the first two kings. The next two books will cover forty to forty-two kings (depending on how they are counted). For the original audience, the pattern of human failure had been set, and it was now just a matter of tracing it out through history. As we have seen, the purpose of these books was not to provide a history of the people—they had that in the books the writers of Samuel, Kings, and Chronicles used as

Read 1 Kings 1:1–3:15.

sources.[22] Rather, the purpose was to show how God was working in the midst of an all-too-human population group to provide a solution for the overall problems of humankind.

As such, the nation of Israel was a step, but not the final one. The goal was the specific seed of Abraham promised about a thousand years earlier. But all the elements were not in place, and the failure of the nation as a political solution would have to be both demonstrated and driven home. The first example was Solomon.

We pick up the story when David was old. Without electric blankets or heating pads, he was unable to keep warm. His servants found a young woman named Abishag to be both nurse and bed warmer. Sensing the end was near, Adonijah, David's fourth son and now the oldest, decided to force matters and make himself king.

Adonijah, developing a coalition that included Joab the general and Abiathar the priest, planned a coronation. Before the plot came to fruition, however, Nathan the prophet found out about it and contacted Bathsheba. He was aware of David's desire (and apparently God's) that Solomon succeed him on the throne. With David's approval, Nathan and Zadok, another priest,[23] anointed Solomon as king, and they proclaimed the event throughout the city. Adonijah and company were celebrating the preliminary dinner when the announcement came, which broke up their party. Running to the tabernacle, Adonijah requested asylum, which Solomon granted on a promise of good behavior.

Near death, David requested that Solomon take care of a few items he had left undone. After this, David died and was buried; the nation mourned and settled in with its new king. Soon afterward, Adonijah requested that Abishag, David's last concubine, be given to him. Solomon saw this as another grab for the throne and had him executed. He pardoned Abiathar the priest because of his role in carrying the ark and sent him home in retirement to Anathoth (later the hometown of Jeremiah). Joab was executed. Shimei was put on probation, which he violated, so he too was executed. Thus, Solomon began his reign in a somewhat bloody manner, handling unfinished business from his father.

DAVID'S TOMB? A tomb in the Kidron Valley that dates from the Bronze Age and is believed to be the tomb of King David.

Other than this, Solomon started out with great promise, going to Gibeon to offer sacrifices to God.[24] There God appeared to him in a vision and offered to grant his desire. Solomon asked for wisdom to rule over the people, and God praised him and granted him that request as well as fame and fortune.

SOLOMON AS A WISE MAN

First Kings gives us one example of Solomon's wisdom in the account of the two prostitutes who lived together. Both had borne sons at about the same time. One woman's child died in the night, and she switched infants. The other mother recognized the switch in the morning, and a ruckus arose with each claiming the living son. Solomon told his guard to cut the living child in half and give half to each. The real mother protested, and Solomon thus discerned the truth of the matter.

Read 1 Kings 3:16–4:34; 10:1–10; 2 Chronicles 9:1–12.

Solomon's wisdom is best demonstrated by two books attributed to him: Proverbs and Ecclesiastes.

Proverbs

The most famous wisdom book is Proverbs.[25] While Solomon wrote many proverbs (1 Kings 4:32 makes reference to three thousand), he also seems to have collected them. Part of this collection is in the book of Proverbs. The book does note that the men of Hezekiah transcribed it (Prov. 25:1) in such a way that what we have today is an edited compilation.

Read Proverbs 1–9.

MEGIDDO. The city gates of Megiddo, one of the three cities Solomon built. Megiddo guarded one of the three choke points along the Coastal Highway.

Individually, proverbs are short general observations about how life works, expressed in an easily remembered manner. Because they are general in character, exceptions do occur. Moreover, observations of this type reflect life across cultural barriers, which is why Solomon and others could collect proverbs from a multitude of sources.

The book of Proverbs is very clear regarding its purpose: it is to teach wisdom. The Hebrew word translated "wisdom" actually denotes skill and can be applied to a number of areas, such as craftsmanship. In the case of the book of Proverbs, wisdom is skill in living—it identifies the best things a person can do to promote a successful life.

In this context, the book of Proverbs is based on two principles. The first is that the basic foundation of a successful life is reverence for God, or "the fear of the LORD." As we read through the book of Proverbs, we soon discover that the writer sees this high reverence for the Lord expressed in obedience to the law of God, that is, the Torah (which, as we saw earlier, indicates divine teaching). In fact, the OT law is an assumed cultural foundation to the book of Proverbs.

The second principle of Proverbs is the nature of humankind. The book points out that basically there are three kinds of people: the simple (or naive), the wise, and the foolish.[26] The simple person is inexperienced and must be shown the ropes. Everyone is born simple. The premise of Proverbs is that all people need instruction to be able to make right decisions. Without that instruction, they will end up making foolish choices and having to learn from their own mistakes. Given good instruction, a simple person can make wise decisions and thus have a fuller, more successful life.

The initial portion of the book (chs. 1–9) was written by a father to instruct an adolescent son. The heart of the book (chs. 10–29) is the collection of individual proverbs that address sundry areas of life and enhance that basic teaching. Assuming that Solomon composed these two sections, they must have been writ-

CONEYS. The animal mentioned in Proverbs 30:26 as small creatures who make their houses in the rocks. They are also known as rock hyrax.

ten before he began to turn away from God. The last two chapters (30–31) incorporate material from two otherwise unknown people, Agur and Lemuel. The latter is termed a king, which suggests that these men were not Israelites. Nevertheless, they feared God too, and their observations of life complement the rest of the book.

Ecclesiastes

Like Proverbs, this book is attributed to Solomon, although there is some controversy over that. If the basic form of the book of Proverbs was written by Solomon as a younger man, then Ecclesiastes was composed when he was older, after he realized the mistakes he had made in being led away from God. He had tried it all and had found that, without God, life is vapid, futile—"vanity of vanities." The point of the book is that God is needed for life to have meaning. While this conclusion is especially evident in the last chapter, where the writer draws his observations together, there are a number of places throughout the book (e.g., 2:24–26) where he begins hinting in this direction. The writer declares that the reader, while still young, should remember God so that in old age he or she will have no regrets—such as the writer himself was expressing.

Read Ecclesiastes 1–3; 12.

Song of Songs

A third book ascribed to Solomon is the Song of Songs (also known as Canticles and Song of Solomon). Historically, there have been two problems with the book. First, as might be expected, there is the question of the author. Again, there

Read Song of Solomon 1–8.

QOHELETH

The title used for the writer of Ecclesiastes is *Qoheleth*, translated "preacher" or "teacher" (1:1). He is also characterized as the son of David, king in Jerusalem; and 1:12 says that he was over all of Israel. This description logically refers to Solomon, who has traditionally been understood as the author.

Critical scholars over the last century have challenged this view, however, arguing for an unknown writer who passed himself off as Solomon. Their arguments fall into two general categories: (1) there are analogies to this type of literature in the later Hellenistic period, and (2) the Hebrew of the book is characterized by a number of Aramaisms (Aramaic being the language of Judea after the Exile). Therefore, they say, the book must have been written at about the time of the Exile or later.

These arguments are inadequate, as shown by Duane A. Garrett in the New American Commentary and by other scholars. The literary analogies are not as close as usually portrayed, and some date back to the time of Abraham. Moreover, linguistic study reveals that many of the features viewed as Aramaisms are attested in older Canaanite languages (which predate Moses) and so may be indicators of greater age, not less. Thus, there is no real reason to deny the traditional authorship.

is no real reason to deny the traditional author. However, the real reason for criticism of this book has been its explicit sexual content—it is definitely R-rated. Consequently, many scholars, both Jewish and Christian, have suggested that it is an allegory portraying the love of God for the nation of Israel or of Christ for the church.[27] It is best to understand the book as a praise of true love, but even so, it is hard to follow. The best interpretation I have seen views it as a series of snapshots showing events in the life of a couple, starting before their marriage through their first year or so together.[28]

SOLOMON AS A SUCCESS

Read 1 Kings 4:1–28;
9:15–28; 10:11–29;
2 Chronicles 8:1–18;
9:13–28.

Solomon was also known as an administrator, international trader, and builder. In a brief overview, the writer gives us a glimpse at the size of the kingdom he had inherited and what he did with it. Early in his career, the nation of Israel peaked, militarily, politically, economically, and most important, spiritually.

As administrator, Solomon redivided the large realm that he had inherited into administrative districts, trying to break down tribal loyalties. It did not work. In terms of international trade, we read of how wealth flowed into the nation from the Arabian peninsula, India, and the east coast of Africa. He built a fleet of trading ships that sailed down the *Yam Suph* (Red Sea) to those exotic locations, making a three-year round trip. He ran an international arms trade, buying horses and chariots from Egypt and Kue (probably an area that is now part of Turkey) and selling them to the Arameans. The text states that the amount of gold that came into his treasury in one year was 666 talents, but that probably reflects a peak year, not an annual event.

In addition to developing a fleet of ships, Solomon built several cities, public buildings, and palaces for his many wives and large bureaucracy. They were lavishly furnished using exotic woods and gold, silver, and ivory in abundance. The text notes specifically the gold shields used for decoration. Clearly, Jerusalem had the potential for becoming a "world" capital.

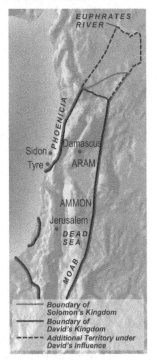

THE KINGDOMS OF DAVID AND SOLOMON.

SOLOMON'S TEMPLE

Read 1 Kings 5:1–9:8;
2 Chronicles 2:1–7:22.

The high point of Solomon's building career and probably the high point of the nation was the construction of the temple. This was the project David had hoped

to accomplish but was denied him. Still, he had done much advance preparation, including procuring the site and buying materials.

Even so, there was a lot of work to be done, and the project took seven years. Eventually, when the job was done, there was a great dedication ceremony. The ark was placed in the Holy of Holies, after which the *Shekinah* glory of God descended on the temple. This was followed by a powerful prayer by Solomon, a national blessing, and then a massive sacrifice (note the types of sacrifice and how they are used in 1 Kings 8:63–64).

God responded to Solomon with a promise (1 Kings 9:3–9) similar to the one He had given to Solomon's father, David. But this promise includes a condition of continued obedience (not found in David's), as well as a severe warning of the consequences of disobedience.

SOLOMON AS A FAILURE

Read 1 Kings 9:9–11:43.

Things went downhill for Solomon from there. We have already read that he married a daughter of Pharaoh, establishing a political alliance with Egypt. Over the years, his political alliances proliferated; and in the midst of many marriages, economic success, and peace in the land, Solomon lost his spiritual zeal. We are told

THE *SHEKINAH*

The *Shekinah* glory of God demonstrated His presence and had originally appeared at the dedication of the tabernacle (Ex. 40:34). We have no record of the *Shekinah* from after the Exodus until this point. We are also not told when it departed the temple (although it likely happened as Solomon began to serve other gods). Both omissions are curious. They suggest that the people failed to notice, which is a tragic commentary. Also noteworthy is that according to both Kings and Chronicles, the ark was still present in the temple at the time of the writing of those books near the end of the Southern Kingdom.

that Solomon had seven hundred wives and princesses and three hundred concubines. Clearly, this goes beyond just political alliances. In fact, the writer tells us that Solomon was drawn away from God by his love for women (1 Kings 11:4–6, 9–10).

Solomon experienced other failures as well. To pay for all the building he did, Solomon had to give some of his land to King Hiram of Tyre. This arrangement created tension because Hiram was not completely happy with the land he got. To provide the manpower for the building projects, Solomon instituted a corvée, mandatory national labor. He differentiated between true Israelites, who became the supervisors, and non-Israelites, who did the hard physical labor. Also, the tremendous trade that Solomon was promoting still did not provide enough income to cover the cost of the lavish decorating of his many buildings, so he imposed high taxes to make up the difference.

The writer tells us that silver became as common in Jerusalem as stones, a situation that would prove to be unhealthy. While the money came in fast, it was spent just as quickly, and most of it, as we have seen, was for ostentatious display. This show of material wealth was one of the things that would prove the undoing of the kingdom.

As Solomon grew older, things became unsettled. Not a warrior, Solomon let the military slide while he concentrated on building. By his later years, several of the lands David had conquered were revolting and breaking away. There were even revolts within Israel itself, a notable one led by a young man named Jeroboam that will be discussed in the next chapter.

GOD'S JUDGMENT

At the end of Solomon's reign, it was clear that the nation was in trouble spiritually. As is often the case with brilliant men, Solomon had not lived up to the standards he knew to be right, apparently thinking himself above them. He built places of worship to accommodate his many pagan wives and then joined them in the worship of those gods. Thus, the evaluation of Solomon is that while he accomplished much, the way he did it was at best questionable; and as a result, the nation suffered.

> At the end of Solomon's reign, it was clear that the nation was in trouble spiritually.

While a number of sociopolitical reasons can be given for the subsequent split of the nation, the real reason was spiritual.[29] Because of Solomon's toleration of, and support for, the worship of other gods, the nation was heading downhill. As in the time of the judges, God punished the nation. It began with a gradual decline as parts of the empire broke off (probably contributing to the economic problems). Finally, God told Solomon that the kingdom would be torn from him as a result. However, because of David's faithfulness (and in reality, for the sake of the promise that God had made to David), God would not tear the entire kingdom from Solomon, and the judgment would not take place until his son ascended the throne.

REVIEW QUESTIONS

1. Describe how David exhibited his faith in times of adversity as Saul pursued him.

2. What is the function of psalms? How do the different types of psalms achieve this?

3. Why was David at first crowned king of Judah only?

4. What are the steps that led to David's becoming king of the entire nation?

5. Why was David not allowed to build a temple?

6. How did David demonstrate his human weaknesses?

7. Describe the process by which Solomon became king.

8. What is the function of Proverbs?

9. Contrast Proverbs and Ecclesiastes.

10. What was Solomon's greatest building project, and why was it so significant?

11. What led to Solomon's failure?

13

CHAPTER

The Failure of the North

OVERVIEW

Soon after the death of Solomon, the united kingdom came to an end. Most of the tribes broke away from the Davidic dynasty and formed a separate entity commonly known as the Northern Kingdom. The biblical narrative characterizes all the kings who ruled in the north as having done what is evil. During its history, God sent various prophets to challenge the nation. After a little more than two hundred years of existence, the Northern Kingdom was conquered by the Assyrians, and the population was carried off into exile.

STUDY GOALS

- ▶ Explain how and why the kingdom of Israel divided.
- ▶ Trace the kings of the Northern Kingdom.
- ▶ Demonstrate the failures of the Northern kings as an entity.
- ▶ Introduce the role of prophets.
- ▶ Contrast the kings and the prophets.
- ▶ Explain the demise of the Northern Kingdom.

Following Solomon, the kingdom split. Our two historians approached their material differently. The writer of Chronicles (writing after the restoration began) ignored the Northern Kingdom and paid exclusive attention to the Southern Kingdom of Judah. From his perspective, the north was already lost—and written off. His focus tended to be on how Jerusalem, though it was the center of worship, failed before God and was destroyed. On the other hand, the writer of Kings (writing at the end of the Southern Kingdom), took a broader approach. Along with the prophets, he recognized that God was now looking to a distant future for the entire nation, but he wanted to show how the nation fared in the meantime and to highlight the work God was doing in its midst. His focus tended to be on the spiritual struggle that encompassed both kingdoms. As such, both writers distilled the data from their sources to present a case. Together the two show the failure of the monarchy to establish a righteous kingdom on earth. At the end, despite God's faithfulness, the people of the covenant had failed. The picture was not hopeless, but the hope had been deferred, as the increased role of God's prophets shows.

Both of our historians take a basic chronological approach, allowing us to trace the action. In Kings, however, the account switches back and forth between the two kingdoms, showing how they were somewhat interdependent. As modern readers, we find that method confusing, and if we are not familiar with the names of the kings, we tend to get lost. To simplify our study, we will discuss the two kingdoms separately. In this chapter, we will deal with the Northern Kingdom, and in the next, we will return to the transition following Solomon's death and discuss the Southern Kingdom.

JEZREEL. A major city in northern Palestine and the site of the winter palace for rulers of the Northern Kingdom. This views shows the path that Jehu would have followed as he approached the city.

Another matter that causes confusion is the terminology. The united kingdom that we have considered up to this point was called Israel. After the split, this name was applied specifically to the Northern Kingdom, while the Southern Kingdom was called Judah.[1] In order to keep the distinction clear, we will use the terms Northern Kingdom and Southern Kingdom instead of the names they were given, and reserve the name Israel for the entire kingdom. In the period after the Exile and in the NT period, we will use the name Judea.

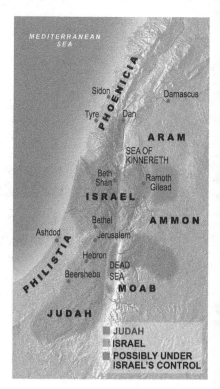

THE DIVIDED KINGDOM.

THE TWO KINGDOMS

Before we start tracing the history, let's take a quick overview of the two kingdoms. The chart on the next page presents a basic comparison between them. The key difference to note is that while the kings of the Southern Kingdom were up and down spiritually, those of the Northern Kingdom were viewed as evil without exception. Furthermore, by the standard count, there were nine "dynasties"[2] in the Northern Kingdom, while the Southern Kingdom retained the dynasty of David for its entire existence.

And there is one other point: individually, each of the two kingdoms was often able to hold its own against the major powers of the day, such as Egypt. Thus, each "half" was about as strong as most of the surrounding nations until Assyria developed as a superpower. This detail is suggestive of what the kingdom as a whole might have achieved had it centered on the worship of God instead of straying from Him.

THE KINGDOM SPLITS

When Solomon died, his son Rehoboam inherited what was left of the united kingdom.[3] He and the people went to Shechem on the slopes of Mount Gerizim for a coronation. There the people requested tax relief. When Rehoboam refused,

Read 1 Kings 12:1–14:20; 15:25–26.

COMPARISON OF THE TWO KINGDOMS

	Dates	Tribes	Dynasties	Capital	Power/Prestige	Spiritual State
Northern Kingdom	931–722 (209 yrs.)	All but Judah/ Benjamin	9	Shechem/ Tirzah/ Samaria	Significant (at times a world power)	Various degrees of evil
Southern Kingdom	931–586 (345 yrs.)	Judah/ Benjamin*	1	Jerusalem	Varied, (less than NK)	Extreme ups and downs

*We think of a 10-2 split in tribes (1 Kings 11:31), but Solomon and Jeroboam were told that the South would retain only one tribe (11:13, 32), which suggests a merger of Judah and Benjamin. Further, the tribe of Simeon was included in the territory of Judah and may have been absorbed by this time, although it may have moved north (2 Chron. 34:6).

the northern tribes revolted and sent for Jeroboam ben Nebat, from the tribe of Ephraim. This is the same Jeroboam who had earlier attempted a revolt against Solomon (1 Kings 11:40) but had to flee when it failed. (That he was given asylum in Egypt sheds some light on the politics of the day.) When Solomon died, Jeroboam was hastily recalled from Egypt by the northern tribes, who made him their spokesman. Now, however, they made him king of a new nation.

Jeroboam quickly set about to organize the Northern Kingdom. He built a new capital at Shechem and established a new religious structure to keep the people from going to Jerusalem. He understood that if the people traveled to Jerusalem to offer their sacrifices, they might also think of shifting their political allegiances. To preclude defection, he had two golden calves set up, one in Bethel and one in Dan.

This action created an overtly syncretistic cult designed to attract people from all backgrounds. The golden calves tied in with the worship of Baal. They also connected the cult with the early history of the nation, when Aaron had made a golden calf at Sinai. Recognizing this connection, Jeroboam told the people, "Here are your gods, O Israel, who brought you up out of Egypt" (1 Kings 12:28). Not only were there ties with the Exodus and with Baal, but also with the historical paganism of the land. We have already seen how the city of Dan had become a center of idolatry during the period of the judges (Judg. 18). Putting one of the new shrines at Dan reinforced that connection.[4]

In addition, there was the convenience factor, for the people no longer had to go to Jerusalem: Bethel was on the same road and not as far away, while for those who lived further north, Dan was closer to home. Moreover, Jeroboam emulated the festivals by establishing a big celebration in the eighth month that copied the festival in Jerusalem. He also established local shrines so that people could worship wherever they wished. Finally, he opened the priesthood to whoever desired to serve, rather than restricting it as God had directed. As we will see later, not everyone in the Northern Kingdom accepted this new religion. Over the years, many of those who still worshiped YHWH would gradually migrate south, although some groups would remain faithful where they were for the next several centuries.

In response to Jeroboam's actions, God sent a prophet from Judah who declared that in the future a man named Josiah would eradicate Jeroboam's false priesthood and defile his altar by burning human bones on it (1 Kings 13:2).[5] The sign or validation given was that the altar would split open, spilling the ashes (v. 3). Angrily, Jeroboam stretched his arm out to demand the seizure of the prophet. As he did so, his arm "shriveled up" so that he was not able to move it, and the altar immediately split open, as had been announced. Humbled, the king asked the prophet to pray that his hand would be restored. The prophet complied and then departed for Judah in accordance with God's directions, although he did not make it home. There were two tragedies in this event. The first was that the prophet of God was misled by the lies of a local prophet, costing the unnamed prophet his life.[6] The second was that despite this powerful demonstration from God, Jeroboam did not change his direction. This stubbornness would cost him the life of his son as well as his dynasty.

One of the powerful messages of this section is the effort God went to in order to leave no question of what people were supposed to do, and how the people rebelled anyway. While the people rejected YHWH, He never rejected them. To drive the message home, the writer tells us about Jeroboam's son Abijah, who became ill. Knowing that true revelation came only from the prophets of YHWH, the king sent his wife in disguise to Jerusalem so that she could consult with Ahijah, the prophet who had met Jeroboam outside Jerusalem several years earlier and told him he would receive ten tribes (1 Kings 11:29–31). Ahijah was now old and blind, and it is unlikely he had ever met Jeroboam's wife. Even so, she went in disguise. But God gave him advance warning, and as she walked through the door, Ahijah told her who she was and gave a harsh message to Jeroboam. Because of his evil acts, his

> Knowing that true revelation came only from the prophets of YHWH, Jeroboam sent his wife in disguise to Jerusalem.

JEROBOAM'S FESTIVAL

The new festival instituted by Jeroboam in the middle of the eighth month (1 Kings 12:32–33) was probably designed to replace Tabernacles (Sukkoth) and Yom Kippur, both of which took place in the seventh month (Lev. 23:34). If so, Jeroboam's festival took place a month after Tabernacles and served solely as a time of celebration, leaving out the need for repentance. Being a month later, it may also have been more convenient for agricultural workers, though that is not completely certain. Although it was later, relative to the completion of the harvest (especially olives), it also tended to put the festival later with respect to the fall rains, possibly interfering with the new cycle of planting.

KINGS OF THE NORTH AND SOUTH

SOUTHERN KINGDOM

Rehoboam (931-913) *Viewed as evil, lost 10 tribes thru stupidity. Suffered invasion from Egypt (Shishak).*

Abijah (913-911) *Evil, followed steps of mother.*

Asa (911-870) *Good, removed grandmother. Defeated Egyptians.*

Jehoshaphat (873-848) *Good. Married son to Ahab's daughter.*

Jehoram (848-841) *Evil. Died early, wife was Athaliah.*

Ahaziah (841) *Evil. Killed by Jehu in process of wiping out Ahab's family.*

Athaliah (841-835) *Evil "queen." Killed off sons/ grandsons. Not counted in king lists.*

Joash (835-796) *Boy king. Began well, but finished poorly. Killed by servants.*

Amaziah (796-767) *Viewed as good king, although brought the idols of Edom to Jerusalem.*

NORTHERN KINGDOM

Jeroboam (931-910) *Viewed as evil. Rebelled with 10 Northern tribes. Instituted new religion with golden calves.*

Nadab (910-909) *Viewed as evil. Assassinated.*

Baasha (909-886) *Viewed as evil.*

Elah (886-885) *Viewed as evil. Assassinated.*

Zimri (885) *Viewed as evil, lasted 7 days, killed by Omri.*

Tibni (885-880) *Viewed as evil, killed by Omri. Never had complete control of nation and is not listed on many king lists.*

Omri (885-874) *Viewed as evil. Major player in international politics, virtually ignored in text.*

Ahab (874-853) *Viewed as evil. Married Jezebel, Sidonian princess. Fought with Elijah, Elisha. Key figure in battle of Qarqar.*

Ahaziah (853-852) *Viewed as evil. Died from fall from second-story window.*

Joram (852-841) *Viewed as evil. Brother of Ahaziah. Assassinated by Jehu.*

Jehu (841-814) *Viewed as evil. Eradicated Baal worship, but returned to syncretistic cult of Jeroboam I. Killed off surviving members of house of Ahab/Jezebel.*

Jehoahaz (814-798) *Viewed as evil. Harrassed by Syrians.*

Jehoash (798-782) *Viewed as evil. Final period of Elisha.*

SOUTHERN KINGDOM		NORTHERN KINGDOM	
Uzziah	(792-740) *Viewed as good king, although tried to burn incense to God and was made a leper. Conquered Philistia.*	Jereboam II	(794-753) *Viewed as evil. Strong point of Northern Kingdom. Jonah served in his court.*
		Zechariah	(753) *Viewed as evil. Final king of Jehu's dynasty. Assassinated.*
		Shallum	(753) *Viewed as evil. Lasted 30 days. Assassinated.*
Jotham	(750-731) *Viewed as basically good king. Did not try to remove idols. Conquered Ammon.*	Menahem	(752-742) *Viewed as evil. Had only part of the Northern Kingdom. Faced resurgent Assyria under Tiglath Pileser.*
		Pekahiah	(742-740) *Viewed as evil. Heir of Menahem. Unable to stand against Pekah. Assassinated.*
		Pekah	(752-732) *Viewed as evil. Held part of kingdom until able to overthrow Pekahiah. Threatened Judah at the time of Isaiah.*
Ahaz	(731-715) *Evil king in every way. Failed to take God's word through Isaiah.*	Hoshea	(732-722) *Viewed as evil. Last king of Northern Kingdom.*
Hezekiah	(715-686) *Good king. Restored all of Ahaz's failures. Celebrated passover in entire nation.*		
			Northern Kingdom in Exile
Manasseh	(695-642) *Evil king. Worst of the bunch, although may have repented near end. Doomed the kingdom.*		
Amon	(642-640) *Evil king. Began like father, assassinated.*		
Josiah	(640-609) *Boy king. Good king in every way. Restored temple, discovered book of Law.*		
Jehoahaz	(609) *A.k.a. Shallum. Lasted 3 months. Taken to Egypt.*		
Jehoiakim	(609-597) *Evil king. Fought with Jeremiah, burned prophecies. Suffered first exile wave after Carchemesh.*		
Jehoiachin	(597) *Reigned but 3 months, taken into exile. Viewed as the last king, living beyond the destruction of city in 586.*		
Zedekiah	(597-586) *Appointed by Nebuchadnezzar. Not really accepted. Tried to play Egypt against Babylon. Caused destruction of Jerusalem.*		

CHRONOLOGIES OF THE KINGS

One of the difficulties in following the chronologies of the Israelite kings is that the Northern and Southern Kingdoms used different methods of reckoning regnal years. Generally speaking, the Southern Kingdom did not count the time from the coronation to the beginning of the next new year (this method is called the accession-year system). The Northern Kingdom did count that time as the first year. Furthermore, the Southern Kingdom celebrated the civil new year on 1 Tishri (September-October), while the Northern Kingdom celebrated it on 1 Nisan (March-April). (See Edwin B. Thiele, *A Chronology of the Hebrew Kings* [Grand Rapids: Zondervan, 1977], 14–19; see also *HBC*, 245–69.)

entire family would be destroyed. The proof would be that as soon as she stepped through the door of her home, the boy would die.

Jeroboam's wife returned home and the child died. We do not see any indications that Jeroboam changed, although his reign lasted twenty-two years (931–910 BCE). He was followed by his son Nadab, whose reign is summed up in brief terms: he did evil, lasted less than two years (910–909 BCE), and died.

THE DYNASTY OF BAASHA

Read 1 Kings 15:27–16:8.

Nadab was assassinated by Baasha. We are told very little about Baasha, but he was apparently a military officer, for he killed Nadab during the siege of Gibbethon. Immediately upon taking the throne, he wiped out the rest of the family of Jeroboam. He then moved the capital to Tirzah. Baasha was not a significant

DAN. The city that Jeroboam I established as one of two alternative religious sites in the Northern Kingdom. The city already had a history of cult worship.

king. He focused on expanding the Northern Kingdom to the south against the Southern Kingdom. Spiritually, he followed the way of Jeroboam. For this reason, God sent a prophet named Jehu ben Hanani, declaring God's judgment against him. He reigned twenty-four years (909–886 BCE), and when he died, he was followed by his son Elah. Elah ruled less than two years (886–885 BCE), and all we are told is that he was drunk when one of his generals, Zimri, assassinated him.

ZIMRI, TIBNI, AND OMRI

After Elah, three people claimed the throne. Zimri, who had wiped out the family of Baasha, moved into the palace in Tirzah, but the people did not support his claim. The army followed Omri, a strong general, whereas the overall population was divided between him and Tibni. Omri and the army went up to Tirzah and surrounded the city. Zimri looked at the situation and, realizing that it was hopeless, burned down the palace about him, ending his one-week "dynasty" (885 BCE). Sometime later the Omri faction prevailed over Tibni's, and Omri established the next dynasty, the fourth, less than fifty years after Solomon.[7]

Read 1 Kings 16:9–28.

Omri was a significant person for two reasons. First, in terms of world politics, he was a major player. He reigned about 885–874 BCE, during the rise of two major powers, Phoenicia and Assyria. Omri arranged a marriage between his son Ahab and a Phoenician princess from Sidon named Jezebel. At this point, the Assyrians were an up-and-coming empire; they so respected Omri that for decades they referred to the Northern Kingdom as *Beth Omri*—the house of Omri. He was also significant because he built a new capital, buying the hill that became the city of Samaria. In many ways, he established the Northern Kingdom. Yet for all of this, his entire twelve-year reign is covered in eight verses in the OT. The slight is clear and intentional. He was like his predecessors and even worse. He died and was buried in Samaria, and Ahab took his place.

THE PHOENICIANS

Phoenicia was a coalition of city-states on the coastal plain north of Israel; the OT refers to it usually as "Tyre and Sidon," its two main cities. Tyre was the city with which David and Solomon (fifty to one hundred years earlier) had working alliances, but that was before the Phoenicians started their major expansion. Jezebel was the daughter of Ethbaal, king of Sidon. The records indicate that at this time the Phoenicians were trading throughout the entire Mediterranean region as far west as Tarshish (in southern Spain) and probably further. This would have been about fifty years before the granddaughter of Jezebel's uncle founded the city of Carthage in North Africa. (See H. Jacob Katzenstein, *The History of Tyre* [Jerusalem: Schocken Institute for Jewish Research, 1973], 116–17.)

HOW COMMON WERE MIRACLES?

By now we should have begun to realize that supernormal events (miracles) were not a regular occurrence during Bible times (a period of about 2,200 years). Scholars have noticed that most of them tend to be clustered in just three periods. The first was the time of the Exodus, a period of about 45 to 50 years. The second was the time of Elijah and Elisha, a period of about 30 years. The third was the time of Jesus and the early church, a period of about 15 years. While we do see some of these supernormal events in other times, such as that of the judges and the late kingdom, they are few and fairly widespread. Even so, the use of the supernormal seems to have been limited to times when God was doing a special work or trying to convey a special message. That is what we see in the ministries of Elijah and Elisha.

AHAB AND JEZEBEL MEET THE PROPHETS OF YHWH

14 ch. of Elijah + Elisha

In contrast to the eight verses covering Omri, the next fourteen chapters (425 verses) cover the ministries of two people who were not kings or even associated with political leadership: the prophets Elijah and Elisha. Beyond the bulk of material covering their ministry, the use of the supernormal emphasizes the significance of their ministry. It was a watershed time for the nation, and the prophets were there to make the choices clear.[8] As we look at this material, we will also see that it was a time when the prophetic office seems to have achieved a greater importance, and the king served as a foil for the lessons God was trying to teach. Thus, Ahab and Jezebel are covered in more detail, not because they did more, but because they demonstrated the direction of the nation at a crucial time.

Ahab (874–853 BCE)

Read 1 Kings 16:29–34; 20:1–22:53.

Ahab was weak in character, a man who tended to blame others for his own shortcomings and who was dominated by his wife. Jezebel was a capable administrator, albeit somewhat ruthless in looking out for her own interests. When the writer introduces Ahab, he tells us up front that Ahab was more evil than his predecessors, for he married Jezebel and served Baal and the Asherah.[9] This is not to say that he was a total failure. We learn from Assyrian sources that Ahab was one of the kings at the battle of Qarqar in 853 BCE. In that battle, Ahab contributed a significant portion of the alliance that forced a draw with the Assyrians, thus stopping Assyrian expansion toward the southwest for a number of years.

Elijah's declaration that there would be no rain until he said so was a direct confrontation with Ahab's new gods.

Ahab is no more than introduced when we read that Elijah confronted him. The prophet declared there would be no rain until he said so, and then he disappeared. Israel depended on rain for agricultural success, so no rain meant famine. The declaration was also a direct confrontation with Ahab's new deities, which were fertility gods supposed to ensure good crops. Elijah was gone for three years, after which he returned with a challenge: YHWH versus the gods of the

THE POWER OF THE NORTH

The alliance against the Assyrian expansion showed the power of the Northern Kingdom with respect to the other nations of the area. According to Shalmaneser's intelligence report, the opposition was as shown:

King or Country	Chariots	Cavalry	Infantry
Hadadezer of Damascus	1,200	1,200	20,000
Irhuleni from Hamath	700	700	10,000
Ahab	2,000	10,000	
Que	500		
Musri (Egypt?)	10,000		
Irqanata	10		10,000
Arvad	200		
Usanata	200		
Shian	30		1(0?),000
Arabia	1,000 (camel)		
Ammon	?,000		

While Shalmaneser claimed victory, so did inscriptions from Egypt, suggesting a draw. (The numbers come from *ANET*, 278–79.)

Canaanites. The challenge was to see which god would answer prayer, specifically to send fire from heaven to burn a sacrifice. The 850 prophets of Baal and Asherah prayed and used every trick they knew to get their gods to answer. After an entire day of futility, Elijah took over. After soaking his sacrifice with water, he gave a short prayer. Following YHWH's victory, Elijah had the people kill the false prophets. Then Elijah prayed again, and it rained.

Although God kept trying, Ahab never got the picture. When Ahab fought against Ben-Hadad out of Damascus, God sent a prophet to assure him of victory (1 Kings 20). Following God's directions, Ahab had several triumphs. He then captured Ben-Hadad and had the opportunity to put his enemy away, but he refused to do so. For that reason, God told him that his own life would be forfeited.[10] Ahab pouted all the way back to Samaria.

The next episode involved a vineyard in Jezreel (apparently the home of Ahab's winter palace). Naboth refused to sell his family property, and again Ahab pouted. In disgust, Jezebel had Naboth executed on a pretext, using perjured witnesses, and gave Ahab his land. For this crime, Elijah told him that dogs would lick his blood and devour Jezebel, and that his house would be destroyed. In response, Ahab went into mourning, and God said that this judgment would be postponed until his son's reign.

The final episode shows Ahab at his charismatic best. He invited Jehoshaphat, the king of the Southern Kingdom, to a conference. Ahab was upset

VINEYARD. A common sight in Israel that eventually became a symbol of the nation. King Ahab showed his disdain for both God and His law when he confiscated Naboth's vineyard after his wife, Jezebel, had Naboth killed.

that the king of Aram (in Damascus) had not yet returned Ramoth Gilead.[11] He wanted to put together an alliance to attack his enemy. Jehoshaphat was willing but wanted God's view of the matter. Here we see a contrast between the prophets of YHWH (represented by Micaiah) and the syncretistic prophets of Jeroboam's cult (whose spokesman was Zedekiah). It is of interest to note that both claimed revelation from the spiritual realm. Micaiah acknowledged that to be the case but maintained that there were two different spiritual sources, and Zedekiah's source was a lying spirit.[12]

Despite revelation from God that he would end up dead on the battlefield, Ahab continued to plan for the battle. He also somehow managed to convince Jehoshaphat to wear his kingly robes, while he went disguised as a common soldier. It didn't matter. An anonymous archer shooting "at random" released an arrow that hit Ahab in a chink in his armor, mortally wounding him. That evening, after the battle had been lost, they returned Ahab's body to Samaria, where he was buried. As they washed his chariot, dogs lapped up the bloody water.

Jezebel

Read 1 Kings 19:1–3; 21:7–15; 2 Kings 9:30–37.

We have already seen how Jezebel brought her pagan gods with her from Sidon and enticed her husband into the active worship of Baal and Asherah. Not only did Jezebel dominate her husband—she intimidated most men. She was not fazed by Elijah's demonstration of the superiority of YHWH at Mount Carmel when he brought down fire from heaven. Her response was to threaten a man who had been successful in hiding from Ahab for more than three years. Even though Elijah had stood fearlessly before 850 prophets of Baal and Asherah in a showdown over whose god was the true God, he ran from Jezebel.

Jezebel's power over men may be one reason why God chose Jehu as the next king. After he had been anointed, Jehu returned to Jezreel, where he killed Jezebel's son Joram, king of the Northern Kingdom, and her grandson Ahaziah, king of the Southern Kingdom, at the vineyard of Naboth. Riding furiously, Jehu continued on into town. Hearing that he was coming, Jezebel put on her makeup, did up her hair, and went to her upper-floor window. Undaunted, Jehu pulled into the palace courtyard. Jezebel insulted him, and he had her thrown out the window. After he drove over her body in his chariot, he went in to dinner. Later he decided that as queen she deserved a burial, but when his people went back out, they found nothing but her skull, feet, and hands. The rest had been eaten by dogs just as God's prophet Elijah had predicted.

THE PROPHETS

We have seen prophets in action even before the nation was formed, although they have not really played significant roles in our accounts. They have served more in the role of advisors, up to now generally behind the scenes. For example, Judges 6 mentions only in passing that God sent a prophet to the people before He called Gideon to be judge. (Note, however, that Deuteronomy 34:10 presents Moses as a paradigm for prophets.) After almost six hundred years of national history, we are entering a phase where the role of the prophets is expanded and they are more significant figures. Likewise, while in the past the prophets had written books kept in the national archives, these writings were not added to the canon, although the authors of canonical books used them for sources (2 Chron. 9:29).

Now, however, we are entering a phase in the history of the nation where prophetic books will be incorporated directly into the canon. The reason seems to be that because of national failure, God would start drawing the attention of the nation toward His long-term work—specifically, the future work of the Messiah and a subsequent transformation of the world. Before we get into that material, we will see what was involved in being a prophet.

In the OT there were two words used for this office: *ro'eh*, translated "seer," and *nabi'*, translated "prophet." They were apparently interchangeable, although "seer" was the earlier (1 Sam. 9:9). It is generally recognized that the term *prophet* means "spokesperson" and probably comes from a verb meaning "to announce." Very early on, we are given a model for the role of prophet. In Exodus 4:15–16, when Moses argued with God regarding his return to Egypt, he protested that he was not an eloquent speaker. God therefore assigned Aaron to be Moses' spokesman ("mouth" in Hebrew). Moses would tell Aaron what to say, and Aaron would tell Pharaoh. A short time later (Ex. 7:1), Aaron's role is specifically described as being a prophet for Moses. After the Fall, human beings have needed these intermediaries for revelation from God.

If a prophet was God's spokesperson,[13] we can now develop a working definition of prophetic literature. It was literature written by God's spokesperson that reveals God's intentions in terms of specific actions in space-time history. These actions may be of two types: they may be God's actions that He has announced He is going to carry out, or they may be expected actions on the part of people in response to God. While prophetic declarations tended to be for the listening audience, when written down, they were understood to have a long-term value.

It would seem that this long-term value would have the primary purpose of showing God's sovereign control over history. One of Isaiah's major points was that YHWH was the only God who could not only act in space-time history, but could announce in advance what He was going to do.[14] Prophecy has three aspects. God's primary program is to reconcile human beings to Himself. This program is the key theme of the entire collection of books we call the Bible, and it was the reason for the calling of Abraham and for establishing the nation, and yet to come,

BILL WILLIAMS MOUNTAIN. Two peaks in Northern Arizona in the U.S. that, appearing to be close together but actually being forty miles apart, symbolize "prophetic perspective"—how a prophet might look to the future and juxtapose two events separated by centuries.

[handwritten margin notes:] prophet ~ spokesperson

3 aspects of prophecy:
1· reconcile human beings to himself

it would be the reason for the sending of the Messiah. This truth was demonstrated in the prophecies we have seen. For example, when God told Abraham that he would have a son in his old age, it was not just to let Abraham know what was going to happen. Isaac was not given to Abraham simply for the sake of his having a son, but as a demonstration of God's special purpose for the line of Abraham.

A second aspect of prophecy was to announce judgment over nations or persons who disobeyed God. Again, we have seen this throughout the OT to this point. A critical issue was rebellion against God. In certain cases, to ensure that the audience understood the judgment factor, the punishment was announced in advance. We saw that in the case of the plagues over Egypt. We saw it also in the death of the son of David and Bathsheba.

The long-term value of prophecy shows God's sovereign control over space-time history.

A third aspect of prophecy was the nature of its fulfillment: a combination of God's intervening in history and God's knowing how created beings would act (that is, His knowing their future actions). This aspect is much more difficult to grasp but can be illustrated in the life of Abraham. In Genesis 15, God comforted Abraham regarding his concern for having descendants. The answer would be Isaac, who was conceived as a result of special intervention by God. God continued by telling Abraham about how his descendants would not possess the land that He had given them until after a period of enslavement, "for the sin of the Amorites [had] not yet reached its full measure" (v. 16). God knew how the Amorites would act over the next several hundred years, and He would wait until they had done so to bring His people back from Egypt.

The encouragement to Abraham was the birth of Isaac, which would be the verification that the long-term prophecy would come about. The OT often calls short-term prophecies "signs"—supernormal events whose purpose was to validate a long-term prophetic declaration. So how did Jacob know that God would bring His people back from Egypt after he went there? Because his father, Isaac, had been born to Abraham in his old age. As the focus began to change in the time of the divided kingdom toward the long-term perspective, short-term

VALIDATING PROPHECY

In Deuteronomy 13:1, Moses gave two criteria by which to validate prophecy. The first was its accuracy; the standard was 100 percent. However, as we will see, some prophecies were contingent on the audience's response, which meant that the people had an opportunity to repent and prevent the judgment. The second standard was the focus of the prophecy. If it did not encourage the people in their worship of YHWH, it was to be viewed as false prophecy. In either case, the punishment was execution of the false prophet.

prophecies became more critical. Not all of the short-term signs were recorded, but enough of them were so that the original audience knew beyond a doubt that the writer was a prophet of YHWH with a pertinent message.

Finally, the message of the prophet was not only pertinent, but it was also designed to promote action. Awareness of God's purposes was to produce hope. Announcement of judgment was expected to produce repentance. Interestingly, this latter element has given us some problems, because we see cases where the repentance occurred and then God did not send the judgment. That looks as if the prophecy was invalid. Jeremiah, however, addressed that question when he told the nation that even though God had pronounced judgment on them, the situation was not hopeless (Jer. 18:7–11). Repentance would bring restoration. Unfortunately, the nation did not repent the way the people of Nineveh did when Jonah came (see the discussion later in this chapter).

Thus, into the heart of the darkest time of the Northern Kingdom, God sent prophets. It is important to remember that all of these were sent by God into a kingdom that had deliberately abandoned Him. But God had not abandoned them.

Elijah

Read 1 Kings 17–19; 2 Kings 1:1–2:11.

We have already noted Elijah's announcement of a drought. This was part one of his prophetic message. Elijah, however, also had to suffer through the drought conditions along with the people he served. Ironically, while fleeing from Ahab, God sent him to the region of Sidon, the home of Ahab's wife. There, operating out of faith, a widow provided for him.

MOUNT CARMEL. The site on the mountain traditionally associated with the prophet Elijah. It may have been near here that he had his showdown with the prophets of Baal and Asherah.

Part two of his prophetic message was the battle on Mount Carmel, which has a number of amusing elements as Elijah ridiculed the gods of the Canaanites. It also is tragic, however, for the people approached the issue totally undecided despite the historical evidences YHWH had provided their ancestors. After bringing down fire and once again demonstrating God's power, Elijah prayed, and it rained—a third demonstration of God's sovereign control. But then he ran from Jezebel and ended up at Mount Horeb (i.e., Mount Sinai). The dialogue between God and Elijah there seems to be an attempt on God's part to show Elijah that he still intended to show mercy (the gentle blowing) to the people Elijah had faced rather than the severe judgment Elijah desired. When Elijah hid his face from this mission, God sent him to find his replacement, Elisha.

But God was not immediately finished with Elijah, for he continued his ministry for some time even after Elisha was called. When Ahaziah succeeded his father, Ahab, on the throne, Elijah was given the responsibility to announce God's judgment on the new king (2 Kings 1:15–17). He was also able to show that YHWH could not be coerced as military commanders marched against him and were destroyed (vv. 9–12). Yes, even if Elijah was fired, that did not mean that he had been discarded. And God's approval of the man who stood firm against the most evil king of the north was shown as he was taken to heaven in the fiery chariot.

Elisha

Elijah was followed by his protégé, the man God had directed him to anoint. At the end of his ministry, Elijah tested the perseverance of his student as they traveled from Gilgal to Bethel to Jericho and then crossed the Jordan. Elisha stuck close and received the double portion of Elijah's spirit he had asked for.[15] After Elijah was taken up by the chariot, Elisha picked up Elijah's cloak (or mantle) that had fallen behind and took his place in the ministry. In addition to performing a

Read 2 Kings 2:12 – 8:14.

ELISHA'S MIRACLES

It has been observed that, in comparison with Elijah's ministry, approximately twice as many supernormal events are recorded of Elisha. These include dividing the waters of the Jordan River, healing the bad water, delivering the armies of both kingdoms from the Moabites, providing oil for the widow, announcing a son to the Shunammite woman and then raising the same son from the dead, purifying a poisonous stew, feeding a hundred men, curing Naaman of leprosy (then placing the leprosy on Gehazi because of his greed), floating an axhead, and foiling the Arameans who had tried to invade Samaria. The one most difficult to understand is the incident when he called down bears on some young men who were jeering at him (2 Kings 2:23–24). This was more than some boys making fun, however. A careful reading indicates that they were almost, if not fully, grown young men. And the fact that forty-two of them were injured by the bears shows that a large mob confronted Elisha, perhaps a hundred or more. Furthermore, their jeer seems to have been a direct assault on the God Elisha served rather than on Elisha himself.

number of supernormal signs to validate his position, Elisha supervised the anointing of the other two people whom God had spoken about to Elijah—Hazael as king of Aram, and Jehu as king over the Northern Kingdom. The latter marked the end of the Omri dynasty. Again, these replacements demonstrated God's sovereign control.

In many ways, Elijah and Elisha are an enigma. Yes, they stood against the most wicked dynasty in the north. Yes, it is obvious that part of their purpose was to show the power and sovereignty of God in an age determined to pick and choose its gods. But why should the writer include so much detail about these two people with obscure origins in an account that otherwise focuses almost exclusively on the political leaders? Probably he intended to send the message that secular power was not the solution to the nation's problem. When we look at the international power and prestige Ahab enjoyed and realize that he and his family were helpless before these prophets, we can grasp the writer's purpose. This truth is reinforced by the last prophetic revelation given to Ahab—which came from another prophet.

Micaiah

Read 1 Kings 22:1–28.

We have already noted this account from Ahab's perspective, but here we need to look at the role played by Micaiah, an otherwise unknown prophet who served in the Northern Kingdom along with Elijah and Elisha. Apparently Micaiah lived in Samaria, close to the seat of power. It would seem that he was protected by Ahab from Jezebel because he not only spoke the truth but revealed things to come. Thus, although Ahab did not like Micaiah's messages, he could not afford to ignore him.

The important thing, however, is the message given on this occasion. Micaiah related two visions. First, he foretold the death of Ahab in the upcoming battle. His declaration shows that Micaiah had received a vision of how the future would play out *should* Ahab go into this battle (although Micaiah understood that he would). More critical, however, is the second vision, whereby the prophet was

[handwritten margin notes: 2 visions: 1. foretold Ahab's death 2. able to foretell spiritual realm]

MICAIAH'S VISIONS

Micaiah's first vision was sharp enough that the prophet was willing to stake his life on the interpretation. It had to be much more than an ambiguous picture of a flock of sheep from which he was able to draw an analogy (as has been proposed). I suspect that he saw something like what we might see in a movie where the director has an aerial camera zoom back from the intense battle. In the process, the picture shows men beginning to drop their arms and flee for their lives. With regard to Micaiah's second vision, I like to use the analogy of "magic eye" pictures that on the surface appear to be a mishmash of shapes or lines. When looked at in the right way, a three-dimensional image pops out. The full picture was there all the time, but one could not see it before. So it is with the spiritual realm. We cannot see it unless we have special insight. This is evident from an episode in 2 Kings 6 where Elisha prayed that his servant's eyes be opened, and when they were, he saw spiritual forces guarding the city.

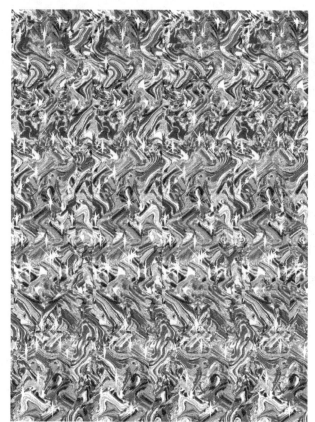

Hold the colored Magic Eye image *right up to your nose* and *stare* through it as if looking off into the distance. The image will be blurry; try not to blink. Move the page *very slowly* away from your face. At a certain point, the hidden object magically appears! In this case, you will see the outline of the angel image shown above.

PROPHETIC INSIGHT. A "magic eye" picture that gives a two-dimensional image or a three-dimensional image, depending on how it is held and viewed. This is an analogy to prophetic insight, in that prophets had the ability to see into the spiritual realm—a realm that is all around us that we cannot normally detect.

able to see into the spiritual realm. Based on what he saw, he maintained that Zedekiah, the leader of Ahab's troop of syncretistic priests, indeed had insight from the spiritual realm, but that this insight came from a lying spirit, not from God.[16]

The lesson of this entire section is clear. There is a spiritual realm beyond the physical, and that is where the real battle is being fought. More than this, God is in control but also very patient and forgiving, desiring to show mercy to all who would receive it. This truth is evident when we are told how Naaman, the enemy general, was cured of leprosy because he humbly obeyed, whereas Gehazi, the servant of Elisha, was struck with the same disease because of his greed and deceit.

Obadiah

The book of Obadiah is problematic. We are told that the author was Obadiah, but we know nothing else about him. The subject of his book is the condemnation of Edom. Scholars disagree on which Obadiah this was and when he lived.[17] If indeed the book was written during this period, as seems likely, it is tempting to identify the author with the Obadiah who served Ahab and met with Elijah (1 Kings 17), although a second Obadiah served Ahab's contemporary,

Read Obadiah.

Jehoshaphat, in the south (2 Chron. 17:7). Regardless of the date, the point of the book is that while God might punish His people, outsiders had better not gloat and jump in, because they then risked facing God's judgment themselves. This is what happened in the case of Edom, and the prophecy was a declaration of a future destruction of that nation—which may be why God's people decided to include this otherwise obscure book in the canon.

THE REST OF OMRI'S DYNASTY

Read 2 Kings 1:1–18; 3:1–27; 6:8–7:20.

After Ahab died, he was succeeded by his son, Ahaziah (not to be confused with his nephew of the same name, son of his sister Athaliah and later king of the Southern Kingdom). We are told little about this man, not even how long he reigned, but by piecing together the data, we estimate that it was less than two years (853–852 BCE). We are given just one episode in his life. After falling through the lattice of an upper-story window and gravely injuring himself, Ahaziah sent messengers to inquire of a pagan god whether he would survive. Elijah, however, intercepted the messengers and sent him God's message: the answer was no. Because he died childless, his brother Joram assumed the throne (852–841 BCE). He is labeled as evil, but not as bad as his father.

The remainder of the incidents involving Elisha took place in the reign of Joram, who seems to have been spiritually clueless. Despite several events in

HITTITE CHARIOT. A chariot depicted in a Hittite frieze that probably resembles the one General Jehu madly drove as he killed the kings of both kingdoms and then Jezebel after being anointed king by Elisha.

which God worked mightily on his behalf, first in a war with the Moabites and then on several occasions with the Arameans, he could not bring himself to worship God. The incident in which Elisha led the blinded Aramean army into the capital city of their enemy and then had God open their eyes is one of the more amusing in the Bible. The following incident of the siege of Samaria and the hunger of its inhabitants is one of the most tragic (and we should note that Elisha was inside the city, suffering with the rest). The end result was that God gave the kingdom to a new dynasty and Jehu was crowned.

THE DYNASTY OF JEHU

Read 2 Kings 9–10.

At the right time, Elisha precipitated action by sending a messenger who anointed Jehu as king. Serving as a loyal general involved in fighting against the Arameans, Jehu initially thought the act was a practical joke initiated by his fellow generals. While they were innocent, they liked the idea. Jehu then quickly drove his chariot to Jezreel, where he killed Joram, king of the north, Ahaziah, king of the south, and Jezebel.

Jehu quickly consolidated power by requiring the leaders of Samaria to defend the house of Ahab. When they desired to capitulate, he demanded that they eradicate the remainder of Ahab's family. After they did so, he pointed out that they were now as guilty of insurrection as he was. He also executed a number of relatives of Ahaziah (king of the south),[18] then proceeded to finish the job Elijah had started of eradicating the leadership of Baal worship. The writer of 2 Kings praises him for this. The one thing Jehu was not able to do was restore the worship to YHWH. While he talked of serving YHWH, he really followed the syncretistic cult of Jeroboam I, for which he was condemned. Unfortunately, that seemed to be about the best the Northern Kingdom could offer.

Jehu is mentioned in the records left by Shalmaneser III. But while Ahab was part of the coalition that fought him to a draw at Qarqar, Jehu is merely noted for bringing tribute.[19] At the same time, the Arameans were gradually taking parts of the Northern Kingdom. Still, Jehu did establish a strong dynasty that lasted eighty-nine years. It was the most solid dynasty that the Northern Kingdom would see during its entire existence. After twenty-eight years (841–814 BCE), Jehu died, and his son Jehoahaz took his place.

Jehoahaz (814–798 BCE)

Like his predecessors, Jehoahaz followed in the cult of Jeroboam I. For this reason, he was viewed as evil, and the Arameans prevailed even further. In response to the prayers of Jehoahaz, God provided for the people a deliverer (a term we have not seen used of humans since Judges 3), who is not identified. But the people did not repent. After a seventeen-year reign, Jehoahaz died and was followed by his son Jehoash.

Read 2 Kings 13:1–9.

Jehoash (798–782 BCE)

Read 2 Kings 13:10–25.

Jehoash followed the footsteps of his father and grandfather. The main item of interest here is that he had one recorded meeting with Elisha, who was now old. In his greeting, Jehoash indicated that he was aware that Elisha as God's intermediary was the strength ("the horses and chariots") of the nation. But Jehoash really did not understand God, nor did he place his faith in Him. Elisha told the king to get a bow and some arrows. Indicating that the arrows represented victory over the Arameans, the prophet told Jehoash to strike the ground. He struck it three times, but Elisha chastised him for his lack of faith and for not going further. He did have the promised three victories, but with greater faith, he actually could have conquered Aram. After reigning sixteen years, he was followed by his son Jeroboam II.

Jeroboam II (794–753 BCE)

Read 2 Kings 14:23–29.

The nation is now in the middle of its longest dynasty. Jeroboam II is noted for three things: he reigned forty-nine years; one of his court advisors was a prophet named Jonah; and he was able to regain lost territory back almost to what the Northern Kingdom had been at the start. The mix in the narrative is interesting. We are told up front that he was an evil king who continued in the ways of his namesake, Jeroboam I. But the writer goes on to show that the reason he succeeded was God's mercy and the honor of His name, "since the LORD had not said he would blot out the name of Israel from under heaven" (2 Kings 14:27). Following that brief overview, we are told that Jeroboam II died and was succeeded by his son, Zechariah.

In many ways, the Northern Kingdom went downhill after Jeroboam II, and there are no real bright spots for the remaining thirty-two years of its existence.

Jonah the Prophet

Read Jonah 1–4.

We have already mentioned that Jonah was an advisor to King Jeroboam II in Samaria. Again this shows that the kings of the north were aware of YHWH and that their rejection of Him was deliberate. It also highlights God's mercy as He dealt with the nation. In addition, it suggests that Jonah was very cognizant of international affairs when God sent him to Nineveh.

COREGENCIES

Jeroboam II is said to have reigned forty-nine years, but about twelve of those years overlapped with the reign of his father, Jehoash. It was not uncommon in the ANE for a king to put his heir on the throne to rule with him for a period. The process is called *coregency*. Normally it was done when a king was involved in war or in some other situation that might put in jeopardy the continuation of the dynasty. We see it in a number of cases in the two kingdoms of Israel. It also shows up in other countries, for example, in the case of Nabonidus and Belshazzar in the Neo-Babylonian Empire, as we will see in chapter 15. (See Eugene Merrill, *Kingdom of Priests: A History of Old Testament Israel* [Grand Rapids: Baker, 1995], 373.)

When we think of Jonah, the first thing that comes to mind is the special fish (it was not a whale). Unfortunately, the overall message of the book sometimes gets lost in the discussion of that issue. The point of the book is that God is the sovereign Creator who is able to judge entire nations and control storms but who also has mercy on the innocent. In that context and understanding of God, a specially prepared fish is a minor issue. Thus, the way we approach the account of the fish really indicates our view of God.

From a historical perspective, the reaction of Nineveh to the message is more important. (While the historicity of the fish episode is significant with respect to the reliability of the reporter, it was important to the nations of Assyria and Israel only insofar as it brought Jonah as messenger to Nineveh.) Historical records indicate that the Assyrian Empire was especially vicious. They led captives away with hooks through their noses and impaled rebels. The biblical writer tells us that the nation repented at Jonah's preaching. Historical records indicate that the period between 770 to 744 BCE was relatively quiet, possibly as a result of this repentance.[20] The message of the book is powerful, showing that the Israelites viewed YHWH as an international God who reserved the right to discipline or forgive even Assyria. This is in contrast to the other nations, who viewed their deities as national gods responsible solely to advance the national cause.

JONAH'S PLANT. A form of castor bean, which most scholars believe is the kind of plant Jonah had for shelter outside Nineveh. It grows rapidly under normal circumstances, becoming a small tree in summer.

THE ASSYRIAN EMPIRE.

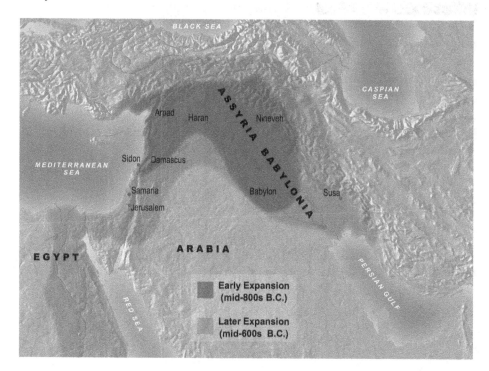

THE DAY OF THE LORD

The phrase "the day of the Lord" is used in a variety of ways throughout the Bible. It is a time of judgment, as shown by passages that list specific nations judged on "the day of the Lord" (e.g., Babylon in Isa. 13:6, Egypt in Jer. 46:10, the Northern Kingdom in Amos 5:18, and the Southern Kingdom in Zeph. 1:18). It is also a time of blessing, as shown from passages such as Amos 9:11, Obadiah 15, and 1 Thessalonians 5:2–4. Some of the judgments have already occurred. Some are yet future, as are the blessings, which means that the "day of the Lord" is more than a single specific time.

Amos the Prophet

Read Amos 1–9.

While Jonah went from the court of Jeroboam II to Nineveh carrying God's message, Amos carried God's message to Jeroboam II. Amos was from a town in the Southern Kingdom called Tekoa, about 6 miles from Bethlehem. It seems ironic that Amos, a shepherd, was called to pronounce judgment on the shepherd of God's people.

The book of Amos begins with a condemnation of seven nations in the region, ending with Judah and Israel (the Southern and Northern Kingdoms). The last nation addressed is the one the book focuses on, the Northern Kingdom. The condemnation is twofold. It is primarily spiritual because of the syncretized worship evident there. It also condemns the social injustice that resulted when the people failed to follow God's teachings. A key term in the book of Amos is "the day of the Lord [YHWH]." This term reflects a period when God intervenes in history to advance His overall program. As such, it can be a time of judgment or a time of blessing, depending on who is involved and when. Amos's warning to the Northern Kingdom is that they can only expect it to be a time of judgment on them because of the way they have acted.

Zechariah (753 BCE)

Read 2 Kings 15:8–12.

Jeroboam's son Zechariah took the throne, but he could not hold it. His rule lasted six months, and he is viewed as evil. An unknown man named Shallum assassinated him in front of the people and took the throne.

THE DYNASTY OF SHALLUM

Read 2 Kings 15:13–15.

The reign of Shallum is another instance where we must put the word *dynasty* in quotes, for it lasted only a month (in 753 BCE), and he was not succeeded by someone in his lineage. His reign was so short that it was not appraised, but we see a pattern. The nation was degenerating into chaos.

THE DYNASTY OF MENAHEM

As we approach the end of the Northern Kingdom, we find the material some-what confusing, apparently because of conflicting claims on the throne and claims of credit for the destruction of the kingdom.[21] Menahem (752–742 BCE) deposed Shallum but did not seem to have total control of the country, with Pekah having a rival claim. Menahem began his reign by cruelly attacking Tiphsah, a city in the Northern Kingdom that refused to submit. He is deemed evil not only because of this horrendous action but also because he followed Jeroboam I spiritually. As the Assyrians restarted their incursions into this area, he bribed Pul (or Tiglath-Pileser III), the Assyrian emperor. This act made Menahem an Assyrian puppet who extorted money from the people to allow him to keep his throne.

After reigning ten years, Menahem died and was followed by his son Pekahiah (742–740 BCE). As is often the case, Pekahiah was not as strong as his father. In less than two years Pekah overthrew him. Pekahiah, like his predecessors, was viewed solely as evil.

Read 2 Kings 15:16–26.

THE DYNASTY OF PEKAH

Pekah (752–732 BCE) apparently had grasped control of part of the Northern Kingdom when Menahem usurped Shallum. While Menahem reigned, neither could defeat the other. After Menahem's death, Pekah was able to defeat Menahem's son Pekahiah. He then gathered all of the Northern Kingdom together again for one brief period.

During his reign, Tiglath-Pileser began making significant incursions into the Northern Kingdom, taking a number of cities. He began the exile of the Northern Kingdom by transporting people from the Galilee and Transjordan regions (2 Kings 15:29). Pekah joined forces with Rezin, the Aramean king in Damascus, to try to formulate an alliance to withstand the growing Assyrian threat. They tried to induce the southern kings (Jotham and Ahaz) to join their alliance but were unsuccessful. As a result, they went up to Jerusalem to attack it. It would appear that the Assyrian invasion came at that time, putting an end to the threat on Jerusalem.

Pekah's "dynasty" ended when Hoshea, supported by the Assyrians, conspired to overthrow him. The final appraisal of Pekah was that he was evil, and as his reign ended, judgment was nigh.

 Read 2 Kings 15:27–31; 16:5–7

THE DYNASTY OF HOSHEA

The last king of the Northern Kingdom was Hoshea. His reign was the last of five "dynasties" in a period of less than twenty-five years. He too was viewed as evil. During his reign, Hosea, the last prophet to the Northern Kingdom, was active.

 Read 2 Kings 15:30–31.

WHEN WAS HOSEA WRITTEN?

One of the challenging things about the book of Hosea is its dating. According to the introduction, he was active during the reign of Hezekiah, who did not even become king until about seven years after the Northern Kingdom had been destroyed (715 BCE). However, while he lists four kings in the Southern Kingdom, he only lists Jeroboam II in the north (who died in 753 BCE, omitting the last six kings we have cited. Thus, although his ministry seems to have focused on the Northern Kingdom, he overlooks the kings he addresses and instead notes a southern king who came later. As we read the book, we note that he uses the term *Ephraim* to refer to the Northern Kingdom as a whole. Ephraim, of course, was one of the ten tribes that split off, and the capital city of Samaria was within its territory. We use a similar figure of speech when we refer to the government of the United States with the name of the nation's capital, Washington.

Hosea the Prophet

Read Hosea 1:1–3:5; 14:1–9.

Hosea was a man whose life exhibited God's message of grace. He began his ministry during the reign of Jeroboam II and actually continued after the demise of the Northern Kingdom. Hosea is an interesting book for several reasons. The first part (chs. 1–3) relates events that took place in his life. He married Gomer, a harlot. They had three children, whose names each carried a prophetic message. Afterward, Gomer ran away, and God told Hosea to go buy her back, which he did. The last part of the book (chs. 4–14) is structured like a legal case—specifically, a writ of divorce. Thus, we find the last prophet of the Northern Kingdom proclaiming the upcoming separation, that is, exile. But that was not the final

GOMER AND HER CHILDREN

Hosea's wife, Gomer, is described as "a wife of harlotry" (Hos. 1:2 RSV; NIV, "an adulterous wife"). The question that has been debated is whether this meant that she was already involved in prostitution or that she would do so once she was married. The primary argument in favor of the latter is the idea that God would not require His prophet to marry a woman who was already promiscuous. That, however, does not follow. The purpose of this marriage was to show the nature of the nation of Israel. As we have seen, the people had been involved in spiritual harlotry from the beginning. We have also seen God's grace to the harlot Rahab. God has never been blind to human nature; thus, I would argue that while He sets high standards, God has never been shocked by our shortcomings.

Gomer's first child was a son, whose name was Jezreel, meaning "YHWH sows." The name also reminds us that it was at Jezreel that Jehu (the founder of the dynasty of which Jeroboam II was the peak) killed the heirs of Ahab and took the throne. The second child was a daughter named Lo-Ruhamah, meaning "no compassion." The final child was a son named Lo-Ammi, "not my people." An interesting nuance of these prophecies is how they foretell both judgment and hope. For example, after declaring that they were "not my people," God talks about how the two nations would be reunited as one people and be called "the sons of the living God."

word. Even as he proclaimed separation, the final plea in Hosea 14 was for repentance and return. And the promise was that, should the nation do so, it would be forgiven and healed.

Hoshea the King

In some ways, the end of the Northern Kingdom is the story of two men: Hosea and Hoshea. In the Hebrew, the two names are identical (the spelling Hosea comes from the Greek and Latin titles of the OT book). But what a difference in the men! Hosea was God's messenger warning of judgment and demonstrating God's compassion. Hoshea was a king who raised the question of whether mental ability was a prerequisite for the throne.

Read 2 Kings 17.

Hoshea was able to get the throne of what was left of the Northern Kingdom by taking it from Pekah—with the help of the Assyrians.[22] Naturally, the expectation was that Hoshea would dance to the Assyrian tune. Instead, he rebelled, but evidently the revolt was suppressed and he was carried off by the Assyrians and put into prison. After several years, however, he was released and put back on his throne.[23] In 725 BCE Samaria (apparently with Hoshea in residence) revolted again, and this time the city was put under siege by Shalmaneser V. The siege lasted three years; in 722 Samaria was captured, and the inhabitants were led off to captivity.[24]

EPITAPH OF A NATION

The final part of this section of 2 Kings addresses the issue of why the Northern Kingdom went into exile. The writer makes it clear that when he was writing, some years after the fact, the Northern Kingdom was still in exile, and the reason was that the people had adopted pagan worship. The warning was primarily for the still-extant Southern Kingdom, but that part of the nation too would soon face God's judgment.

THE TEN LOST TRIBES?

Because there is no record of a return of the Northern Kingdom, we sometimes hear references to the "Ten Lost Tribes of Israel." However, a careful reading of the text reveals that the "ten tribes" were never lost. Over the years, many people who served the true God migrated south. More important, while the writer talks about how the northern tribes were removed, this does not mean that every person was carried off. In fact, we soon learn that some of the people had been left behind, generally the poorer classes (and interestingly, often those who truly served YHWH). A few years after the destruction of Jerusalem, we read of Hezekiah's great reformation and learn that people from all of the northern tribes were still living in the land and that many came south (2 Chron. 30). However, this movement does not seem to be the unification that the prophets referred to, for writers like Isaiah talked about such a restoration in the future tense.

REVIEW QUESTIONS

1. Why did the northern tribes leave the kingdom of Israel?

2. What steps did Jeroboam take to establish a separate identity for the Northern Kingdom?

3. Why is Omri largely ignored in the biblical record?

4. What did Ahab do that showed the direction the Northern Kingdom was going?

5. What is the significance of Jezebel?

6. What was the function of a prophet, and how was that function fulfilled?

7. Compare the ministries of Elijah and Elisha.

8. What is the significance of Micaiah?

9. Who was Jehu?

10. What was the distinctive mission given to Jonah?

11. Summarize the message of Amos.

12. How did Hosea try to convey his message to the Northern Kingdom?

13. How did the Northern Kingdom end?

14

CHAPTER

The Roller-Coaster South

OVERVIEW

The Southern Kingdom, unlike the Northern, enjoyed one dynasty throughout its history. Its kings, however, were a mixed lot—some very spiritual and some as evil as the worst in the north. In time God brought prophets to the Southern Kingdom, and we find in their records anticipations of an exile (and a return) and of the future Messiah. The Davidic dynasty met its demise at the hands of the Babylonians.

STUDY GOALS

- Trace the kings of the Southern Kingdom.
- Describe the spiritual diversity of the southern kings.
- Trace the decline of the Southern Kingdom.
- Show how the role of prophets increased as the nation declined spiritually.
- Trace the three waves of exile of the Southern Kingdom culminating in the destruction of Jerusalem.

After the split of the kingdom following Solomon, the two nations took separate paths spiritually. We have already seen the downward spiral of the Northern Kingdom. Now we want to look at the Southern Kingdom and see how it fared. As we do so, we will divide its history into periods.

THE AFTERMATH OF SOLOMON

The first group of kings in the Davidic dynasty begins with Solomon's son Rehoboam. These kings had to adjust to a truncated kingdom consisting of only two tribes, Judah and Benjamin; however, its area was about a third of the overall territory, because the region occupied by the tribe of Simeon was apparently absorbed into that of Judah. Naturally there was strife between the two kingdoms. As the smaller portion, the Southern Kingdom experienced decreased political power and economic viability. The leaders also had to adjust to migration from the north as Levites and true believers in YHWH came south. This development probably produced more stress, because many of those originally in the south were less than sincere in their own worship.

Rehoboam (931–913 BCE)

Read 1 Kings 12:1–20; 14:21–31; 2 Chronicles 10:1–12:16.

The surface reason that Rehoboam lost the northern tribes was that he not only refused to cut taxes, but also threatened to raise them.[1] When the northern tribes abandoned him at Shechem, Rehoboam fled for his life. After arriving safely in Jerusalem, he gathered troops from Judah and Benjamin, the tribes faithful to

BETHLEHEM. Known as the city from which David came and as the birthplace of the Messiah as foretold by the prophet Micah—but a small, insignificant town during all those times.

him, with plans to attack the Northern Kingdom.[2] God sent the prophet Shemaiah to warn against this action. To his credit, at this point Rehoboam listened.

He did fortify what was left of the nation against a possible attack from the north. In the meantime, the Levites who were unemployed under Jeroboam's syncretistic religion came south. More important, the chronicler observes: "Those from every tribe of Israel who set their hearts on seeking the LORD, the God of Israel, followed the Levites to Jerusalem" (2 Chron 11:16). This was the beginning of what apparently was a constant flow of true worshipers of God to the south. For the first three years, things went well. Then Rehoboam began to slip.

> Rehoboam's reign saw the beginning of what apparently was a constant flow of true worshipers of God to the south.

We are told that Rehoboam had eighteen wives and sixty concubines—fewer than his father, Solomon, but more than his grandfather, David. The one he loved the best was Maacah, identified as daughter of Absalom (2 Chron. 11:20–21; some believe she was his granddaughter). Consequently, he arranged his family affairs so that her oldest son (instead of his own firstborn) would become the next king. Rehoboam must have accomplished this with wisdom, for there appears to have been no controversy in the succession. During this process, Rehoboam and the national leadership began to decline spiritually. Consequently, God allowed the Egyptian pharaoh Shishak (also referred to as Sheshonk and Shoshenq), to attack the country and sack Jerusalem. Because the people repented when Shemaiah the prophet proclaimed judgment, God told them that it would not result in destruction (2 Chron. 12:5–8). Indeed, Shishak looted the city (taking the gold that Solomon had amassed) but did not burn it.

In summary, Rehoboam was spiritually ambivalent. He tended to go his own way and thus was deemed "evil." But when condemned, he humbled himself. He also worshiped YHWH in the temple.

Abijah (913–911 BCE)

Abijah (spelled Abijam in the Hebrew text of 1 Kings) did not display the wisdom and restraint of his father, Rehoboam. He instigated the war against the Northern Kingdom that Rehoboam had stopped after receiving a warning from God. Before

Read 1 Kings 15:1–8; 2 Chronicles 13:1–22.

RAIDERS OF THE LOST ARK

Shishak's looting of Jerusalem occurred in 925 BCE and is the premise behind the movie *Indiana Jones and the Raiders of the Lost Ark*. It is argued that the ark of the covenant was stolen by the Egyptians at this time. The argument assumes that the treasures of the house of the Lord necessarily included the ark. There are two problems with this premise. The first is the textual evidence that the ark was still present at the end of the kingdom (2 Chron. 5:9). The second is the theological problem of whether God would allow the ark to be so lightly treated (see 1 Sam. 5 for an account of what happened when the Philistines captured the ark).

the battle, Abijah gave a fine speech against his enemy, blasting the spiritual foundations of the Northern Kingdom, but he was then surprised by an ambush Jeroboam had set. Trapped, the men of the Southern Kingdom cried out to God, who delivered them. They were then able to expand the kingdom's borders to the north of Bethel. Spiritually, this was Abijah's high point. He too was viewed as ambivalent and was condemned for not being true to God. There are some indications that he was dominated by his mother, who overtly served pagan gods. After a short reign, Abijah died (with no cause given), and his son Asa took his place.

Asa (911–870 BCE)

In contrast to his three predecessors, Asa was spiritually strong—but not quite measuring up to David. He began well. Apparently, early in his reign, Zerah "the Cushite" invaded the Southern Kingdom. Asa gathered his troops and then called upon God to provide the deliverance. God did so, and the Southern Kingdom drove off the invaders.

Amid the joy of the victory, Asa was visited by a prophet named Azariah ben Oded. Azariah recalled the turmoils of the nation in the past and exhorted the young king to start a revival. Asa did so, removing the idols and repairing the altar at the temple. He then gathered the people of the kingdom for worship (and note that, according to 2 Chronicles 15:9, people from the tribes of Ephraim, Manasseh, and Simeon were part of that gathering). They performed a large sacrifice and made a national covenant to return to God. He also removed his grandmother, Maacah, from her position of power because she was a primary instigator of the idolatrous worship.

As a result of these actions, God ensured peace for part of Asa's reign—there was no war until the thirty-fifth year.[3] Then Baasha of the Northern Kingdom began to erect fortifications in Ramah, which was only about 5 miles north of Jerusalem—an overt incursion into territories claimed by Asa. Baasha's apparent purpose was to prevent further migration of people moving south (1 Kings 15:17). The fact that Asa did not himself attack indicates that he was not militarily strong at this time. Instead, he bribed Ben-Hadad of Damascus to attack the Northern Kingdom (thus violating a treaty between Ben-Hadad and Baasha).

God sent Hanani, a prophet, to condemn Asa's lack of faith in that he trusted Ben-Hadad and not God. The result would be war for the rest of his reign. Asa

Read 1 Kings 15:9–22; 2 Chronicles 14:1–16:14.

ZERAH THE CUSHITE

Zerah the Cushite (sometimes translated "the Ethiopian") is often associated with the Egyptians under Osorkon I. What is not clear is whether we are looking at mercenary Arabian troops stationed in Gerar or possibly troops from Upper Egypt (i.e., the southern area, modern Sudan). The account in Chronicles notes that it included Libyans, which suggests that we have an account of the actual Egyptian army under Zerah as general (John Bright, *A History of Israel*, 4th ed. [Louisville: Westminster John Knox, 2000], 234–35).

threw Hanani in prison, showing that he had lost his spiritual sensitivity. He oppressed his people and was struck by God with a foot disease. Still he did not return to God, and he eventually died after a reign of forty-one years. Overall he was still given credit for the positive reformations he had made, and the writer of Kings views him as one who "did what was right in the eyes of the LORD."

INTERTWININGS WITH THE NORTH

By the time Asa died, Omri had established his dynasty in the north and had passed the throne on to his son Ahab. Jehoshaphat, Asa's heir, took his throne a year after Ahab began to reign, and the two seem to have been about the same age. For the next several years, the two dynasties not only became close but also intermarried.

Jehoshaphat (873–848 BCE)

In many respects, Jehoshaphat was a bright spot in the history of the nation. The writer of Kings described his rule by saying, "In everything he walked in the ways of his father Asa and did not stray from them; he did what was right in the eyes of the LORD" (1 Kings 22:43). As we look at his overall record, however, we find that while his heart attitude was right, he made several mistakes.

Read 1 Kings 22:41–50; 2 Chronicles 17–20.

On the positive side, he fortified the country and went through the land removing pagan shrines that had either not been removed by Asa or had crept back in. He sent teachers throughout the land teaching the law. He organized the country militarily, and the power was evident enough that he had peace with his neighbors.

But on the negative side, Jehoshaphat arranged a marriage between his son, Jehoram, and Athaliah, the daughter of Ahab and Jezebel. This decision was extremely unfortunate, because Athaliah was like her mother in virtually every respect. Then Jehoshaphat made the well-known visit to Ahab we discussed in chapter 13. Micaiah warned the kings that Ahab would be killed, and Jehoshaphat agreed not only to go into battle with him but also to wear his royal robes while Ahab went disguised. It almost cost him his life. When Jehoshaphat returned, the prophet Jehu ben Hanani (not to be confused with King Jehu of the Northern Kingdom) told him that he would be judged for helping the wicked, although his zeal for God would stand him in good stead.

GRAINERY OF MEGIDDO. A grainery showing how food can be stockpiled. One concern of any city was the protection of food and water supplies.

Subsequently, a large army of Moabites, Ammonites, and Meunites came through Edom to attack the Southern Kingdom. Jehoshaphat demonstrated his character as he proclaimed a national fast and prayer meeting at the temple in Jerusalem. God

JEHOSHAPHAT'S REVIVAL

In some respects, Jehoshaphat's revival was very similar to the much more familiar revivals that occurred later during the reigns of Hezekiah and Josiah. The key here is that the revival was based on the reading and teaching of the Book of the Law to the people (2 Chron. 17:9). This passage presents problems to those who assert that there was no real Book of the Law prior to Josiah.

answered their prayer, and although they led the army into the field, they did not have to fight the battle. Before they reached the enemy, the coalition forces had begun fighting among themselves, and no one was left standing on the battlefield. Jehoshaphat's forces had only to pick up the spoil.

Not learning from the past, Jehoshaphat made an alliance with Ahaziah, Ahab's son. They planned a joint trade expedition out of Ezion Geber (on the Red Sea), but God intervened, destroying the ships. Later Jehoshaphat joined with Joram, Ahab's other son and heir, on an expedition against Moab (2 Kings 3:1–27). They recruited the king of Edom to go with them, and in the wilderness they despaired when they ran out of water. Elisha, who was with the army, intervened, and God provided the water.

After this we are told that Jehoshaphat died and was replaced by his oldest son, Jehoram. The final analysis is that Jehoshaphat was a strong man spiritually but not always discerning regarding the people around him. While he personally was judged a good king, his legacy would prove harmful to his family and to the kingdom.

Jehoram (848–841 BCE)

Read 2 Kings 8:16–24; 2 Chronicles 21:1–20.

Jehoshaphat's legacy emerged soon after his death. His oldest son, Jehoram, killed all of his brothers (six are listed) to eliminate any possible rival claims to the throne. He was evaluated as an evil king who emulated his in-laws in the north. Because of this, God judged him severely. There were external problems as Edom, Libnah, the Philistines, and the Arabs rebelled and fought against the Southern Kingdom. In the process, they carried off his entire family, leaving only one son, Ahaziah.[4] The preservation of Ahaziah is evidence of God's desire to maintain the line of David. Then Jehoram received a letter written by Elijah telling him that he would die of a horrible intestinal disease. He died two years later at the age of forty.

WHO WERE THE MEUNITES?

The Meunites (sometimes referred to as Meunim) apparently were a tribe associated with, but not part of, Edom. The Edomites themselves were not part of the army that marched against the Southern Kingdom. The unsuccessful attack may reflect a tie-in with the judgments pronounced in the book of Obadiah, but this is not clear, especially since during the reign of Jehoshaphat's son Jehoram, Edom successfully rebelled against the Southern Kingdom and Obadiah foretold its destruction. The Meunites show up again later in the conquests of Uzziah.

Ahaziah (841 BCE)

Jehoram was followed by his youngest and only surviving son, Ahaziah, who was viewed as evil. Enamored with his mother's relatives in the Northern Kingdom, he was visiting his uncle in Jezreel when Jehu came through. As a descendant of Ahab, he was killed less than a year after taking the throne.

Read 2 Kings 8:25–29; 2 Chronicles 22:1–9.

Athaliah (841–835 BCE)

The death of Ahaziah opened the way for Athaliah, his mother, to take control. Athaliah is not called "queen," although she is described as having "ruled the land" for six years (2 Kings 11:3). In fact, from the perspective of the historians, Athaliah seems to have been more of a gap-filler than a legitimate claimant to the throne—and for good reason. As soon as she heard that her son was dead, she proceeded to kill off the rest of the males in the royal family so that she could rule. She missed one: Joash. He was but an infant when his father died, and the circumstances of his rescue are amazing.

Read 2 Kings 11:1–16; 2 Chronicles 22:10–23:15.

One of Athaliah's own daughters, Jehosheba (sister of King Ahaziah and thus aunt to the boy), who was married to the priest Jehoiada, slipped Joash out of the royal nursery before the purge. The priest and his wife kept the boy hidden for six years, after which they planned a coronation in the temple. Gathering their forces, they surrounded the temple and began the ceremony.[5] When Athaliah heard the commotion, she went to where the people were gathered, and seeing the newly crowned boy king in the temple, she screamed, "Treason! Treason!" In order not to profane the temple, Athaliah was dragged outside before she was executed, ending this tragic period in the history of the nation.

Joel the Prophet

Joel is another undated book of prophecy, and scholars disagree on the most appropriate date. A number of factors point to a time before the Exile, not the least of which is the idea that it was given as a warning of future invasion and exile.[6] The fact that the leadership of the nation is characterized in the book as consisting of elders and priests suggests a time when there was no king. This feature would seem to reflect the time of Athaliah.

WHEN WAS JOEL WRITTEN?

Three possible periods have been suggested as the setting for the book of Joel (see the arguments for each in David A. Hubbard, *Joel and Amos: A Commentary* [Downers Grove, Ill.: InterVarsity, 1989], 23–27). A late date after the exile is primarily based on the use of the term "Greeks" (Joel 3:6). An intermediate date of about 597–587 BCE finds support in the comment that Israel was scattered among the nations (3:2). An early date of about 841–835 BCE, during the youth of Joash and Athaliah's rule, is based on 2:16–17, which suggests that the leadership of the nation was in the hands of elders and priests rather than a king. (Gleason L. Archer, *A Survey of Old Testament Introduction* [Chicago: Moody Press, 1994], 338–41, gives the strongest presentation of this third view.)

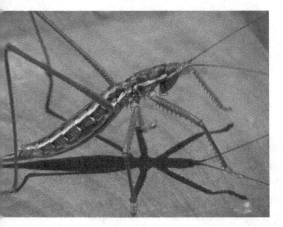

LOCUST. A variety of grasshopper that was the focus of Joel's prophecy about a locust plague. This species undergoes a physiological change and then breeds very rapidly. When a swarm of them develops and migrates, the results are devastating.

Joel's message is one of condemnation and judgment on the nation for continuing apostasy. It seems to be predicated on the disaster caused by a large locust swarm, which Joel argues was no accident. In fact, it was only the foretaste of far worse things to come. The invasion of insects portended a coming military invasion in a time called "the day of the Lord." The key to the book is Joel 2:12–14, which pleads for the nation to repent because God is a God of compassion who might yet relent. In the process, the prophet slips beyond contemporary events, giving hints about the overall outcome of the historical process that we have been following. There will come a time of judgment characterized by supernormal events that will anticipate God's final judgment, when He sets up His rule on the earth.

A TIME OF HOPE

With the execution of Athaliah, a new age dawned for the Southern Kingdom. The new king, Joash, had been well trained by the priests. In the Northern Kingdom, Jehu had begun eliminating the worst elements of pagan worship (although he could only return to the syncretistic worship developed by Jeroboam I). The next four rulers in the south are all evaluated by the writer of Kings as men who "did what was right in the eyes of the LORD," although this evaluation was qualified because they did not measure up to David. It would seem that here was the opportunity for the nation to be what God intended.

Joash (835–796 BCE)

Read 2 Kings 11:17–12:21; 2 Chronicles 23:16–24:27.

Joash was seven years old when he was crowned king. Following the execution of Athaliah, the priests purified the temple, eradicating the worship of Baal from the Southern Kingdom. Sometime after this, Joash repaired the temple, restoring the worship and sacrificial system.

Unfortunately, Joash was solid only as long as his stepfather, Jehoiada, was alive. Once Jehoiada died, leaders who disagreed with the reforms that had been made began to advise the king, and they turned his heart away from God. A number of prophets warned the people, but this did not faze them. It all came to a climax when Zechariah, the grandson of Jehoiada,[7] proclaimed God's message in the temple and Joash ordered that he be stoned on the temple grounds.

A small Aramean army invaded Judah and with God's empowerment was able to conquer Jerusalem. Many leaders were killed, and Joash was wounded. Upset over the death of God's prophet, Zechariah, two men finished off Joash on his sickbed, ending his forty-year reign.

JOZABAD AND JEHOZABAD

Interestingly, the two officials who killed King Joash (2 Kings 12:21) were sons of foreign women. According to 2 Chronicles 24:26, Jozabad (here called Zabad) was the son of Shimeath, an Ammonite woman; and Jehozabad was the son of Shimrith (Shomer), a Moabite woman. Most likely their fathers were men of the Southern Kingdom (otherwise mention of their nationality would probably have been made). Apparently some of the men of Judah were intermarrying with foreign women, and at this point, they were pious in their worship of YHWH.

Evaluating their action, as well as their subsequent execution by King Amaziah, is difficult. On the one hand, the two officials were zealous for God in killing the one who ordered the murder of God's prophet. On the other hand, we see in the history of the nation a strong disapproval of those who killed kings. The text does not evaluate either action but merely reports what happened. The writer makes it clear, however, that in sparing the children of the killers, Amaziah followed "what is written in the Book of the Law of Moses" (2 Kings 14:6). This is yet another passage that creates difficulties for those who maintain that the Book of the Law was not written until the time of Josiah (about 175 years later).

Amaziah (796–767 BCE)

Amaziah followed his father on the throne. One of his first acts was to execute the two officials who had killed his father, but the point is made that he followed the law in not executing their children. He is viewed as a man who did good—not quite like David, but more like his father, Joash, that is, allowing personal pride and poor logic to get in the way.

Read 2 Kings 14:1–22; 2 Chronicles 25:1–28.

We see this ambivalence when he attacked the Edomites. He assembled his army and then hired troops from the Northern Kingdom to augment them. A prophet of God told him that what he was planning was a mistake and that he should send the northern soldiers back home. When he worried about the loss of the payment, the prophet reminded him that God could repay more than he lost by doing what was right. Amaziah listened and sent the northern troops home. They were angry and looted cities in the Southern Kingdom en route. In the meantime, the army of the Southern Kingdom had a great victory over the Edomites. In celebration, however, he brought back their idols and set them up in Jerusalem to worship them there. Of course, this deed violated the covenant principles of the nation, but when one thinks about it, it was also very foolish. After all, the gods of the Edomites were unable to defend Edom, so why use them in place of the God who had given him the victory?

Amaziah's pride showed up in two other incidents in which he disregarded warnings. First, when a prophet was sent to castigate him for bringing back Edom's idols, Amaziah tried to dismiss God's spokesman by asking who had made him a royal advisor. Then, in self-exultation over the victory in Edom, he picked a fight with Jehoash the king of the Northern Kingdom. Jehoash warned him against following through with his threat, but Amaziah did not listen. His army was routed at Beth Shemesh, and he was captured. Jehoash came up to

HOW LONG DID AMAZIAH REIGN?

One of the difficulties in OT chronology is the statement that Amaziah lived fifteen years after the death of Jehoash (2 Kings 14:17; 2 Chron. 25:25). Jehoash died in 782 BCE and then Amaziah in 767, but Amaziah's son Uzziah (Azariah) began to reign in 792, when he was sixteen years old (2 Kings 14:21; 2 Chron. 26:1). Two alternatives have been proposed. The first puts the battle of Beth Shemesh about 792 and argues that Uzziah was appointed to the throne as acting king. The other proposal puts the battle of Beth Shemesh in 783 or 782 and views the reference to Amaziah's continued life span as a subtle reference to the death of Jehoash during, or shortly after, the battle, resulting in the release of Amaziah (Eugene H. Merrill, *Kingdom of Priests: A History of Old Testament Israel* [Grand Rapids: Baker, 1995], 372).

Jerusalem, where he tore down 600 feet of the wall and looted the temple and palace. Amaziah retained his throne but at a high price.

Unfortunately, Amaziah seems to have drifted further from God as he got older. Because of this, a conspiracy developed among the leaders. He fled Jerusalem but was tracked to Lachish, where he was put to death, leaving his son Uzziah on the throne.

Uzziah (792–740 BCE)

Read 2 Kings 15:1–7; 2 Chronicles 26:1–23.

Although Uzziah (usually called Azariah in 2 Kings) had an exceedingly long reign of fifty-two years, he spent most of it sharing the throne, first with his father and then with his son. It would appear that he was placed on the throne with his father when he was but sixteen and ruled with him for about twenty years.[8] He became sole ruler when his father, Amaziah, was killed. Uzziah was distinguished as being a good king—like his father. In effect, this comparison suggests that he started out spiritually strong but faded as he got older. This is evident in the expanded report in Chronicles, where we read that Uzziah sought after God only as long as his spiritual advisor Zechariah was alive.

Uzziah was successful against several of the traditional enemies of the Southern Kingdom, especially the Philistines, although he had success against the Arabs and Meunites as well. He also rebuilt the fortifications of Jerusalem and other areas of the country. Like his father, however, he was most noted for allowing his pride to get the better of him. He went into the temple to burn incense, something only the priests were to do. The high priest Azariah and eighty other priests confronted the king, but he was not willing to listen. Before they could do anything, God intervened and struck him with leprosy. So, ironically, because of his pride and misplaced zeal in worshiping God, he was rendered unfit even to enter the temple.

Not only was Uzziah unable to enter the temple, he even had to live in a separate house; and although he was king, he could not perform any royal duties. His son Jotham shared the throne for the last ten years of his life. Thus, Uzziah was king in his own right only twenty-two of the fifty-two years he was viewed as king. The death of Uzziah is an important date in the biblical record, for it was during that year that Isaiah was commissioned as prophet.

Jotham (750–731 BCE)

After ten years of sharing the throne with his father, Jotham became sole regent of the kingdom. It appears, however, that during the last four years of his reign, his son Ahaz joined him on the throne, possibly because of the increased threat from the north. During Jotham's rule, the Assyrian Empire restarted its expansion to the west. In response, Pekah, the king of the Northern Kingdom, and Rezin, the Aramean king in Damascus, tried to form an alliance to stand against the growing Assyrian threat. When the Southern Kingdom did not join in, they perceived that as a threat to their rear. Pekah and Rezin then conspired to erase this threat from the south before the Assyrians grew any stronger. These events apparently occurred about 735 BCE, when Ahaz began sharing the throne with his father. Ahaz was an Assyrian sympathizer, perhaps seeing the Assyrians as an aid against the alliance between the Northern Kingdom and Aram.[9]

Read 2 Kings 15:32–38; 2 Chronicles 27:1–9; Isaiah 7.

We are not told much more about Jotham except that he was as good as his father and did not make the mistake of improperly entering the temple. The only other point of note was that he was able to collect tribute from the Ammonites for three years.[10] He died at the relatively young age of forty-one.

A TIME OF EXTREMES

The next three kings were spiritual extremes. Ahaz hit bottom; his son Hezekiah soared, perhaps equaling David; and his grandson Manasseh was even worse than Ahaz. This period also saw the proliferation of prophets, a phenomenon that, as we have already noted, pointed to a spiritual watershed for the nation. As a result, by the time Manasseh died, the coming exile was unavoidable—it was only a matter of time.

Ahaz (731–715 BCE)

We have already seen Ahaz in action in face of the Pekah/Rezin alliance. In about 735 BCE, apparently the time when Ahaz joined his father on the throne as coregent, Isaiah foretold that the enemy alliance would not last and gave the king two time markers. Within sixty-five years, the Northern Kingdom would be shattered (Isa. 7:8), and within ten to thirteen years, the two kingdoms would be forsaken (v. 16).[11] The first date would be after he died, but it represented the final stage of population removal by the Assyrians. The second date represented the fall of the Northern Kingdom to the Assyrians. To show God's control of the situation, Ahaz was given the opportunity to ask for any proof he desired (a sign). Ahaz refused, showing his lack of faith.

Read 2 Kings 16:1–20; 2 Chronicles 28:1–27.

Spiritually, it was downhill from there. Turning from YHWH, Ahaz served the pagan gods, including Baal, and apparently even performed child sacrifices.[12]

AHAZ AND GOD'S SIGN

When Isaiah told Ahaz to ask God for a sign, the king answered, "I will not put the LORD to the test" (Isa. 7:12). On the surface, this response sounds pious. In reality, it disobeys a direct command from God and hints that Ahaz did not believe God could act. We might paraphrase his response as, "I'm not willing to give God a chance." As a result, God gave a sign that went beyond Ahaz ("you house of David," v. 13) and addressed a much bigger issue, the Messiah.

As a result, God, instead of providing deliverance from Pekah and Rezin, gave the Southern Kingdom into their hands. Over the next couple of years, the alliance was able to defeat the southern army, take prisoners (although prophets in the north warned the army to release them), and kill one of Ahaz's sons (Maaseiah). Ahaz asked the Assyrians for help, and Tiglath-Pileser came, though in the process, Ahaz got more trouble than help. The northern alliance was broken, and by 732 both of the kings he feared were dead; but Ahaz had to pay dearly for the "help," because beyond the extortion, the Southern Kingdom was next in line to be annexed.

> Ahaz served the pagan gods and apparently even performed child sacrifices.

As Damascus succumbed to the Assyrian might, Ahaz was in the area meeting with his new "protector," Tiglath-Pileser. There he saw an altar that he liked and sent its design to Jerusalem so that a copy could be made. He closed the temple Solomon had built for the worship of YHWH, preferring his new altar and the gods of Damascus.

Through a combination of international politics and God's intervention, the Southern Kingdom was not annexed by Assyria. Ten years later, Ahaz watched as Samaria was destroyed and the Northern Kingdom was carried off into exile, which should have been a warning. But again it was a word from God that he ignored. Consequently, he was viewed not only as an evil king but as one of the worst in the Southern Kingdom.

ASSYRIA AND THE SOUTHERN KINGDOM

The political relationship between Assyria and the Southern Kingdom is difficult to sort out. Tiglath-Pileser must have demanded a high price and in essence made Ahaz a vassal. At the same time, he seems to have been very aggressive militarily and anxious to capture other nations. He was followed in 727 BCE by Shalmaneser V, who seems to have been less aggressive against Ahaz. From the spiritual perspective, it appears that God was still giving the Southern Kingdom a chance to turn around, probably because of the heir apparent. Ahaz would be followed by Hezekiah, who through the help of Isaiah, Micah, and other prophets did promote a national revival. We will see later, however, that it was a short-term repentance.

Hezekiah (715–686 BCE)

The contrast between Ahaz and Hezekiah is amazing. Hezekiah was as good as his father was evil. He cleaned out and opened the temple that Ahaz had closed. He rejected the foreign gods and showed great trust in YHWH. He looked to Isaiah for advice. He was one of two kings in the Southern Kingdom who is compared favorably to David (the other is Josiah). He also receives more coverage in the OT than any of the kings after the kingdom split. Even so, we are not given a detailed history of his reign, only several snapshots—events that show his character.

Read 2 Kings 18–20; 2 Chronicles 29–32; Isaiah 36–39.

Perhaps the most flattering event took place during the first years of his reign. In the first month of his reign, the writer of Chronicles tells us, he opened the temple and began making repairs (2 Chron. 29). The temple was cleansed and rededicated with burnt offerings and with the praise psalms that had been composed by David and Asaph (v. 30). This was followed by a celebration of the Passover a month later.[13] For this celebration, Hezekiah sent messengers throughout the region of what had been the Northern Kingdom, inviting those who would to participate. Some ridiculed, but many came (2 Chron. 30:10–11).[14] The writer observes that there had not been a celebration like it since the days of Solomon.

Following the celebration, the people cleansed the land. They destroyed the pagan shrines in both the southern and northern regions. The spiritual renewal carried over into the bringing of tithes and offerings to the temple. And for what may have been the first time since Solomon, the priests had plenty.

After this, we see Hezekiah's faith being tested. First, in 712 BCE Sargon's army came back through and attacked Ashdod and parts of Egypt (Isa. 20:1–6). While this event is not mentioned in the historical books, Hezekiah apparently followed Isaiah's advice and did not get involved. As a result, he and Jerusalem were not affected.

Perhaps anticipating the next step, Hezekiah began to strengthen Jerusalem for a siege. This was the time when he built a tunnel to bring the water supply

WHEN DID HEZEKIAH BEGIN TO REIGN?

According to 2 Kings 18:1, Hezekiah began to reign in the third year of Hoshea king of the Northern Kingdom, that is, about 729 BCE. Verse 2, however, states that he was twenty-five when he became king and that he ruled twenty-nine years. Working back from Manasseh, this would mean that Hezekiah's reign began in 715 rather than 729. Apparently verse 1 refers to his initial accession at the age of eleven, so that he shared the throne with Ahaz for about fourteen years, whereas verse 2 marks the beginning of his sole reign. As a youth, he would have had no real say in the running of the kingdom and certainly could not have instituted the Passover and reopened the temple. The overlap does show that he would have been very aware of what happened to the Northern Kingdom in the year 722, for at that time he was about eighteen. Ahaz would have died then when Hezekiah was twenty-five. Only then did Hezekiah assume complete control.

HEZEKIAH'S TUNNEL

An inscription was discovered in 1880 just inside the Siloam pool end of the tunnel that explains how the engineers started at both ends of the 1,777-foot-long tunnel and met in the middle. While there has been debate regarding whether the tunnel followed a crack in the rock (of which no evidence has been found), it is clear that the tunnel has a carefully sloped floor that provides a smooth flow from the springs into the pool. (See Simon B. Parker, "Siloam Inscription Memorializes Engineering Achievement," *BAR* 20, no. 4 [July/August 1994]: 36–38.)

HEZEKIAH'S TUNNEL. A tunnel constructed by King Hezekiah between the springs of Gihon and the pool of Siloam, giving the city a more secure water supply.

inside the city. Hezekiah's tunnel, which connected the springs at Gihon with the pool of Siloam, was a masterpiece of engineering that is still used today.

After Sargon died in 705 BCE, various regions tested his successor, Sennacherib, by withholding tribute and overtly rebelling (a norm throughout the ANE). Sennacherib led his army into that region, intent on reestablishing control of what had earlier belonged to Assyria. This time, Hezekiah was affected. His religious reformations, which the Assyrian overlords viewed as a lack of support for the empire, had finally come to Sennacherib's attention, and Jerusalem was surrounded and besieged.

While Sennacherib focused on the destruction of Lachish, he sent his general to Jerusalem to demand surrender. Hezekiah listened to the proud claims and demands of the Assyrians. Disconsolate, he took the issue directly to God. He laid out the Assyrian letter before God in the temple and prayed for deliverance, pointing out that only YHWH, the living God of Israel, was able to help in this situation. God sent Isaiah with a message that all was under control. Overnight, His angel visited the Assyrian army, killing a recorded figure of 185,000 troops. All Sennacherib recorded was that he did not capture the city.

At approximately the same time, Hezekiah was stricken with a serious physical ailment.[15] God sent Isaiah with the warning that Hezekiah was going to die. When Hezekiah repented, God sent Isaiah back with a grant of fifteen more years of life.

In terms of politics, Hezekiah did make mistakes. He tried to bribe Sennacherib. Later Merodach-Baladan, the leader of Babylon, sent representatives to Jerusalem ostensibly to congratulate Hezekiah on his "miraculous recovery." Apparently another agenda was to discuss possible revolt against Assyria. While Hezekiah did not join in any overt rebellion, he did show off all of his treasures to the representatives. Isaiah told him that he had been foolish and that all he had shown would be taken by the Babylonians.[16] Hezekiah's pride seeped through

HEZEKIAH AND SENNACHERIB

There is an interesting and complex relationship involved in Hezekiah's loyalties. Trust in God required that the king not trust in bribes and tribute: being the vassal of YHWH precluded being Sennacherib's. Hezekiah vacillated. In the beginning, he looked to God. When crunch time came, however, he gave in and sent the bribe (2 Kings 18:13–16). As is often the case, the amount was inadequate, and Sennacherib demanded more. Hezekiah realized that he could not comply and turned to God.

In keeping with ANE practice, Sennacherib does not record the loss of his army. On a large prism inscription, however, he gives an account of how he conquered all of the cities in the area except Jerusalem. The text takes special interest in Hezekiah: "As to Hezekiah, the Jew, he did not submit to my yoke, I laid siege to 46 of his strong cities, walled forts and to the countless small villages in their vicinity, and conquered (them).... I drove out (of them) 200,150 people.... Himself I made a prisoner in Jerusalem, his royal residence, like a bird in a cage.... Thus I reduced his country, but I still increased the tribute." Sennacherib continues on to boast about how Hezekiah was brought to heel (*ANET*, 287).

The number of Assyrian soldiers killed, as recorded in the biblical text, is large, but it is in line with the number of captives Sennacherib claims. While modern archaeology raises questions regarding such numbers in the light of ancient population figures, its estimates derive from known tels and excavations. Sennacherib notes "countless small villages," which may be suggestive. The OT account claims that Sennacherib left because of divine intervention. Interestingly, the Greek historian Herodotus also states that Sennacherib had to leave through strange circumstances: field mice ate the Assyrian bow strings, quivers, and thongs by which they held their shields, leaving many of them helpless in the battle (*The Histories* 2.141). We do know from Assyrian accounts that this was Sennacherib's last campaign in that region, even though his control there was tenuous at best for the last twenty years of his reign (Hallo, "From Qarqar to Carchemish," 184). In 681 BCE, Sennacherib was murdered by two of his own sons in a temple while worshiping his god, Nisroch.

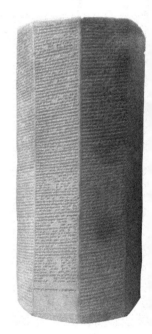

Sennacherib's prism. A monument on which Sennacherib boasts of destroying forty-two cities in Canaan—but with regard to Jerusalem he could only say that he besieged the city.

HEZEKIAH'S ILLNESS AND MANASSEH'S BIRTH

The story of Hezekiah's illness and restoration is a clear example of the premise stated in the last chapter that a prophetic message was expected to instigate action. Hezekiah took the appropriate action of repentance and was granted a reprieve of fifteen years. It should also be noted that Manasseh was twelve when he took the throne. Some have suggested that he must have been born after his father's illness; thus, had Hezekiah not been given an extension of life, Manasseh would not have been born. That is not clear, however, for Manasseh appears to have shared the throne with his father for nine of those fifteen years. If that was the case, then he was about six at the time of his father's illness.

again when he thought to himself that such a punishment would be fine, for there would be peace during his own lifetime.

Hezekiah was important for another reason not addressed directly in these historical accounts: as he promoted the spiritual revival, his advisors probably reviewed and updated the canon. We have observed how this collection had been expanded through the years. Because the last several chapters have dealt primarily with historical issues following the time of the judges, this process has not stood out clearly. We did note how Hezekiah's spiritual leaders edited the book of Proverbs (see Prov. 25:1). I would suggest that they also prepared a revised edition of Psalms and a first edition of Kings (which probably ran up only through 2 Kings 17 and the fall of the Northern Kingdom).[17] The purpose of this first edition was to remind the people that God was in the midst of what they were seeing as tremendous problems. The key lesson from Hezekiah would be that God was not yet through with the nation, as shown by the acts He was performing.

The overall evaluation of Hezekiah was positive. Despite his mistakes, the writer of Kings put it this way: "Hezekiah trusted in the LORD, the God of Israel. There was no one like him among all the kings of Judah, either before him or after him. He held fast to the LORD and did not cease to follow him; he kept the commands the LORD had given Moses" (2 Kings 18:5–6).

Isaiah the Prophet

Read Isaiah 1:1–12:6; 52:13–53:12; 61:1–2.

Isaiah is one of the most familiar and beloved of the prophets. His book is also very profound, and this brief overview cannot do full justice to it. Isaiah ministered during the reign of four kings: Uzziah, Jotham, Ahaz, and Hezekiah (Isa. 1:1), although predominantly during the time of the last two (he apparently lived on into the reign of Manasseh, but that period is not covered in the book). This means that he was active when the Northern Kingdom was carried off into captivity. It also means that he saw the worst and the best that the Southern Kingdom had to offer. Isaiah was both a prophet and a historian. Part of the book we call Isaiah records events in the lives of the kings. We have already noted some of these, such as his confrontation with Ahaz (ch. 7), Sennacherib's attack (ch. 36), Hezekiah's illness (ch. 38), and the visit of the Babylonians (ch. 39).

The writer of Chronicles apparently used other works of Isaiah as a source (see 2 Chron. 32:32).[18] The community of believers, however, selected one of the prophet's writings to be included in the canon, the book we call Isaiah. This complex book gives us some of our most powerful anticipations of the Messiah, as well as pictures of how God will eventually reign on earth. As such, it shows a transition in the role of the nation. It highlights the national failure and points to God's future work in a person, the Messiah.

Isaiah is also a controversial book. Many scholars suggest that it is really a compendium of two works, which they call Isaiah (chs. 1–39) and Deutero-Isaiah or Second Isaiah (chs. 40–66), the latter viewed as an anonymous author who wrote in the sixth century BCE or later. (Some maintain that chs. 56–66 constitute a separate third work, which they call Trito-Isaiah; a few scholars have divided the book still further.) This division is based primarily on two factors: prophetic content and literary style.

The most important consideration in many minds is that the last portion of the book contains some very specific prophetic announcements regarding the period of Babylonian captivity. The most specific prediction is the declaration that Cyrus would end the captivity (Isa. 44:28). The real issue is the nature of prophecy. Can God's spokesperson give true prophetic declarations that reveal specific aspects of the future? Those who accept the possibility of prophetic revelation see no problem in the claim that Isaiah wrote about Cyrus some 175 years prior to the event. Those who rule out that possibility must then see this passage as having been written after the fact, sometime after the return from exile.[19] The context of Isaiah's statement is crucial to the issue. The declaration about Cyrus is at the climax of a passage that contrasts YHWH with the pagan gods. The contrast is how YHWH not only acts in space-time history but proclaims in advance what He is going to do. As such, the declaration about Cyrus is a specific example of YHWH's ability not only to know the future but also to control it.

The issue is even more complex, however, for several passages in both halves of Isaiah give declarations about the Messiah that the NT applies to Jesus. No one contests that all these statements were written several centuries before Jesus' birth. We will note just three of them. The first is the anticipation of the birth of the Messiah. The NT understood Isaiah 7:14 to reflect a virgin birth, that is, one without a human father (Matt. 1:18–25; note that, according to Luke 1:34, Mary

THE GREAT ISAIAH SCROLL

The basic authenticity of the book of Isaiah has been confirmed by the Dead Sea Scrolls. In particular, the Great Isaiah Scroll, which is one of the most significant finds, contains the entire book of Isaiah with very few substantial differences from the text of our modern Hebrew Bible. Scholars agree that it should be dated to about 150–175 BCE, long before Jesus' birth. One other point should be made here. In the Great Isaiah Scroll, the entire book is written sequentially without a break: chapter 40 follows immediately after chapter 39 in the middle of a column.

protested to the angel that the pregnancy was not possible, for she had never had sexual relations). This was apparently also the understanding of the Israelite people prior to Jesus.[20] Sometime after this prophecy, Isaiah anticipated the marvelous birth of a boy who would be called "Mighty God" and "Everlasting Father" (Isa. 9:6).

Second, Isaiah includes four passages that are called "Servant Songs" because they all are about "my servant." These are Isaiah 42:1–4; 49:1–6; 50:4–9; and 52:13–53:12. The fourth one is the most significant for our purposes. Just as Isaiah 7 gave a "snapshot" of the birth of the Messiah, so Isaiah 52:13–53:12 gives a snapshot of his death. This passage reveals a number of NT themes, such as the Messiah's bearing the sins of His people (53:3–6), His death (53:3, 8–9), and even His resurrection (53:10–12).[21]

The third passage is Isaiah 61:1–2, which Jesus would later read in the synagogue in Nazareth (Luke 4:16–22). At that time, Jesus stopped in the middle of a sentence and declared that the part He had read had been fulfilled in the hearing of the people. The part that had not been fulfilled was the phrase "the day of vengeance of our God." This distinction would become one of our first clear indicators of two comings of the Messiah, although Isaiah gives hints as he points to two roles—one of suffering and one of reigning.

The second issue used to argue for two (or more) authors of Isaiah is the matter of style. Some scholars claim that there are significant stylistic differences in the various sections of the book, showing multiple authors at work. Those who hold to the unity of the book argue that the stylistic differences simply indicate different purposes. They also maintain that the distinctions in style are not as sharp as is often thought.[22]

It seems, rather, that the key stylistic difference focuses on a dual theme: the first theme is judgment, and the second theme is restoration. As we look at the issue of judgment, we must put it in the perspective of Deuteronomy 28–30. In chapter 28 Moses declared that God's judgment on the nation would be a progressive matter. He listed a series of judgments, each stronger than the last. The final step in this progression would be exile. However, the entire purpose of the judgment sequence was to bring the nation to its senses, as shown by the subsequent declaration in chapter 30, where Moses related what would happen after all of the curses had occurred. This text tells of the restoration of the nation to the land.[23]

GOD'S SERVANT IN ISAIAH

Historically, there has been much debate on who is "my servant." Part of the problem is that the term is used in a number of ways in the text. For example, sometimes the entire nation is addressed as God's servant (cf. Isa. 41:8–9). However, it is clear as we read through the four Servant Songs that there is a contrast between the nation in this role and an individual also referred to as God's servant. The point is that this Servant would be the one who fulfills the role the nation was to have fulfilled.

It would appear, then, that Isaiah picked up the same theme and applied it to the current situation. First there was a warning of judgment (explaining why), culminating in Isaiah 39:6–7, where Hezekiah was told that the Exile would come. Then there was the promise of restoration, beginning two verses later with the poignant cry, "Comfort, comfort my people, says your God. Speak tenderly to Jerusalem, and proclaim to her that her hard service has been completed, that her sin has been paid for, that she has received from the LORD's hand double for all her sins" (Isa. 40:1–2).

Isaiah's picture of restoration, however, goes beyond the return from the Exile. He looks also at the restoration of the world from the effects of the Fall. Thus, his restoration theme is at least threefold. The nation of Israel would be restored from the upcoming exile. The purpose of this national restoration would be to provide redemption through the Messiah in His role as the Suffering Servant. Then the Messiah would provide ultimate redemption in reversing the effects of sin in a final glorious age.[24]

> Isaiah's picture of restoration goes beyond the return from the Exile and looks at the restoration of the world from the effects of the Fall.

Therefore, for the original audience there was both a warning and a hope. The warning was straightforward—if the nation did not repent, it would suffer even worse than before (and the Northern Kingdom was held up as an example). In this sense, the book is pessimistic; based on human nature, it reflects a certainty that judgment would come. The hope, however, was that out of all that, God would provide a redeemer and a future age when all humankind would serve Him—and this is a crucial theme of the book.

But that future age was far off. Tradition tells us that Isaiah died at the hands of Hezekiah's son Manasseh. The story is that after Manasseh had the throne to himself, he pursued Isaiah out of Jerusalem. When Isaiah hid in a hollow tree, the king had the tree sawn down with Isaiah inside (see Heb. 11:37).

Micah the Prophet

Micah was a contemporary of Isaiah and Hezekiah. He and Isaiah preached similar messages, which is not surprising, for they addressed the same issues in the same age. However, their focuses were different. Both agreed that the underlying problem was spiritual—worshiping false gods. But while Isaiah focused on how spiritual apostasy produced poor political leadership, Micah focused on how it translated into social injustice.[25]

Read Micah 1–7.

Like his contemporary, Micah also understood that God would solve the problem with a person, the Messiah. In a very familiar passage, Micah told the nation about the birth of the Messiah—He would come from Bethlehem (Mic. 5:2, quoted in Matt. 2:6).[26] Interestingly, Micah then went on to tell the people that this Messiah would be a very special person whose "origins are from of old, from ancient times" (lit., "his goings forth are from old, from the days of eternity"). Like Isaiah, Micah seems to be hinting that the Messiah would be more than just a human being.

We know little more about Micah, although we learn later from Jeremiah that his message did have an effect on the national situation. On one occasion, Jeremiah was being condemned by the leadership (priests and "prophets") for daring to foretell bad things about the nation; but the people (the elders and popular leaders) argued that Jeremiah should not be condemned for that reason, and they cited the case of Micah (Jer. 26:1–24). They pointed out that when Micah foretold the destruction of Jerusalem (Mic. 3:12), Hezekiah and others took it to heart and prayed for God to relent. Interestingly, the Micah passage is in a context in which the prophet anticipated the destruction of the city because of the corrupt leadership of the priests.

Manasseh (695–642 BCE)

Read 2 Kings 21:1–18; 2 Chronicles 33:1–20.

Manasseh was the exact opposite of his father. In fact, he was viewed as being as evil as his grandfather, Ahaz, and perhaps more so. Since with his reign the nation bottomed out spiritually and exile was now inevitable, it is not too much to say that Manasseh was the worst king in the Southern Kingdom.

Manasseh was put on the throne as coregent with his father, Hezekiah, in 695, about nine years before Hezekiah's death. He was twelve at the time and thus had missed out on the greatest works that God had done during his father's life (he would have been six at the time of Sennacherib's siege). Even so, we have no real understanding of why he went so far in the opposite direction from his father.

Although he had a long reign, Manasseh did little of significance outside of his acts of apostasy. The writers of both Kings and Chronicles report how he reversed Hezekiah's reforms, began false worship, set up idols, and even per-

VALLEY OF GEHENNA. A region near the heart of present-day Jerusalem, known in the time of the prophets (and later, in Jesus' day) as the location of the city dump. It was apparently also used for child sacrifices.

formed child sacrifice. The writer of Kings records the announcement from multiple prophets (unnamed) that as a result of his acts, the Southern Kingdom would go into exile.

The writer of Chronicles records one other event. Probably near the end of his reign, the king of Assyria came up to Jerusalem and led Manasseh off into captivity bound with chains and with a hook through his nose. In his Babylonian prison (the location is a hint to the date) Manasseh came to realize what he had done and repented. After prayer, he was returned to Jerusalem, where for his last few years he reversed some of the worst of what he had initiated.

Nahum the Prophet

Nahum was another prophet whose focus was on international affairs. Like Jonah, he addressed the nation of Assyria and its capital Nineveh. The entire theme of the book is that both would be destroyed. The book of Nahum must have been written after 663 BCE, for it describes the destruction of Thebes (Heb., *No Amon*) in Egypt as an example of what would happen to Nineveh (Nah. 3:8). This reference could place the writing of the book either at the end of Manasseh's reign, during Amon's brief rule, or during the early part of Josiah's reign. It was most likely during the earlier period, for both Manasseh and Amon seem to have been loyal to Assyria. The point of the book is that while the Assyrians had repented under Jonah, this time there was no repentance. The destruction came as anticipated in 612 BCE. As such, the message for the original audience was that the leadership of the Southern Kingdom should not give its allegiance to Assyria, because God would destroy it. And within fifty years, that was the case.

Read Nahum 1–3.

Amon (642–640 BCE)

Manasseh was followed by his son Amon. He was like his father at his worst. As a result, some of his servants assassinated him after a reign of less than two years. As we have seen earlier, the Hebrew people did not take kindly to the assassination of royalty, regardless of the depravity of the king. They executed those responsible and placed Josiah, Amon's eight-year-old son, on the throne.

Read 2 Kings 21:19–26; 2 Chronicles 33:21–25.

Josiah (640–609 BCE)

Read 2 Kings 22:1–23:30; 2 Chronicles 34:1–35:27.

Josiah was another boy king who began well. Unlike his predecessor Joash, however, he finished strongly as well, although his death was a tragic result of interfering in international politics.

Like his great-grandfather Hezekiah, Josiah is best noted for his religious reforms. When he was only sixteen, he started seeking God personally, and at the age of twenty, he began to clean up the country by removing the places of idolatrous worship (2 Chron. 34:3). It is interesting to note that this religious reformation extended into the former region of the Northern Kingdom—the tribal territories of Manasseh, Ephraim, Simeon, and as far as Naphtali (v. 6).[27] Six years later he initiated a restoration of the temple. *age 22*

While workers were cleaning out the temple, they found a copy of the "Book of the Law." This discovery raises several questions. Was this book what we call the Pentateuch, or was it just Deuteronomy? Does this mean that all of the other copies had been destroyed? Without the written book, on what basis were the people accomplishing their reform? How did they verify that this copy was indeed the Book of the Law that had been given to Moses? We don't have answers to all of those questions. While it seems likely that there were other copies of the material hidden away in various parts of the realm, the point is that the temple and palace did not seem to have a copy.

> Josiah's returning the ark of the covenant to the temple is the last explicit reference to the ark in the historical accounts.

It appears that the national leadership got its spiritual guidance from prophets. As Josiah and the leaders read the text, they realized that the passage dealing with condemnation applied to their context, and Josiah sent the priests to ask God what this meant. They went to Huldah, a prophetess, to get the answer.[28] She told them that God had announced that indeed all of the curses would come about, but not in the lifetime of Josiah, because of his repentant heart.

Josiah then covenanted before God to obey His commandments. After the priests and Levites cleansed the temple, they celebrated a great Passover feast.

THE BOOK OF THE LAW

The discovery of the Book of the Law has promoted much debate. At one point, many scholars thought the text was composed during the reign of Josiah, although that view seems to have been abandoned. It is likewise not necessary to suppose that the book represented an idealism developed in the Northern Kingdom in the aftermath of its fall. Although international politics surely was a factor, this incident cannot have been merely a political ploy, as has been suggested by Siegfried Herrmann (*A History of Israel in Old Testament Times* [Philadelphia: Fortress, 1979], 263–73). It seems likely that the priests were familiar with the work, although they may not have had a readily available copy of the text when they started the reform. In fact, the text seems to suggest that Hilkiah recognized it as a copy and knew what it was immediately (2 Kings 22:8). When the scroll was read to the people, it was called the Book of the Covenant (23:2), showing that they recognized what the book represented.

THE ROLE OF THE ARK IN ISRAEL'S WORSHIP

One issue that raises concerns among scholars is the sparseness of references to the ark in Kings and Chronicles. The assumption seems to be that if the ark was as central to the worship of God as the earlier books represent, then it would have a more prominent role in the literature. That does not follow, given the purposes of the written accounts. The nation was judged, not because of its treatment of the ark, but because it did not worship and serve God. Still, Jeremiah notes that at his time the ark continued to play a major role in the religious thinking of the people (Jer. 3:16), although it seems to have been more of a holy relic than the meeting place of God.

Josiah attempted to encourage the priests in the performance of their duties and told them to put the ark back in the temple where it belonged. This is the last explicit reference to the ark in the historical accounts. Second Kings amplifies some of the specifics of how Josiah purified the nation and notes in passing how he destroyed the altar of Jeroboam I in Bethel, fulfilling an earlier prophecy (1 Kings 13:2).

Josiah was spiritually solid, but he also was involved in the international politics of his day—and not completely to his advantage. During his reign of thirty-one years, the Assyrian Empire began to disintegrate. Ever since the days of Sennacherib, the Assyrians had struggled to maintain control of the entire empire. The southern portion of Mesopotamia under Babylon was determined to break free. The Assyrians tried to incorporate Egypt, but they had sporadic, short-lived successes at best. At the same time, to the east the Medes were developing their own expansionistic ideas. Under increasing pressure from them, the Assyrians focused less and less on the western portion of their realm. This change, of

PLAINS OF JEZREEL. The region where Josiah, the last good king of the Southern Kingdom, was killed when he tried to stop Neco of Egypt from helping the Assyrians. The plain also figures into the prophecies of Revelation as the location of the battle of Armageddon.

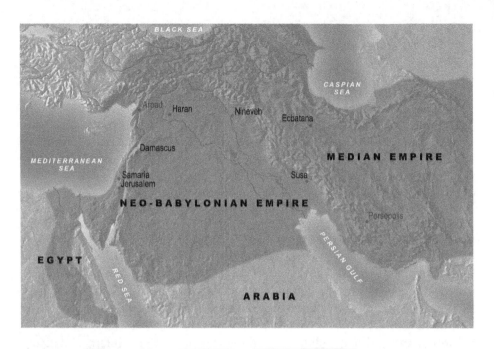

course, gave Josiah more freedom, but we must not assume that his actions were all politically motivated.[29]

Under Ashurbanipal (668–627 BCE), Assyria was barely able to keep control, even though his own brother Shamash-shum-ukin was the ostensibly subservient ruler of Babylon. After the death of Ashurbanipal, it was downhill for Assyria. Many of the peripheral powers began to repudiate the authority of Nineveh. By 626 Nabopolassar had taken the throne in Babylon and begun to consolidate power. In 612 he and forces from the Median Empire to the east and the Scythians to the north attacked and destroyed Nineveh.[30] This did not quite destroy the empire, because Ashur-uballit II was able to regroup in Haran. But that merely staved off the inevitable.

In 609 the Assyrians were forced to abandon Haran. At that time, the Egyptians, led by Pharaoh Neco, tried to come to their aid, but Josiah led his army out to stop them. At Megiddo he engaged the Egyptians in combat and lost his life as a result. In some respects, he achieved his goal. The Egyptians were too late to help, and the Assyrians retreated to Carchemish, where they held out for four more years. But the death of Josiah spelled the end of the Southern Kingdom.

Zephaniah the Prophet

Read Zephaniah 1–3.

Zephaniah was another obscure prophet who wrote a short book. At the beginning of the book, he writes that his ministry was during the time of Josiah. He also gives his own genealogy, showing that he was a great-great-grandson of Hezekiah.

The message of Zephaniah is one of judgment following on the heels of the wicked reigns of Manasseh and Amon. The judgment, which would occur during the day of the Lord, was viewed as multinational, encompassing the Southern Kingdom, their neighbors, and Assyria.[31] It appears that this judgment came about fewer than fifty years later, during the Babylonian expansion. As such, Zephaniah's message was amplified by Habakkuk.

Like many of the prophets, Zephaniah also had a message of hope in the last portion of his book, which speaks of a time of national restoration. This restoration would build on a remnant of true worshipers at a time when it could be declared of the nation that YHWH, the King of Israel (referring to the entire nation), was in their midst (Zeph. 3:15). The overall description of that event suggests that from our perspective it is yet future.

THE END IS NIGH

The end of the Southern Kingdom involved a couple of decades filled with a series of kings and prophets. The kings were minor from our perspective, more involved in international political intrigue than in spiritual understanding. The prophetic books vary in length and intensity, but the message is always the same: God's judgment is coming, but His compassion remains.

Jehoahaz (609 BCE)

After Josiah was killed in the battle with the Egyptians, the people of the Southern Kingdom put his twenty-three-year-old son Jehoahaz on the throne in his place. However, after three months, Jehoahaz was captured by Pharaoh Neco and held captive in Riblah of Hamath and died in exile.[32] Although on the throne only a short time, he was judged to be evil like many of his predecessors.

Read 2 Kings 23:31–33; 2 Chronicles 36:1–4.

Jehoiakim (609–597 BCE)

Having military control of the region, Neco put Jehoiakim, another son of Josiah, on the throne. He lasted eleven years and was viewed as evil. While not much is told about Jehoiakim in the historical books, he shows up also in the book of

Read 2 Kings 23:34–24:7; 2 Chronicles 36:5–8; Jeremiah 25–26; 36.

POLITICAL INTRIGUE

The politics of this period are very obscure, but it should be noted that Jehoahaz was a younger son. According to the text, he was two years younger than his brother Jehoiakim, who later took his place as king. These events would indicate a populace that was divided in its allegiance. It is also possible that Neco's subsequent placing of Jehoiakim on the throne was at the instigation of the latter, who may have sold out for the kingship. But the evidence is not clear.

ALMOND TREE. The object in a vision of the prophet Jeremiah, as related in Jeremiah 1. This involved a word play, since the same root word denotes one who watches, showing that God was watching over Israel.

Jeremiah. There we see him from God's perspective as a man who sought personal advancement and who, in the end, sold out both God and the nation.

The first event recorded about Jehoiakim is in Jeremiah 26, in the first year of his reign. God told Jeremiah to go to the temple and proclaim that because of its wickedness, the Southern Kingdom was going to end up like the Northern Kingdom. Key people among the leadership were furious at the negative message and demanded execution of the messenger. Others saw Jeremiah as a true prophet of God who proclaimed truth, and they rejected the demand. They used Micah and his message to Hezekiah as an example, perhaps hinting to the leadership that Jehoiakim should respond like his ancestor. Here Jeremiah interjects the account of the prophet Uriah, his contemporary who fled this evil coalition and sought exile in Egypt. Jehoiakim had him pursued and executed. Jeremiah remained in Jerusalem and was preserved by God through loyal friends. This incident set the pattern for Jehoiakim's reign.

Four years later (in 605 BCE), Jeremiah became especially active as events heated up on the international scene. The Egyptians (who had put Jehoiakim on the throne) tried to stop the expansion of the Babylonians at Carchemish, to the north of Israel. The Babylonian victory there tilted the power balance in the ANE, eventually leading to the exile of the Southern Kingdom. It also set the stage for the first wave of the Exile. As Nebuchadnezzar followed up his victory and pursued the Egyptians south, he took a number of political hostages from the aristocracy of the Southern Kingdom, including Daniel and his friends Hananiah, Mishael, and Azariah (Dan. 1:6). Under this pressure, Jehoiakim switched his allegiance to Babylon.

Jeremiah picked up on the victory at Carchemish when he proclaimed to the leadership that Nebuchadnezzar (the leader of the Babylonians) would come against the Southern Kingdom and destroy Jerusalem (Jer. 25).[33] This was the first announcement that the Exile would last seventy years (25:11). Jeremiah also delivered an "oracle" or declaration regarding the fate of Egypt (ch. 46) designed to warn Jehoiakim not to count on Egypt for help. Beyond the defeat at Carchemish, Egypt itself would be invaded and lost.

TIMELINE OF THE BABYLONIAN EXILE

605   Small number of hostages (Dan. 1:3–4)
      Included: Daniel, Hananiah, Azariah, Mishael

597   Major exile of 10,000 (2 Kings 24:14)
      Included: Jehoiachin, Ezekiel

586   Destruction of Jerusalem (2 Kings 25:11)
      Most of remaining people either went into exile or fled to Egypt
      Included: Jeremiah (taken to Egypt)
      Remnant of poor left behind

In December of that year, Jeremiah, who was under house arrest, sent his scribe Baruch to the temple to read a prophetic declaration about the nations (including both the Northern and Southern Kingdoms). Eventually this scroll was brought to Jehoiakim, who listened while sitting in his winter palace. As the scroll was read, Jehoiakim cut off several columns of writing at a time and burned them, reflecting his opinion of Jeremiah's proclamations (Jer. 36:23). God's response was to have Jeremiah redo the scrolls—with a few extra announcements regarding the king who felt he was beyond God's judgment (vv. 28–32).

Three years after Carchemish, internal turmoil in Babylon seemed to indicate a weakening, and Jehoiakim turned to Egypt—which, as Jeremiah had predicted, was a mistake. Nebuchadnezzar put down the local uprising and returned to Palestine where he attacked Jerusalem and captured it. Jehoiakim did not live to see that. He had died three months earlier, and his eight-year-old son was put on the throne in his place. The appraisal of Jehoiakim was that he was evil.

Habakkuk the Prophet

Habakkuk is a short book with a powerful message packed in it. The writer tells us virtually nothing about himself and little about the occasion. The book antic- *Read Habakkuk 1–3.* ipates the Babylonian conquest, which would seem to date its prophecy prior to 605 BCE. It reflects a national situation where injustice and wickedness prevail. The time would seem to be after Josiah, because it was during his reign that the timing of the Exile was announced.[34] Thus, it was probably written early within the reign of his son, Jehoiakim.

The book presents a dialogue between the prophet and God, followed by Habakkuk's response in the form of a prayer. Habakkuk first questioned God as to why He let injustice prevail in the land. God responded that He was bringing the Babylonians to judge the Southern Kingdom and eradicate the injustice. Habakkuk then raised a more serious question: How could God judge His people by using a nation that was even worse than the Southern Kingdom? God's response was that there was a bigger picture that involved an appointed time—"the end." In essence, God's response had two aspects: (1) His overall goal for history, and (2) the Babylonians' just deserts. The Babylonians would get what they deserved. That is, although God would allow the Babylonians a victory as part of His overall goal, they would still be accountable for their actions.

> How could God judge His people by using a nation that was even worse than the Southern Kingdom?

The most moving part of the book is Habakkuk's response (ch. 3). As he reflected on what he knew of God, he realized that understanding how He works was beyond him. However, despite the circumstances, he would put his trust wholly in God and rejoice as a result.

Jeremiah the Prophet

Read Jeremiah 1; 37–45.

Jeremiah began his ministry during the reign of Josiah, but the bulk of his written work is from the reigns of Jehoiakim, Jehoiachin, and Zedekiah. Jeremiah was a priest called by God to be a prophet even before his birth. Although he was born in Anathoth, a town northeast of Jerusalem in the tribal area of Benjamin, his ministry was in Jerusalem in the presence of the king. He had a most difficult ministry, for he served in a time when the people refused to hear God. In fact, like Micaiah and others, Jeremiah had the challenge of ministering during a period when prophetic declaration was rife, most of it people-pleasing prophetic declaration instead of honest revelation from God.[35]

Jeremiah is noted for his various acts of role-playing. Today he would be considered a master teacher—or an eccentric. We may suppose that "desperate times called for desperate measures." Some of his more significant messages included burying a linen sash near the Euphrates River to signify the Exile (Jer. 13); watching a potter remake a flawed item, illustrating how God would remake the nation (ch. 18); breaking a large pot before the leadership, demonstrating how God would destroy the Southern Kingdom (ch. 19); redeeming a piece of land, showing confidence that God would preserve the people even through exile (ch. 32); remaining single because of the anticipated hard times (ch. 16); and wearing a yoke to symbolize upcoming bondage (ch. 27).

Jeremiah's book is clearly an anthology put together near the end of his ministry. The material is usually dated but is not in chronological order, and it has no clear-cut organization that can be followed.[36]

Isaiah was noted for his observations regarding the Messiah and how YHWH was a God who acted in space-time history. Jeremiah provided further insights on both of those concepts. With regard to the first, Jeremiah pointed out that the Messiah would be involved in redoing the covenant between God and the nation (Jer. 31:31). For the first time, it is called the "new covenant," although, as we saw earlier, this notion was hinted at, at the end of the Exodus (Deut. 30:1; the term *new covenant* was used by Jesus when He instituted the Lord's Supper, Luke

THE NEW COVENANT IN JEREMIAH

Note that the covenant prophesied in Jeremiah 31:31–34 was to be with both the Northern and Southern Kingdoms and that it would replace the covenant at Mount Sinai. It would also be an *internalized* covenant, as opposed to the one written on the stone tablets. Moreover, the role of the Messiah is added a couple of chapters later when Jeremiah addresses the "righteous Branch" of David's line (33:15).

22:20). Picking up on Isaiah's term *Branch*, Jeremiah also emphasized that the Messiah would be from the line of David (e.g., 23:5; 30:9; 33:15).

Relating to God's role in history, Jeremiah added the idea of how personal actions affect the outcome. In chapter 18 he reported how God would make prophetic declarations based on a nation's actions but would either follow through or cancel them based on how the people responded. He gave the nation specific alternative futures and opportunities to repent (e.g., Jer. 7:3–7; 17:24–27; 22; 38:17). At the same time, Jeremiah was not reticent to declare when the opportunity to repent was past. For example, King Zedekiah asked Jeremiah to request God's intervention, but Jeremiah declared that while God would intervene, it would be *against* Zedekiah (see ch. 21).

Generally speaking, as we read through the book, we find that the people did not respond well and Jeremiah tended to complain about their response. He also showed extreme concern about the spiritual state of the nation, and consequently, he is often called the weeping prophet. Because he anticipated the coming destruction, he is viewed as pessimistic. Like the other prophets, however, Jeremiah foresaw a restoration and revival of the nation's fortunes in the distant future.

Jeremiah advised the king to capitulate to the Babylonians and alleviate the inevitable. For this reason, he was viewed as a traitor and was thrown into a prison and then into a muddy cistern (Jer. 37–38). While not a Babylonian sympathizer, he was given special treatment by Nebuchadnezzar when he captured Jerusalem in 586 BCE (ch. 39). Jeremiah also told the people not to fear the Babylonian captors. When they refused to listen and decided to flee to Egypt instead, they forcibly took Jeremiah with them (43:6). Jeremiah's ministry essentially ends with the destruction of Jerusalem, which validated his long-term message. Based on the last verse of the book, it appears that Jeremiah lived for approximately another twenty-five years, most likely in Egypt, although he did not record any more prophetic revelation after Jerusalem was destroyed.

Jehoiachin (597 BCE)

After Jehoiakim revolted, Nebuchadnezzar moved west again with his armies to attack Jerusalem. Jehoiakim died, leaving his son Jehoiachin to take the throne and face Nebuchadnezzar's wrath. After a reign of only three months, the city was subdued and Jehoiachin was led off into exile with his mother, his wives, and a large

Read 2 Kings 24:8–16; 25:27–30; 2 Chronicles 36:9–10.

CISTERN. A large pit dug into rock designed to save water. Jeremiah used a broken cistern to illustrate the insecurity of their false religions—they just wouldn't hold water. At one point as punishment, Jeremiah was thrown into a cistern partially filled with water.

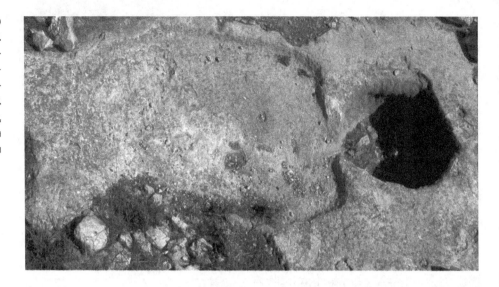

number of skilled artisans and the aristocracy. The priest Ezekiel, who will be significant later, was part of this second wave of exiles.

Jehoiachin survived in the Exile, as noted by the last three verses of 2 Kings, and apparently raised his family there. One of his descendants would help lead the first group of returning exiles in 538 BCE.

Zedekiah (597–586 BCE)

Read 2 Kings 24:18–25:26; 2 Chronicles 36:10–36:21.

Although Jehoiachin was still alive and considered by many still to be the king, he had no say in the rule of the kingdom. Back in Jerusalem, Nebuchadnezzar put Zedekiah, Jehoiachin's uncle (and brother of Jehoiakim), on the throne. He served in this position for eleven years. The first nine years were essentially status quo, but then Zedekiah revolted against his overseer. Nebuchadnezzar led his armies west again and put Jerusalem under siege. The siege lasted until the summer of 586 BCE, when the famine was becoming unbearable, and then the walls were breached.

Zedekiah and some of his leaders sneaked out at night but were captured near Jericho. Nebuchadnezzar then executed Zedekiah's sons before his eyes and had his eyes gouged out. This apparently happened on about July 18. On the tenth of Ab (August 17), 586 BCE, the city and temple were burned.[37] Zedekiah, along with a number of the inhabitants, was taken to Babylon in the third wave of exiles. With that he was lost to history and apparently died there.

CRY FOR THE CITY

Read Lamentations 1–5.

Perhaps the most fitting ending for this chapter is the book of Lamentations. The author, Jeremiah, was viewed by King Jehoiakim and other Southern Kingdom leaders as a traitor and as one who hated Jerusalem because he dared to foretell

HOW MANY EXILES?

Jeremiah lists a total of 4,600 captives in three waves, suggesting that the leadership was either exported or killed, while the rest of the people remained (Jer. 52:28–30). However, when we look at the dates, we realize that these three waves do not include the first group of 605 BCE. There was also a fourth group about 582, after the city had been destroyed and perhaps in response to the assassination of Gedaliah (2 Kings 25:25). Moreover, it is difficult to correlate these numbers with 2 Kings 24:14, which lists 10,000 for the wave in 597 alone. One possible explanation is that Jeremiah was looking only at the inhabitants of Jerusalem, while the writer of Kings had in mind the entire land. Another possibility is that Kings looked at the total number of captives, while Jeremiah referred only to adult males. In addition to the deportees to Babylon, we know that many inhabitants fled to Egypt (Jer. 43:5–7). This all points to a major depopulation of the land.

disaster. In reality, Jeremiah was filled with tough love as he tried to prevent the disaster from coming. He recognized that real love seeks what is truly good even when it requires one to say harsh things and demand rigorous acts—and even in the face of personal rejection and persecution.

> Jeremiah recognized that real love seeks what is truly good even when it requires one to say harsh things.

The book of Lamentations is a collection of five songs structured in the form of a lament. They all focus on the city of Jerusalem and its destruction. It seems as if Jeremiah was sitting on the Mount of Olives watching his beloved city burn as he wrote. Although he felt extreme sorrow, Jeremiah admitted throughout the book that the reason for the destruction was the sin of the people. But in true lament fashion, he ended with a prayer: "Restore us to yourself, O LORD, that we may return; renew our days as of old unless you have utterly rejected us and are angry with us beyond measure" (Lam. 5:21–22).

Eventually, but not during Jeremiah's lifetime, it would become clear that God had not utterly rejected the people.

REVIEW QUESTIONS

1. How did Rehoboam manage to lose most of his kingdom?

2. Why is Asa viewed as a good king but given a mixed review?

3. How did Jehoshaphat show piety on the one hand but political naivete on the other?

4. What is most memorable about Athaliah?

5. How did Joash bring hope to the Southern Kingdom? What did he do that caused him to be assassinated?

6. In what way did Uzziah demonstrate spiritual foolishness? What were the consequences?

7. What is most memorable about Ahaz?

8. Compare and contrast Hezekiah with his father, Ahaz, and with David.

9. What was the role of Isaiah in the Southern Kingdom?

10. What key prophecies did the prophets of this period give regarding the Messiah?

11. What is most memorable about Manasseh?

12. In what ways was Josiah the last hope for the Southern Kingdom?

13. Trace the decline and fall of the Southern Kingdom.

14. Describe the different ways by which Jeremiah tried to convey his message to the people.

15. Why was Lamentations written?

15

CHAPTER

The Nation in Exile

OVERVIEW

Exile came for the Southern Kingdom as God had announced. Some of the people fled to Egypt, but most were exiled to Babylon, where they settled in for the predicted seventy-year stay. God continued to work with His people, however, as evidenced by Daniel, Ezekiel, and Esther. This period saw the rise of apocalyptic literature, which showed that God was still in control.

STUDY GOALS

▶ Evaluate conditions of the Israelites in exile.

▶ Describe God's continual control of history.

▶ Introduce apocalyptic literature.

When we think of Israel in exile, we often picture a displaced people, basically destitute and homeless, who barely eke out sustenance in temporary, cramped quarters. Perhaps the current situation of the Palestinians would be a close approximation. While I am sure there was a lot of that during the period of exile, especially at the beginning, the picture on the whole was not so bleak.

There are likely a number of reasons for this. First, from the Assyrian and Babylonian perspective, the design of the exile process was only partially punishment. We see their approach expressed in the speech of Rabshakeh, the Assyrian general, to Hezekiah and the people of Jerusalem (2 Kings 18:31–35; Isa. 36:16–21). The Assyrian leader told the people that if they surrendered, they would be able to live in peace until he returned to take them to a land like their own—"a land of grain and new wine, a land of bread and vineyards." Naturally, a good portion of the speech was political propaganda, but there was also some truth to it. The Assyrians (and later the Babylonians) had conflicting objectives for their empire. On one hand, they wanted people in the various regions to be self-sustaining, which required that the exiles be productive and organized. On the other hand, they needed loyalty to the empire, and this goal required that local allegiances be broken down and replaced with a different organization.

The method those empires used to accomplish their objective was to shift people groups. But they tended not to move complete groups. Rather, they shifted the leadership—the aristocracy, the skilled artisans, the priests. In other words, the people who were moved were those who were most likely to organize uprisings. The poorer people, such as the small-scale farmers, tended to be left behind,

ELEPHANTINE ISLAND. An island in the Nile River that was the home of a large Israelite settlement during the time after the destruction of Samaria. A temple was established there, probably by syncretistic Jews. It may have been where Jeremiah was taken when he was carried off to Egypt.

and new foreign leadership groups were brought in. This is the situation we see in the Northern Kingdom in 2 Kings 17:24–41. It is interesting that later, in the case of the Southern Kingdom, the Babylonians did not bring in any new regional leadership but left the people under local control.

A second reason the Exile was not so dire seems to be that at least some of the people listened to the prophets. Jeremiah ran counter to the false prophets who were maintaining that the people would be back from exile in just a few years.[1] He told them that it would be a seventy-year period and that they were to buy houses, plant gardens, get married and have children, plan for grandchildren, and "seek the peace and prosperity of the city to which I have carried you into exile. Pray to the LORD for it, because if it prospers, you too will prosper" (Jer. 29:7). The evidence suggests that they did exactly that.

A third reason seems to be coupled with the people's following this instruction. God blessed the people even while they were in exile. When we looked at the word *bless* in chapters 4 and 5, we noted that God's blessing is oriented toward an objective or mission. Thus, even in a time of exile, the people were being given the wherewithal to accomplish their task, which would be to return to the land and work toward the coming of the Messiah. We will see this truth demonstrated as we note some of the people who were in exile. We need to recognize, however, that the biblical writers have given us only a few snapshots (although we do have other pictures of this period in the Apocrypha). When we go through the material, we will also discover a new genre of literature known as apocalyptic. One question we will address is, Why this type of revelation now?

OBJECT LESSON. A jar such as Jeremiah would have used for safekeeping of the deed (a scroll) when he purchased property from his uncle (Jer. 32:1–15).

God blessed the people even while they were in exile.

DANIEL, PRINCE AND PROPHET

The first wave of exiles, in 605 BCE, was most likely the smallest. Its primary purpose was to provide political hostages to ensure that the king of the Southern Kingdom followed the Babylonian party line. As such, the people in that wave were primarily members of the aristocracy and relatives of the king (Dan. 1:3). Those hostages were "young men," probably in their middle to late teens. The group included Daniel, Hananiah, Mishael, and Azariah (we normally remember the last three by the pagan names given to them by the Babylonian king: Shadrach, Meshach, and Abednego).[2] They were taken to Babylon, where they were put into a three-year training program to learn the Babylonian language and literature and to be inculcated with the Babylonian culture. At the end of this time period, they would become advisors to the king.

Read Daniel 1–6.

A VEGETARIAN DIET?

The decision on the part of Daniel and his friends to eat "nothing but vegetables" (Dan. 1:12) is not an argument for vegetarianism. It reflects instead a desire to maintain the food standards set forth in the OT law. The key is the statement that Daniel "resolved not to defile himself" (v. 8), showing that the issue was uncleanness. Clearly the ten-day period of the test would not have been enough in and of itself to have a significant effect on their physical appearance. Rather, it demonstrated God's honoring their desire to please Him in difficult circumstances. We should note also that Daniel and his friends were just part of the group taken hostage from the Southern Kingdom, yet they apparently were the only ones who made this stand. While they are commended, the others are not condemned for not doing so, although at the same time, we never hear of any of the others again. Of course, that in itself may be a subtle condemnation.

From the Babylonian perspective, there were several astute reasons behind this policy. Of course, there was the political pressure such a policy would put on the king back in Jerusalem. By educating the young men, the Babylonians hoped to influence their thinking and make them more "pro-Babylonian." In the process, the Babylonians would learn about the Israelites, thus gaining knowledge on how to better rule that region of the empire. Moreover, by bringing in young men from all over the empire, they were developing a more cosmopolitan atmosphere in Babylon.

The first part of the book of Daniel gives us several insights into this process. There is, of course, the account of Daniel and his three friends deciding not to eat the Babylonian food. They found approval from the chief official for two reasons. First, they approached the matter courteously, willing to put their proposal to the test. This consideration allowed the official, who was caught in the middle, viable alternatives. Second, at the end of the ten days of testing, Daniel and his friends were so healthy that the chief official had no qualms in granting their desire.

A year or so later (while Daniel and friends were still in their training), the second episode occurred. Nebuchadnezzar had a dream that he wanted interpreted. So he called all the advisors together and asked them what it meant—and, oh, by the way, they had to tell him the dream also. Of course, this stipulation ran counter to the dream interpretation process, as the advisors reminded Nebuchadnezzar. But he informed them that this way he would be able to verify their

A BILINGUAL BOOK

The text of the book of Daniel changes from Hebrew to Aramaic at 2:4. By this time in history, Aramaic had become the international trade language, having replaced Akkadian sometime earlier (the book of Ezra has Aramaic sections as well). A possible reason for this switch is that the prophetic message of chapters 2 to 7 focuses on the nations of the world rather than Israel. The focus then turns again to Israel when the text switches back to Hebrew in chapter 8.

interpretation. The advisors left his presence in despair, doomed to failure and death.

As people in training for advisory roles, Daniel and his friends had not been part of the audience before the king, but they were still subject to the death decree. The first they heard of the episode was when Arioch, the commander of the king's guard, showed up at their house and announced that they were to be executed. Daniel asked for and received a stay of execution in order to try to get an interpretation. He and his friends held a prayer meeting, and God answered their prayers. After praising God (a declarative praise psalm—see above, ch. 12), Daniel went to the king and reported the results. He informed him that the vision was a statue made of four metals. These represented four successive world kingdoms, beginning with the Babylonian Empire. They would be followed by God's kingdom, represented by a stone cut out without hands, which would fill the earth. Finally, Daniel told Nebuchadnezzar that God was giving him this message as a broad outline of the future (Dan. 2:28).

The book of Daniel presents several other incidents that show the spiritual integrity of Daniel and his friends. We see his friends thrown into the fiery furnace because they failed to worship Nebuchadnezzar's gold statue, but they were rescued by God.[3] Later, after the Medes and the Persians took over the kingdom, Daniel was thrown into the lion's den because he dared to pray to the God in heaven rather than to Darius, but he also was delivered by God.

NEBUCHADNEZZAR'S DREAM

We saw in our discussion of Joseph the process by which dreams were interpreted in the ANE (see ch. 5, above). In the case of Nebuchadnezzar, the question is whether he really had forgotten the dream. The advisors had to assume that he had, but they did not dare bluff him. If he had not forgotten the dream, they would flunk the test. Even if he had forgotten the dream, there was a good chance that something they said might bring it to mind. As such, their dream catalogs were useless. The fact that later Nebuchadnezzar grants a stay of execution shows that he was most concerned with understanding the message rather than with getting rid of his advisors. It may also indicate that he had really forgotten the content, although he was genuinely troubled by the dream.

Why didn't Nebuchadnezzar object to Daniel's interpretation, which indicated that there would be other kingdoms besides his? First, Daniel alone was able to tell him the dream, so the interpretation must have come from a divine source. Second, the subsequent kingdoms were presented as inferior to Nebuchadnezzar's, an evaluation that would stroke his ego a bit. Finally, those kingdoms would come after his death, and the sequence would end in a kingdom established by God. Nebuchadnezzar could see divine control over a process that would occur primarily after he himself was long gone.

Matching the interpretation to history raises questions. Those who do not accept predictive prophecy argue that the book must have been written during the Maccabean period; in their view, the fourth kingdom was the Greek Empire founded by Alexander. That would mean that the second and third kingdoms were those of the Medes and the Persians respectively. In the book of Daniel, however, these are not viewed as two distinct kingdoms but are always presented as one, the Medo-Persian Empire. Therefore, those who allow predictive prophecy generally put the Medo-Persian Empire as the second kingdom, Greece as the third, and then the Roman Empire as the fourth.

A very important incident took place at the end of the Babylonian Empire, when Belshazzar was the king. By this time, Daniel was old and retired. The king had a big party while the Persian armies were surrounding the city. When he was drunk, Belshazzar decided to drink a toast to his gods with the cups taken from the temple in Jerusalem.[4] While they were drinking, a hand appeared and wrote on the wall opposite him: "*Mene, Mene, Tekel, Parsin.*"[5] Belshazzar was terrified. Eventually, through the advice of the queen, he called for Daniel and asked him to translate. While he refused the king's offer of a reward, Daniel did translate the words, telling the king that it was all over for him and for Babylon. That night—the text adds almost as an afterthought—the Persians took Babylon.

In the last part of the book, Daniel relates several visions he received that supplement Nebuchadnezzar's dream of the statue, and then the book ends. While the first wave of exiles returned to Jerusalem about the time of his last vision, Daniel was apparently not part of it. He was probably in his mid to late eighties at the time, but we are told no more about him.

The book of Daniel carried powerful lessons for its original audience, who included it in their canon. It showed how a pious man could serve in the court of a pagan king with integrity. It demonstrated how God could protect His servants when they were attacked because of their beliefs.[6] Most important, it showed how God was in control of history, and it could even lay out the flow of future history (although it was explained in very broad terms). Finally, the book finishes with a promise that God would provide justice and that there would be a future restoration of the righteous. When Daniel asked when that would be (Dan. 12:8), he was basically told to mind his own business.

APOCALYPTIC LITERATURE

In Daniel we are introduced to apocalyptic literature. We find apocalyptic material also in Ezekiel, Zechariah, the Gospels,[7] and Revelation. In addition, several other books that belong to this genre, such as 1 Enoch, have never been included in the canon.[8]

In terms of style and content, apocalyptic literature is related to prophetic literature, but it has several distinctives. While prophetic writings serve to show God's sovereign control over history, apocalyptic literature serves to show God's sovereignty over the future. The significance of this difference lies in the fact that prophetic literature is oriented toward the audience receiving the message, and

DANIEL'S VISIONS

The first vision recorded in the last part of the book is of four beasts that parallel the four metals of the statue (Dan. 7); it amplifies Nebuchadnezzar's dream in giving some details, especially relating to God's kingdom at the end. The vision in Daniel 8 focuses on the second and third of the four kingdoms, Medo-Persia and Greece (explicitly named as such in this account). Daniel 9 is a response to Daniel's concern about the future of his people as he looked at Jeremiah's prophecy of the seventy years, which was nearing completion. Here, after a powerful prayer of confession, Daniel was given information about the Messiah (or Anointed One, v. 25), showing that the point of the future for Daniel's people centered on the Messiah. The final vision, given between October 537 and October 536 BCE (the third year of Darius), concerned what would happen to Daniel's people in the future (Dan. 10:14). We are not told what precipitated this revelation. The timing might tie it with the first return from the exile. In 10:1 Daniel notes that the focus was a "great war" or conflict. This section is the most controversial in Daniel because of its great detail corroborated by history, at least up to the time of Antiochus Epiphanes (c. 215–163 BCE). Again, how one views this material depends on whether one accepts the possibility of predictive prophecy. This extended section ends in Daniel 12 with an anticipation of an end-time resurrection.

THE BLIND GIRL. A nineteenth-century painting by Sir John Everett Millais that offers an analogy to the difficulty a prophet seeing into the spiritual realm would have in trying to explain what he saw to someone who had never had that experience.

there is an expected response from the hearer. Apocalyptic literature seems to be less concerned with a response and more focused on what God is going to do—regardless. As such, we might say that prophetic literature is more contingent than apocalyptic literature, that is, the foretold event might not occur, depending on the response of the people (Jer. 18:7–12).

Apocalyptic literature also tends to be more visually oriented than prophetic literature. In many prophetic passages, we read of the prophet reporting revelation given by "the word of the LORD." Apocalyptic passages tend to be visual scenes, often with the prophet being in the middle of them. While on occasion a voice is heard, verbal revelation is more often given by an angelic being.

A third distinction lies in the use of symbols. While prophetic literature has some symbolic representation, apocalyptic is very rich in the use of symbols. For example, there are some that represent nations, like a ram for Medo-Persia and a goat for Greece (Dan. 8). Interestingly, most of the symbols are interpreted in the text for us. Those that are not interpreted are either common symbols or are explained in other, earlier texts.

These distinctives give us a hint as to why apocalyptic literature arose during this period. The nation was in exile, and many of the questions people asked now went beyond the nation of Israel and its role as provider of the Messiah. God was starting to instill a vision for the world, although that would not start to come to

fruition until the Messiah came. Furthermore, because of specific declarations by God (e.g., a return after seventy years), key elements of the future had been determined. That is, it was determined that the nation would go back to Jerusalem and that this return would take place seventy years after the people had been taken captive. So since a path was determined, part of the function of the apocalyptic prophets was merely to declare this message rather than to demand a response (although clearly a response of faith and hope would be expected). Finally, God was now pointing to the far future. Hints were being made as to how He would be working so that observant people could "get on board" with His program.

This long-term view was evident in the first apocalyptic vision in Daniel 2. As we have already noted, Daniel told Nebuchadnezzar that God had given him a broad outline of the future. However, since the revelation was included in Scripture, this broad outline was also given to *all* future generations. This would seem to be why, when Jesus was born, many people in Judea were expecting Him. It may also explain why the magi (a later generation of one of Nebuchadnezzar's advisor groups in Dan. 2:2) came to Jerusalem after the birth of Jesus looking for the king of the Jews.

But much of the long-term view of apocalyptic literature seems to be yet future even from our perspective. This element is amplified for us in the NT in

WAS DANIEL A PROPHET?

One point of curiosity is that while the book of Daniel was included within the canon, it was not placed among the prophetic books in the Hebrew OT. Rather, it is included within the third section, called the Writings. This section includes most of the poetic and wisdom works as well as Chronicles and the postexilic works of Ezra and Nehemiah (interestingly, it also includes the early book of Ruth). The most probable reason for this location is that Daniel was not a prophet by profession; although sometimes he functioned as one, his position was that of government official.

Revelation and passages such as Matthew 24. One of the tensions scholars face is how to put those two aspects together. A good example is Isaiah 61. Today we now understand that passage shows that there would be two comings of the Messiah. The original audience, however, would not have been able to grasp that application. But even though the perspective was long-term, the reader would come away from the apocalyptic work with hope, recognizing that God was in control.

JEHOIACHIN, KING IN EXILE

Jehoiachin was the key figure in the second wave of exiles in 597 BCE. We have already noted how after his initial imprisonment Jehoiachin was treated well in Babylon. According to the historian, after Nebuchadnezzar died, his son Evil-Merodach released Jehoiachin from prison, although he was kept in Babylon. The date would have been approximately 560 BCE, long after the city of Jerusalem had been destroyed. The succinct report in Kings seems a bit boastful when it says that he ate at the king's table and was honored over all the other kings. But it has been somewhat corroborated by material from the Babylonian archives, which list some of the rations given to Jehoiachin. Not only was Jehoiachin still called King of Judah in the Babylonian documents, but his sons shared in the provisions.[9] Thus, although the king was in exile, God was preserving David's royal line, and Jehoiachin came to enjoy some favor with the king of Babylon. One has to

Read 2 Kings 25:27–30.

wonder if some of the benefits he received were a result of the good work his countrymen were doing during the same time period.

EZEKIEL, PRIEST AND PROPHET

Read Ezekiel 1–10.

Ezekiel was a priest who was carried into exile during the second wave with Jehoiachin the king. His book opens five years later, when he was thirty years old and had a vision of God. At the time, he was in Babylon along the Kebar, or Chebar, River (apparently a canal that split off from the Euphrates northwest of Babylon, and rejoined it 60 miles later to the south). While it was unusual for a prophet to record his initial meeting with God, it was not unique (see Isa. 6). It may be that Ezekiel spends as much time as he does addressing his calling to validate his position, given that he was in exile at the time.

> Like his contemporary Jeremiah, Ezekiel would be considered eccentric by most people.

Like his contemporary Jeremiah, Ezekiel would be considered eccentric by most people. He performed a number of object lessons to show what was about to happen, some of which were personally degrading. He made a model to show a besieged Jerusalem (Ezek. 4:1–8).[10] He ate bread made from a mixture of grains and baked on a fire of dried dung to symbolize the famine associated with a siege (4:9–27).[11] He shaved his beard and head with a sharp sword and then divided the hairs to symbolize the various ways the people of Jerusalem would be punished (5:1–17). He packed his baggage and crawled through a hole he had dug under the wall of his home to show how the rest of the nation would be scattered into exile (12:1–16). He had to watch his wife die to show God's feelings regarding what was happening in Jerusalem (24:15–27).

Ezekiel also told a number of parables. He compared Jerusalem to the wood of a vine that was only good for burning (15:1–8). He compared the nation to an adulterous woman (16:1–63). He compared the politics of the day to a cedar twig (the kingly line) caught between two eagles (Babylon and Egypt). Interestingly, this parable contains a promise that another twig from the same tree would be

THE TEMPLE IN EZEKIEL

The description of the temple is given in very explicit detail, and it is clear that no actual temple seen to date matches it. The question is, then, Was the vision symbolic, or did it anticipate a temple yet in the future? The key problem with a symbolic interpretation is that there are no guidelines for interpretation, especially of the very detailed measurements. If the numbers are symbolic, we are given no help to understand their meaning. This would seem to indicate that Ezekiel was looking at an actual building that is yet future. On the other hand, the meticulous measurements are tied into the detailed tribal distribution of the nation that he gives in this section, which produces a rather stilted layout of the land. Charles H. Dyer gives several diagrams of both in his discussion of this section (*BKC*, 1:1303–17).

PROBLEMS IN EZEKIEL

Although the book of Ezekiel was included in the canon, questions were raised regarding its use in the liturgy of worship and public reading. Some rabbis included it among a group of books that were regarded as disputed (Lamar Eugene Cooper Sr., *Ezekiel*, The New American Commentary [Nashville: Broadman, 1994], 30–31). One significant difficulty lay in apparent contradictions to the Torah in the last section of the vision of the temple (chs. 40–48), which contributed to modern critical scholarship's attack of the book. The most radical of those attacks have said that Ezekiel wrote only a small portion of the book (170 to 251 of the 1,273 verses, depending on who made the analysis). The subjectivity of these evaluations renders their validity suspect.

replanted back in Israel (17:1–24). He compared the two kingdoms to two sisters, both of whom became harlots (23:1–49).

Ezekiel was also a man who had visions. Some of these showed insight into the spiritual realm, such as we saw in the case of Micaiah. His initial vision was of God upon His throne being carried by cherubim (1:4–28). This passage is difficult to follow, but it is clear from the comparisons that he was struggling to explain what he saw in terms his people would understand. Later he was transported within a vision to the temple in Jerusalem, where he saw the true nature of worship (8:1–18; this vision was dated to the year 591 BCE and thus was about five years before the destruction of the temple in 586).

The most notable visions Ezekiel had were of the future. In chapter 37, he records his famous vision of the valley of bones. This passage is undated, but it points to a future restoration of the nation. It follows immediately after a prophetic declaration (ch. 36) of a future period of restoration when God would place His Holy Spirit within the people.[12] The other major vision was of a restored temple. It took place in 572 BCE, fourteen years after the destruction of Solomon's temple. The fascinating thing about this vision is the amount of detail it includes, which shows how the temple he describes differs from both the one built by Solomon and the second one built after the Exile. The description of the temple and its environs takes nine chapters (40–48).

Finally, Ezekiel was a prophet in the classic sense who pronounced judgments as God's representative (chs. 25–32). Because both of the Israelite kingdoms were already being judged, these judgments were pronounced on Israel's neighbors: Ammon, Moab, Edom, Philistia, Tyre, and Egypt.[13]

WOULD-BE MODERN PROPHET. A self-proclaimed prophet standing in London's Hyde Park proclaiming his own explanation of how Ezekiel's visions were being fulfilled—in 1973.

Thus, we see that the book of Ezekiel is a challenging book containing material that is difficult to understand. Even though it was written in Babylon, it seems to have been accepted by Israelites who devoutly believed God, and it was incorporated into the canon. It was likely taken back to Jerusalem by those who returned from the Exile.

ESTHER, QUEEN AND SERVANT

Read Esther 1–10.

One of the most fascinating figures in the OT is Esther, a woman whose family had remained in Babylon long after the nation's return from exile (see ch. 16, below). According to the text, the book begins in the third year of the reign of Xerxes I, who ruled Persia 486–465 BCE. This places it about fifty years after the majority of the returnees had made it back to Jerusalem. The book of Esther really consists of two parts. The first is the "beauty contest," which shows how she became queen. The more important part is the defense of the Jewish people from an attempt to exterminate them.

As the book begins, Xerxes is giving a big, extended, party.[14] During the festivities and while under the influence of alcohol, Xerxes "invites" his wife, Vashti, to come before the crowd "in order to display her beauty to the people and nobles." As worded in our text, the invitation seems innocent enough, but Vashti dared to refuse and so incurred the king's anger. This might suggest an R-rated (or even X-rated) party. Angry at her refusal, Xerxes divorced her. Because he took this action through an official edict, he was unable to nullify it.[15]

When the king sobered up, he realized what he had done, but it was too late. His attendants suggested that a search be conducted for a new queen, to which he agreed. Promising young women were brought to the palace, where they spent a night with the king. At the end, he found Esther the most pleasing, and she became queen.

Esther had not disclosed her Jewish ancestry (by now Israelites were being identified as Jews, a name derived from the name of the Southern Kingdom, Judah). Her guardian, Mordecai, was a descendant from the tribe of Benjamin; his great-grandfather was among those who had been carried into exile (Est. 2:5–6).[16] Mordecai worked in the palace and was very loyal to the king, as shown by an incident noted in passing: he had once uncovered and reported a plot against the king's life (2:21–23).

NO GOD IN ESTHER?

One of the interesting points of the book of Esther is that God is never mentioned in the text. However, it is clear from several passages (e.g., Est. 4:13–14) that the characters depended on God to defend them, and most scholars seem to understand that the book makes subtle allusions to God's omniscience and power as that which provided deliverance for the Jewish people. No one really understands why the book was written in the way it was written. However, the fact that it was accepted as part of the canon indicates how the early audiences perceived it.

PERSEPOLIS. A capital of the Persian Empire. Its construction began during the reign of Darius I.

The heart of the story, however, is about a second plot, this time against Mordecai and his people. This episode begins about four and a half years after Esther became queen.[17] The instigator was Haman, a high official who was honored for some unspecified reason. He got trapped by pride in his position and resented the fact that Mordecai refused to bow down to him. When he learned that Mordecai was a Jew, he decided to get revenge for his perceived slight by killing off all the Jewish people.

Through his contacts, Mordecai learned of the plot and sent word to Esther, telling her that she needed to act. Since Esther had managed to keep her ethnic background hidden, she must have felt safe in the palace. To reveal herself to the king at this point put her personally at risk along with her people. However, Mordecai warned her that even being in the king's palace could not protect her. He was confident that God would provide deliverance for His people, and the only question for her was what part she would play (Est. 4:13–14). The rest of the book describes how Esther took the risk, outwitted Haman, and thus saved her people.

> Mordecai was confident that God would provide deliverance for His people, and the only question for Esther was what part she would play.

One outcome of the book of Esther was the festival of Purim (or "lots"), a name derived from the lots Haman had cast to decide when to initiate the plot. He probably thought that his process of selection was guided by spiritual beings, but ironically the time he felt was best for his purposes actually turned out to be the most propitious for his own destruction. The implication is that God was controlling or overruling whatever the lots indicated. And it is suggestive that the date Haman thus chose to initiate his efforts at genocide became a holiday celebrating the deliverance of the Jews.

LOOKING AHEAD

As demonstrated by Esther's family, when the time for the return from the Exile came, many did not go back. In fact, as we will see in the next chapter, the leaders of the second and third waves of return were themselves members of families who had remained "in exile." Since the fall of Jerusalem, most of the Israelite people have lived in places other than the land that had been promised to them. Historically, this Jewish dispersion has been known as the Diaspora. There was a gradual regathering over the next several centuries, but this process collapsed with the destruction of the temple in 70 CE. Even today most Jews live in places other than Israel, which seems to point to a yet future fulfillment of the prophetic declarations. But before we discuss that topic, we need to look at the first return.

REVIEW QUESTIONS

1. What are some reasons that the Exile was not as severe as it might have been?

2. Summarize both the incidents and the visions recorded in the book of Daniel.

3. What is apocalyptic literature, and how is it different from prophetic literature?

4. What makes the book of Ezekiel distinctive?

5. What is the significance of Esther?

16

CHAPTER

Home Again

OVERVIEW

As predicted by Jeremiah and others, the nation returned from exile. The attempt at restoration had its ups and downs. The people began to rebuild the temple and then stopped, but Haggai got the people back on track while Zechariah pointed to a future temple. Then the rebuilding of the walls stopped, but the people were encouraged by Nehemiah and Ezra. At the end, Malachi noted that the people still did not have the spirit of worship they needed, and he also pointed to a future Messiah.

STUDY GOALS

▶ Trace the three phases of the return from exile of the Southern Kingdom.

▶ Show how the nation resettled in the land and rebuilt the temple and the city of Jerusalem.

▶ Explain the challenge facing Ezra and Nehemiah of maintaining national godliness and obedience to the Law.

▶ Set up the transition to the New Testament as the Old Testament is completed by Malachi.

I n 538 BCE, approximately sixty-seven years after he had gone off into exile, Daniel began looking for his people to return to the land of Israel. Then the Persian king Cyrus, during the first year of his reign (sometime between the conquest of Babylon on 12 October 539 and the anniversary of that event in October 538), issued a decree allowing *all* captive peoples to return to their native lands. While some, like Daniel, would have been hoping for this event, it still probably took a while to complete all of the arrangements. They would have to dispose of their property, organize the returning group, and then make the arduous journey. Thus, it is not surprising that the first of the returnees did not arrive in the area of Jerusalem until about 536.

THE FIRST WAVE OF RETURNEES

Read Ezra 1–4.

In his first few chapters, Ezra recounts the events surrounding the return of that first group of exiles. Ezra himself lived sometime later and thus had not been part of that group. But this information is a necessary background to his story. As he describes the preparation of the initial group, he makes several interesting points. According to Ezra 1:5, the group included family heads from the tribes of Judah and Benjamin as well as priests and Levites. More important, he noted that the group included "everyone whose heart God had moved." This comment clearly suggests a divine sifting of the people. Even more interesting, many who did not go back provided monetary support to those who did.[1] They also brought back to

WALLS OF POST-EXILIC JERUSALEM. Walls that date to the time of King Hezekiah and therefore probably the walls that Nehemiah rebuilt after the exile.

Jerusalem many of the utensils that Nebuchadnezzar had taken from the sanctuary. This act anticipated the rebuilding of the temple.[2]

Once the group was organized, 42,360 returned along with 7,337 servants. There were two key leaders, a prince and a priest. The prince was Zerubbabel, a grandson of Jehoiachin, the king taken into exile (see 1 Chron. 3:17–19). The priest was Joshua. Because this group was from the remnant of the Southern Kingdom, or Judah, they began to be called Jews. From here on, we will use that name.

Once the Jews had reached the land, they gathered in Jerusalem, where they erected and dedicated an altar. They began offering sacrifices on the altar as part of a renewed national worship, although the temple was not yet rebuilt. This service took place on the first day of the seventh month, the day of the Festival of Trumpets. Today it is known as Rosh Hashanah, or the beginning of the new year. Two weeks later they also celebrated the Feast of Booths (Sukkoth), the feast that reminded the people of the work God had done to bring them out of Egypt (Lev. 23:34–44). The people had made a good start. Their journey had been successful, and they were safely in the land. Worship was reinstituted. The temple had not yet been rebuilt, but that was the next item on the agenda.

Seven months later they had contracted for the supplies (rations for the builders and cedars from Lebanon for beams) and had begun work on the temple. Joshua the priest organized the workers into teams, and the foundation was laid. It was a bittersweet moment. On one hand, it was a time of triumph, and the people cheered and sang praise songs as the temple orchestra accompanied them. On the other hand, those who recalled the original temple wept for what had been lost.[3]

ZERUBBABEL AND JOSHUA

While Chronicles shows Zerubbabel to be the son of Pedaiah—a younger brother of Jehoiachin's oldest son, Shealtiel—Ezra and Nehemiah both present him as the son of Shealtiel. It would appear that this was a case of levirate marriage; while biologically the son of Pedaiah, Zerubbabel was legally the son of Shealtiel. As for Joshua the priest, his name is spelled Jeshua in Ezra and Nehemiah, but the fuller form Joshua is used in Haggai and Zechariah (Heb. *Yeshua'* is a short form of *Yehoshua'*, meaning "YHWH is salvation"). It would seem to be one of those ironies of history that both the military leader of the first movement into the land and the spiritual leader of the second movement were named Joshua, the given name of the one the NT views as the Messiah, whom we call Jesus.

With success, however, came opposition. Some of the inhabitants of the region that had been the Northern Kingdom offered to help build the temple. From his later perspective, Ezra characterized them as enemies of Judah and Benjamin, although the specifics are not explained. The primary reason their offer was rejected seems to have been that they followed the syncretistic cult that had been established by Jeroboam. As we noted in chapter 13, those involved in such a cult claimed to serve YHWH, but their worship was actually a form of idolatry rejected by God. This syncretistic process had apparently been aggravated by the foreign peoples the Assyrians had settled within the land, for these intermarried with the remaining Israelites.[4] They naturally would have merged some of their pagan beliefs into the local cult, although we have little data to show exactly what they believed or practiced. Because these people were centered at the old northern capital, Samaria, they became known as Samaritans.

Joshua and Zerubbabel decided that they were better off without the help of the Samaritans and refused to allow it. From our perspective, the reason is not clear. However, recognizing our lack of good records, we need to allow that they may have had good reason to do so. Regardless, this act initiated antagonisms that would last for centuries. In response to this rejection, the local leaders expressed their hostility against the Jews through slander and threats. As the intensity of threats increased, work on the temple stopped.[5]

IMPURE WORSHIP

Jeroboam's cult was not the only one that claimed to serve YHWH but was in fact idolatrous. One of the struggles throughout the history of both the Northern and Southern Kingdoms was the effort to preserve the purity of the worship of God. We have seen this concern throughout the Prophets. An interesting illustration of the problem is a colony of Jews in Egypt that settled on an island called Elephantine at the first cataract on the Nile. Late in the nineteenth century, a number of papyri were found that shed light on this colony—including the fact that they had their own temple (*ANET*, 491–92). These papyri date from the period between the return and Nehemiah's work.

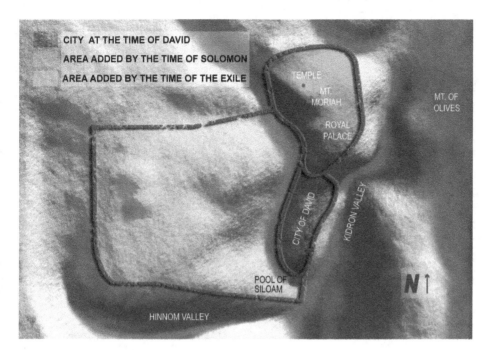

CITY AT THE TIME OF DAVID

AREA ADDED BY THE TIME OF SOLOMON

AREA ADDED BY THE TIME OF THE EXILE

TEMPLE

MT. MORIAH

ROYAL PALACE

MT. OF OLIVES

CITY OF DAVID

KIDRON VALLEY

POOL OF SILOAM

HINNOM VALLEY

N ↑

THE EXPANSION OF THE CITY OF JERUSALEM, from David to Nehemiah.

SAMARITANS

The introduction of foreign people into the area that had been occupied by the Northern Kingdom is the background of the schism between the Samaritans and the Jews that we see in the Gospels. Some seem to feel that there were two or more groups, one of which consisted of the descendants of the nondeported Israelites, while the other descended from the people imported by the Assyrians. More likely, there was one group that had subcategories. One of the powerful effects of Christianity would be to bridge the gap between the groups centered in Samaria and the Jews.

SAMARIA. Like Jerusalem, a city rebuilt after the Exile. That Samaria became a Hellenistic-Roman city had a profound influence on the Judean settlers.

From the little material we have, we understand that the Samaritans centered their worship at the dual mountains of Gerizim and Ebal. They also had their own version of the Pentateuch that emphasized the role of these mountains, but they did not seem to accept any of the other canonical books. Beyond that, our knowledge of their beliefs is limited. It does appear from what we read in the Gospels that by that time they agreed with the Jews with regard to belief in a single God and with regard to their history. They differed, of course, on where to worship and likely on what caused the split between the two groups.

THREE PHASES OF RETURN

537   Reason: Decree of Cyrus
       Led by Sheshbazzar, Joshua, Zerubbabel
       Included: about 50,000
       Built houses and the temple
          Ezra 1–6
458   Reason: To provide law
       Led by Ezra
       Included: about 1,800
       Started a revival
          Ezra 7–10
444   Reason: To rebuild city walls
       Led by Nehemiah
       Included: small number along with Persian soldiers
       Rebuilt city, promoted revival
          Nehemiah 1–13

THE PROPHET HAGGAI

Read Haggai 1–2.

Haggai was a prophet with a specific agenda—get the temple rebuilt. His book is a series of four short messages, dated over a period of less than four months, that address that agenda. He began fifteen years after the work on the temple had stopped. In the interim, Cyrus and two subsequent kings had died, and Persia was now being ruled by Darius I.[6] Haggai and his contemporary Zechariah told the people it was time to get on with the job at hand. Under their prodding, the work began again.

> Haggai was a prophet with a specific agenda—get the temple rebuilt.

FINISHING THE JOB

Read Ezra 5–6.

Soon after the Jews began the rebuilding process, word reached Tattenai, the Persian governor who ruled the province west of the Euphrates River. Tattenai and several colleagues went to Jerusalem where they challenged Joshua and Zerubbabel, asking them by what authority they were doing that work. They replied that it was based on a decree from Cyrus.

Tattenai sent a letter back to the capital asking Darius what should be done. Since the Jews claimed to have authority from Cyrus, the Persians searched the archives at Ecbatana. Soon they found the official copy of the decree showing that the Jews were indeed authorized to build their temple. Darius then sent a new

IRON AGE HOUSE. A house that probably reflects the typical architecture for the upper class during the post-exilic period. This house in the southern part of Judea had a large cistern beneath it.

decree back to Tattenai telling him not only to allow the Jews to continue but also to fund the rest of the project out of his budget.

Because of the threats in the letter, Tattenai hastened to comply, and the Jews worked with more zeal. The project was completed in four years, and the new temple was dedicated on March 12, 515 BCE (that is, just a few months past the seventieth anniversary of the destruction of the temple, which occurred on August 17, 586). Significantly, the dedication ceremony included twelve male goats—one for each tribe of the united nation. A few weeks later, they celebrated a Passover and Feast of Unleavened Bread, showing that they were back into the full worship cycle.

THE PROPHET ZECHARIAH

Zechariah was a contemporary of Haggai who had a similar concern regarding the worship of God but who focused more on future issues: while Haggai presented his message in the style of the traditional prophet, Zechariah's message was more apocalyptic (see ch. 15, above). Zechariah was a priest, apparently born in Babylon, and had traveled back to Jerusalem with Zerubbabel and Joshua.[7] His first message is dated in the eighth month of Darius's second year (520 BCE), so he began his ministry between Haggai's second and third proclamation (Hag. 2:1, 10).

Read Zechariah 1–14.

above, left to right

OLIVE PRESS. An underground press that gently squeezed the oil from ripe olives. Being underground helped keep the oil from becoming rancid.

MILL. A grain mill in southern Judea that was part of the same underground complex as the olive press.

Zechariah begins his book like a classic prophet. He reports "the word of the LORD" that had come to him—a cry for the people to return to God. He draws on history that the people would know and understand. God had told their ancestors to repent and had sent prophets to warn them. These measures had not worked, and God's judgments had overtaken the people. That was the reason the nation was in the fix it was in now. It was back in the land after a long exile, but the temple was not yet built. The people's faith in God was still lacking. At this point in the book, Zechariah begins reporting his visions.

The visions of Zechariah are difficult to understand, but fortunately, angelic messengers tell him (and us) the salient points of each. Thus, while many details are not clear, the main lesson is. For example, Zechariah's second vision (1:18–21) consists of four horns. In Daniel we read of horns associated with particular beasts representing the strength of specific kingdoms. Here, however, the angel tells Zechariah that the four horns represent the four powers or forces that scattered Judah, Israel, and Jerusalem. The craftsmen in the vision were said to be counter-forces that would throw down the powers represented by the horns.

The point of these visions seems to lie in Zechariah 1:16–17. God had been angry at Israel and had used foreign nations to exact punishment. However, those powers had gone beyond what they should have. Therefore, they would now be punished. Zechariah's visions tie all of this with the coming Messiah and the purification of Israel.[8] While no date was given for those events, the nation apparently took them to heart as soon-to-be-fulfilled promises. Based on the spiritual encouragement of Haggai and Zechariah, they plunged into the work, and in a few years, the temple was finished.

A couple of years later, with the construction of the temple in full swing, representatives from Bethel came to Zechariah and asked a profound question. Now that the people had returned and the temple was being rebuilt, should they continue to fast? God's reply was that they had been fasting for the wrong reason. They were in mourning for the loss of the temple rather than because they had displeased God. Instead of fasting, the people should have been making sure that they were living righteous lives as shown by justice, kindness, and compassion toward one another.

The last part of the book is undated, but its message clearly was given during the time of construction. Its purpose was to be an encouragement to the builders. For example, the Lord said in Zechariah 8:9, "Let your hands be strong so that the temple may be built." He also told the people to listen to the prophets in this regard. Yet the real encouragement was for the long term. God would judge the nations round about, but more important, the Messiah was coming. Through Zechariah, the Lord encouraged the people by telling them that Zion's king would come riding on a donkey (9:9).[9] Later we read of how He would be sold for thirty shekels of silver, which would then be thrown "into the house of the LORD to the potter" (11:12–13). Still later we read that the nation would look at the Messiah they had killed and mourn "as one mourns for an only child" (12:10).[10] The book culminates in a proclamation of a future time when the nation would be restored and in a holy state.

> Through Zechariah, the Lord encouraged the people by saying that He would judge the nations round about and, more important, that the Messiah was coming.

THE FOUR HORNS

While the angel explains that the horns represent four forces that scattered the Israelites, no national identities are given. Some have suggested Assyria, Egypt, Babylon, and Medo-Persia (Charles Ryrie, *Ryrie Study Bible*, note on Zech. 1:18–21). Others see a parallel with the four kingdoms of Daniel: Babylon, Medo-Persia, Greece, and Rome (C. F. Keil, *The Minor Prophets* [Grand Rapids: Eerdmans, 1977 reprint], 238). Others argue that no specific forces are intended; rather, the term *four* represents the cardinal points of the compass and thus the picture is one of total opposition (Joyce Baldwin, *Haggai, Zechariah, Malachi* [Downers Grove, Ill.: InterVarsity, 1975], 104). Another possibility, since no "beasts" are presented with the horns, is that they represent the spiritual forces behind the scenes causing the scattering. The fact that the four were viewed as existing in the present (at the time of Zechariah) but that their actions had occurred in the past supports this interpretation.

EZRA AND THE LAW

Read Ezra 7–10. Skipping over the story of Esther and Mordecai (which we looked at in the previous chapter), we come now to the time of Ezra. The temple had been completed in 515 BCE (Ezra 6:15), and we jump to about 457, which was the seventh year of the reign of the Persian king Artaxerxes I. We learn that Ezra led a small group from Persia to Judah. The families are listed in Ezra 7 with a total of approximately 1,772 males.[11]

Although we are not told why Ezra decided to go, nor why Artaxerxes offered such generous support, we can find some hints. The text stresses that Ezra was knowledgeable in the law, and the decree that Artaxerxes sends also stresses observance of the law.[12] As a pagan king, Artaxerxes most likely would not have been concerned about observing God's laws, although that was what the decree mandated. However, he would have been concerned if a given region of the empire was lawless. This consideration seems to suggest that the key purpose of sending Ezra and his associates was to bring order to a region that was somewhat chaotic. The best way to restore stability was to send leaders who would be accepted by the group to teach law. In this case, they would teach a higher law, which would bring about the desired results.

As he did so, Ezra was presented with the challenge of intermarriage among the Israelites. It was not so much the intermarriage per se that was the issue, but the fact that the foreign wives were bringing their "detestable practices" (Ezra 9:1).[13] Confronted by the evidence, the people admitted their sin. After a prayer of confession, they called an assembly at which the leadership investigated all of these marriages on a case-by-case basis. The process took about three months. The book ends with a list of the men involved: it includes 113 men, of whom 27 were priests and Levites.[14] The outcome is not clear. The stated purpose of the assembly was that the foreign wives would be divorced and sent home (along with their children). According to some scholars, however, the text states only that the first four in the list did this (Ezra 10:18–19), leaving open the possibility that the

EZRA AND NEHEMIAH

During the past century, some scholars have questioned whether Ezra and Nehemiah were contemporaries. Because of papyrus documents found on Elephantine Island in Egypt, Nehemiah is considered firmly dated in the reign of Artaxerxes I; therefore, it is argued that Ezra must have lived at a later date, that is, during the reign of Artaxerxes II (404–359 BCE). There are several apparent anomalies in the text, such as Nehemiah's seeming lack of awareness of Ezra's handling of the divorce case, that cause these scholars to restructure the entire account. These are adequately addressed in Derek Kidner, *Ezra and Nehemiah* (Downers Grove, Ill.: InterVarsity, 1979), 146–58.

others did not. The book ends abruptly here. Ezra had apparently accomplished what he had come to do.

NEHEMIAH AND THE WALLS

Nehemiah was another Jew whose family had remained in exile. He personally was a highly trusted member of King Artaxerxes' court. It was approximately 445 BCE when he received information from his brother, Hanani, concerning the Israelites living in Judah. We are not told what Hanani's role was, but the report he brought was apparently unexpected.[15] The bombshell as far as Nehemiah was concerned was that the walls of Jerusalem were still unbuilt.

Read Nehemiah 1–7.

It is not completely clear from the material we have why Nehemiah would have expected the walls to have been rebuilt. Haggai, Ezra, and Zechariah all concentrated on the temple. Ezra 4:21 does note a decree by Artaxerxes to stop building the city, but this was in the beginning of his reign (c. 464 BCE); Nehemiah's trip was twenty years later. Ezra 9:9, however, seems to suggest that

DARIUS INSCRIPTION AT BEHISTUN. An inscription by Darius the Great, written in three languages, which proved to be a key to deciphering cuneiform. Behistun was a town in what is now western Iran.

one of Ezra's tasks after he arrived in 457 was to rebuild the walls.[16] If that was the case, Nehemiah may well have been surprised that the task was incomplete. Regardless of the cause, clearly he was dismayed at the state of Jerusalem.

At this point, Nehemiah began to show excellent management and leadership skills. He had just been presented with a problem. The first step he took was to pray about it. As is the case in many of the great prayers of the Bible, his was a prayer of confession in which he included himself as part of the problem. His requests were purely for the glory of the God he served. After the prayer, he continued in his tasks but continued to ponder the situation.

Although Nehemiah resolved not to allow his personal sorrow to affect his work, the king noticed his sad demeanor and asked him the cause (Neh. 2:2). Nehemiah stated his problem succinctly. When Artaxerxes asked him what he wanted to do, he quickly breathed another prayer, then took a risk and stated his proposal. Clearly, he had spent the intervening time working out a possible solution, for he could give the king specific details regarding what resources he would need and how long the project would take. With this, Artaxerxes granted his request and sent him to Jerusalem for a twelve-year term as governor. Nehemiah then gathered the forces he needed to travel as the king's emissary. En route he presented himself to the leaders of the opposition and showed his credentials. While they were irate, there was nothing they could do.

> Nehemiah gave evidence that his solution regarding the wall would work by showing how God had worked to that point.

When Nehemiah arrived at Jerusalem, he spent three days surveying the lay of the land before taking any action. Then he made a night trip around the city to assess the situation. It was only after this that he approached the leaders of the community with the job he had in mind. As he did so, he presented it as a problem of which he was part and proposed a common solution. He gave evidence that his solution would work by showing what God had done to that point.

Once he got agreement on the proposed solution, Nehemiah organized the forces in such a way that each of the groups felt an identity in their part of the project. Each family or professional group worked on the section of the wall closest to their houses or places of work. The different groups appear to have been set in competition with one another. As the work progressed and opposition arose, Nehemiah never lost sight of the objective.[17] As a result, they were able to build the walls in fifty-two days.

REDEDICATION AND BACKSLIDING

Read Nehemiah 8–13. After the walls were complete, Nehemiah and Ezra gathered the people for a covenant renewal ceremony.[18] At that time, the Law was read and explained. This explanation likely consisted of two parts. First the Law was translated into Aramaic, a language closely related to the Hebrew in which the Law was writ-

NEHEMIAH'S COVENANT

While several times throughout the history of the nation we read of the people agreeing to observe the Law, the ceremony described in Nehemiah 10 puts a new twist on it. It is the first time we read of the leaders signing their names (affixing their seals) to a document. In this case, eighty-four men are listed, beginning with Nehemiah. Interestingly, Ezra is not one of them, apparently because those who signed were the heads of the families. In Nehemiah 12:13, we read that the head of Ezra's family was Meshullam, who did sign the covenant.

ten. During the Exile, it had become the spoken language of the people. Then the leaders explained the practical ramifications of the individual laws.

As they did so, the people realized that they needed to celebrate Sukkoth, which was supposed to begin on the fifteenth day of the seventh month (Lev. 23:39). They spent the next two weeks gathering the requisite branches to build the booths and otherwise preparing. After the festival, which celebrated both Sukkoth and the completion of the walls, the people repented. This repentance would have been expected for the tenth of the month (Yom Kippur), but apparently the leaders did not wish to dampen the positive spirit.[19] Here the festival set the stage for a new phase in the life of the people as they dedicated the newly completed city walls.

The dedication was led by the Levites. It was initiated by a declarative praise psalm that succinctly recited the history of the nation. The leaders then signed a pledge to God to observe the Law God had given to them through Moses (Neh. 10). The text gives us the basic criteria of the oath: they would not intermarry with the surrounding peoples; they would keep the Sabbath day and Sabbath year; they would ensure that the one-third shekel temple tax would be collected and used properly; and they would ensure that the firstfruits, the firstborn, and the tithes were brought to the temple. After the city walls were dedicated, Nehemiah and others realized that the city of Jerusalem was grossly underpopulated. They then drew lots to move a tenth of the overall population of Judea into the city (11:1).

When Nehemiah had completed his twelve-year term as governor, he returned to Susa. Later he went back to Jerusalem for a second term. While he was gone, things had apparently not gone well. He discovered that the portion for the Levites was not coming in and that the Sabbath was not being honored. More critically, he discovered that the priest Eliashib had given a room in the temple court to Tobiah. Not only was Tobiah an Ammonite (who according to the law of Moses was expressly forbidden from entering the assembly), but he also had been one of the adversaries to the construction of the wall.

Nehemiah had Tobiah evicted. He cleansed the rooms in the temple, reinstituted the tithe to the Levites, and reestablished the closing down of the city on the Sabbath. Once again he addressed the issue of mixed marriages.[20] It is in this last account that we learn that the problem of the mixed marriages was that the children were not even learning to speak "the language of Judah" (Neh. 13:24). If they were unable to speak the language of the people, they certainly could not read God's law—and apparently they did not.

MALACHI: THE CLOSING OF THE BOOK

Read Malachi 1–4. The OT wraps up with one final word from God. The book of Malachi is written in the style of a classic prophet bringing the word of the Lord to Israel. Malachi's message was simple and straightforward. While the people of Judea had gotten the external form of their worship right and were avoiding idolatry, they had missed the heart of worship. This is evident in the Lord's accusations that the people were bringing inferior animals as sacrifices. They complained that the entire process was a burden. They also robbed God by not bringing their tithes and offerings. Although they went through the rituals, they really did not worship God, and yet they complained that God did not listen to them. More than that, in their arrogance they stated that it was vain to serve God.

HELLENISTIC INFLUENCE. A cave near Caesarea Philippi that is associated with the worship of Pan, a Greek god over pastures, flocks, and forests. While the earlier returners from exile strove diligently to purify their worship of God, Hellenistic influences permeated the land after Alexander's conquest.

THE AUTHOR AND DATE OF MALACHI

The name Malachi means "my messenger." As such, some have suggested that the author of the book wished to remain anonymous. Malachi was more likely the prophet's name, but nothing else is said about him in the OT. The date of the book is uncertain, although there are several indications that it was written sometime after the Exile. For example, the title "governor" in Malachi 1:8 is a Persian term applied to both Zerubbabel (Hag. 1:1) and Nehemiah (Neh. 5:14). Furthermore, it is clear from the context that the temple worship was in full swing, indicating a period after the construction of that building. Some scholars go further and point to Daniel 9:25, which says that from the decree to restore and rebuild Jerusalem (which is commonly understood to be the decree to Nehemiah mentioned in Neh. 2:5–8) there would be two periods of time: seven sevens (49 years) and sixty-two sevens (434 years) until the Messiah. It has been demonstrated that the total period of 483 years correlates to the time from the decree to the crucifixion of Jesus (see ch. 19, below). No one is sure why the period is divided, though some suggest that the first time frame would mark the conclusion of God's written revelation to the nation in what we call the OT. If so, Malachi as the last OT book would have been written in approximately 397 BCE, which would correlate well with the traditional date of composition (c. 400).

However, as was the case with the other prophets, Malachi also had words of promise. First, he assured the people that God would be sending a messenger to prepare the way. That future event would be a time of testing when the false and unfaithful would be burned up but the true and faithful would be proven, healed, and victorious. This would be the time known as "the day of the LORD."

Malachi then gave a final promise that before that "day" occurred, God would send Elijah. His ministry would be one of restoration and healing. With that declaration, the OT canon closed. The community of believers somehow understood that no more books were to be forthcoming, although there would be other prophets (e.g., Simeon and Anna, who had revelations from God in the temple; see Luke 2:26, 36). With this understanding, the Jewish people began a conversation that would last several hundred years. The focus of their discussion was on what they should do to keep the Law.

> While the people of Judea had gotten the external form of their worship right and were avoiding idolatry, they had missed the heart of worship.

REVIEW QUESTIONS

1. What allowed the people initially to return to their land?

2. What was the function of Haggai?

3. How was Zechariah's ministry different from that of Haggai, his contemporary?

4. What was Ezra's role in the return?

5. How did Nehemiah help the struggling community in Jerusalem?

6. What is the significance of Malachi?

PART

2

THE BLESSING

INTRODUCTION

Not long ago, I listened as a well-meaning woman asked a friend of mine in his Sunday school class, "Why do we bother to study the Old Testament? Christ did away with it all, so it's irrelevant." I trust that by this point we have begun to realize that the OT is not irrelevant. It lays a solid prophetic, historical, and theological foundation for the work Jesus did. Without the OT, we would have no idea of what Jesus meant when He claimed to be the Messiah.

We have now laid that foundation. We are ready to explore the claims of Jesus based on it. We have jumped four hundred years from the time when the OT closed. The language of the biblical text is Greek now, not Hebrew. As a result, some of the terms have changed. For example, in the OT, we talked about the Messiah; in the NT, we read about (the) Christ. They mean the same thing. To show the continuity between the two books, we will use some of the same Eng-

lish terms to bridge the gap. Thus, we will call Jesus the Messiah rather than (the) Christ.

A number of points of continuity could be listed. The process of inspiration discussed with the OT has remained the same. The criteria for acknowledging books as canonical have remained the same. The problems in the world were also the same, and we will see the same wide spectrum of reactions to God's Word.

We observed in chapter 3 that the root problem of the world was the Fall. We have seen how the national covenant with the nation of Israel proved to be inadequate to resolve that spiritual problem. That is the reason Jesus came—to provide a solution for humankind's basic problem. But before we get to Jesus, we need to understand how the world had changed during the four-hundred-year gap between the two parts of our Bible, what we call the Old Testament and New Testament.

17

CHAPTER

Bridges to the New Testament

OVERVIEW

During the four hundred years between the OT and the NT, a number of changes took place within the Judean culture. In terms of religion, we see many books being written but not added to the canon; these include the collections we know as the Apocrypha, the Mishnah, and the Pseudepigrapha. We see the development of the religious groupings of the NT: the Pharisees, Sadducees, and Essenes, among others. In terms of political structure, we see the nation go from serving Persia to serving the Greeks—first under Alexander and then under either the Ptolemies or the Seleucids—then achieve independence, and finally end up serving Rome.

When we left the Jewish community at the end of what is called the OT (about 400 BCE), we noticed several key points. While a significant number of the Jews had returned to their land, many had opted to stay in the lands of their dispersion (the Diaspora). The Jews who were back in the land were fairly united as they struggled to maintain their religious heritage against both internal and external enemies. Ezra, Nehemiah, and the last group of prophets guided the community of believers as they discussed what it meant to be faithful to God. The discussion was couched in terms of keeping the Law. Those Jews were also looking for the Messiah whom God had promised to send, but they seemed to anticipate that the event was far off.

The dominant world government was the Persian Empire, whose capital was about a thousand miles east. Under the Persians, what had been the Southern Kingdom of Judah became the province of Judea, which enjoyed a fair degree of self-government—after all, it was the Persians who had allowed them to return and to rebuild the temple. The international trade language was Aramaic, a language related to Hebrew; because of this, two of the last books added to the canon (Ezra and Daniel) include sections written in Aramaic. After Malachi was added to the canon, no more prophets arose whose works measured up. So somewhere during the following centuries, the Jewish community came to the conclusion that God had nothing more to say to them.

In most of our English Bibles, we turn a page or two, and we find ourselves in the NT, approximately four hundred years later. We don't see it immediately, but we soon learn that many of the Jews were still dispersed throughout the

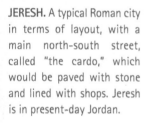

JERESH. A typical Roman city in terms of layout, with a main north-south street, called "the cardo," which would be paved with stone and lined with shops. Jeresh is in present-day Jordan.

world, although there was now a sizable population in Judea. We discover that there were several religious-political parties vying for power. The discussion that had begun shortly after Ezra and Nehemiah had become an intense debate. Most Jews were still looking for the Messiah, but by this time there was an underlying expectation that He might come soon. The dominant world government was now the Roman Empire, whose capital was about 1,500 miles west. Under the Roman government, Judea enjoyed a degree of self-government but less than it had experienced under Persia. The international trade language was now Greek, and many of the Jews in the Diaspora used it instead of Hebrew or Aramaic.

It was into this milieu that Jesus was born. After His time on earth, new books were written that many considered canonical. We call their collection the NT. Before we look at Jesus, however, we need to set the stage by looking at how the geopolitical situation had changed. In doing so, we will look at three bridges that take us from the OT to the NT. Each of the bridges consists of several "arches" moving us from one side of the four hundred "silent years" to the other.

THE LITERARY BRIDGE

The part of the canon that we call the OT is the same collection of books the Jews at the time of Jesus viewed as authoritative. The last books the Jewish community considered canonical had been written about 400 BCE. This did not mean, however, that the Jewish people stopped writing books. In fact, many books were written during this period, some of which we still have today. But these other books were not accepted as canon. Today we place these other books into three basic categories: the Apocrypha, the Mishnah, and the Pseudepigrapha and other works.

The Apocrypha

The Apocrypha is the collection of books that is found between the OT and NT in some Bibles.[1] The Greek word *apocryphon* (plural, *apocrypha*) means "hidden" or "secret." Apparently the collection got this title because it was not to be read to the congregation (in ancient and medieval times many people could not read). The early church fathers knew that the Apocrypha had not been accepted by the Jews and the apostles, and thus they never included these books in the canon. Some have argued that the reason was that most of the apocryphal books were written in Greek and not Hebrew. More likely, the Jewish faithful who read the works when they came out agreed that they did not measure up to the standard of canon. As such, this decision would reflect the guiding work of the Holy Spirit. Regardless of the reason, the community of believers drew a distinction between the canon and the Apocrypha at a very early stage, it would seem from the outset.

SCROLL. The medium used by Israelites to record important works, including the text of the canon. They were probably developed before the Exile, but our earliest copies date from about 200 BCE, during this transition period. Passages were not always easy to find (see Luke 4:17).

THE JEWISH BIBLE

Some scholars have argued that the Hebrew Bible of the Jews at the time of Jesus was different from what we call the OT. This point has been argued on two fronts. First, there are differences between the Masoretic Hebrew text (MT) and the Greek of the Septuagint (LXX). Second, some Hebrew texts with differences have been found in various places such as Qumran (the Dead Sea Scrolls). However, the Jewish scholar Lawrence Schiffman argues convincingly that what we now call the MT was the accepted canon (*Reclaiming the Dead Sea Scrolls* [New York: Doubleday, 1995], 161–80). A less technical overview of this position is provided by Randall Price (*Secrets of the Dead Sea Scrolls* [Eugene, Ore.: Harvest House, 1996]). He suggests that the Jews considered the LXX a translation and thus less authoritative, somewhat like one of our modern paraphrases.

The Apocrypha included a wide variety of books. For example, 1 Maccabees is a good historical account of the Maccabean revolt, which we will cover below as part of the political bridge. On the other hand, the story of Susanna and the elders, which intends to show how wise Daniel was and carries a great message, probably never happened; we would place it today in the category of some of the legendary accounts of our own founding fathers, such as Washington chopping down a cherry tree. Ecclesiasticus is a wisdom book similar to Proverbs. Bel and the Dragon reminds one of a Hardy Boys mystery story.

The exact origin of these books and their status through the ages is widely debated by scholars. While Apocryphal books are included in copies of the Septuagint, these were all copied by Christian scribes. There is no evidence that the Jews ever viewed them as canonical.[2] It is evident that the early church, along with the Jews, never regarded the Apocryphal books on a par with the OT canon.[3] After Jerome included the Apocrypha as part of the Latin Vulgate, they were held in higher esteem, especially in the Western church, which adopted the Latin version as the official version. During the medieval period, some points of theology, such as the idea of purgatory, were developed from the Apocrypha.

At the time of the Protestant Reformation, the Reformers noted the differences in quality and declared that the Apocrypha was not canonical. In reaction the Roman Catholic Church declared at the Council of Trent in 1546 that it was deuterocanonical. The exact meaning of this term (which often is interpreted as "second canon") is debatable.

The Mishnah and Talmud

A second, less familiar arch to the literary bridge dealt with the OT law. After the Jews decided that God had nothing more to say, they began concentrating on how to apply the revelation He had already given. Because of the Exile, their focus was on how to live up to the Torah ("law") on a daily basis. Thus, around the year 400 BCE, the Jewish religious leaders began a discussion regarding what was needed to keep the law. This growing oral tradition was written down about 200 CE. in a multivolume work called the *Mishnah* (meaning "repetition," that is, "study or teaching by repeated recitation"). In some respects, the Mishnah is a commentary on the Law, but it is also a record of the debate and the conclusions the Jewish rabbis reached.

For example, one of the chief concerns of the Jewish leaders of the period was observing the Sabbath. Everyone agreed that keeping the Sabbath meant that people were not to work. The problem was that not everyone agreed on what constituted work. After centuries of debate (and if you look carefully, you will see that Jesus was right in the middle of it), the rabbis reached an agreement that is recorded in a tractate of the Mishnah entitled *Shabbat* (Sabbath). It is this final agreement that is the foundation of modern Jewish law.

> After the Jews decided that God had nothing more to say, they began concentrating on how to apply the revelation He had already given.

After the destruction of the temple in 70 CE, many of the rituals and laws were put into abeyance. Without a temple, one could not sacrifice. Then in 110 CE, the Roman emperor expelled the Jews from Palestine. While the Mishnah debate continued, the Jewish community soon turned to a new discussion. This discussion was eventually recorded in the *Gemarah* (meaning "completion, the learning of oral teaching, tradition"), which is basically a commentary on the Mishnah, explaining how it can be carried out away from the land and without a temple.

The Mishnah and the Gemarah together constitute the *Talmud* ("teaching, learning"). This composite work, which was completed about 500 CE, is the heart of modern Judaism. In fact, in many respects, modern Judaism depends more on the Talmud, the commentary, than it does on the Torah.

More obscure to Christian audiences are *Targumim* and *Midrashim*. These were interpretive translations of the Hebrew text designed to make the text more understandable to Jews who did not read Hebrew. Targumim were generally in Aramaic but also in Greek. Their main purpose was to make the text more understandable. Midrashim were more expository. Both give some insight into how certain portions of text were understood during the period of Mishnah (about 200 BCE–200 CE).[4]

There is quite a bit of discussion about why Christianity and Judaism split, but the data suggest that several factors were involved. Of course, the primary issue was the question of whether Jesus was the Messiah. A second factor was this entire debate on the keeping of the Law. As the temple was destroyed and the Mishnah was completed, a reaction against Christian understanding of the OT seems to have set in.[5] This reaction is evident in the Gemarah.

OSSUARY. A decorated box made of stone in which the bones of a person were reburied a year or so after a body had been allowed to decay. The practice began during the intertestamental period. In 2002 an ossuary was discovered that is labeled "James, son of Joseph, brother of Jesus," but scholars disagree as to whether it contains the bones of Jesus' brother.

THE TALMUD

There are two versions of the Talmud. The Palestinian Talmud was developed primarily in Tiberias, a town in Galilee. Here a number of Jewish scholars settled after they were expelled from Jerusalem and continued their scholarly discussions. The second version is the Babylonian Talmud, written primarily in Babylon, where a large number of Jews still resided after the exile of the Southern Kingdom and continued to reside even after NT times. Ironically, the Babylonian Talmud became the dominant version and is the one primarily used by Jews today.

The Pseudepigrapha and Other Works

Our third arch is a catchall category that includes many works produced by Jewish writers. Some of these were written prior to the NT period, while others originated in the last part of the first century and beyond. The Greek word *pseudepigraphon* means "written under a false name," and the plural *Pseudepigrapha* was first applied to works attributed to someone other than the actual writer, usually a noted prophet. As additional Jewish writings were identified, however, they were placed in the same category even if they were not written under an assumed name. Moreover, the Dead Sea Scrolls (DSS) include not only copies of the biblical books but also a number of other works that shed light on the culture of the period between the testaments.[6]

Other works help shed light on the period. One is that of Philo, a Jewish philosopher who lived in Alexandria about the time of Jesus (c. 20 BCE–50 CE). Another is the historical work of Josephus, who lived late in the first century (37 CE–c. 100 CE). However, they did not directly contribute to the transition in religious thinking that led to the NT milieu. Periodically, some Pseudepigrapha will be presented as "lost books of the Bible." This is a misnomer, because they have never been lost. The church has known about most of them throughout its existence—and rejected them as forgeries. In the same vein, some have suggested that the delay in publication of the DSS was because of explosive secrets that scholars were trying to hide. Now that the scrolls have been published (at least in preliminary form), it is clear that this is not the case. The primary delay was a failure of the scholars concerned to make the publication a priority.

Summary

The literary bridge in general reflects the trends and changes we have already observed. The early texts are in Hebrew; the later texts, in Greek. In the DSS especially, there is a significant focus on prophecy, especially relating to the Messiah. Coupled with this, while in the early works we find a basic acceptance of the Persian government, toward the end we see increasing opposition to Roman rule. More important, we sense a greater hunger for holiness, which is evidenced by the change from the tendency toward idolatry in the OT to the increasing legalism of later Jewish literature. This brings us to our second bridge, the religious setting.

CAVE 4 AT QUMRAN. The place where the Dead Sea Scrolls were discovered in 1947. These scrolls, dating from 200 BCE, are a thousand years older than any previously known manuscripts of the OT text.

THE RELIGIOUS BRIDGE

The religious bridge moves us from a fairly homogeneous social and religious structure[7] shortly after the return from exile to a society that was divided into several strong parties. In some respects, these were religious segments, but because the religious leaders really ran the country, they also were political. The key groups were the Pharisees, Sadducees, and Essenes; also significant were the scribes who identified themselves with different parties.[8] In essence, the various groups derived from different ways of addressing the same issue: How do we tie together our faith and our culture?

During the centuries following Ezra and Nehemiah, two totally different primary thought processes emerged that divided the Jews into two basic camps. The first may be considered a conservative view. The mind-set was, "We must return to our roots." Those who followed this view could be called *traditionalists*. The second thought process might be considered a more liberal view. This mind-set was, "How do we accommodate our Judaism to a different culture and new ideas?" Those who followed this view could be called *accommodationists*. While the Jewish society was divided into these two major viewpoints, there seemed to be a tremendous amount of disagreement *within* the two camps. So what we are really

NEW TESTAMENT APOCRYPHA

The terms Apocrypha and Pseudepigrapha are most frequently applied to Jewish books associated with the OT. During the first centuries of the Christian church, however, many works were also falsely attributed to the apostles. These Christian pseudepigrapha, and other similar works, are usually placed under the category of NT Apocrypha (see Wilhelm Schneemelcher, ed., *New Testament Apocrypha*, rev. ed., 2 vols. [Louisville: Westminster John Knox, 1992]). In addition, an important collection of Coptic writings was found in Nag Hammadi in Egypt in the late 1940s. These books include a work called *The Gospel of Thomas*, which has been significant in the Jesus Seminar discussions. However, because these works are gnostic, it would appear that they had been rejected by the church as a whole long before they were buried in the late 300s (see James M. Robinson, ed., *The Nag Hammadi Library in English*, 4th ed. [Leiden: Brill, 1996]).

looking at is a spectrum between two extremes, with about twenty different distinct groups evident.[9]

The traditionalists could also be called Hebraists, because they wanted to maintain a Hebrew culture, using the Hebrew language, following a rigid interpretation of the Jewish law. For the most part, they seem to have been located in Palestine or Babylon. In time they came to be known as the *Asideans* or *Hasideans* (a name derived from the Greek form of the Hebrew term *Hasidim*, which means "pious ones"). Their goal was to revive Jewish ritual, to study the Jewish law, and to root out paganism. In this respect, they may be seen as the followers of Ezra and Nehemiah. They became the nucleus of the Maccabean revolt.

The accommodationists were also called Hellenists. In contrast to the Hebraists, the Hellenists were more widely dispersed and tended to accept the cultures of the various lands in which they lived more willingly. After Alexander, the Greek language and culture united his empire, and the key ideas now were Greek or Hellenic. Consequently, these Jews learned to speak Greek, the new international trade language, and used that as their means of communication.

The development of these two groups is not well understood, and the following is an oversimplification. The Hebraists drew on the *oral tradition* to substantiate their position. This oral tradition was basically a method of interpretation passed from one generation to the next that validated their legalistic interpretations of the Law. They argued that they were passing down a second law given by Moses after the written law given at Mount Sinai. There is nothing to substantiate this position. However, no one really knows how this verbal record originated. A key problem with this concept is the Mishnah itself. If there was a true "oral tradition," why was so much dissension and disagreement recorded in the Mishnah?

The Hellenization process stood in opposition. Did the concept of oral tradition arise as a reaction to the Hellenization process, or did the two opposite strands arise at the same time? Or is it possible that the Hellenization process arose as a reaction to what some saw as a too-strict legalism? These are questions to which we have no answer.

Sadducees

We will begin with the Hellenistic side. The Sadducees developed from a Hellenization movement sometime after the Maccabean revolt. Apparently the group was named after the priest Zadok. It became the party of the Jerusalem aristocracy and the temple priesthood. The Sadducees and Pharisees seem to have arisen at about the same time as the Jews tried to sort out several issues and had to take sides.

The Sadducees got a great boost under John Hyrcanus (see below) when he espoused their cause and promoted their secular and pro-Hellenistic philosophy. Their primary concern seems to have been to avoid confrontation with the secular "powers that be." As a result, they were often viewed by the people as selling out—first to the Syrians and then to the Romans. Ironically, they were strict in the sense of "law and order" but not in adherence to the distinctive qualities of the OT law.

The Sadducees seem to have built their understanding of the Law on Greek (Hellenistic) philosophical speculation. For example, on the issue of man's free will and God's sovereignty, they opted for a strong position of free will.[10] They argued against any resurrection of the dead and any future life (whether one of joy or sorrow). They argued that the soul perished with the body, and they tended to be very materialistic (which perhaps accords with their aristocratic status). They also rejected any belief in angels or demons, denying the spirit realm and viewing God as a very limited being. Their legal positions, while supposedly drawn from a strict understanding of the *written* Mosaic law, were developed through this grid. Because of their emphasis on the written law, they rejected the rigid interpretations based on the oral tradition or oral law as developed by the Pharisees.

Pharisees

The Pharisees probably owe their existence both to the foundation that Ezra and Nehemiah laid and to a reaction against the cultural syncretism of the Sadducees. Apparently coming out of a movement known as *Hasideans* or *Hasidim* ("pious ones"), one strand of the Hebraists became known as the *perushim* or "separated ones." At first this term was apparently intended as an insult, but later it was

---

THE DIASPORA

When Zerubbabel and Ezra led the exiles back to Palestine, most of the Jews did not return. Instead, they remained in Babylon, Persia, and other locations where their parents and grandparents had been forcibly resettled. Many also remained in Egypt, where they had fled to avoid captivity. Later, either as a result of persecution or other pressures, they dispersed throughout the world. As a result, by the time of Jesus, we have record of Jewish settlements as far west as Spain and as far east as India. There may have been settlements as far east as China, but the sources are unclear about how early Jews arrived there (see Sidney Shapiro, *Jews in Old China* [New York: Hippocrene Books, 1988]).

proudly accepted by this group itself. Because of the confrontations Jesus had with the Pharisees, we tend to view them negatively. However, it would appear that Jesus only argued with a minority that was viewed by the rest of the Pharisees as extremely legalistic.

In contrast to the Sadducees, the Pharisees were largely middle or lower class, both businessmen (predominantly) and priests (or Levites). Their chief concern was following the Law and, more specifically, how to apply the Law to various day-to-day issues. The Pharisees tried to follow a strict adherence to the OT law—as supplemented by the *oral law* (oral tradition). Doctrinally, they looked toward an eschatological future centered on a messiah who would lead Israel to greater glories than it had ever enjoyed in the past. This would be a time of righteousness, which would include those who had died (a general resurrection). They viewed humans as having a free will, but they also understood God to be a Sovereign God who was ultimately in control. They were very cognizant of the spirit world and the hierarchies of angels. They also argued for a general equality of all human beings.

Essenes

The third important religious party was the Essenes, a much more conservative group than the Pharisees. Although the Essenes made up one of three parties mentioned by the Jewish historian Josephus, at the time of Jesus it played an insignificant role. Apparently the Essenes split off from the Hasideans (who became the Pharisees) about twenty years before the Maccabean revolt (thus about 180 BCE). As might be expected from an origin common to that of the Pharisees, many of the doctrines of the two groups are similar. The origin of the name is uncertain, and many suggestions have been made, none of which is satisfactory. The most likely is that it is derived from the Greek *hosiōtes*, meaning "holiness."[11] More significantly, they never referred to themselves as Essenes. Apparently they called themselves "Sons of Zadok" (sometimes referred to as "Covenanters of Damascus").

Because they were a minority party and because of conflicts with the Pharisees, they had essentially abandoned Jerusalem by the time of Herod and were dispersed throughout the rural countryside. Many scholars think that Qumran was an Essene community, although this is debated.[12]

While doctrinally the Essenes were linked to the Pharisees, they followed a much stricter lifestyle, one we would call ascetic. They followed a strict daily regimen, beginning with early prayer. They worked long hours at assigned jobs and participated in frequent ritual cleansing, communal meals, and study of Scripture and group rules. They also gave all their possessions to the community. Admission to the group was by trial. First, a one-year period determined whether the candidate had the desired characteristics. After that was passed, there was a two-year probation period. Only then was a candidate admitted to full membership. After that, there was strict punishment for violation of a number of rules. Most

Essenes were celibate, although at least one group used marriage strictly for reproduction, thus insuring succession.

Estimates indicate that there were about four thousand Essenes in the first century. Since most of the Essenes were dispersed in small towns and villages, their influence in Jerusalem was minimal at this time. This may explain why there is no overt mention of them in the NT.

Scribes

One other group we find in the NT is the scribes. *Scribe* was a professional title, a generic term that could include both Pharisees and Sadducees. Scribes traced their office back to the time of Ezra "the scribe" (Ezra 7:11 NRSV). Their primary functions were to *copy* the Law, to *read* it, and then to *interpret* it to the people. This latter function was to become critical for what became rabbinic Judaism. This was the process that produced the Mishnah and later the Gemarah (which together made up the Talmud). When the scribes challenged Jesus, it was not on account of the OT law, but on the traditional *interpretations* of the Law, which had already acquired a legal authority by this time.

Zealots

One last group that should be mentioned is the Zealots. The Zealots were the extreme nationalists. According to Josephus, the movement started in reaction to Herod the Great.[13] Their goal was to rid Israel of any outside rulers, so as to serve only YHWH. As a result, they refused to pay taxes, they murdered officials, and they rejected Greek as a means of communication. In many respects, they functioned as a terrorist organization as they fought for the liberation of Judea.

Summary

These religious groups also dominated the social and political environment at the time of Jesus. As can be seen even in this cursory overview, the scene was complicated. It is very likely that the distinctions between the various groups, as in the case of our political parties today, were not as sharp as we have presented them and that there was some overlap of positions.

THE POLITICAL BRIDGE

During the same time frame (after 400 BCE), a number of world events occurred outside of Israel that profoundly affected the Jews and, ultimately, Christianity. This is our third bridge from the Persian Empire of the OT to the Roman Empire of the NT. As in the case of the other bridges, there are several arches.

When we left the OT, the nation had returned to the land, but it was still under the domination of the Persian Empire. Even school children know from the Christmas story that the birth of Jesus took place under the Roman Empire (ruled by Caesar Augustus). How did the nation get from the Medo-Persian

Empire, which was the second of the four world empires Daniel talked about, to the Roman Empire, which was the fourth?

Alexander the Great

The first arch is the Greek Empire. At the end of the OT period, the Persians were the world rulers. Their empire stretched from Egypt to the borders of India. At about the time of Esther, various Persian kings, including Darius and Xerxes, decided to expand to the west.

They were able to conquer Greek colonies in the western region of modern Turkey, but when they crossed the Bosporus, it was a different story. Each time, they suffered defeat when the Greeks used brilliant strategy and tactics to delay or beat forces that vastly outnumbered them. Even today the battles of Marathon (490 BCE), Thermopylae, and Salamis (the latter two in 480 BCE) are used around the world to train military officers.[14] These battles stopped the expansion of the Persians and allowed the Greeks to develop their civilization. We see the results of this development in the Greek classics, including the philosophical contributions of Socrates (c. 470–399 BCE), Plato (427–347 BCE), and Aristotle (384–322 BCE). Greek civilization, however, was really a loosely affiliated collection of city-states, such as Athens and Sparta, that cooperated only when necessary. After the threat of Persia was gone, the city-states squabbled for about

THE EMPIRE OF
ALEXANDER THE GREAT.

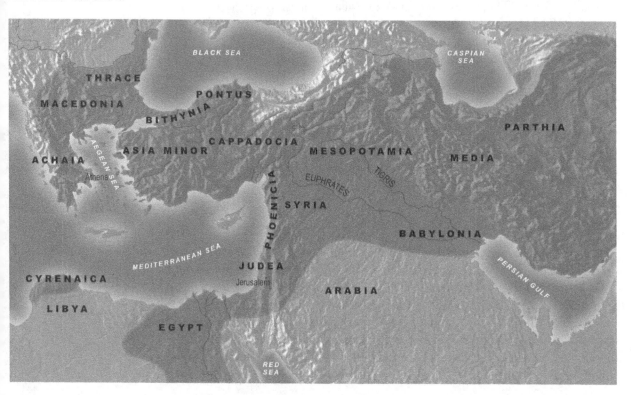

ALEXANDER'S ARMY

After Alexander conquered an army, he gave the defeated troops the opportunity to join his forces or die. Many of the soldiers were mercenaries and immediately went over to the higher bidder. This allowed his army to increase in size by more than 400 percent, despite casualties. The original troops from Macedonia and Greece became the officer corps, getting higher positions as the army grew.

fifty years. This broke out into outright warfare from 431 to 404 BCE, a conflict called the Peloponnesian War.

Coming out of this divided environment, Philip, a general in the northern region, unified the region of Macedonia in 358 BCE. His initial goal was access to the sea. But after he had done that, not content to rest, he went on to unite most of the Greek peninsula to the Peloponnesian or Bosporus straits. In 336 Philip was assassinated, and his son Alexander took over at the age of twenty. Alexander had already had four years of experience as a general, having assumed that role at the age of sixteen under his father. Because of his earlier successes, the Macedonian army quickly acclaimed him as Philip's successor. First, Alexander wrought vengeance on those thought responsible for Philip's death. He then reinforced his control over the regions that his father had conquered.

By 334 BCE, Alexander was ready for his real objective—the Persian Empire. With an army of 30,000 foot soldiers and 7,000 cavalry, he crossed the Dardanelles in the spring of that year. During the next three years, he went through Asia Minor, down through Egypt, and then took on Babylon. In 330 BCE, he marched northeast into what is now Iran and worked his way through what is today Afghanistan and Pakistan. By 327 BCE, he had moved into India with a force of 120,000, crossing the Indus River the following year. He desired to press on, and it is likely that he had the Ganges River and its civilization (that of the Buddha Gautama) in mind. After eight years of conquest, however, his troops had had enough and mutinied. Alexander worked his way back to Babylon in 325 BCE.

During the next two years, Alexander struggled with military and political unrest, and there are many questions as to what his policies really involved. He settled in Susa, the Persian capital. Many of his Macedonian followers felt that he was "going native." They wanted him to go back to Macedonia and rule from there. On the other hand, it might be argued that he developed an enlightened governmental process that amalgamated the various peoples under his rule. He gave land for new cities to his troops, and they held positions of leadership in these cities. As a result, his Greek-speaking army became a new ruling class. What effect this would have had on an empire that stretched from Greece to the Indus River is unknown, for Alexander was not able to enjoy the fruit of his labors for long. In 323 BCE, after

> Alexander the Great's Greek-speaking army became a new ruling class.

a prolonged banquet and drinking bout, he suddenly took ill; ten days later, on July 13, Alexander died.

Because Alexander had not appointed a successor, his generals struggled among themselves for position. After years of struggle, four key leaders predominated, and by 301 BCE the empire had been divided up as follows: Lysimachus had Thrace and Asia Minor; Cassander had control of Macedonia (including Greece); Ptolemy controlled Egypt (also Palestine and various other regions); and Seleucus ruled the Persian heartlands. The latter eventually gained control of Asia Minor, so the Seleucid and Ptolemaic Empires became the key forces in that region of the world. It must be noted that later several other forces began to erode the Seleucid region from the east.

At this time (c. 300 BCE) in the west, the Romans had just embarked on their campaigns to unite the Italian peninsula. During the next decade, they began to enjoy some success, although several significant powers, such as Carthage, were arrayed against them.[15] The outcome would be an open question for decades. In fact, it would be a few centuries before the Roman expansion reached empire status.

Thus, in terms of geopolitics, after 300 BCE the two major powers in the world were Ptolemy over Egypt and Seleucus over Syria (including Asia Minor in the west and Mesopotamia in the east). Their successors vied for dominance, and over the next 250 years, until the time of Cleopatra and Mark Antony, there was a constant power struggle between these two realms. After the death of Cleopatra, the Romans absorbed the last of this region. For about 150 years of that period, unfortunately, Judea with the returned exiles was caught in the middle. We read about this period in several of Daniel's visions of the future. The culminating vision is in Daniel 11, where the two opposing regions are called "the king of the South" (Egypt) and "the king of the North" (Syria) because of their geographic relationship to Israel.

SARCOPHAGUS OF ALEXANDER THE GREAT. A sarcophagus found in Sidon (and now housed in Istanbul), whose name comes from the scenes of Alexander's battles carved on the side. The occupant was unidentified, and Alexander's tomb has never been located.

Rulers of Egypt (Kings of the South)

Ptolemy I, one of Alexander's generals, founded the dynasty that ruled the southern part of Alexander's empire. This is our second arch, Egypt. Ptolemy also gained control of other areas, including the island of Cyprus and some footholds in southern Asia Minor, as well as Judea and southern Syria. He was followed by a series of fourteen rulers with the same dynastic name (Ptolemy). During this period, there were also a number of Cleopatras, although most were wives of Ptolemies. The Cleopatra of Shakespeare and movie fame was Cleopatra VII.

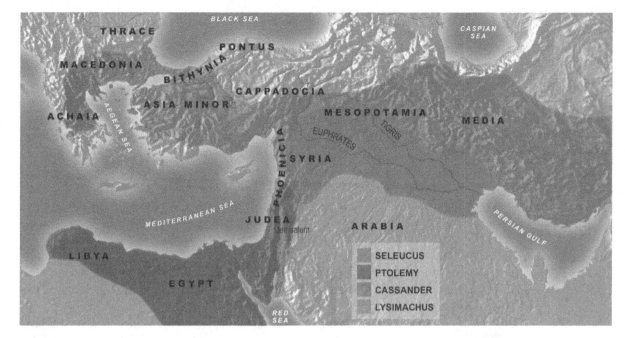

In 305 BCE, after sixteen years as a nominal "satrap" or governor, Ptolemy I took the title of "King of Egypt." One of his most significant acts was to establish a major library in Alexandria, a city founded by Alexander the Great and named after him. Alexandria also became a major settlement for Hebrews who did not go back to Judea.[16] His son, Ptolemy II Philadelphus (284–246 BCE), organized his father's library and instituted major expansions and settlements. Manetho, a major Egyptian historian who provided records of the Egyptian dynasties, worked for him. It was during this time that the Septuagint (a Greek translation of the OT) was made.

Wars between the Seleucids and the Ptolemies began during this period, but a tenuous peace was established when Philadelphus gave his daughter in marriage to Antiochus II of Syria. Just before Philadelphus's death, she and her son were murdered. This act led to further conflicts for Ptolemy IV and V. Ptolemy V, a

DANIEL AND THE EMPIRES

The age of empires during the intertestamental period is shown by the four beasts in the vision of Daniel 7. Many scholars correlate the third beast (the leopard with four heads) with Alexander's empire, which divided into several Greek-speaking kingdoms. It is seen in more detail in the vision of the goat and the ram in chapter 8, where Daniel is told specifically that the ram represents Media and Persia, and the goat, Greece. The conflict between Syria and Egypt is traced in significant detail in Daniel 11 (for which reason scholars who do not accept prophetic revelation argue that it must have been written after the Maccabean revolt).

THE SEPTUAGINT

There seems to have been a twofold reason for producing a Greek translation of the OT. Because Ptolemy Philadelphus was gathering copies of all the great books of the world into the library of Alexandria, this translation would allow the Hebrew Scriptures to be included in a form accessible to Hellenistic readers. A more practical reason was that already we see Hebrews of the Diaspora using Greek as the lingua franca. The translation would allow them to read their own Scriptures in a language in which they were more comfortable. (Of course, having the Bible in Greek made it easier for them to ignore their national language.) The Greek version made at this time probably included only the Pentateuch. Even so, the other books of the OT had been translated by 132 BCE (Henry Barclay Swete, *An Introduction to the Old Testament in Greek* [New York: KTAV, 1968 reprint], 24). As Phillip Sigal points out, the Septuagint is an interpretive translation and may be viewed as Targum (*Judaism: The Evolution of a Faith* [Grand Rapids: Eerdmans, 1988], 100).

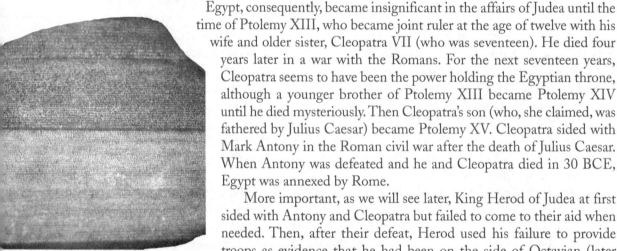

mere child when he assumed the throne in 205 BCE, was actually more the focus of political infighting than the ruler. Weakened by this internal political intrigue, Egypt lost several significant possessions, including Judea, which became part of Syria.[17]

Egypt, consequently, became insignificant in the affairs of Judea until the time of Ptolemy XIII, who became joint ruler at the age of twelve with his wife and older sister, Cleopatra VII (who was seventeen). He died four years later in a war with the Romans. For the next seventeen years, Cleopatra seems to have been the power holding the Egyptian throne, although a younger brother of Ptolemy XIII became Ptolemy XIV until he died mysteriously. Then Cleopatra's son (who, she claimed, was fathered by Julius Caesar) became Ptolemy XV. Cleopatra sided with Mark Antony in the Roman civil war after the death of Julius Caesar. When Antony was defeated and he and Cleopatra died in 30 BCE, Egypt was annexed by Rome.

More important, as we will see later, King Herod of Judea at first sided with Antony and Cleopatra but failed to come to their aid when needed. Then, after their defeat, Herod used his failure to provide troops as evidence that he had been on the side of Octavian (later Caesar Augustus) all along.

THE ROSETTA STONE. Found near Rosetta, Egypt, in 1821, a large piece of basalt expressing a decree of Ptolemy V inscribed in three languages. Now in the British Musem, it provided the basis for deciphering Egyptian hieroglyphics.

Rulers of Syria (Kings of the North)

The third arch of the political bridge was Syria. The ruling Syrian dynasty was named Seleucid after its founder, Seleucus I, who had been a general under Alexander. Six kings were named Seleucus; thirteen of the kings in the Seleucid dynasty, however, bore the name of Seleucus I's father, Antiochus (e.g., Seleucus I's son was Antiochus I).

There are two key figures for our purposes. The first was Antiochus III (242–187 BCE), known as Antiochus the Great. He regained a large amount of the land that had been lost in the east and then expanded his empire. He was also the Syrian leader credited with taking Palestine from the Egyptians in 198 BCE. After this change, the Hebrews were allowed to continue with their religious rituals for thirty-one years (up to 167 BCE). Antiochus III was the first Seleucid king to have a confrontation with the expanding Roman Empire. The Romans defeated him in battle at Magnesia in western Asia Minor (modern Turkey) in 190. That victory gave Rome control of Asia Minor.

Antiochus IV or Antiochus Epiphanes (215–163 BCE) was the third son, who took the throne in 175.[18] He attempted a strong program of Hellenization to unite the kingdom. A critical aspect of this program was an effort to force the worship of his favorite god, Zeus, on his subjects. By 169 Antiochus was encouraging his people to worship *him* as the human manifestation of Zeus. He took the title *Theos Epiphanes* (God manifest), but his enemies called him *Epimanes* (the mad man).

Antiochus took the title "Theos Epiphanes" (God manifest), but his enemies called him "Epimanes" (the mad man).

During the early part of his reign, he contented himself with playing Jewish factions against one another (even in the priesthood, there were pro-Ptolemy and pro-Seleucid parties). In 169 BCE, Antiochus attacked Ptolemy VI in Egypt. While he was there, trouble broke out in Jerusalem. Perceiving this internal struggle to be rebellion against his own authority, Antiochus desecrated the temple when he, a Gentile, entered it. He then plundered it.

To ensure that Judea would remain "loyal" over the next two years, Antiochus accelerated his Hellenization program and decided to eradicate the Jewish religion. His ultimatums included forbidding the observance of the Sabbath and the customary festivals, abolishing the sacrificial system, stopping the circumcision of children, and ordering the destruction of copies of the Torah. This program culminated on December 16, 167 BCE, when a statue of Zeus was set up in the temple and swine were sacrificed on an altar to this god. In addition, pagan altars were set up in every village in Palestine.

This desecration precipitated the Maccabean revolt, which eventually resulted in independence for Judea. Following the death of Antiochus in 163 BCE, his general, Lysias (who had already suffered two defeats attempting to take Jerusalem), established a truce with the Jews so that he could take control of the Seleucid Empire. Syria became politically unstable and was conquered by the Romans under Pompey in 64–63 BCE. At that point, it became a Roman province.

The Maccabees

The program that Antiochus instituted actually backfired, for he grossly underestimated the values and strength of Judaism. Instead of forcing the Jews down in obedience, his program ignited the Maccabean revolt.[19] This uprising, which was as much religious as political, began in the village of Modein, 17 miles northwest of Jerusalem.

Antiochus had sent out agents to enforce paganism throughout Judea, but in Modein a priest named Mattathias refused to offer the required sacrifice. When another Jew volunteered to do so, Mattathias killed both him and Antiochus's officer. He then fled to the mountains with his five sons and a number of other followers. Thus began a revolution that ultimately led to independence for Judea and began changing Judaism.

One of the first significant results of the Maccabean revolt occurred after a group of more than a thousand Judeans were slain because they refused to fight on the Sabbath. Mattathias and his followers realized that the Syrians were taking advantage of this policy by using this day to attack the Jews. They decided that it was God-honoring to defend themselves, even on the Sabbath.[20]

When Mattathias died in 166 BCE, his third son, Judas, took his place. He was given the nickname Maccabeus (which probably means "The Hammer"). Judas was a credible general, and he gathered his forces carefully. The first phase was guerrilla warfare, but gradually his men were able to execute carefully planned battles. Twice (in 165 and 164 BCE), Lysias, the Syrian general, led armies against Jerusalem, only to be defeated both times by Judas Maccabeus and the Jews. After the second defeat of the Syrians, Judas and the Jews occupied Jerusalem. They cleansed the temple, and on 25 Chislev (December 14) 164 BCE, the temple was rededicated. This event is recalled in the festival of Hanukkah.

> Judas Maccabeus and the Jews occupied Jerusalem and cleansed the temple, an event recalled in the festival of Hanukkah.

Although Judea was now basically free, the goal was to secure independence for all of Palestine. To accomplish this, Judas campaigned against the Idumeans (or Edomites) and the Ammonites south and east of Judah. His brother Simon led campaigns in Galilee. In the south, however, events did not go as well as they had earlier.

Then Antiochus Epiphanes died in 163 BCE. His son was only nine, so two generals, Philip and Lysias, struggled to see who would be the real power. Because of this internal struggle, Lysias negotiated a peace with the Jews, granting them religious freedom but retaining their political subordination to Syria.

The Syrians, through their Hellenizing surrogates, continued the struggle against the Maccabeans, but now they worked internally. In the process of attempting to get political independence and fighting the Hellenizing party, Judas asked for help from Rome. The Romans sent an ultimatum to Syria but at this point were unable to back it up. Judas was killed in battle in 160 BCE.

Judas's youngest brother, Jonathan, was his first successor. The Maccabean struggle was helped at this time by internal strife in Syria as a certain Alexander Balas, who claimed to be the son of Antiochus Epiphanes, fought for the throne. Jonathan used guile, audacity, and military cunning, playing both Syrian factions against each other to win Samaria as part of Palestine. He also continued the negotiations with the Romans begun by Judas. Jonathan walked into a trap in 143

BCE and was killed by the Syrians. He was followed by an older brother, Simon. The two are noted for three key accomplishments: they merged the priesthood and the throne; they achieved independence from Syria; and they entered into an alliance with Rome. Simon also started a dynastic succession. The family became known as the Hasmonean dynasty after the great-grandfather of Mattathias, Hashmon (in Greek, Asamonaios).

Jonathan became high priest under the auspices of Syria. Under his brother Jonathan, Simon had become governor of the Philistine coastal cities and then high priest upon Jonathan's death. Because of his actions, the Jewish people recognized both positions (1 Macc. 14:35). Initially there was some contention regarding this. Mattathias had been a Levite, but not of the high priest's family. Two factors contributed to Simon's position. One was his wise rule. The second was that the previous high priestly family, that of Onias, had fled to Egypt. This was interpreted as a renouncement of any claims they had on the position. As a result, Simon and his descendants were named as high priests "forever, until a trustworthy prophet" should arise (1 Macc. 14:41).

While Judea had already achieved a degree of independence, Simon was able to play the two Syrian factions against each other. As a result, he was able to stop the tribute payments. By 142 BCE, Judea had received full independence.

After Jonathan's death, Simon continued the negotiations with Rome. While it may seem strange that Rome would ally itself with an upstart state like Judea, we must recall that Rome was still developing as an empire[21] and was striving to consolidate its power. Although Rome had defeated Syria once, a strong Syria and a strong Egypt were both obvious threats. At the time of the Maccabean conflict, Rome was in the middle of its wars with Carthage. Rome was not secure until Carthage was burned in 146 BCE.[22] Greece had been conquered just a short time before in 168 BCE. At this point, Syria was still a potentially strong empire in the east and a definite concern to the Romans. In fact, Syria was not finally conquered until the campaigns of Pompey around 65 BCE.

John Hyrcanus was the third son of Simon, who survived after his father and two brothers were murdered in 135 BCE. Under John Hyrcanus, Syria formally

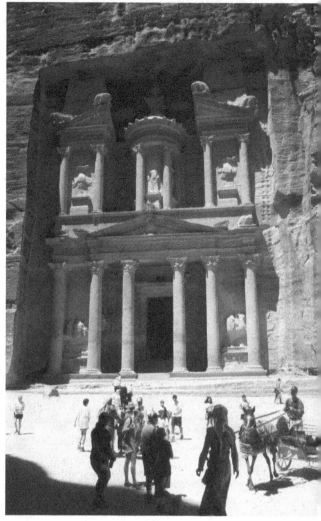

PETRA. The major city of Edom during the intertestamental period, and the region Herod the Great came from (and near where he later imprisoned John the Baptist). Petra flourished in its secure location adjacent to the King's Highway in the Trans-Jordan region.

recognized the independence of Judea, although as part of the agreement most of the coastal strip (except for Joppa) was returned to the Syrians.

After Antiochus VI was killed in 128 BCE, leaving the Syrian throne uncontested for the first time in several years, John Hyrcanus began a program of expansion. In this program, he was able to conquer and annex Edom (or Idumea). He forcibly converted the Edomites to Judaism. He also destroyed the Samaritan temple on Mount Gerizim. As a result, Judea encompassed much of the land that had been possessed by David, but it was predominantly a military rule, not an actual possession by the Jewish people.

As is usually the case with ruling dynasties, the family structure was complicated, and there was a history of intrigue, most of which is not directly relevant for our purposes. Significant rulers include the ruthless Alexander Janneus (son of Hyrcanus) and his wife Salome Alexandra, who succeeded him upon his death and under whom the nation prospered. Their son, John Hyrcanus II, was high priest from about 76 to 40 BCE and supreme civilian authority from 67–57 BCE. During his rule, Antipater II was appointed governor over Edom (Idumea).

Antipater was noted for his political astuteness. When John Hyrcanus II became involved in a civil war with his brother, Aristobulus II, Antipater supported him. Both brothers appealed to Rome for help. At first Rome held back, but in 63 BCE Pompey was ordered in to restore peace. Antipater aligned himself with the Romans and impressed them such that in 47 BCE he was allowed to appoint his two sons as military governors: Phasael over Judea and Herod over Galilee.

Herod had been educated in Rome, where he became friends with key Romans, including Mark Antony and Julius Caesar. After Antipater was poisoned and Phasael committed suicide, Herod was promoted over John Hyrcanus II in 42. This meant that an Edomite was now in charge of the semi-independent Jewish state.

ROMAN RELIGION. A partially reconstructed Roman temple in Jeresh in present-day Jordan, symbolizing the Roman influence in the spreading of the worship of the various Greco-Roman gods and then emperor worship.

HEROD THE IDUMEAN

Herod married Mariamne primarily to develop a political alliance with the Hasmonean line. She was merely the third of what ultimately were ten wives. Although initially he seems to have loved her, later he had her killed along with the son she had borne him. This and other crimes were part of the reason the Jews hated him. Other factors included his policy of promoting Hellenism and the fact that he was Edomite (Idumean). Because of the Jews' animosity, Herod undertook the renovation of the temple to win them over. This project would take more than eighty years. But soon after its completion, the temple was destroyed in 70 CE.

In 40 BCE, Herod fled to Rome when the Parthians (who came from a region corresponding to modern northeast Iran) invaded Galilee. There he persuaded the Roman senate to appoint him king of Judea. He returned with a Roman army, claiming his position. In 37 BCE, he solidified the throne by marrying Mariamne I, the daughter of John Hyrcanus II. Herod's position was reaffirmed by Caesar Augustus after Herod "helped" him in his war against Antony and Cleopatra. Herod maintained his kingship until his death in 4 BCE; the realm was then divided among his three sons.

Rulers of Rome

The last arch of the political bridge is the Roman Empire. Rome was originally a republic. It transitioned to a dictatorship and an empire during the century between 133 and 31 BCE. The key period was about 70–60 BCE, when three generals, Pompey, Crassus, and Julius Caesar struggled for dominance. Pompey achieved his power base in the far east, Julius in Gaul, and Crassus in Italy, where he had defeated the slave uprising led by Spartacus. The three initially formed a triumvirate by which they were able to win positions as consuls that the Roman senate tried to block. After Crassus was killed in battle, Julius and Pompey started a serious power struggle. The key event was when Julius took his army south into Italy, crossing the Rubicon River, and thus in essence invading Italy. The civil war that followed merely determined which general would have absolute power. Julius Caesar gained control after Pompey was murdered in Egypt. He then won out over several other would-be rulers. However, he was killed on the Ides of March in 44 BCE, less than a month after being appointed dictator for life.

CAESAR AUGUSTUS. Found in Corinth, a statue of Caesar Augustus, the Roman emperor at the time of Jesus' birth.

THE ROMAN EMPIRE.

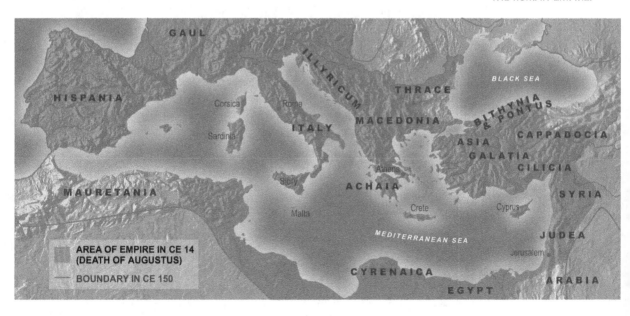

AREA OF EMPIRE IN CE 14
(DEATH OF AUGUSTUS)

BOUNDARY IN CE 150

BUST OF CAESAR. A bust of emperor Marcus Aurelius that is typical of many busts found in the territory of the Roman Empire. Once the Romans had established their empire, the world became Roman.

Following Julius Caesar's death, the "empire" faced civil war for thirteen years, with the prime competitors being Mark Antony, Octavian (an adopted son of Caesar), and several other generals, including Brutus and Cassius. After Antony and Cleopatra committed suicide in 30 BCE, Octavian had undisputed control. The senate gave him the honorary title of *Augustus* in 27. This event is held by many to mark the beginning of the actual empire.

With this, the Roman world settled into a period of relative quiet and tranquility. One of the exceptions was a backwater province called Judea. Because of its troubles, in 6 CE it ceased being a client kingdom and became a Roman province. Discontent brewed and bubbled to the surface off and on until the temple was destroyed in 70 CE. Even that did not solve Rome's problems. Finally, in 135 CE, all the Jews were exiled from the land.

Summary

As we look at the political bridge, we find a number of ironies. Rome became an empire merely a few decades before the birth of Jesus, setting up the situation for the decree and census that would take Mary of Nazareth to Bethlehem with her espoused husband, Joseph. Likewise, during the youth of Jesus, the semi-independence of the nation was revoked, and Judea became a Roman province, subject not only to the laws but also to the legal system of Rome, setting up the trial situation in which the Roman governor had to be asked to execute those criminals that the Jewish rulers condemned—doing so by means of a Roman cross. Furthermore, it was as this Roman Empire was reaching its peak that the gospel was promulgated and began to spread.

The expansion of the Roman Empire in the west stopped with the battle of Teutoburger Forest in 9 CE. It continued to expand in the east under Trajan, with the taking of Armenia, Assyria, and Mesopotamia from the Parthians. After the death of Trajan in 117, Hadrian gave back these three territories to establish peace with Parthia. This concession began the long-term disintegration of the Roman Empire. By that time, Christianity was a solid movement. How it began is the subject of the next chapter.

REVIEW QUESTIONS

1. Why did the OT canon end with Malachi?

2. What is the Apocrypha, and how was it viewed by the Jews at the time of Jesus?

3. What is the Mishnah? How is it different from the Talmud? Why are they important?

4. What are Pseudepigrapha?

5. How did the Sadducees develop?

6. How did the Pharisees develop?

7. Who were the Essenes, and why are they important?

8. Who were the scribes, and what role did they play in Judean society?

9. Trace the rise and demise of Alexander the Great.

10. What happened to Alexander's empire after his death?

11. Who were the Ptolemies and the Seleucids, and why are they important?

12. Who were the Maccabees, and what did they do for Judea?

13. How did Herod, an Edomite, become king of Judea?

14. How did Rome make Judea part of the Roman Empire?

18

CHAPTER

Who Is Jesus the Messiah?

OVERVIEW

According to the NT, two unique births occurred in Palestine about six months apart. These infants were John, a prophet-evangelist, and his relative, Jesus, who was none other than the Messiah. Four books, called the Gospels, serve to demonstrate the validity of their claims. In this chapter, we look at the recorded events in their lives from their births to the height of Jesus' popularity. We also consider some of the questions that have been raised about the gospel documents.

STUDY GOALS

▶ Explain the concepts of Messiah (or Christ) and gospel.

▶ Introduce the Synoptic problem.

▶ Evaluate the purpose of the four gospels.

▶ Review the births of John the Baptist and Jesus.

▶ Trace the early ministry of Jesus (up to the feeding of the five thousand).

pproximately four hundred years after the OT canon was closed, Judea bubbled with excitement and expectation. But it was also a time of frustration and fear. The Roman Empire ruled with an iron hand through an Idumean (Edomite) king, Herod. But while the Judeans chafed, they also had hope. For centuries they had looked for the Messiah—the person who was specially anointed. According to the prophets, He would deliver them from their oppressors. He would restore the glory of the nation that had been briefly glimpsed under David. Some of the more spiritually perceptive understood from the prophetic books that the time was at hand. But there were also many obstacles.

Given the different religious and political factions of the time, there were significant disagreements within the leadership of the nation. The Judeans who occupied leadership positions, especially those of a more Hellenistic bent, had a vested interest in the status quo.[1] Moreover, Herod had been placed on the throne by the Roman senate, and thus both he and the Romans also were interested in retaining the current state of affairs. Herod would have been especially concerned about any talk regarding a "king of the Jews." It was a threat to him not only as the current king, but especially as an Idumean ruler. So as we begin the NT, we find that not everyone was eager for the Messiah God had promised.

MACHAERUS. One of Herod's several palace-fortresses. Lying east of the Dead Sea, it is believed to be where John the Baptist was imprisoned and beheaded.

As a result, anyone who claimed to be the Messiah would have to demonstrate it before a somewhat hostile audience. The evidence would necessarily consist of several strands. First, there would be the *genealogical requirement*. He would have to be a descendant of Abraham, from the tribe of Judah and the line of David. This criterion left many people out, including Herod. Second, there was the *prophetic strand*. A number of prophecies would have to be fulfilled. For example, He would have to be born in Bethlehem. His mother would have to be a virgin. And He would flee to Egypt and be called back by God. The prophetic strand

THE ANOINTED ONE

Anointing was both a literal and a symbolic ritual. It was literal in that the person who was anointed had a small amount of olive oil poured over his head. It was symbolic in that the process represented both personal dedication and the special work of the Holy Spirit within the person (so that the external act was a visible representation of something that was supposed to occur within). In the OT, the ritual was conducted for kings, priests, and prophets. The Hebrew word used for "anointed" has been transliterated into English as *messiah*. In the Greek, it was *christos*, transliterated into English as a title or name, "(the) Christ." As the prophetic books looked forward to *the* Anointed One (the Messiah), the focus tended to be on His kingly role as He led the nation in righteous service of God, although priestly and prophetic roles also were evident. Naturally, the kingly role dominated the people's thinking, especially during times of oppression.

MESSIANIC PROPHECIES

Some of the prophetic elements regarding the Messiah were clearly understood and waited for. For example, the prophecy from Micah 5:2 (quoted in Matt. 2:6) was clearly understood by the Jews, as evidenced by the response the Jewish leaders gave to Herod at the visit of the magi. It is interesting to read the next phrase in Micah, which describes a messiah "whose origins are from of old, from ancient times." Here is a hint of His divine nature.

Other prophecies were more obscure and could be understood only after the fact. Even today we look at some of the statements that the gospel writers noted as fulfilling OT prophecies and realize that we probably would not have understood them in that way. For example, Matthew states that Joseph's move to Nazareth after leaving Egypt "fulfilled what was said through the prophets: 'He will be called a Nazarene'" (Matt. 2:23). We do not find such a statement in the OT, and scholars have debated its origin. The most commonly accepted suggestion is that Matthew was thinking in terms of Isaiah 11:1, where the Messiah is referred to as the shoot *(netser)* of Jesse.

Another prophetic fulfillment that we would not see as obvious is Matthew's use of Hosea 11:1, which talks about the Exodus and the subsequent development of the nation. When Matthew 2:15 quotes this declaration as being fulfilled, there is a double nuance. The first is the reference to the journey to Egypt. The second is the use of the word *son*, which again seems to be an allusion to the Messiah's divine nature.

Especially controversial has been the use of Isaiah 7:14 as a prophecy of the virgin birth. As noted earlier (see the discussion of Isaiah in ch. 14, above), some have argued that the Hebrew word *'almah* does not refer to a virgin. Questions have also been raised as to whether the Jews at the time of Jesus understood Isaiah to foretell a virgin birth of the Messiah (see Robert H. Stein, *Jesus the Messiah* [Downers Grove, Ill.: InterVarsity, 1996], 66). Given the different characteristics of the Pharisee and Sadducee parties (see ch. 17, above), we should be leery of assuming that there was a single "Jewish understanding" of prophetic declarations. However, both Matthew and Luke, who addressed the birth of Jesus in their gospels, clearly understood Mary to have been a virgin at the time of the birth. They both saw that event as prophetic fulfillment.

was stronger, but clearly not all of it was a matter of public record.[2] Third, there would be the *physical evidences*. By this we mean the actions He did, such as healing the sick. Such evidence would be the strongest strand, for it would involve public actions and many eyewitnesses.

So the NT begins with this question: Was Jesus the Messiah? It was to answer this question that a number of books were written in the decades following His life. In the NT, we find four of them. We call them the Gospels: Matthew, Mark, Luke, and John.

THE GOSPEL OF JESUS THE MESSIAH

Many of us are frustrated by what we read about Jesus in the NT—there just isn't enough there. We would like to know more about His life. He lived more than thirty years, but all the recorded events put together cover just a few weeks of that time. In fact, more than a third of the material in the Gospels focuses on the last week of His life.[3] Just a quick reading of any of the gospel accounts demonstrates that we are not looking at a biography. As we evaluate the issue, we need to address two questions. The first is one of definition: What is a gospel?

Jesus lived more than thirty years, but all the recorded events put together cover just a few weeks of that time.

The word itself gives us a hint. It comes from a Greek word that means "good news." The book of Mark begins as follows: "The beginning of the good news about Jesus the Messiah, the Son of God" (my translation). This statement indicates that the good news about Jesus was tied to the question of whether or not He was the Messiah. It also suggests that part of the good news about Jesus was His special relationship to God, which we will address in more detail later. With this beginning, we might suggest the following as a working definition: *A gospel is a document that proclaims that Jesus was the promised Messiah, and gives evidence to demonstrate that claim.*

This definition gives insight into the structure of the books. The primary proof that Jesus was the Messiah and the Son of God was the resurrection (cf. Rom. 1:4, "[Jesus Christ] was declared with power to be the Son of God by his resurrection from the dead"). Consequently, the Gospels focus on that event. But the resurrection needs a context, which is primarily the crucifixion, the method the Roman Empire used to execute criminals. The reader needs to understand why the Jewish Messiah was being executed like a criminal. More than this, one needs to understand that the life Jesus lived was truly messianic. Enough data is given to show it in broad brushstrokes—and to whet our appetites.

The second question addresses the relationship of the four gospels collected in our NT, primarily focusing on the first three (Matthew, Mark, and Luke): Why are they so similar but at the same time have so many differences? At some points, Matthew and Mark follow the same order of material as opposed to Luke,

HOW SIMILAR ARE THE SYNOPTICS?

The similarities among Matthew, Mark, and Luke are often expressed by saying that they have 221 verses in common. Some might infer that the verses are identical. When we examine the material, however, we find that they actually share topics, with varying numbers of verses and words. One example is the healing of Simon Peter's mother-in-law (Matt. 8:14–15; Mark 1:29–31; Luke 4:38–39), a commonly used sample (e.g., Fredric R. Crownfield, *A Historical Approach to the New Testament* [New York: Harper & Row, 1960], 57–59). Matthew and Luke cover the event in two verses, whereas Mark (the shorter gospel) takes three. The number of words in the Greek are 30 for Matthew, 44 for Mark, and 38 for Luke. Mark (viewed as the less embellished gospel) includes additional information, such as the detail that the house also belonged to Andrew and that James and John were present. In comparing the wording, I find only four phrases containing eight words common to all three. When we look at these three gospels by topic (incidents reported), we find that they share 30 out of 68 topics in Matthew, 60 in Mark, and 71 in Luke. Deciding what is a "topic" is somewhat arbitrary, but it is clear that there are many more differences than similarities. Of course the issue is more complex than presented here. For example, another major concern involves items shared by two of the three.

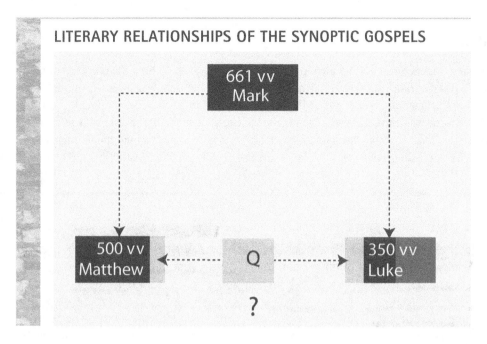

LITERARY RELATIONSHIPS OF THE SYNOPTIC GOSPELS

661 vv
Mark

500 vv
Matthew

Q

350 vv
Luke

?

SYNOPTIC PROBLEM. The relationship of Matthew, Mark, and Luke. In each, some verses contain information similar to one or both of the others. This graphic shows the relationship as often presented, although part of the problem is an oversimplification, since if the verses (a late, somewhat arbitrary division) contain similar information, they are labeled as "the same."

and at other points, Luke and Mark follow the same order of material as opposed to Matthew. This commonality has suggested that Mark is somehow tied into the composition of the other two.[4] Historically, this has been called "the synoptic problem."[5] The question then is, was Mark used as a source (often called Marcan priority), or did Mark use the other two as sources (often called Matthean priority)? This "problem" has been a focus of modern critical scholarship, and several explanations have been generated.

Prior to the eighteenth century, scholars had tried to harmonize the accounts of all four gospels, seeking to find a smooth chronology of the life of Jesus. Johann Griesbach (1745–1812) initiated a major shift in thinking when he argued that John should be viewed separately, and the Synoptics could not be harmonized. He also argued that Matthew was written first (Matthean priority). This "Griesbach Hypothesis" dominated until the twentieth century, although it was challenged. In 1894 William Sanday convened the first of several seminars on the synoptic problem. Out of these came the "Oxford Hypothesis," which argued for Marcan priority. It has held dominance through most of the twentieth century but again is being challenged.

During the twentieth century, following the acceptance of Mark as the first written gospel, the most popular explanations were the "two-source theory" and the "four-source theory." Both theories began with the same premises.[6] An important premise addresses the dates that the Gospels were written. During the eighteenth and nineteenth centuries, it was felt that these dates were late, that is, several generations after Jesus lived.[7] Following the work of H. S. Reimarus (1694–1768), a largely German school of scholars arose who rejected the super-

SOURCE CRITICISM

Source criticism is a process that begins with the premise that a given book of the Bible was compiled from different sources (whether written or oral) and seeks to identify which parts came from which source. In the OT, we saw it demonstrated in the Documentary Hypothesis of the Pentateuch, which was developed primarily by Julius Wellhausen. In the NT, the focus was on the Gospels, and no one individual dominated. The struggle was twofold. On one hand, the scholars grappled with the question of which gospel was written first, and the writings of the early church fathers provide conflicting evidence (William R. Farmer, *The Synoptic Problem* [Dillsboro, N.C.: Western North Carolina Press, 1976], 1–5). On the other hand, there is also the complicated issue of similarities between Matthew, Mark, and Luke.

normal aspects of the Gospels. In essence, the assumption was not only that supernormal events did not occur, but that Jesus was a normal human being just like everyone else. It might be said that He felt a special calling. It might even be granted that He was very gifted. However, He was just human. Reimarus was a deist who argued that the apostolic teaching about Jesus was based on their theology, not history. This Jesus without supernormal elements, that is, the Jesus of history without any "myths" enveloping him,[8] is the Jesus of the Jesus Seminar, as well as of the musical *Jesus Christ Superstar*.

D. F. Strauss (1808–74), especially, argued that the Gospels were largely mythological in the way they presented Jesus. However, after the studies of J. B. Lightfoot (1829–89), the dates of composition have been pushed back into the first century but only as early as about 65 CE for the first written gospel.

The second premise focuses on the length of the Gospels. The argument is that it is unlikely that a gospel writer would omit items that were included in an earlier gospel, and since Mark is so much shorter, it must have been the original.[9]

Third, as these writers looked at the three accounts, they noticed that the three accounts had some things in common. Matthew and Luke also shared a number of items that were not found in Mark, such as genealogies and the Sermon on the Mount.

In critical study of the Gospels, it is important to remember that Q is purely hypothetical.

The two-source theory was based on these observations and premises.[10] According to its proponents, Mark was one of the sources the other two gospel writers used. The second source contained the material common to Matthew and Luke but absent in Mark. It is normally referred to as Q (from the German word *Quelle*, "source"). It is important to remember that Q is purely hypothetical, even though a number of books refer to it as though it were an attested document, some even claiming to reconstruct its text.

This solution has a number of problems. One of the most significant is that if Q was so important, why has it not survived? Although we have more than five thousand manuscripts of the NT, not a single scrap that can be identified as Q has been discovered to date. Another very significant problem is that a Q source does

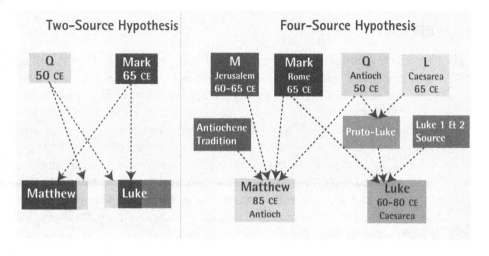

Two-Source Hypothesis

Q 50 CE
Mark 65 CE
→ Matthew
→ Luke

Four-Source Hypothesis

M Jerusalem 60–65 CE
Mark Rome 65 CE
Q Antioch 50 CE
L Caesarea 65 CE
Antiochene Tradition
Proto-Luke
Luke 1 & 2 Source
→ Matthew 85 CE Antioch
→ Luke 60–80 CE Caesarea

TWO-SOURCE THEORY. The theory that Matthew and Luke derived from two sources, Mark and Q.

FOUR-SOURCE THEORY. A more complex theory that was developed because of the inadequacy of the two-source theory. It maintains that Matthew and Luke derived from four separate earlier sources with additional material added. At this point one starts to ask whether the authors were "copying" or making reference to a common body of knowledge.

not explain the places where Matthew and Luke differ. For example, we might consider the differences in the Sermon on the Mount (Matthew 5–7) and the Sermon on the Plain (Luke 6:23–49).[11]

To resolve this latter problem, a more complicated four-source theory was proposed. In addition to Mark and Q, two other sources (called M and L) are hypothesized to explain the places where Matthew and Luke differ.[12] Because of the complications, some recent scholars have taken a fresh look at the material and concluded that the synoptic problem has been overblown.[13]

One problem with both theories as traditionally presented is that they seem to make the gospel writers merely compilers who copied material from other sources. This is sometimes called "literary dependence."[14] Today almost all scholars realize that this view is too simplistic. The term we use today for a person who copies the material but then puts it into his own words is *redactor*. It would seem, however, that this is not too different from a writer who has done research.

SOME EARLY FATHERS

Clement of Alexandria (c. 150–215) is quoted by the historian Eusebius (*Ecclesiastical History*, 6.14.5–6) as saying that the gospels with genealogies, Matthew and Luke, were written first, followed by Mark, which was written at the request of friends in Rome while Peter still was alive but apparently in prison (see *ANF*, 2:580). An earlier Christian theologian was Irenaeus, who lived from about 130 to 200 CE. He was a student of Polycarp, who in turn had been a student of the apostle John. In his work *Against Heresies* (3.1.1), Irenaeus asserts that Matthew first wrote a gospel in the "dialect" of the Hebrews while Peter and Paul were in Rome (the reference may be to the Hebrew or Aramaic language, or perhaps to a style of writing). Mark wrote down Peter's testimony. Luke recorded Paul's testimony, and later John wrote down his own (*ANF*, 1:414). Even earlier we have a report from Papias (recorded in Eusebius, *Ecclesiastical History*, 3.39.15–16), who lived from about 60 to 130 CE and was a student of John. Papias reports that Mark wrote down Peter's testimony, although it was not entirely in chronological order. He also reports that Matthew wrote in "the Hebrew dialect."

REPEATED TEACHINGS

We tend to visualize the teaching ministry of Jesus as something that was continually new, giving fresh insights and deeper teachings each time. In an age where there was no media in the sense we think of today, He was beginning afresh in every town to which He came. It is true that some merely came for the signs—the spectacular demonstrations He gave. Others, however, came to see if this man was, indeed, the Messiah. In that sense, the signs helped, but the people also had deep spiritual needs, as shown by the ministry of John (see Matt. 3:5–6). As such, it is likely that the disciples heard the same basic teachings from Jesus dozens of times. Clearly, He gave them amplifying information as they stayed with Him, but the deeper teachings were in private and were given to the disciples gradually as they became ready for them.

So then, how should we approach the issue? Is literary dependence the only explanation? In the case of the NT, we actually have testimony from early church writers that points to a probable explanation. This is the traditional view of the origin of the Gospels. Based in part on 1,900 year-old evidence, the following process for writing the Gospels is suggested.

THE ORIGIN OF THE GOSPEL ACCOUNTS

The early church began with several basic convictions. The first was the conviction of the eyewitnesses, totally contrary to common experience and their expectations, that Jesus had arisen from the grave. The second conviction was that Jesus would return—soon. When He returned, Jesus would establish the kingdom that God had promised and for which the Israelites had been waiting for centuries. A third conviction was that there was a need to promulgate this message, "the gospel of the kingdom," to as many as possible.[15] Because of these three convictions, the early eyewitnesses gave their testimonies verbally. These testimonies are sometimes referred to as "oral traditions."

> As an itinerant preacher, it is likely that Jesus had a basic message that He taught in every town He visited.

Actually, the practice began with Jesus. In Matthew 4:23 we read that early in His career Jesus was proclaiming the "gospel of the kingdom" (KJV). Matthew 5–7 seems to give a summary of that message. As an itinerant preacher, it is likely that Jesus had a basic message that He taught in every town He visited. Those who became His regular followers would have heard that message repeatedly (although they would also have had private amplifying teaching).

More important for the development of the Gospels were certain key events in the life of Jesus. As we have already noted, the primary events were those that took place during the last week of His life, culminating in the crucifixion and resurrection. Even here the writers differed in the specific actions and teachings they reported. When we look at His earlier ministry, it is likely that many of His followers had been strongly impressed by the same major events, such as the feeding of the five thousand (one of few events included in all four Gospels: Matt. 14:13–21; Mark 6:30–44; Luke 9:10–17; John 6:1–14). Other incidents they recorded would be of a more personal interest, such as Mark's story of the young man in the garden who fled naked (Mark 14:51–52). These events are "unique" to specific gospel writers.

For our purposes, the promulgation of the gospel by the disciples began on the day of Pentecost with the testimony of Peter (Acts 2:14–41).[16] Following his testimony, the number of those who accepted that Jesus was the Messiah (or the Christ) jumped from the handful who had gathered in the upper room after the crucifixion to more than three thousand. For the next few years those who had seen Jesus continued to give testimony. Those who had heard Him teach shared with others the implications of that testimony (Acts 6:4). As the church expanded, the eyewitnesses likely honed their testimony as they repeated it from town to town. With a sense of urgency, they focused on the essentials. New converts listened to and memorized the eyewitness accounts. This process continued for about twenty to twenty-five years.

In 44 CE, James the brother of John was executed by Herod (Acts 12:2)—the apostles were not invulnerable. Four years later Paul and Barnabas went on their first missionary journey (Acts 13–14). In 49 CE, the Jerusalem Council was held to discuss the place of the Gentiles in the church (Acts 15). With these events, Acts shifts its focus almost entirely to Paul. However, we start seeing indications that the other apostles were also beginning to go on missionary journeys. Tradition tells us that Matthew remained in Judea about fifteen years, but then he left and traveled mostly to the east, including Syria and Persia. Tradition also says that Matthew first wrote down his gospel in Hebrew (or Aramaic) and that sometime later he produced a Greek version of it.

WHEN WERE THE GOSPELS WRITTEN?

The date of the original "composition" of the Gospels (that is, putting the account down in writing) is problematic. Luke's gospel seems the easiest to date because it precedes Acts, which can be dated to Paul's Roman imprisonment (59–61 CE). According to the church fathers, Matthew was first, and Mark would then have been third, writing down his account near the death of Peter (c. 64). Early church tradition states that Matthew remained in Jerusalem about fifteen years before he went out preaching the gospel. One of the places he went to was Mesopotamia, which still had a large Jewish population. He then apparently died in Persia (*ANF*, 5:255). In that region, Aramaic was likely the primary language the Jews would have used, which explains why this first gospel was written in Aramaic, probably around 48–50 CE. Jerome states that in his time the Aramaic form was still extant (*NPNF*, Series 2, 6:472). While there is extensive evidence among the church fathers that Matthew wrote in Aramaic, this is questioned today, primarily because the Greek of Matthew is viewed as reflecting not a translation but a Greek original. However, that could be a matter of translation philosophy and style.

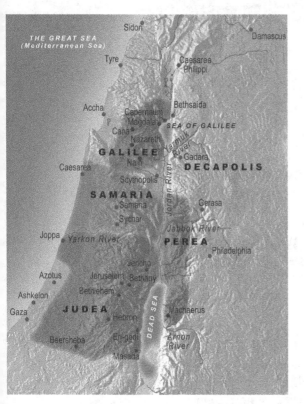

THE REGION OF ISRAEL IN THE TIME OF JESUS. The Romans named this region Palestine. All the political entities, such as Judea, were under Roman rule.

Under this scenario, Matthew was followed by Luke in the late fifties. Luke states explicitly that others prior to him had written down an account of what had happened. He also states that he had researched the matter carefully (Luke 1:2–3). It is likely that this research took place while Paul was in prison in Caesarea (57–59 CE; see Acts 24:27). By this time, the first letters to the churches were beginning to be drafted and collected.[17]

Finally, according to the church fathers, Mark wrote down Peter's testimony (either shortly before or shortly after Peter's death in Rome about 64 CE), because he had been a student of the apostle and was familiar with his message. If these dates are correct, the first three gospels were written down within a period of thirty years or so after the resurrection. This would still have been soon enough that many other eyewitnesses were available to verify or refute their testimonies.

The final gospel kept by the church was John. It was written at a later date, apparently around 90 CE. At this point, John was an old man, and the church was in its third generation. Few if any other eyewitnesses were left. John's purpose was to provide not just a testimony but also an explanation. As such, his gospel is much more theological, relating not only what he saw but what the events meant. John is also much clearer in his layout, showing that Jesus' ministry probably lasted just over three years, and he gives expanded discussion of certain key events. John cites fewer miracles, but he puts them in a more expanded context. (The gospel of John is discussed further below, ch. 28.)

LUKE-ACTS

The authorship and dating of Luke-Acts may be inferred from the texts themselves. The two books were written by the same author, as shown by the introductions of each. Acts appears to have been written during Paul's imprisonment in Rome, for it records his arrival in that city and then abruptly stops. The statement that Paul was in prison two years seems almost to be an afterthought. The key indicator of authorship is what are called the "we passages" (specifically Acts 16:10–18; 20:5–21:15; and 27:1–28:11). It is clear from those that the writer was a traveling companion of Paul but was not with Paul during all of his journeys. A careful comparison of the known itineraries of Paul's companions leaves Luke as the most likely candidate. The gospel of Luke would have been written earlier, and since it seems to have involved eyewitness accounts, it was likely researched and written in the Judean area. Paul's imprisonment in Caesarea was one occasion when Luke did not seem to be with him; this period would likely have been the time of composition. Given the context of Paul's being in prison and the content of the two works, it is tempting to see them as briefs drafted for Paul's defense attorney in Rome.

Thus, when we look at the four gospels together, we have four eyewitness accounts. As would be expected, there are some similarities but also some differences. In fact, if we analyze the accounts, we see that even when they talk about the same events, they use different terminology and often provide unique slants. With this background, what we really want to see is what they have to say about Jesus.

THE MESSIAH ARRIVES

As we have already noted, the NT does not give us a biography of Jesus, but only the highlights of His life and career. We will cover part of those in the rest of this chapter, saving the events of the last months of His ministry for the next chapter. The material is presented as a compilation gathered from the four gospels.[18]

The Birth of the Forerunner

We begin the account in Luke with a priest named Zechariah. He and his wife, Elizabeth, were old and childless. The story picks up when he was serving in the temple, burning incense. While he was inside the Holy Place, the angel Gabriel appeared to him and announced that Elizabeth would have a baby. This child was to be a Nazirite, and he would come in the spirit of Elijah, fulfilling prophecy. Because Zechariah expressed disbelief, he was told that he would be speechless until the boy was born.

Read Luke 1:1–25, 57–80.

THE SECOND TEMPLE. A model of Jerusalem and the temple of the time of Jesus, based on the descriptions of writers such as Josephus. This model can be seen in the Holyland Hotel in Jerusalem.

When the boy came, Zechariah, following God's direction, named him John. As instructed by God, John was a lifelong Nazirite, and when he reached adulthood, he served in a prophetic role, calling for the repentance of the nation.

The Birth of the Messiah

Read Luke 1:26–56; 2:1– 39; Matthew 1:1–2:12.

Jesus' birth is probably the most familiar story in the Bible, for we hear it every Christmas in a variety of forms. After Elizabeth was pregnant with John, Gabriel appeared to a young woman named Mary. When Gabriel told her she was going to have a child, Mary asked how that could be possible when she had never had sexual relations.[19] Gabriel explained that the child would be special, one who was conceived by the Holy Spirit. Mary was then told about her relative, Elizabeth, who was pregnant in her old age. After agreeing to God's call, Mary journeyed south to visit Elizabeth. The moment Mary walked in the door, Elizabeth confirmed the special nature of the coming child.

However, when Joseph discovered that Mary, his fiancée, was pregnant, he was understandably upset. Being a just man, he decided to quietly divorce her.[20] But God sent an angelic messenger to tell Joseph not to go through with the divorce. Joseph listened and married her. Even so, they did not have sexual relations until after the birth of the baby she was carrying.

As Mary's pregnancy approached full term, she journeyed to Bethlehem with Joseph to be registered for a census.[21] There the child was born. The time was approximately 5 BCE. Shepherds visited the family after they received an announcement from angels. Mary and Joseph dedicated Jesus at the temple, where Simeon and Anna both noted His special position.[22] Sometime later, magi from Mesopotamia visited. Following this, Joseph took Mary and Jesus to Egypt to escape Herod.[23]

After Herod died, the family returned to Nazareth, where the boy was raised and learned the trade of His father, a carpenter. As would be the case with all Jewish males, He not only learned a trade but also attended the synagogue each Sabbath and studied the Scriptures with the other boys in the community.[24] We are told very little about His youth outside of a general observation that He grew up mentally, physically, and spiritually ("in favor with God and men," Luke 2:52). When He was twelve, He went with His family up to Jerusalem for the Passover. On the return trip, He went missing, and His parents backtracked to the temple. There they found Him talking

> **WHEN WAS JESUS BORN?**
>
> The Christian calendar was devised in 525 by a monk named Dionysius, who calculated that Jesus was born in December of the year 753 after the founding of Rome. That year was thus designated as 1 BC (before Christ; or BCE, before the Common or Christian era), and the following January as marking the beginning of AD 1 (from Latin *Anno Domini*, "year of [our] Lord"). We know now that those dates were off. It is generally agreed that King Herod died in 4 BCE (but see *HBC*, 300, for the view that it was 1 BCE), and Jesus had to have been born before then.

STONE MANGER. A manger from Megiddo probably similar to the one in which Jesus was placed—made of stone despite being commonly portrayed as made of wood.

with the teachers of the nation. Although He was asking questions, He also had answers that astounded everyone.

THE MESSAGE OF THE MESSIAH

The gospel writers omit everything else about the childhood and youth of Jesus.[25] In fact, both Mark and John begin their books with John the Baptist preaching and Jesus starting His ministry. According to Luke 3:23, Jesus was *about* thirty years of age.[26] There are two indications that Jesus' ministry lasted about three and a half years. The first is from John's gospel, where John tells of at least three (probably four) Passover celebrations Jesus observed. The second is based on comparing the historical anchors we have for the beginning of His career and the crucifixion. The former appears to have been in the fall of 29 CE, the latter in the spring of 33.[27]

THE MAGI

The magi were part of a guild that had been in existence for some centuries. They were associated with Daniel during the Exile, which may explain why the magi mentioned by Matthew were looking for the king of the Judeans. The exact nature of the star is highly debated, and we do not know the number of magi (the traditional number of three derives from the three gifts). They visited Herod in his palace first, assuming that a king would be born in the royal court. Herod, an Edomite, was mystified and concerned. His Jewish advisors, however, quickly gave the response that the expected king would be born in Bethlehem. Since they did not seem to be surprised by the announcement, there must have been some awareness that the time of the Messiah was near. After the magi returned to Mesopotamia by a different route, Herod killed all the male children in the Bethlehem region under the age of two, which suggests that Jesus could have been as old as two at that point.

JORDAN VALLEY. The region where John the Baptist began his ministry. Here, at the southern end, the river meandered through dense vegetation such as these tamarisk trees.

The Ministry of John

Read
Matthew 3:1–17;
Mark 1:1–11;
Luke 3:1–22;
John 1:1–34.

The Gospels portray John as a fulfillment both of Isaiah's figure of one crying in the desert (Isa. 40:3) and of Malachi's Elijah (Mal. 4:5–6). They also portray him as preaching a message of repentance based on the nearness of the kingdom of heaven (Matt. 3:1). The people naturally wondered if this meant that John was the Messiah. John said no, but the Messiah was right behind him.

It was probably in the fall of 29 CE that Jesus showed up at the Jordan River somewhat north of Jericho, where John was baptizing, and asked to be baptized. According to Matthew's testimony, John recognized Him and suggested that Jesus should instead baptize him. Jesus did not deny this point but nevertheless told John to baptize him "to fulfill all righteousness." After the baptism, the Holy Spirit descended on Jesus, and God spoke from heaven commending Jesus as His beloved son.[28] With this, John moved offstage, and the focus shifted to Jesus.

JOHN AND ELIJAH

All four gospels, quoting the LXX, note that the ministry of John the Baptist fulfills Isaiah 40:3 (Matt. 3:3; Mark 1:3; Luke 3:4; John 1:23). Likewise, all four tie John to the fulfillment of Malachi's prophecy regarding Elijah (Matt. 11:14; 17:10–14; Mark 1:2; 9:11–13; Luke 1:17; John 1:21). It is interesting that Luke uses the phrase, "he will go on before the Lord, in the spirit and power of Elijah," which would seem to indicate that there is yet to be a reappearing of Elijah. If so, this allusion, in our further understanding of the nature of the Messiah, probably coincides with Jesus' second coming. This interpretation then would coincide with Matthew 11:14, where Jesus says that John was Elijah, "if you are willing to accept it."

The Temptation

Immediately after the baptism, Jesus was led into the desert by the Holy Spirit. This would be the desolate area between the central plateau and the Jordan River. Mark notes that wild animals were there. All three synoptic writers note that He fasted for forty days. He was tempted repeatedly during this entire period, and this testing seems to have culminated in the three major temptations that Matthew and Luke record.[29] Jesus successfully resisted this temptation, using Scripture to battle Satan. By the time the ordeal ended, it would have been well into the winter of 29/30 CE.

Read
Matthew 4:1–11;
Mark 1:12–13;
Luke 4:1–13.

An Expanding Ministry

What happened next is somewhat problematic. The gospel accounts are generally, but not rigorously, chronological. And here the synoptic narratives skip over significant time periods. Matthew and Mark jump immediately to some time after John the Baptist was put into prison, which was at least several months later. While we are not given the date of John's imprisonment, we learn from John 3:24 that several other things occurred before that happened.

Read
John 1:1–5:47;
Matthew 4:12–14:12;
Mark 1:14–6:44;
Luke 4:14–9:17.

After His time in the desert, Jesus returned to the Jordan region. This would have been late winter in 30 CE. There He called His first disciples (John 1:35–51). While all were from Galilee, they were at that time in the Jordan Valley, where John was preaching. Andrew was one of two men listening to John when he proclaimed that Jesus was "the Lamb of God." They followed Jesus and stayed with Him that day. Andrew went to get his brother, Simon, who was nearby. His message was, "We have found the Messiah." Jesus gave Simon the nickname "Peter" (which means "rock"). On the next day, while in the same area, Jesus talked to Philip. Philip went to get his brother, Nathanael, for he too was convinced that Jesus was the Messiah. Nathanael had a somewhat cynical view and was shocked when Jesus was able to tell him what he had been thinking.

With this entourage, Jesus returned to Galilee. Shortly afterward, He attended a wedding in Cana, a town probably about 8 miles north of Nazareth. There John records that He performed His first miracle—turning water into wine. While this was done at the request of His mother, John implies that the purpose was so that His new disciples would believe in Him.

Following the wedding, Jesus, His family, and His disciples went to Capernaum. This trip may have been a relocation.[30] Moreover, several of those who were becoming His disciples lived there as well. Apparently, during this period, these disciples went with Jesus on some of His trips, but they also spent periods of time on their regular jobs. For example, we later see that Jesus calls Peter and Andrew while they are fishing. When that call comes, they leave the boats and go with Him.

At the time of the Passover (spring of 30 CE), Jesus went up to Jerusalem, taking some of His new associates with Him. According to John, while Jesus was there, He cleansed the temple. Two issues were involved in this incident. The first was the selling of sacrificial animals, which was allowed by OT law (Deut. 14:24–26) as a help for people who lived a long distance away from the temple. What was not allowed was charging exorbitant prices because of the increased demand; also prohibited was the selling of these animals in the temple complex itself. The second issue was the role of the money changers. Jews came from all over the known world (both inside and outside the Roman Empire) and brought a variety of currencies. To pay their temple tax, those foreign coins had to be converted to temple coins—for a fee. It is estimated that the money changers made from $400,000 to $500,000 in today's dollars each year from this practice. But the temple also got a cut, and that totaled about $3,750,000 per year.[31] In terms of buying power, both represented much more. With the vested interest of the temple authorities, it would be surprising if the money changers were not back in the temple courtyard almost as soon as Jesus left.

In the process of the controversy that arose from Jesus' actions, we find Him making an allusion to His coming death and resurrection. He declared to His adversaries that if they destroyed "this temple" (referring to His body), He would raise it again in three days. They understood Him to be referring to the physical edifice near which they were standing.[32]

This trip to Jerusalem was also the occasion when Nicodemus came to Jesus by night. It is within the context of that discussion that we find the famous verse describing God's love (John 3:16).

After the Passover, Jesus remained in Judea for a while teaching, and His disciples were baptizing people who came for repentance, probably in the Jordan River, although we are not told. At the same time, John the Baptist was still in the Jordan Valley baptizing. Some of the Jews tried to stir up trouble between the two by telling John about his "competitor." John reiterated his position as forerunner, noting that they were not in competition. When Jesus knew that the Pharisees were aware of the shift in popularity, He decided to go back to Galilee. This would have been late spring of 30 CE.

For some undisclosed reason, Jesus headed north through Samaria rather than taking the usual route Jews took up the eastern side of the Jordan.[33] At Sychar, He met a woman at a well. After challenging her spiritually, He told her He was the Messiah. When the people of Sychar invited Him, He remained two more days,

THE CLEANSING OF THE TEMPLE

The synoptic writers describe a cleansing of the temple during the last week of Jesus' ministry. This difference between their accounts and the Gospel of John has been viewed by some as a "contradiction." Others have suggested that the different writers chose to put the account in different places for thematic reasons. A third alternative proposed is that Jesus cleansed the temple twice, once at the beginning of His ministry and once at the end. Considering human nature, we would have no reason to doubt that if He indeed cleansed it at the beginning of His ministry, the people later may well have reverted back to form, especially in view of the profits involved.

teaching. He then returned to Galilee, where He traveled and ministered through the summer of 30 CE. It was apparently during this summer that John the Baptist was thrown into prison (Mark 1:14).

In Cana, the same city where Jesus had turned the water to wine, He met a high official whose son in Capernaum was sick. Jesus told him to go home, that his son would live. On his way home, the official met some of his servants, who joyfully told him that his son was well. Upon inquiry, he learned that the boy was healed at the same time Jesus told him the boy would live, although the conversation had taken place about 20 miles away.

The next year and a half are most obscure. The Synoptic Gospels include only a few items, and their relative chronology is not clear; John includes even less. Apparently Jesus maintained His home base in Capernaum and traveled as appropriate. Luke notes that He went from Capernaum to Nazareth, where He read from Isaiah 61 in the synagogue (Luke 4:14–30) and proclaimed that Isaiah's prophecy was fulfilled in their hearing.[34] Matthew seems to interject here a sample of a basic teaching that Jesus proclaimed, namely, the famous Sermon on the Mount (Matt. 5–7). Luke reports a similar sermon "on the plain" (Luke 6:16–49), although he places some of the teaching elements in other contexts. These seem to be typical of the "sermons" Jesus preached when He had any new audience.

The next clear time indicator is in John 6:1, which ties the feeding of the five thousand with a Passover. This Passover was most likely in 32 CE, for events after that started cascading toward the crucifixion. Another indicator, in John 5:1, is the mention of a festival of the Jews. The festival is not named; however, it seems likely that it was the Passover of 31 CE.[35]

During this first portion of Jesus' career, prior to 32 CE, Jesus started giving indications of what He was really about. Two key incidents are reported. The first was the healing of a leprous man. Leprosy made the person "unclean." By heal-

AN OVERVIEW OF JESUS' MINISTRY

(The probable sequence of major events, based on the chronology of this book.)

Time of Inauguration (29–31 CE)
Baptism (autumn 29)
Temptation in the wilderness
Initial calling of the disciples
Miracle in Cana
Passover (30 CE)
Trip through Samaria
Ministry in Galilee
Passover (31 CE)

Year of Popularity (31–32 CE)
Healing ministry/Sabbath controversy
Sending out of the Twelve
Feeding of the 5,000
Passover (32 CE)

Year of Opposition (32–33 CE)
Trip to Phoenicia
Ministry in Galilee
Feeding of the 4,000
Transfiguration
Three trips to Jerusalem
Sukkoth (September 32)
Hanukkah (December 32)
Passover/crucifixion (March/April 33)
Resurrection
Ascension (May 33 CE)

THE SERMON ON THE MOUNT

Two themes vie for dominance in Matthew 5–7. First is the kingdom. Immediately prior to this sermon, we are told that Jesus proclaimed the gospel of the kingdom. The coming of the kingdom was something the Jews had been anticipating for at least a thousand years. Thus, as Jesus proclaimed this message, in their minds, it was a reference to an empire that would displace Rome. Although the term *kingdom* appears ten times in these three chapters, at no time does Jesus redefine that term. He does give it certain new nuances by focusing on morality or ethics, his second theme, and He ties these to abstract qualities such as character traits and prayer. In essence, in this section, He lays out the characteristics of a life within the kingdom much as the Mosaic law laid out characteristics for a person living within the covenant with God.

above left to right
CHURCH OF THE BEATITUDES. A twentieth-century building located near the traditional site of the Sermon on the Mount.

COVE OF THE BEATITUDES. A cove near the Church of the Beatitudes where a speaker can stand along the coast and be heard clearly up the side of the mountain.

ing the man, Jesus was demonstrating not only power to heal but also power over cleanness and uncleanness. The second was the healing of a paralytic man. The text relates that Jesus was in a crowded house. Unable to get in, four men lowered a paralytic man down through the roof.[36] Jesus told the man that his sins had been forgiven. This statement caused consternation among the listeners, for they understood that only God could forgive sins. Thus, Jesus was assuming divine prerogatives. Jesus knew the unspoken (or perhaps murmured) question, and He responded, "Which is easier: to say, 'Your sins are forgiven,' or to say, 'Get up and walk'?" Of course, to say "your sins are forgiven" would be easier, for there would be no way of verifying that assertion. For this reason, He gave a sign that could be verified: He had the man get up and walk home. Thus, He was demonstrating His power to forgive sins and, in the understanding of the Jews, to do what only God could do.

> Jesus demonstrated His power to forgive sins—to do what only God could do.

It was also during this period in Galilee that Jesus started calling specific people to follow Him on a more regular basis. Here we see the account of the call of two sets of brothers, Peter and Andrew, and James and John (Matt. 4:18–22;

Luke 5:1–11). Peter and Andrew, of course, had already met Jesus, but they were now back fishing.[37] They were also living in Peter's house with Peter's mother-in-law. Jesus healed her of a fever after a Sabbath service in the synagogue. Matthew was called later (Matt. 9:9–13). These and other men were designated "apostles" ("sent ones") or sometimes "the Twelve," to distinguish them from the larger group of disciples or followers.

Matthew records several other events that seem to have occurred in this period. Jesus raised the daughter of a synagogue official from the dead (9:18–26); He healed two blind men (9:27–31); and He healed a man who was mute (9:32–34). These supernormal acts had a pur-

PETER'S HOUSE IN CAPERNAUM. The likely location of Peter's house, according to archaeologists. (It later became a church.) After beginning his ministry, Jesus moved his base of operations to the city of Capernaum on the coast of the Sea of Galilee.

pose. They were to validate His claim to be the Messiah. At this point, John the Baptist had been in prison for some time (probably about a year) and was discouraged. Perhaps he expected Jesus to do more for him in his situation. Or perhaps he expected an overthrow of the government. In any case, he sent some of his followers to Jesus to ask whether He was really the Messiah (Matt. 11:2–19). Jesus told them to report to John what they had seen: "The blind receive sight, the lame walk, those who have leprosy are cured, the deaf hear, the dead are raised, and the good news is preached to the poor." In this claim, Jesus was alluding to the promises of Isaiah 35:5–6 and 61:1.

During this period, we also see a growing pattern of confrontation between Jesus and the religious leadership. The main issue was the observance of the Sabbath, but this merely symbolized the rigid guidelines that were being developed to "fence in" or protect the law.[38] One example occurred when the disciples of Jesus walked through a field and plucked grain on the Sabbath (Matt. 12:1–8; Mark 2:23–28; Luke 6:1–5). The problem was not the taking of the grain, for the Mosaic law stated that a person walking through a field might pick fruit or grain to eat as long as he didn't put it in a basket (Deut. 23:24–25). However, the disciples were doing it on the Sabbath. When they rubbed the grain between their hands, which removed the chaff, they threshed the grain. Both of these acts were

DID JESUS HAVE A HOME?

In connection with the healing of the paralytic, Matthew indicates that Jesus was back in Capernaum (Matt. 9:1). Mark 2:1 says that Jesus "had come home," which may suggest that He was in His own house. The primary argument against that view is the quotation in Matthew 8:20 and Luke 9:58: "Foxes have holes and birds of the air have nests, but the Son of Man has no place to lay his head." However, it is not clear if this expression was used to reflect the time of His traveling, or even a later phase of His career. While Matthew quotes this saying prior to the healing of the paralytic, Luke's citation is some four chapters later. Clearly, at one point, Jesus had a home. We just don't know when He stopped living in it.

considered violations of the Law according to the standards agreed upon by the rabbis.

When confronted, Jesus responded with a curious illustration of how David violated the Law by eating the consecrated bread of the tabernacle (1 Sam. 21:4–6). The point would seem to be that David, supposedly on the king's business, was viewed as functioning in the Lord's service. As such, he was authorized to use the portion dedicated to the priests—those in the Lord's service.[39] Since the disciples were following Jesus, who was greater than the temple, they also were ministering and thus able to eat.

A MUSTARD TREE. A tree, growing by a wall, identified as the kind of tree Jesus referred to in the parable of the mustard seed.

Another "violation" of the Sabbath was the healing of the man with the withered hand (Mark 3:1–6). Jesus had a direct confrontation with the Pharisees over this issue in the synagogue. He called the man up front where everyone could see and began the healing with a question, "What is better to do on the Sabbath, good or evil?" No one wanted to answer the question because they knew the implications. They could not say evil. But if they said good, then Jesus would heal, which was contrary to their interpretations. Jesus healed the man anyway.

Perhaps the culminating "violation" of the Sabbath during Jesus' early ministry was the healing of the lame man at the pool of Bethesda (John 5:1–47). Tradition had developed that an angel would occasionally stir up the waters of this pool, and the first one in at that point would be healed. While in Jerusalem for a feast (probably Passover in the spring of 31 CE), Jesus saw a man lying there who had been waiting for thirty-eight years for healing. Jesus asked him if he wanted to be healed, whereupon the man noted that he was helpless and did not have anyone to put him in the water. Jesus then told him to pick up his pallet and walk.[40] The man obeyed; he picked up his pallet and apparently headed for home. En route he met some of the Jewish leaders, who were aghast that he would carry a load on the Sabbath. He replied that whoever healed him gave him authority to carry the pallet.

There is a pattern to what the writers report. First, it is clear that there was a major disagreement between Jesus and the rabbis regarding how the Law should be understood. And He kept challenging them on this issue—not by debate but by action. The actions were not routine, however. As Jesus tried to convey to John, they were demonstrations of His position as Messiah. As such, these challenges were intended to shift the focus of the rabbis from the Law to the fulfillment of the Law in the person of Jesus. But they were more concerned about their rules, and as a result, they missed the message.

It was for this reason that Jesus used many parables in His teaching. Parables are often defined as "stories with a heavenly meaning." More properly, we should view them as analogies in which spiritual truths are presented through familiar incidents.

BETHESDA. A model of the pools of Bethesda in Jerusalem that shows the five colonnades, or porticos, mentioned in John 5:2. The lower pools have been excavated and found to be some twenty feet deep.

Probably one of the favorites is the parable of the sower (Matt. 13:1–23; Mark 4:1–20; Luke 8:4–18). In this parable, a man sows seed, which lands on a variety of surfaces. Some seeds are eaten by the birds, some sprout and die, and some produce fruit. While Jesus admonished His listeners to pay attention to the message, it is clear that they didn't get it. Even His closest disciples did not, and when they got Jesus aside, they asked Him what it meant and why He used that method of teaching. Jesus told them that the reason He used parables was so that those who were insensitive would be hardened, while those who were sensitive to spiritual teaching would understand. In the process, He quoted from Isaiah (Matt. 13:14–15; cf. Isa. 6:9–10).

One point that we should keep in mind is that if our chronology is correct, the point at which we see Jesus starting to use parables significantly was almost two years after His baptism by John. In the interim, He had busily given demonstration after demonstration of His power and position. Instead of being hailed as the Messiah, however, He was being condemned because He helped people on the Sabbath. It is for this reason that so many of the parables begin, "The kingdom of heaven is like. . . ." Their function was to obscure Jesus' message of the kingdom to those who weren't really interested. Pages 394–95 show a summary chart of most of Jesus' parables.

The second year of Jesus' ministry concluded with several notable events. First, His mother and brothers came to visit Him (Matt. 12:45–50; Mark 3:31–35; Luke 8:19–21). Their visit is mentioned in conjunction with the time when the Pharisees inferred that Jesus was able to perform miraculous signs because He was Himself demon-possessed.[41] Apparently even His family was concerned that He was possessed (Mark 3:21). Unable to reach Jesus in the house where He was

A LAMP. An oil lamp such as the one Jesus spoke of in a parable.

THE PARABLES OF JESUS

Jesus makes a number of comparisons. Many are parables, many are not. Some are difficult to determine. The following list focuses on comparisons that are explicitly identified in the text as such. Those in bold type are parables that describe the kingdom of heaven.

OBJECT LESSION		MEANING
New Patch on Old Garment	(Matt. 9:16; Mark 2:21; Luke 5:36)	Justifies Jesus' disciples not fasting.
New Wine and Wineskins	(Matt. 9:17; Mark 2:22; Luke 5:37)	Justifies Jesus' disciples not fasting.
The Sower	(Matt. 13:1-23; Mark 4:1-20; Luke 8:5-8)	People respond differently to God's Word.
The Lamp*	(Mark 4:21-25)	The purpose of light is to reveal, not to hide.
Growing Seed	(Mark 4:26-29)	The kingdom of heaven grows mysteriously.
The Wheat and Tares	(Matt. 13:24-30)	An enemy is sowing counterfeits within the kingdom.
Mustard Seed	(Matt. 13:31-32; Mark 4:30)	The kingdom of heaven begins small but gets big.
Leaven	(Matt. 13:33)	The kingdom of heaven grows like leaven secretly.
The Good Samaritan**	(Luke 10:25-37)	A neighbor is whoever has a need.
Rich Man with Full Barns	(Luke 12:16-21)	A warning against greed.
Slaves Waiting for Bridegroom	(Luke 12:35-40)	Everyone is to be ready for the coming of the Son of Man.
Unfruitful Fig Tree	(Luke 13:6-9)	The nation of Israel would be judged for lack of fruit.
Hidden Treasure	(Matt. 13:44)	The kingdom of heaven is a hidden treasure.
The Pearl of Great Price	(Matt. 13:45-46)	The kingdom of heaven is worth everything someone has.
The Dragnet	(Matt. 13:47-50)	At the end of the age, people will be sorted and the wicked rejected.
The Householder	(Matt. 13:51-52)	Disciples of the kingdom of heaven have new insights.

Blind leading the Blind	(Matt. 15:14; Luke 6:39-40)	The Pharisees were poor teachers because they did not understand the truth.
The Prodigal Son	(Luke 15:11-32)	God's love will accept anyone.
The Dishonest Steward	(Luke 16:1-13)	Jesus' disciples were to use material goods to win friends.
The Rich Man and Lazarus***	(Luke 16:19-31)	If people did not listen to the OT, they would not believe even when Jesus rose from the dead.
Debt of Ten Thousand Talents	(Matt. 18:23-25)	People should forgive.
Working in the Vineyard	(Matt. 20:1-16)	God admits people to the kingdom without favoritism and rewards all generously.
The Unjust Judge	(Luke 18:2-8)	Disciples should pray ceaselessly.
Prayers of Tax-collector and Pharisee	(Luke 18:10-14)	People should not trust in themselves.
Two Sons Asked to Work	(Matt. 21:28-32)	People who obey will be admitted to the kingdom of heaven.
The Rented-out Vineyard	(Matt. 21:33-44; Mark 12:1-13; Luke 9-18)	The leaders of Israel would be responsible for the national rejection.
Wedding Feast	(Matt. 22:2-14; Luke 14:7-24)	Many are called to the kingdom of heaven, but they must get there the right way.
Fig Tree	(Matt. 24:32-35; Luke 21:29-36)	As the blooming of a fig tree foretells summer, so various signs foretell the coming of the Son of Man
The Ten Virgins	(Matt. 25:1-13)	People not prepared will not be able to enter the kingdom of heaven.
The Talents	(Matt. 25:14-30; Luke 19:12-27)	Preparation for the kingdom involves using the abilities God has given.

*   The context of Mark puts this as part of Jesus teaching in parables. Matthew includes the comparison in the Sermon on the Mount.

**   While commonly viewed as a parable, it is not labeled as such.

***   It is debated whether this is a parable. It is not labeled as such, but the primary argument against that is the fact that it contains a specific name.

teaching, they sent for Him. Jesus responded that His mother and brothers were those who did God's will.

The second event occurred as Jesus and His disciples were crossing the Sea of Galilee in a fishing boat (Mark 4:35-41; Luke 8:22–25; Matthew records this incident earlier in his book, Matt. 8:23–27). Jesus was sleeping in the stern when a sudden storm arose. The men with Him (even the expert sailors) feared for their lives. They awakened Jesus, who first rebuked them for their lack of faith and then rebuked the elements. The storm stopped.

When they reached the opposite side of the lake, they encountered a demoniac in the tombs. Jesus cast out the demons, although He allowed them to go into a herd of pigs on the hill. When this occurred, however, the pigs ran down the hillside into the lake and drowned. This incident frightened the local people enough that they asked Jesus to leave.[42]

> The people of Nazareth felt that because they knew Jesus as a boy, He could not be the Messiah.

Jesus returned home (Matt. 13:53–58; Mark 6:1–6), where He did not get a good reception. The people of Nazareth felt that because they had known Jesus as a boy, He could not be the Messiah. Because of this lack of faith, Jesus was unable to work and left.

Approximately at this time, Herod was enticed to kill John the Baptist (Matt. 14:1–12; Mark 6:14–29).[43] The account in the Gospels is given after the fact, in connection with Herod's reaction to reports of the Twelve being sent out by pairs and performing miracles. He suspected that John had been raised from the dead.

The Peak of Popularity

This brings us to the high point of Jesus' career from a human perspective, and the only miracle recorded in all four gospels (Matt. 14:13–21; Mark 6:30–44; Luke 9:10–17; John 6:1–40). Near the time of the Passover in 32 CE, shortly after John's death, a large group gathered out in the hills of Galilee near Bethsaida

*Read
John 6:1–71;
Matthew 14:13–36;
Mark 6:30–52;
Luke 9:10–17.*

FISHING BOAT. A fishing boat from the first century, buried beneath the Sea of Galilee and uncovered by archaeologists during a dry spell. This gives insight into the kind of boat Jesus and his disciples would have used.

to listen to Jesus. As He finished His teaching, the people were not prone to leave. The disciples wanted Jesus to send them home. He challenged them to feed them, but they remarked that they didn't have the money to buy food. Jesus took the five small loaves of bread and two fish that a young man had, and with that He fed the entire group. As they organized the people into groups of fifty, they discovered that there were five thousand men in addition to women and children. Not only were all fed, but the disciples collected leftovers.

John takes the incident a step further as he relates the aftermath. The people noted this tremendous power and decided to try to force Jesus to be king. He sent His disciples back across the sea, and then later that night, He walked across the water, where He met the boat in the middle of the lake. Peter cried out, asking Jesus to allow him to walk across the water also. Jesus invited him, and Peter was all right as long as he was not distracted by the wind. As soon as he became aware of it, however, he began to sink. Jesus kept him from going under and then rode back with the disciples in the boat.

The next day, the people Jesus had fed began looking for Him. They finally found Him across the lake, in Capernaum, and wanted to know when He got there. Jesus rebuked them, saying that they really didn't want Him, they were just interested in being fed. They attempted to dodge the issue by asking for a sign to verify His message. To justify their request, they cited Moses and the manna, the bread that came down from heaven. Here Jesus gave the conversation a spiritual focus by asserting that He was bread come down out of heaven. This statement totally lost the people, who were upset both because He refused to perform more miracles and because He claimed to have come down out of heaven. Unable to follow or accept the spiritual truths Jesus taught, the audience grumbled and then began to leave in disgust.

Following this discussion, many of His so-called disciples stopped following Him. They were not prepared for a Messiah who had a mind of his own and who was not interested in being king. Following this, Jesus asked the Twelve if they would leave also. Peter got it right when he replied, "Lord, to whom shall we go? You have the words of eternal life" (John 6:68).

However, with this event, the tide of popularity had turned. Jesus generally avoided Judea because of the animosity of the Jewish leadership. Events were beginning to come together that would result in His execution.

REVIEW QUESTIONS

1. Why would someone who claimed to be Messiah have to prove it?

2. What is the genre called "gospel"?

3. What is the synoptic problem?

4. What is the difference between the two-source and the four-source theory?

5. What is Q, and why is it significant?

6. How does this book suggest that the gospel accounts originated?

7. How and why was the birth of John unique?

8. How and why was the birth of Jesus unique?

9. Trace the activities of Jesus up to the peak of His popularity.

10. What are parables, and why did Jesus use them?

11. Why did many people stop following Jesus after He fed the five thousand?

19

CHAPTER

An Empty Tomb

OVERVIEW

After the feeding of the five thousand and about a year before the crucifixion, we see Jesus carefully arranging His activities. Many people were disappointed that He refused to be king on their terms and left. The Jewish leaders wanted to execute Him, but He stayed out of their way. During the summer, He went north as far as the region of Tyre and Sidon. He also gave His closest followers hints of what was to come. In the fall, He went to Jerusalem for the Feast of Taber-nacles, but on His terms. That winter He stayed in the Jordan Valley. Twice He went to the Jerusalem area, once for Hanukkah, and once to raise Lazarus from the dead. Finally, a week before Passover, He presented Himself to the people as Messiah in a triumphant entry. Less than a week later, He was crucified, coinciding with the sacrifice of the Passover lamb. Buried, and placed under armed guard, three days later He was resurrected.

STUDY GOALS

▶ Trace the later ministry of Jesus.

▶ Demonstrate how Jesus anticipated and moved toward the crucifixion.

▶ Show how the date of the crucifixion may be determined.

▶ Trace the events of the last week of Jesus' life up to His crucifixion.

▶ Demonstrate the historicity of the resurrection.

The last year of Jesus' life seemed especially to be carefully choreographed. His confrontations, His travels, His signs, and even His teachings worked to place Him in Jerusalem during the correct Passover celebration at exactly the time the Jewish leaders reached the point of open hatred and the Roman leaders were ready to acquiesce in a lynching. In other words, Jesus knew where He was going, when He would get there, and what would happen next.

We pick up with the aftermath of the feeding of the five thousand. As we noted in chapter 18, after that miracle, Jesus' disciples (that is, those who followed Him) began to leave.[1] Some left for material reasons—they discovered they would not be able to get a steady supply of free meals. Others left for political or social reasons—they discovered they would not be able to make Jesus king under their terms. Still others left for theological reasons—they discovered they could not put Jesus into a neat little box that they had all figured out, whether as a prophet or as a king.

But some were beginning to understand that there was more to Jesus than to any other man. Peter expressed it well when he said, "You have the words of eternal life" (John 6:68). After this event, the Twelve followed Jesus on a regular basis, although when the transition point from "sometimes" to "full-time" occurred is not clear.

A SUMMER OF HIDE-AND-SEEK

Read Matthew 15:1–17:27; Mark 6:53–9:32; Luke 9:45.

During the summer of 32, Jesus avoided Jerusalem. John skips over that period, jumping instead to the fall Feast of Tabernacles. The Synoptic Gospels, however, record several significant events as Jesus began teaching His closest followers, the

GARDEN TOMB. A tomb discovered in 1883 by General Charles George Gordon, who was impressed by the location. It is most likely not the tomb of Jesus. The traditional site of the burial is covered by the Church of the Holy Sepulchre.

RITUAL WASHING

Two aspects of ritual washing became a point of contention between the Pharisees and Jesus (Matt. 15:1–20; Mark 7:1–23). The distinction lies in the word *unclean*. On the one hand, there was the hygienic aspect, although we know from history that many people have ignored that. Uncleanness could make one sick. It does not seem that Jesus was ignoring this element. However, since the time of Ezra and Nehemiah, there had been more concern with *how* one washed. For the Pharisees, *unclean* did not have to do with sickness but with method. The issue seems to be that the disciples were not following the prescribed ritual in their daily activities. (It is not clear whether the problem was a failure to wash at all or a failure to wash "properly.") For the Pharisees, the process had become a form of obsessiveness (William L. Lang, *The Gospel According to Mark* [Grand Rapids: Eerdmans, 1974], 242–49). Jesus countered their position by saying that while dirt can make a person sick, it cannot make a person unclean. The outside—the ritual—doesn't matter. Uncleanness comes from what is inside, from a heart attitude.

Twelve, about His upcoming death (and, if they had been listening, they also would have heard "hints" about His resurrection).

After several healings (Mark 6:53–56) and the discussion in the Capernaum synagogue (John 6:25–65), we read of another confrontation with the Jewish leaders. This time the issue was cleanness. The concern was that Jesus' disciples did not perform the ritual cleansings that the Pharisaic tradition dictated. Jesus responded that cleanness was an issue of the heart. He said that heart attitudes produced evil actions. Thus, a clean heart was more important than clean hands.

He also declared at this time that the Pharisees, because of their traditions, had nicely set aside God's direct revelation. For example, they dishonored their parents by declaring that what would have supported their parents in their old age was to be regarded as Corban, that is, a gift to God (Mark 7:11).[2] After this rebuke, even Jesus' disciples were concerned. They approached Him and asked if He was aware that the Pharisees were offended. Jesus pointed out that a time of judgment was coming, and the Pharisees were the blind leading the blind. He was more concerned, however, that the disciples did not understand His point.

From Capernaum, Jesus and His cadre moved north into the region of Tyre and Sidon. The writers mention this trip only in passing, and its purpose is not clear. Mark describes it as an attempt to seek solitude and rest. However, His reputation had preceded Him. We are told of the faith of a Canaanite woman who asked that her daughter be healed. Jesus asserted that His mission was to the Jews, and He used the term "dogs" when referring to Gentiles (outsiders).[3] Unoffended, she replied that even dogs ate crumbs that fell from the table. Because of her faith, He healed her daughter without leaving where He was.

Jesus then returned to the region of Galilee, apparently to the southeast side of the lake. There He healed a deaf man who could hardly speak. He also fed another large group of people, this time about four thousand.

Then a group of Pharisees arrived and demanded a sign. Instead of giving in to their demand, He assured them that the only sign they would see would be that of Jonah the prophet (Matt. 16:1–12).[4] This incident set the stage for another lesson for the Twelve. They were crossing the Sea of Galilee again and realized that they had forgotten to bring bread. As they journeyed, Jesus chose to use the travel time for teaching. He warned them to beware of the yeast of the Sadducees and Pharisees. Jesus was warning against philosophical blinders that would keep them from seeing what was before them. But the disciples were thinking about the fact that there was no physical food in the boat. Jesus reminded them of the two times they had observed Him feed multitudes with scraps. He was trying to drive home the point that with God physical needs were not an issue. They should thus be more concerned with spiritual needs.

> Jesus was warning the disciples against philosophical blinders that would keep them from seeing what was before them.

When they landed at Bethsaida, Jesus healed a blind man and then moved further north to Caesarea Philippi. There He began to quiz His disciples on their perception of what was happening. "Who do people say I am?" He asked them (Mark 8:27; cf. Luke 9:18).[5] This would have been a diagnostic question—did they perceive what was happening in the culture? Their reply showed a variety of answers being bandied about. Clearly the people were confused. They understood that Jesus was special, but they couldn't quite place Him in a niche. Was He Jeremiah? Or John the Baptist? Or Elijah? Or just one of the prophets?

Jesus then asked the Twelve, "Who do you say I am?" Peter responded with his famous declaration, "You are the Messiah, the Son of the living God" (Matt.

CAESAREA PHILIPPI. A Roman city at the northern edge of Palestine, near the headwaters of the Jordan River and on the slopes of Mount Hermon.

THE BLIND MAN IN BETHSAIDA

Jesus' healing of a blind man in Bethsaida (Mark 8:22–26) is one of the more inter-esting healings in the gospel accounts. Jesus healed the man in two stages. In the first stage, He restored the man's physical vision. The second stage may then have involved correcting the parts of the brain required to interpret what the man saw. Following on Jesus' warnings to the disciples against the teachings of the Sadducees and Pharisees, there would seem to be a lesson here indicating that physical sight was not all that was involved in "seeing."

16:16).[6] His answer has two parts. The first part is clear. It would be expected that at this point in Jesus' career, the disciples would have understood that He was the Messiah. That was the purpose of all the signs that had been done. That was why Jesus had been so exasperated with the Pharisees. Seeing Him as Messiah would have been the minimum understanding. What would not be clear to His disci-ples was His relationship to God, which Peter expressed as the "Son of the living God." Jesus Himself noted that Peter had received divine revelation and that his declaration would be the foundation stone of the yet-future church. It also showed that the understanding of who Jesus really is was starting to come together for the Twelve, although they still had a long way to go.

This is evident in the aftermath. Following Peter's declaration, Jesus told them about His upcoming death. Even though He also was telling them about His res-urrection, it must have been baffling. When Peter, somewhat impetuously, began to rebuke Jesus for such a thought, Jesus confronted him, stating that he was spouting the ideas of men, not God.[7] Jesus then continued to explain that the secret to eternal life was for people to follow Him. One of the most perplexing items in this section is the statement, "I tell you the truth, some who are stand-ing here will not taste death before they see the Son of Man coming in his king-dom" (Matt. 16:28). The context suggests that this prediction refers to the next

WHEN IS A ROCK NOT A ROCK?

Matthew 16:18 records Jesus as observing, "You are Peter [Petros] and on this rock [petra] I will build my church." The former Greek term means "rock" or "stone," while the latter refers to solid rock as in bedrock. In the former case, "Rocky" might be analogous. The latter would be "the foundation of an impregnable position or a rocky fortress" (BDAG, 660). Another point is that the church at this point is yet in the future. Although there had been many who had a special relationship with God, the collection of people called "the church" would not come about until some-time afterward.

One other point needs to be observed. The expression "gates of hell" refers to defenses, not offenses. Attack-ing armies do not have "gates," but bastions do. Therefore, when Jesus said that the gates of hell would not win over them, He was stating that hell would not be able to stand against the onslaught of this new entity called the church.

event recorded—the transfiguration of Jesus, probably as a foreshadowing of the resurrection.

Less than a week later, Jesus took some of those standing there, Peter, James, and John, up on a high mountain, where He was transfigured before their eyes. His clothing and face became radiant, and Moses and Elijah appeared with Him.[8] Overwhelmed, Peter suggested building three tabernacles or booths as memorials. Immediately, they heard a voice from heaven saying, "This is my Son, whom I love. Listen to him!" (Mark 9:7). When they looked up, only Jesus was there. As they descended from the mountain, He advised them not to tell what they had seen until after His resurrection.[9]

MOUNT HERMON. Probably the mountain where the transfiguration took place.

Coming down from the mountain, they encountered a crowd. At the center was a man who had a demon-possessed son. He told Jesus that the boy had had numerous seizures as a result of the evil spirit and was unable to speak. He had brought the boy to Jesus' disciples, but they were unable to help. Jesus cast out the spirit, and the people were amazed.[10]

Jesus once again passed through Galilee. He continued to travel covertly because He was trying to convey an important lesson to the disciples: He was going to be betrayed, put to death, and then resurrected on the third day (Matt. 17:22–23; Mark 9:30–32; Luke 9:43–45). However, as Luke observes, "They did not understand what this meant . . . and they were afraid to ask him about it" (Luke 9:45).

After they had returned to Capernaum, local tax collectors stopped Peter and asked whether Jesus paid the temple tax (Matt. 17:24–27). Without consulting Jesus about the issue, Peter asserted that of course he did. When Peter returned home, Jesus greeted him with a question regarding whether the kings of the world collected taxes from their own sons or from strangers. When Peter replied, "Strangers," Jesus told him that the sons were then free. The idea was that Jesus, as king, should be exempt—and His specially chosen followers also. However, to

LESSONS IN HUMILITY

Jesus' instructions on humility include at least three aspects. First, there is the matter of humility and openness in accepting Jesus' teachings. Second, there is an aspect of servitude—serving others rather than just looking out for ourselves. Then, tucked into Mark's and Luke's accounts is the added element of tolerance of those who may not be doing things exactly as we are. This aspect is seen in the Lord's response to John after the latter expressed concern regarding the man who was casting out demons in Jesus' name (Mark 9:38–41; Luke 9:49–50).

CAPERNAUM. A synagogue in Capernaum that was actually built about the fourth century but may have been on the same site as a synagogue Jesus attended.

avoid offending, He sent Peter out to catch a fish. Peter was told that in the mouth of the fish he would find a coin with which to pay the taxes. Apparently Peter did so.[11]

While still in Capernaum, the disciples got into an argument about who was the greatest. This issue likely had become an ongoing point of debate. Mark notes that they had been discussing it along the road. Matthew reports that they actually asked Jesus about it. In response, Jesus stood a child in their midst and asserted that they needed to become like little children to enter the kingdom of heaven.

AUTUMN IN JERUSALEM

Jesus seems to have remained in Capernaum until autumn. When it was time for the pilgrimage to Jerusalem in conjunction with the Feast of Tabernacles or Booths (Sukkoth), Jesus' brothers encouraged Him to go with them. He demurred. But it was the method that was at issue, not the trip. They encouraged Him to "show yourself to the world" (John 7:4). Jesus told them that it was not the right time. They left, and He continued His practice of traveling in as much secrecy as His public position would allow.

Read
Matthew 19:1–12;
Mark 10:1–16;
Luke 9:51–11:54;
John 7:1–10:21.

As they traveled, Jesus again used the time for teaching. In this section, we see instructions regarding the cost of discipleship (Luke 9:51–56), living with our neighbors (Luke 10:25–37), divorce (Matt. 19:1–12; Mark 10:1–12), and humility and wealth (Matt. 19:13–26; Mark 10:13–16). Also during this trip, Jesus sent out a group of seventy by pairs into the cities ahead of Him. While He gave them a number of directions, their message was very simple. They were to heal the sick and tell them, "The kingdom of God is near you" (Luke 10:9).[12] He was bringing people to an awareness of His person and preparing the nation for a decision.

En route to Jerusalem, Jesus went back through Samaria (Luke 9:51–56). This time the greeting was not as warm as we saw earlier in John 4. The people of a specific village "did not welcome him," showing anti-Jewish bias. His disciples were ready to call fire down from heaven, but Jesus rebuked them for failing to understand the spiritual issues and went on to another village.

From there they crossed the Jordan into the eastern region of Judea. The challenges and questions continued. It was there that the Pharisees asked Him about divorce and the wealthy man was told to sell all he had.[13] It was also the place where the lawyer asked Jesus who his neighbor was (Luke 10:29). In answer, Jesus told him the story of the Good Samaritan, showing that a neighbor was whoever one came into contact with.

As He neared Jerusalem, Jesus stayed at the house of Martha in Bethany.[14] Martha's sister Mary sat at the feet of Jesus listening, while Martha was busy preparing for Jesus and His entourage. When Martha complained because Mary wasn't helping, Jesus told her that Mary had chosen the "better" thing (Luke 10:42)—spiritual teaching—implying that Martha should have made simpler plans.

Luke now reports several items that Matthew presented earlier in his record, including teaching on prayer (cf. the Sermon on the Mount, Matt. 6:9–13; 7:7–11) and a confrontation with the Pharisees over the source of His power (cf. Matt. 9:34; 12:24–29). These differences have caused considerable controversy. They are often viewed as discrepancies or as items "out of order." This view assumes that each gospel was supposed to be in strictly chronological order. I have suggested a general chronological but also topical order. There is also a tendency to assume that each teaching or confrontation of Jesus had occurred only once in His ministry. These are probably not valid assumptions. For example, would Jesus teach on prayer only once? As a traveling teacher, it is probable that He taught a number of times on the same subjects. It is also likely that each teaching occasion included some different nuances; that is, He did not make "canned" speeches, but taught genuinely. This means that each gospel writer could well have picked one occasion to report, reported it accurately, and thus have some differences in the same message. The Lord's Prayer is a major theme of the Sermon on the Mount,

WHOSE HOUSE?

We tend to assume that Martha, Mary, and Lazarus as sisters and brother still lived in the same house. That does not seem to be the case. When we look at a later incident involving Martha and Mary in John 12:1–8, and compare it with Matthew 26:6–13 and Mark 14:3–9, the following picture emerges. They are at the house of Simon the Leper, and Martha is serving. Most English translations and many Greek manuscripts for Luke 10:38 state that Martha welcomed Jesus into her home. This suggests that Simon and Martha are married. Lazarus is reclining at the table, apparently as a guest. Mary also is apparently a guest. This incident does not seem to be the same occasion that Luke talks about in 7:36–50, where the setting is the house of Simon the Pharisee.

CELEBRITY WITHOUT MASS MEDIA

Amid the heightened tensions surrounding Jesus, we need to keep in mind the demographics of the country. It was a time without mass media. As a result, few would have known what Jesus looked like. The exceptions would have been those who had personally listened to Him. However, they also would have reported on what they had seen and heard (the reason for the "signs" and the stories was to give the people something to pass on to their neighbors as validation of His message). Jesus' reputation would therefore have spread widely within Judea and in the surrounding environs. Given the short term of His ministry, the word probably would not have gone much beyond that.

a larger message on kingdom living. In Luke, this model prayer is a result of a request from "one of his disciples" for teaching on this subject (Luke 11:1). The same observation would be true of the confrontations. Jesus had a message that ran counter to the teachings of the Jewish leaders. Pharisees would have tended to react similarly, regardless of where they lived, so it would not be surprising if several different groups made the same accusations (e.g., that He was possessed by demons). Of course, some confrontations would be key. It is suggested that given the writers' freedom to insert material topically, different writers would put events in different literary contexts.

At some point during this trip, Jesus was invited for lunch to the house of a Pharisee (Luke 11:37). Jesus surprised the man by not following ritual in washing His hands before the meal. He probably surprised him even more by His response to the criticism. Once more He addressed the fundamental issue of internal cleansing, but as He did so, He was rather strong in His condemnation. A lawyer at the luncheon took offense and told Jesus that He indicted the lawyers as well. Jesus was unapologetic and proceeded to blast the lawyers even more strongly. The basic criticism of both groups was the same—hypocrisy. They set high standards for others but then excused themselves when they fell short. As might be expected, this episode heightened tensions, and the Jewish leaders began plotting to kill Him.[15]

As Luke 12:1 expresses, a crowd had gathered, apparently having heard that Jesus was in town. Jesus, as He regularly did, began teaching, using this episode as a warning. When a person in the crowd asked Jesus to intervene in family affairs (a role for a judge or higher civil leader such as a king), Jesus began teaching in parables. The point made in these parables was that people should not be focused on material things. Rather, they should be focused on spiritual matters and prepared for when God's kingdom erupted into the human sphere. Somewhat confused, Peter asked for whom the parable was intended: the Twelve or people in general? Jesus seemingly dodged the issue by talking about how important it is that servants wait for the return of their master. He was pointing them toward His second coming, although the disciples did not realize it at the time.

"LIVING WATER"

Part of the ceremony for Sukkoth involved taking a pitcher of water each of the seven days of the festival and pouring it into a basin by the altar of burnt offering. This was not done on the eighth day (Lev. 23:36), the day Jesus cried out (John 7:37–38). His offer of "living water" would then have been a new item and not part of the OT covenants. The OT uses a Hebrew equivalent phrase in a number of passages that talk about cleansing (Lev. 14–15; Num. 19), which the NIV translates as "fresh water," and the KJV and NASB translate as "running" or "flowing" water. As such, the offer of "living water" within this context should have been understood as a symbolic reference to cleansing.

In Jerusalem the Jews who had gathered for Sukkoth were wondering whether Jesus would come. He did not make His presence known until midway into the feast, when He began to teach in the temple.[16] Jesus' knowledge amazed those who heard Him (John 7:15). It also attracted the attention of the Jewish leaders. As the crowds gathered, Jesus began to confront them about their plot to kill Him. They played dumb, asking who could be seeking to kill Him. However, some of the common people knew there was a plot under way. They asked, "Isn't this the man they are trying to kill?" (v. 25).

Over the next three days, the debate continued. Finally, on the last day of the feast, He stood in the temple and offered "living water." This offer precipitated an even greater debate and varied reactions within the crowd. The Sanhedrin sent troops to take action. They returned empty-handed, however, because they were amazed at Jesus' teaching.

> The Sanhedrin troops returned empty-handed because they were amazed at Jesus' teaching.

Included in this section of John is the account of the woman caught in adultery (John 7:53–8:11).[17] Jesus had been on the Mount of Olives, and when He returned to the temple courts, some Jewish leaders brought her to Him. They said that she had been caught in the act of adultery. Pointing out that the OT punishment for this act was execution by stoning, they asked for His recommendation. Jesus did not respond, but He stooped down and wrote on the ground. When they persisted, He stood up and said, "If any one of you is without sin, let him be the first to throw a stone at her." He then stooped down and wrote again. When He arose, the mob had dispersed and the woman was left alone. When He asked where her accusers were, she said that no one remained. He then told her not to sin again (showing that He knew that she was guilty but was inadvertently part of a trap).[18]

After this incident, the Pharisees confronted Jesus over the validity of His testimony (John 8:12–59). The next day, Jesus was in the treasury teaching. There He began one of those conversations that do not fit well with our image of a meek, nonconfrontational Jesus. He started out by declaring that He was the "light of the world" and anybody who followed Him would not be in darkness (a rather arrogant claim from their perspective). The Pharisees immediately challenged His claim, stating that He testified about Himself. He then asserted that His Father also testified about Him, and that made two witnesses (as required by the Law, Deut. 17:6; 19:15). The Pharisees then asked, "Where is your Father?" Jesus responded that they didn't know His Father. As the conversation progressed, He raised the ante by asserting that He was not of this world—and they would die in their sins unless they believed in Him (an even more arrogant claim). To this the Pharisees asked, "Who are you?" Jesus continued by asserting that those who were disciples would be set free by knowing the truth. The Pharisees stated, "We are Abraham's descendants and have *never* been slaves of anyone. How can you say that we shall be set free?" (John 8:33, italics added). Jesus replied that they were the slaves of sin and sought to kill Him. He also told them that if they were descendants of Abraham, they should do what Abraham would have done.

Following that comment, the Pharisees started getting nasty. They asserted that they were not born of fornication (probably implying, "unlike someone who is present"), and that God was their Father.[19] At this Jesus proclaimed that if God was their Father, they would love Him, for He was from God. Rather, their father was the Devil. At this point, He made one of the boldest challenges possible. He challenged His enemies to point out even one sin that He had committed. Their response was that He was demon-possessed.

> Jesus challenged His enemies to point out even one sin that He had committed.

Jesus replied that He was not demon-possessed, for He honored God (His Father). However, He turned the conversation again by asserting that whoever kept His word would never see death (another very arrogant claim). With this, one senses disgust in the Jews, who now proclaim that Jesus' claim proves that He has a demon. Abraham and the prophets all died, so how dare He promise that His followers would not taste death? Basically they were asking, "Who do you think you are?" Jesus did not answer directly but pointed out that Abraham rejoiced to see His day. By now the Jews were totally mystified. How could this man, who was not even fifty years old, have seen Abraham, who had died nearly two thousand years earlier? At this Jesus replied, "Before Abraham was born, I am!" Jesus was claiming to be God (as arrogant a claim as one can make), and the

THE BLINDNESS OF THE PHARISEES

The claim of the Pharisees that as Abraham's descendants they had never been slaves illustrates their blindness. The temple was in the shadow of the Antonia, a Roman fortress that housed Roman troops who served the Roman governor, the actual ruler of the land. Less than two hundred years earlier, the Maccabean revolt had freed the Jews from the rule of Syria. Two centuries before that, they had been in exile in Babylon, from which most Jews had not come back. Before the Exodus, they had been slaves in Egypt. So to say that as Abraham's descendants they had never been enslaved shows a poor grasp of history. However, Jesus does not address that issue but points toward more important spiritual matters.

WHY NOW?

Two interesting philosophical questions arise out of the account of Jesus' healing of the blind man in John 9:1–12. The first is, How many times had Jesus passed this man if he was put in that place to beg every day? Why did Jesus not heal him earlier? It would seem that Jesus was waiting for the right time in terms of the testimony the healing would provide. The other question is the one the disciples asked—"Who sinned, this man or his parents?"—which tied physical problems to sin. In the case of a birth defect, who was the sinner causing the problem? The cause of sin, as we saw earlier, was the focus of the book of Job.

Pharisees knew it. Their immediate reaction was to pick up stones and stone Him, even on the temple grounds. But Jesus "hid himself" and left.

After leaving the temple, Jesus passed a man blind from birth, and He healed the man. When the formerly blind man returned to his family and friends, they took him to the Pharisees.[20] It just happened to be the Sabbath when Jesus performed this healing, and the Pharisees were upset about the violation.[21] Try as they might, however, they could not shake the man's testimony.

Jesus was claiming to be God (as arrogant a claim as one can make), and the Pharisees knew it.

So they kicked him out of the synagogue. Jesus then told the Pharisees that they were the blind ones and gave a speech in which He claimed to be "the door" (or gate, John 10:7), that is, the only means of access for salvation, and "the good shepherd" (v. 11) who gave His life for his sheep (again, arrogant claims). After this Jesus apparently left Jerusalem, but the debate He left behind continued.

WINTER IN JUDEA AND GALILEE

Read
John 10:22–11:57;
Matthew 19:16–20:28;
Mark 10:17–45;
Luke 12:1–18:34.

During the next six months, Jesus remained in the outlying reaches of Judea and Galilee, although He made two trips up to the Jerusalem area. The first was in December at the Feast of Dedication, or Hanukkah (John 10:22–39). There He was challenged by the Jewish leaders, who asked Him point-blank whether He was the Messiah. Jesus told them to look at what He did, and then He asserted that He and God (the Father) were identical. Again they started to stone Him. But once more He challenged them to look at His works, and then left.

Jesus went out into the Jordan Valley. While teaching there (the time would have been between January and March), word came that Lazarus was sick. Jesus continued about His business for two more days, then announced to His disciples that He was going to Judea. They were aghast because of the death threats, but He told them not to worry. He also remarked that Lazarus had fallen asleep (John 11:11). Knowing that restful sleep is good for a serious illness, the disciples exclaimed that then he would recover. Bluntly, Jesus told them that Lazarus was dead.

As they headed up toward Bethany, the disciples fully expected to die. When they got to Bethany, Jesus was met by the two sisters, Martha first and then Mary. Both knew that if Jesus had been there, He could have healed Lazarus. In their

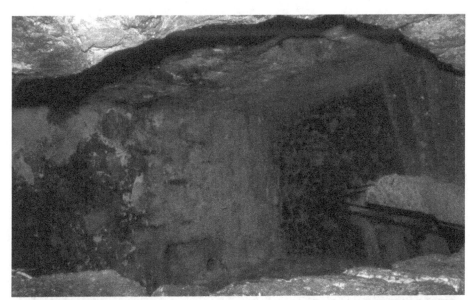

LAZARUS'S TOMB. According to tradition, the site hewn from rock where Jesus raised Lazarus from the dead in Bethany.

TOMB WITH STONE. A first-century tomb that shows what Lazarus's tomb might have looked like from the outside.

minds, however, it was now too late. He asked to be taken to the tomb, where He ordered the sealing stone to be rolled away. Martha protested, knowing that her brother had been dead for four days and that under normal circumstances the decomposing body would stink. Jesus prevailed, crying out for Lazarus to come forth—and he did.

Word quickly got back to Jerusalem, and the Jewish leaders were alarmed. In council they noted that if things continued, "the Romans will come and take away both our place and our nation" (John 11:48). This remark showed their true motives and concerns. Caiaphas, the high priest, prophetically announced that it was expedient that one man should die for the nation (vv. 49–50).[22] Before anything could be done, however, Jesus again left the region.

Little is recorded about the next few months. Jesus probably continued teaching and healing. Apparently it was during this time that the rich young man came to Jesus and asked how to obtain eternal life. Jesus told him to follow the Law, which the man asserted he had kept from childhood. In response, Jesus told him to sell all he had and follow Him.[23] The man was upset because of his wealth.

More parables and healings followed. Jesus healed a woman who had been crippled for eighteen years—on the Sabbath (Luke 13:10–17). He also healed a man of dropsy—again on the Sabbath (14:1–4).[24] Luke records even more parables (see chart, pages 394–95). The focus of the parables was on the kingdom of God and the coming of the King. Some of the most beloved parables illustrate God's love, such as the lost sheep and the prodigal son (Luke 15).

PREPARING FOR CRUCIFIXION

Read
Matthew 20:29–34;
Mark 10:46–52;
Luke 18:35–19:27.

As spring and the Passover approached, Jesus made plans to go up to Jerusalem. Repeatedly He told His disciples what was going to happen, although they never seemed to grasp it. His route brought Him out of the Jordan Valley through Jericho. On His way, He healed two blind men at Jericho.[25] He also met with Zacchaeus in this city.

As noted earlier, the last 30 to 40 percent of the Gospels covers the last week of Jesus' ministry. We will not go into the detail that the gospel writers do but will highlight the events as we read about them. Before we do that, however, let's take a look at some of the historical evidence used to determine the date of the crucifixion, for this detail will affect how we look at the last week as a whole.

The Day of the Week of the Crucifixion

Traditionally the church has observed Friday as the day of the crucifixion. This view, however, has come under criticism, primarily based on the statement that Jesus was in the ground three days and three nights (Matt. 12:40). Those who reject Friday disagree on whether Jesus was crucified on Wednesday or on Thursday. But without the statement in Matthew, a Friday crucifixion fits well. Moreover, the phrase "three days and three nights" need not be interpreted as an exact period of time, for we know that in that culture, any part of a day counted as a day. The evidence lends support to the traditional understanding of Friday as the day when the crucifixion took place.

THE BIBLICAL ANCHOR POINTS

Both testaments have historical anchor points. That of the OT is the Passover event. That of the NT is the crucifixion/resurrection event. These are the events that serve as the foundation for later writers. For this reason, it is most important that we understand their historicity, that is, that they are portrayed as historical events and are indeed part of world history. In this light, we will look back at how the crucifixion fits into our own history.

HOW LONG IS THREE DAYS?

The biblical evidence is clear that the resurrection occurred on Sunday, the first day of the week (e.g., Matt. 28:1). It is the other end of the period, Jesus' death and burial, that is in question. Some argue, on the basis of the phrase "three days and three nights" (Matt. 12:40), that Jesus had to have been in the grave a full three days and three nights, or ninety-six hours. However, His death was in the afternoon, and the resurrection occurred at about dawn. Certainly that phrase must have some figurative quality.

Several other passages state that Jesus would rise on the third day (e.g., Matt. 17:23; Luke 9:22), which also correlates with the expectations of the Jewish leaders. This language usage may clarify what Luke was thinking of in chapter 2 when he relates that the boy Jesus was found in the temple. Luke states that after three days they found Him, and we tend to think of that as three days of searching the city of Jerusalem. It is more likely that since they had gone one day's journey out, and a day's journey back, on the third day they found Jesus at the temple.

Several OT passages show that in Jewish reckoning any part of a day counted as a day. One of the clearest instances is in Leviticus 7:16–17, which gives directions regarding the votive, or freewill offerings. The people might eat the meat the day of the offering and the day after, but "any meat of the sacrifice left over till the third day must be burned up." We might also note that the Pharisees asked for a guard only up to the third day, as opposed to a full three days and nights (Matt. 27:64). In addition, there are several references in the Talmud that show the same thing. For example, the Babylonian Talmud records that "part of the day is as the whole of it" (*Pesaḥim* 4a; 55a). All of these point to a common use of the term "three days" as meaning less than three full days.

The Day of the Month of the Crucifixion

On the surface, determining the day of the month is easier. We are told that Jesus ate the Passover at a meal that became known to us as the Last Supper (Luke 22:15). Passover was celebrated on 14 Nisan. Since the meal took place the night before the crucifixion, Jesus was crucified on 15 Nisan. However, we are told in John that the reason the priests did not go into Pilate's palace on the morning of the crucifixion was so that they would not be made unclean for the Passover (John 18:28; note also that the Sabbath after the crucifixion is referred to as a "high day," 19:31 KJV).

John's statement creates a problem, for it suggests that Jesus had already eaten the Passover but the high priests had not. A number of attempts have been made to explain this difference, such as that Jesus and His disciples ate their Passover dinner a day early, or that the Last Supper was not really the Passover, or that the gospel writers were confused on the issue. The conclusion of most conservative scholars, however, is that the meal was the Passover. If so, then how do we explain the apparent discrepancy?

The answer seems to be that the Jews had two ways of measuring a day: from sunset to sunset (Ex. 12:18) and from sunrise to sunrise (Matt. 28:1).[26] If that was the case of the Passover, when one ate the dinner depended on when the day began. The Mishnah indicates with respect to working habits that the Galileans (and probably the Pharisees) observed the sunrise-to-sunrise day, while the Judeans (and probably the Sadducees) used the sunset-to-sunset method.[27]

According to the sunrise-to-sunrise schedule, then, Jesus and His disciples slaughtered their Passover lamb the afternoon of 14 Nisan. Assuming a Friday crucifixion, 14 Nisan began at sunrise on Thursday for them. They ate the dinner that evening, still on 14 Nisan. The high priest, following the Judean calendar, had 14 Nisan begin at sunset on Thursday evening. He then slaughtered his Passover lamb the next afternoon (on 14 Nisan) and ate the dinner Friday evening (thus actually on 15 Nisan after sunset).

The Year of the Crucifixion

The gospel writers help us narrow down the possible year. Caiaphas, the high priest when the crucifixion took place, held that post between 18 and 37 CE. Likewise, Pilate was governor of Judea between 26 and 36 CE. These limit the possible period to between 26 and 36. Assuming a Friday crucifixion and a Judean calendar, we can find when 14 Nisan fell on Friday to determine the date of the crucifixion. Three dates fulfill all of these requirements: 30, 33, and 36.

Since Luke 3:1–2 places the beginning of John the Baptist's ministry in the fifteenth year of Tiberius (who succeeded Augustus in 14 CE), that means that John began his work in 28–29. This information would eliminate the year 30 as too early.[28] Likewise, the year 36 would be too late, for it would require a six-year ministry for Jesus. Thus, we conclude that Jesus was crucified on 14 Nisan (April 3 on our calendar), 33 CE.

THE TRIUMPHANT ENTRY

Read Matthew 21:1–11; 26:6–16; Mark 11:1–11; 14:1–11; Luke 19:28–44; John 12:1–19.

The defining event of Jesus' last week occurred when He proceeded into Jerusalem to the acclamation of crowds. Traditionally this event is thought to have taken place on the Sunday before the crucifixion. We call it Palm Sunday because of the palm fronds the people cut and placed on the path before Him.

All four gospels agree in the general outline of what happened. However, it is not clear how the procession fits into the events around it. The Synoptic

WHAT HAPPENED WHEN?

Harold Hoehner argues that Jesus' triumphant entry took place on Monday, not Sunday, to allow for the dinner in John 12 (*Chronological Aspects of the Life of Christ* [Grand Rapids: Zondervan, 1978], 90–91). A major advantage of this view is that it eliminates the apparently empty day of Wednesday. The problem is the notation in John 12:1 that Jesus arrived in Bethany six days before the Passover. The trip from Jericho was about 15 miles, almost all of it uphill; on foot, it would have been at least a five-to-six-hour trek. Hoehner's proposal would seem to have Jesus traveling to Bethany on Saturday. While Jesus was not particularly observant of the detailed regulations of the Pharisees, this does not mean that He did not observe the Sabbath. It is unlikely that He would have transgressed this observance by traveling up from Jericho on Saturday. He more likely traveled to Bethany on Friday and then continued to Jerusalem on Sunday, after the Sabbath.

Gospels imply that it occurred during the journey from Jericho. But John places a dinner in Bethany (between Jericho and Jerusalem) the night before.

It is likely that the events developed as follows: Jesus' entourage arrived in Bethany on Friday, six days prior to when they celebrated Passover according to their calendar. He remained with His friends, Lazarus and his sisters, on the Sabbath. On Saturday evening the Judeans, Lazarus, Mary, and Martha had a dinner, inviting a number of neighbors. As pointed out earlier, the text suggests that this dinner was at Martha's house and that Lazarus was a guest.

After the meal, Mary took some costly perfume and anointed Jesus' feet. Many at the table were indignant with the extravagance of this act. Some said that the perfume should have been sold and the money used to help the poor. Jesus accepted her act as the homage that was intended and asserted that she was anointing Him for His burial. He was clearly anticipating the events of the next few days. Judas was especially upset, and as a result, he sought out the Jewish leaders so that he could betray Jesus.[29]

ALABASTER JAR. The kind of jar—often inset with semi-precious stones and having household uses such as holding perfume—that Mary of Bethany may have used to anoint the feet of Jesus.

The next day was the triumphal entry. According to our chronology, on Sunday, March 29, Jesus and His entourage traveled from Bethany toward Jerusalem (about a two-mile distance). He sent two men ahead for the purpose of finding a donkey and her colt that were tied up and bringing them back to Him.[30] At Bethphage they got the donkey and her colt, and Jesus rode into Jerusalem on this colt to present Himself to the nation as the Messiah, a clear fulfillment of prophecy. The gospel writers note both the excited, jubilant reception of the people and the critical reception of the religious leaders. When the leaders demanded that Jesus restrain His followers, Jesus replied that if the people were silent, the stones would cry out. It was now the right time.

EASTERN GATES INTERIOR. The gate through which Jesus would have made his triumphal entry into the temple area in Jerusalem. When Jerusalem was rebuilt after the Roman destruction, the gate was sealed to prevent any would-be messiahs from going through it.

Jesus and His disciples then came down the Mount of Olives where others would have seen and heard them and rushed out to see what was going on. Two reactions occurred. Those who had already concluded that He was the Messiah were exuberant that at last He was proclaiming Himself. Those who had already concluded that He was not the Messiah were angry and upset. It was decision time for the nation.

Because of the crowds, the procession went slowly. By the time Jesus arrived at the temple, it was late. He looked around and then left. That night He returned to Bethany with the Twelve.

THE REST OF THE WEEK

*Read Matthew
21:12–26:6;
Mark 11:12–13:37;
Luke 19:45–21:38;
John 12:12–12:50.*

On Monday Jesus and the disciples returned to Jerusalem. As they entered the city from Bethany, Jesus went to a fig tree to get fruit. When He found it barren, He cursed it. This was symbolic of the nation of Israel and reflected an upcoming judgment. Once Jesus arrived in the city, He went back to the temple, where He drove out the money lenders and the animal sellers (as we noted earlier, this would have been the second cleansing of the temple). That evening they left the city, going back to Bethany.

On Tuesday they again went into Jerusalem. When they passed by the fig tree, the disciples saw that the fig tree had withered, and they remembered the curse. Jesus used that to teach His disciples about faith. He also stressed forgiveness.

Jesus returned to the temple, where He began teaching. There He was challenged by the Jewish leaders. The gospel writers record a number of controversies as Jesus and the Jewish leaders sparred verbally. It was clear that they were trying to trap Him. Not only did they not succeed, but Jesus continually exposed their false motives. First, the leaders asked Him by what authority He acted (referring to the events of the cleansing). He replied by asking where John got his authority. They dared not answer, because if John's authority was from God, they should have listened to him. However, if they said it was from men, they would have to face the crowd, which viewed him as a prophet of God. They said they could not answer, and Jesus said He would not answer either.

Another challenge was the question of the Pharisees about Roman taxes. If Jesus said they should pay the hated taxes, He faced the wrath of the crowd. But if He said they should not, then He could be accused by the Romans of sedition. Instead, Jesus asked them to show the Roman coin. Pointing out Caesar's image, He told them to give Caesar what was his and give to God what was His.

The Sadducees asked an involved question about the resurrection (which they did not believe in). Based on the OT levirate marriage concept, they posed a hypothetical case of a woman who was married in turn to seven brothers, each of whom died without children. In the resurrection, whose wife would she be? Jesus went to the heart of the matter (their disbelief in the resurrection) and told them they erred, not knowing Scripture or the power of God.[31]

At this point a scholar in the OT law asked a question: Which is the greatest law? Instead of one of the expected Ten Commandments, Jesus picked two other laws: "'Love the Lord your God with all your heart and with all your soul and with all your mind.' This is the first and greatest commandment. And the second is like it: 'Love your neighbor as yourself'" (Matt. 22:37–39). The point was that the rest of the laws merely illustrate how love of God and man might be manifested in specific instances. Jesus also told a number of parables that focused on the judgment that would come to the nation and its leaders. The leaders got the point but could do nothing at the time. He also gave a scathing indictment of the Pharisees.

"RENDER UNTO CAESAR...."
A coin dating from the first century that shows the likeness of the emperor who issued it. Jesus used a coin such as this as an illustration on the question of taxes.

PREPARING FOR PASSOVER

One of the more mystifying aspects of Jesus' directions to the disciples is that they were to follow a man carrying a pitcher. It would appear that Jesus was preventing Judas from disrupting that last meal, for it was to serve as a model for future generations. As it was, Judas did not know ahead of time where the dinner would be held. In terms of the preparations, several things would be involved, beginning with sacrificing a lamb at the temple, roasting it, and setting the table with all of the elements for the meal.

That afternoon as they headed back toward Bethany, Jesus and His disciples crossed over to the Mount of Olives. There several of His disciples noted the beauty of the temple on the hill opposite them. Jesus gave a prophetic discourse that discussed His second coming. This talk is sometimes called the Olivet Discourse (because of where it was given). It is also sometimes called the Little Apocalypse, for it addresses some of the same issues covered in the book of Revelation (the Apocalypse).

It seems that Jesus' disciples asked Him three questions, but He answered only two of them. They asked Him when those events would be, what the signs of His coming would be, and what the signs of the end of the age would be. He never told them when. In fact, He asserted that no one knew when those events would take place. Rather, the point was that each man and woman was to live his or her life in readiness at all times. To illustrate this principle, He gave His disciples several more parables, including the parable of the wise and foolish virgins and the parable of the talents.

If our chronology is correct, we have no record of what happened on Wednesday.[32] This could have been a day of prayer and meditation, or it could have involved further teaching in the temple. In any case, either our chronology is a day off, or the gospel writers saw nothing of significance to report.

About this time in the week, John reports, several Greeks were present.[33] When they asked to see Jesus, He viewed their request as another sign that His hour was near. At about the same time, the Sanhedrin began planning how they might covertly dispose of Jesus, whom they saw as a problem. Their plan was to wait until after the festival because of the crowds. However, as will be seen, God had other plans.

On Thursday Jesus sent Peter and John into Jerusalem to prepare for the Passover meal. After a second day about which nothing is recorded, Jesus and His disciples went to the designated room that evening. Once there, they celebrated the Passover dinner.

A NIGHT OF BETRAYAL

Passover was a time of celebration commemorating what God had done for the nation centuries earlier. As such it would normally be a joyous affair. However, for Jesus and His followers, there were several dark clouds. Jesus knew the events that

Read Matthew 26:17–56; Mark 14:12–52; Luke 22:1–53; John 13:1–18:11.

were coming and must have dreaded them. The Twelve had been told over and over that Jesus would be betrayed but still seemed clueless. Judas, like any double agent, dreaded being found out but was convinced that he was doing what was best. And still the ritual went on.

When they had gathered in the upper room, Jesus took a towel and basin and washed the feet of His disciples. Normally that would be a service provided by the host, either by supplying the utensils or, in a more well-to-do home, by making a servant available to the guests. If Peter and John, who had made the preparations, were considered hosts, then Jesus' action reflects an oversight on their part.[34] This detail may explain why Peter objected to Jesus washing His feet. However, Jesus insisted, because such an act was not only to be symbolic but also a model for His disciples to serve one another.

> Following the custom that had endured for about fourteen centuries, Jesus' Passover dinner would have included lamb, unleavened bread, bitter herbs, and wine.

After this, they began the meal. Following the custom that had endured for about fourteen centuries, they would have had lamb, unleavened bread, bitter herbs, and wine. As the meal progressed, Jesus announced that one of the Twelve would betray Him. This comment created a stir, and the disciples were buzzing with speculation—who could it be? Each person denied that it would be him. According to Matthew, even Judas questioned Jesus whether it could be him (Matt. 26:25). Jesus replied somewhat enigmatically (lit., "You have said") but in the affirmative. As the meal progressed, Peter nudged John ("the disciple whom Jesus loved") and asked him to find out who the betrayer would be (John 13:23–24). John coaxed Jesus, who told him that it would be the person to whom He gave a special morsel. He then gave a morsel to Judas. John

THE WORK OF THE HOLY SPIRIT

Jesus' talk with the disciples on the night before the crucifixion contains some of the most important teaching in the Bible on the work of the Holy Spirit. There are four key elements.

- The Holy Spirit would teach the disciples all things and remind them of what Jesus had spoken to them (John 14:26). This truth is important as we evaluate their outreach and their writing of NT Scripture.
- The Holy Spirit would comfort those whom Jesus was leaving behind (John 14:27; 16:7).
- There was to be an aspect of conviction toward the *world*, not the disciples (John 16:8–11). The purpose of the conviction was threefold. It was to be of sin—specifically, a failure to believe in Jesus. It was to be of righteousness (which is tied to the issue of sin). Because Jesus was about to go to the Father, the Holy Spirit would convict the world about the inability to be righteous before God without Jesus Christ. And it was to be of judgment—judgment of the ruler of this world, Satan (see 12:31). Because of Jesus' death and resurrection, Satan has been condemned, even though the judgment has not yet been executed.
- The function of the Holy Spirit was to work in believers to instruct them in the truth of who Jesus is, what He did, and the implications of that. As such, His role even today is to bring glory to Jesus.

states that at that point Satan entered Judas.[35] Jesus told him to do quickly what he had to do.

After Judas left, the other disciples figured he had some business to conduct on their behalf. They also began to debate about who was the greatest (Luke 22:24). Jesus again used this occasion to teach His disciples, this time reminding them that greatness was measured by service (the lesson of the foot washing had been forgotten already).

As they approached the end of the traditional Passover, Jesus added a new tradition. He took the unleavened bread and the wine and imbued them with new symbolism. They were now to remind His disciples of the upcoming sacrifice that He would be performing.

Jesus also tried to comfort His disciples by telling them that He was going away but would return, but they did not grasp the concept. When Peter asked where He was going, Jesus seemed to dodge the issue by asserting that they couldn't follow Him. Peter claimed that he would go anywhere with Jesus, even to death. But Jesus responded that before the night was over, Peter would deny Him three times. Jesus then comforted His disciples by asserting that He would return under better circumstances after having prepared a place for His followers. And because He was going, He said, the Holy Spirit would come and be another comforter.

After praying for His disciples and Himself,[36] Jesus led them out into the garden of Gethsemane. There He spent more time in prayer. This prayer was an emotional response to the agony He knew was coming. But He also accepted the will of the Father in this matter. While He prayed, His disciples kept falling asleep (it was now very late).

WHO WAS LEADING WHOM?

Although Jesus was arrested and bound by the soldiers, He made it plain that He was the one in control of the situation. When the crowd fell back at His declaration "I am," their response reflected His divine power. He chastised the leaders for not taking Him earlier in the temple. He stopped the resistance of His followers and healed the right ear of Malchus, the servant of the high priest. He reminded His followers that if He wanted, He could call more than ten legions of angels to His defense. He went calmly, without resistance.

Finally, Judas arrived with a large crowd of Romans, Jewish leaders, and others. It is unlikely that any had been in the crowd that welcomed Him to Jerusalem a few days earlier. That group was probably all asleep at this point. Judas pinpointed their man with a kiss. Jesus asked who they were looking for. When they said, "Jesus the Nazarene," Jesus replied, "I am," alluding to God's name, YHWH (John 18:5, literal translation; most versions render, "I am he"). The crowd fell back. After repeating that He was the one they were looking for, Jesus told them to let the disciples go. As some of the crowd moved to arrest Jesus, Peter jumped into action and cut off the ear of the high priest's servant. Jesus stopped the resistance and healed the injured man. He then went with the crowd. His disciples, however, fled.

A MOCKERY OF TRIALS

Read Matthew 26:57–27:26; Mark 14:53–15:15; Luke 22:54–23:25; John 18:12–19:15.

The rest of the night and morning were a series of rigged and illegal trials. First, Jesus was presented to Annas (Caiaphas's father-in-law) in a preliminary hearing; ostensibly retired from the high priesthood, he was still part of the ruling inner circle, but in that position he had no real legal authority to interrogate Jesus. Then He was tried before Caiaphas, the high priest. This action was illegal because it was at night and in Caiaphas's palace instead of the council chambers. Also, the testimony was contradictory. The best "evidence" they could find was two men reporting Jesus' claim to rebuild the temple in three days (cf. John 2:19; Jesus' words were really an anticipation of the resurrection). Frustrated, Caiaphas asked Jesus if He was the Messiah, the Son of the Blessed One. Jesus replied that He was and quoted a messianic passage from Daniel 7:13.

> Caiaphas understood Jesus' claim to be the Messiah and declared it blasphemy.

Caiaphas understood the claim and declared it blasphemy.[37] The rest agreed and condemned Him to death. This sentence was illegal, for a verdict for execution could not be given until the next day. As such, a capital crime could not be tried on the day before a festival or Sabbath. Of course, under Roman law, they did not even have authority to give a death penalty. Following the sentence, the members of the court began beating Jesus. Then they led Him away.

Judas, who had been part of the arresting party, apparently had not anticipated this result. After the sentence was pronounced, he tried to return the money to the leaders. Flinging the blood money at their feet, he fled. Outside of town, he hanged himself. The priestly leaders were puzzled about how to handle the money, which they recognized as tainted by blood. They decided to buy a field used by potters as a source of clay and turn it into a graveyard for the poor. Thus, inadvertently, they fulfilled prophecy (Matt. 27:9–10).

While Jesus was inside, Peter and another disciple (probably John) had followed at a distance. As the night wore on, they worked their way into the crowd in the courtyard of the high priest. There Peter was recognized and challenged. Three times he denied that he was a follower of Jesus, just as Jesus had predicted. When Peter heard the cock crow, he realized what he had done and left weeping.

The cock crow also signaled the coming dawn (a little later John 19:14 says that it was "the sixth hour," about 6:00 a.m), and the Jewish leaders led Jesus over to the palace of Pilate. There they asked Pilate to find Him guilty of treason against Rome so that they could have a facade of legality for an execution. Pilate waffled because, as he interviewed Jesus, he could find nothing that substantiated their charge. He told the Jewish leaders that the man was not guilty. Learning that Jesus was a Galilean, he sent Him to Herod Antipas.

PILATE INSCRIPTION. An inscription uncovered in Caesarea that mentions the name of Pontius Pilate as governor of Judea.

Herod questioned Jesus but learned nothing. Mockingly, he had a royal purple robe put on Jesus' back and sent Him back to Pilate. Having been warned by his wife that he should distance himself from this case, Pilate tried to find a way out. Following the custom for the upcoming festival, he offered to free Jesus. He gave the people a choice of Him or Barabbas, a noted robber and murderer.[38] The crowd gathered by the Jewish leaders yelled for Barabbas and demanded that Jesus be crucified. Finally, washing his hands of the issue, Pilate gave Jesus to the priests to be crucified.

> Finally, washing his hands of the issue, Pilate gave Jesus to the priests to be crucified.

THE CRUCIFIXION

Crucifixion was a Roman penalty normally reserved for the worst criminals. It was probably the most excruciating death process devised by man. Before Jesus was crucified, He was further beaten and humiliated. He then was forced to carry the crossbeam of His cross through the streets of Jerusalem to the execution site. This processional may have been the first time that many of those who were pro-Jesus were aware of the situation. When Jesus, who had been beaten and whipped, faltered and fell under the load of the heavy beam, the Romans drafted a passerby, Simon of Cyrene, to carry it for Him.

Read Matthew 27:27–65; Mark 15:16–47; Luke 23:26–56; John 19:16–42.

The procession reached Golgotha, the place of execution, about 9:00 a.m.[39] By now Jesus had been up for more than twenty-four hours. At Golgotha He was

THE NAILS AND THE CROSS

Many artists' representations of the crucifixion show the nails through the palm of Jesus' hands. However, such a procedure would not sustain the weight of the body. The nails would have been placed through the wrists, between the ulna and radius of the forearm. There seems to have been more variation in the nailing of the feet. They could have been nailed to a small platform attached to the upright. Probably one nail held both feet, with one foot in front of the other. An alternative would be to drive the nail through the heels.

nailed to the cross. This grisly process consisted of placing a nail through each wrist, anchoring the arms to the crossbar. The crossbar was then raised to the upright already in the ground. The feet were nailed to the upright, anchoring them there. The weight of the body suspended by the arms forced air out of the lungs. To inhale, the victim had to push the body up by putting weight on the nailed feet. Of course, the rough upright would rub the scourged bare back raw. Normally death came as a result of asphyxiation as the legs cramped up and the victim was unable to lift his body to breathe. This could take as long as two to three days.

To provide one last dig at the Jewish leaders, Pilate put an inscription on the cross: "Jesus the Nazarene, the King of the Jews." The Jewish leaders protested, for they had already claimed that Caesar was their king; nevertheless, Pilate was unrelenting.[40] On either side, two criminals were crucified at the same time.

With their work done, the soldiers had nothing to do but wait for the inevitable. In the meantime, they served as crowd control and ensured that no one attempted to take the victims down early. To pass the time, they divided up the remaining clothing of the victims. In Jesus' case, they divided the four pieces of outer garments but gambled for His tunic.[41]

While Jesus was on the cross, several significant interchanges took place. Seeing His mother and John in the crowd, Jesus gave responsibility for her care to this close friend. The crowd abused Him, but He asked God to forgive them because of their ignorance. The criminal hanging on one side of Jesus became bitter and taunted Him, asserting that if He truly was the Messiah, He would save Himself (and them as well). The other criminal asked Jesus to remember him when the kingdom came. Jesus promised that by the end of the day they both would be in paradise.

From noon to about three in the afternoon ("the ninth hour," Mark 15:33), darkness was over the land. Jesus cried out in agony, "My God, my God, why have you forsaken me?" This line from Psalm 22:1 reflected continuing fulfillment of prophecy. Then Jesus said that He thirsted. One of the soldiers soaked a sponge in sour wine (vinegar). Putting it on a stick, he reached it up to Jesus' mouth, but Jesus merely tasted it, fulfilling another prophecy (Ps. 69:21). Because it was the middle of the afternoon, the high priest was in the temple sacrificing Passover lambs. The darkness left the land. All three Synoptic Gospels record that the temple veil that blocked off the Holy of Holies tore in two, from top to bottom. Jesus cried out, "Father, into your hands I commit my spirit" (Luke 23:46). Shortly afterward, He proclaimed, "It is finished" (John 19:30). With that He gave up His spirit and died.

The observers were convinced that they had witnessed something unparalleled in history. The centurion in charge of the crucifixion is recorded as saying, "Surely this man was the Son of God" (Mark 15:39). As the day wore on, several other items had to be taken care of. Because it was the day before the Sabbath, the Jewish leaders did not want the bodies left on the crosses overnight, because that would "profane" the land. They asked Pilate to have the legs of the victims broken. With broken legs, they would not be able to push up on the cross to breathe and would die much more quickly. Soldiers were sent to do that, and they broke the legs of the two criminals on either side. Jesus, however, appeared to be dead, for His body hung limp and He clearly was not breathing. However, to make sure, one of the soldiers ran his spear between the ribs into the heart. Out ran a mixture of serum and blood, showing the man was dead.

Joseph of Arimathea, a rich Pharisee who had accepted Jesus' claims, asked for the body. It surprised Pilate that Jesus was already dead, but this was confirmed by the centurion in charge of the execution party. Permission was granted, and Joseph took down the body and moved it to his own newly carved tomb located nearby (again fulfilling prophecy, Isa. 53:9). He was trailed by several of the women who had followed Jesus. They observed where the body was laid, and with that information, they went back home and began to prepare the proper spice mixture so that after the Sabbath, they could finish the burial process. Joseph was assisted by Nicodemus, who brought about seventy-five pounds of myrrh and aloes.[42]

They rolled a large stone in front of the tomb entrance and then left to observe the Sabbath. The Jewish leaders went to Pilate and noted the claims that

DARKNESS OVER THE LAND

We don't know the actual cause of the darkness during the crucifixion, but it could not have been an eclipse for three reasons.

- The ancients understood eclipses and would have reported this event as such.
- A solar eclipse lasts only a few minutes, while this event lasted for three hours.
- Solar eclipses can occur only at the new moon (when the moon is between the sun and the earth); this was the day of the full moon (Passover).

The closest analogy would seem to be the ninth plague back in Egypt, when the darkness lasted three days (Ex. 10:21–23).

INTERIOR OF THE GARDEN TOMB. The interior, showing how the body of the occupant would have been positioned.

Jesus had made regarding His own resurrection. To prevent Jesus' disciples from stealing the body and claiming a resurrection, they asked for a squad of soldiers to guard the tomb. Pilate provided them. They sealed the tomb with the seal of Rome and then camped in front of it. The request of the Jewish leaders is ironic, because it suggests that they paid more attention to Jesus' claims than did His own disciples. However, no one believed that He would really rise. And so the Sabbath passed.

THE RESURRECTION

Read Matthew 28:1–15;
Mark 16:1–14;
Luke 24:1–49;
John 20:1–21:25.

About dawn on Sunday morning, Mary Magdalene, Mary the mother of James, Joanna, Salome, and other unnamed women went to the tomb carrying the spices they had prepared to finish the burial process. As they got closer, they began to wonder who would roll away the stone. Thus, they knew about the stone, but they apparently did not know about the Roman guard.[43]

When they arrived at the tomb, they were surprised to find the stone already rolled away. Apparently the soldiers had already noted the missing body and trekked back into the city to inform the leaders. The Jewish leaders told them to spread the story that they had fallen asleep on duty and the disciples had stolen the body. The Jewish leaders then bribed the Roman leaders to smooth things over. So the women found no one there except two angels. The angels told them that Jesus was not there, that He had risen.

This message apparently did not register. The women went back to the city, and Mary Magdalene went to tell Peter and John that the body was missing. They rushed to the tomb to find it empty, just as Mary had told them. Mystified, they left, leaving Mary there weeping, convinced that the body had been stolen. Jesus then appeared to Mary, and she went back to the city, a witness to the resurrected Jesus.

That afternoon Cleopas and another of Jesus' followers were traveling to Emmaus when they were joined by Jesus. He traveled with them and discussed the events, but they didn't recognize Him. At their house, He revealed Himself to them and then disappeared. They rushed back to Jerusalem to share the news.

That evening the disciples were gathered in a locked room to discuss events. So much had happened since they had last gathered on Thursday evening! It was clear that the tomb was empty—both Peter and John attested to that. But they still did not know what it meant. Now several of the women claimed that they had seen Jesus alive. While they discussed this, Jesus appeared in their midst, showing His battered body as proof that it was Him.

> It was clear that the tomb was empty, but the disciples still did not know what it meant.

Thomas was not present that evening, and he questioned their testimony. A week later, when the disciples were again gathered, Thomas was with them. Jesus appeared again. This time Thomas believed.

Following an unspecified number of appearances to disciples and relatives in Jerusalem, Jesus sent them to Galilee, where He met them. John records a powerful dialogue with Peter that carried two messages. First, it restored Peter after his denial (John 21:15–18). In the process, Jesus warned Peter of how he would die (apparently it was a comfort that he would indeed follow Jesus). As they were doing so, Peter looked back and saw John. He asked Jesus what was going to happen to John. Jesus told him that it was no concern of his, even if He decided to

WHEN IS EASTER?

Virtually everyone knows that the date of Easter varies from year to year. The main reason for this is the transition from the Jewish calendar to our solar calendar. But it is much more complicated than that. First, we have already seen the relationship between the crucifixion and Passover. Passover takes place on 15 Nisan, the first month of the Jewish *religious* calendar. But the Jewish calendar really begins with *Rosh Hashanah*, in the fall, which means that Nisan could begin prior to the spring equinox. However, the modern Jewish calendar uses a very complicated system to adjust for the differences between the lunar and solar calendars. As such, in the modern era, Passover is generally viewed as the full moon following the spring equinox. This would put Easter from late March to late April.

Second, technically Easter could be any day of the week, but from an early date, the church celebrated it on Sunday. The problem was that there was no real agreement on which Sunday was to be observed. As a result, Easter was being celebrated on different dates in different places. For example, in 387 CE, Easter was being celebrated on March 21 in Gaul but not until April 18 in Rome and April 25 in Alexandria. In an effort to standardize the liturgical calendar and to separate the Christian Easter from the Jewish Passover, the Roman church developed a method of calculating which Sunday would be celebrated as Easter. The current Western date is basically the first Sunday after the first full moon falling on or after the spring equinox, which allows Easter to fall between March 22 and April 25 inclusively. The Eastern church uses a different model that allows its Easter date to fall up to five weeks later.

A STOLEN BODY?

Although the tale that the disciples stole Jesus' body is widely believed by those who are unwilling to accept a physical resurrection, several items make it implausible. First, it is unlikely that an entire squad of trained soldiers would fall asleep at once. Even granting that, however, it is unlikely that the disciples would have been able to roll away a large stone and remove the body without disturbing the sleeping soldiers. Also, if the Roman soldiers had really fallen asleep on duty, they would have been subject to execution (not to mention that they would not have observed the theft). Execution would have been especially the case, for they lost the body they were supposed to be guarding. And the Jewish leaders would not have been so casual about such a state of affairs.

leave John until He came. As a result, the rumor started that John would remain alive until Jesus' second coming. Fifty-some years later, there appeared to be some merit to the idea. So John, in writing his gospel, emphasized that that would not be the case (John 21:23).

The Messiah had been rejected, but He had not gone away. He had been killed, but He was now resurrected. That fact would be the foundation stone of the kingdom of God. The reality was that the kingdom would not be implemented the way the Jews—and the disciples—had thought. So, in Galilee, Jesus spent several weeks with the disciples, teaching them about the kingdom of God.

REVIEW QUESTIONS

1. Why did Jesus refuse to give a sign to the Pharisees when He returned to the region of Galilee?

2. What was the Mount of Transfiguration, and why was it significant?

3. Why did Jesus refuse to travel with His brothers to the festival of Sukkoth, but went by Himself later?

4. Why did Jesus wait three days before going to the home of Lazarus when He heard Lazarus was sick?

5. How do we determine the date of the crucifixion?

6. What was the triumphal entry?

7. Trace the events of Jesus' last week.

8. Describe the last night of Jesus' life.

9. Why were the trials of Jesus mockeries?

10. How do we know that Jesus really died?

11. What are the evidences that Jesus was resurrected?

12. What did Jesus do after the resurrection?

20
CHAPTER

The First Church Was Jewish

OVERVIEW

During the forty days following the resurrection, Jesus appeared to a number of people and spent much time giving further teaching to His disciples. At the end of that time He unexpectedly ascended to heaven, leaving the disciples with the directive to wait in Jerusalem. Ten days later, during the Festival of Pentecost, the Holy Spirit descended. Some three thousand people accepted Jesus as the Messiah, and the church was born.

Over the next few years there were growing pains as it became obvious that the Jewish people as a whole were not going to place their faith in Jesus the Messiah, causing a schism between believing and nonbelieving Jews. There were also problems within the church. After Stephen was executed, the church scattered. One of the leading persecutors, Saul, was himself converted while he was pursuing believers to Damascus.

STUDY GOALS

▶ Show how the church was established after Jesus' ascension.

▶ Trace the development of the early church in Jerusalem.

▶ Show the expansion of the early church out of Jerusalem into Judea and Samaria.

▶ Explain the conversion of Saul of Tarsus (Paul).

A fter the resurrection, the disciples experienced a paradigm shift. They had respected Jesus as a great teacher, a prophet, and the Messiah. They had even called Him the Son of God, but they never really grasped His true identity. Ironically, it seems that Thomas the doubter was the first to grasp the meaning of the resurrection. After Jesus appeared to him and showed him His wounds, Thomas cried, "My Lord and my God!" (John 20:28). These were words that no Jew would say to another human being. But it is through this new understanding that we now read the Gospels and the rest of the NT.

EXPECTING THE KINGDOM

Read
Matthew 28:16–20;
Mark 16:14–20;
Luke 24:50–53;
Acts 1:1–11.

For forty days after the resurrection, Jesus made a number of appearances to verify that He had indeed risen from the dead. The physical evidence was very plain: the tomb was empty, and the body was missing. Yes, a story circulated that the disciples had stolen the body, but the disciples were nowhere to be seen. Besides, there was that sticky element about the Roman guard supposedly falling asleep. When the disciples did meet, it was behind locked doors. Then they left Jerusalem to go to Galilee. But the reports of a resurrected Jesus kept cropping up from a variety of sources.

In addition to the witnesses already noted, Paul mentions several more in 1 Corinthians 15:3–8. Many other witnesses are not mentioned by name. On one occasion Jesus appeared to a group of more than five hundred. Only a few appearances are listed, but there must have been others. Jesus also continued His teaching to the inner circle, the Twelve minus one. We don't know what His itinerary was. Part of the time they were in Galilee, and part of the time in the Jerusalem area. Only two aspects of His postresurrection teaching are recorded (aside from

THE REGION OF GALILEE. An aerial shot of the Arbol cliffs, with the Sea of Galilee in the background. This shows that there would have been many places where Jesus and His disciples could have met in private after his resurrection.

the restoration of Peter, noted in the previous chapter; that episode probably occurred very early during this period).

The first aspect is what we call the Great Commission (Matt. 28:18–20). According to Matthew, it was given in Galilee. This directive is a single command—"Make disciples." The rest of it explains how that was to be done. The disciples were to go out to the nations. They were to baptize. They were to teach. Our impression from Matthew and the longer end of Mark[1] is that this was one of the last things that Jesus told His disciples. When we look closer, however, we see that was not the case. As Luke points out, Jesus and the disciples returned to the Jerusalem area afterward, although he doesn't explain why.

Luke also notes that the focus of the teaching during this period was on the kingdom of God. This was same subject that Jesus and John the Baptist had begun proclaiming about three and a half years earlier. While we are not given any further information, it would be expected that Jesus was now explaining to His disciples concepts they had not grasped before the crucifixion. The resurrection was a new lens through which to view things. It changed the focus on all of His teachings. In the process, there were probably a number of times when the disciples said, "Oh, so that is what you meant!"

THE SLOPES OF GALILEE. The region where Jesus conducted much of His earthly ministry, and where He may have met the disciples after the resurrection, as suggested in Matthew 26:32 and 28:16.

At the end of the forty-day period, Jesus and His disciples were on the Mount of Olives in the Bethany area (less than two miles from Jerusalem). Luke ended his gospel with an account of this event and then began his follow-on book, Acts, by amplifying the same event. According to Acts 1:6, the disciples on this occasion asked the question, "Lord, are you at this time going to restore the kingdom to Israel?" Why did they ask that question now? First, they had been taught about the kingdom for forty days. Then there was the location: the Mount of Olives is mentioned in Zechariah 14 as the place where the Messiah would initiate His kingdom.

Jesus was back!

From the disciples' perspective, not only was the question logical, but so was the timing. On the night of His betrayal, Jesus had told them that He was leaving but would return for them. Then He died (He left) and now was resurrected (He returned). So all the OT prophecies that anticipated two comings could make sense. Jesus was back, and so it must be time for the events of the "second coming," that is, the kingdom. Then, after moving the disciples to Galilee, where they had some safety from the Jewish leaders, He had brought them back to the Jerusalem area. Was this the time for the kingdom?

It is interesting that Jesus did not chastise them for the question. Nor did He tell them they had totally misunderstood the nature of the kingdom. Rather, He told them that it was not for them to know the *time* of the kingdom (that is, it would be yet future). In the meantime, they had a job to do. They were to be witnesses throughout the world. That is, they were to carry out the Great Commission mentioned earlier. But, Jesus said, the starting point was Jerusalem. With that, He ascended into heaven.

This event caught the disciples totally off guard, and they stood staring at the sky where Jesus had disappeared. While they stood there, two angels appeared and told them to get on with their business. They also told the disciples that Jesus would return the same way He had ascended (fulfilling the prophecy from Zechariah). The disciples then returned to Jerusalem to the upper room, where they had celebrated Passover almost six weeks earlier.

MOUNT OF ASCENSION. The Mount of Olives, where Jesus ascended to heaven and where it was proclaimed He would return. This accords with the prophecies in Zechariah regarding the arrival of the Messiah. For this reason, many Jews and Christians have been buried on its slopes, as seen by the tombs in the foreground.

LUKE'S TESTIMONY IN ACTS

The Gospels, in keeping with their purpose (see above, ch. 18), end with a brief discussion of the appearances of Jesus after the resurrection. The Epistles and the book of Revelation address some of the problems the church experienced as it spread throughout the Roman Empire. The book of Acts bridges between the Gospels and the rest of the NT.

Many Bibles, following an ancient manuscript tradition, entitle this book, The Acts of the Apostles. As such, it is really mislabeled. The first twelve chapters focus mainly on Peter, while the rest of the book focuses on Paul. The book ends abruptly with Paul in jail in Rome. These features hint at both its authorship and its purpose.

The key indicator of authorship is an interesting change of pronoun as the writer talks about Paul's missionary journeys. Most of the time, the author describes the journeys in the third person plural, "they." In several places, however, it uses the first person plural, "we." When we compare other mentions of Paul's traveling companions with these changes, it appears that the most likely author is Luke. This inference also correlates with early church tradition.

carry out the Great Commission!

The abrupt ending of Acts is thought to point to the time the book was written, that is, during the period Paul was in jail in Rome, approximately 60–62 CE. As such, the book's primary purpose seems to be to show what brought Paul to that situation. This hints at its being a brief prepared for the defense of Paul before Caesar. But long before that, Acts relates how the church was founded.

WAITING FOR THE SPIRIT

Back in Jerusalem, the eleven remaining disciples met on a regular basis with others to whom Jesus had appeared after the resurrection. These were all Jews from various walks of life, totaling about one hundred and twenty. They had followed Jesus in varying degrees during His earthly ministry. They were now convinced that He was the Messiah. Included in this group were several of the women, Mary

Read Acts 1:12–26.

UPPER ROOM. The place, renovated in medieval times, that is traditionally considered the place where the disciples had gathered for the Last Supper and then met together after Jesus' ascension.

the mother of Jesus, and His brothers.[2] This was a period of prayer, although we are not told what they prayed about.

At some point following the ascension, Peter stood up and made reference to OT prophecies that Judas should be replaced. He then proposed that they choose a successor, picking from the group that had followed Jesus since John's baptism.[3] The rest agreed, and Joseph Barsabbas (or Justus) and Matthias were presented as candidates. They prayed, then cast lots, and Matthias was selected. Neither is heard of again.

THE FOUNDING OF THE CHURCH

Read Acts 2:1–47. The date of the founding of the church is significant. We have already pointed out that Jesus died at the time the Passover lamb was being sacrificed; the day of His resurrection was the Feast of Firstfruits (Lev. 23:10–11). The next holiday in the Jewish spring schedule was Pentecost or Weeks, the second of three festivals (the first being Passover and the third Tabernacles) when all Jews were directed to appear before the Lord at the central sanctuary. So on this date Jerusalem would be full of Jews from all over the known world. Pentecost was also known as the Festival of Ingathering, representing the beginning of the harvest.

In retrospect, it all seems obvious, given the significance of these festivals. Jesus had promised that they would be baptized with the Holy Spirit in a short while. He told them to wait in Jerusalem for it to happen. Although they probably did not know what "baptized with the Holy Spirit" meant, they knew that Jesus kept His promises. It was now ten days after the ascension. Jerusalem was jammed with Jews from all over the known world. So they should have suspected something, but apparently they didn't.

It was early in the morning. They were sitting in a house, probably in prayer. Without warning, the sound of a strong wind filled the house and the neighbor-

DISTINGUISHING THE FESTIVALS

The Feast of Firstfruits is very little understood and usually not treated as a separate festival. It is often confused with the Feast of Weeks (Pentecost), which is called "the day of firstfruits" (Num. 28:26). Leviticus 23:10–11 directs that Firstfruits—the offering of "a sheaf of the first grain"—be the day after the Sabbath after the Passover. Although Leviticus uses the term "firstfruits" (cf. NASB/KJV), it does not name the holiday. Since Jesus was raised on that day, Firstfruits was Resurrection Sunday. Paul seems to point to this connection when he declares in 1 Corinthians 15:23 that Christ was the firstfruits of the resurrection. A more perplexing celebration that began with Passover and overlapped with Firstfruits was the Festival of Unleavened Bread. This celebration lasted eight days. Its symbolism is not as clear, although we suggested in chapter 6 that it had the very pragmatic purpose of providing food during the period of flight from Egypt, when the Israelites did not have time to allow bread to rise before baking. For further information on the celebration of the festivals and their meaning, see Kevin Howard and Marvin Rosenthal, *The Feasts of the Lord* (Orlando, Fla.: Zion's Hope, 1997).

hood. A tongue of fire appeared in the room, separated into smaller pieces, and rested above each head. With this, they began speaking in other languages.[4]

The sound of the wind brought many curiosity seekers to find out what was happening. When they got there, they heard the disciples speaking in their own native languages. This was surprising, since the men were Galileans and not highly educated. Fifteen different ethnic groups are identified, from as far west as Rome and as far east as Parthia and Media.

Some of the more cynical (perhaps native Judeans who heard it as babble) suggested that they were drunk. Peter took the lead and addressed the crowd.[5] The sermon began by addressing the charge of drunkenness. Peter denied it since it was only nine o'clock in the morning. Rather, he asserted, it was a prophetic fulfillment. He cited Joel and the promise he had made regarding the last days. In that time, God had promised that He would pour out His Spirit on all humankind. Peter saw the events on

> The sound of the wind brought many curiosity seekers to find out what was happening.

Pentecost as an initial step in that prophecy. However, the real issue in Peter's mind was the crucifixion of Jesus. He noted the signs that Jesus had done (which had been widely talked about), and the crucifixion (which was common knowledge), and then the resurrection (which would have been widely rumored). Peter then referred to David and the prophecies he had made. His conclusion drove the point home: "God has made this Jesus, whom you crucified, both Lord and Messiah" (Acts 2:36).

This message convicted the crowd.[6] What they could do now? Peter was very clear. Collectively, they were to repent. Individually, they should be baptized to show their personal repentance. They would be forgiven their sins and would receive the gift of the Holy Spirit. Teaching continued through the day, and the core group of one hundred twenty in the upper room earlier swelled to over three thousand who accepted Jesus as Messiah. Today we see this event as the beginning of the church, although that term is not used in Acts 2. On Pentecost, they

THE SIGNIFICANCE OF BAPTISM

The disciples placed a strong importance on the ritual of baptism. However, its exact significance and degree of importance are debated today. Clearly, some of those who believed and were saved were not baptized. The prime example was the thief on the cross. We are never told that the apostles and the 120 with them prior to Pentecost received water baptism. The Greek text behind the phrase "for the forgiveness of your sins" (Acts 2:38) may be interpreted to mean that this act was something that accompanied or demonstrated belief. Apparently the early church used the term *baptism* as an outward expression of an internal change. We use other phrases today, such as "walking the aisle" or "making a profession of faith," in a similar manner.

were merely Jews who had embraced their Messiah. Luke calls them "believers" (Acts 2:44; the term *church* first appears in 5:11). Their acceptance of Jesus as the Messiah affected their actions. They listened to the teaching of the apostles (the Twelve). They met regularly to be together, to share meals, and to pray. As a result, the apostles performed many signs to validate the message. We are not told how long this went on, but it probably lasted for almost two years.[7]

Many of the first group of believers were from other regions of the Roman Empire and beyond. We are not told what they did after Pentecost, but two options were possible. Some no doubt returned home, sharing the good news that the Messiah had come. Others probably remained for further teaching. It is likely in this latter group that material needs arose, so the native Judeans helped out, even selling their own property to take care of the non-Judeans with needs (Acts 2:44–45).[8] As a result, others were accepting the message of the Messiah on a daily basis, swelling further the size of a church that already was over three thousand.

THE CHURCH GROWS

Read Acts 3:1–4:37.

Even so, these believers continued to follow many of the Jewish rituals they had grown up with. The next incident recorded begins with Peter and John going up to the temple to pray at the appointed time for prayer, three in the afternoon.[9] On this occasion, they noticed a man who had been lame from birth.[10] Apparently, the Holy Spirit spoke to both Peter and John, since they both looked at the man (Acts 3:4). Peter was the one who told him to get up and walk in the name of Jesus the Messiah. Peter reached out his hand to help the man up, and immediately his withered limbs were healed. The three went on into the temple, and the healed man was literally jumping for joy. This quickly caught the attention of others. Some recognized the man, and the story quickly went out—Peter and John had healed, just like Jesus.

As the crowd gathered, Peter used the opportunity to preach another sermon. Again he touched on the issues at hand while focusing on the resurrection of Jesus. Interestingly, Peter had noted in his first sermon that Jesus ascended to the right hand of God. Now he stated that Jesus must remain in heaven until it was time to restore everything as prophesied. The disciples were starting to realize that His second coming might take longer than they had thought. Another interesting point of the sermon is the concluding comment that God had raised up His servant for the Jews first so that they would turn from their wicked ways (Acts 3:26).[11]

Some of the priests overheard this sermon and became upset with the proclamation of the resurrection of Jesus. They threw Peter and John into jail. But the message had already had its effect with even more people coming to belief in the messiahship of Jesus.

The next day, Peter and John were brought before Caiaphas and the leaders of the Sanhedrin. The question was very simple: "By what power or what name did you do this?" (Acts 4:7). Peter quickly cut to the heart of the issue. The source of the power was Jesus the Messiah, whom they had rejected. Now the Jewish leadership was in a quandary. They dared not admit the truth of the claim of the resurrection. But they could not deny the healing of the crippled man—too many people knew about it. Nor could they explain the courage and articulateness of two men who had been with Jesus. Their only hope was to try to stop the message from spreading. So, as leaders of the Jewish people, they commanded the two Jewish men not to teach in the name of Jesus again.

Peter and John told the leaders that they could be the judge as to whether Jewish people should obey men or God. The apostles could not stop telling what they had seen and heard. Because of the magnitude of what had been done, however, the leaders were able to do nothing more than make additional threats. So Peter and John were released.

They went back to the group of believers and reported what had happened. As a result, the group prayed, giving praise to God for what had been done and asking for boldness to proclaim that Jesus was the Messiah. After the prayer, the

SANHEDRIN. A model of the meeting place of the Sanhedrin, which was apparently located on the second floor, over Solomon's colonnade on the grounds of the temple in Jerusalem.

HOW LARGE WAS THE EARLY CHURCH?

The phrase "about five thousand" (Acts 4:4) is ambiguous. It can be understood either as a total of five thousand (as suggested by the NIV and NASB) or as an additional five thousand (which seems to be the way the KJV and NRSV understand it). The church already consisted of over three thousand as a result of the first sermon (2:41), so if people were being added on a daily basis, a five thousand total might be low. We also need to keep in mind that throughout this period many of the new believers were probably returning to their homes in the Diaspora, but what effect that had on the numbers is not clear.

place was shaken, and they were all filled with the Holy Spirit and boldly spoke the word of God.

At this point, Luke inserts a comment about the unity of the church. This really serves to preface the actions of Barnabas, who in the same spirit of unity sold a field and gave the money to the apostles.[12]

PROBLEMS IN THE CHURCH

The church has always been very human. Remember the premise it was founded upon—Jesus was the Messiah, the Son of the Living God. The messianic concept takes us back not only to the OT prophets but also to Moses and the organization of the nation of Israel. Actually, it takes us back even further to Abraham,

> It should not surprise us to discover that problems arose in the church not long after it was founded.

who was called by God to have "seed." As Paul noted, this seed was not only many descendants; it was also an individual (Gal. 3:16). Ultimately, though, it takes us back to Eve and the garden. After she and Adam sinned, God told her that her "seed" would defeat Satan. It is the fallenness of mankind that produced the need for the Messiah. Those fallen people who accept Jesus as Messiah become part of the universal church.[13]

Ananias and Sapphira

Read Acts 5:1–11.

With this background, it should not surprise us to discover that problems arose in the church not long after it was founded.[14] The account begins when a married couple offered to give the money from the sale of property to the apostles. However, they decided to tell the apostles that they had sold it for less than the actual amount and pretend that they were giving everything to the church. Both were struck dead for the lie. As Peter told them, it was their property to dispose of as they wished, and the money they got from it was theirs. It was not their failing to give all the money that was the problem, but their trying to lie to God. As would be expected, this judgment produced a healthy fear and respect for God both in and out of the church.

The Apostles in Jail

Read Acts 5:12–42.

With this increasing respect, the apostles were able to perform more validating signs. They were also able to teach openly in Solomon's court around the temple.

ANCIENT CHUTZPAH

It is amazing how the Sadducees conveniently ignored the blatant supernormal act that had released the apostles from jail. It is also amazing, in that context, how they thought they could order those men around. This confrontation shows the Sadducees as badly shaken men who were far beyond their depth, trying to bluster their way out.

However, this could not last. After a few weeks or a couple of months or so, the Sadducees, led by the high priest, decided to get into the act. Luke says it was out of jealousy. The message of the resurrection also did not sit well.

The apostles were arrested and put into jail (Acts 5:18; the text implies that it was the entire group of the Twelve). However, an angel opened the doors and brought them out. So the next morning they were back at the temple preaching. In the meantime, the Sanhedrin sent officers to bring them in from the jail. When they got there, the jail was securely locked and the guards were in position, but the prisoners were gone. Then they heard that the apostles were preaching in the temple.

Very courteously, they invited them to meet with the Sanhedrin. The leaders chastised them for disobeying their orders. Peter and the others reiterated to the religious leaders that they needed to obey God rather than men. The Sadducees were ready to kill them. Gamaliel, a well-respected Pharisee, warned them against it.[15] If this movement was purely human, he said, it would soon die out. However, if it was of God, then they might find themselves fighting God. His warning carried the day. The leadership had the men flogged, warned, and released. The apostles, however, kept teaching and preaching, and the church kept growing.

HASIDIC JEWS. Members of the largest group of legalistic Jews today, in some respects the spiritual descendants of the Pharisees, who in their scrupulousness to observe the details of the Law often came into conflict with the Apostles.

Overlooking the Widows

Sometime afterward, a controversy arose over the daily distribution of food to widows. Hellenistic (or Greek-speaking) Jews complained that their widows were being overlooked. This incident raises a number of questions for which we do not have answers. Who were those Hellenistic Jewish widows? Apparently they had come from the Diaspora, but at what point had they been widowed? And at what point did they become believers (if indeed we are only addressing believers here)? How did the church start taking care of them, and what did they do prior to the establishment of the church? Who was handling the distribution? How long was the distribution going on before the problem arose, and how long did the problem persist before it came to the attention of the apostles? Any answers we give to these questions are pure speculation.

Read Acts 6:1–7.

When it did come to the apostles' attention, they called together the disciples, apparently the entire assembly of several thousand believers. Their point was very strong. The people were squabbling over what was really a secondary issue. As a result, the apostles were being asked to intervene. This was not seemly, since it took them away from their real responsibilities, the ministry of the word. Thus they suggested that the congregation select seven men to handle this issue. This solution would allow the apostles to continue in prayer and teaching. The people

THE SEVEN "DEACONS"

There is an interesting word play in Acts 6:2–4. The apostles argued that they should not serve or *minister* tables (the Greek verb is *diakone*o) but rather pay attention to the *ministry* of the word (the noun is *diakonia*). One should also note the related term *diakonos* ("servant, minister"), from which we get the English word *deacon* (Phil. 1:1; 1 Tim. 3:8–12). Thus the seven men chosen at this time are usually referred to as "deacons," although the term does not appear in this passage.

It has been noted that the Seven all have Greek names, suggesting that they or their families had come from the Diaspora. This detail suggests that a large number of the believing Christian Jews in Judea were from other countries. It is likely that some of them had been visiting Jerusalem for Pentecost when the church was founded. If so, then they had stayed on for teaching. It may well be that some had come to Jerusalem for other Jewish holidays after the founding of the church and that they too had stayed on. We should also note from this passage that there was no distinction in the church leadership at this time between the Greek-speaking and the native Aramaic-speaking Jews.

selected seven men "full of the Holy Spirit": Stephen, Philip, Prochorus, Nicanor, Timon, Parmenas, and Nicolas. Of these Jerusalem Seven, only Stephen and Philip play significant roles in the subsequent narrative.

Challenging the Priests

Read Acts 6:8 – 7:60.

As a result of such wisdom and concern, the church kept growing. Luke notes that even a number of the priests were becoming believers. This undoubtedly caused tension within the Sanhedrin. The account picks up with Stephen, one of the seven chosen to minister to the widows. He was noted as being full of the Holy Spirit and a very articulate communicator. He also was performing supernormal

MIKVEH. A special kind of basin used in Judaism for ritual baths during the time of Jesus. This *mikveh* is at Masada.

acts as validation. All of this made him a point of controversy with nonbelieving Jews.

Specifically, a group of men from the Synagogue of the Freedmen began to argue with Stephen. When they were unable to refute his arguments, they decided to get rid of him. They bribed false witnesses who gave twisted testimonies. They claimed to have heard Stephen teach that Jesus the Nazarene would destroy the temple and change the customs Moses had passed down.[16] Stephen was brought before the Sanhedrin to answer these charges. When they looked at Stephen and waited for his answer, they noticed that his face glowed like an angel's. He responded to this challenge with a powerful sermon that recapitulated the early history of the nation. He concluded with the harsh charge that they were stiff-necked and had uncircumcised hearts just like their ancestors.

His hearers were furious, and Stephen then cried out that he saw the "Son of Man standing at the right hand of God" (Acts 7:56).

With this, the sophisticated higher court of Judea mobbed Stephen and dragged him out of town. There they proceeded to stone him. One of the observers was a young rabbi, a student of Gamaliel, named Saul of Tarsus (again, a Jew from the Diaspora). The witnesses left their coats at his feet.

> Stephen became the first actual martyr for the cause of Jesus the Messiah.

Stephen, then, became the first actual martyr for the cause of Jesus the Messiah. The probable time was spring in 35 CE. This would then have been about two years after the resurrection. The evidence is that the Roman leaders merely looked the other way.

THE CHURCH IS SCATTERED

The death of Stephen started the first real persecution of the church as Jew attacked Jew over the issue of whether Jesus was really the Messiah. As a result, many of the believing Jews were driven from Jerusalem. A key exception was the apostles. One of the most fervent in the nonbelieving camp was Saul. With great zeal he gathered up whatever believing Jews he could find and threw them into prison.

Read Acts 8:1–40.

THE SYNAGOGUE OF THE FREEDMEN

A synagogue was basically a group of Jews with a corporate religious identity, comparable to a local church. In this case the members of the synagogue were *freedmen*, normally a term used to refer to former slaves or prisoners of war. For Luke and his original audience, it was apparently a significant group that everyone would know. Today it is very obscure. What is known is that they would have been considered Hellenistic Jews, having come from the cities of Cyrene and Alexandria in North Africa, and from the provinces of Cilicia and Asia in southern Asia Minor (modern Turkey).

THE SAMARITANS RECEIVE THE SPIRIT

The Samaritans did not receive the Holy Spirit until Peter and John prayed and laid their hands on them (Acts 8:14–17). The significance of this event has been debated, but the best answer seems to be that by this subsequent act, the Samaritan believers received the Holy Spirit in the same way the Jewish believers did, that is, through the work of the apostles. This process would put the two groups on a par. The only other place where an analogous situation occurred was when the first Gentiles became believers (Acts 10).[17] Again, this event took place through the work of Peter, and again it showed that the three groups were equal.

As a result of the persecution, one of the Jerusalem Seven, Philip, left Jerusalem and went to Samaria. This development marks a transition in the book, which follows a structure indicated in Acts 1:8.[18] In Samaria, Philip proclaimed Jesus as the Messiah and large crowds gathered. He performed a number of validating signs, creating joy as people believed. As word got back to Jerusalem, the apostles sent two emissaries—Peter and John.

When Peter and John arrived in Samaria, they found a group of believers who, unlike the believers in Judea, had not yet received the Holy Spirit. Laying their hands on the Samaritans, Peter and John prayed for the new believers and they received the Spirit.

A man named Simon who lived in Samaria had collected quite a following because of his magical powers. He professed belief in Jesus as the Messiah and watched Philip with amazement (and perhaps some jealousy). When he saw the work of Peter and John, he tried to buy their power. Peter rebuked him strongly for his wrong attitude, since he thought he could buy the power of God with money. Simon repented immediately.

Their work completed, Peter and John headed back to Jerusalem. En route they preached the good news of the Messiah to each village they went through.

In the meantime, the Holy Spirit directed Philip to leave and head toward Gaza. On the way there, he saw a chariot carrying an official from Ethiopia who was returning to his country after visiting Jerusalem to worship in the temple.[19] On his way back, he was reading from the book of Isaiah. At the prompting of the Holy Spirit, Philip ran up alongside the chariot and asked the official about his reading. The Ethiopian invited him into the chariot and asked him to explain Isaiah 53. As Philip explained the prophetic declaration of the crucifixion and resurrection shown in that chapter, the man believed that Jesus was the Messiah. He then asked to be baptized as they passed a body of water.

After being baptized, the man headed back to Ethiopia, where presumably he founded a church among the Jewish people there. Philip suddenly found himself transported to Azotus, about twenty miles north of Gaza. He proceeded up the coast to Caesarea, preaching in each city en route.

THE CONVERSION OF SAUL

Luke now turns his attention back to Saul in Jerusalem. Zealous for Judaism as he understood it, Saul became a leader of those trying to eradicate what he perceived to be a cult. The group of those who believed in Jesus was now being called "the Way" (Acts 9:2), and it was continuing to grow. After the death of Stephen, the disciples had been scattered. Some of them ended up in Damascus, about 150 miles northeast of Jerusalem.[20] Apparently, they had become part of the synagogue in Damascus and continued to teach that Jesus was the Messiah. Saul asked for letters from the high priest to the synagogue leaders there so that he could bring those "heretics" back to Jerusalem for trial. The letters were given, and Saul set out with an entourage of like-minded men.

Read Acts 9:1–31.

As they approached Damascus, suddenly a bright light from heaven shone around him. Saul fell to the ground, where he heard a voice asking, "Saul, Saul, why do you persecute me?" (Acts 9:4). When Saul asked who was speaking, he was told that it was Jesus. He was also told to go on into the city, where he would be given guidance. Those with him had heard the voice but did not see anyone.

Saul was now blind and had to be led into Damascus. For three days, he remained blind and did not eat nor drink. It was clearly a time for inner reflection. The words he had heard outside the city must have haunted him. Did he also think of Stephen? Had Saul been in Jerusalem at the time of the crucifixion two years earlier, and did he think about that? Did he think about the reports of the resurrection?

While Saul was reflecting, a disciple named Ananias, living in Damascus, had a vision. God told him to go to Saul and through prayer restore his sight. Ananias balked. He had heard many reports about Saul and wanted nothing to do

THE HOUSE OF ANANIAS. The church in Damascus located in the place that has traditionally been regarded as the site of the house of Ananias, who ministered to Saul.

STRAIGHT STREET. The street in Damascus on which Ananias lived, where Saul was sent after his conversion.

with him. God persisted, telling Ananias that Saul was chosen for a purpose. So Ananias went to Saul and prayed for him. As he laid his hands on Saul, something like scales fell from his eyes, and he regained his sight. When he got up, he was baptized as a believer in Jesus as the Messiah.

Almost immediately he began to proclaim that message to his fellow-Jews in the synagogues of Damascus: Jesus is the Messiah and the Son of God. This change in Saul amazed everyone who knew his original intent in coming to Damascus.

Apparently it was during this time that Saul went to Arabia to be by himself.[21] His experience changed everything, including his understanding of the OT. He needed to think through the implications. By Saul's testimony (Gal. 1:16–17), he was given special revelation of God during this period. As a Pharisee and a rabbi, he probably spent much time evaluating the prophetic declarations in the OT. After about two years, he returned to Damascus.

> Paul's experience in Arabia changed everything, including his understanding of the Old Testament.

Saul's demonstrations of the messiahship of Jesus were so convincing that he started collecting students. At the same time, the nonbelieving Jews decided to get rid of him. Saul's students got him out of town by lowering him in a basket through an opening in the city wall.

Saul went back to Jerusalem, his first return there as a believer. He tried to become a part of the assembly of believers, but they were not ready for this, not trusting a man who had earlier been trying to kill them. It was Barnabas who broke the ice. He took Saul to the apostles and shared the story of his vision near Damascus. He also shared how Saul had argued for the messiahship of Jesus in

HOW MANY APOSTLES DID SAUL SEE?

According to Acts 9:27, Barnabas took Saul (Paul) "and brought him to the apostles," but in Galatians 1:18–19, Paul states that he met only with Peter and James at this time. Two explanations are possible: (1) he met Peter and James as representatives of the entire group; or (2) he was presented before all the apostles, but as a relatively new believer, really had nothing else to do with the group as a whole. Paul's main point in Galatians was to show that he had not received teaching from the Twelve, but from Jesus Himself. We tend to see Paul's early ministry in light of his later fame. It would have taken several years before he was accepted on a par with the apostles.

the synagogues. With this, Saul was accepted. He then proceeded to argue for the messiahship of Jesus in Jerusalem, especially with the Hellenistic Jews. This created even more tension. The Jews were looking for a repeat of what they had done to Stephen several years before.

Instead, Saul was sent out of town, first to Caesarea and then to Tarsus, his home town.[22] With this, Luke notes that the church in Judea, Galilee, and Samaria enjoyed peace and continued to grow. So a little over four years after the crucifixion the church had spread throughout the entire region of what had once been Israel. The Jewish people were split, but a significant number of them were now believers. Moreover, pockets of believers were cropping up in the Jewish settlements of the eastern Mediterranean region. While there were Samaritans in the group, at this point there were no Gentiles. It would be several years (until after Cornelius) before that changed.

REVIEW QUESTIONS

1. Why was the last question the disciples asked Jesus about the kingdom?

2. Trace the events of Pentecost.

3. Describe the conflict between the Jews who accepted Jesus as the Messiah and those who did not.

4. What are some of the problems the early church faced?

5. Why was Stephen stoned?

6. What led to Saul's conversion?

21
CHAPTER

Reaching Out to Gentiles

OVERVIEW

To this point the church was entirely Jewish. Two events were instrumental in changing this condition. The first was Peter's visit to and conversion of Cornelius, a Roman centurion. After this incident, the church expanded tremendously in Antioch. Barnabas was sent there and recruited Saul to help. Subsequently these two men went out on their first missionary journey, which predominantly connected with Gentiles after Jews refused to listen. During this period we also see the first of the letters of the NT being written, including the Epistle of James.

STUDY GOALS

▶ Demonstrate how God moved the church to evangelize Gentiles.

▶ Contrast the arrests of James and Peter.

▶ Show how the church began using epistles for communication and teaching.

▶ Develop the message of the epistle of James.

▶ Follow Paul and Barnabas through their first missionary journey.

When God called Abraham, He told him that he would be a blessing to the nations, that is, to all the families of the earth (see above, ch. 4). The immediate content of that promise was that his own family would grow throughout future generations. And, as we have followed the history from that point, the focus has been on that one family—traced through Abraham's second son, Isaac, and through Isaac's second son, Jacob. The latter, whose name was changed to Israel, fathered the family and nation known by his new name. Over the years a few outsiders were brought in, but in general the focus was on the nation of Israel as Abraham's family. However, the nation of Israel did not accomplish its intended goal, which was to represent the true God to the nations, that is, being a kingdom of priests (Ex 19:6).

Bringing the Gentiles to the true God was one of the purposes of the Messiah and was part of the message of Jesus. He Himself claimed to be the Messiah and gave proof of it. He also told His disciples to take His message to the world—first to Jerusalem, then to Judea and Samaria, and then to all the nations of the earth. It had taken about two years and the death of Stephen to get to Samaria. Now, the disciples were spreading throughout the nations—sort of. They were going to pockets of Jews in the various nations of the world. Christianity was still a segment of Judaism and was giving no indications of moving beyond this culture. As we will see, it took another act of God to change that.

CAPPADOCIA. The region in the heart of the central plateau of Asia Minor that became the focus of Paul's first missionary journey. In Paul's day it was politically part of the province of Galatia, but today it is known as Cappadocia.

PETER AND THE GENTILES

As He did twice before, God used Peter.[1] Up to this point, the entire group of twelve apostles had remained in Jerusalem. By 40–41 CE, approximately seven to eight years after the resurrection, Peter traveled through western Judea.[2] Luke records two specific events of those travels. First, in Lydda (between Jerusalem and Joppa) Peter healed Aeneas, who had been paralyzed for eight years. While he was there, a disciple named Tabitha, or Dorcas, died in Joppa. Other disciples there had heard that Peter was in Lydda about eleven miles away. Because of her renown for doing good works, they sent for Peter, who came down to Joppa. After prayer, Peter told her to arise, and she did. These events helped draw others to belief in Jesus as the Messiah. Peter then remained in Joppa for some time, staying with a Simon who tanned leather.

While Peter was staying at Simon's house, an angel appeared to a Roman soldier in Caesarea, about thirty-five miles to the north. Cornelius was a centurion in the Roman army. He was also what was called a God-fearer; that is, he believed in the God of Israel and served Him in a variety of ways, but had not undergone the conversion process to Judaism (which would have included circumcision). It was the middle of the afternoon when an angel appeared to Cornelius and told him to send messengers to Joppa to get Peter.

The next day the three messengers that Cornelius sent were approaching Joppa at about noon. Peter was waiting for lunch and had gone up on the roof to pray while waiting. During his prayers, he had a vision of a large sheet lowered from heaven containing all sorts of mammals, birds, and reptiles listed in the OT law as unclean. A voice told him to get up, kill, and eat. Peter was aghast and protested that he had never eaten any unclean meats. The voice replied that he was not to call unclean what God had cleansed.[3] This interchange was repeated three times, and then the sheet returned back to the sky. Peter was puzzling about the meaning of the

Read Acts 9:32–10:48.

UNCLEAN ANIMALS. An important issue for observant Jews, with the criteria given in Leviticus 11. The reasoning behind the criteria is debated, but the criteria themselves were very clear. Thus a rabbit would have been an unclean animal for the apostle Peter.

CORNELIUS THE CENTURION

The Latin term *centurion* (and its Greek equivalent in Acts 10:1) originally indicated a commander in charge of one hundred men. The responsibilities of Cornelius would have been comparable to those of a modern (U.S.) army captain, although he did not have the same status as a modern captain (he would be considered a noncommissioned officer). His troop was part of the Italian Regiment or Cohort stationed in Caesarea. The cohort, or one-tenth of a legion, would have consisted of 600 to 1,000 men and thus was roughly equivalent to a modern battalion.

vision when Cornelius's messengers knocked on the door asking for him. The Holy Spirit told him who they were and why. He went down, listened to their story, and then understood the meaning of the vision.

The next day Peter accompanied the messengers to Caesarea. He went into the house of Cornelius and shared his vision; Cornelius then shared his. With this, Peter presented the testimony he had of who Jesus was. While he was speaking, the Holy Spirit fell on this group of Gentiles in the same way He had fallen upon the Jews and the Samaritans. The Jewish believers who had come with Peter were amazed. Based on this clear evidence of God's work, Peter baptized that group of Gentiles. He then remained there for several days, discussing what had happened and what it meant.

REPORTING IN JERUSALEM

Read Acts 11:1–18. The word quickly got back to Jerusalem to the rest of the apostles, and Peter soon went up to Jerusalem to report what had happened. However, he was immediately met with a hostile response from a segment of the believing Jews who saw Jesus in a very Jewish mode.[4] This reaction clearly delineated two growing divisions. The first was between those believers who maintained that Christianity was a Jewish group (so that all who came to Jesus had to become Jewish also) and those who did not think Gentiles had to submit to Jewish ritual. The second division was between what would become Christianity and what would become Judaism.[5]

Peter was called on the carpet before the rest of the apostles to explain his decision to eat with unclean men. Peter recounted his vision and the events that followed. He concluded by stating, "So if God gave them the same gift as he gave us, who believed in the Lord Jesus Christ, who was I to think that I could oppose God?" (Acts 11:17). This answer satisfied those who were present, and they withdrew their objections.[6]

THE CHURCH IN ANTIOCH

Read Acts 11:19–30. Luke now turns his attention to Antioch. First, he reiterates how the stoning of Stephen spread the church out, bringing believers to Antioch. There a church was

---

ANTIOCHENE AND ALEXANDRIAN INTERPRETATION

In the fourth century CE, Antioch became the center of a major school of biblical interpretation (hermeneutics) that took a fairly straightforward, literal approach. A second major school of thought came out of Alexandria, home to the first-century CE Jewish writer Philo, who took a more allegorical view of the Bible and whose writings influenced Christians in that city in the second and third centuries. (This topic will be discussed further in chapter 28.)

founded that would become very significant over the next several centuries. The next few chapters give hints to its increasing importance.

The church in Antioch was the first to follow Peter in sharing the good news about Jesus with Gentiles.[7] Soon word about this move reached Jerusalem. The leaders there (the apostles) sent Barnabas to Antioch to find out what was going on. When Barnabas reached Antioch, he became excited about what he found—the Holy Spirit was working in a mighty way. Barnabas was soon busy encouraging the new believers. After a while, he decided he needed help. So about two years after he arrived in Antioch, Barnabas went to Tarsus to get Saul. For the next year they worked together in the church at Antioch, teaching the new disciples.

ANTIOCH OF SYRIA. A city that became a major Christian center with both Jewish and Gentile believers. From here Paul began his missionary journeys, and he returned here between them. This church, however, is named after Peter.

With the new Greek population in their midst, the disciples acquired a new title—"Christians." This was a Greek term for followers of the Messiah, since Christ is the Greek word for Messiah.

The growth of the church in Antioch was demonstrated by the next event. Several prophets came from Jerusalem, and one of them, named Agabus, proclaimed that the Holy Spirit had foretold a famine. Foreseeing a need in Jerusalem, the Antiochene believers decided to send a contribution. The party carrying the relief funds was headed by Barnabas and Saul. Apparently, Titus was also part of the group.[8] But that trip was future, and it took some time to organize. In the meantime, significant events were transpiring in Jerusalem, which Luke seems to place between Acts 11:30 and 12:25.

THE ARREST OF PETER AND JAMES

In the spring of 44, Herod Agrippa had several of the disciples arrested, including James, brother of John and son of Zebedee.[9] James was executed, which pleased the non-believing Jewish leaders. Herod then arrested Peter and put him in jail to await a trial.

Read Acts 12:1–24.

However, while God's plans allowed for the physical death of James, He still had other plans for Peter.[10] That night an angel appeared in his cell, where he was sound asleep, bound by chains to two guards (with two more guards at the locked cell door). When the angel appeared, he woke up Peter and told him to leave. Peter's chains fell off and the angel led him out. Peter thought he was dreaming, especially since the guards seemed totally unaware of what was happening. After they went through the locked doors and reached the streets of Jerusalem, the angel disappeared. At this point Peter realized it was no dream and headed for John Mark's house.[11] When he got there, he found a large number of believers inside praying.

Peter knocked on the gate, and a servant girl named Rhoda came to answer, asking who was there. When Peter answered, she was so excited, she ran to tell the others, leaving Peter standing in the street. The group, which had been praying for Peter, refused to believe it was actually him. She insisted and Peter kept knocking. Finally they let Peter in. When they had calmed down, he explained what had happened, and told them to send word to James (the half brother of Jesus) and the other believers. He then left to an undisclosed location.

The next morning Herod was irate. The guards were interrogated, but their story did not make sense.[12] So he had them executed. He then went down to Caesarea. There the crowds proclaimed him a god. Accepting this blatant flattery and lie, Herod was struck down by God.[13]

THE CHURCH HAS MAIL

Most of the books of the NT have traditionally been called "epistles,"[14] which means "letters"—the term we more commonly use today. The dictionary also notes that epistles are communications "especially of formal or didactic character."[15] The most important thing to remember regarding the interpretation or

DUAL AUTHORSHIP

The truth that each biblical book has both a human and a divine author is critical, but we struggle with the concept. How did it work? On the one hand, the idea that the Holy Spirit merely implanted concepts that the human author put into his own words seems too loose. On the other hand, the idea that the Holy Spirit dictated the letter to the human author word for word seems too tight. Part of the problem may be that we have condensed the issue down to the few hours that the person worked on the letter, omitting the overall context. I would suggest that inspiration is a process whereby God worked with the human author *over an entire lifetime*, so that when it came time to create the letter, the human author was working with a reservoir of experience and a vocabulary that allowed him to convey exactly the point that God intended.

ANCIENT LETTER-WRITING

In ancient times, the usual writing material was made from the stalk of the papyrus reed. This stalk is hollow. It would be cut open and laid flat, producing a veneer about an inch wide. A sheet of papyrus would consist of two layers, one vertical and one horizontal. They would be about the size of a sheet of modern typing paper—about 9 to 10 inches wide and 11 to 12 inches long. The ink was made from carbon suspended in a fluid (probably water) that would evaporate. Letter-writing was fairly common in the Roman Empire even though there was no postal service. Messengers would carry letters to the recipient. As such, most letters addressed items of importance, often of a commercial or official nature. Standard formats for letters developed. The NT letters follow that form, although they tend to be much longer than most letters from other sources. (For more information on letters, see John E. Stambaugh and David L. Balch, *The New Testament in Its Social Environment* [Philadelphia: Westminster, 1986], 39–40.)

We have been fortunate to find copies of some of the early NT manuscripts (that is, hand-written documents) in the desert areas of Egypt and Israel. These have helped show both how early the NT documents were written and how accurately they were preserved. While the copyists did make errors, the vast majority of the mistakes are very evident and easily explained. By the second century, churches were putting their collections of letters into books made of parchment, a more durable material. (See Bruce M. Metzger, *The Text of the New Testament*, 3rd ed. [New York: Oxford University Press, 1992], ch. 1.)

study of the biblical epistles, or letters, is that they were "occasional writings."[16] That is, they were written on a specific occasion to a specific local church, usually to deal with a specific issue. This feature has a number of implications.

First, the letter writer had a specific agenda in mind. This seems to go without saying, given our definition, but it is amazing how often this point is overlooked. However, very often we need to infer that agenda from the text. Usually it can be determined by the responses laid out within the body of the letter. For this purpose, the organization and overall content of the letter is very important. It also helps to have the historical background of the letter, but that is sometimes not clear to us. We also

PAPYRUS MAKING. The practice of slicing the stalk of the papyrus reed into thin slices and producing a writing material. It is still practiced today, although only for the tourist industry.

need to keep in mind that there were two authors for each book—the human author and the divine behind-the-scenes author.

As the NT writers wrote to churches, the churches that received the letters sometimes kept them for future reference and teaching. Churches in nearby towns would make copies for their use. Over time, more and more churches had copies. These letters were generally written on papyrus. While relatively inexpensive, papyrus degraded with age and use. After a few years, even the original churches no longer had the original letters but only copies.

After a few decades, many churches had copies of most of the letters we include in the NT. When heretics began questioning those letters, the church gathered to establish which letters were to be included in the canon, but that was sometime later. But that was after the NT period, and first the letters had to be written.

WISDOM IN THE FACE OF PERSECUTION

Read James 1–5. The first NT letter to have been written seems to be the epistle of James. We have just noted how, after his special deliverance from prison, Peter sent word to James, the half brother of Jesus, as a leader of the church. Traditionally, this James is credited with writing the letter that bears his name.

The letter was written to Jewish believers (the twelve tribes). The context of the letter was persecution. The primary period of persecution of a predominantly Jewish church was the period following the death of James bar Zebedee reported in Acts 12. Peter had fled Jerusalem, or at least was in hiding. Although Herod died shortly afterward, his action apparently precipitated a more widespread per-

THE NT LETTERS AND THE CANON

We are not sure of the exact process whereby the church accepted certain letters as canonical, but there seem to be several key points. First, the writers were supported by the events they reported. Second, they were also corroborated by others: many witnesses of the events were still alive at the time of the writing, lending an opportunity to each of the early writers to be checked out. Third, they were often substantiated by supernormal events. This issue is often totally ignored today, but to do so is a product of a philosophical presupposition rather than an unbiased view of the data.

As we trace the early history of the church, we find a very interesting pattern. Early in church history, the apostles and disciples performed miracles to demonstrate the point they were trying to make. What is even more interesting is that about halfway through the book of Acts (chs. 15–16, during the period from about 50 to 55 CE), we find the reports of these supporting miracles dying out. As we superimpose a chronology of the writing of the NT on this pattern, however, we find that as the written revelation appears, the need for supernormal events seems to disappear.

While we do not have an explicit record of the development of the NT canon, we can see its evidence. About 140–50 CE, Marcion of Pontus published his list of accepted books. He was excommunicated as a heretic in 144 because of his docetism (a gnostic view that asserted that Christ did not have a truly human body). Marcion was also anti-Jewish and tried to expurgate the NT of any OT residues. Furthermore, he tried to separate the OT view of God as exacting and just from the NT view of God as love. A few years later Irenaeus (120–202) asserted that Marcion gave his followers "merely a fragment" of the gospel. He also stated that Marcion "dismembered the Epistles of Paul" (*Against Heresies* 1.27.2; see *ANF*, 1:352). This shows that Irenaeus recognized a collection of Paul's letters as part of the canon. Thus, although the church as a whole did not formalize the canon until the Synod of Hippo in 393, at that point it merely made official what the churches collectively had already recognized.

JAMES WHO?

Four men named James are mentioned in the Gospels, but only two have significant claims to be the author of the letter that bears that name: (1) James bar (i.e., son of) Zebedee, who was one of the Twelve and the brother of John, and (2) James the half brother of Jesus. James the brother of John would likely have used his title of apostle rather than just "the servant of God" (James 1:1); moreover, he was martyred very early (Acts 12:1–2), before the letter was likely written. Thus the probable author of the epistle of James is Jesus' half brother.

Were the "brothers" of Jesus (Matt. 13:55 et al.) the children of Mary? At some point in the ancient church, the view arose that these brothers were children of Joseph by an earlier marriage. This theory seems to have been a corollary of the view that Mary remained a virgin her entire life. The obvious and most likely explanation, however, would be that these were children that Mary and Joseph had after Jesus was born.

James didn't believe his half brother was the Messiah at first (John 7:5), until Jesus appeared specially to Him after His resurrection (1 Cor. 15:7). Acts 12:17 suggests that by 44 CE he had become one of the church leaders (see also Acts 15:13; Gal. 1:19).

secution. The immediate context of the letter seems to be that persecution. The writer asserts that suffering is really something to rejoice in, since it produces spiritual growth.

More than this, the letter addresses several specific issues that would have arisen among the messianic Jews throughout the Roman Empire. As such, the letter of James reads more like a book of wisdom than a letter. The author uses the term *wisdom* four times, beginning with a directive to ask for wisdom. More important than the actual use of the word are the practical ramifications. The letter gives the readers insight into how to conduct their daily lives if Jesus is really the Messiah.[17] As such, it is addressed to individuals that the writer assumes are believers.

Historically, the book has been somewhat controversial. Some have seen a conflict between it and the writings of Paul (cf. James 2:24 NRSV, "a person is justified by works and not by faith alone," with Rom. 3:28 NRSV, "a person is justified by faith apart from works"). Closer examination, however, shows that the two are actually saying the same thing but focusing on different aspects. Paul focuses on how one is reconciled with God and then secondarily mentions aspects of lifestyle. James is primarily concerned with the lifestyle of one who is reconciled with God.[18] But even as James was writing, Paul and the church in Antioch were demonstrating their faith.

FAMINE AND RELIEF

We saw in Acts 11:30 the anticipation of the famine by Agabus. This took place approximately 47 CE.[19] Paul and Barnabas made their trip to Jerusalem with relief funds and then returned to Antioch, a trip that Luke just mentions. Now he picks them up as they return from Jerusalem and take John Mark back to Antioch with

Read Acts 12:25.

AN INTERESTING GROUP

The leaders of the church in Antioch included a very interesting group. There was Barnabas. There was Simeon, called Niger (a Latin name meaning "Black"). This man may have been the Simeon from Cyrene (a city in Libya) who was "recruited" to carry the cross of Jesus (Mark 15:21). He is also named as the father of Alexander and Rufus. In Romans 16:13 Paul mentions Rufus and his mother, a possible reference to Paul's staying at their house while in Antioch. There is Lucius of Cyrene. One wonders if he and Simeon were some of those from Cyrene mentioned in Acts 12 who began evangelizing the Gentiles in Antioch. There was Manaen, who had been brought up with Herod Antipas the tetrarch (some believe that the Greek term translated "brought up with" indicates that he was a foster brother). And there was Saul.

them. John Mark was a cousin of Barnabas (Col. 4:10). The group remained at Antioch for several months.

PAUL'S FIRST MISSIONARY JOURNEY

Read Acts 13:1–12.

When Luke picks up the account in Acts 13, the leaders of the church of Antioch are fasting and praying. This was the practice used by pious Israelites throughout the OT to seek God's leading. While they prayed, the Holy Spirit indicated that Barnabas and Saul were to be set aside for a special work. This was a journey of outreach, and Barnabas was apparently to be the leader. After prayer, the group that stayed behind laid their hands on Barnabas and Saul and sent them on their way. They took John Mark along as a helper. This is considered Paul's first missionary journey. The time was approximately spring of 48 CE.[20]

Journey to Cyprus

We are not told why Barnabas and Saul chose Cyprus, but there are hints. First, this was Barnabas's home (Acts 4:36). Second, there had already been evangelistic work done in Cyprus, although it had been limited to Jews (11:19).

PAPHOS. A church in Paphos, the last city Paul and Barnabas visited on the island of Cyprus.

Barnabas and Saul began at Salamis on the east coast of Cyprus and worked their way across the island to Paphos. They focused entirely on Jewish synagogues. We are given no record of any response until they got to Paphos.[21] There they encountered both a positive and a negative response.

The positive response was from a Gentile. He was Sergius Paulus, the proconsul. He was the Roman who was responsible for the province, that is, the entire island. He heard of Barnabas and Saul and sent for them to explain what they were doing.

The negative response was from a Jewish magician and would-be prophet named Elymas (or Bar Jesus), who worked with Sergius Paulus. He did not want Sergius

Paulus to accept the message of Barnabas and Saul and kept interfering as they tried to explain the gospel. As this went on, the Holy Spirit filled Saul. He turned to Elymas, chastised him, and declared that he would be physically blind for a period of time.[22] When Sergius Paulus saw this miracle, he proclaimed his belief in Paul's message of Jesus as Messiah. Saul's overpowering of a magician was the turning point in the proconsul's life.

Jews were not open to the message about the Messiah, but Gentiles were.

This event seems to have set a general pattern that would become more and more evident. Jews were not open to the message about the Messiah, but Gentiles were. This response would have profound effects on the church, but it would take several years before it was recognized.

Interestingly, at this point Luke notes Saul's alternative name of Paul, a Roman name. Luke will use it from here on. Also, following this event, Paul is mentioned first—he seems to have assumed the leadership. The proconsul's conversion then may have marked a change in Paul's thinking, making him more open to direct evangelism of the Gentiles.

Journey to Galatia

Paul and his companions left Paphos by ship. They sailed north to the port of Perga on the southern coast of Asia Minor (modern Turkey). There John Mark decided to return to Jerusalem.[23] Paul and Barnabas headed on north to Antioch of Pisidia, about a hundred miles north of Perga (this Antioch is to be distinguished from Antioch of Syria, where Paul's own church was). The city was on the southern edge of the central Turkish plateau and lay at a major crossroads. By this time, it was a cosmopolitan city that included not only native Phrygians, but also Greeks, Romans, and a large Jewish element.[24] In terms of political divisions, Antioch was in the Roman province of Galatia. There, they visited the synagogue on the Sabbath, as was their custom. As guests and educated Jews who had studied in Jerusalem, they were asked if they had a message to share during the service. Paul did, and Luke records his message.

Paul began with the Exodus event and showed God's faithfulness in bringing their ancestors to the land promised to Abraham. He focused on the heart attitude of David, the greatest king, but from there he jumped to the promised heir of David. The rest of the message focused on Jesus and how He fulfilled the OT prophecies, showing Him to be the Messiah. When the leaders in Jerusalem refused to acknowledge this claim and had Him crucified, He rose again on the third day, as documented by many witnesses. Paul concluded with a challenge to the Jews who were listening so that they might not have prophetic judgments come upon them for failing to believe.

Read Acts 13:13–14:25.

PAUL'S FIRST MISSIONARY JOURNEY.

This message won at least a willingness to hear more. Paul and Barnabas were invited back the following Sabbath to share further details. However, the message did more than that. It became the talk of the town. By the next Sabbath, a large crowd had gathered.[25] Unfortunately, this response created tension. Some of the Jews were jealous and tried to contradict everything Paul and Barnabas said. Finally, Paul and Barnabas declared that their hearers had lost their chance. They cited Isaiah 49 as their authorization to go to Gentiles.

Following this incident, a large number of Gentiles became believers. But the issue had not been laid to rest. The jealous Jews became even more

PERGA. The city gates that Paul and company passed through in the small city that was their entryway into Asia Minor. John Mark left Perga to return to Jerusalem while Paul continued on his journey.

irate. They sowed discontent, using a number of key figures who are described as devout women and leading men. A wave of persecution arose against Paul and Barnabas, who were driven out of the city and the region. These issues would eventually become a controversy involving all the believers in the known world.

Paul and Barnabas shook the dust off of their sandals and headed east, traveling about eighty miles to Iconium (modern Konya). Here they followed the same pattern, with similar results. The Jews initially believed, and some Gentiles heard and believed also. Those who did not, however, stirred up the uncommitted against Paul and Barnabas. As a result, the two again fled, heading southeast through Lycaonia, a subregion of the Galatian province.

The first city they went to was Lystra. Their visit to Lystra was an apparent disaster. First, they encountered a man who had been lame from birth, and Paul healed him. However, the observers decided that he and Barnabas were visiting Greek gods. Barnabas was equated with Zeus, and Paul with Hermes (the spokesman).[26] Even the priest at the temple of Zeus got into the act. He brought

GALATIA

The region of Galatia had originally been settled by Gauls who had migrated from Europe to Asia Minor about 278 BCE. Here they established a country that retained its boundaries until about 25 BCE, when the region was incorporated into the Roman Empire. At that time, the Romans established the province of Galatia, but a section south of the traditional region was incorporated into it. This southern section included the cities of Antioch (of Pisidia), Lystra, Derbe, and Iconium.

up oxen to offer sacrifice to them and garlands of flowers to place around their heads.

When Paul and Barnabas understood what was going on, they were visibly distraught.[27] They tore their clothes and rushed into the excited crowd, trying to get them to stop. Paul tried to preach a sermon that was powerful in its attestation of "natural revelation." Through this they were barely able to restrain the offering of sacrifices on their behalf.

As Luke recounts the events, about this time Jews from Antioch and Iconium showed up. They incited the crowd into a riot. After all, if they weren't gods, they must be imposters. As a result, Paul, the spokesman, was stoned, dragged out of the city, and left for dead. In fact, even the disciples with him thought he was dead.[28] They were standing around what they supposed to be his dead body when Paul got up, and they went into the city.

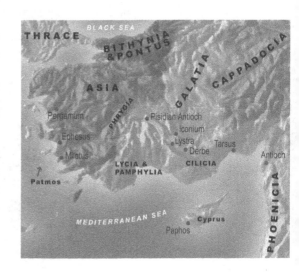

IHLYA GORGE. An area (also called Ihlara) in the Cappadocia region that for centuries after Paul remained a stronghold of Christianity and became the home of monasteries and churches carved into canyon walls as shown here. This influence lasted well into the Muslim era.

This event points out that not everyone in the city had taken a position either for or against the proclaimed message. The growing group of Christians was still a peripheral movement. While we are not told explicitly, there must have been a small group of believers even in this city. The next day Paul and Barnabas went to Derbe.

Derbe was different from Lystra. People listened and believed. Apparently Paul and Barnabas remained there through the winter. They then retraced their steps back through Lystra, Iconium, and Antioch. In each city they encouraged those who had become disciples. They also prayed, fasted, and appointed leaders for the fledgling churches.

They spent more time at Perga, which they had apparently just passed through on the way out. This time they preached. Although no results are mentioned, it may be assumed that another fledgling church was founded. From there they returned to Antioch of Syria.

THE ROMAN PROVINCES OF ASIA MINOR.

ELDERS

The Greek word translated "elder" (Acts 14:23) is *presbyteros*. The concept came out of the synagogue, but in the Christian churches at this time the elders seemed to acquire more prestige and duties, including teaching the word of God. Part of the reason for this development may have the increasing persecution. Part of it may have been the fact that there was yet no NT for the churches to work with. At this point, all that was available was the letter from James, and probably most churches did not have that yet. Consequently, while we are not told so, it is likely that most of the new elders were Jewish believers. They would have had a background in the OT scriptures, which was all that Paul and Barnabas had at this point. They would have been able, then, to look at the implications of the messiahship of Jesus within that context. Once the church began reaching to communities that were entirely or even predominantly pagan (without a solid OT background), the question of leadership would be an entirely new problem. That is when we begin seeing Paul and others writing letters to give guidelines.

Return to Antioch

Read Acts 14:26–28.

Paul and Barnabas probably arrived back in Antioch of Syria during the fall of 49 CE. Their first journey had taken about a year and a half. In Antioch they reported what God had done during the trip. All in all, it had been a success. There were a number of new groups of disciples in the areas where Paul and Barnabas visited. It is possible that there had already been some scattered individuals or even cells of believers as a result of Pentecost. Acts 2 does mention people from Pamphylia (where Perga was located), Phrygia (Antioch of Pisidia was near here), and Cappadocia (near Derbe) in Jerusalem on the day the church was founded. However, we are not given information on when or if those people in Jerusalem returned home.

More importantly, the good news about the Messiah was definitely being shared in Gentile communities. Many Gentiles were becoming believers. And that was going to raise questions that had not been anticipated.

CAPPADOCIA. A region of eastern Asia Minor known for its unusual geology, an area that Paul might have traveled through on one of his journeys to Galatia.

REVIEW QUESTIONS

1. Describe the conversion of Cornelius.

2. Why did Peter have to go to Jerusalem to defend his ministry to Cornelius?

3. How did James die, and what happened to Peter at the same time?

4. Why was the letter of James written?

5. How did Paul end up as a missionary?

6. Describe Paul's first journey as a missionary.

22
CHAPTER

What about the Gentiles?

OVERVIEW

After Paul's first missionary journey, dissent arose over the process by which Gentiles would be included in the church. Some wanted Gentile believers to go through the process of adopting Judaism and to practice Jewish ritual. This issue was addressed in the letter to the Galatians and at the Jerusalem Council. As a follow-up, Paul and Barnabas planned to retrace their steps from the first journey. Because of a controversy over John Mark, they split up. Barnabas and John Mark went to Cyprus; Paul and Silas went to Asia Minor.

STUDY GOALS

▶ Evaluate the question of Gentile circumcision that led to the Jerusalem Council.

▶ Develop the message of the epistle to the Galatians.

▶ Explain the Jerusalem Council in terms of both its conclusions and its significance for later doctrine.

▶ Show how Paul's disagreement with Barnabas led to a missionary journey with Silas.

It does not seem to have been too long after Paul and Barnabas returned to Antioch in Syria that they realized things were not quite right. We saw earlier that after Peter preached the gospel to Cornelius, controversy arose in Jerusalem. Some who believed that Jesus was the Jewish Messiah maintained that everyone who accepted this proclamation had to follow Jewish ritual. Others did not think Gentiles had to submit to such ceremonies. After the first missionary journey, two things seem to have happened concurrently that brought the issue to a head. One was in Antioch. The other was in Galatia. In both cases, Jewish elements began maintaining that in order to follow Jesus the Messiah, one must become a Jew. In other words, anyone who claimed to be a Christian must also submit to Jewish conversion ritual, including circumcision.

The two events are addressed in two places in the NT. As a result, scholars debate their sequence and timing. While the reports are fragmented, they seem to be intertwined, and we will address them as such. The precipitating event appears to have been in Antioch around the time of Paul's return from his first journey in 49 CE. This incident is reported in Acts 15:1. By now there would have been a number of Gentile believers in Antioch. When Judeans arrived in Antioch, they began telling them that they had to follow the custom of Moses and be circumcised. That is, they had to follow Jewish ritual if they truly believed in the Jewish Messiah. Luke tells us that Paul and Barnabas argued with them sharply.

Then Paul received word of the same problem in Galatia. He addressed that problem in a letter that he sent to the churches he had planted. After writing the letter, Paul and Barnabas went up to Jerusalem to clarify the issue with the apostles.[1] After that meeting, he returned to the churches in Galatia to personally share the results. These three events—the writing of Galatians, the visit to Jerusalem, and the second missionary journey—will be addressed in this chapter.

CAVE OF CHARON. A cave near Antioch of Syria that is associated with Charon, the god in Greek mythology who ferried dead souls across the River Styx into elysium. The Greeks had a fascination with death and the underworld, perhaps because they lived in a region active tectonically. This fascination may have contributed to the open hearing many gave Paul and other early witnesses to the resurrection.

THE LETTER TO THE GALATIANS

As in the case of the letter of James, the letter to the Galatians addressed a point of concern in the church. James dealt with persecution. Galatians addressed the question of circumcision and Jewish ritual for Gentile believers. Everyone agrees that the letter deals with this topic and that it is addressed to "the churches in Galatia," but not everyone agrees on the identity of the Galatians. Who they were may affect the date it was written. One view identifies the Galatians as inhabitants of the northern portion of the province of Galatia (see map, page 472).[2] Paul certainly did not visit that area during his first missionary journey. According to this view, however, he did travel there during the second journey (cf. Acts 16:6, but see sidebar on next page), so the letter must have been written subsequent to this time and probably about 57–58 CE (that is, during the third journey). The other view identifies the recipients as the inhabitants of the cities in the southern part of the province, which he had just visited during the first journey, and dates the letter to about 49 CE. There are several clues that point to the earlier date. For example, there is no record that Paul ever visited the cities in northern Galatia (such as Pessinus, Ancyra, and Tavium). But the strongest clue is the letter's failure to mention the decisions taken in the Jerusalem Council.[3]

As we will see, this council gave an apostolic final answer on the issue of circumcision. It would seem strange for Paul to fail to mention this strong declaration in his letter on the issue unless the council had not yet met. Moreover, the tone of the letter is sharp, which could be expected at a time when Paul was in the middle of a strong debate on the same issue in Antioch. If Galatians was written on this occasion, it appears that this document would have been Paul's first letter and the second oldest letter in the NT (after James).

The letter consists of three parts. The first part (Gal. 1:1–2:21) is a recapitulation of Paul's ministry. In this section we learn a few more details about what he did after his conversion. The main thrust was that through this entire time his message had been the same, one he had gotten from God. More than this, he had consulted with some of the apostolic leaders privately, and they had agreed with his understanding of the gospel.[4] This understanding was that salvation was a

Read Galatians 1–6.

THE PAULINE CORRESPONDENCE

As we start looking at the letters of Paul, we must note that they are true letters. The word *epistle* is defined as a formal written communication, especially one of a didactic or teaching nature. Paul's letters followed the style of the day (with a greeting, thanksgiving and prayer, main subject, and farewell). They were written for the purpose of teaching. Some of them (like Galatians) deal with only one or two issues. Others cover a whole gamut of problems. The NT indicates that Paul wrote other letters that were not retained by the church (cf. 1 Cor. 5:9; Col. 4:16). Those that were retained were accorded canonical status, suggesting that the issues involved in them were of a type that affected many churches. Thus, the churches not only saved but also shared the letters (by allowing them to be copied or by having them copied and sent to other churches).

NORTH OR SOUTH?

There are two main reasons to take the view that Galatians was addressed to churches in the southern part of the province of Galatia. First, Paul's habit was to use the Roman province names, as opposed to the names of ethnic groups. We see this tendency in his use of such names as Achaia, Asia, and Macedonia. The latter is an excellent example, since the people of Philippi and Thessalonica were ethnically Thracian, but Paul refers to the region as Macedonia, the Roman province (e.g., 1 Cor. 16:5). Second, Luke gives us a specific, carefully laid out history of the founding of the churches in South Galatia (in Acts 13–14). The North Galatian view assumes, on the basis of Acts 16:6 (lit., "they went through the Phrygian and Galatian region"; cf. 18:23), that Paul visited the northern part of the province during the second journey. But that verse more likely refers to the part of Phrygia included in (the southwestern area of) the province of Galatia (see F. F. Bruce, *The Epistle to the Galatians: A Commentary on the Greek Text* [Grand Rapids: Eerdmans, 1982], 11–13). Even if Paul had any contacts with North Galatia, these would have been minimal at best.

GREEK TEMPLE AT HIERAPOLIS. One of what would have been a number of temples dedicated to a Greek god or goddess in Hierapolis, a city near Laodicea and Colosse in southern Galatia in Asia Minor.

result of faith in Jesus the Messiah, not of obeying the OT law, and Paul uses the word *justification* several times to describe this.

The second part of his letter (3:1–5:12) is an appeal for the Galatians who were believers in Jesus as the Messiah to live a life of faith. Paul urged them to follow the example of Abraham, who lived prior to the law but was still viewed as the model believer. Thus, in many respects, the issue of Galatians was not really one of salvation but of sanctification. As such, it addressed the question of the proper lifestyle for a Christian. Specifically, it was an issue of whether following the rituals of the Law was necessary in order to demonstrate true salvation.[5] Paul's contention was that such a practice was not the gospel they had received and accepted. In essence, they were trying to prove their worth (or really to be "justified") by following the rituals of the OT law. But, while Paul asserted that the Gentiles were free from that obligation, he warned them not to let freedom become license.

In the final part of the letter (5:13–6:18) Paul warned the Galatians that there *were* lifestyle implications to believing that Jesus was the Messiah. But these were matters of relationships and holiness— not religious ritual. James agreed with this message: there is nothing in his letter regarding ritual observations. An interesting exercise is to compare the lifestyle admonitions that Paul makes in the last two chapters of Galatians with those that James makes. There are many similarities, but they take different approaches. James addresses what should be evident in that lifestyle. Paul concentrates on how it should be done, that is, through the work of the Holy Spirit guiding a believer's heart and mind.[6]

> In many respects, the issue of Galatians was not really one of salvation but of sanctification.

THE JERUSALEM COUNCIL

Read Acts 15:1–35.

The church in Antioch appointed Paul and Barnabas to lead a party up to Jerusalem to raise the question with the apostles. This trip was apparently made in the fall of 49 CE. As they traveled south, they stayed with "churches" in towns along the way. At this point, we are still looking at what are called house churches, small groups of believers that met in individual homes. Still, the number of locations does indicate continuing growth during the previous fifteen years. As they passed through both Phoenicia and Samaria, they related the purpose of their trip. To do this they had to tell what God had been doing among the Gentiles. This report was received with great joy.

In due course they arrived at Jerusalem, where they presented their case. This gathering is usually called the Jerusalem Council.[7] Over the centuries, other councils would be held to discuss various issues that arose. The meeting described in Acts 15 set the pattern for future church councils. First, a question would arise regarding the implications of the messiahship of Jesus or the church He founded. Generally, this would happen when a small group started teaching something that was different from what the church as a whole had been teaching.[8] As the matter reached a point of controversy within the church as a whole, church leaders would gather to discuss the matter. Both sides would give their arguments. The church leaders would then make a decision as to what was, indeed, the orthodox or true position.

In the case of the Jerusalem Council, the issue was the relationship of Gentiles to Jesus the Messiah. We have already seen from the evidence of Peter and Paul that the church as a whole was not requiring the Gentiles to be circumcised.[9]

That is, the Gentiles could accept the messiahship of Jesus directly without having to follow Jewish conversion ritual. In essence, the question was whether a person could have a covenant relationship with God without becoming part of the national covenant of the nation of Israel.

Paul and Barnabas started with a straightforward report about what had happened. However, their conclusions were challenged by believers who had come from the party of the Pharisees. This group argued that the new Gentile converts had to follow Jewish ritual exemplified by circumcision. There seems to be an analogy here to an incident in the book of Numbers where a Levite named Korah challenged the authority of Moses (Num. 16). He began with a point of truth, but then through faulty logic arrived at false conclusions.[10] The point of truth that these Pharisees began with was that Jesus was a Jewish Messiah. The faulty logic lay in how this truth carried over to non-Jews. Here the testimony of Peter was crucial.

> They began with a point of truth, but then through faulty logic arrived at false conclusions

Luke tells us that there was much debate before Peter gave his testimony (how unlike Peter to keep silent so long). Peter testified how God had poured out the Holy Spirit on Cornelius and his household when they believed. This was the crucial element, and the Gentile believers had received the Holy Spirit in the same way the original Jewish believers had. Peter's conclusion was that God

THE ORIGINS OF ORTHODOXY

The impression is sometimes given that the church councils of the ancient church created "orthodoxy." Historically, this was not the case. As far as I can tell, the controversies always arose when someone began giving a new twist that changed the nature of Christianity, that is, departed from commonly held positions, or "orthodoxy." Another false impression, which is especially evident in our postmodern age, is that these other views were merely different ways of looking at things and were generally accepted—or at least tolerated. Again, this was not the case historically. The controversies usually represented an attempt to use current philosophical thinking as the core of a syncretistic form of Christianity. This tendency was not new, but it was already evident throughout the history of the nation of Israel. We saw it in the cult of Jeroboam I (see above, ch. 13). We also saw it in the development of the theology of the Sadducees (ch. 17). For more information on how doctrine was established by church councils, see Louis Berkhof, *The History of Christian Doctrines* (1953; reprint, Grand Rapids: Baker, 1975); or Ted M. Dorman, *A Faith for All Seasons* (Nashville: Broadman and Holman, 1995).

CHRISTIANS AND THE LAW

The status of Gentiles in the church raised a question that is still being debated today: How should Christians approach the OT law? As we have traced the biblical teaching, it would appear that the nation of Israel had been under a national covenant. Through the crucifixion/resurrection event, a new covenant was established. This new covenant was no longer a national covenant, but a universal covenant with all mankind through the Messiah. The Messiah was the fulfillment of God's covenant with Abraham, the "seed" through which all the families of the earth would be blessed. He was also the culmination of the covenant with the nation through Moses, so there were national connotations to the Messiah. But the nation rejected the messiahship of Jesus. The question then arose, What about the nation of Israel? That is a profound question and lies beyond the scope of this work. However, there are currently two dominant answers. One argues that the church has permanently replaced the nation, and thus it tries to apply the OT law directly to the church. The other argues that the church has only temporarily replaced the nation, and even that is only with regard to certain spiritual aspects. This view applies only the principles underlying the OT law to the church.

"made no distinction between us and them, for he purified their hearts by faith" (Acts 15:9).[11] He then challenged the Pharisaic party regarding what they were doing. He called it placing a yoke on the neck of the disciples. Moreover, it was a yoke the Jewish nation had found to be impossible to bear. With this, he reiterated that both the Jewish and the Gentile believers were "saved through the grace of the Lord Jesus." This is an important testimony, since it shows us that Peter had the same view of salvation that Paul had. It was a logical implication of what Jesus had done as the Messiah.

At this point, the council returned to the testimony of Paul and Barnabas. This time the two explained the "signs and wonders" God had performed among the Gentiles. This testimony removed the discussion from an intellectual matter to a question of what God had demonstrated.

JEWISH TOMBSTONES AT PERGAMUM. Evidence that Jewish settlement and influence in northwest Asia Minor, which began in the time of Alexander, continued well into the Muslim age. The Jewish presence was one reason that Paul traveled through Asia Minor on his missionary journeys.

Clearly the Gentiles, just as they were, had been accepted by God. The question now was, what were the implications of that? We have already seen that both James and Paul in their letters had indicated that there were lifestyle issues. We have also noted that they were relational issues, not matters of ritual such as circumcision.

Finally, James, the half brother of Jesus, who was the leader of the council and who according to my understanding had already written a letter to the scattered believing Jews, gave his conclusions. He began by noting Peter's testimony. He tied that to OT teaching, citing a passage from the book of Amos.[12] He

THE DECREES

The principles (sometimes called "decrees") laid out by the Jerusalem Council seem to involve factors in pagan worship services: (1) *Idols.* Obviously one can't worship idols if he worships the true God. This was the critical issue addressed by the OT prophets. (2) *Fornication.* This item relates to two areas. First, and the most obvious in our thinking, is that of an overall culture that had a rather free sexual lifestyle. Equally important might be the issue of temple prostitution, which would fall under the category of fornication. (3) *Strangled animals.* This is the area where Jews had a problem with Gentile eating habits. The law was very clear regarding the procedures for sacrifice and how the blood was to be drained (see Lev. 17). More than this, strangled animals probably denoted pagan sacrifices. (4) *Blood.* This item is the more obscure and thus controversial one today. The question is whether the apostles were suggesting that the Gentile Christians avoid blood in the same sense as the Jews do so that they would have kosher-prepared meat, or whether the issue was bloodshed, as in murder. Given the context, it would seem to be the former.

then concluded: "It is my judgment, therefore, that we should not make it difficult for the Gentiles who are turning to God" (Acts 15:19). Based on that premise, James advocated four lifestyle principles for the believing Gentiles: they should abstain from things contaminated by idols; from fornication; from what is strangled; and from blood.[13] These denoted the key areas where worship of the true God must affect the lifestyle and where Jewish sensitivities were most acute.

These guidelines are somewhat similar to those given in the OT for what are called sojourners, non-Jews who desired to live in Israel.[14] Thus, the overall suggestion seems to be a standard whereby the Gentiles were not under Jewish law but would avoid specific practices that offended the Jewish believers. This principle allowed the Gentile believers freedom in religious ritual but would make it possible for the two groups to be unified in their faith. It also allowed the Jewish believers freedom to continue to go up to the temple when in Jerusalem or to worship in the synagogues elsewhere.[15]

James seems to have spoken for the apostles, and his judgment was accepted by the council. There is no mention of any opposition, at least within the council. It does become evident later that not all of the Jews accepted the council's conclusions. What is not clear is whether those later disagreements were from Jewish believers or from Jews who were unwilling to accept Jesus as the Messiah.[16]

The final act of the council is very important. They drafted a letter that expressed the council's conclusions. Luke includes the text of this letter in Acts. The original was likely signed by all of the apostles. They also selected two of the elders of Jerusalem (men who were part of the council) to return to Antioch with Paul and Barnabas. They were Silas and Judas Barsabbas (that is, the son of Sabbas).

The letter was addressed to Gentile believers in Antioch, Syria, and Cilicia. It notes that those who had been teaching the requirement to follow Jewish rites had come from the Jerusalem church, but they did not have the authority of the

apostles (something that Paul and Barnabas did have). It also mentions the witnesses being sent back with Paul and Barnabas. Finally, it lists the four requirements for Gentiles.

The party returned to Antioch, where they read the letter to the church. There was general joy at the news. This decision removed a point of concern and verified that they were, indeed, worshiping properly. This was corroborated by the testimony of Judas and Silas. They spent some time teaching in the church at Antioch. Judas Barsabbas then returned to Jerusalem, while Silas remained in Antioch. He, along with Paul, Barnabas, and others had a very fruitful outreach ministry.

SYRIA AND CILICIA

It is important to realize that there were a large number of Gentile believers in the regions to which the letter of the Jerusalem Council was addressed (Acts 15:23). Antioch was the capital of Syria, a province just north of Galilee. Cilicia was the region between Syria and Galatia. One puzzling question is, Why did the letter not include the Gentile believers in Galatia? We don't have a good answer to that. Regardless of our understanding of the letter to the Galatians, this council took place after Paul's first missionary journey where he evangelized Gentiles. The best solution is that Paul and Barnabas were really representatives of the listed regions, and the policy established for them would carry over to Galatia.

PAUL'S SECOND MISSIONARY JOURNEY

Read Acts 15:36–16:10.

The first missionary journey of Paul began when he and other leaders of the church were praying and fasting. We do not find a similar impetus for the second journey. Rather, it seems that Paul was concerned for the people he had already evangelized. He approached Barnabas and suggested that they return to the converts in cities they had visited and "see how they are doing" (Acts 15:36). The text says that this was after "some days." A close examination of various time indicators suggests that it was the following spring, around April in 50 CE.

Barnabas agreed that this was a good idea but suggested that they take John Mark with them. Paul objected strenuously because John Mark had left them on the first journey, about two years earlier. Both became emphatic in their positions, to the point that Luke calls the incident a "sharp disagreement" (Acts 15:39). The end result was that the team split.[17] Barnabas took John Mark, and they went back to Cyprus. Paul took Silas and headed toward Galatia, this time taking the land route north out of Antioch.

The first leg of Paul's second journey was through Syria and Cilicia. Luke tells us that they strengthened the churches. This work probably included two things. First, they gave teaching and encouragement. Second, since the letter from the Jerusalem Council was addressed to the churches in those regions, they gave a copy of it to each church.

Paul and Silas passed through Derbe, the furthest stop on their original trip. They continued on to Lystra, where on the first journey Paul had been stoned after being mistaken for a Greek god. There is no record that the pagan leadership recognized him or were even aware of his return. However, we learn that among the believers there was a Jewish woman who was married to a Greek (a Gentile). According to 2 Timothy 1:5, her name was Eunice, and her mother, Lois, was also a believer. Between the two of them, they had raised Eunice's son Timothy well, and he too was a believer. Apparently his father was not, as he is not mentioned again.

Paul found that Timothy had a good reputation among the believers not only in Lystra but also in Iconium, so he wanted to have this young man join his party. Because Timothy had not been circumcised, however, Paul made arrangements for him to go

PAUL'S SECOND MISSIONARY JOURNEY.

WHAT HAPPENED TO BARNABAS AND MARK?

We hear little about Barnabas and John Mark after they split from Paul. In time, Paul apparently made up with both of them. In 1 Corinthians 9:5-6, written about five years later, he discusses taking a wife on a missionary journey and asks whether only he and Barnabas did not have that right. Likewise, in Philemon 24 he calls Mark a fellow worker, and in 2 Timothy 4:11 he asks that Mark be brought to him because he was helpful.

through this ritual. While Paul and the apostles did not require that of Titus (Gal. 2:3), they did ask it of Timothy, which seems strange, given the recently completed Jerusalem Council. The difference was that Timothy had a Jewish mother.[18] As such, he should have access to the Jewish synagogues and various activities. Apparently, Paul desired to use Timothy as part of his outreach to Jews.

As will be seen later, Paul's practice was still to visit the synagogues first in any new city. Even though he had told the Jews in Antioch of Pisidia that they were turning to the Gentiles, Paul never lost his heart for his own countrymen. This is evident both by his later ministry and by his words in Romans 10. This outreach would have been risky for Timothy as an uncircumcised Jew. Thus, for practical ministerial reasons, Paul practiced the very thing he had argued strenuously was not necessary for salvation. (We might also note that Paul never objected to circumcision for Jews, which he viewed as a different issue.)

> Paul never lost his heart for his own countrymen.

Paul and Silas continued to deliver copies of the letter from the Jerusalem Council to each city they visited. The result was a strengthening of the believers in their faith. It also helped in reaching out to other Gentiles. Consequently, many more were learning of and accepting Jesus as the Messiah.

As they continued west through southern Galatia, the natural route would have been west toward Ephesus on the Aegean coast. However, that was in the province of Asia, and the Holy Spirit forbade them to go in that direction.[19] Consequently, they headed northwest through the region of Phrygia. Based on their standard procedures, they must have continued to proclaim the good news of the messiahship of Jesus as they went. But no results are cited, again reminding us that Luke is giving a selective record.

Based on normal travel times, it was likely the middle of summer when they arrived in the region of Mysia.[20] Their desire was now to go northeast into Bithynia, another Roman province that bordered the Black Sea. However, they were again forbidden. We are not told why

ICONIUM. A city of Paul's day now covered by the modern, major industrial city known today as Konya, known for its Muslim mystics (especially Mevlana) and the sect called "Whirling Dervishes." The ancient city in south central Asia Minor is now a large mound on which the city hall of Konya is built, precluding excavation.

APHRODISIAS. A major cultural and economic center in southwestern Asia Minor—one of a number of cities Paul could have visited, but did not, on his journeys through the region. The reconstruction of this Tetrapylon—an ornamental gate so named because it has four groups of four columns—was completed in 1990.

Paul was forbidden from going either to Asia or Bithynia. On his next journey, he would spend a large part of his time in Asia (specifically in Ephesus). It may be that these two regions already had churches planted. In Acts 2, we read that Jews from five areas of modern Turkey were present in Jerusalem on Pentecost: Cappadocia, Pontus, Asia, Phrygia, and Pamphylia. Pontus was associated with Bithynia. Thus, it is likely that these regions already had groups of believers as others were effectively serving as missionaries.[21]

With travel to the northeast and west now blocked, they worked their way northwest to Troas. Located near the ancient city of Troy at the mouth of the Hellespont, Troas was in a strategic location. We are not told that they founded a church there, but later we will see Paul visit a church in Troas while on his way back to Jerusalem (Acts 20:5).

While they were preaching in Troas, Paul had a vision during the night. A man from Macedonia appeared to him and said, "Come over to Macedonia and

THE EXPANSION OF CHRISTIANITY

When we consider the foundational events of Christianity, its rapid expansion is an item that must be evaluated. It is clear from the Roman records that by the middle of the first century the growth of Christianity was capturing notice from the secular authorities. The only other comparable expansion of a religious movement was that of early Islam, which however was virtually entirely military and by force (see Michael A. Harbin, *To Serve Other Gods* [Lanham, MD: University Press of America, 1994], 167–85). This development stands in total contrast to the expansion of Christianity in the first three centuries, which took place not only through nonviolence but also in the face of significant persecution.

help us" (Acts 16:9).[22] As far as we can tell, the team had never before been given any guidance of this type. Still, when Paul relayed the account to his companions the next day, they decided that this vision represented God's direction. With that they decided immediately to leave Troas and go to Macedonia.

This region would have been totally uncharted territory for Paul and Silas. We often think of this move as the initial expansion of the gospel into Europe, but that is not quite accurate, for we will soon find Paul meeting other believers who were coming from Rome (Acts 18:2). On the day of Pentecost as described in Acts 2, Rome is mentioned as one of the locations from which people had come to Jerusalem for the feast. Thus, the first church in Europe would likely have been in Rome. But there was a lot of untouched territory between Rome and Troas, where Paul was.

While Luke focused his history only on Paul, a number of other unmentioned missionaries were also carrying the good news from city to city, and these were largely responsible for the rapid expansion of Christianity.[23] Within a generation it went from a handful of witnesses on the day of the resurrection to a major force within the Roman Empire. However, the move from Troas to Macedonia was indeed a significant step, and the start of another chapter.

HELLESPONT SUNSET. A view across the strait known today as the Dardanelles, the body of water by which Paul and his companions would have stood as they prepared to enter Europe, their new mission field.

REVIEW QUESTIONS

1. What factors indicate the date and audience of the letter to the Galatians?

2. What was the purpose and process of the Jerusalem Council?

3. How did the Jerusalem Council end?

4. Why did Paul and Barnabas split up for their second journey?

5. Why did Paul and company at this stage plan on going to Europe?

23
CHAPTER

Moving into Europe

OVERVIEW

After passing through Asia Minor, Paul and company ended up at Troas, uncertain where to go. After a vision, they moved on to Philippi, in Europe, where they continued their journey through Thessalonica, Berea, Athens, and then Corinth. While in Corinth, Paul sent messengers to various churches and wrote letters to the Thessalonians. From Corinth, Paul returned to Antioch to check in with his home church.

Throughout the history of Christianity there have been significant events and locations marking changes in the direction of its growth. Philip's trip to Samaria was one. Peter's trip to Caesarea was a second. Barnabas's trip to Antioch was a third. Paul's vision at Troas was a fourth. Following this, Paul's ministry circled the Aegean and moved westward toward Rome. While there was already a church in Rome itself, Paul started filling the spaces in between.

FIRST CONVERTS IN PHILIPPI

Read Acts 16:11–15.

PARTHENON. The most famous temple in Athens. It is actually part of a large complex of temples atop a large rock outcropping near the center of the city.

As soon as Paul's companions agreed that his vision was a direction from God, the team took action. They caught a ship and sailed directly to the island of Samothrace and then to Neapolis, a coastal town in Macedonia. Their choice of a direct route indicates that they took advantage of a southeast wind. These ideal conditions would seem to confirm the choice they had made. From Neapolis, they traveled to Philippi.

Luke notes that Philippi was both a Roman colony and a major city of the region. As a colony, it tended to follow carefully the leading of Rome. Since Claudius, the emperor, had cast the Jews out of Rome in 49 CE. (see Acts 18:2), it is possible that a similar decision was made in Philippi.[1] Consequently, when Paul and Silas arrived in the fall of 50, they did not find a synagogue in which they could follow their standard process. So on the Sabbath, they went outside the city, looking for "a place of prayer."

When they got to the banks of the Gangites River, where they expected to find a gathering of Jewish men, they found only a group of women. Never one to let an opportunity go by, Paul talked to them about Jesus. One of the women was a merchant of purple fabrics from Thyatira.[2] Her name was Lydia. The nature of her profession shows that she was a part of the upper socioeconomic group. She is also termed "a worshiper of God" (Acts 16:14).

PHILIPPI

This city, originally called Crenides, was founded in the fourth century BCE and then named after Philip II, king of Macedonia. It was reestablished by Mark Antony in 42 BCE after a battle that he and Octavian fought against Brutus and Cassius. Because of Roman expansion toward Thrace and incorporation of the Scythian tribes along the Black Sea (ca. 46 CE), it was a garrison city on the edge of the empire at the time of the emperor Claudius.

LYDIA OF THYATIRA

The phrase used to describe Lydia, "a worshiper of God" (Acts 16:14), is analogous to the term "God-fearer" (applied to Cornelius, Acts 10:1–2) and is often used to indicate a Gentile who worshiped the God of Israel without converting to Judaism. Given her socioeconomic status, Lydia probably had a fairly large house of two stories built around a courtyard. The building would have included her shop on the ground floor, and several rooms for family living quarters on both stories.

After Lydia listened to Paul, she accepted the message of Jesus as Messiah and was baptized, along with her family. She then prevailed upon Paul and his companions to stay in her house. Paul and his companions did so, and this was the beginning of the church of Philippi. Undoubtedly, there was significant teaching within the house as Lydia and her family learned about the implications of following Jesus the Messiah.

CONFLICT WITH PAGANS IN PHILIPPI

Paul and his companions remained in Philippi for about two months.[3] They regularly slipped out of town on the Sabbath and went to the place of prayer at the riverside. On one occasion they were followed by a slave girl who was demon-possessed. In this condition she engaged in fortune telling and brought much money to her masters. She began crying out, "These men are servants of the Most High God, who are telling you the way to be saved" (Acts 16:17). This behavior became a pattern. After a number of days, Paul became annoyed and commanded the spirit to leave in the name of Jesus.[4] The spirit did so immediately, taking away the fortune-telling ability of the slave girl. This irked her owners, who responded by grabbing Paul and Silas and dragging them to the market place, where the city authorities were located. Their accusers basically had three charges: Paul and Silas were creating confusion; they were Jews; and they were teaching customs that were not "lawful" for Romans to accept.[5] From our perspective, the only true "accusation" was that they were Jews.

Perhaps for that reason, their "trial" was a sham. The crowd erupted into an uproar. The magistrates had Paul and Silas stripped of their outer garments and beaten. Following the beating, they were thrown into jail. The jailer was told to watch them carefully. With those instructions, he placed them in the innermost cells and put their feet in stocks.

Read Acts 16:16–40.

OMPHALOS AT DELPHI. A stone shrine, supposedly marking the center of the earth, that also covered a volcanic vent producing narcotic gases. When a priestess breathed the gases, they supposedly gave her revelations from the gods. The term used for the demon-possessed girl is the same word used for the priestesses at this oracle on the slope of Mount Parnassus in Greece.

above left to right

LION BRIDGE. The monument that marked the Egnatian Way bridge over the Strymon River near Philippi in Macedonia. It may have been along the banks of this river that Paul met Lydia when he did not find any Jewish men to consult with.

AGORA AT PHILIPPI. The agora, or central shopping and business area. This was where Paul was harassed by a demon-possessed slave girl.

That night Paul and Silas were praying out loud and singing. About midnight, there was an earthquake that shook the foundations of the prison. The doors of the prison broke open, and the chains of all the prisoners fell off. Awakened from his sleep, the jailer saw the result and despaired. With the prison doors opened, there was no question in his mind but that the prisoners had escaped. Since his life was forfeit, he planned to avoid the embarrassment of the trial and commit suicide. However, Paul cried out for him not to do it since they were all present.

Getting a light, the jailer inspected the prison and found Paul's statement to be true. Saved from execution for dereliction of duty, the jailer asked Paul and Silas what he needed to do to be saved. Paul's reply was that salvation is only through believing in Jesus. As a result, the jailer and his household were saved. He took the men up into his quarters at that late hour, washed their wounds, and gave

MIRACLE AT THE JAIL

This supernormal event at the jail in Philippi consists of three parts. First, there was the earthquake, which could be considered a natural phenomenon, except for the timing and the precise location. Second, the chains of the prisoners fell off: this is mystifying, since it would not be the result of an earthquake. Finally, the prisoners all remained in place despite their sudden freedom in a chaotic situation; apparently, they were restrained by something supernormal.

THE PHILIPPIAN JAILER

Clearly the jailer was aware of the message that Paul and Silas had been proclaiming. He may have heard it during the days before the arrest. Or he may have heard it during the praying and singing of the evening. Whatever his reaction to the message earlier, the clear hand of God on the activities of the night led him to accept the message that Paul taught. We are not really sure, however, what Luke means when he says that the jailer "believed in God with his whole household" (Acts 16:34 NASB; cf. also the reference to Lydia's household being baptized, v. 15). The best understanding seems to be that the members of the household also expressed their personal faith based on the leadership of the household leader. In each of these cases, it appears that each individual had heard the preaching of Paul and thus made personal decisions.

them food to eat. The rest of the night Paul and Silas shared with them what it meant that Jesus was the Messiah.

When daylight came, the magistrates sent some officers to the jailer telling him he could release the prisoners. The jailer, apparently pleased that the case had been resolved, took the word to Paul and Silas and asked them to leave in peace. Paul, however, decided to make a point of the issue. He told the jailer to send word back to the magistrates that what they had done was illegal, since he and Silas were Roman citizens. When this word got back to the magistrates, they were very concerned. So they went to the jail and apologized to Paul and Silas, begging them to quietly leave town.

Paul and Silas returned to the house of Lydia. By this time, there must have already been a solid group of believers, for they were gathered at Lydia's place. After a time of encouragement, Paul and Silas did leave town. Apparently Luke remained in Philippi, however, since this section ends one of the "we passages."

PRISON AT PHILIPPI. According to tradition, the place where Paul was imprisoned before the earthquake freed him.

CONFLICT WITH JEWS IN THESSALONICA

Read Acts 17:1–9.

Paul and Silas headed west following the Egnatian way.[8] After passing through several cities and towns, they stopped at Thessalonica, about seventy miles to the west. Thessalonica, founded about 315 BCE by Cassander (one of Alexander's generals; see above, ch. 17), was by this time a major port and a regional capital. It also had a sizable Jewish population (it is likely that some of those had come from Philippi if there had been a deportation).

As was Paul's custom, he began preaching in the synagogue. According to Luke, he was able to teach there for three Sabbaths.[9] His efforts had a significant effect, for a number of Jews and God-fearing Gentiles accepted that Jesus was the Messiah.

This created jealousy and conflict with Jews who did not accept the messiahship of Jesus. They gathered their forces, including a number of "bad characters" from the marketplace, and started a riot. Paul and his company were staying with a person named Jason, and the mob went to his house in search of them. When they did not find Paul and the others, they took Jason instead. They dragged him and some Thessalonians who had believed in the messiahship of Jesus and brought them before the city officials.

Again they essentially accused Paul and Silas of advocating beliefs that were "un-Roman." Jason was considered guilty by association, since they were staying at his house. The apparently clinching argument was that these men viewed Jesus as king. Although the city was in turmoil, the officials required Jason and the brothers to post bond and then allowed them to go.

That night, Paul and his company were encouraged to leave town. Leaving the Egnatian way, they traveled to Berea, about fifteen miles south. Founded apparently in the fifth century BCE (during the times of the Persian wars), Berea was not a significant town for several centuries, but by NT times it had become one of the more populous cities in the region.

THE JEWS IN BEREA CHECK PAUL'S STORY

Read Acts 17:10–14.

At Berea, Paul again began at the synagogue. Here he met a positive reaction. It was not that the Jews accepted Paul's teaching. Rather, they went back to the OT to evaluate whether what Paul said was true. Because of this response, Luke states that they were more commendable than their fellow Jews elsewhere. Based on this validation, they did accept Paul's message, and many of the Jews became believers in Jesus as the Messiah. This was quickly accompanied by a similar pattern of belief among leading Greek citizens, both men and women.

However, this positive situation was not to last long. Word got back to Thessalonica, and the dissident Jews there came over to Berea, determined to stop Paul. Their agitation began to stir up the crowds there. With riots threatening, the believers in Berea got Paul out of town. At the coast, he boarded a ship to Athens.

While Paul went ahead, accompanied by an escort from Berea, Silas remained behind.

Paul's escort took him and Timothy as far as Athens. Then Timothy was directed to return to Thessalonica to encourage the believers. With Luke still in Philippi, Silas in Berea, and Timothy in Thessalonica, we see Paul's team dispersed throughout the region, teaching those who had come to believe that Jesus was the Messiah.

> The Berean Jews are commended because they went back to the OT to evaluate whether what Paul said was true.

THE GREEKS IN ATHENS CHALLENGE PAUL

Athens had a long history. During the Persian period it was noted for its military leadership and its schools of philosophy. Although past its prime, the city was still considered a major cultural center. Here Paul continued his ministry. As was his practice, he visited the synagogue, where he discussed the messiahship of Jesus with the Jews and God-fearing Gentiles. On a daily basis, he taught in the marketplace, proclaiming the same message. He even engaged a number of philosophers belonging to both the Stoic and the Epicurean camps. Since his teaching was new, they took him to the Areopagus (or Mars Hill), and he was asked to share his teaching with the various thinkers who met there to discuss philosophical concepts.

Read Acts 17:16–34.

Paul used this opportunity to tell them about Jesus. He began his presentation with an observation about how religious Athens was. He had noted one altar

TEMPLE OF ZEUS. One of the magnificent and well-designed temples in Athens that would have impressed Paul and his companions, this one dedicated to Zeus, the supreme god of the ancient Greeks, and located about a kilometer from the Parthenon (in the background).

inscribed "to an unknown god" (Acts 17:23). Paul began his speech with reference to this inscription and asserted that he represented that God who was the Creator of the entire cosmos and everything within it. Thus, he used the knowledge that the Athenians had and proclaimed to them that there was now a way to salvation that everyone was expected to take.

It seems that his audience was with him until he reached the topic of the resurrection. Some of the Athenians sneered at the idea of a person being resurrected from the dead. Just as is the case for many today, the concept was philosophically unacceptable, so they rejected it without evaluating the evidence. Others, however, wanted to delve deeper into the matter before they made a decision. Still others believed Paul's testimony, and a church was formed in Athens. We are not told how long Paul remained in Athens. Luke does mention the names of two converts, one of them a philosopher (Acts 17:34). After establishing the new church, Paul left Athens to go to Corinth, about sixty miles west. This was the fifth city where Paul preached and planted a church in his sweep through Greece.

MARS HILL. A view, looking from the Parthenon, of the place where philosophers gathered in Athens.

STOICS AND EPICUREANS

These groups represented the two dominant philosophical schools in Athens. The founder of the Stoic school was Zeno (342–270 BCE). His philosophy was an offspring of that of the cynics. It was a complex, comprehensive worldview, but only a couple of items are important here. First, the Stoic school had a strong sense of divine determinism (or fate). They tied this principle to a strong sense of responsibility, arguing that if an action was determined to occur, it required the effort of the actor to make it occur (that is, it didn't happen by itself). In this light, they stressed virtuous actions. The Epicurean school was founded by Epicurus about the same time. This philosophy too was wide-ranging in scope. It was apparently a reaction against licentiousness. The Epicureans advocated that the aim of life was pleasure, a position that has been misunderstood as reflecting hedonism. Epicurus himself defined pleasure as a tranquil mind and the absence of pain. Excessive drinking, gluttony, and so forth were not viewed as yielding pleasure, since they produced pain. At the other end of the scale, however, the Epicureans viewed the supposed gods who punished evildoers as the largest obstacle to a tranquil mind. Consequently, Epicureans were irreligious. Overall, both schools advocated a form of piety, though the Stoics certainly tended to be more ascetic than the Epicureans.

A NEW MINISTRY IN CORINTH

Paul arrived in Corinth in late winter of 51. Corinth was an important city in a strategic location. It had an estimated population of about a half million people. Soon after he arrived, Paul met a Jewish believer named Aquila and his wife, Priscilla.[10] They had just recently arrived from Rome because Claudius had expelled the Jews out of the city (49–50 CE). Because they were tentmakers, like Paul, the apostle worked with them for several months. He used that occupation to cover expenses while waiting for the rest of his team to come from Macedonia. Every Sabbath he went to the synagogue, where he presented Jesus as the Messiah. He gave the same message to any Greeks (Gentiles) who would listen. In the process, he waited anxiously for word from Macedonia on how things had been going after he left. Sometime later in the spring, both Silas and Timothy arrived with their reports. These precipitated Paul's second letter, the one we call 1 Thessalonians.

Read Acts 18:1–5.

CORINTH

Originally Corinth was one of the major Greek cities. It enjoyed an excellent position on the isthmus that joined southern and northern Greece. Historically, this placed it directly between the two major Greek powers, Athens and Sparta.

In addition, the isthmus was an excellent transition point for trade between the east and west, since it was easier to travel across it than to go around the peninsula (saving more than 200 nautical miles or 375 kilometers of sea travel, depending on how closely one followed the coast). One method of traversing it was to unload the ship and cart the material across. Another method was to drag the entire ship across with rollers (a distance of about seven kilometers). Nero attempted to dig a canal across it but was unsuccessful.

Corinth was destroyed in 146 BCE by the Romans. When it was rebuilt about a century later, it was as a Roman colony and was virtually shunned by the Greeks. Corinth grew rapidly as a cosmopolitan city, attracting people from all over the Roman Empire, rather than as a Greek city, although Koine Greek was the language of communication. Estimates of the population at the time of Paul have ranged from a very conservative 100,000 to more than 700,000 (200,000 free and 500,000 slaves). Although accurate figures are impossible, a higher estimate is more likely, suggesting at least 500,000.[11] (*ZPEB* I:961).

CANAL AT CORINTH. The dream of many generations, but not built until the 1800s. In Paul's day, cargo had to be transported overland between the port cities of Corinth and Cenchrea in Greece.

PAUL'S FIRST LETTER TO THE THESSALONIANS

Read
1 Thessalonians 1 – 5.

Paul's first letter to the church in Thessalonica expresses both relief and encouragement. He was relieved and pleased at how the believers there had remained steadfast in the face of the persecution that had continued after it drove him out of town. When he had left, he was uncertain how the new Christians would react to adverse circumstances, and he sent Timothy back to check on them. Timothy brought a good report to Corinth in this respect.[12] However, the Thessalonian community felt some discouragement, apparently because they misunderstood a crucial point of doctrine. It was important enough that Paul had to correct their views on that issue.

> Paul wove through 1 Thessalonians three principles that became the focus of most of his letters: faith, hope, and love.

In the process, Paul wove through his letter three principles that became the focus of most of his letters. These principles are faith, hope, and love. As we read through Paul's letters, we realize that these facets of the Christian belief reflect areas of what we call spiritual growth. In the case of the Thessalonians, they were strong in faith (although even that could grow). Their love was solid but needed work. The real concern was their hope. When Paul left Thessalonica, he was chased out by jealous Jews and leading Gentiles. Apparently, after Paul left, the persecution continued and became more ferocious. It was in that context that a question about hope arose.

In the last part of this letter, Paul addressed two areas. First, he discussed several practical areas of lifestyle (1 Thess. 4:1 – 12). The Thessalonians were to avoid sexual immorality. They were to express their love to one another in practical manners. They were to work at their jobs quietly and conscientiously so that they would have assets to help others.[13]

The more important concern was the question of what happens to "those who fall asleep" (1 Thess. 4:13). Paul's discussion indicates that a number of the believers in Thessalonica had died; possibly some of them had been killed in the ongoing persecution. The believers apparently had learned from Paul that when Jesus the Messiah returned, He would set up His kingdom on earth (1 Thess. 2:12). While Paul does not specifically talk about God's kingdom on earth in this sec-

FAITH, HOPE, AND LOVE

These three items reflect different implications of believing that Jesus is the Messiah. Faith is the historical aspect and reflects acceptance of the eyewitness testimonies of those who saw Jesus resurrected. Hope is the future aspect. It reflects both an anticipation of the return of Jesus and the ultimate victory of God in terms of the conflict introduced in Genesis 3. Love is the present aspect. It illustrates that the very present implication of Christianity is the relationship of believers with one another. In this sense, Christianity reflects the fulfillment of the covenant relations introduced in the OT, especially within the outline of the Mosaic covenant presented in the Ten Commandments. Faith and hope highlight our relationship with God, and love highlights our relationships with our fellowmen.

tion, this seems a logical inference given the circumstances and his reference to the Day of the Lord (5:2). We saw in chapters 13 and 14 that this was a favorite term of the prophets referring to God's program. The Thessalonians had been taught this by Paul when he was there. However, they mistakenly assumed that those who had already died could not be a part of that kingdom.[14]

Paul wanted the Thessalonians to understand that their death was not a matter of grief without hope. Rather, he maintained that those who died before the return of Jesus would come back with him. Those who were still alive at the time of the return would meet Christ in the air.

As Paul addressed the question of Jesus' return, he amplified what he had already taught them. The time of that return ("the day of the Lord") would be as unexpected as a thief slipping in to rob a house at night. But Christians were anticipating Jesus' return, so they should be prepared for it even if they did not know when it would be.

With this, Paul wrapped up his letter with more practical observations regarding lifestyle. These are interesting, since many of them are short, snappy directives. His final directive was that the letter be read to "all the brothers." This shows that Paul had a sense of authority in what he wrote.

PAUL'S SECOND LETTER TO THE THESSALONIANS

Several months later, Paul wrote a second letter to the Thessalonians. This letter corrected another misunderstanding, this time about the day of the Lord. It derived from a forged letter that some had read and others were talking about. This letter claimed that the day of the Lord was already present. We reach this

Read
2 Thessalonians 1–3.

THE RESTRAINER

Paul says regarding the man of lawlessness that the Thessalonians "know what is holding him back, so that he may be revealed at the proper time" (2 Thess. 2:6). There is discussion among scholars as to who the restrainer is. Some have suggested that it is government, which restricts "lawlessness" in society in general. Others say the restrainer is the Holy Spirit. The latter is more likely. If so, then when the Holy Spirit is removed from the world, those who are indwelt by Him will leave also.

conclusion from the responses that Paul made, although we do not have the questions they were asking.

Picking up on his three principles, Paul says he was pleased to see that their faith and love were growing (2 Thess. 1:3). This commendation suggests that they still had problems with their hope. The persecution was continuing, and Paul was aware of their endurance. However, he needed to clarify their understanding of the day of the Lord.

First, they were to be encouraged about what would happen. At that time, God would judge those who were persecuting them. More importantly, they needed to be aware that the day of the Lord had not yet come (2 Thess. 2:1–3).[15] Paul's point was that although no one knew when Jesus would return, they did know from OT teaching that the "man of lawlessness" had to come first. However, he could not come until that which restrained him was removed. This probably is a reference to the Holy Spirit who indwells believers. Only after that occurred would the man of lawlessness institute his program and portray himself as God. Paul reminded the Thessalonians that these are the very things he taught when he was there.

Following this major point, Paul wrapped up his letter with prayer requests and some admonitions. Paul's main prayer request was that the ministry in Corinth would be fruitful as God opened doors for Paul and his fellow-workers. The admonitions build on directives he gave in his first letter. There he had told the Thessalonians to work at their jobs (1 Thess. 4:11). Here he amplified this instruction by asserting that those who did not work should not be given meals (2 Thess. 3:10).[16]

Finally, Paul pointed out that he signed the letter with his own hand. This signature was to be an identifying sign to avoid forgeries. Paul states that signing letters was his regular practice, although we only have record of three letters by Paul at this point. This comment would suggest that he wrote many other letters the church did not preserve.

Paul's comment about his signature suggests that he wrote many other letters the church did not preserve.

A CHURCH GROWS IN CORINTH

Read Acts 18:5–17.

After Timothy and Silas returned from Macedonia, Paul began spending more time in his teaching (Acts 18:5).[17] As happened in previous cases, some of the Jews in the synagogue rejected the idea that Jesus was the Messiah. They became abusive. In response, Paul "shook out his clothes in protest" (v. 6). He told them that they had now incurred their own guilt and that he would now go to the Gentiles.

On the one hand, this seems to be a major shift in policy, even though Paul would always have a special place in his heart for his fellow Jews (see Rom. 10:1–10). On the other hand, there were a large number of Jews in the new church he was building in Corinth. Luke tells us that Paul began working out of the house of Titus Justus, a Gentile who worshiped God. At the same time, Crispus, the leader of the synagogue, became a believer along with his family. God gave Paul a special encouragement regarding his ministry in Corinth, which included a promise of protection. As a result, Paul remained there for about a year and a half.[18]

One more incident is recorded that illustrates God's protection. During the time that Gallio was proconsul of Achaia, the Jews attacked Paul through legal action.[19] Their accusation was again more of an innuendo: "This man is persuading the people to worship God in ways contrary to the law" (Acts 18:13). Paul was about to give a defense when Gallio interrupted. He told the Jews that the matter was an internal religious issue and not one for the court, so he dismissed them. In anger, the Jews turned on the synagogue leader, Sosthenes, and beat him up in front of the proconsul.[20] Gallio considered even that an internal matter and ignored the confrontation.

RETURN TO ANTIOCH

After a year and a half in Corinth, Paul decided it was time to return to Antioch and report in. When they left Cenchrea, the sister city of Corinth on the Aegean, Luke tells us that Paul got a haircut because he had been keeping a vow. This would seem to be a Nazirite vow, which serious Jews would take as they looked to God for special protection.[21] Since God had protected him during his stay in Corinth, he completed the vow at this time.

Read Acts 18:18–28.

It is interesting to note that Luke does not record that any of Paul's traveling companions (Luke, Timothy, and Silas) went with him back to Jerusalem and Antioch. He does note that Priscilla and Aquila left Corinth with Paul. When they arrived at Ephesus, they stopped in at the synagogue. Paul received a warm welcome and was asked to stay. He refused, wanting to get back to Antioch before winter closed the sea lanes. He did promise to return, should God allow it. However, he left Priscilla and Aquila there to minister in that important city.

Luke adds an addendum to this section regarding the ministry of Priscilla and Aquila in Ephesus. They met a Jew named Apollos there who knew of the early ministry of Jesus and of John's baptism of repentance. As such, he would have been aware of Jesus' claims to be the Messiah but might not have heard of the resurrection. Apollos was teaching in the synagogue in Ephesus and having a good influence. When Priscilla and Aquila heard him, they took him aside and filled

APOLLOS'S PARTIAL KNOWLEDGE

The fact that Apollos knew little about Jesus raises the very interesting question of where he had received his information and where he had been for the previous twenty years. We can do no more than speculate on this. If he had been in Judea, he must have left that area while John was still alive. It is possible that he was a merchant who traveled through other parts of the Mediterranean region and was simply unaware of the changes that had occurred after he left. Some suggest that he learned of John in Alexandria. This incident also illustrates the problems of communication in the Roman world.

in the gaps of his learning. Following this, he decided to return to Greece, where Paul, Priscilla, and Aquila had been earlier. There he was accepted and became a powerful teacher. In Corinth, he helped refute some of the Jews who denied that Jesus was the Messiah.

From Ephesus, Paul sailed to Caesarea. After disembarking, he went up and "greeted the church." Luke clearly is referring to the church in Jerusalem, since from there Paul went to Antioch. Luke does not tell us all he did there, since describing the visit was not important for his purposes. However, we can draw inferences from Paul's other trips. He probably checked in with the apostles, reporting on the work done. He may have offered a votive sacrifice in thanksgiving for God's protection and grace on the journey.

Leaving Jerusalem, Paul returned to his home church in Antioch, where he reported on the results of the trip. In the meantime we can but infer the location of his companions. Priscilla and Aquila were in Ephesus. Timothy and Silas were probably still in Corinth. The last we heard of Luke, he was in Philippi. Paul remained in Antioch for some time before starting another journey.

REVIEW QUESTIONS

1. Why were there apparently no synagogues in Philippi, and what did Paul do as a result?

2. Why did Paul get into trouble with some businessmen in Philippi?

3. What happened while Paul and Silas were in prison?

4. Why did Paul have trouble with the Jews in Thessalonica?

5. What distinguished the Jews in Berea?

6. What did Paul do in Athens while he was waiting for his friends?

7. Whom did Paul meet in Corinth, and how did they work together?

8. Why did Paul write two letters to the Thessalonians? What was their content?

9. What did Paul and Silas do at the end of their stay in Corinth?

24

CHAPTER

Tentmaker and Troubleshooter

OVERVIEW

After a few months in Antioch, Paul and his company headed back toward Ephesus and Greece. Paul spent more than two years in Ephesus. While there, he communicated with the other churches he had founded, apparently making several short trips and writing several letters, especially to Corinth. We will look at the two letters to Corinth that are in the canon.

STUDY GOALS

▶ Follow Paul's return to Ephesus and the time spent teaching there.

▶ Show how Paul's message of 1 Corinthians highlights problems that are common in churches today.

▶ Develop the message of 2 Corinthians as a balance to the Corinthians' overreaction to his first letter.

aul probably remained in Antioch through the winter of 52/53. This gave him a chance to catch up on what had been going on, and he likely talked about a number of issues with the leaders of the church. Luke skips over this period. Knowing Paul, however, we should not suppose that he did nothing. Then, during the spring of 53, Paul started out again to go back through the churches he had planted.

RETURN TO EPHESUS

Read Acts 19.

The account of Apollos seems to interrupt our narrative. In Acts 18:23 we read that when Paul left Antioch, he retraced his steps through Galatia and Phrygia. He strengthened all of the disciples, which means that he spent time at each of the churches he had founded. This would have been a time of teaching when he expounded on the implications of the messiahship of Jesus. It is likely that much of his teaching paralleled the concepts we find in his letters to churches.

The "upper country" that Luke mentions (Acts 19:1 NASB; "interior regions," NRSV) would be the central plateau of Asia Minor (modern Turkey). The most direct road from that region to Ephesus went through Colosse and Laodicea. If Paul went that way, he did not start churches in those cities.[1] His destination was Ephesus, where he arrived in the early fall of 53 CE.[2]

One of the first challenges Paul encountered in Ephesus was a group of disciples who knew only of John's baptism (Acts 19:1–3). This would appear to have been a group that had been taught by Apollos prior to his understanding of the resurrection (Apollos is mentioned in the preceding passage, 18:24–28). When Paul asked them about the Holy Spirit, they said they had never heard of Him. Paul taught them about Jesus and how He was the one that John had stated was coming after him. When they learned about Jesus, they were baptized in His name. Then they received the Holy Spirit, and they spoke in tongues and prophesied.

Paul entered the synagogue in Ephesus, continuing his pattern of going to the Jews first, and discussed and debated the question of whether Jesus was the Messiah and what that meant regarding the kingdom of God.[3] This lasted for three months until Paul's teachings drove a wedge among the Jews. Some refused to accept his mes-

EPHESUS. The main street of Ephesus, looking toward the library.

sage and became hardened. They "spoke evil" of the believers (Acts 19:9 NASB, NRSV);[4] since they could not refute their arguments, they resorted to slander.

When this occurred, Paul left the synagogue group and began to meet with the disciples in the lecture hall of Tyrannus. This ministry continued for more than two years. Luke notes that as a result many heard the message. Just as important, those who heard learned of the implications of the message. At the same time Paul was teaching in the school of Tyrannus, Priscilla and Aquila continued to host a church in their own home in Ephesus (1 Cor. 16:19). Timothy was apparently back in Macedonia, continuing his ministry there (1 Cor. 16:10; Acts 19:22). Luke was probably still in Philippi where he had remained on the second journey. Titus may have been in Ephesus with Paul at least part of the time, since he is labeled Paul's partner to Corinth and messenger (2 Cor. 8:23).[5] These joined Paul later when he headed back to Jerusalem at the end of this journey.

Corroborating his teaching, Paul performed a number of supernormal signs. These included healing and casting out demons. Apparently, a number of Jews were using the name of Jesus as part of their exorcisms. However, this tactic

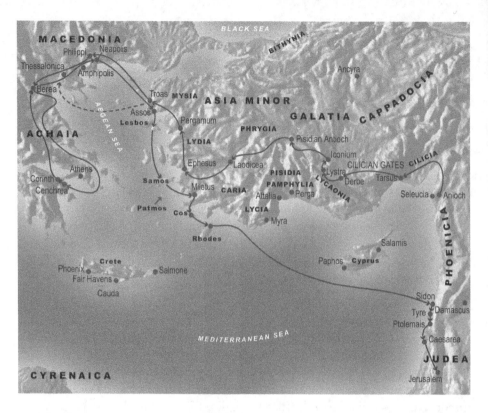

backfired on one group, the seven sons of a priest named Sceva. When they tried to cast out a spirit, the spirit replied, "Jesus I know, and I know about Paul, but who are you?" (Acts 19:15). With that, the man who was possessed attacked the would-be exorcists. He beat them and drove them, wounded and naked, out of the house. As a result, the name of Jesus was held in higher respect within the entire community.[6]

These events caused those who had become believers in the messiahship of Jesus to get serious. A number confessed their evil deeds, specifically their syncretizing their worship of God through Jesus with their former practices, including the practice of magic. As the revival grew, they burned their books on magic. This must have been an impressive fire, for the text estimates the value of the books at 50,000 drachmas (a drachma was approximately a day's wage).[7]

ARTEMIS OR DIANA?

Artemis was the Greek name of a goddess that the Romans identified with their own deity, Diana. Ephesus was a center for her worship. She was a fertility goddess, and her worship may have been associated with the mother-goddess cult that had been prevalent throughout the ANE. Thus, her worship may have some connections with that of the Canaanite goddess Asherah (see above, ch. 9). The worship of Artemis in Ephesus was associated with a meteorite encased in her temple (see Acts 19:35).

But the magic and book-selling industries were not the only ones being affected. A man named Demetrius was a silversmith who made a living making silver shrines or idols for Artemis. Seeing his business drop off, he compared notes with the other silversmiths and concluded that Paul had caused the local recession. They became irate and stormed into the local stadium, where they had a pep rally for "Artemis of the Ephesians."

Paul wanted to go before the assembly, but he was held back by his companions, who feared for his life. Apparently most of the crowd was there because of the spectacle, not because they understood what was going on. Finally the town clerk was able to get their attention and told them that the gathering was illegal. If Demetrius had a valid complaint, he could go to court. Otherwise they were facing Roman intervention. With this, he dismissed the assembly.

This incident seems to have been near the end of Paul's stay in Ephesus. As such, it may have precipitated Paul's leaving the city, which had already been planned.

TWO REPRESENTATIONS OF ARTEMIS
A statue of the goddess Artemis associated with Ephesus, and in Acts with Demetrius and the silversmiths.

A second image of Artemis discovered at Ephesus, showing that the image-makers were allowed some artistic license.

PAUL'S FIRST LETTER TO THE CORINTHIANS

While Paul was in Ephesus, he had frequent contact with the church in Corinth. He personally made at least two visits to Corinth (2 Cor. 12:14 and 13:1–2). In addition, there were visits and letters by the Corinthians to Ephesus and letters that Paul wrote back to them. The evidence seems to indicate that Paul wrote at least four letters to the church in Corinth, of which we have two.

Read 1 Corinthians 1:1–9.

In the document we call 1 Corinthians, Paul refers to a previous letter (1 Cor. 5:9). In that earlier communication he had given them directions, which they had misunderstood. Now he was correcting them. This passage suggests that what we

THE CHURCH IN CORINTH

Both Ephesus and Corinth were major seaports and there was regular trade between the two; the distance between them, by way of the port of Cenchrea, was about 230 nautical miles (or 430 km; a trip took one or two days each way, depending on wind and sea conditions). Thus it would have been easy for Paul to maintain contact with the Corinthians while he was in Ephesus. In reading 1 and 2 Corinthians, we need to remember that "the church in Corinth" refers to the entire group of believers within a given city. It was not a single group, but a collection of small groups of believers scattered throughout the city. They met in various houses, and we are not sure how much connection they had with one another, especially in a city as large as Corinth. To what degree they were organized is very unclear.

WHERE IS THE SORROWFUL LETTER?

Twice in 2 Corinthians, Paul refers to a difficult letter that he had written to the church in Corinth: it had caused him anguish (2:4) and it had made the Corinthians sorrowful (7:8). Because there is a change in tone in 2 Corinthians itself beginning with chapter 10, some scholars have suggested that this document combines two different letters and that chapters 10–13 are really (part of) that earlier sorrowful letter. However, the tone of this last portion, although sometimes stern, is not really sorrowful. To make this argument work, one has to conclude that part of the sorrowful letter was lost and the other part was put on the end of a later letter. It is more likely that the entire letter was not saved. A likely reason is that Paul gave some very direct admonishment, perhaps even naming people.

ACRO-CORINTH. A mountain towering over Corinth that had several temples with as many as a thousand temple prostitutes in them. This would have been a daily reminder to Corinthian Christians of their pagan past.

call 1 Corinthians was really Paul's second letter to the church. Then, in the letter we call 2 Corinthians, Paul makes reference to a letter that caused sorrow or grief to the Corinthians (2 Cor. 2:4; 7:8). Because that description does not seem to fit 1 Corinthians, most scholars believe that this communication, sometimes called "the sorrowful letter," was written between 1 and 2 Corinthians. If so, 2 Corinthians is actually Paul's fourth letter to this church.

When we look at 1 Corinthians, we find that Paul responded to a number of issues that had arisen in the Corinthian church. Some of these problems were mentioned in a letter the church had sent to Paul (1 Cor. 7:1). Others were personally communicated to him by Chloe's household, a group that had come from the Corinthian church to Ephesus (1:11). These two communications probably took place at the same time; that is, Chloe's representatives themselves likely brought the letter from the church. The time was spring of 56 CE, about five years after Paul's first arrival at Corinth. This means that it would be unlikely that any in the church had been believers more than five years.

As we read the letter, we soon learn that the church in Corinth had many problems. In fact, the letter sounds very contemporary in some of the issues it addresses. The problems were so severe that one may wonder if these church members were really believers. In this light, it is worth noting that Paul addressed them all as Christians.

The Problem of Church Divisions

Paul plunged into his concerns rather quickly. The first and perhaps primary issue was division within the church. Paul initially addressed the symptoms of the division and then its causes. In terms of symptoms, he noted that there were four factions: people who claimed to follow Paul or Cephas (Peter) or Apollos, and others who just claimed to follow Christ.[8] Paul placed the source of the factions in pride and boasting. This was just the opposite of the way Christians should think and act. True Christian thinking was based on principles totally opposite of those of society. Paul characterized the foundational principle as "Christ crucified: a stumbling block to Jews and foolishness to Gentiles" (1 Cor. 1:23). Working out the implications of this truth should produce humility and unity. Paul asserted that his first visit to Corinth exemplified that point. In essence, Paul was telling the Corinthians that their weak area was love. That would become evident by what he taught in 1 Corinthians 13.

Read 1 Corinthians 1:10–4:21.

To further stress the distinction between Christianity and culture, Paul talked about two types of people—the natural and the spiritual (1 Cor. 2:14–15 NASB). We illustrated this concept in chapter 3, which includes a simple model showing human beings (or man, to use Paul's term) before the Fall, after the Fall, and after faith in Jesus the Messiah, which results in the infusion of the Holy Spirit. Paul's terminology here refers to the last two images (see pages 72–73). The "natural man," or the person without the Spirit, is born into this world as a fallen person. The spiritual man is a person after he or she has placed trust in Jesus the Messiah. However, Paul told the Corinthians that there is a third category (some people prefer to call this a subcategory). He called this category "carnal man" or "man of flesh" or "worldly"

SHOPS IN CORINTH. A commercial part of the city, where Paul, as a rug maker, probably worked in a shop. Other shops sold meat that was left over from sacrifices from the many temples throughout the city.

LEADERS IN CORINTH

The woman named Chloe (1 Cor. 1:11) was apparently a local Christian leader in Corinth who had a house church meeting in her home. One of her representatives may have been Sosthenes, whom Paul lists in his opening as being present when he wrote (1:1). We saw earlier that he had been a leader in the synagogue in Corinth and quickly became a believer when Paul came to town (Acts 18:17). He then assumed a position of leadership in the Corinthian church. At the end of his letter, Paul also mentions three others who came from Corinth to Ephesus: Stephanas, Fortunatus, and Achaicus. Stephanas was definitely another leader, probably of his own house church. However, it is not clear whether these others were associated with the report Paul had received or whether they had come earlier. It would appear that they also brought some financial aid to Paul.

BUILDING ON THE FOUNDATION

In 1 Corinthians 3:10–15, Paul uses the idea of the foundation as the principle underlying life. His assertion is that placing one's trust in Jesus provides a solid foundation for all of life. He then mentions various things we can use in the lives we build on that foundation. Some are worthwhile and lasting, like gold, silver, or precious jewels. Others are temporal and easily destroyed, like wood, hay, and stubble. A lifestyle built on God's principles produces lasting results. A lifestyle built on cultural standards is easily destroyed.

(1 Cor. 3:1–3). These are people who have placed their trust in Jesus (i.e., they are still spiritual) but still try to live in the same lifestyle as the pagans around them. Paul's concern was that the Corinthians were adopting that type of lifestyle.

Paul asserted that their divisions illustrated that they were worldly. He then gave several analogies to show how foolish such a lifestyle was. Perhaps the most powerful was the illustration of preparing a foundation for a tremendous house and then building a flimsy structure on it. At the time of judgment, this flimsy structure will be devoured as by flame (1 Cor. 3:10–15). Paul's plea was that the Corinthians would turn away from that lifestyle. In fact, he asked them to follow him just as he followed Jesus.

The Problem of Tolerating Immorality

Read 1 Corinthians 5–6.

In the next section Paul tackles three problems that contributed to the divisions. The first was a man in the Corinthian church who was living with his father's wife (1 Cor. 5:1).[9] While sexual intimacy between a man and his father's wife was forbidden in the OT law (Lev. 18:8), Paul did not use this prohibition as a criterion of judgment. Rather, he noted that even the pagans did not tolerate this act. This comment suggested that the church of Corinth was worse than the pagans. Paul gave the church explicit directions on how to handle the issue. This case would be important in later communications with the church.

The second problem contributing to division was lawsuits. Believers were taking fellow believers to court.[10] Paul noted that they were letting pagans judge between them, which was not a good situation. More than this, they were defrauding each other and showing themselves to be unrighteous. Paul asserted that the unrighteous would not inherit the kingdom of God. Furthermore, he asserted, they used to be that way, but as believers were not anymore.[11]

Paul states in a different way what James had addressed in his letter about ten years earlier—there is a wise way of living when one believes that Jesus is the Messiah.

The third problem that contributed to divisions was sexual immorality. This was being rationalized within the church by several slogans: "Everything is permissible for me" (1 Cor. 6:12); "Food is for the stomach and the stomach is for food" (v. 13 NASB); "Every sin that a man commits is outside the body" (v. 18, literal translation).[12] After he quoted each slogan, Paul gave

SLOGANS THAT RATIONALIZED SIN IN THE CORINTHIAN CHURCH

SLOGAN	REBUTTAL
"Everything is permissible for me."	"Not everything is beneficial."
"Food is for the stomach and the stomach is for food." (Although this saying refers to food, it apparently was used to justify all physical appetites, especially the sexual one.)	"I will not be mastered by anything." "God will destroy them both."
"Every sin that a man commits is outside the body."	"The body is not meant for sexual immorality, but for the Lord, and the Lord for the body." "He who sins sexually sins against his own body." "Your body is a temple of the Holy Spirit, who is in you, whom you have received from God." "You are not your own; you were bought at a price."

several rebuttals to each. These are shown in the chart above. Paul's overall conclusion is that Christians are to honor God with their physical bodies. This is another way of stating what James had addressed in his letter about ten years earlier—there is a wise way of living when one believes that Jesus is the Messiah.

Questions about Marriage
At this point, Paul turned to questions that the Corinthians had asked him, as is clear from the initial statement, "Now for the matters you wrote about" (1 Cor. 7:1; the abbreviated form "now concerning" or "now about" is repeated in 7:25; 8:1; 12:1; 16:1). His responses to those questions cover the bulk of the book (chs. 7–14). The first topic was marriage. Paul addressed seven different questions on that topic.[13] The bottom line, according to Paul, was that marriage was good. It would be better to be single, if a person were able, for the purposes of ministry. But that was true only if he or she could be single without falling into immorality. If not, it would be better to be married.

Read 1 Corinthians 7.

Rights and Responsibilities
The next two sections address the need for the Corinthians to have consideration of others. In the first, Paul responded to questions relating to what may be called "gray areas." That is, they are issues where there is freedom, depending on how one perceives them based on past experience ("psychological baggage") and faith. The key area of concern was "food sacrificed to idols."

Read 1 Corinthians 8:1–11:1.

We have already noted in the OT section how the sacrifice system worked for the Israelites. That is, many of the sacrifices were designed to be meals shared within the community. A similar process occurred within the pagan communities, with one added twist. While a pagan might make a sacrifice and bring home the meat for a celebration, at times the meat left over from the pagan sacrifice might be sold in the meat market. This practice placed early Christians in an awkward situation. Should they ask where the meat came from? This problem would arise especially when dining at a pagan acquaintance's place. Did his friend make a special sacrifice that day to Poseidon? Did he buy the meat in the marketplace, which secured food from the temple of Athena? What about a Christian? Should she buy her meat at the marketplace, where she might not know the source?

Paul responded that it depended upon two issues. How strong was the faith of the person buying and preparing the meat? If she had no problem recognizing that the pagan gods were really nothing, then by all means she could buy, cook, and eat the meat. However, if that brought back harmful associations, then Paul asserted that it would be better to avoid it. The second issue was whether she was having a guest for whom that was an issue. Even if the one buying and preparing the meat had no problems, she should avoid using questionable food out of consideration for her neighbor.

Taking this one step further, Paul asserted that while we have freedom in Christ, that does not mean that there are no limits. Rather, the limits are self-imposed, much like an athlete in training. Paul's warnings against letting liberty become license remind us of the guidelines of James.

Issues of Worship

Read 1 Corinthians 11:2–14:40.

Paul's next area of concern revolved around issues of worship. There were three questions. What was the role of women in worship? What was the proper way to celebrate the Lord's Supper? How should spiritual gifts be used in worship? Each of these is controversial even today.

Paul's answer regarding the role of women in worship seems to be misinterpreted in two different ways. On the one hand, it is argued that women should have no role in leading worship. On the other hand, it is argued that there should be no restrictions. Both seem overly simplistic. Part of the problem is that we are not really sure what question was being asked. Was it a question regarding the *role* of women in worship or of *decorum* for women in worship?

First, Paul clearly did not visualize women having no role in worship. In 1 Corinthians 11:5, he assumed that they would be participating in public prayer and prophecy.[14] However, there seems to be another issue here, since Paul talks about how a woman was to do these. Paul's terminology about having the head covered is difficult. Was he saying that women should have hats or scarves on their heads? If so, then what did he mean when he said that a woman's long hair sufficed as a covering (v. 15)? More than that, why does Paul use a word that may suggest "hairdo," or at a minimum points to "long" hair? The issue becomes even

EQUALITY

One of the big problems of our age is its confusion over the issue of equality. First, we confuse equality before God with equality of ability and productivity. Second, we confuse equality with sameness. There seems to be an assumption that if we are equal, we are basically the same and interchangeable. This is the opposite view of the NT, where there is a strong sense of equality before God, but also a very definite recognition that all people are not given the same gifts or abilities, attributes, or positions. More than this, we see an analogous situation in the relationship between God the Father and God the Son (see Phil. 2:6–11). Further, when we begin dealing with the issue of attributes or gifts given by God, we need to recognize that one of these is our distinct sexual identity, or gender.

more difficult with the expression "because of the angels." Apparently, there are some issues involving angelic beings that transcend our cultural understanding.[15]

The bottom line seems to be that when women participate in the worship, they are to visibly demonstrate respect. But why does Paul make this distinction between men and women? That is an especially sticky question because Paul, although he stresses authority here, balances it with a focus on equality and mutual dependence in verses 11–12. Paul seems to argue that while there is a situation of equality and interdependence between male and female, there is also a question of role and authority, which Paul sees as determined by the created order. How his instructions should be worked out is still a subject of debate.[16]

WOMAN WEARING A SCARF. An illustration of how some cultures have an expectation that women will wear head coverings, which apparently was an issue in Corinth.

The second aspect of worship involved the Lord's Supper, or communion. In the Corinthian church it was more than just a ceremony added on to the worship service. It was an actual dinner, perhaps similar to what we call a "potluck." Each family or individual brought their own food, and an enormous disparity was evident. While some had plenty and actually got drunk, others went hungry. Paul makes the observation that as a consequence of abusing the Lord's Supper, some of the Corinthians were sick and some had actually died.

The third area Paul addressed was that of spiritual gifts, still a very controversial issue today. One reason is that we tend to focus on one or two of the gifts. The issue was a real problem in the Corinthian church, as shown by the fact that Paul devoted considerable space to it (three chapters according to the divisions in our Bibles). In the process, he used three different criteria by which to measure gifts.

Paul's first argument was that God provided a variety of gifts to the church. All of them were given for a common purpose—edification of the body. As such, the Holy Spirit decides who gets which gift. Consequently, there should be no

God provided a variety of gifts to the church; the Holy Spirit decides who gets which gift.

boasting in the gift received and no looking down on someone who has another gift. Likewise, the recipient should be willing to use her gift for the overall good of the body, not for self-advancement.

Interestingly, Paul asserted that there was a hierarchy of value in the gifts. But when he listed his hierarchy, the tongues—which were the point of controversy—were at the bottom of the list. So Paul encouraged the Corinthians to ask God for gifts, but especially for what he called the "greater gifts" (1 Cor. 12:31; 14:1).[17] Within this context, Paul then advocated something better than tongues. He pointed out that while the Corinthians were using tongues to show that they were Spirit-filled, in reality, love did that (1 Cor. 13). Finally, Paul gave guidelines on using the gifts. Since they were to be used for the edification of the church, Paul showed how the church could be best edified.[18] One important item stands out in this section: the people who possessed the gifts had the ability to control them—and Paul directed those who had them to do so.

The Question of the Resurrection

Read 1 Corinthians 15.

The third question that Paul addressed was the resurrection. Apparently some in Corinth were challenging the doctrine of the resurrection.[19] Paul used an interesting piece of logic to demonstrate that believers would be raised from the dead. First, he established the historicity of the physical resurrection of Jesus. Based on that, he argued that those who believed in Jesus would also be resurrected.[20] After this extensive argument, he presented one more point, one he had included in his letters to the Thessalonians. Here, he terms it a mystery: not all Christians will die, but all Christians will be changed into a new spiritual body, in an instant, at the last trumpet.

Collecting Money and Other Issues

Read 1 Corinthians 16.

The final issue Paul addressed was about money that was being collected for the relief of the believers in Jerusalem. Several important points derive out of this passage. First, the believers in Jerusalem were undergoing persecution, and believers elsewhere were collecting money to help. Second, Paul was already laying down foundations for financial integrity. He planned that men from the churches that raised the money would deliver the money. He, personally, would not be involved. Finally, the money was to be collected each Sunday. This is one of the first indicators of a change from the OT tradition of Saturday worship to the Sunday worship of Christians.[21] Paul wrapped up his letter with his travel plans and personal matters. While he planned to come to Corinth, he wanted to remain in Ephesus until after Pentecost. These plans did change later, as we will see.

First Corinthians gives us a vivid picture of a particular church (that is, all the congregations within a given city) about twenty-five years after the resurrection. As we have seen, it is not a pretty picture. It shows us a church that had divisions, controversy, and members living in gross sin. In some respects, the church has not

changed over the past two thousand years. Overall, these problems validate the message about the nature of people and their need for Jesus.

PAUL'S SECOND LETTER TO THE CORINTHIANS

The letter we call 2 Corinthians followed 1 Corinthians after about six to eight months. During the interim, Paul had made a quick trip to Corinth (often called "the painful visit"; see 2 Cor. 2:1; 12:14; 13:1–2) and returned to Ephesus. There he left town earlier than planned as a result of the riots led by Demetrius the silversmith (Acts 19:24–41; cf. 20:1; 2 Cor. 1:8–11). He journeyed to Troas and back into Macedonia (probably Philippi), where he met Timothy (cf. Acts 19:22 and 20:4). There he also met Titus, who had carried "the sorrowful letter" to Corinth (2 Cor. 7:6). Titus brought the report that the church in Corinth had turned around. Thus, Paul wrote this letter to express his joy, but he also addressed other issues. Titus then carried it back to Corinth.

Paul's Change of Plans

Part of Paul's purpose for this letter was to clarify what had happened in Ephesus ("Asia," 2 Cor. 1:8–11). Paul had quickly left the city, and it is likely that rumors of some type had gotten back to Corinth. Now that he was safe in Macedonia, he needed to let them know he was all right.

Read 2 Corinthians 1:1–2:4.

Beyond that, Paul explained here the reason why he had not traveled through Corinth on his way to Macedonia. Previously he had indicated that he would, and apparently some criticized that change of plans (2 Cor. 1:15–18).[22] Paul explained that the painful reception some of them had given him during his previous trip had caused him to reconsider (2 Cor. 1:23–2:1). He determined not to come again until some of the issues had been resolved. Then he would be able to visit them with a positive spirit.

Restoring the Repentant

Read 2 Corinthians 2:5–13.

Another reason he wrote was to encourage them regarding the restoration of a sinner who had repented. Apparently, this was the man who Paul noted in 1 Corinthians 5 as living in sin.[23] Despite Paul's admonition there, the church had not taken action. Then Paul wrote a much stronger letter. This had hurt some people. Perhaps, in that letter, Paul had gone so far as to suggest that the reason for his change of plans was that he could not fellowship with the Corinthians again until they settled this issue. These factors may be one reason why "the sorrowful letter" was not preserved in the canon. Then, as a result of this third letter, which is now lost, the church got serious about the situation. The believers stopped meeting with the man, who then repented. Paul stated that he had been confident that they would do the right thing, and now they had.

> Paul's encouragement was that the purpose of strong action within the church is to promote repentance, not to punish.

Unfortunately, whatever the circumstances that precipitated the issue, the man who repented was not accepted back into fellowship after his repentance. This problem prompted 2 Corinthians, urging reconciliation. Paul's encouragement was that the purpose of strong action within the church is to promote repentance, not to punish. Now that the sinner had genuinely repented, he must be accepted back into fellowship.[24]

Paul Explains the New Covenant

Read 2 Corinthians 2:14–7:16.

Paul then subtly transitioned to an explanation of the new covenant and its superiority to the old covenant. The situation that may have prompted this discussion is not clear, but there seems to have been a challenge to the message he proclaimed, probably from Jewish elements. The key contrast in this section is between the first covenant of Moses and the new covenant that Paul had been proclaiming. In the process, he suggested that he was not like Moses, trying to hang on to the glory of something fading away.

The tone of this section is interesting. It appears that Paul was tired of the problems created by the factions in the church in Corinth. He was really ready to go home to God (in heaven), but he recognized that God still had a purpose for him in that church. Despite his frustrations, Paul was still willing to work with the Corinthians. However, he warned them that they were in danger of having made their profession of faith in vain because they were not following through on it.

This section is somewhat difficult to follow for two reasons. We really don't know the issues that caused Paul's response. Moreover, it is very heartfelt and follows an emotional rather than a logical flow. The bottom line of the discussion was that the gospel Paul proclaimed had much to commend it and that the Corinthi-

A LESSON IN LEADERSHIP

In 2 Corinthians 8–9, Paul demonstrates a leadership trait that I was taught in the navy. Even though he knew of many problems in Corinth, when he talked about the Corinthians to others, he only talked about their strong points (he bragged on them). He then gave them every chance to live up to those positive words. He took his criticisms to them personally and basically in private.

ans were overlooking this truth. Furthermore, everything Paul did was for them, whether they realized it or not. He then gave them an exhortation to walk with God and with other believers, not with those who were worldly. Finally, he expressed again his joy that they were now taking the right steps.

Preparing the Offering

Paul now addressed a very practical issue. The Corinthians had made some promises regarding the offering they were going to make for the believers in Judea who were suffering. Paul wanted them to follow through. More than this, he was giving them an advance warning that when he came to Corinth, some men from Macedonia would be with him, and he did not want them to be embarrassed.

Read 2 Corinthians 8–9.

Defending His Apostleship

As was often his practice, Paul saved the most important issue for last. There had been hints throughout the letter regarding opposition to his authority. Now Paul addressed it directly. Apparently, some self-appointed leaders in Corinth were challenging Paul on theological issues.[25] Paul called them false apostles and even suggested that they were of Satan.

Read 2 Corinthians 10:1–12:18.

Conclusion

Paul wrapped up the letter with a plea for repentance on the part of the Corinthians. This was coupled with a warning. He was coming a third time, and he anticipated that if necessary he would come with judgment. As such, he warned the Corinthians to examine themselves to see if they were truly Christians.

Read 2 Corinthians 12:19–13:14.

But Paul did not end on that negative note. Rather, he encouraged the Corinthians, saying that he was confident that they were indeed believers. As such, he exhorted them to grow to maturity in Jesus: "Aim for perfection, listen to my appeal, be of one mind, live in peace. And the God of love and peace will be with you."

PAUL RETURNS TO CORINTH

After Titus delivered the letter we call 2 Corinthians, Paul continued through Macedonia to Achaia. He remained there (in Corinth) for several months. This

Read Acts 20:1–3.

was probably the winter of 56–57, the season when travel on the Mediterranean was too risky. Paul probably used this time to wrap up various issues with the Corinthian church. He left Corinth to travel to Jerusalem the following spring. With him was a party of men from Achaia and Macedonia who carried the offering for the church in Jerusalem. Before he left, he wrote a letter to the church in Rome. But those are both the subject of another chapter.

REVIEW QUESTIONS

1. What pattern of evangelism did Paul use in every new city, including Ephesus?

2. What were the results of the time Paul spent in Ephesus?

3. Why were there schisms in the Corinthian church?

4. What were Paul's conclusions on the issue of marriage as discussed in 1 Corinthians?

5. What did Paul conclude about Christian liberty in 1 Corinthians?

6. What were the issues of worship that Paul addressed in 1 Corinthians?

7. What was Paul's view on the resurrection as expressed in 1 Corinthians?

8. Why did Paul change his plans before he wrote 2 Corinthians?

9. What was the concern Paul expressed in 2 Corinthians about the person who had repented?

10. Why was Paul asking for an offering, and how did he plan on collecting it? Why?

25
CHAPTER

The Road to Rome

OVERVIEW

Before Paul left Corinth, he wrote a letter to the church in Rome letting them know of his desire to come there on his way to Spain. First, he needed to go to Jerusalem. When he got there, however, his presence caused a riot, and he was taken into custody by the Romans. Because he was a Roman citizen and there were threats on his life, he was taken to Caesarea. After two years awaiting a trial, Paul appealed to Caesar. He was then taken to Rome, suffering shipwreck en route.

STUDY GOALS

▶ Develop the message of Romans as a preparation for Paul's visit to that church.

▶ Summarize basic church doctrine as expressed in Romans.

▶ Follow Paul's return to Jerusalem.

▶ Trace the events leading to Paul's arrest by the Romans.

▶ Follow Paul's drawn-out journey to Rome.

We don't know when Paul set his heart on going to Rome and Spain. It may have been during his first visit to Corinth in 51 CE in his talks with Priscilla and Aquila, who had come from Rome. It may have been even earlier. But it is clear that it was a priority for him when he was in Corinth in 56–57. Late that winter he had an opportunity to send a letter to the church in Rome, which we call the Epistle to the Romans. In it, he expressed his longtime desire to visit that city (Rom. 15:23). But he also indicated that his main desire was to go to Spain, and he would be using Rome as a stepping-off place.

THE LETTER TO THE ROMANS

Read Romans 1:1–15;
16:1–27.

Phoebe, a leader of the church in Cenchrea, apparently carried this letter to Rome (Rom. 16:1). Cenchrea was the sister city of Corinth, about four miles away across the isthmus. Since it was a part of Achaia, that church would have been considered part of the audience addressed in the letters to the Corinthians (2 Cor. 1:1). As such, she would have been part of the discussions involved in those letters. We are not told why Phoebe was traveling to Rome, but Paul took advantage of her trip.

PHOEBE

In the Greek text of Romans 16:1, Phoebe is called a *diakonos*, "servant, minister, deacon" (for the latter, English has the feminine form, *deaconess*). Both the NIV and the NASB translate it as "servant." There is debate whether this designation means that she was the wife of a deacon, or that she was a female who occupied the position of a deacon within that church. It is most likely the latter.

COLISEUM IN ROME. The prominent edifice in Rome that after New Testament times would become a symbol of persecution. It was built about fifteen years after the death of Paul.

The final chapter of the letter lists a number of people to whom Paul sent special greetings. He included Priscilla and Aquila, who were now back in Rome, along with a number of other believers, both Jewish and Gentile. Some were even relatives of Paul. He also mentioned at least five house churches.[1]

The reason for the letter was at least fourfold. First, there was the opportunity. Phoebe was going to Rome and thus was a ready messenger. Then there was the greeting of old friends. The list in Romans 16 contains twenty-four names of personal friends and relatives. Third, there was his need to introduce himself to the Roman church.[2] Paul wanted to visit Rome and go on from there to Spain. But for most Romans he was just a name they might have heard from the lips of a few other believers. The fourth reason involved the importance of Rome. As the capital of the empire, it was an obvious goal. Furthermore, as far as we can tell, at this time no apostle had yet visited Rome.[3] Since they had no previous apostolic teaching, Paul desired to give the Romans a solid theological foundation on which to build.

> In Romans, for the first time, we have a carefully developed written analysis of what the claims of Jesus mean.

The church there had a good start. Many Romans were becoming believers, and it had a good reputation (Rom. 16:19). But Paul wanted to make sure that it continued. To that end, he gave a detailed presentation of the gospel and its implications in Romans, which is certainly the most theological of the books in the NT. In fact, we might say that here, for the first time, we have a carefully developed written analysis of what the claims of Jesus mean. In this respect, we may assume that the letter to the Romans is a condensation of Paul's teaching. That is why this letter is considered so important today.

The letter to the Romans might be divided into three sections. The first section lays out the basic principles of Paul's message (Rom. 1–8). We might call this Paul's gospel message. The second section addresses certain questions brought up by that message (chs. 9–11). The key question has to do with the implications of the Jerusalem Council. If the Gentiles do not have to follow the law to have a relationship with God, then what does that say about the Jews?[4] The final section (12:1–15:22) ties together the two previous ones by addressing practical implications of lifestyle that result from understanding and accepting that Jesus was the Messiah.[5] In addition, there is a closing chapter addressing friends and relatives.

PAUL'S GOSPEL

Twice in Romans (2:16; 16:25) Paul uses the expression "my gospel." While his message was distinctive, this should not be construed to say that his teaching differed from that of the other apostles. We have already noted how Paul had checked with them on several occasions to verify that they were in agreement. We have also seen how Paul's message in Galatians correlated with James's message in his letter. What we see is that Paul had a much greater awareness of the implications of that message. As a result, his teaching was deeper. Peter observed this quality himself (2 Pet. 3:15–16), noting that some of what Paul taught was difficult to understand. Peter also pointed out that "ignorant and unstable people" distorted Paul's teaching.

Who Was Jesus?

Read Romans 1:1–15.

Even in his greeting, Paul began addressing his topic. He introduced himself as a servant and an apostle of Jesus the Messiah. In this role he proclaimed the good news about that Messiah. This good news was anticipated by the prophets. It involved the descendant and heir of David's kingly line. But more importantly, this Jesus the Messiah, the Lord of Paul and the Romans, was demonstrated to be the Son of God, through the Holy Spirit, by the resurrection. Although tucked away in the introduction, this may be the most important point of the book.[6] Here Paul pointed to the historical need for the resurrection. He then observed how his entire career and ministry developed out of that historical fact.

As he turned to his audience, Paul noted that they were "saints" (Rom. 1:7 NASB). They were loved by God. They also had a worldwide reputation for their faith. Consequently, Paul prayed for them regularly. He also had wanted to visit them for some time.

Sin Separates from God

Read Romans 1:16–3:20.

Paul segued into his first topic in a marvelous manner. Beginning with his desire to visit Rome, he noted that he had an obligation to the Romans as well as to the rest of the Gentiles. As such, he wanted to preach the gospel to them because he was not ashamed of it. Rather, he knew that it showed God's power both to the Jews and the Gentiles. These comments led him to explain why the gospel showed that power and why everyone needs the message he preached.

Paul began with the observation that everyone in the world has an awareness of God. But because of the fallen nature of man, everyone also has rejected the knowledge he or she has. This is the basic concept of sin. This rejection is reflected in ungodly lifestyles, which precipitate God's wrath. Because of the all-encompassing nature of the consequences of rejecting God, everyone on earth faces judgment. Moreover, because everyone knows about God, no one has an excuse. Even if someone could truthfully say that he or she was not aware of God's standards (a possibility Paul denied), that person could be judged on the basis of the standards

No one lives up to his or her own standards, let alone God's.

BELIEVERS AS SAINTS

The word *saints* means "holy ones." This is a challenging term, since it presents a twist on lifestyle that is different from the OT. The word *holy,* as used in both testaments, reflects a concept of moral purity (in the sense that God is holy), and God's people are then to be morally pure. As a consequence of that, God's people in both testaments are to be different from (or set apart from) the standards of this world. The difference, however, lies in how that worked out. Although the OT occasionally refers to Israel as a "holy" people, it is generally in the context of a reason the nation was forbidden to do certain things (e.g., worship other gods, Deut. 7:6). Usually the "holiness" of the nation was a standard to strive for based on obedience (Ex. 19:5–6). In the NT, God's people are given the title "holy ones" and then encouraged to live up to that title.

by which he or she viewed others. In other words, no one lives up to his or her own standards, let alone God's.

As a result, everyone is guilty before God. Here Paul pointed out that this truth applied to both Jews and Gentiles. While the Jews had greater revelation, they also then had higher standards to live up to. And as such, in some respects, they were more guilty, since they fell short by a greater amount. But Paul's point really was that all are guilty before God. In their guilt, they have no hope but are deserving of death.

Salvation Provides Access to God

But if there is no hope, then what is mankind to do? This is where the significance of Jesus' claim to be Messiah really came in. The OT gave testimony of how God had been working in history to resolve the problem that surfaced in Genesis 3.

Read Romans 3:21–5:21.

VIA SACRA. The "holy way" in Rome leading to the Arch of Titus. In Paul's day, Rome was a large city with many temples.

After centuries of preparation, the plan culminated in the life of Jesus, who presented Himself as the promised Messiah. As we have already seen, He did what no one else could do. He demonstrated His position by His deeds, including a variety of supernormal signs or miracles. He challenged His enemies to point out any sin He had committed. They responded by killing Him. He then validated His claims by His resurrection. As such, Jesus became the substitute to take the punishment for the sin of humankind. To put it in OT terms, He was the sacrifice who atoned for human sin.

Jesus validated His claims by His resurrection.

In view of this truth, Paul wrote, all who placed their trust in Him were reconciled to God. He described this act as being "justified freely by his grace through the redemption that came by Christ Jesus" (Rom. 3:24). This redemption process was available to both Jew and Gentile on an equal basis. Paul called the result "salvation."

To demonstrate how it worked, Paul used the example of Abraham. He was a perfect example, since he lived several centuries before the Law was given to Moses. Thus, the Jews who claimed Abraham as their ancestor had to recognize that he had not followed the Law. Yet he had been pronounced righteous because of his faith in God's promises. Theologians call this "justification." Paul pointed out that this event in Abraham's life occurred years before he was circumcised.[7]

In the last part of this section, Paul talked about the implications of the relationship believers have with God through Jesus the Messiah. They have peace with God. They have cause for rejoicing, even in times of suffering. They have hope. They have faith. They have love.

What Does It Mean to Be Saved?

Read Romans 6–8.

But Paul did not stop there. He argued that it was not enough to have faith in the redemption of Jesus. He expressed it in the form of a question: Since God displayed grace in forgiving our sin, shouldn't we continue to sin so God can show more grace? His response (Rom. 6:2) was as strong a "No way!" as the Greek language allowed.

SALVATION

The term *salvation* is used in a dual sense in the Bible. Part of the problem for the Jews who did not accept Jesus as the Messiah was that they viewed the term with the wrong focus. *Salvation* was used to reflect deliverance from sin. But it was also used to refer to deliverance from a military or other physical threat, such as the Roman occupation. This aspect is seen even in Zechariah's praise song at the birth of John. He talked about salvation from Israel's enemies (Luke 1:71). But he also talked about salvation in the deliverance from sins through the Messiah who would follow John (1:77). As Paul developed his argument, he focused on salvation in the latter sense, at least as far as the First Coming was concerned. The Jews understood and looked for salvation primarily in the former sense, looking for deliverance from Rome. Many did not understand that the rituals they had been following did not provide salvation in the sense of reconciliation with God.

He used three analogies to illustrate why not. The first was death: in Jesus, Paul asserted, believers have died to the old lifestyle. The second was slavery: nonbelievers are slaves to sin, but believers are freed from that slavery and are no longer *required* to act as though they are in bondage. The third analogy was marriage: one is married only until his or her spouse dies, so after the death of the spouse, there are no longer any legal requirements regarding the relationship (in this analogy, the dead spouse is the sin nature).

Paul recognized that, unfortunately, these truths are not easy to implement. Believers still have physical bodies. Our minds were programmed while we were living in sin. We continue to live in a fallen world that is in rebellion against God. We have to make choices all the time, and we often make the wrong ones. However, Paul asserted that the difference is the Holy Spirit, whom we have within us, changing our lives. Because of that, we are not under an obligation to live out the unbridled passions of the physical bodies (which he called "the flesh"), but have control over them.[8] This difference is seen in a variety of ways. We see it in the way we are led (Rom. 8:14). We see it in our spirits (8:16). We see it in our prayers (8:26). Finally, we see it in our ultimate confidence: because the Holy Spirit dwells within, nothing can separate us from God (8:38–39).

But What about Israel?

Paul's final assertion immediately brings questions to mind. If nothing can break the covenant relationship we have with God, then what about Israel? Hadn't the nation been rejected?[9] Wasn't that covenant broken? Didn't that set a precedent? In his next section, Paul addressed those very questions.

Read Romans 9:1 – 11:32.

Paul recognized that the nation of Israel illustrated a problem. His response was complicated, and this section is probably the most challenging in the book. Paul's overriding thought was that God has the right to chose whom He desires. But in response to that, Paul noted, if God makes the choice, why is Israel then held responsible? To this, Paul argued that there were two aspects to the problem—individuals and corporate identity. As such, Paul really had two answers: one regarding the individuals, and one regarding the corporate identity.

Part of the problem with this passage is that Paul's distinction—which involves defining what is meant by Israel—is difficult to follow. First, Paul noted that while the OT covenant was given to the nation (i.e., the corporate entity called Israel), individuals were responsible to live up to covenant responsibilities (Rom. 9:4–6). As such, Paul seemed to assert that the problem was with the individuals who failed (i.e., they did not believe, cf. Rom. 10:3–4). But as Paul developed his argument, he seemed to assert that while these individuals who failed were physical descendants of Israel (the man), they were not part of Israel (the corporate entity), even through physically they were part of the national entity. The terms "true Israel" or "spiritual Israel" are sometimes used for this new concept.

Paul demonstrated this in several ways. First, he noted that not everyone who has a physical tie to Abraham was part of the nation, as illustrated by the cases of

THE ROLE OF THE LAW

Paul's discussion of righteousness and the Law is very complicated and intensely debated. Part of the reason is the difficulty in understanding his terminology (complicated by two thousand years of explanations). For example, when Paul talks of "law" in Romans 9:31, is he referring to the Ten Commandments, the collective commandments of Exodus, Leviticus, Numbers, and Deuteronomy, or to the concept of *torah* as teaching? Or was he just using it to refer to a general concept of "rules?" It seems that he used the word in different senses at different places. In this case, he seems to be using it to refer to a rule, that is, if you do this (work), you will get that (relationship) in return. In essence, Paul seems to argue that this approach is a reversal of what God intended, which was: because you have a relationship, you do the work. The Torah gave guidelines on how the established covenant relationship could work best within the nation (see above, ch. 7).

Isaac and Ishmael, and Jacob and Esau. He used the phrase "children of promise" (Rom. 9:8) to point out that some of the individual physical descendants were not part of the corporate (or spiritual) promises. As such, even Gentiles could be (and historically were) part of those promises.[10]

Thus, Paul divided the nation of Israel into two parts: a majority who had rejected God and His Messiah through unbelief, and a "remnant" who had accepted God and His Messiah through faith or belief. As such, he argued that God's covenant with Israel had not failed because many individuals were part of the new covenant (e.g., Paul himself; see Rom. 11:1). Based on his earlier discussion, Paul used the term *salvation* to reflect this new relationship.

Paul's desire was that the Israelites (the individuals) would be saved (Rom. 10:1). He had come to recognize, however, that their salvation would have to be through individual faith, not in trying to keep corporate guidelines.[11] Paul's development of this concept is really the heart of this entire section. In the process, he pointed out that both Gentiles and Jews were reconciled to God through faith (reconciliation seems to be what Paul had in mind when he speaks of "establishing righteousness") with the key being the intermediary work of Jesus. Anyone who attempted to force reconciliation by what they did was doomed to failure. Rather, reconciliation came as a result of a heartfelt belief and a confession of the mouth regarding the messiahship of Jesus.[12]

Unfortunately, not all Israelites had believed in Jesus, Paul recognized. But the next question is, Was the judgment on Israel a corporate rejection? Or to put it another way, did God reject the nation because *individuals* had rejected God? Paul's adamant answer here was, "No way!" (Rom. 11:1; in the Greek, this is the same phrase used in 6:1 in response to the suggestion that believers may continue in sin). In other words, there was still a corporate or national aspect.

As we looked at the OT, we noted how Moses told the people they could live as vassals in obedience to the covenant, or they could live as vassals in disobedience. In the first case, they would be blessed. In the second, they would suffer judgment (curse).[13] Paul showed this principle to the Romans through historical evidence. It was very clear that some Jews (or Israelites) had not been rejected by

God. Paul himself was an excellent case in point. Throughout history, God had preserved a remnant of true Israelites (heirs of promise) within a nation that constantly rebelled. We have seen how many Israelites had indeed accepted Jesus as the Messiah. Through this remnant the corporate identity was preserved. But Paul seems to have in mind more than just a preservation of a remnant.

Here Paul used the metaphor of an olive tree. The corporate body was the olive tree. Wild branches (i.e., believing Gentiles) were grafted in. Dead branches (nonbelieving Israelites) were purged. But Paul warned that the Gentiles should not be arrogant against the Jews, because he saw that there was more in the future. More believing Jews would be grafted in. Ultimately, there would indeed be national restoration, which would fulfill that aspect of prophecy. Paul termed all of this a "mystery" (Rom. 11:25).

> Paul recognized that there are implications to the relationship established between the believer and God.

Then What about Lifestyles?

As always, Paul recognized that there are implications to the relationship established between the believer and God. These implications are necessarily reflected in lifestyle. In a general sense, Paul argued that the lifestyle of a believer should be different from that of the pagan culture surrounding him or her.

Read Romans 12:1–15:22

Paul then addressed specific issues. Most of them have to do with relationships. For example, he talked about how believers should relate to one another in the church. He also addressed how believers should relate to their societies and their governments. Then he discussed personal relationships. Many of these comments are very similar to what Paul had written to the church in Corinth. The bottom line, from Paul's perspective, was that believers should model their lives after Jesus.

Conclusion

Read Romans 15:23 – 16:27.

Paul concluded his letter with an outline of his plans. After going to Judea with the offering from the believers in Macedonia and Achaia, he would be coming to Rome. He asked for prayer for protection during the journey, especially from the Jews who did not believe.

Paul then sent greetings to those he knew in Rome. At the end he noted those whom the Romans knew who were with him in Corinth. These included Timothy, along with Lucius, Jason, and Sosipater, relatives of Paul. Other were Gaius, Erastus, the city treasurer, and Quartus. Finally, we learn that Tertius was the scribe who actually wrote the letter for Paul.

PAUL'S RETURN TO JERUSALEM

Read Acts 20:3 – 21:14.

Paul probably left Corinth in April of 57 (note that the traveling party appears to have spent Passover and the Feast of Unleavened Bread in Philippi, Acts 20:6). His original plan had been to sail directly from Cenchrea to Syria (20:3). However, they learned of a plot of the Jews to kill him. As a result, Paul and his companions changed plans and took a land route north through Macedonia. Eight men from several different churches went with him, although the entire party didn't meet until they reached Troas.[14]

In Troas, Paul spent a week teaching before leaving. On Sunday when the church had gathered, Paul spent a long time teaching because of his plan to leave the next day. The group met in a third-story room, and a young man named Eutychus was sitting in the window. As Paul talked on and on, Eutychus went to sleep and fell out of the window. When the group, including Luke the doctor, reached him on the ground, he was pronounced dead. Paul embraced him, and he came back to life. They returned to the third-story room, where they ate, and then Paul continued teaching until dawn.

From Troas, Paul and his company traveled by ship to Miletus, south of Ephesus.[15] Paul was in a hurry to get to Jerusalem before Pentecost. So rather than stopping at Ephesus, he arranged for the elders of the Ephesian church to meet him in Miletus. There he gave them an exhortation on how to manage the church. When they parted, they feared that they would not see him again in this world.

Paul and company caught another ship to Tyre. They stayed with a group of believers in Tyre for a week. Several who had prophetic insight warned Paul not

EPHESUS. The city that was so prominent in Paul's ministry, but was bypassed by him on his journey back to Jerusalem. Instead, he stopped at the next port, Miletus, and the Ephesian elders came down to meet him there.

to go up to Jerusalem. However, Paul was determined. The group prayed on the beach, and then Paul and his friends continued down the coast.

After stopping at Ptolemais, they continued to Caesarea, where they met Philip the evangelist, whom we last saw more than twenty years earlier coming to Caesarea (Acts 8:40). Philip had four virgin daughters who were prophetesses. They and a prophet named Agabus (apparently the same man who foresaw the worldwide famine, 11:28) predicted that Paul would be bound and delivered to the Gentiles if he went up to Jerusalem. Again, Paul expressed his determination, and the journey continued.

PAUL CAUSES A RIOT IN JERUSALEM

Accompanied by some of the believers from Caesarea, Paul and his group made it to Jerusalem. They stayed at the house of a believer named Mnason, who was originally from Cyprus (like Barnabas). The next day Paul and his friends went to see the leadership, James and the elders. As usual, Paul reported on the results

Read Acts 21:15–23:11.

SHORT-TERM PROPHECY

The believers in Tyre, speaking "through the Spirit," urged Paul not to continue his trip to Jerusalem (Acts 21:4). This warning is an example of a short-term prophecy in which the prophetic revelation merely states what would happen if a certain course of action were followed (see above, ch. 13). Paul was still given the freedom to choose which course of action to take. In this case, he may have also had encouragement from the Holy Spirit that while he would be bound and imprisoned, his life would be preserved.

CAESAREA. The port city where Paul arrived on his way to Jerusalem at the end of his third journey.

of his work. The leadership rejoiced to see what God was doing among the Gentiles.

At the same time, a number of Jews in Judea were accepting Jesus as the Messiah. Many of them, however, were adamant that all believers had to fit within the national covenantal structure, that is, follow the OT law. In the process, the misconception had come up that Paul, in his ministry to Gentiles, was advocating that Jews abandon their culture. The elders expected that word would soon circulate that Paul was back, and trouble would be the result.

These leaders decided that the solution was for Paul to show by his own actions that he was not advocating a wholesale abandonment of the Jewish culture. He had just come from a long journey where he apparently had been under a Nazirite vow, similar to what we saw in Acts 18:18. Four local believing Jews were also completing similar vows. They suggested that Paul not only accompany those others but also pay the expenses involved in completing their vows. He agreed to do so.

The next day, Paul went up to the temple with the other four to give notice of their "purification" as they completed their vows. They had their heads shaved. They prepared for the sacrifice of the votive offerings, which would take place a week later. However, before the week was complete, some of the Jews who had come from Asia saw Paul in the temple. They had seen him talking to a Gentile, Trophimus from Ephesus (one of the men who had come with Paul to deliver the offering raised by believers in the Aegean region, Acts 20:4), and they assumed that Paul had brought him into the temple. Jumping to this false conclusion, they yelled for help as they grabbed Paul. The rapidly growing mob dragged Paul out of the temple, and some of the priests shut the doors.

THE JERUSALEM LEADERSHIP

Luke's use of the term "elders" rather than "apostles" in Acts 21:18 is interesting. This language seems to reflect a transition in the leadership of the church in Jerusalem during the forties. From Acts 1 through 14 (that is, from Pentecost in 33 to the Jerusalem Council in 47 CE), the church leadership is almost always referred to as "the apostles." (The one exception is Acts 11:30, which uses the word *elders* in a very general sense.) Then at the Jerusalem Council, the leadership is referred to as "the apostles and elders" (15:4). The next reference to the leaders is 21:18. Extrabiblical evidence suggests that by this time most of the apostles had followed the lead of Peter and Paul and were evangelizing foreign lands on their own.

Some of the crowd wanted to kill Paul; others were content to beat him. Because of the chaos, the situation did not get beyond that. Hearing the uproar, the Roman commander deployed some troops and they waded into the fray. Under the scrutiny of the armed Roman soldiers, the Jews stopped the beating. Clearly, Paul was the center of the fracas, so the Roman commander had him bound in chains and started asking questions. The result was bedlam, with everyone making accusations. Unable to understand anything, the commander ordered that Paul be taken to the barracks for interrogation. The mob was so great that the soldiers had to carry Paul.

At the top of the stairs, Paul could finally make himself heard and asked to talk to the Roman commander. The Roman was surprised that Paul knew Greek,

ANTONIA. A model of the Roman fortress adjacent to the temple in Jerusalem. After the riot started in the temple courtyard, Roman troops from the Antonia rescued Paul.

supposing that Paul had been an Egyptian who had caused problems before. Paul identified himself and asked to speak to the crowd. The commander gave Paul permission, and the soldiers set him down. He stood on the top of the stairs to quiet the crowd and began talking to them in Aramaic.[16]

When they heard Paul speak in their own language, the crowd became even quieter and listened to what he had to say. Paul shared his testimony of how he had been very zealous in persecuting followers of "the Way" until his experience on the road to Damascus. The crowd listened carefully until he shared how God told him that he would be sent to the Gentiles.

> When Paul shared how God told him that he would be sent to the Gentiles, the Jewish crowd exploded with disgust.

With this, the crowd exploded with disgust. Not understanding what was said, but sensing that the situation was about to get out of control, the Roman commander had Paul brought into the barracks. There the intent was to interrogate him, with the assistance of a scourging.

As they stretched him out for the lashings, Paul asked them whether it was lawful for them to do that to a Roman citizen. This put a new face on the situation, so the soldier in charge of the interrogation reported back to the commander. The commander asked him about his citizenship (his own had been bought by a high price) and discovered that Paul was born a citizen.[17] With this they untied him and released him the next day.

However, the commander wanted to know what had caused the riot. So he ordered the Sanhedrin (the ruling council of the Jews) assembled and brought Paul before them. Paul began his testimony with an assertion that he was a Jew in good conscience. At this Ananias, the high priest, ordered that his mouth be slapped. Paul responded angrily, asserting that God would strike Ananias because of his hypocrisy: he claimed to try Paul by Jewish law but violated the law in ordering him to be slapped.

The observers were aghast. They asked Paul how he dared to revile the high priest. Paul asserted that he was not aware that the man was high priest and then quoted Exodus 22:28, which states that Jews should not speak evil of their leaders.[18] Since Ananias was high priest, that meant that he was a Sadducee. Paul recognized other Sadducees and also Pharisees in the group, even though it had been

PAUL AND THE SANHEDRIN

As a rabbi, Paul had been a student of Gamaliel, one of the leading Pharisees of the day. As such, it is likely that he had attended a number of sessions of the Sanhedrin. The most evident was the session that had condemned Stephen (Acts 6:12). In the narrative of Acts 23, there are several points that Luke does not cover. One is the question of how many members of the Sanhedrin at this time had accepted the messianic claims of Jesus. Those who had were most likely of the party of the Pharisees. Beyond that, there would be the question of how those believing Pharisees viewed the issue of the Gentiles. It is likely that the Sanhedrin at this time was very divided and that every meeting was very tense.

more than twenty years since he had been privy to the Sanhedrin. Noting this division, Paul turned to his fellow Pharisees and cried out, "I am on trial for the hope and resurrection of the dead!"

This declaration put the issue into a different context. The disagreement on the question of life after death was a major one between the two parties (see above, ch. 17). This issue created an uproar in the Sanhedrin, as some of the Pharisees began to argue that it was possible that Paul had indeed seen an angelic vision, something else the Sadducees denied. As the council dissolved into a melee, the Roman commander decided to get Paul out before he was torn to pieces.

The Romans kept Paul in protective custody.[19] That night God gave Paul a vision. It was to encourage him that he would, indeed, go to Rome.

PAUL GOES TO CAESAREA

The next day a group of more than forty Jews formed a conspiracy against Paul. They vowed that they would neither eat nor drink until Paul was dead.[20] The subterfuge they developed was that the high priest was to ask the Roman commander to bring Paul in the following day for further questioning. They would attack the group before they arrived at the council spaces.

Read Acts 23:12–24:27.

However, Paul's nephew overheard the plans and went that night to tell Paul.[21] Paul sent him to the Roman commander. After the commander heard the story, he directed that a large detachment of troops (two hundred soldiers, two hundred spearmen, and seventy mounted soldiers) be prepared to take Paul down to Caesarea, the Roman administrative center on the coast. The entire group left that night and took him halfway. There the infantry returned, and Paul and the others on horses continued to Caesarea. They took with them a letter to the

CAESAREA AQUEDUCT. The aqueduct that brought water from the mountains about twenty miles away to the city of Caesarea, where Paul was in prison for two years as he awaited trial before the governors Felix and Festus.

governor noting that Paul was both a Roman citizen and innocent of violating any Roman laws that would require him either to be imprisoned or executed. The issue was entirely an internal Jewish issue.

When Felix, the governor, read the letter, he told Paul that he would wait for his accusers to arrive. He kept him in protective custody in the Praetorium, a palace that had been built by Herod. Five days later Ananias arrived with several leaders of the Sanhedrin and Tertullus, a lawyer.[22]

Tertullus was the spokesman for the group. After trying to flatter Felix, he accused Paul of being "a real pest" (Acts 24:5 NASB; the NIV translates the word as "troublemaker"). He also claimed that Paul stirred up riots all over the world as a ringleader of the Nazarenes and that he had tried to desecrate the temple.

> When Paul gave his defense, he pointed out that he was ceremonially clean (having followed the purification rituals of Judaism) when they had found him in the temple.

When Paul gave his defense, he pointed out that all he had done was to go up to the temple to worship. He did not argue with anyone and had not done any debating in any of the synagogues in Jerusalem. He also noted that he was being accused of being part of a sect because he believed everything in the Law and the Prophets, including a resurrection of the dead. Furthermore, he pointed out that he was ceremonially clean (having followed the purification rituals of Judaism) when they had found him in the temple. There was no one with him, and the disturbance was caused by false accusers—who really should be there to make a case if they had one.

Felix deferred judgment, waiting for Lysias the Roman commander. After several days, Paul was called before Felix again. During the interview he talked about righteousness, self-control, and the judgment to come. This convicted Felix, and he responded by sending Paul away.[23] However, Luke states that he really hoped Paul would give him a bribe to dismiss the case. Felix also wanted to do the Jews a favor, so Paul was kept in prison. Over the next two years, Felix would talk with Paul but would not release him.

PAUL IS ARRAIGNED BEFORE FESTUS

Read Acts 25–26.

After two years (in 59 CE) Porcius Festus replaced Felix as governor. Soon after taking office, he had occasion to go up to Jerusalem. The Jewish leaders had not forgotten the case. Frustrated with Felix's handling of the situation, they began accusing Paul as soon as they had an audience with the new governor. They suggested that Paul be brought up to Jerusalem for trial (planning an ambush en route).

Festus responded wisely that Paul was safely locked up in Caesarea. Since Festus would be returning there shortly, he suggested that the Jews come down to Caesarea with him. When they got back to Caesarea, Paul was brought before him. This time the accusers showed up, and they made a number of wild accusations that were impossible to prove.

Like his predecessor, Festus wanted to win the favor of the leaders he governed. At the same time he wanted to be just in his administration (or at least appear so). Apparently, he thought that a trial in Jerusalem would resolve the issue. So he asked Paul if he would be willing for a trial in Jerusalem with Festus as the judge.

It may be that Paul had been given further revelation from God on what the Jews planned. It may be that he was just tired of the games being played. It may be that he had been talking to a Roman lawyer about his rights. In any case, he demanded his right as a Roman citizen for a trial before Caesar. This request took the case out of Festus's hands. After conferring with his advisors, he forwarded the case to Caesar.

A few days later King Agrippa and his wife, Bernice, arrived.[24] Festus talked about the case with Agrippa, since it somewhat affected his realm. Interestingly, Festus observed that the only accusations the Jewish leaders had were religious matters, including the question over whether Jesus had been resurrected. With this simple statement, Festus drove to the heart of the matter (see 1 Cor. 15:12–19). Agrippa stated that he would like to talk to the man, and a meeting was arranged.

Paul was brought before Agrippa. Festus publicly recapped what had happened, noting that while the case was going to Caesar, he didn't know what to write regarding "charges." So the purpose of the hearing was ostensibly to draft a letter about the case to send to Caesar.

In his speech, Paul addressed Agrippa. It was basically a reiteration of his testimony, explaining how he went from being a zealous Pharisee who persecuted followers of "the Way" to being a follower himself. He culminated his defense with the observation that he was on trial solely for asserting what Moses and the prophets had said—"that the Christ [Messiah] would suffer and, as the first to rise from the dead, would proclaim light to his own people and to the Gentiles" (Acts 26:23).

Because he had appealed to Caesar, Paul needed to go to Rome.

At this point Festus exclaimed that Paul was mad. Paul responded that he was not mad, and he was sure that Agrippa was aware of the truth of what he had said. Agrippa dodged that question by asserting that Paul was trying to make him a Christian. Paul agreed, and actually stated that he desired that everyone who was listening would become Christians.

The assembly recessed, and Agrippa told Festus that Paul had done nothing that required further imprisonment. Because he had appealed to Caesar, however, he needed to go to Rome.

PAUL SAILS TO ROME

After this, it was just a question of arranging transportation. Julius, the Roman centurion in charge, seemed to show special favor toward Paul although he had a number of other prisoners. Somehow Luke went along as did Aristarchus from

Read Acts 27:1–28:16.

FAIR HAVENS. A harbor on the south side of Crete where Paul stayed during his journey to Rome, although— despite the name—it was not a safe place to stay during the winter. Paul's ship tried to reach Phoenix, also in Crete, to stay there instead.

Thessalonica (see above, n. 14). But we are not told if any of the others who came to Jerusalem with Paul were still there. Most likely Timothy and the rest had returned to their ministry positions in Asia, Macedonia, and Achaia.

Finally, in late summer of 59 CE, the group set sail. They took the route up the coast, touching in at Tyre, passing Cyprus, and then disembarking in Myra in Lycia, along the southern coast of modern Turkey. There they caught a ship from Alexandria headed for Rome. Because of headwinds, they did not make the desired progress, and they ended up at a place called Fair Havens in Crete. As the bad weather continued, they were delayed further. Sailing season ended, and still the crew endeavored to continue on.[25] Paul warned them that he had been given revelation that the ship and cargo would be lost if they continued, although there would be no loss of life.

The ship's crew disagreed. The harbor they were in was too small to winter over, and the crew felt they could still beat the winter storms at least for a short trip. Julius listened to the crew rather than to Paul. So they decided to sail on to Phoenix, a distance of about fifty miles and normally a one-day sail. They would have liked to spend the winter there.

However, even though they sailed close to the shore, they got caught by what Luke called a "northeaster" (Acts 27:14; NASB, "Euraquilo"). Caught by strong winds, the ship could only sail before them. Soon they were in a storm. They had to jettison some of the cargo to keep afloat. Later, they threw over the tackle to make the ship as light as possible. For fourteen days they were driven by the storm. Everyone but Paul feared for their lives. He told them that an angel had come in the night to assure him that he would indeed stand trial before Caesar.

After two weeks the seasoned sailors began to suspect that they were near land. They took soundings and found that to be true. They then thought to sneak off in the ship's boat under the guise of setting a sea anchor, but Paul warned

Julius. The centurion and soldiers cut away the boat. Paul encouraged all to eat something. When daylight arrived, they finished jettisoning the cargo and tried to drive the ship into a bay. Instead they hit a reef. As the ship began to break up, the soldiers planned to kill the prisoners. But Julius would not allow that because he wanted to protect Paul. So all 276 on the ship made it safely to shore—some by swimming, others by holding on to boards or other debris.

Ashore, they found that they were on Malta, a small island south of Sicily. The inhabitants of the island were very helpful and built a large fire where the survivors could warm up from the cold and the rain. Everyone must have pitched in to gather wood, including Paul. While he was bringing in some wood, a viper bit his hand. The natives thought that this was the judgment of God showing that he had committed a horrendous crime, but Paul shook the snake off into the fire and suffered no ill effects. With this, they began to think that he was a god.

Their admiration increased when he healed the father of Publius, one of the leaders of the island. Others were brought to Paul for healing, and he cured them all. Because of this, they honored Paul and his associates, meeting all of their needs.

PAUL'S VOYAGE TO ROME.

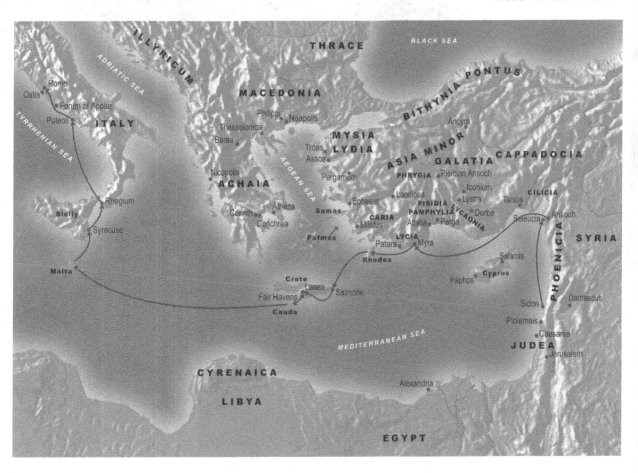

ROMAN HOUSE. An excavated structure in Pompeii, near Naples, which is very likely more elegant than the place where Paul spent two years in house imprisonment in Rome.

After three months, they caught a ship to Sicily and then up the Italian coast to Puteoli. There they found some believers and spent time with them. They traveled by land from there, arriving in Rome about the end of February in 60 CE.

PAUL'S FIRST STAY IN ROME

Read Acts 28:17–31. After two years in prison and a long arduous journey, Paul had reached his destination. However, he was still a prisoner. He called for local Jewish leaders, who came to visit him. He told them why he was there. They had received no word from Jerusalem so were willing to listen to him. They came back on a later date when he gave his full gospel presentation. Some believed, but others refused. Paul warned them that the gospel would be going to the Gentiles as a result.

With this, Luke abruptly concludes his book with a summary statement that Paul was in prison in Rome for two years. We do have some evidence for what happened during that period and after his release, although it comes from Paul's letters and early church sources.

REVIEW QUESTIONS

1. Why did Paul write the letter to the Romans?

2. What did Paul have to say in Romans about sin, salvation, and what it meant to be saved?

3. Why is Israel an issue in the book of Romans?

4. Why did Paul go to Jerusalem?

5. Why was there a riot in Jerusalem?

6. Why did Paul end up in Caesarea?

7. Why did Paul appeal to Caesar?

8. Trace Paul's journey to Rome.

26

CHAPTER

Rome and Beyond

OVERVIEW

Paul remained in Rome for two years as a prisoner. During that time he wrote a number of letters, of which four are in the canon. We begin this chapter with overviews of Philemon, Colossians, Ephesians, and Philippians and then discover what happened to Paul and the rest of the apostles.

STUDY GOALS

▶ Summarize Paul's two-year imprisonment in Rome.

▶ Develop the message of Philemon.

▶ Develop the message of Colossians.

▶ Develop the message of Ephesians.

▶ Develop the message of Philippians.

▶ Trace the fate of Paul and the other apostles, which brought the apostolic age to an end.

L uke ended Acts abruptly with a summary statement that Paul was in prison in Rome for two years, probably from February of 60 to March of 62 CE.[1] This gives us an approximate date for the writing of the book.[2] It also suggests that Luke's purpose for writing the book of Acts was associated with Paul's imprisonment. If so, it likely contained information that was to be used in Paul's defense before Caesar.

However, that trial evidently did not take place. Paul was in prison for two years and then released.[3] Apparently, Paul was released without a trial. Paul was taken to Rome by the Roman guard. The trial could not be conducted, however, until the accusers arrived. They were the leaders of the Jewish hierarchy. It would seem that they had already learned before Felix and Festus that the Romans did not think they had a case. Therefore, it would not have been to their benefit to have a trial—especially an early one. So it is presumed that they stalled and eventually just didn't show up. Although this meant that Paul was released, he had been out of circulation for about four years.

Although Luke does not tell us much about this time in prison, we can glean a few pieces of information from other sources. This is enough to suggest that Paul was basically under house arrest rather than in a cell. Roman soldiers guarded him, and he had to rent the quarters, but he was able to receive visitors freely. He was also able to write letters. Apparently, he wrote a number of letters to different churches over the two-year period. Four of those were preserved and became part of our canon. Because they were written during this period of imprisonment, they are often called the Prison Epistles. They are Ephesians, Colossians, Philemon, and Philippians. The first three seem to have been written at the same time, since they were sent to the same geographical area (Asia) and mentioned the same

A LEGAL BRIEF

Several factors suggest that the material in the book of Acts was used to defend Paul in Rome. The book focuses on only two apostles, Peter and Paul. It clearly has an agenda, showing that what we call Christianity began with the ascension of Jesus and gradually spread throughout the world. But it basically covers only the efforts of Paul and ignores the other apostles except where they directly intersect Paul's work. In the process, Acts illustrates how the conflict between Paul and the Jewish leaders was over the question of whether Jesus was the Messiah. It also points out how the messiahship of Jesus was not a conflict with Caesar. Rather, those who followed "the Way" were hardworking, solid citizens. It shows how the civil problems associated with Christianity really developed from the conduct of others who misunderstood or resented Christians.

Finally, Acts is the last half of an interesting dual work. If Luke was written while Paul was in prison in Caesarea, it may well have given information for a trial before the governor. In contrast, Acts was written in Rome during the imprisonment of Paul. In Acts, Luke carefully presented data about Paul as the representative of Jesus up to the time of his Roman imprisonment, where he awaited his trial. When the trial did not occur, he added a hasty addendum to explain what Paul did while he was in Rome (Acts 28:30–31). With that, copies of the book were made for the benefit of churches who wanted to know more about how the church began.

courier. Philippians was written near the end of the imprisonment as Paul anticipated his release.

PAUL'S LETTER TO PHILEMON

Given the circumstances, the letter to Philemon provided the opportunity for the letters to the Ephesians and Colossians. In terms of content, it certainly is the shortest and the most straightforward. Its purpose was specific—to reconcile Philemon with his slave Onesimus. It was probably written late in 61 CE.[4] The letter was addressed to Philemon, a wealthy man who lived in Colosse. Paul also addressed the letter to Apphia and Archippus as well as to the house church that met in Philemon's house. Apphia was probably Philemon's wife, and Archippus was possibly his son. The subject matter seems somewhat private, but since the entire house church was included as addressees, we may conclude that they read it also. In actuality, the letter conveyed an important practical implication of the messiahship of Jesus. As such, its message is timeless.

Read Philemon 1–25.

The primary purpose of the letter was to intercede on the behalf of a runaway slave. In the Roman Empire at that time, there were millions of slaves. Onesimus was one who had run away from his owner, Philemon. He had made it to Rome, where he met Paul. Through Paul, Onesimus became a believer in the messiahship of Jesus. Now he was returning to his master, carrying Paul's letter. He and his traveling companions probably also carried the letters to the Ephesians and the Colossians en route.[5]

Onesimus was taking a physical risk in returning. In the Roman world the standard treatment for runaway slaves was execution. Paul asked Philemon to treat the willingly returning slave humanely, recognizing that he was now a brother in Christ. In the process, he never asked for Onesimus to be released.[6] In fact, the letter to Philemon must be read in the context of both Ephesians and Colossians, which were written at the same time. In both letters

> In the Roman world the standard treatment for runaway slaves was execution.

WHO WAS ARCHIPPUS?

The relationship of Archippus to Philemon is very uncertain. The two most likely suggestions are that he was Philemon's son and that he was a pastor. The former is more likely, given the structure of the letter's opening. It is clear that Archippus had some type of leadership position or pastoral relationship, as mentioned in Colossians 4:17, "Tell Archippus: 'See to it that you complete the work [diakonia] you have received in the Lord.'" However, we are not really sure what Paul meant. The word he used is related to the term for deacon. If Archippus was a pastor, we would have expected Paul to have used one of the words denoting the work of overseeing (cf. the terms presbyter and elder). Moreover, at this time the concept of pastor had not developed in the strong professional sense that we think of today.

he instructed slaves to obey their masters and masters to treat their slaves humanely (see sidebar below).

Although all he asked of Philemon was to take Onesimus back, there were two points of grace attached. The first would be that, in the process, Philemon would have to overlook the act of running away. Second, he would be taking Onesimus back as a fellow believer in the messiahship of Jesus, that is, as a spiritual brother. In a broader perspective, the first point of grace put Christian slave owners on notice that within the context of their relationship with God, they would be expected to live up to higher standards in their treatment of slaves. This second point of grace would ultimately lead to the abolition of slavery. Unfortunately, it would take centuries for it to actually become effective.

SLAVERY AND CHRISTIANITY

Slavery was a major social force in the Roman Empire, just as it has been for most cultures throughout history. For the Roman aristocracy, manual labor was considered demeaning, but they had large villas and farms that were labor intensive. As such, slavery was a key driving force of the economy. Many of the slaves were military captives, although there were slave markets and a slave trade. How did Paul approach the situation of slaves who were part of the church?

To the church in Ephesus, he wrote: "Slaves, obey your earthly masters with respect and fear, and with sincerity of heart, just as you would obey Christ. Obey them not only to win their favor when their eye is on you, but like slaves of Christ, doing the will of God from your heart. Serve wholeheartedly, as if you were serving the Lord, not men, because you know that the Lord will reward everyone for whatever good he does, whether he is slave or free. And masters, treat your slaves in the same way" (Eph. 6:5–9). Similarly to the church in Colosse he wrote: "Slaves, obey your earthly masters in everything; and do it, not only when their eye is on you and to win their favor, but with sincerity of heart and reverence for the Lord. Whatever you do, work at it with all your heart, as working for the Lord, not for men, since you know that you will receive an inheritance from the Lord as a reward. It is the Lord Christ you are serving. Anyone who does wrong will be repaid for his wrong, and there is no favoritism. Masters, provide your slaves with what is right and fair, because you know that you also have a Master in heaven" (Col. 3:22–4:1). While Paul argued that if a slave had an opportunity for freedom, he should take it (1 Cor. 7:21), in general terms he maintained that slaves should continue in the position in which they came to belief in Jesus and be the best persons they could be under those circumstances.

Slavery per se seemed to virtually disappear in the Roman world under the influence of Christianity once it became the official religion. However, there have been hints of it throughout the medieval period. The feudal system often became a de facto slavery in that peasants were tied to the land. True slavery returned within certain venues with the expansion to the New World, but that was in the context of a world slave trade. The abolishment of slavery in the nineteenth century came about largely from looking at the implications of the claims of Jesus as the Messiah—one of the results of the revivals in England and America under Jonathan Edwards, John and Charles Wesley, and George Whitefield. Generally speaking, the abolition of slavery has been a peculiarly Christian phenomenon.

PAUL'S LETTER TO THE COLOSSIANS

The letter to the Colossians was written to believers in Colosse, a city in Asia Minor that lay about a hundred miles to the east of Ephesus. A number of people are mentioned in both Colossians and Ephesians as sending greetings. This correlation suggests that the two letters were written about the same time.[7] While the return of Onesimus provided an opportunity for delivering correspondence, the letter was prompted by news from a messenger named Epaphras. He had carried to Paul in Rome news of a "false gospel" that was hurting the church in Colosse. Paul told the church how to respond.

Read Colossians 1 – 4.

> Paul was concerned that the Colossians clearly understand that Jesus was divine

Although Paul had never visited the city, it would appear that the church there was founded during or shortly before Paul's ministry in Ephesus, almost ten years earlier. The probable founder was the same Epaphras who was now in Rome (see Col. 1:7).

The issue of the book of Colossians was the nature of Jesus the Messiah. Paul focused on the hope we have in Jesus (see Col. 1:4 – 5, where Paul noted that he had heard of the Colossians' faith and love, and that while their hope was laid up in heaven, it seemed weak). Paul was concerned about their hope in the light of the false or "new gospels" that were springing up.

The "new gospels" that were becoming a concern in Colosse included three key features. First, they proposed a false view of Jesus. Paul was concerned that the Colossians clearly understand that Jesus was divine (Col. 1:15 – 19). He was a physical manifestation of the invisible, spiritual God. He was the creator of the entire cosmos, including all the power structures. Interestingly, Paul included here the invisible, behind-the-scenes spiritual forces. Jesus was also the one who

COLOSSE. One of the cities to whom Paul sent a letter. Today the city is just an unexcavated mound.

held the entire cosmos together. He was the head of the church, and through His resurrection had reconciled the world to God. Because of this, Paul assured the Colossians that while they had formerly been alienated from God, they now had been reconciled by the physical body of the Messiah (note the emphasis on the physical reality).[8] Paul warned the Colossians that if they went after this false gospel, they would not have hope.

Second, false gospels placed an emphasis on philosophy, that is, on human logic (Col. 2:8). Actually, rational inferences are not wrong if valid logical processes are followed and correct premises are used as a foundation. Here the false teachers were using invalid premises. Paul warned against those wrong assumptions, which he called "human tradition and the basic principles of this world."[9] Some of the basic premises that the Colossians needed to watch out for included a failure to recognize the deity of the Messiah, and a supposition that there were no lifestyle implications to one's belief that Jesus was the Messiah.

However, having said that, Paul hastened on to the third problem of the false gospels: a supposition that the lifestyle implications were imposed from the outside rather than expressing an inner reality. These outside impositions included strains of legalism, mysticism, and asceticism (2:16, 18, 20). There is perhaps a fine distinction between (a) realizing that life as one who believes in Jesus as the Messiah has lifestyle implications and (b) putting rules on life to define belief.

Paul asserted that the antidote to these false gospels was twofold. The antidote to false philosophy and teaching was a correct understanding of who Jesus the Messiah was. The antidote to the various "isms" was a correct understanding of the implications of that belief in their lifestyles. Because of the nature of the problem, the first half of Colossians is more theoretical than some of Paul's other letters.

The last half of Colossians is very practical. It addresses the implications of Jesus the Messiah as Redeemer for a believer's own life and relationships with others (3:1–4:6). Paul argued for what we might call mindset. Rather than focusing on the things of this world, like jobs, wealth, and so forth, the believers should be maintaining an eternal perspective. With this mindset, the believer would eradicate everything that would draw him or her away from God. Obviously this includes issues of immorality. But Paul also included things such as anger, lying, and filthy language. This was not a negative picture, since Paul asserted that believers should put in their place things such as compassion, kindness, humility, gentleness, and patience. In other words, believers are to become the type of people that everyone really admires.

> ### NO DISTINCTIONS?
>
> The point that Paul seems to be making in Colossians 3:11 is that in terms of humankind's approach to God and characteristics of a new life in relationship to Him through the Messiah, there were no distinctions. However, in terms of roles, there were and would continue to be differences. This approach would seem to add insight to what Paul stated in Galatians 3:28, where he included "male/female" among distinctions that do not exist in Jesus. This would be an important principle that Paul would use later in his pastoral epistles when he addressed questions of church leadership.

This theme provided Paul his transition to areas of relationship. He addressed three basic areas: husband/wife; parent/child; and slave/master.[10] Interestingly, in each he only addressed responsibilities, which differed for each role. One might have expected some mention of advantages. When we look at these relationships, we should also note that Paul laid down those role requirements right after he asserted that there are no distinctions in the Messiah (Col. 3:11). Clearly, there were and are differences in roles, and differing responsibilities within those roles.

Paul suggested that much of what he was addressing fell under what he called "the mystery of the Messiah." The idea of mystery was something that had been unclear (perhaps only partially revealed) in ages past. Now, however, Paul asserted

that it had been clarified by the coming of the Messiah. That was the content of his message. He asked for prayer that God would continue to open a door for this message so that others might hear it (we need to remember that Paul was still in prison). Paul would expand on this concept in his letter to the church in Ephesus.

PAUL'S LETTER TO THE EPHESIANS

Read Ephesians 1–6.

As we have already noted, the letter to the Ephesians was probably written at the same time as Colossians and Philemon, and carried by the same messengers.[11] Its message was somewhat similar to that of Colossians, but there were significant differences.

Paul had a special relationship with the church in Ephesus. He had essentially founded the church during his third missionary journey almost ten years earlier. He had also spent more than two years working with the believers there. Perhaps as a consequence, the church in Ephesus seemed to have had a more solid foundation than many of the other churches.

Most of the letters we have seen addressed major problems within the churches. That was not the case in Ephesians. Rather than correcting error, Paul in this letter encouraged a congregation whose founding pastor was in prison for his faith. He did so by reviewing the Christian hope. This aspect is evident in Ephesians 1:15–18, where Paul stressed the soundness of their faith and love but emphasized his prayer that they might know their hope.

While the church had a solid foundation, there was still room for improvement. We remember that the last time Paul had been in Ephesus (about five years earlier), he left after the riot of Demetrius and the silversmiths. That social unrest surely had an influence on the church. Paul also anticipated encroachment of the false gospels coming in from the region of Colosse. So even as he encouraged, Paul exhorted. The letter was designed to be a circular letter passed among the various house churches in the Ephesus area.[12] It would also subsequently be copied by other churches, illustrating the process by which the NT canon was developed.

Paul included two key concepts in the book. The first is the phrase "in the heavenlies," which is used at least five times.[13] The term refers to the spiritual realm where Paul saw the hope of the church. That is where Jesus is now located. As such, it was where the church was now established because he was the foundation of its hope. The second key phrase of the book is unity. This theme is coupled with the admonition in Ephesians 4:14–16, where Paul stresses increased love. This feature would suggest that if the primary purpose of the letter was to increase hope, a secondary issue was to demonstrate increased love and thus unity.

> Rather than correcting error, as he did in most of his letters, Paul in Ephesians encouraged a congregation whose founding pastor was in prison for his faith.

Paul began with praise to God. In the process he expounded tremendously on who God is. This initial passage is very close to an OT descriptive praise psalm.[14] The praise of God naturally flowed into praise of Jesus the Messiah. Paul then declared that he thanked God for the Ephesians because of the position they had in Jesus, which he had just described.

From here, Paul reminded the Ephesians of their past. Historically, they had been just like the rest of the world, dead in their sins and subject to the ruler of this world.[15] As such, the key work of Christ was a new creation. This was the hope that Paul wanted the Ephesians to be aware of (1:18). In the process, Paul emphasized two key points of this new creation: it was by grace through faith (2:8–9), and it was to lead to a fruitful lifestyle (2:10). The two were intertwined.

This new creation, the church, incorporated both Jews and Gentiles. As such, the barrier between the two was broken down (2:14). The result should then be a unified church, one that demonstrates a unity far beyond anything the world could comprehend. Paul described this entire process as a mystery, namely, that the Gentiles will become fellow heirs of the Jews. We saw this theme in Romans and will see it again elsewhere.[16]

As was the case with Colossians, the last half of the book addresses the implications of the theological truths contained in the first half. These are all lifestyle issues in three general areas. First, within the church, he exhorted that there be unity (Eph. 4:1–16). This unity would be based on an understanding of the Holy Spirit and His works. It focused on the use of spiritual gifts, which reminds us of 1 Corinthians 12 and Romans 14.

Second, he exhorted the believers to pursue a holy lifestyle (Eph. 4:17–5:21). As Paul presented this instruction, it was a reminder that they were to be different from their culture. Their lifestyle would be characterized by a new mindset (that is, positive values) and a resistance to evil or sin. Personal holiness was

RACETRACK. A racetrack in the city of Aphrodisias in Asia Minor, symbolic of Paul's frequent use of the image of an athlete running a race. Note that the track is a straight line, not an oval, as is common today.

crucial to the unity of the church. This theme again reminds us of what he had to say to the Romans (Rom. 12).

Third, Paul addressed personal relationships (Eph. 5:22–6:20). He set forth four areas where these concepts are to be exhibited. Three of those were relationships mentioned in Colossians—husband/wife, parent/child, and slave/master—and these same concepts were repeated in Ephesians. The fourth was very important, and that was the relationship of the individual believer with the spiritual forces of Satan. Paul stressed the warfare aspect of that relationship. In the process, he used the illustration of a well-fitted Roman soldier to describe the resources that a believer has. The key weapon was prayer, and he again asked for prayer for his own ministry.

PAUL'S LETTER TO THE PHILIPPIANS

Read Philippians 1–4.

Sometime later, Paul wrote a letter to the church in Philippi. A man from that church named Epaphroditus had delivered a contribution to Paul on behalf of the Philippians. He was now about to return. Paul used that occasion to write a thank-you letter to the Philippians for their help, not only for their financial aid but also for "lending" Epaphroditus to him.

Epaphroditus had become sick during the journey or visit, and Paul also addressed the concerns of the church regarding his health (Phil. 2:26–27).[17] A secondary motive was to encourage that church to continue in its growth. He talked about their love (1:9) and their faith (1:27). He did not mention the term *hope*, apparently seeing that as solidly based (for an example, see Philippians 1:6, where he expresses his confidence in them).

Near the end of his imprisonment, Paul seems to have been encouraged. His imprisonment had actually helped the promulgation of the gospel, and for that he was thankful and content. Interestingly, he acknowledged that some of the gospel proclamation was a result of wrong motives. But Paul did not worry about their motives. Rather, he suggested that the motive was not as crucial as the result of men and women being saved. But at the same time, he pointed out that his prayer was that the Philippians would all continue to grow in love.

Like always, as he encouraged the church to continue to grow in love and to progress in the faith, Paul gave them exhortations regarding lifestyle. First, he encouraged them to have the right motivation, which came out of humility. Paul saw that motivation illustrated by Jesus the Messiah when He became a man.[18]

THE DATE OF PHILIPPIANS

At the time of writing Philippians, Paul seemed to anticipate his release from prison (see Phil. 1:19), although he also recognized that his position continued to be precarious. In 1:20–26, he prepared the Philippians for either possibility, yet even there he seemed to be confident of his release. If indeed this letter was written relatively close to the time when he was freed from prison, the probable date is the spring of 62 CE.

Here Paul very clearly states that prior to the incarnation, Jesus the Messiah had preexisted in the form of God. Even so, He not only stooped to became a man but also endured the death on the cross. Consequently, some day everyone would acknowledge His sovereignty, including both human and spiritual beings.

After Paul exhorted the Philippians to model the same humility, he turned their attention to Timothy and Epaphroditus. Epaphroditus was now healthy, and Paul was sending him back with his thanks. Timothy would be coming as soon as Paul knew the outcome of his legal issues.

When Paul had been in Philippi initially, his problems had been with the Gentiles. Subsequently Judaizers had begun to oppose the gospel the Philippians had heard from Paul.[19] Paul was very strong in his opinion of them. He called them "dogs" and "mutilators of the flesh" (Phil. 3:2; for the latter expression, the NASB has "the false circumcision"). He placed them in the same category as he had placed the Judaizers of Galatians. However, after fifteen years of debate, he now used much stronger terminology. To prove his point, Paul gave a brief biographical sketch. This account showed that if anyone had reason to be confident about his security as an observant Jew, it was Paul. But he had come to realize that all of his credentials were worthless compared to the value of knowing Jesus as the Messiah, who provided righteousness through faith.

For this reason, Paul had set his goal to know Jesus more perfectly. He recognized that in this world that would involve persecution and suffering. He also recognized that he was imperfect and that improvement was a lifelong project. Paul encouraged the Philippians to join him in common pursuit of that goal because there were many who opposed the entire concept. Their destiny, however, was destruction, since they were focused on this world, which would be destroyed.

Drawing on the same ideas that he had conveyed to the Ephesians, Paul reminded the Philippians that they were really citizens of a heavenly realm. They eagerly awaited for Jesus to return. But in the interim, they were to live lifestyles deserving of that title. Here Paul gave several specific examples. Euodia and Syntyche were to stop fighting. The Philippians should rejoice. They should be gentle to others. They should not worry. They should guard their thoughts and concentrate on more noble things.

Paul was glad because of what the gift represented in the lives of the believers in Philippi.

Finally, Paul got around to thanking the Philippians for their gift. God had been supplying Paul's needs, and he was not worried. However, he was glad because of what the gift represented in the lives of the believers in Philippi.

WHAT HAPPENED TO THE APOSTLES?

Probably in the spring of 62, Paul was released from prison. He returned to Asia and Greece and then apparently made it to Spain. He again returned to Greece, where he was again arrested.[20] During the same year Peter arrived in Rome. He apparently spent the rest of his life there.

THE EXPANSION OF CHRISTIANITY IN THE FIRST CENTURY CE. The areas marked indicate the regions where the apostles are reported to have worked and ministered. Mesopotamia and India are not shown.

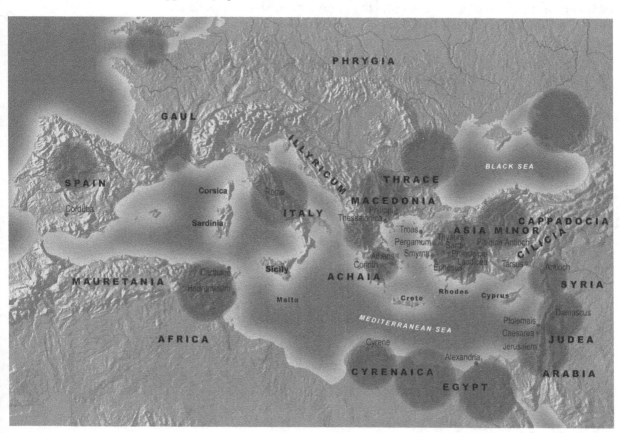

About this time, James, the half brother of Jesus who had been heading up the church in Jerusalem, was executed. Apparently this was a result of a plot by the Sanhedrin after Festus died and before the new governor arrived in Judea.[21]

In fact, the decade of the sixties was a crucial one for the church. Persecution increased tremendously under Nero. Most of the remaining apostles were martyred. The Judeans revolted against Rome, and Jerusalem was burned. Most of this is recorded outside the NT, but some of the effects show up in the books that were yet to be written. Before we look at those last books, we want to present an overview of the rest of the apostles.[22]

> The decade of the sixties was a crucial one for the church: persecution increased under Nero, apostles were martyred, the Judeans revolted against Rome, and Jerusalem was burned.

Peter

From the book of Acts, we know that Peter was the early leader of the church. He was also probably the first apostle to leave Jerusalem. We saw that he left the area during the persecution after Stephen's death. Around 40 CE. he went to Lydda, Joppa, and Caesarea, where he saw God reach out to the Gentiles. He returned to Jerusalem but left after James, the brother of John, was executed in 44 (Acts 11:2; cf. 12:1–3; 12:17). Sometime during the next five years or so, he made it up to Antioch. Then in 49, he was back in Jerusalem at the Jerusalem Council. There he defended the incorporation of Gentiles into the church. Later, while Paul was in Ephesus, he journeyed to Corinth. In the late fifties he apparently traveled east into Babylonia, home of many of the exiled Jews. Finally, he made it to Rome, where he was executed in about 64 CE.

BUST OF NERO. One of the first Roman emperors to persecute Christians. This bust from Corinth is of the young Nero.

James Son of Zebedee

This James was the brother of John. The two of them were sons of Zebedee and were fishermen together. Jesus called them Boanerges, which means, "Sons of Thunder." They, along with Peter, constituted a special inner circle. For example,

---

FROM BABYLON TO ENGLAND?

William Steuart McBirnie places Peter's trip to Babylon in the forties. This may be possible, but it seems more likely that Peter went later in his ministry. As McBirnie notes, there is unified evidence from the eastern churches that Peter ministered in Mesopotamia (*Search*, 56–57). He also discusses the possibility that Peter actually made it to England. There is strong anecdotal evidence to that effect, but nothing solid. Still, he concludes that "there certainly is no reason why Peter could not have visited Great Britain. Many believe he did" (*Search*, 61). His major point in favor of the idea is that Britain had long had a strong civilization (dating back to the Phoenicians). However, the available evidence does not seem strong enough to include it in Peter's itinerary.

they were the three who went with Jesus to the mountain where He was transfigured (Matt. 17:1). Perhaps it was because of this close relationship that their mother asked that they sit on Jesus' left and right hand in His kingdom (Matt. 20:20–28).

We have little information about James's activities after the resurrection of Jesus. He was part of the eleven in Jerusalem. There is some tradition that after the persecution resulting from the stoning of Stephen, he traveled to Spain.[23] James and Peter were arrested in 44. Herod had James put to death, after which an angel delivered Peter (Acts 12:1–12). James was thus the first of the apostles to be martyred.

John Son of Zebedee

John was the brother of James, and the third member of the inner circle. He also had a close relationship with Jesus and was called "the disciple that Jesus loved."[24]

HIERAPOLIS. The major city between Colosse and Ephesus in Asia Minor, not far from Laodicea.

When Jesus was on the cross, He had John take over the responsibility of caring for His mother (John 19:25–27).

After the resurrection, John and Peter were closely associated in the early activities of the church. For example, they were the two involved in the healing of the lame man in the temple (Acts 3).

After some time in Jerusalem, he moved to Ephesus.[25] There he supervised the Ephesian church (which means that he took the place once occupied by Paul and then Timothy). There he spent most of his later years before being exiled to Patmos. After the exile was over, he returned to Ephesus. There is no record of how John died. Given the time frame, it was probably of old age.

Andrew

Andrew was the brother of Peter. According to John 1:40, Andrew followed Jesus first, and brought his brother to him. He was soon outshone by his more outgoing brother. In the gospel accounts, he does not hold a significant role. Both he and Peter were fishermen and seemed to travel together. According to John 6:8, Andrew was the one who brought the lad with the loaves and fishes to Jesus. That lunch became the meal for the five thousand. In John 12:22, Andrew and Philip brought the Greeks to Jesus in the week before the crucifixion.

After the resurrection, Andrew's life is obscure. Eusebius[26] states that Andrew had a ministry to Scythia, the region north of the Black Sea (in what is now

southern Russia/Ukraine). Other evidence points to Greece or Macedonia. Both are likely. The main traditions have him dying in Patros, Greece, as a martyr in about 69.[27]

Philip

According to John 1, Jesus found Philip the day after He met Peter and Andrew. He was from the same hometown, Bethsaida. Jesus asked Philip to follow Him, and at that point Philip went to get Nathanael (who was probably a friend). He is not mentioned in the Gospels much beyond that. According to John, Jesus asked Philip, "Where shall we buy bread for these people to eat?" before He fed the five thousand (John 6:5). Philip the apostle should not be confused with Philip the evangelist, one of the deacons who left Jerusalem and then preached to the Samaritans and to the Ethiopian eunuch and settled in Caesarea.

Legend has it that after leaving Jerusalem, Philip the apostle traveled to Scythia, north of the Black Sea, where he preached for twenty years; there is other evidence that he traveled to South France (Gaul).[28] From there he moved into Asia Minor in Phrygia, settling in the city of Hierapolis, about six miles from Laodicea and twelve miles from Colosse. Papias is quoted as visiting Philip's daughters there (see *ANF*, 1:154). He apparently died in Hierapolis as a martyr at the age of 87.[29] This would place his death near the end of the first century (ca. 85), assuming that he was in his thirties when called by Jesus.

Bartholomew (Nathanael)

He is listed as Bartholomew in the Synoptic Gospels and in Acts but is not mentioned again in the NT. His name is always associated with Philip. In John's gospel we see Philip associated with Nathanael, who is not included in the other lists. These details suggest that Bartholomew and Nathanael are the same. Beyond his introduction to Jesus by Philip, the only other occasion he is noted is when he went fishing with Peter (John 21:2).

In terms of tradition, Bartholomew has been credited with going to India.[30] One of the more interesting items attributed to him was that he took a Hebrew (or Aramaic) Gospel of Matthew with him. After returning from India, he is credited with ministering in Armenia (south of the Caspian Sea—modern Azerbaijan). He was beheaded there in about 68.[31]

Thomas (Didymus)

The name Didymus means "twin," but we have no information about his sibling. He is most noted for his questioning attitude, which was evident especially after the resurrection. From this we get the epithet "Doubting Thomas."

After the resurrection, Thomas traveled east. According to some accounts, he visited Babylon with Bartholomew and Judas Thaddaeus. At this time Babylon still had a large Jewish community, although little is known of Christian activities there. While Bartholomew traveled either to Persia or western India, Thomas continued on to Malabar in South India in approximately 50 CE. Apparently he died in Mylapore, near Madras, as a martyr (spear-thrust). The date was probably 63.

Matthew (Levi)

Because Matthew was the writer of a gospel, we seem to have somewhat more information about him than about many of the apostles. Called later than the initial disciples, Matthew was a tax collector before he became an apostle. Mark 2:14 calls him Levi son of Alpheus, so he may have been the brother of James the Less (cf. 3:18).

After Jesus' resurrection, apparently Matthew remained in Palestine for about fifteen years (until about the time of the Jerusalem Council). He then seems to have traveled extensively, being credited with having gone to Ethiopia, Macedonia (Greece), Syria, and Persia (Iran).[32] Apparently he died in Egypt, probably in Alexandria, upon his return from Ethiopia, but the date is unknown.

THOMAS THE TRAVELER

When early Portuguese explorers reached Malabar in the late fifteenth century, they found Christian churches that traced their origin back to Thomas. Unfortunately, the explorers deemed the group heretical and destroyed their historical records (McBirnie, *Search*, 168). Some accounts suggest that Thomas may have reached as far as China (ibid., 159). This would be feasible, since there is serious evidence of Jewish communities in China at the time (Sidney Shapiro, *Jews in Old China* [New York: Hippocrene Books, 1984]). There is no solid evidence of when Thomas died. The closest estimate places his death in the thirtieth year of "the promulgation of the gospel." Given that the resurrection and beginning of the church were in 33, that would place his death in 63.

James Son of Alpheus (James the Less)

This James was apparently the brother of Matthew and the same James described as "the less" (Mark 15:40 KJV; the NIV translates, "the younger"), probably to distinguish him from the more renown James son of Zebedee. Beyond this, we know very little about him. He apparently ministered in Syria, but there is no indication of the location. It seems that he died by stoning. The date is unknown.

Judas (Thaddaeus)

Judas (the Greek form of Judah) was a fairly common name, and there were two disciples among the Twelve who bore it: Judas Iscariot and Judas son of James (Luke 6:16; Acts 1:13). The latter is apparently the same disciple that Matthew and Mark call Thaddaeus. He is noted in the Gospels for one incident. During the Last Supper, when Jesus was encouraging His disciples, he was the one who asked, "But, Lord, why do you intend to show yourself to us and not to the world?" (John 14:22, where he is identifed as Judas "not Judas Iscariot").

There is not much information about him. Early traditions suggest that he traveled through Armenia, Syria, Arabia, Mesopotamia, and Persia. He was martyred in Syria in about 66.

Simon the Zealot

This Simon was viewed as a radical patriot of Judea. Not much is said about him in the NT. The tradition is that when he left Jerusalem, he headed southeast to Egypt. He then went to Libya and across North Africa. There is strong tradition that he went on to Britain and that he made this journey with Joseph of Arimathea.[33] He returned to Persia, where he traveled with Judas (Jude) son of James. He was martyred either in Persia or Syria in about 66.

LOOKING AHEAD

It is evident that, in spite of the information provided by the church fathers and tradition, we do not have a detailed picture of the early spread of Christianity. However, two points seem clear even from this quick overview. First, by about 70 CE the gospel had already spread extensively. Within approximately thirty-five years after the resurrection, the early apostles had taken the gospel to the extremities of the then known world: from Spain and Great Britain in the west, to India and possibly as far as China in the east.

Second, most of the apostles had been martyred by the sixties. The only two who seemed to be still alive by the time Jerusalem was destroyed were Philip and John. Thus the decade of the sixties marked a major transition period. This feature is more evident in the letters that were written then. But that is for another chapter.

REVIEW QUESTIONS

1. Why did Paul write to Philemon, and what did he ask him to do?

2. What was happening to the church in Colosse that caused Paul to write to it?

3. How is Paul's letter to the church in Ephesus different from the one to the Colossians? Why?

4. What were the key issues underlying Paul's letter to the Philippians?

5. What happened to Paul after he was released from prison?

6. Trace the key events in the lives of the remaining apostles.

27
CHAPTER

The End of the Apostolic Age

OVERVIEW

We have very little historical data in the NT about the end of the apostolic age. Most of the information that has survived comes from the early church fathers. The NT, however, does include a number of letters dated during the decades of the sixties to eighties. In this chapter we look at 1 and 2 Peter, Hebrews, 1 and 2 Timothy, Titus, and Jude.

STUDY GOALS

▶ Summarize the purpose of each letter.

▶ Develop the messages of Peter's "catholic" letters (1 and 2 Peter).

▶ Develop the messages of Paul's "pastoral" letters (1 and 2 Timothy and Titus).

▶ Develop the message of Hebrews.

▶ Develop the message of Jude.

We are approaching the end of the apostolic age in our study. We have already noted how the book of Acts not only stops about midway through that period, but it also leaves out most of the apostles. Our records about Paul after he was released from prison in 62 are very incomplete. We do know that he wrote several more letters near the end of his life. Likewise, Peter and Jude wrote letters that were included in the canon. There is also the letter to the Hebrews, which is anonymous. To wrap up the apostolic age, we need to look at those last letters.

THE "CATHOLIC" LETTERS AND THE PASTORAL LETTERS

As we approach the end of the apostolic age, we note a change in the letters. Outside of James, the letters we have seen thus far were written to individual churches, that is, to all the believers within a given city. By contrast, the letters written in the sixties or later were written either to larger geographical regions or to specific individuals. This change indicates several things. First, it shows how Christianity had grown. Second, it shows how the needs had changed. The church leaders realized that the needs addressed were common to all believers, not just to specific cities. Likewise, those who believed were recognizing their commonality, which led to the collection of works that we call the canon. Third, there are thematic changes. In the earlier letters, the major problems were lifestyle issues—the implications of the believers' faith. The key theological question was the relationship of belief in Jesus as the Messiah and Judaism. In the later letters, the

MASADA. A palace-fortress of King Herod in the Judean desert, famous as the last stand of the Jews in 70 CE. The Romans built a ramp in order to assault the fortress. Rather than submit, the Jews committed mass suicide. Masada has become a symbol of the Jewish will to survive.

struggle was against false teaching. Beginning with Colossians, we see pagan philosophy infiltrating the church. It began to supplant the understanding of God developed through the nation of Israel. This movement resulted in a new syncretism. The dominant philosophical concept being fought came to be known as Gnosticism.

Those letters written to larger geographical regions are often called Catholic or General Epistles because they were written to believers in general, not to a specific individual or city. Of the letters written to individuals, three stand out: Paul's two letters to Timothy and his letter to Titus. Both men were pastors to whom Paul was giving pointers. These three are called the Pastoral Epistles. But first we want to look at Peter's letters.

PETER'S FIRST LETTER

The two letters attributed to Peter received differing responses in the ancient church. First Peter was one of the first letters that won virtually universal acceptance by the church. Second Peter was one of the last.

Read 1 Peter 1–5.

Based on the internal and external evidence, we may infer that both books were written late in the life of Peter. First Peter mentions suffering but does not seem to suggest martyrdom. This would seem to place it earlier than the persecution instigated by Nero beginning about 64 CE. There are some topical similarities to Paul's letters. Based on these, some have argued that all of Paul's letters must have been written first. This does not necessarily hold true.

Peter's first letter states that it was written from Babylon, which many scholars take to mean Rome.[1] Since Peter is reported to have arrived in Rome in 62, that is a good possibility. To allow for his writing 2 Peter before his death, this view would require that 1 Peter was written shortly after his arrival. However,

---

WHEN DID PETER WRITE HIS LETTERS?

Peter's letters are usually dated to about 62–67, that is, in the last three to four years of his life (he was executed as early as 64 or as late as 67). The date is based on various correlations with other letters and hints at historical events.

During the nineteenth century, Peter's reference to persecution was viewed as supporting a late date for 1 Peter and thus a different author. Alan M. Stibbs argues that the suffering or persecutions mentioned in the letter were common throughout the first century (*The First Epistle General of Peter* [Grand Rapids: Eerdmans, 1959], 57). While that may be somewhat of an overstatement, it does allow for dating the book to almost any time after the martyrdom of James. With the solid testimony of Petrine authorship from the early church, a date in the early sixties is preferred.

Because 2 Peter 3:15–16 refers to Paul's letters, the assumption is sometimes made that Peter had to have written after all of Paul's letters had been collected. This is a non sequitur. A related argument for a late date, developed in the nineteenth century, is based on similarities between the theology and terminology of Peter's and Paul's letters. More likely they reflect a "common apostolic pattern of exhortation for believers" (Stibbs, *First Epistle*, 45–48).

there are also strong arguments that the term refers to the actual Babylon in Mesopotamia. While Babylon was often used as a code name for Rome, that was more usual after John wrote Revelation, some thirty years later. It is unlikely that Peter would be using a false name at this point.[2] If the letter was written from geographical Babylon, it must have been written about 60 CE or sooner.

Peter wrote his letter to a church that was suffering persecution. We are not told exactly how intense its suffering was.[3] However, it was a regional, not a universal letter. The addressees were believers in Pontus, Galatia, Cappadocia, Asia, and Bithynia, all regions that are now within modern Turkey (see map on page 529; it is likely that Peter listed these areas in the order that he anticipated they would receive the letter, which suggests that Silvanus was traveling from the east). There is good documentation of persecution going on in the Asia Minor region during the early part of the sixties.

> Peter wrote his letter to a church that was suffering persecution.

Peter addressed what would be a natural question to ask at a time like that. The one suffering would begin to wonder, Have I done the right thing? Is this Christianity thing for real? Peter's first point was to assure the Christians that suffering was the process by which the church was refined. He used an analogy of gold being purified by fire to show that there would be a positive result.

In other words, the Christian's ultimate expectation should be spiritual purification. Peter then turned to the practical implication of how this attitude should affect the believer's life. Or, to use the phrase Francis Schaeffer borrowed some years ago, "How should we then live?" (cf. Ezek. 33:10 KJV). Peter explored a

SUFFERING PERSECUTION. Walkers strolling along the oval depression that was once the *Circus Maximus*. During the first century, Roman emperors were "entertained" as they watched the games—which included the persecution of Christians—from the Palatine Hill above the arena.

LIFE AFTER THE FALL

Peter's words about suffering reflect an understanding of the Fall. Given the breakdown in relationships, everyone will have desires and needs that are not met, expectations that are thwarted, and disappointments in life. At best, life will be filled with frustrations. More likely, there will be deep hurts because of competition and lost opportunities. As these mount up, they produce suffering in our lives. Then there will be occasions of overt persecution when others deliberately hurt us for a variety of reasons.

number of issues, which can be divided into two general categories that we have seen repeated several times in the various letters.

The first general category is *personal holiness.* This addresses the issue of how believers should conduct themselves personally. In general, Peter suggested that they are to be holy as God is holy (1 Pet. 1:15–16). More specifically, they are to focus on living for long-term abiding values rather than fading worldly ones. The picture he used was of strangers and aliens living in a land not theirs. In fact, it was because they were aliens that believers were being persecuted by the world.

The second general category focuses on *relational issues.* We have seen most of these before. They include the believer's relationship with the government, slave and master relationships, and husband and wife relationships. Peter's conclusions are very similar to those of both Paul and James.

But Peter's main concern was persecution. His premise was that everyone is going to suffer to some degree in this world. Therefore, he concluded, it is better to suffer while doing good for God than for doing evil. With this in mind, we are to be aware that the end is in sight because God is in control. Therefore we should especially persevere.

Finally, Peter addressed the issue of leadership in the church as well as church conduct. Leaders should serve in a manner worthy of God. Believers should live godly lives. In all of this, we are to be aware that the real cause of our persecution is Satan, who seeks to destroy us. But God will preserve us forever.

PETER'S SECOND LETTER

There are a number of contrasts between the two letters attributed to Peter. When we compare them, we find that they have different themes as well as somewhat different styles. Consequently, some scholars have questioned whether they had the same author. The different themes could be based on different needs from different occasions. The different styles could be based on a number of factors, including being written down by two different scribes.[4] Nevertheless, although there are some stylistic differences, we also find a number of similar phrases common to both books. More importantly, both of these letters show

Read 2 Peter 1–3.

strong similarities to the speeches of Peter that Luke summarized in the book of Acts.

Those who view 2 Peter as authentic seem in agreement that it was probably written from Rome shortly before Peter's death, which would place its composition in 63–64 CE. In contrast to 1 Peter, its audience is specified. While 2 Peter 3:1 suggests the same audience as 1 Peter, this is not a given. Asia Minor is still viewed as the general region.[5]

Thus, Peter's two letters were written from different locations on different dates, about different subjects, probably to different audiences, using different scribes. This would explain the stylistic variations. It would also explain why there was a difference in acceptance of the two through church history, because the circumstances surrounding their circulation and collection differed.[6]

While 1 Peter addressed persecution, 2 Peter primarily dealt with false teachers. We have already seen from Paul's letter to the Colossians that such teachers were beginning to infiltrate the church. These were the first strains of what would later be called Gnosticism. While Gnosticism did not gain full sway until the next century, several strands were already beginning in the middle of the first century. Gnosticism derives from the Greek word *gnosis*, meaning knowledge. It was primarily an intellectual movement. A number of factors were involved, and of the several strands that arose, some actually seem contradictory. They all had in common the concept that there were hidden secrets (knowledge) to which only the initiated could have access.[7]

A philosophical principle that lay at the foundation of Gnosticism was a sharp distinction between spirit and matter called "dualism." More important, matter was considered evil and spirit good. This principle seems to have come from Greek philosophy.[8] As applied to Christianity, Gnostics argued that God was spirit and man was matter. Based on this premise, they concluded God could have no direct contact with evil man. The solution was that between the two were intermediary beings called *aeons*. More significantly, there was a secondary divine being called the *Demiurge*. This being was identified as the *Christ*, or *Logos*, which tied the entire concept to Christianity.

The danger of Gnosticism was twofold. First, the distinction between the spirit and matter was crucial. This manifested itself in two forms. One form of gnostic thinking became licentious and hedonistic. Since the spirit could not be

GNOSTICISM

The development of Gnosticism is a very complicated subject. Like Greek philosophy in general, Gnosticism was more of a collection of ideas and teachings than an organized school of thought. Moreover, it changed radically over the next century and a half. Much of modern scholarship on Gnosticism has looked primarily at the mature forms found in the second century. Only during the past fifty years has serious work shown that the strains that became Gnosticism were already developing early in Hellenistic Judaism, perhaps as early as the Qumran period (cf. K. Rudolph, *Gnosis: The Nature and History of Gnosticism* [San Francisco: Harper & Row, 1984], 280).

affected by what the physical body did, this school of thought argued that bodily appetites could be fulfilled without restriction. The other form went to the other extreme and argued for asceticism. The effort here was to purify the body. The first form seems to have been the more prevalent.

The more critical danger of Gnosticism lay in the idea that knowledge was associated with the spirit. As long as a person had the right knowledge, it didn't matter what he or she did in the body. The crux was the concept of knowledge. Only masters of the mysteries had the right knowledge. To get the knowledge, initiates had to pass "tests." But this only admitted them to the next level. This made the "masters" the ones who controlled their eternal destiny.

> The more critical danger of Gnosticism lay in the idea that as long as a person had the right knowledge, it didn't matter what he or she did in the body.

For this reason, one of the key words of 2 Peter is _know_. Peter used it in various forms sixteen times in this short letter. He claimed that true knowledge is the knowledge that _all_ Christians already have. This knowledge came from the prophetic message validated by the historical facts of the resurrection of Jesus the Messiah and the presence of the Holy Spirit. Thus, for Peter the key part of knowledge was the resurrection.

Having a knowledge of the resurrection, a believer did not need to listen to the false teachers. Likewise, a believer could "participate in the divine nature and escape the corruption in the world caused by evil desires" (2 Pet. 1:4). Thus, Peter argued that there was no need for levels of knowledge or special initiations. Rather, he argued that the false teachers were the same sort that had been evident throughout the ages, dating even back to Noah.

key knowledge & RESURRECTION

CRETAN PALACE. A palace at Knoss, built several centuries before the time of Paul and Titus, an indication that the city was still a sophisticated cultural center when they traveled on Crete.

At this point Peter gives two key characteristics of the false teachers. First, they followed "the corrupt desire of the sinful nature" (2 Pet. 2:10). Thus, Peter argued that true belief would have an effect on one's lifestyle. Believers, especially leaders, should be highly moral. If they are not, then their position is suspect. Second, the false teachers were arrogant and "despised authority." They were even so bold as to claim the authority to revile angelic beings.

Apparently, one of the features of the false teachers was to ridicule the idea of the return of Jesus (His second coming). Peter assured his readers that although it had been some time (about thirty years) and Christ had not returned, God had a reason. The purpose was to allow more people to come to God. But they needed to understand that Jesus *would* return, and it would be *suddenly*. When that happened, the world would be destroyed. As such, believers should be prepared by the way they lived.[9]

PAUL'S FOURTH MISSIONARY JOURNEY

After he was released from prison in 62 CE, Paul continued his travels. Tradition has it that he did finally make it to Spain.[10] His letters to Timothy and Titus indicate that he also returned to Greece and Asia Minor. What is not clear is when he did what.

The most plausible solution seems to be that following the expectations he had expressed to the Philippians, Paul went back to Asia Minor and Macedonia first. This trip would be to encourage the believers of those cities who had expressed concern during his imprisonment. From there he went to Spain. That

WAILING WALL. The only portion of the temple still standing after the Romans destroyed Jerusalem and the temple in 70 CE, after the Jews revolted against Rome. Officially named the Western Wall, it is a place where Jews and pilgrims today gather to pray and lament. Judaism was rethought and changed after the destruction of the temple.

would have taken him to Spain about 64–66, at the time Nero's persecution was starting to erupt. Leaving Spain in 66, he returned to Crete, Asia, Macedonia, and Greece. During this last trip, he was arrested and returned to Rome in the fall of 67. The following summer, he was executed.[11]

We can only wish that Luke had written a sequel to Acts. But we are confident that Paul *was* released from prison and that his last letters (the Pastoral Epistles) were written after the events recorded in Acts. This view is based on comments in those letters that point to various circumstances different from Paul's situation in Rome as related in Acts 28.[12] While Paul was on this last extended trip, he left Timothy and Titus as overseers of the churches in Ephesus and Crete, respectively. The three letters written to them reiterate the guidelines he had given them as overseers.[13] Today we use those letters as directives on church governance.

PAUL'S FIRST LETTER TO TIMOTHY

We met Timothy in Lystra while Paul was on his second missionary journey in 50 C.E. (Acts 16:1–3). He was described as a young man of mixed Jewish-Greek parentage. He became a believer and traveled with Paul through Macedonia and Greece. Timothy served as a messenger, traveling back and forth between Macedonia and Greece to encourage the Macedonian churches and to keep Paul informed on what was happening. For a while, he was left in charge of the church in Corinth (cf. Acts 18:5 with v. 18) and then in Macedonia (19:22; cf. 20:4). On this fourth trip, Paul left him in Ephesus while he went to Macedonia (1 Tim. 1:3).

Read 1 Timothy 1–6.

Paul, then, was writing Timothy from Macedonia, giving some directions on how to manage the churches in the city of Ephesus. The time was probably late 62. While the letter was addressed to Timothy, it seems to have been designed for the churches collectively (1 Tim. 3:13–15; 5:7). From it, they would see that Timothy had Paul's authority. Paul also gave clear apostolic backing for specific guidelines for church leadership and worship. This emphasis might suggest that as Timothy had worked with the churches in Ephesus, he started encountering the same false teachers that had begun showing up in Colosse when Paul wrote Colossians, about a year earlier.

The tone of the letter suggests that Timothy was feeling overwhelmed by the task at hand. False teachers were advocating either extreme asceticism or hedonism. Some women were introducing false teaching, apparently using their sexuality to manipulate others. Some of the older men felt it demeaning to be taught anything by the young Timothy. In other words, the church (the collection of individual house churches) in Ephesus was developing a number of problems.

After greeting Timothy, Paul immediately plunged into his topics. He first warns against false teachers. The abrupt way he delves into this issue suggests that it was foundational to all the other problems. The heresies involved here

FALSE TEACHING IN EPHESUS

It seems that some of the false teachers in Ephesus used genealogies to buttress their positions, that is, they had heritage and tradition on their side. This claim was coupled with an attempt to use the law to justify their position. In contrast, others went to the opposite extreme and tolerated all types of unrighteous behavior in the context of claims for a freedom in Christ (antinomianism). Paul countered these ideas by noting that there was a purpose for the Law. He had covered this matter before in Galatians, where he called the Law a "tutor" or "guardian" (Gal. 3:24). Here, he reflects that the purpose of the law is for the lawless and rebellious. That is, the Law was given not to tell the righteous that their conduct is righteous, but to tell the unrighteous that what they are doing is out of line.

apparently were the same as or very similar to what we saw already in the letter to the Colossians. Heresies have a way of spreading, so it is not surprising that the Colossian heresy should now show up in Ephesus.

Paul encouraged Timothy to hang in there, noting that he had been told in advance that there would be problems (1 Tim. 1:18–19). He reminded Timothy that there were those who had rejected the faith and suffered "shipwreck." This implies that they or similar people were present in Ephesus.

> The tone of the first letter to Timothy suggests that he was feeling overwhelmed by the growing number of problems in the house churches at Ephesus.

Paul then moved into key issues on managing a church. He began with two general guidelines. The men were to be occupied with prayer. United in prayer, they would not be divided by anger and argument. It is interesting, in light of the increasing persecution, that Paul directed the church to pray for "kings and all those in authority, that we may live peaceful and quiet lives in all godliness and holiness" (1 Tim. 2:2).

In this context of church management, Paul turned to women. This is a very controversial section (1 Tim. 2:9–15). It is made more so because it is often taken out of context, and the last verse is often misunderstood.[14] Paul first directed that women be modest in their dress. The fact Paul felt impelled to give this instruction suggests that some women were immodest. That is, they were distracting men from prayer and proper worship. This issue and the problem of false teaching provide the context for Paul's directives on how women were to conduct themselves.

Paul had two arguments. First, based on the order of the creation of male and female, Paul suggested a hierarchy, or level of authority. Although distorted in the Fall and subject to abuse, Paul saw this hierarchy as still valid.

More importantly, Paul seems to address tendencies within each gender. Reflecting back on the issues of the Fall, we recall that the woman (Eve) complemented the man (Adam). That is, she had strengths that matched his limitations. The text hints that the strong points of the two genders match what psychologists have observed as tendencies. Women tend to be more relational and emotive than men.[15] However, this is both a strength and a weakness. It is a strength in building relationships, in helping people, and in ministering in certain ways. On the other hand, it may be a weakness when it comes to probing into truth and discerning deception. Likewise, men tend to be more dialectical and direct. This tendency can be a strength in the area of discerning false teaching or teachers, but also a weakness when it comes to other aspects of ministry.[16] Given what was happening in Ephesus, Paul seemed to be concerned that certain women were moving the church in a wrong direction as they listened to the false teachers.[17]

This passage then set the stage for Paul's guidelines for church leadership. Paul recognized two levels of leadership. The first was "overseer." The Greek word here (1 Tim. 3:1–2) and in Titus 1:7 is *episkopos*, which seems to be used interchangeably with *presbyteros*, "elder" (1 Tim. 5:1, 17, 19; Titus 1:5). Overseers or elders served as spiritual leaders of the church. The second level consisted of "deacons." Both levels appear in the book of Acts. Deacons were first selected in Jerusalem (Acts 6). Elders or overseers were selected for each city (e.g., Acts 14:23). Elders in Jerusalem worked with and then replaced the apostles (Acts 15:2; 21:18). Because Timothy needed to select qualified leaders within the context of the church problems, Paul pointed out to him the criteria he was to use.

At this point Paul went back to the theological issues that prompted his writing of the book. Timothy should not be surprised at apostasy, since it had been anticipated. Here Paul encouraged the young man, who seems to have been discouraged. In the process, he gave a series of guidelines for relationships. These included some we have seen before, such as slave-master relationships. There were others also, such as guidelines to the rich.[18]

HIERARCHY OR EQUALITY?

What Paul says about women in 1 Timothy 2:11–14 needs to be handled carefully. In 1 Corinthians 11—and Timothy was present with Paul in Ephesus when he wrote 1 Corinthians (see Acts 19:22)—Paul used a similar argument. There he noted that woman was originally created for the sake of man, but he then went on to observe that man was born from (or comes from) woman. Also in that letter, Paul acknowledged that women prayed and prophesied in the church. These qualifications are a reminder that a man should not be arrogant and that equality in Christ exceeds what is often given culturally.

Because what Paul said in 1 Timothy addressed a specific situation in Ephesus, some have argued that Paul intended these guidelines to apply only to that church. However, he uses universal principles as the foundation of his conclusions, suggesting he intended universal application. Still, this is an area where we really wish Paul had told us more about what was going on in the church of Ephesus. Some scholars have argued that, as in Corinth, some women were being disruptive of the services as they asked questions of their husbands. Thus, it is argued, Paul was telling them to wait until they got home to ask those questions (cf. 1 Cor. 14:33–35). This seems to read too much into the text and does not do justice to the overall context. Rather, it appears that Paul was addressing authoritative statements that would be associated with the gift of prophecy.

Paul told Timothy that he hoped to return to Ephesus soon. The letter was written to help him in the meantime. Paul was very concerned that Timothy not fail in his responsibilities.

PAUL'S LETTER TO TITUS

Read Titus 1–3.

The letter to Titus was written between the two letters to Timothy, probably in the summer of 66, after Paul's return from Spain. At the time, Paul was in Greece, either at, or more likely en route to, Nicopolis on the west coast of Greece (Titus 3:12). His plan was to spend the winter in Nicopolis, and he wanted Titus to join him there. He probably wanted to discuss his ministry in Crete personally. Paul seemed aware that time was running out for him. Early church historians indicate that he was arrested that fall and taken to Rome, where he was subsequently executed. We do not know if the meeting with Titus took place.

As was the case of 1 Timothy, the focus of the letter to Titus was on practical aspects of ministry, specifically the development of leadership in the church. Just as Paul had left Timothy in Ephesus to manage the development of that church, so also he had left Titus in Crete. There is a very close correlation between 1 Timothy and Titus in their emphasis on developing leadership.[19]

> There is a very close correlation between 1 Timothy and Titus in their emphasis on developing leadership.

Again, as was the case of Timothy in Ephesus, Titus was running into opposition within the church. There, however, instead of overt false teaching, it was more a problem of human nature. Paul quoted a Cretan philosopher who had stated, "Cretans are always liars, evil brutes, lazy gluttons" (Titus 1:12).[20] Agreeing with that assessment, Paul encouraged Titus to be strong as he rebuked and exhorted the Cretans. With this, Paul gave Titus guidelines of

ROMAN SIEGE MACHINERY. Replicas of the machinery the Romans used when they besieged the Jews on Masada. The machine at left heaved large rocks atop the mountain. The machine at right enabled troops to dig under walls.

what was needful for various groups in the church. After giving directions on how to build relationships within the church, Paul told Titus of his plans and then signed off.

PAUL'S SECOND LETTER TO TIMOTHY

This was apparently the last letter Paul wrote. It was probably written in the fall (cf. 2 Tim. 4:21) of the year 67, during his second imprisonment in Rome, before he was executed the following spring.[21] The primary purpose of the letter was either to ask Timothy to visit or to give guidelines and convey a note of urgency regarding an already expected visit. It was more likely the latter. It seems likely that Timothy was still in Ephesus and Paul had sent Tychicus to Ephesus to take his place (2 Tim. 4:12).[22]

Read 2 Timothy 1–4.

This imprisonment apparently was sudden, since Paul had left several items behind—a coat, some books, "especially the parchments" (2 Tim. 4:13).[23] As he came, Paul wanted Timothy to pass through Troas to pick them up. In addition to the request for the items left behind, Paul again encouraged Timothy. He also warned him regarding the general situation, which had worsened. One of the indications of this development was that some Christians, such as a metalworker (coppersmith) named Alexander, were defecting. On his way to Rome, Paul expected that Timothy would be seeing Onesiphorus, and Priscilla and Aquila, and he sent greetings to them.[24]

The tone of the letter is somber. In some respects, Paul seems to have written to encourage Timothy. But it seems to be the type of encouragement given by someone who knows that he is dying yet turns around and encourages others. Paul knew that he was near the end, and this affected his outlook even though he did his best to keep upbeat. To compound the issue, Paul saw a wide-scale desertion by people he cared for, which depressed him even more.

Perhaps because of this, the theme of the book is endurance. As such, Paul used the analogies of a soldier and an athlete. He also used Jesus as a model. He warned that worse times were to come "in the last days." The reason was predominantly human nature. People, even believers, tended to look out for selfish ambitions rather than working for an eternal reward.

Paul's exhortation was that Timothy had learned better. Based on what he had learned from childhood, he was to both stand fast and to preach the good news.

We don't know if Timothy made it to Rome that fall. Records suggest that Paul died the following spring.[25] As a Roman citizen, he was beheaded.

THE LETTER TO THE HEBREWS

Near the end of the apostolic era, the epistle to the Hebrews was written. It is somewhat unique among the NT letters in that it does not have a stated author. This detail has created quite a bit of discussion as different scholars have

Read Hebrews 1–13.

conjectured his or her identity. Despite this question, the letter was accepted as canonical by the early church. The Western church (that is, the church of Italy, North Africa, Spain, and France) hesitated, but after consideration, accepted it.[26]

A number of possible authors have been suggested. Interestingly, many of the suggestions have been made by modern scholars rather than by early writers. Most of the early church fathers viewed Paul as the writer. Origen, who lived from about 185 to 254 referred to Paul as the author a number of times. Still, there was some question since the church fathers knew that Paul had very clearly marked his authorship of the other thirteen letters which are ascribed to him. Clement of Alexandria (ca. 150–215) made two suggestions as to why Paul, if he was the author, may have omitted his name. First, he suggested that it was because the letter was written in general to the Hebrew Christians. Paul was not held in high regard among Jews in general, even by a number of Jews who professed to be Christians. Therefore, Clement said, Paul did not attach his name to allow the letter to speak for itself. Second, Clement suggested that Paul wrote the letter orig-

below left to right

ARCH OF TITUS. An arch built in Rome by the Roman general Titus to commemorate his victory in Jerusalem.

DETAIL OF THE ARCH. A carving in the Arch of Titus that shows Roman troops carrying off loot from the Jerusalem temple.

inally in Hebrew (for his Jewish audience), and what we have today is a Greek translation done by Luke.[27]

The other early suggestion that has significant merit is that the writer was Barnabas. As a contemporary of Paul associated with the apostles, Barnabas would have been well acquainted with Timothy, who is the only person mentioned by name in the book (Heb. 13:23).[28] Tertullian (ca. 160–215), who lived in North Africa, held the position that the writer was Barnabas (although that was contrary to the opinion of many of his contemporaries).

Modern scholars have generally concluded that Paul could not be the author, but there is no agreement on who the author might be. Besides Barnabas, other suggested authors have included Luke, Apollos, Silvanus (or Silas), Philip, Priscilla, and Clement of Rome.

The concerns raised include the fact that it is anonymous, with differences of style from the other letters attributed to Paul, such as the "absence of the characteristic Pauline spiritual experience," and theological differences with Paul's letters.[29]

Those who hold to Pauline authorship acknowledge these problems. They argue that the original greeting may have been lost, or that the author deliberately omitted the opening in consonance with his purpose following the thinking of Clement of Alexandria. Stylistic differences are problematic, although as Zane Hodges acknowledges, they are "notoriously subjective."[30] The failure to include allusions to his own experience may have been due to the subject matter, and the apparent doctrinal differences "do not exclude Pauline authorship."[31]

Even so, the authorship of this anonymous book is an open question, even as Origen stated, "Who wrote the epistle, in truth, God knows."[32] However, given the early tradition, especially of the Eastern church, it seems best to continue with an assumption of Pauline authorship.

Surprisingly, the date seems relatively easy to establish. The writer spends much time examining the issue of the sacrificial system and pointing out how the Jewish sacrifices performed in the tabernacle or temple were inferior to the sacrifice that Christ had performed. Since he wrote about the sacrifice in the present tense, this suggests a date before 70 CE, when the temple was destroyed. If the temple had already been destroyed, the writer would surely have mentioned that fact as supporting his argument. On the other hand, it was after an imprisonment of Timothy, who was noted as having been released in Hebrews 13:23. This detail would seem to place the letter toward the end of the decade of the sixties.[33] A probable date then would be about 67 CE.

The audience was a group of Jews who had become, or had at least professed to have become, Christians. There are indications that some of this group were trying to bring the church back into Judaism. The entire point of the book was a comparison between the Messiah (the "Christ" and thus Christianity) and the

> Since the author of Hebrews wrote about the sacrifice in the present tense, this suggests a date before 70 CE, when the temple was destroyed.

THE RECIPIENTS OF HEBREWS

Where was this letter originally sent? Proposals include Jerusalem, Rome, Alexandria, and Syria. There has not been much support for the latter two. Robert H. Gundry presents fairly strong arguments for Rome (*Survey of the New Testament*, 423). But there are some problems. First, he refers to Hebrews 2:3 as indicating that the recipients had not heard Jesus. However, this verse does not specifically state that; rather, it affirms the testimony of eyewitnesses. And even if the verse suggests that the recipients as a whole had not been eyewitnesses, that could have been an essentially true statement for Jerusalem (the letter was written some thirty-five years after the resurrection). Likewise, we should not infer that just because the Judean believers had been through times of need themselves, they were incapable of the generosity named in Hebrews 6:10. One of the most telling points against the view that Hebrews was addressed to the Roman church is the later hesitancy of that church to include it in the canon: if it had been sent to Rome, it likely would have been acknowledged much sooner there.

inferior aspects of Judaism. Perhaps a better way of expressing it would be that in the Messiah, Judaism was fulfilled. While applicable to Jewish believers in general, the original recipients were probably localized. The two prime candidates were Jews in Jerusalem and Jews in Rome. Because of the focus on the issue of sacrifice, it is likely that Jerusalem was the original recipient of the letter.

The overall theme of the book can be succinctly stated as "Jesus is better." The flow of the book was a series of comparisons to show that Jesus as Messiah was better than any aspect of Judaism. This argument is very evident in the opening section.

First, Jesus was better than the prophets because of the nature of revelation. The intial verses serve as an introduction, pointing out that the revelation of Jesus was better than that of the prophets, who were merely anticipating the Messiah. This assertion sets the stage for the other points. Interestingly, there was no effort on the part of the writer to prove that Jesus was either the Messiah (or Christ) or the Son of God. This would suggest that his audience had at least intellectually accepted this point. The key of the letter, however, was that these people did not understand the implications of that identification and thus were prepared to throw it all away for matters of lifestyle.

At this point, there is an extensive argument to point out the superiority of Jesus to the angels. The length of time spent on the contrast between the Messiah and the angels suggests that there was some awareness on the part of the original audience that angels have a powerful position and are involved in the affairs of men.

After that the author compares Jesus to Moses,[34] Joshua, and the OT high priest. This last comparison provided the writer with a smooth transition into the priestly and then the sacrificial systems. The writer broke off his thought regarding the priestly system at 5:10. He observed that at this point he feared he was losing his audience because the material was so theologically sophisticated. This is the most difficult part of the book. The writer observed that the audience had been in a rut regarding issues of "repentance" and "dead works" and as a result was not going on to deeper teachings.[35]

This section is very difficult and highly debated. There are primarily three views. Some argue that the passage refers to Christians who have actually lost their salvation. However, that creates problems, because the writer then says it is impossible "to be brought back to repentance" (Heb. 6:6). Others suggest that this refers to individuals who have made a verbal profession but have not made a true faith decision. In this argument, the falling away is just a rejection of intellectual knowledge (vv. 4–5). This also presents a problem since the writer seems to assume that the recipients have true faith (e.g., vv. 9–11). A third view is that this is a hypothetical situation, since it is impossible for a genuine believer to fall away. The problem with this view is why the writer would use an impossible situation for an example. Moreover, the Greek seems to suggest that the writer was aware of cases of apostasy and was not presenting a hypothetical situation.[36] In any case, after presenting this warning, the writer quickly assures the recipients that he is convinced that they are not of this category. As such, they should "go on to maturity" (v. 1) and "make [their] hope sure" (v. 11). Beyond this, the writer points out that our salvation is really not an issue of our faithfulness but of God's unchangeable nature (vv. 16–17).

The point was that once a person places his faith in Jesus as the Messiah, he needs to build on his salvation.

THE BETTER PRIEST

The earthly priests ministered in physical tabernacles or temples, which were copies of the spiritual or heavenly ones. Jesus ministers in the heavenly original. Moreover, the earthly priests died and had to be replaced. Because of the resurrection, Jesus is a perpetual priest.

After showing that Jesus was a better priest, the writer says that Jesus instituted a better covenant. This was a reference to Jeremiah 31:31, which anticipated the new covenant, and the Last Supper, where Jesus announced it (e.g., Luke 22:20). Jesus was also better than the tabernacle. In the earthly tabernacle, people could approach God only once a year and then only after very careful preparation. In Jesus, people have access to God regularly, since He has entered the heavenly tabernacle where God dwells.

MELCHIZEDEK

In his discussion of the priesthood, the author of Hebrews introduces Melchizedek, a non-Israelite priest who received an offering from Abraham (Gen. 14:18–20). The key point in Hebrews 7:1–6 is that Melchizedek appears to us in Scripture virtually out of nowhere. There is no mention of ancestor or descendant. In a number of ways He was greater than Abraham, the ancestor of the Jewish nation, and thus, by correspondence, greater than Levi and Aaron, both of whom were descendants of Abraham.

The writer argues that Jesus provided a better sacrifice. Under the old sacrificial system, the blood merely put off judgment, but it could not cleanse. This inadequacy was demonstrated by the fact that the sacrifices had to be performed regularly. In contrast, Jesus performed one sacrifice good for all time.

Finally, the writer asserts that as a result of what Jesus did, there were lifestyle implications. This is the focus of the last section of the book. These implications fall into three areas. First, believers are to be faithful by holding fast to their confession, challenging one another to love and good works, meeting together regularly, and forsaking sinning. Second, believers are to be encouraged by the testimony of those who have gone before. He illustrates this by the faith of saints from the history of Israel who expressed their faith by their actions. Third, believers should regard persecution as a purifying process. The result should be that one is drawn closer to God.

In Hebrews 11, the writer defines faith. He then illustrates it and gives the reader practical ways of expressing it. Following this, the letter ends with a typical conclusion.

THE END OF THE APOSTOLIC ERA

As we saw earlier, Judea came under Roman rule reluctantly (see above, ch. 17). Because the Judeans never really accepted it, the province was a constant trouble spot for Rome. The situation worsened in the sixties. In 66 CE they began another revolt. This one resulted in the destruction of Jerusalem and the temple.

Determining the cause of the war seems to depend on who recorded it. According to Josephus, the Jewish historian, the cause was an unprovoked massacre instigated by the governor Florus; but according to Tacitus, the Roman historian, the cause was the failure of the Jews to submit to Roman government.[37] At first the Jews had some success. They captured the Roman fortress of Masada. But soon Roman legions marched against Judea. In reality, the only reason the war lasted for several years was that there was a civil war in Rome in 68–69. The general, Vespasian, left Judea to fight in Rome. When he succeeded in becoming emperor, his son Titus destroyed Jerusalem, burning the city and the temple in 70 CE.[38] The forces at Masada held out until 74. When it was about to be captured, they committed mass suicide rather than submit.

When Jerusalem was destroyed the first time, the prophets made it clear that this was God's punishment for failing to uphold the covenant. We have no prophetic record clearly showing such a correlation in the second destruction.[39]

After the destruction of Jerusalem, Christianity and Judaism were headed in diverging directions. As a result, Christianity was becoming increasingly Gentile. Judaism would become more focused on rabbinic tradition (eventually codified in the Mishnah and further developed in the Talmud).

THE LETTER OF JUDE

Read Jude 1–25.

Jude is a small book, tucked into the back of the NT. Since it is not long enough to be divided into chapters, it is easily overlooked. This letter is somewhat controversial for two reasons. First, verses 17–18 are very similar to 2 Peter 3:2–3. The question is, who borrowed from whom? Some argue that 2 Peter borrowed from Jude, meaning that it had to be written later. As Guthrie points out, neither assertion is demonstrated.[40] While it is possible that 2 Peter and Jude reference a common source, it seems more possible that Jude quoted Peter. Jude should be dated about a decade after Peter's death, thus around 75 CE.

The second point of controversy involves the writer's use of noncanonical books. The material in Jude 9 probably derives from the ending (now lost) of a document known as *Assumption of Moses* or *Testament of Moses*, and Jude 14–15 is clearly a quotation from *1 Enoch*. However, both the OT and other NT writers quote from noncanonical books.

According to verse 1, the author of this letter was Jude (Greek *Judas*) the brother of James. It is generally agreed that this James was the half brother of Jesus, who became the leader of the Jerusalem church in the forties. The Gospels list Judas as the fourth or third of the four half brothers of Jesus (Matt. 13:55; Mark 6:3). Since there were also sisters, Judas/Jude would probably have been at least ten years younger than Jesus.[41]

It was now more than four decades after the resurrection and the promise of Jesus' return. Many had given up.

The location of the writer and the audience are both undetermined. His topic, however, was very straightforward. Like the other letter writers near the end of the apostolic age, he addressed false teachers, contrasting true knowledge of Jesus Christ with the false teachings that were arising. This emphasis suggests that he was addressing an even more organized form of gnostic thinking. The writer is very quick to compare those false teachers with the very worst the OT record had to offer. These included the people of Sodom and Gomorrah, Cain, Balaam, and Korah. His point was that there was really nothing new in their teaching. Rather, it reflected a long stream of rebellion against God.

NONCANONICAL QUOTATIONS

The quotation from *1 Enoch* in Jude 14–15 is often regarded as something unusual. The OT, however, quotes frequently from books never included in the canon (e.g., both Josh. 10:13 and 2 Sam. 1:18 quote from the *Book of Jashar*). Paul even quotes from pagan writers (Aratus in Acts 17:28; Menander in 1 Cor. 15:33; Epimenides in Titus 1:12). Quoting from a noncanonical source did not elevate that source to some inspired, quasi-canonical level. It merely addressed a particular statement made by the other author.

He also focused on the certainty of the return of Jesus the Messiah. It was now more than four decades after the resurrection and the promise of Jesus' return. Many had given up. There was increasing persecution, and those who accepted Jesus as the Messiah were being killed. The remaining eyewitnesses were very few, although they had left written records. Jude's purpose was to encourage those who were starting to doubt whether it was really true, and to warn those who were promoting false teaching.

LOOKING AHEAD

We have seen how the pattern had continued: God's message was rejected, contradicted, and twisted. For fifteen hundred years prophets had told about the Messiah. And then He came. But He was rejected and crucified. He proved His point and identity by the resurrection. But that too was rejected. Now, the question was, What next? God had one last message for His people.

REVIEW QUESTIONS

1. What is a catholic epistle?

2. What is the focus of 1 Peter?

3. How is 2 Peter different from 1 Peter, and why is this important?

4. What is Gnosticism, and what effect did it have on the early church?

5. What is a pastoral epistle?

6. How do 1 Timothy and Titus reinforce each other?

7. How is 2 Timothy different from 1 Timothy, and why is this important?

8. Who are the possible authors of Hebrews, and what are the arguments for each?

9. What is the primary focus of the book of Hebrews?

10. What important event happened in Judea in 70 CE?

11. What is the focus of the book of Jude and how does it relate to 2 Peter? Why is this important?

28 CHAPTER

But What about John?

OVERVIEW

John outlived his entire generation and most of the next. The rumor was that John would be alive at the time of Jesus' second coming. As John ministered, he addressed that issue, first in his gospel and then in the book of Revelation. In this chapter we look at the writings attributed to John at the end of the first century, which bring the apostolic age to its conclusion.

STUDY GOALS

▶ Show how John marked the end of the apostolic age.

▶ Demonstrate that John was the author of the gospel and the three epistles bearing his name as well as the book of Revelation.

▶ Develop the messages of 1, 2, and 3 John.

▶ Introduce the problems of interpreting the book of Revelation and the key interpretational methods.

▶ Develop the message of Revelation.

The church was approaching the end of an era. All of the apostles whom Jesus had called had died—except for John. Most, if not all, of the eyewitnesses to Jesus' resurrection had died, some as martyrs, some in old age—except for John. Rumor had gone throughout the world that John would be alive until Jesus returned, and John was now an old man. Surely the time must be soon. After all, it had been more than fifty years since the resurrection. The church was now seeing the third generation of Christians become leaders. There had been several waves of persecution. The city of Jerusalem and the temple had been destroyed. The gospel had been carried to the ends of the earth. Surely the time of salvation was near.[1] What could God be waiting for?

We still do not know the answer to that question. Peter had stated more than twenty years earlier that God is not willing that any should perish. This, he stated, is the reason that the return of Jesus was delayed (2 Peter 3:9). As John neared the end of his life, he had a bit more to say about this topic. The final words of John completed the NT canon; these words are recorded as three letters, a gospel, and a book of prophecy.[2] Then the church sat back to wait, convinced that God had given adequate revelation with which to function in the world.

John apparently moved to Ephesus about the time of the destruction of Jerusalem in 70 CE. (Tradition says that he took Mary, the mother of Jesus, with him and that both died there.) He became the leader of the Ephesian church. As a witness to the resurrection, he continued to tell his version of the good news, the gospel. As a church leader and apostle, he passed on the teachings he had received from Jesus. He taught and trained a number of the leaders who ministered late in the first century and early in the second. Finally, as an apostle he put some of his knowledge and wisdom into writing for future generations.

BASILICA OF ST. JOHN. The church built on the traditional site of an early church pastored by the apostle John.

The material John wrote is undated. Moreover, there is no mention of secular or religious events with which to correlate it. Church tradition places it late in the first century. Most likely John wrote around 85–95 CE.

JOHN'S GOSPEL

Tradition has it that John's gospel preceded his other writings.[3] Tradition also holds that John the apostle is indeed the author, and the internal evidence points in the same direction. The Synoptic Gospels show that there was an inner circle of three disciples—Peter, James, and John—who often met with Jesus alone, as at the Transfiguration (Matt. 17:1–8), and the author apparently was part of that group. The author also presents himself as "the disciple whom Jesus loved." Since James died early (Acts 12:1–5) and Peter is clearly other than that disciple (John 21:7), John is the only one left.[4]

Many early church fathers who were contemporaries or near-contemporaries of John quote or allude to his gospel as Scripture, suggesting an early and rapid acceptance of the book. They include Polycarp (ca. 69–155) and Papias (60–130), both students of John; also Ignatius (35–107), and Irenaeus (ca. 130–200), who was a student of Polycarp.

So some fifty years after the resurrection (about 85–90 CE), John wrote down his own account of the gospel. It supplemented the three Synoptic Gospels in several ways. It is preeminently a thoughtful evaluation, after a half-century of contemplation, of the implications of all that Jesus said and did. Apparently in reaction to increasingly strong false

> The gospel of John is preeminently a thoughtful evaluation, after a half-century of contemplation, of the implications of all that Jesus said and did.

REVISING DATES

The dates and the sequence of the three letters of John and the gospel of John are widely debated because there are no historical anchors. In the *Zondervan Pictorial Encyclopedia of the Bible,* Huber L. Drumwright Jr. argues that the gospel of John was likely written in about 85 and the letters a couple of years later (3:651). In the very next article, George Turner proposes that the gospel must have been written before 70 (3:672). Tradition since the early church fathers has placed the writings in or near the last decade of the first century.

John's authorship of the fourth gospel came under critical attack in the nineteenth century, primarily because of the way the book presents Jesus and His claims. John strongly portrays Jesus as divine, and critics say that such a concept developed rather slowly in the early church, which was responsible for deifying Jesus. Proponents of this view dated the gospel no earlier than 150 CE so as to allow the "myths" enough time to develop. This theory was devastated by the discovery of the John Rylands Papyrus—a small fragment of the gospel of John that has been dated to about 125–35, barely forty years after the traditional date of writing (ca. 90). Because the fragment was discovered in Egypt, one must allow time for the copying and distribution of the document. Critical scholars have thus revised the date of composition and almost all of them now recognize that the gospel of John must have been written by the end of the first century.

teachings, John wrote to demonstrate the deity of Jesus. One important way to do this was the use of "I am"—the title God used to introduce Himself to Moses (Ex. 3:14). John also introduces many other titles,—such as "the only begotten," "the Lamb of God," "the Son of God," "the true bread," "the light," "the shepherd," "the door," "the way, the truth, and the life," "the resurrection," and "the vine"—with the phrase, "I am."

In many respects John was saying, "I saw this happen, and based on what I now know, this is what it meant." He did not try to "correct" synoptic accounts of events he wrote about; we regard their views as complementary (as would be expected from four different witnesses). However, John did give greater insight into some issues.

John had a very clear purpose for his gospel, and he expressed it near the end when he stated, "Jesus did many other miraculous signs in the presence of his disciples, which are not recorded in this book. But these are written that you may believe that Jesus is the Christ, the Son of God, and that by believing you may have life in his name" (John 20:30–31). Interestingly, John recorded only eight miracles, six of which are unique to his account.[5] This feature again points out that he was building on the Synoptics.

As noted earlier, John is the only gospel that reports the early Judean ministry of Jesus. The account gives us a sense of the overall ministry of Jesus. John also records several Passover celebrations, indicating the length of Jesus' ministry. Yet John covers only about twenty actual days in the life of Jesus. Chapters 13–19 cover one day.[6]

John included one other important point in his gospel. We noted earlier how the rumor had gone out that John would remain alive until Jesus returned (see above, ch. 19). Now, approaching the end of his life, John had to address this rumor, since Jesus had not returned. So John pointed out that Jesus had not said that John would not die.

WHY JOHN WROTE TO THE CHURCHES

At about the time he wrote his gospel, John also wrote several letters. He followed the pattern of Paul and Peter, sending written documents to regions, cities, and individuals to address specific issues. Third John makes reference to another letter (3 John 9), which we do not have.[7] This information suggests that John wrote a number of letters that have not been preserved. Three of them were kept by early believers and included in the canon. These were written to three different audiences for three different purposes at three different times.

The letters give us some insight into the church at large at the end of the first century. It had grown, but it was running into opposition. It depended on traveling teachers, who moved from city to city. Thus there was considerable interaction among churches through correspondence and personal visits. In these circumstances, the believers had to be cautious, because there were also many false teachers who passed themselves off as the real thing. John called them "antichrists." There was also at this time a transition in leadership. With the departure of the apostles, the church was developing the pattern that Paul had laid out in 1 Timothy and Titus.

> John's three letters give us some insight into the church at the end of the first century.

FALSE MESSIAH. A person in Hyde Park, London, claiming to be Jesus. By definition that makes him an antichrist.

THE FIRST LETTER OF JOHN

John's first letter is a general or circular letter. As such, it does not contain the normal introduction and conclusion we have come to expect in NT letters. John plunges right into his subject.

Read 1 John 1–5.

John picks up on an issue that Peter (in his second letter) and Jude had dealt with—an increasing manifestation of false teaching. What specific teaching John has in mind is not clear, but his warnings seem directed toward an encroaching Gnosticism. One gnostic teacher in Ephesus was the heretic Cerinthus. John had confrontations with him, suggesting that his letter is directed against Cerinthus' or similar teachings.

CERINTHUS

Irenaeus records that on one occasion John entered a public bath house in Ephesus, saw Cerinthus there, and rushed out without bathing, crying, "Let us fly, lest even the bath-house fall down, because Cerinthus, the enemy of truth, is within" (*Against Heresies* 3.3.4; see *ANF*, 1:416). Cerinthus held a view called "docetism," taken from a Greek verb meaning "to seem." Docetists said that the incarnation was in appearance only. Specifically, Cerinthus maintained that the "Christ" descended upon Jesus at the time of His baptism and then left Jesus before the crucifixion (Irenaeus, *Against Heresies* 1.26.1; see *ANF*, 1:352). Thus, the Christ did not suffer but kept the purity demanded of a spiritual being. John's admonition that believers "test the spirits" as to whether they accepted the incarnation suggests that he was writing against docetic or similar views (1 John 4:1–3). As presented by Irenaeus, the Cerinthian teachings do not exactly correlate with the warnings John gives. However, those systems were complex enough that either John or Irenaeus may not have addressed all the issues.

John, like Peter earlier, proposes that the solution to this false teaching—which would eventually develop into full-fledged Gnosticism—is the knowledge that comes from the resurrection of Jesus the Messiah and the presence of the Holy Spirit. For John, this knowledge results in righteous living and love among believers. The point of his letter is that these three things—the resurrection, the work of the Spirit, and right living—are adequate for discerning false teaching.

THE SECOND LETTER OF JOHN

Read 2 John 1–13. John's second letter is addressed to "the chosen lady." Most likely this term indicates a specific local church. John sends greetings from her "chosen sister" and her children, suggesting the church in Ephesus.

Apparently John is responding to news he had received from a specific community. He is encouraged to hear that in spite of false teaching, the believers were following the truth. This was a period when teachers traveled from city to city, and many believers (who also gave them hospitality) were dependent on them for instruction. In verse 10, John warns them about infiltration by false teachers.

The letter is short because John planned to visit "the lady" in person. At that point, he said, he would expand on what he had written.

THE THIRD LETTER OF JOHN

Read 3 John 1–14. Although it is the shortest book in the NT, 3 John contains several significant points. The book is addressed to a person, Gaius, and deals with the issue of false teachers. As with the other letters, we have no indications of date.

In the letter John cites three teachers—two good (Gaius and Demetrius) and one bad (Diotrephes). He praises Gaius himself for his hospitality, specifically to teachers from Ephesus. They had told John of the warm welcome they had received.

This response was in contrast to Diotrephes. John had written a letter to the church as a whole (a letter we do not have). Apparently, Diotrephes refused to accept the contents of the letter and perhaps would not even allow it to be read. All in all, he was making a play to become a leader among the local house churches. It appears that Gaius and Diotrephes were in the same city but in dif-

THE CHOSEN LADY

According to some Latin fragments of a work by Clement of Alexandria (ca. 150–215), 2 John was written to a specific Babylonian woman named Electa (Latin for "chosen woman"). Most scholars, however, hold that in verse 1 the Greek term *eklektai* (the feminine form of the word "chosen one") refers to a church, not a person.

ferent house churches. John apparently had doubts about Diotrephes' gifts (or perhaps spiritual integrity) for a higher position. As a result there was tension, and Diotrephes tried to reject John's apostolic authority. One way was to refuse to lodge any traveling teachers. Because of this, John hoped to visit and straighten things out.

In the final section, John praises Demetrius, who was probably a traveling teacher carrying the letter to Gaius. This missive would serve to introduce Demetrius to believers. Again, as in his second letter, John saves much of what he wants to say for a hoped-for personal visit sometime in the future.

THE APOCALYPSE (THE BOOK OF REVELATION)

John's last work is the last in the Bible: the book of Revelation. Unlike the letters attributed to John, Revelation claims John as its author and gives a location of writing, the island of Patmos off the west coast of Asia Minor. These facts suggest the date. John had been sent to Patmos as a prisoner in the early nineties under the emperor Domitian. John was released shortly after Domitian's death in 96 CE, so the book was probably written around 95.

The book was accepted into the canon in the Western church quickly for several reasons.[8] First, it was written to seven churches, and there were multiple copies. John may have sent separate copies to each church. It may have been a circular document that traveled from city to city, in which case believers in each place probably made a copy before passing it on. Either way, the existence of multiple copies gave it widespread distribution as part of the process of canonization.

PATMOS. The island where John lived in exile. While he was there, he had the vision that has been recorded as the book of Revelation.

CAVE ON PATMOS. The building that now covers the cave where, tradition says, John had his vision.

A second reason for the book's rapid acceptance is its authorship. This was John, after all, the last of the apostles. Unlike the letters 2 and 3 John, Revelation was intended for general distribution and probably got passed around quickly.

A third reason is the content. The book addressed some major concerns of the day—concerns that persist so as to make Revelation one of the most familiar books of the Bible to people who never read the Bible.

The book's purpose seems to be to answer four key questions. First, when is the kingdom going to be established? We noted in the book of Acts that this was the last question the disciples asked on the day of ascension. Jesus deflected the question, saying it was not for them to know the time. Now the last of the apostles was nearing death. The church was experiencing more and more persecution. Because of the declarations of Jesus recorded in the Gospels, the timing of the kingdom had again become a burning question. Paul had addressed the issue in some of his letters (notably 1 and 2 Thessalonians); he had given some signals to look for, though he never suggested a timetable. Peter had observed that the purpose of God's delay was to allow time for repentance; the delay was not because of any misunderstanding on the part of the apostles. Now, almost thirty years later, John addresses the same question.

Second, what about the Lord's return? As early as the fifties, naysayers questioned the return of Jesus, as Paul mentions in 1 and 2 Thessalonians. Now sixty years have passed since the ascension. All during that time, the church (including the apostles) had been looking for an imminent return of her Lord. After three generations, Jesus had still not returned. The church was becoming increasingly Gentile, with tremendous evangelistic outreach in the northern and western regions of the Mediterranean.

This change in the demographics of the church was affecting the outlook of Christians. A predominantly Jewish church had naturally looked to Jesus as the Messiah who was to establish the kingdom. As the second generation faded into the third and Gentiles became dominant, attention to this imminent return began to fade. The idea of the kingdom of the Messiah became less important, even though the OT record indicated that the messianic kingdom would be for the benefit of *all* the world. Instead, the church began to attempt reconciliation with the political power that was Rome. This was especially true among the increasing numbers of Gentiles who were Roman citizens.[9] It was also true in the western part of the empire, where the church was growing rapidly. Those believers were farther away from the land where Jesus had lived and its reminder that the messianic kingdom had both a spiritual and physical aspect.

> As the second generation faded into the third, the idea of the kingdom of the Messiah became less important to the church.

Third, what about the situation of John? The author was possibly the very last of his generation—the generation that had followed Jesus and witnessed the resurrection. It was rumored that John would live until Jesus' second coming (see John 21:23). Now he was growing old. Had he died without further revelation, there would undoubtedly have been tremendous discouragement within the church, which had been undergoing persecution. Without an explanation, many would have fallen by the wayside.

Fourth, what in the world is happening? The previous sixty years had been a period of persecution and tribulation for the church. In some respects, this was expected. As Jesus had said and Paul had written, the world hates God's truth. In another respect, questions had arisen regarding the course of history (see 2 Peter, notably chapter 3). How was the world going to end? Was evil going to win?

HOW OLD WAS JOHN?

John might have been in his twenties when he became a follower of Jesus. If so, he would have been in his late eighties when the book was written, a credible lifespan for the time. As we have seen, Clement of Rome may have lived seventy years, Polycarp ninety, and Papias at least eighty.

The first century was a very corrupt time in the Roman Empire and consequently in the civilized world. Only in the realization that God was not only in control of history but had already planned the ultimate final defeat of Satan was there any real encouragement. As such, the book would provide answers to the concerns of the first-century church. More than this, it would also provide hope to every generation that came afterward. John gave us a book that is uniquely addressed to the needs of all ages.

WAYS OF INTERPRETING REVELATION

The book of Revelation is controversial. Because of the material, there is much disagreement about what it means. We have already addressed both prophetic literature (see above, ch. 13) and apocalyptic literature (ch. 15). John's book of Revelation can be classified under each of those categories. But it is not entirely prophetic, and it is not entirely apocalyptic. Rather, it blends both types.

The book of Revelation has become the focus of prophetic studies for a variety of reasons. It is the most clearly organized and detailed work that addresses the return of Jesus. It seems to focus on the church and what will happen to it, whereas OT prophetic and apocalyptic literature focuses on the future of the nation of Israel.[10]

Differences of opinion arise over whether we should follow what is often called a *literal* method of interpreting these prophetic books, or take what is often called an *allegorical* method. In theory, the differences are really just matters of degree.

Views on how to interpret prophecy lie along a spectrum between two poles. At one end is an allegorical approach. At the other end is a totally literal approach. However, no one interprets prophecy at either extreme. All who follow an allegorical method of interpretation recognize that some parts must be taken literally. Likewise, all who follow a literal method of interpretation recognize that figures of speech and symbols are used. Thus a key issue in prophetic interpretation is "how much of prophecy is to be interpreted literally, and how much symbolically."[11]

In this light, Berkhof's first rule for interpreting prophecy is very helpful: "The words of the prophets should be taken in their usual literal sense, unless the context of the manner in which they are fulfilled *clearly* indicate that they have a symbolic meaning."[12] One problem is that interpreters do not agree on what clearly indicates a symbolic meaning.

LITERAL OR ALLEGORICAL?

It is unfortunate that some writers—on both sides of the interpretative spectrum—have set up straw men or used ad hominem arguments to support their positions. Some of those in favor of a more allegorical approach have accused those at the other end of the spectrum of being woodenly literal. Some scholars at the more literal end have accused those at the other of excessive allegorizing. A very basic question that needs to be decided is, Does the interpretation of prophetic literature require a "special hermeneutic"? I would argue that it does not. Tied to that question are two subordinate issues: How does one handle figures of speech? Who determines the meaning of the symbol? Anyone attempting to interpret Revelation must first answer these questions.

A literal approach (as advocated in this book) seeks to understand figures of speech as the writer intended. This is a normal procedure followed in any literary analysis. We intuitively understand how figures of speech work, although most of us think in terms of only a few types. As a result, we sometimes overlook a proper analysis of them. The authoritative work for evaluating figures of speech used in the Bible is E. W. Bullinger, *Figures of Speech Used in the Bible* (Grand Rapids: Baker, 1968, reprint of 1898 edition). While some of his distinctions are rather fine, he lists more than two hundred types of figures of speech.

Likewise, the approach I advocate seeks to interpret symbols either from the context or other places in the Bible where similar symbols are defined. While this does not answer all of the questions, it is felt that this provides a logical foundation leading to the interpretation of other symbols.

Perhaps more importantly, even after agreeing on what is a symbol, interpreters do not agree on how to interpret it. Some interpreters argue that the symbols should be taken in the most straightforward manner possible. Others argue that they represent spiritual truths.

This distinction can be important. For example, in Revelation 13:1, the writer states that he saw a beast coming out of the sea. A "literal" view might argue that the beast was a symbol of a specific nation or empire (based on similar imagery from Daniel). At the other end of the spectrum, an "allegorical" view might argue that the beast represented "any governmental system at any time that opposes the kingdom of God."[13]

BUST OF DOMITIAN. A bust of the Roman emperor Domitian, who imprisoned John. It is part of a larger-than-life statue uncovered in Ephesus—the head is about six feet tall—and may have been used in emperor worship.

There are a number of passages in Revelation on which all the interpreters agree. For example, everyone agrees that the Lamb in Revelation 5:6 is a symbolic picture of the ascended Jesus. Likewise, virtually everyone agrees that the woman described in Revelation 12:1 is a symbol of the nation of Israel. Moreover, her pregnancy represents the struggle to bring forth the Messiah. As such, this passage would be an allegory.[14] So, the real question is not whether one follows a literal or an allegorical view, but how "literally" and how "allegorically" does one interpret the material? That is, the question comes down to which visual images represent symbols (i.e., of more abstract systems or concepts), and which visual images just represent actual physical items.

There are no clear-cut answers for this, even with a given "school" of interpretation. For example, among "literal" interpreters, there is disagreement as to which of the items discussed in the various judgments (i.e., the seals, trumpets, or bowls) are actual physical events and which represent more abstract judgments. Likewise, in various allegorical views, there is disagreement on which represent spiritual issues, and which merely symbolically represent physical judgments. Overall, it is important to remember that the differences between interpreters and schools of interpretation are of degree, not absolute criteria.

> The one who determines the meaning of the symbol determines the meaning of the text.

We would make one observation. When a symbol is interpreted, the one who determines the meaning of the symbol determines the meaning of the text. However, it would appear that many of the symbols have interpretations given to us. For example, in Revelation 12, we are introduced to an enormous red dragon. In 12:9, the writer tells us that the dragon was the "ancient serpent called the devil, or Satan, who leads the whole world astray."[15] Thus, the symbol is defined for us. Many of the symbols draw upon OT imagery. For example, the woman in the same section is described as having twelve stars on her head. This description apparently alludes back to Joesph's dream in Genesis 37. Consequently, one who studies the book of Revelation needs to be well acquainted with the OT. While John gives an interpretation of many of his symbols, he also frequently draws a lot on symbols that the OT has already interpreted.

With this in mind, we note what four basic schools of thought have arisen over the past almost two thousand years: idealist, preterist, historical, and futurist. We will look at them where they tend to fall on the spectrum beginning with the most allegorical. We must recognize that within each basic position, there would also be a variety of perspectives, some more allegorical or more literal.

Idealist

The most allegorical of the four is what is often called the idealist view. This view would see few if any literal qualities in the book. This school of thought arose in the Alexandrian school of theology demonstrated by the writings of Clement of Alexandria and Origen.[16] Egypt had become the home of many Jews in exile following the times of Jeremiah. After the city of Alexandria was founded by Alexander the Great, many Jews settled there. They enjoyed the cosmopolitan atmosphere that allowed the Jewish community freedom not found in the more tradition-bound areas of ancient Egypt. This city became the home of the Septuagint, the Greek translation of the OT.

Alexandria was famous for several schools of thought that arose around the time of Jesus. The most significant for our purposes was founded by a Jewish philosopher named Philo. He developed a theory of interpretation of the OT that was highly allegorical. One of the more significant Christian followers of this method of interpretation was Origen (180–254 CE), who was noted for his practice of allegorizing, including prophetic literature.[17] While we lack much of Origen's work, he seems to have laid the foundation for the idealist school.

The idealist school seemed to be relatively minor until the barbarian invasions of Rome. Emperor Constantine had prohibited persecution against Christianity within the Roman Empire with the so-called Edict of Milan in 313. During the following century, the empire became increasingly Christianized. It would not be surprising then, that many began to confuse the empire and the kingdom of God. As such, when the barbarians burned Rome in 410, the Christians were shocked. How could this happen to God's kingdom?

ALEXANDRIA AND ANTIOCH

Philo of Alexandria (also known as Philo Judaeus) lived about the same time as Jesus and was noted, among other things, for representing the Jews before Caligula in 40 CE. He developed and advocated a highly allegorical method of interpretation of the OT accounts. Philo's theory of interpretation was adopted by several church fathers who lived in the area, including Clement of Alexandria and Origen. In contrast, an alternative school of interpretation developed in Antioch of Syria (which we will recall was the home church of Paul and Barnabas). Less is known about the history of this school of interpretation, except that it was more "literal" (Milton S. Terry, *Biblical Hermeneutics* [Grand Rapids: Zondervan, 1974], 644–48).

CHRISTIANITY AND THE ROMAN EMPIRE

There is some debate as to the significance of the Edict of Milan in 313. This event stopped short of making Christianity the official religion of the Roman Empire, but it did put it on at least an equal footing with other religions. It also provided some restoration of property lost during the persecutions. However, as the emperors professed Christian faith, Christianity did gain a dominant position politically.

The fall of Rome a century later raised serious questions for those who had come to identify the empire with God's kingdom. Many were dismayed to think that the kingdom had come to an end. There was also an attempt to defend Christianity from the ultimate blame for the sack of Rome in 410. Some of the pagans were arguing as follows: Rome became Christian; Rome got sacked; therefore, it was the Christians' fault.

In this context, a North African scholar proposed a solution. In his book *The City of God* (written between 413 and 427), Augustine redefined the terms. He argued that the victory and kingdom described in Revelation was a spiritual one. As such, even though the barbarians had burned a "Christian city," it was not the city of God. His work laid the foundation of modern allegorical interpretation of Revelation, which argues that this NT book is purely a symbol of the struggle between good and evil.

Preterist

The preterist (from Latin *praeteritus,* "past") argues that the book is symbolic, but symbolic in a very narrow sense. That is, it represents a record of the spiritual conflict between the early church and Judaism and paganism. The exception is the closing chapters (Rev. 20–22), which constitute a symbolic picture of the contemporary triumph of the church. Historically, this view seems to have been developed in the late Medieval period following Luis de Alcázar (1554–1613).[18]

The typical preterist argues that the primary focus of the book is on the early church. The conflict contained within its pages was the conflict of the first century. The book was written solely to encourage first-century Christians, and thus there are no directly predictive elements in it. Beyond this, since the book described the battle between Christianity and its foes, in some respects the preterist view is similar to the idealist.

Historicist

The third view is the historical approach. Proponents of this view tend toward a literalistic approach in that they see a qualified historical fulfillment. That is, they see the book as an outline of future history. Each event is really a symbol of a future event in the history of the church. For example, the pouring out of the first bowl (Rev. 16:1–2) is seen as representing the French Revolution.[19] It then would culminate with the second coming of Jesus at the end.

Joachim of Fiore (ca. 1135–1202) is credited with developing this school of thought in his *Exposition of the Apocalypse.* He is noted as being a mystic philosopher of history. A native of Calabria, Italy, he became a Cistercian monk and later founded the order of San Giovanni in Fiore, Italy. While there, he claimed to have at least two mystical experiences that he said gave him the gift of spiritual intelligence, enabling him to understand the inner meaning of history. He taught that there would be three ages: the OT period (the age of the Father), the NT period (the age of the Son), and the coming age of the Holy Spirit. He calculated the latter to begin in 1260 (after forty-two generations of thirty years each).

There are two problems with this view. First, interpreters from this perspective have tended to see the second coming of Jesus as being very soon. They thus would take the history up to that point. This approach would then require rewriting of the interpretative scheme in every generation that Jesus has not come. The symbolism also points to past events. Thus, there is no way to look at a symbol and anticipate any given event. As such, if there is a yet future section in a historicist's interpretation, it tends to be very nebulous.

Futurist

The futurist approach argues that the heart of the book of Revelation (Revelation 4–19) portrays a distinct period of judgment that is yet to come, because the judgments listed there are associated with the second coming of Jesus.

Futurists maintain that their view derives directly from the text when it is read as literally as possible. This apparently was the view of the early church, at least into the third century (if not the time of Augustine).[20] Even after Augustine, a small minority of scholars throughout history have apparently held this view. It became a very popular view beginning in the middle to late 1800s.

One weakness of this view would seem to be that it applies the book only to the generation that would be associated with that second coming. However, the

PERGAMUM. One of the seven cities of Revelation. Situated in a mountainous region, it resisted Roman conquest longer than other cities in northwest Asia Minor, and when it finally fell, it became the chief Roman city in the region.

assurance of God's ultimate victory would be a comfort to all generations. Moreover, it appears that aspects of the book speak directly to all generations.

WHAT IS THE MILLENNIUM?

We have observed that one of the major questions of the first-century period was that of the kingdom. This theme was built on OT teaching that the Messiah would establish God's kingdom on earth. Revelation talks about that reign, but not in a detailed sense. In fact, much of the book still anticipates the kingdom. It is not until Revelation 20:4 that we read about Jesus the Messiah establishing His reign or kingdom. At that time, those who died as believers will be resurrected and will join those still alive as part of the reign of the Messiah on earth.[21] The time period for this reign on earth is described as a thousand years—that is, a millennium.

> One of the major concerns in the first century was that the OT taught that the Messiah would establish God's kingdom on earth.

How one interprets that thousand-year period and its relationship to the coming of Jesus determines how one views prophecy in general. In fact, three derivatives of that word are used to characterize a person's views on prophecy.

The first view looks at the book of Revelation as a generally chronological sequence. In that case, the second coming of Jesus, which is described in Revelation 19, precedes the kingdom, which is described in chapter 20. This view is called *premillennialism*.[22]

The *amillennialist* view argues that this one-thousand-year period is symbolic, representing a long period of time. Those who hold this view argue that the kingdom of God is predominately a spiritual one, that is, it represents the rule of Jesus over His people in the world today. The phrase in Revelation 20 then represents Christians who have died as reigning with Christ in heaven.[23]

The third view, called *postmillennialism*, maintains that the church will become the means of establishing the kingdom of God and will manage it, followed by the return of Christ. In essence, it still holds for an actual kingdom. But based on its interpretation of the Bible, it is solely a spiritual one, "a golden age of spiritual prosperity."[24]

POSTMILLENNIALISM

The basic concepts of postmillennialism have been attributed to Daniel Whitby (1638–1726). This approach, however, flourished with the development of science and technology. It has emerged in history in a variety of places and slogans. For example, in American history the Puritans came to America to establish God's kingdom. American expansion in the nineteenth century followed the same theme, characterized as "manifest destiny." The British Empire carried the concept under the guise of "white man's burden." Basically, there was an identification of a given culture with Christianity, and the expansion of one became the expansion of the other.

THE VISIONS OF REVELATION

The book of Revelation consists of three sections, which are clearly defined. Chapter 1 is a vision of the resurrected Jesus. Chapters 2 and 3 are letters to be written to seven churches in Asia. The last nineteen chapters consist of a series of visions into the spiritual realm.

A Guiding Outline.

Revelation 1:19 provides an outline of the intent of those three major sections. There John says he was told to write of the things that he had seen (ch. 1), the things that are (chs. 2–3), and the things that are to follow, or things that will take place after these things (chs. 4–22). As such, it would seem that while the things that are (the seven churches) related to John's era, the last section was in the future.

The Vision of the Resurrected Jesus

Read Revelation 1.

The book is written as a letter, addressed to the seven churches.[25] John indicated at the beginning of his book that while he was on Patmos he had a vision. In this vision, he saw the resurrected Jesus. The vision set the stage for the subsequent messages in chapters 2 and 3. As he looked at Jesus, he noted certain characteristics (e.g., a two-edged sword coming out of His mouth). Each of those characteristics would be specifically appropriate to what was said to each church. At the end, Jesus told John to write to each of the churches about current conditions and what was to come.

The Vision of the Seven Churches

Read Revelation 2–3.

Jesus dictated to John what he was to write to each church. The structure of each letter was basically the same. They all began with a command to write to the specific church. The content of each was a message from the resurrected Jesus. However, it was associated with a specific characteristic of the sender as listed in chapter 1. Each message began with a commendation for something the church was doing right (except for Sardis and Laodicea). This was followed by criticism or citation of something that could be done better (except for Smyrna and Philadelphia). It was emphasized by a specific admonition. The letters each con-

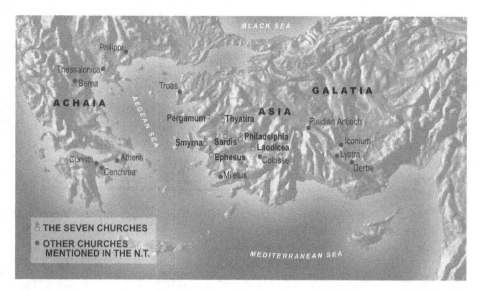

cluded with a nonspecific challenge keyed to the phrase, "He who has an ear, let him hear."

It is generally accepted that the seven churches were seven specific locations that did exhibit those characteristics. That is, by the time of John's last days there were some churches that were strong. Some churches struggled with specific issues, usually associated with false teaching. Then there were some churches that were already dying (or dead). Beyond this, however, there has been debate. Why those seven churches? Was it because they represented seven possible types of churches that would be present throughout history? Or was it because they

THE SEVEN CHURCHES OF REVELATION

ORIGINAL	TYPE	AGE*
Ephesus	Losing its fervor	33–100 (Pentecost-Last Apostle)
Smyrna	Persecuted	100–316 (Edict of Milan)
Pergamum	Compromised	316–787 (Nicean Council)
Thyatira	Syncretistic	787–1517 (Reformation)
Sardis	Sleeping	1517–1792 (Missions movement)
Philadelphia	Faithful	1792–Rapture (Hour of testing)
Laodicea	Dead	Rapture–Kingdom

*The dates set here are somewhat arbitrary as are all stages in history. The advantage of this layout is that while we might say that we are in the next-to-last "age" and there is an ending event, there is no way to anticipate the exact end.

represented dominant characteristics of different ages? Or is it possible that there were aspects of both? If the latter is true, the chart on page 589 shows a possible pattern.

Visions into the Spiritual Realm

Read Revelation 4–20.

The heart of the book of Revelation is a series of visions. The first (chs. 4–5) puts John in heaven, where he saw God on the throne.[26] He also saw the resurrected Jesus, addressed as the Lion of Judah, but in appearance as a Lamb. He was given a scroll sealed with seven seals. As He broke the seven seals, judgments occurred on earth (chs. 6–7). After the sixth seal, John saw the multitudes of believers from every nation.[27]

When the seventh seal was broken, a second series of judgments followed (chs. 8–11). These were introduced by seven angels blowing seven trumpets. As was the case of the first series, there was a pause after number six. In this case, John records

> **The heart of the book of Revelation is a series of visions.**

that he was given a book, which he ate. It was sweet, but bitter in the stomach. He was told that he had to prophesy. He then was told of two messengers in the Holy City who would be martyred, then resurrected. Subsequently the seventh angel sounded his trumpet. Angelic beings praised God for subduing the nations of the world and making them into the kingdom of the Messiah. Then God's temple in heaven was opened and the ark of the covenant was seen.[28]

At this point, John records a long interlude where he saw a vision that served as an allegory of the coming of the Messiah and the spiritual warfare associated with that (chs. 12–14). It culminated with Jesus on Mount Zion with 144,000.

BEMA AT CORINTH. The platform where the judge sat. The word *bema* is used for the place where Jesus will sit and judge when He returns.

He continued with a description of a "harvest" on earth as God executed judgment.

This vision was followed by a third cycle of seven plagues poured out from seven bowls by another seven angels (chs. 15–16). This cycle was culminated by judgment on, and the fall of, Babylon (chs. 17–18).[29]

With the judgment of Babylon, victory was declared. Jesus rode in on a white horse symbolizing victory (ch. 19). The last of Satan's forces gathered on the plains of Megiddo to oppose Him. They were killed by "the sword that came out of the mouth of the rider on the horse" (v. 21).[30]

The last part of this section relates the judgment of Satan's forces. Satan himself is cast into a pit for the thousand years of the Messiah's reign. He then is released to deceive future generations. This attempt also fails, and Satan is cast into the lake of fire. At this point, all of those who have never established a relationship with God through the Messiah are raised from the dead. Because their names are not found in the book of life, they too are cast into the lake of fire.

Ever After

The final section of the book relates the renovation of the cosmos. This event apparently removes the last taints of the curse. John described it as a new city of Jerusalem. What he saw is very difficult to comprehend. According to the explicit measurements he gave, it was a cube, a thousand miles on an edge. To us, that does not make sense. According to our understanding of physics, such a cube would throw a rotating earth into dynamic imbalance. We can only say that John was try-

Read Revelation 21–22.

ing to describe in physical terms something that transcended the material universe and belongs in the spiritual realm.

As John tried to convey the beauty of that city, there are three significant points. First, it was noted for the presence of God (and the Lamb). Second, the tree of life (which we saw in Genesis 3) was there. Third, finally, there was no more curse.

Finally, there was no more curse.

John wrapped up the book with a warning from Jesus. He would be coming soon. As such, every reader should be aware of his or her lifestyle and live expectantly. The book gave fair warning to all of the judgment that Jesus would bring with Him. To this John responded, "Amen. Even so, come, Lord Jesus" (KJV).

THE FINALE

And so the Bible ended more than fifteen hundred years after it started. The final writer was in a foreign country some seven hundred miles from Palestine. He wrote in an entirely different language. But the theme had not changed. Just like Moses, John was writing about God's relationship with His people. Moses had anticipated the coming of the Messiah. John was there when it happened, and it wasn't quite what anyone expected. Even so, John was confident that was not the end of the story. Rather, as Jesus had promised, He would return and finish fulfilling the prophecies that God's prophets had given. But that is another story for an undisclosed future.

To be continued . . .

REVIEW QUESTIONS

1. Why is John's gospel so significantly different from the Synoptic Gospels?

2. What is the focus of John's first letter?

3. How are John's second and third letters different from his first letter and from each other?

4. What are the purposes of the book of Revelation?

5. What are the four main schools of interpretation of Revelation, and what is the key premise on which they disagree?

6. What is "the Millennium," and why is it important?

7. What are the three main sections of Revelation?

8. What passage seems to provide a basic outline of the book?

9. How is the ending of the Bible different from its beginning? What theme do they have in common?

GLOSSARY

The number in parentheses following a term indicates a page where a significant reference (not necessarily the first reference or the only significant one) can be found in the book.

allegorical hermeneutic (582) A method of interpretation that takes the text as having a deeper, spiritual meaning behind the straightforward meaning of the words. This spiritual meaning needs to be extracted by skilled teachers who then determine what the text really means. These teachers also determine which parts of the biblical text need an allegorical interpretation and which may be understood literally. This method seems to have originated in Alexandria, and it gradually displaced the literal hermeneutic of the early church. See *literal hermeneutic.*

amillennialism (587) A school of prophetic interpretation that understands the term millennium (Revelation 20) to be symbolic, but disagrees on what it symbolizes. The dominant view is that "millennium" represents how blessed the current Christian experience is. Amillennialists look for a glorious return of Jesus Christ followed by judgment and the destruction of the evil world. See *premillennialism* and *postmillennialism.*

antinomianism (560) Technically, it suggests opposition to law. Primarily it views moral law as nonbinding upon Christians. It often reflects an antiauthoritarian attitude that argues there should be no restrictions on personal freedom.

Apocrypha (48) A term meaning "hidden" (singular *apocryphon*). It is used to refer to a number of books written after the OT canon was closed. They were highly valued by many and were declared canonical in the sixteenth century by the Roman Catholic Church (which calls them *Deuterocanonical*), but the Protestant Reformers did not accept these books as authoritative. Some Bibles include the Apocrypha between the OT and the NT.

apodictic (143) A term meaning "clearly established, incontrovertible." An apodictic law is a decree based on the authority of the person or body that promulgates it (sometimes viewed as "do this because I said so"). See *casuistic.*

apostle (53) A term meaning "sent one," used primarily to refer to members of the group that Jesus selected for special mentoring during the last part of his ministry. This group is also known as "the Twelve." Later, Paul was listed as an apostle.

asceticism (538) The idea that spirituality or moral purity can be attained by extreme self-denial. It goes beyond self-control and discipline both in terms of cause and effect and in the degree of denying physical needs.

canon (52) A standard that something else is measured against (from a Greek term meaning "rod, rule"). In biblical terms, the canon is the collection of books that are viewed as Scripture.

casuistic (143) Derived from the Latin *casus,* meaning *case,* it reflects the use of case studies to set forth legal principles or applications. Most ANE law was *casuistic.* See *apodictic.*

Catholic Epistles (553) NT letters written to general audiences rather than individuals or specific churches (from a Latin word meaning "universal").

codex (54) An ancient manuscript in the form of a (modern) book, distinguished from a rolled manuscript or scroll (from a Latin word meaning "block [of tablets]," later "book").

communal lament (162) A psalm that expresses concern about misfortunes affecting the entire nation.

communal offering (151) A sacrifice performed to show gratitude to God. The burnt meat provided a meal of celebration for all who were present.

consecratory offering (151) A sacrifice performed as part of an act of dedication.

conservative (28) A very loose term used to describe scholars who approach the biblical text with such presuppositions as acceptance of the traditional view on the origin of Scripture and the existence of the supernatural.

coregency (276) Joint rule. In the ANE a king sometimes would make his son joint ruler to help ensure succession.

critical scholarship (30) Sometimes called "higher criticism," a form of biblical criticism that attempts to interpret Scripture through reason (based on naturalistic presuppositions). It includes several approaches, such as source criticism (or historical criticism), which looks for "sources" behind the biblical text. This is in contrast to "lower criticism," which looks at the different manuscripts of the biblical text and evaluates how they relate and determines which is closest to the original.

cuneiform (37) A form of writing using wedge-shaped marks, the most common form of writing throughout the ANE (except for Egypt) up until the time of Moses.

Dead Sea Scrolls (54) Manuscripts discovered in the region of the Dead Sea beginning in 1948. These manuscripts, which date from about 150 BCE to 100 CE, include portions of all the books of the OT except Esther (as well as many other documents). They often verify the accuracy of the later manuscripts from which our modern Bibles have been translated.

declarative praise psalms (151) Psalms written to tell of the deeds God has done in history, especially in the life of the poet.

descriptive praise psalms (236) Psalms written to describe God's goodness and power.

Diaspora (357) The dispersion of the Israelite people (whom we today collectively call Jews) throughout the world as a result of the exile of the Northern and Southern kingdoms. While part of the Southern Kingdom returned for a few hundred years, the Diaspora is still considered ongoing.

docetism (454) An early Christian heresy that argued that the incarnation was in appearance only (from a Greek verb meaning "to seem"). That is, it denied the human nature of Jesus Christ, arguing that he was a spiritual being who only appeared to be human.

documentary hypothesis (30) See *JEDP theory*.

Essenes (358) A Jewish religious-political party during the second temple period. In many ways they, like the Pharisees, sought a society that had a strong commitment to a strict Jewish lifestyle based on the covenant, but they were even more rigorous in their piety.

expiatory offering (149) A sacrifice performed as part of a sinner's demonstration of repentance.

four-source theory (379) A theory that the three Synoptic Gospels actually developed out of four original sources: Mark, an otherwise unknown source called Q, and two other otherwise unknown sources called L and M. See *two-source theory*.

freewill offering (151) A communal offering offered spontaneously, that is not given as a response to any specific events in life.

futurist school (586) A school of interpretation of Revelation that argues it is a prewritten record of the actual conflict between God and Satan that will occur at the end of the church age. This view recognizes many symbols but tries to look at the text as literally as possible.

Gemarah (353) An Aramaic term meaning "traditional learning or teaching" and applied to the rabbinic commentaries and debates on the Mishnah (the Mishnah and the Gemarah make up the Talmud). It is a centuries-long discussion on how to carry out the law while not in the land with a temple. See *Mishnah*.

Gnosticism (556) A religious current (from Greek *gnōsis*, "knowledge") that placed strong emphasis on the attainment of divine knowledge and drew a sharp distinction between the physical (evil) and spiritual (good) realms. While gnostic tendencies are evident in Hellenistic influences on Judaism, they became significant in Christianity late in the first century and especially in the second century.

go'el (211) A Hebrew word translated "kinsman-redeemer," referring to the closest relative of a man who had died, this relative being responsible for securing his inheritance. If the man was murdered, the relative was also responsible for pursuing justice.

gospel (375) The distinctive Christian message (from Old English *gōd*, "good," and *spel*, "story," used to translate Greek *euangelion*, "good news"). The term is also applied to the NT documents that proclaim Jesus as the promised Messiah and give evidence to demonstrate this truth.

Graf-Welhausen hypothesis (60) See *JEDP theory*.

Hanukkah (366) A Jewish festival commemorating the cleansing of the temple under the Maccabeans in 164 BCE. The Hebrew word means "dedication," and the event is called either the Feast of Lights or the Feast of Dedication. According to tradition, there was only enough consecrated oil for one day, but the lights burned the entire eight days of the cleansing. John 10:22–23 records Jesus' celebration of this festival.

hedonism (484) A philosophy that argues that pleasure or happiness is the chief end of life (from Greek *hēdonē*, "pleasure"). While as a philosophy it originally reflected moderation, as a lifestyle it aimed toward self-gratification.

Hellenization (356) The process of adopting Greek culture and even the Greek language (from *Hellas*, "Greece").

hermeneutics (9) The science of interpretation, particularly applied to the study of the Bible (from Greek *hermeneuō*, "to interpret, explain").

ḥerem (178) A Hebrew term meaning "devotion, ban, extermination," used especially in relation to the Israelite conquest of Palestine. Cities under the ban were given over to or devoted totally to God. While this often involved destruction, specific guidelines are given in most cases.

ḥesed A Hebrew word variously translated "lovingkindness, mercy, steadfast love"; it relates to faithfulness to a covenant relationship. While especially evident in God's care for His people, it is also evident in human relations, for example in Ruth's actions (Ruth 3:10).

historicist school (585) A school of interpretation that argues that the book of Revelation is a record of the spiritual conflict throughout the entire church age. As such, it is viewed as future history portrayed in symbolic form.

idealist school (584) A school of interpretation that argues for a highly allegorical view of the book of Revelation, suggesting it really addresses only spiritual truths of the battle between God and evil and does not depict a physical struggle.

immanence (60) The attribute of God that reflects that he is close to his creation and thus always nearby, in contrast with *transcendence*.

individual laments (235) Psalms that express concern about misfortune in the life of the writer.

JEDP theory (31) The theory that the Pentateuch originally came from four different sources (Yahwist/Jehovist, Elohist, Deuteronomistic history, Priestly tradition) and were put together during the postexilic period to produce the Pentateuch we have today. See *critical scholarship*.

justification (466). An act of God that pronounces guilty sinners as righteous and just, based on the atoning death of Jesus the Messiah. According to the NT, sinners are justified by faith (Rom 3:21–30).

kenōsis A Greek word meaning "emptying" and used to refer to the incarnation of the Second Person of the Trinity as Jesus. In Philippians 2:7 Paul states that Jesus "emptied Himself" (NASB) or "made himself nothing" (NIV). Theologians debate what this really means, but the key point is that because of this example, Christians are not to look for self-advancement.

Kings of the North (364) The term used in the book of Daniel for the Seleucid dynasty, that is, the rulers of the Syrian portion of Alexander the Great's empire after it broke up.

Kings of the South (362) The term used in the book of Daniel for the Ptolemaic dynasty, that is, the rulers of the Egyptian portion of Alexander the Great's empire after it broke up.

legalism (538) The idea that spirituality (that is, salvation) can be attained by following a list of rules and regulations that tends to become more detailed with time. In the process, the person becomes more concerned about obeying rules than having a relationship with God.

liberal (29) A very loose term used to describe scholars who approach the biblical text with such presuppositions as rejection of the supernormal and skepticism regarding the origin of the text. See *critical scholarship.*

lingua franca (47) An Italian phrase (literally meaning "Frankish [French] tongue") referring to a language used by different cultures as a common medium for trade or diplomacy.

literal hermeneutic (582) A method of interpretation that takes the biblical text in a straightforward manner as saying exactly what the author intended. In this view, figures of speech are understood as standard methods of conveying ideas. This was the interpretational method of the early church, especially in Antioch. See *allegorical hermeneutic.*

Maccabeans (365) Followers of Judas Maccabeus, a key leader of the Jewish revolt against the Syrians in the mid-second century BCE. This successful uprising led to independence for Judea and a cleansing of the temple and is celebrated in the festival of *Hanukkah.*

manuscript (53) A handwritten document. We have manuscripts of parts of the Bible dating from several hundred years before Jesus was born (for the OT) up to and beyond the time that Gutenberg began printing the Bible in the fifteenth century CE.

Messiah (51) A Hebrew and Aramaic word meaning "anointed one" that can refer to any person who is anointed for a purpose. When capitalized, however, it refers to a specific person who would be sent from God and serve an intercessory role for the nation of Israel and the world. The Greek form of this word is *Christos,* from which we get "Christ."

millennium (587) A Latin term meaning "one thousand years" and applied to the time that Jesus would have a kingdom on earth (Rev. 20:4).

Mishnah (352) A collection of early rabbinic traditions that were written down ca. 200 CE (the Mishnah and its commentary, the Gemarah, make up the Talmud). It is basically a recorded discussion between the rabbinical leaders (during the period of about 300 to 400 BCE to 100 CE) over the meaning of the law for specific details of day-to-day life.

mysticism (538) The idea that spirituality can be attained or demonstrated by glimpses into the spiritual realm. These glimpses are deemed to be through direct spiritual contact between the individual and God or other spiritual beings and not through the normal physical senses.

myth (29) In modern criticism, a narrative that involves interaction with a deity or in some other way with the spiritual realm. In this usage the term does not say anything about the historicity of the account. However, an underlying assumption of modern criticism rules out spiritual intervention in the physical realm, which makes a "myth" at best one's interpretation of a physical event. Most contemporary critical scholars suggest that the Bible does not contain actual "myths" (in the normal sense) but appropriates mythical motifs.

Nazirites (160) Also spelled "Nazarites." People who made a promise to God and for a set time changed their lifestyle, which was marked by three elements: they did not cut their hair, they could not touch anything unclean, and they could not use alcohol or any grape product. At the end of the period, a votive offering was required. A very few, such as Samson and Samuel, were Nazirites for life.

oral tradition (356) The transmission of sayings, beliefs, or events by word of mouth. In rabbinic thought, it refers to the authoritative interpretation of the OT law, supposedly given originally (like the written law) to Moses on Mount Sinai but not written down until the publication of the *Mishnah.* Much of this tradition was traced back to the time of Ezra and was used by the Pharisees to justify their understanding of the OT law.

parable (392) An analogy whereby spiritual truths are presented through familiar incidents. According to Jesus, His parables are deliberately obscure so that those who are spiritually insensitive will not understand them (Mark 4:11–12).

parallelism (235) The matching or balancing of corresponding ideas in successive lines; it is the key indicator of Hebrew poetry.

peace offering (150) A communal offering to thank God for some benefit.

Pentateuch (30) The first five books of the OT (from the Greek words for "five" and "book").

Pharisees (357) A Jewish religious-political party during the second temple period. Viewed as the conservatives of their day, they resisted Hellenization through their interpretation of the OT law, using an oral tradition to help them.

poetry (234) A form of literature that uses the sounds of the language to enhance the meaning of the piece. In contrast with classical and English poetry, which places more emphasis on rhyme, rhythm, alliteration, and other literary features, the most distinctive feature of Hebrew poetry is *parallelism*.

polemic An argument against an idea or position. Sometimes the opposite viewpoint is referred to indirectly. An example is the suggestion that Genesis 1, by showing God as the Creator of everything, argues against multiple gods.

postmillennialism (588) A school of prophetic interpretation espousing that God's kingdom on earth is currently spreading by the preaching of the gospel and the work of the Holy Spirit, and that Jesus will not return until the end of a long period of peace and righteousness. See *amillennialism* and *premillennialism*.

premillennialism (587) A school of prophetic interpretation that understands that Jesus will return prior to the establishing of God's kingdom on earth, based on the chronology of Revelation 20. See *amillennialism* and *postmillennialism*.

preterist school (585) A school of interpretation that argues for a narrowly allegorical view of the book of Revelation, suggesting that it is a record of the conflict between the early church and Judaism on the one hand and paganism on the other. As such, most of the events of Revelation have already occurred.

Protevangelium (76) A term derived from two Greek words meaning "first" and "gospel." It refers to God's announcement to Eve of "the seed of woman," which is viewed by theologians as the first anticipation of the Messiah (thus the first proclamation of the gospel).

proverb (248) A short, general observation about how life works, expressed in an easily remembered manner.

Pseudepigrapha (48) Books that claimed to be written by well-known Bible figures but were not. The term is also applied more broadly to a variety of other Jewish works. These books were never accepted by the church, which has been aware of them from the beginning. On occasion they are called "lost books" of the Bible.

radiometric dating (36) Dating the age of an artifact by comparing the amount of radioactivity left in it with how much it began with. Radioactive carbon is the most common means of dating in archaeology. Other forms include potassium-argon and uranium-lead, which are used in geologic records.

royal psalms (237) Psalms that address the human king as God's representative but also see God in his role as the great King over the nation. Many address the ideal King or Messiah and are called messianic psalms.

Sadducees (357) A Jewish religious-political party during the second temple period. Sometimes viewed as the religious liberals of their day, they interpreted the OT law in a way that accommodated it to a Hellenistic worldview.

sanctification (466) The process of a believer's becoming more Godlike. The key is that while salvation reestablishes the proper relationship between a person and God, it takes time to change from a sinful lifestyle.

scribe (359) A professional title for scholars in the intertestamental and NT periods whose primary job was to copy the Law, read it, and interpret it to the people.

second temple (383, Illustration of Second Temple Model) The temple built in the postexilic period (520 BCE) and destroyed in 70 CE. This edifice replaced the first temple, built by Solomon but destroyed by Nebuchadnezzar. The second temple, originally finished under the instruction of Haggai, was renovated and expanded by Herod the Great.

Septuagint (48) The early Greek translation of the OT, often abbreviated LXX. The word comes from the Latin word for "seventy," based on tradition about the number of scholars who translated the Pentateuch. This was probably the version of the OT used by most NT writers.

Shekinah (148) A term that comes from the Aramaic and means "dwelling" or "royal residence." It was used by Jews after the Exile to describe the glory that demonstrated the presence of God in the tabernacle or temple.

source criticism (378) A form of higher criticism that looks for various literary and oral sources behind the biblical documents. Many source critics assume that few of the biblical books were written by the authors to whom they are traditionally ascribed. In biblical studies, modern source criticism originally began with the Pentateuch (see *JEDP theory*).

suzerain-vassal treaty (142) An ancient treaty form that joined two nations, one as an overlord (or suzerain) and the other as a subordinate (or vassal).

synoptic problem (377) The question of why the gospels of Matthew, Mark, and Luke are very similar but at the same time have many key differences.

Talmud (353) A Hebrew word meaning "learning"; it denotes a two-part work Jews use to give guidance on how to live a righteous lifestyle. The two parts are the Mishnah and the Gemarah.

teraphim (109) A Hebrew term commonly understood to denote household idols. While associations with worship (and probably idolatry) are clearly implied, to date we are not really sure what they were.

theocracy (214) The type of government the nation of Israel had before it became a monarchy (the latter beginning with King Saul). The idea was that God was the direct ruler, and the people were to obey Him without the intermediary of a human sovereign.

theophany (71) An appearance of God on earth in a physical form, usually human.

toledot (58) A Hebrew word usually translated "the account of" in the NIV or "the generations of" in the NASB. It serves as a structural indicator for the book of Genesis, and a better translation may be "this is what became of."

Torah (141) The Hebrew word that is often translated "law" but literally means "teaching." It generally refers to the Pentateuch, the first five books of the OT.

transcendence (60) The attribute of God that indicates that He is totally beyond His creation.

two-source theory (378) A theory that the three Synoptic Gospels actually developed out of two original sources, Mark and an otherwise unknown source called Q. See *four-source theory*.

votive offering (51) A communal offering performed in thanksgiving to God for answering a request that was expressed in terms of a vow or promise.

"we passages" (433) Passages in Acts where the writer indicates his presence with Paul by using the pronoun "we." This is the key indicator that Luke wrote Acts.

BIBLIOGRAPHY

This overview is a product of more than thirty years of study, research, and teaching of both the Old and New Testaments. The following are works that contributed significantly to the writing of this book or that the reader may find helpful in providing different perspectives. It is by no means exhaustive in either aspect.

Albright, William F. *From the Stone Age to Christianity*. New York: Doubleday, 1953.

_____. *Proto-Sinaitic Inscriptions and Their Decipherment*. Cambridge, Mass.: Harvard University Press, 1969.

Alden, Robert L. *Job*. New American Commentary. Vol. 11. Nashville: Broadman, 1993.

Allis, Oswald T. *The Unity of Isaiah*. Phillipsburg, N.J.: Presbyterian and Reformed, 1980.

Andersen, Francis I. *Job: An Introduction and Commentary*. Downers Grove, Ill.: InterVarsity, 1976.

Anderson, Bernhard W. *Understanding the Old Testament*, 2nd ed. Englewood Cliffs, N.J.: Prentice-Hall, 1966.

Archer, Gleason. *A Survey of Old Testament Introduction*. Chicago: Moody Press, 1994.

Armerding, Carl E. *The Old Testament and Criticism*. Grand Rapids: Eerdmans, 1983.

Arnold, Bill T., and Bryan E. Beyer, *Encountering the Old Testament*. Grand Rapids: Baker, 1999.

Aune, David E. *The New Testament in Its Literary Environment*. Philadelphia: Westminster, 1987.

Baker, David A. *Obadiah: An Introduction and Commentary*. Downers Grove, Ill.: InterVarsity, 1988.

Baldwin, Joyce. *Haggai, Zechariah, Malachi*. Downers Grove, Ill.: InterVarsity, 1975.

Barnes, Albert. *Notes on the Book of Revelation*. Edinburgh: Gall & Inglis, 1852.

Berkhof, Louis. *The History of Christian Doctrines*. 1953; reprint, Grand Rapids: Baker, 1975.

_____. *Principles of Biblical Interpretation*. Grand Rapids: Baker, 1950.

Bierling, Marilyn, ed. *The Phoenicians in Spain*. Winona Lake, Ind.: Eisenbrauns, 2002.

Bimson, John J. *Redating the Exodus and the Conquest*. Sheffield, UK: Almond, 1981.

Black, David Alan, and David S. Dockery. *New Testament Criticism and Interpretation*. Grand Rapids: Zondervan, 1991.

Blair, Joe. *Introducing the New Testament*. Nashville: Broadman & Holman, 1994.

Block, Daniel I. *Judges, Ruth*. New American Commentary. Vol. 6. Nashville: Broadman, 1999.

Boettner, Loraine. *The Millennium*. Philadelphia: Presbyterian and Reformed, 1957.

Boyd, Greg. *God at War*. Downers Grove, Ill.: InterVarsity, 1997.

Brackman, Arnold C. *The Luck of Nineveh*. New York: Van Nostrand, Reinhold Co., 1981.

Bright, John. *A History of Israel*. 4th ed. Philadelphia: Westminster, 2002.

Bruce, F. F. *The Acts of the Apostles: The Greek Text with Introduction and Commentary*, 3rd ed. Grand Rapids: Eerdmans, 1990.

_____. *Commentary on the Book of Acts*. Grand Rapids: Eerdmans, 1954.

_____. *The Epistle to the Galatians: A Commentary on the Greek Text*. Grand Rapids: Eerdmans, 1964.

_____. *New Testament History*. Garden City, N.Y.: Doubleday, 1972.

_____. *Paul: Apostle of the Heart Set Free*. Grand Rapids: Eerdmans, 1977.

Bullinger, E. W. *Figures of Speech Used in the Bible*. 1898; reprint, Grand Rapids: Baker, 1968.

Cassuto, Umberto. *A Commentary on the Book of Exodus*. Jerusalem: Magnes, 1987.

_____. *A Commentary on the Book of Genesis: Part 1, from Adam to Noah*. Jerusalem: Magnes, 1978.

_____. *A Commentary on the Book of Genesis: Part 2, from Noah to Abraham*. Jerusalem: Magnes, 1984.

_____. *The Documentary Hypothesis and the Composition of the Pentateuch*. Jerusalem: Magnes, 1961.

Ceram, C. W. *Gods, Graves, and Scholars*. Rev. ed. Toronto: Bantam Books, 1967.

_____. *The Secret of the Hittites*. New York: Schocken Books, 1973.

Černý, Jaroslav. *Ancient Egyptian Religion*. London: Hutchinson's University Library, 1952.

Childs, Brevard. *Introduction to the Old Testament as Scripture*. Philadelphia: Fortress, 1979.

Clouse, Robert G., ed. *The Meaning of the Millennium: Four Views*. Downers Grove, Ill.: InterVarsity, 1977.

Connick, C. Milo. *The New Testament: An Introduction to Its History, Literature, and Thought*. Encino, Calif.: Dickenson, 1972.

Craigie, Peter C. *The Book of Deuteronomy*. Grand Rapids: Eerdmans, 1976.

Cranfield, C. E. B. *A Critical and Exegetical Commentary on the Epistle to the Romans*. 2 vols. Edinburgh: T. & T. Clark, 1975.

Culver, Robert D. *Daniel and the Latter Days*. Chicago: Moody Press, 1954.

Custance, Arthur. *The Doorway Papers*. 10 vols. Grand Rapids: Zondervan, 1975–79.

Davids, Peter H. *The Epistle of James: A Commentary on the Greek Text*. Grand Rapids: Eerdmans, 1982.

Dillard, Raymond B., and Tremper Longman III. *An Introduction to the Old Testament*. Grand Rapids: Zondervan, 1994.

Donfried, Karl P., ed. *The Romans Debate*. Rev. ed. Peabody, Mass.: Hendrickson, 1991.

Dorman, Ted M. *A Faith for All Seasons*. Nashville: Broadman & Holman, 1995.

Edersheim, Alfred. *The Life and Times of Jesus the Messiah*. 1896; reprint, Grand Rapids: Eerdmans, 1971.

Eissfeldt, Otto. *The Old Testament: An Introduction*. New York: Harper & Row, 1976.

Elwell, Walter A., and Robert W. Yarbrough. *Encountering the New Testament*. Grand Rapids: Baker, 1998.

Farmer, William R. *The Synoptic Problem*. Dillsboro, N.C.: Western North Carolina Press, 1976.

Fee, Gordon. *The First Epistle to the Corinthians*. Grand Rapids: Eerdmans, 1987.

Feinberg, Charles Lee. *The Minor Prophets*. Chicago: Moody Press, 1976.

_____. *The Prophecy of Ezekiel*. Chicago: Moody Press, 1969.

Fensham, F. Charles. *The Books of Ezra and Nehemiah*. Grand Rapids: Eerdmans, 1982.

Ferguson, Everett. *Backgrounds of Early Christianity*. Grand Rapids: Eerdmans, 1987.

Finegan, Jack. *Handbook of Biblical Chronology*. Rev. ed. Peabody, Mass.: Hendrickson, 1998.

Finley, Moses I. *Early Greece: The Bronze and Archaic Ages*. Rev. ed. New York: Norton, 1981.

Frankfort, H. *Ancient Egyptian Religion*. New York: Columbia University Press, 1948.

Freedman, David Noel, and Edward F. Campbell Jr., eds. *Biblical Archaeologist Reader*. 2 vols. Cambridge, Mass.: American Schools of Oriental Research, 1975–78.

Freeman, Hobart E. *Introduction to the Old Testament Prophets*. Chicago: Moody Press, 1977.

Garrett, Duane A. *Proverbs, Ecclesiastes, Song of Songs*. New American Commentary. Vol. 14. Nashville: Broadman, 1993.

Garstang, John, and J. B. E. Garstang. *The Story of Jericho*. London: Hodder & Stoughton, 1940.

Gelb, I. J. *A Study of Writing*. Chicago: University of Chicago Press, 1963.

Glickman, Craig S. *A Song for Lovers*. Downers Grove, Ill.: InterVarsity, 1976.

Godet, Frederic Louis. *Commentary on Romans*. 1883; reprint, Grand Rapids: Kregel, 1977.

Grant, Robert M. *A Historical Introduction to the New Testament*. New York: Harper & Row, 1963.

Gray, George Buchanan. *A Critical and Exegetical Commentary on the Book of Isaiah I–XXVII*, International Critical Commentary. Edinburgh: T. & T. Clark, 1912.

Gregg, Steve. *Revelation: Four Views, a Parallel Commentary*. Nashville: Thomas Nelson, 1997.

Grimal, Nicolas. *A History of Ancient Egypt*. New York: Barnes and Noble, 1997 reprint.

Grosheide, F. W. *Commentary on the First Epistle to the Corinthians*. Grand Rapids: Eerdmans, 1953.

Gundry, Robert H. *A Survey of the New Testament*. 3rd ed. Grand Rapids: Zondervan, 1994.

Guthrie, Donald. *New Testament Introduction*. 4th ed. Downers Grove, Ill.: InterVarsity, 1990.

Hallo, William W., and William Kelly Simpson. *The Ancient Near East: A History*. New York: Harcourt, Brace, Jovanovich, 1971.

Hanson, Paul D. *The Dawn of Apocalyptic*. Rev. ed. Philadelphia: Fortress Press, 1979.

Harbin, Michael A. *To Serve Other Gods: An Evangelical History of Religion*. Lanham, Md.: University Press of America, 1994.

Harris, R. Laird. *Inspiration and Canonicity of the Bible.* Grand Rapids: Zondervan, 1969.

Harris, Stephen L. *The New Testament: A Student's Introduction.* 2nd ed. Mountain View, Calif.: Mayfield, 1995.

Harrison, R. K. *Introduction to the Old Testament.* Grand Rapids: Eerdmans, 1969.

Heidel, Alexander. *The Gilgamesh Epic and Old Testament Parallels.* Chicago: University of Chicago Press, 1963.

Helyer, Larry R. *Yesterday, Today, and Forever: The Continuing Relevance of the Old Testament.* Salem, Wis.: Sheffield, 1996.

Hengstenber, E. W. *The Prophecies of Ezekiel Elucidated.* 1869; reprint, Minneapolis: James Publications, 1976.

Herodotus. *The History.* Trans. by George Rawlinson. The Great Books of the Western World. Vol. 6. Chicago: Encyclopaedia Britannica, 1952.

Herrmann, Siegfried. *A History of Israel in Old Testament Times.* Philadelphia: Fortress, 1979.

Hill, Andrew E., and John H. Walton. *A Survey of the Old Testament.* 2nd ed. Grand Rapids: Zondervan, 2000.

Hoehner, Harold. *Chronological Aspects of the Life of Christ.* Grand Rapids: Zondervan, 1978.

Hoekema, Anthony A. *The Bible and the Future.* Grand Rapids: Eerdmans, 1979.

Hoerth, Alfred. *Archaeology and the Old Testament.* Grand Rapids: Baker, 1998.

House, Paul R. *1, 2 Kings.* New American Commentary. Vol. 8. Nashville: Broadman, 1995.

_____. *Old Testament Survey.* Nashville: Broadman, 1992.

Howard, David M., Jr. *An Introduction to the Old Testament Historical Books.* Chicago: Moody Press, 1993.

Howard, Kevin, and Marvin Rosenthal. *The Feasts of the Lord.* Orlando, Fla.: Zion's Hope, 1997.

Hubbard, David Allen. *Joel and Amos: A Commentary.* Downers Grove, Ill.: InterVarsity, 1989.

Jeffers, James S. *The Greco-Roman World of the New Testament Era.* Downers Grove, Ill.: InterVarsity, 1999.

Josephus. *Complete Works.* Trans. by William Whiston. Grand Rapids: Kregel, 1960.

Jukes, Andrew. *The Law of the Offerings.* Grand Rapids: Kregel, 1966 reprint.

Kaiser, Walter C., Jr., and Moisés Silva. *An Introduction to Biblical Hermeneutics.* Grand Rapids: Zondervan, 1994.

Katzenstein, H. Jacob. *The History of Tyre.* Jerusalem: Schocken Institute for Jewish Research, 1973.

Kaufmann, Yehezkel. *Christianity and Judaism: Two Covenants.* 2nd ed. Jerusalem: Magnes, 1996.

Keil, C. F. *The Minor Prophets.* Commentary on the Old Testament. Vol. 10. Grand Rapids: Eerdmans, 1977 reprint.

Kenyon, Kathleen M. *The Bible and Recent Archaeology.* Atlanta: John Knox, 1978.

Kidner, Derek. *Ezra and Nehemiah.* Downers Grove, Ill.: InterVarsity, 1979.

_____. *Psalms 1–72.* Downers Grove, Ill.: InterVarsity, 1973.

_____. *Psalms 73–150.* Downers Grove, Ill.: InterVarsity, 1975.

King, Philip J., and Lawrence E. Stager. *Life in Biblical Israel.* Louisville, Ky.: Westminster John Knox, 2001.

Kitchen, Kenneth. "The Patriarchal Age: Myth or History?" *Biblical Archaeology Review* 21, no. 2 (March–April 1995), 48–57, 88–99.

Klein, Ralph W. *Textual Criticism of the Old Testament.* Philadelphia: Fortress, 1974.

Kramer, Samuel Noah. *The Sumerians: Their History, Culture, and Character.* Chicago: University of Chicago Press, 1963.

Lachs, Samuel Tobias. *A Rabbinic Commentary on the New Testament.* Hoboken, N.J.: 1987.

Lane, William L. *The Gospel According to Mark.* Grand Rapids: Eerdmans, 1974.

Lapide, Pinchas. *The Resurrection of Jesus: A Jewish Perspective.* Minneapolis, Minn.: Ausgburg, 1982.

LaSor, William Sanford, David Allan Hubbard, and Frederic William Bush. *Old Testament Survey: The Message, Form, and Background of the Old Testament.* Grand Rapids: Eerdmans, 1982.

Lindsay, F. Duane. *The Servant Songs.* Chicago: Moody Press, 1985.

Linnemann, Eta. *Is There a Synoptic Problem?* Grand Rapids: Baker, 1992.

Livingston, G. Herbert. *The Pentateuch in Its Cultural Environment.* Grand Rapids: Baker, 1974.

Lohse, Eduard. *The New Testament Environment.* Nashville: Abingdon, 1976.

Long, V. Philips. *The Art of Biblical History.* Grand Rapids: Zondervan, 1994.

Manton, Thomas. *An Exposition on the Epistle of Jude.* 1658; reprint, Minneapolis: Klock & Klock, 1978.

Marcus, David. *Jephthah and His Vow.* Lubbock: Texas Tech Press, 1986.

Marshall, I. Howard. *The Epistles of John.* Grand Rapids: Eerdmans, 1978.

_____. *Luke: Historian and Theologian*. Grand Rapids: Zondervan, 1971.

Matthiae, Paolo. *Ebla: An Empire Rediscovered*. Garden City, N.Y.: Doubleday, 1981.

Mays, James Luther. *Hosea: A Commentary*. Philadelphia: Westminster, 1969.

McBirnie, William Steuart. *The Search for the Twelve Apostles*. Wheaton, Ill.: Tyndale House, 1973.

McDowell, Josh. *Evidence That Demands a Verdict*. Arrowhead Springs, Calif.: Campus Crusade for Christ, 1972.

_____. *More Evidence That Demands a Verdict*. San Bernardino, Calif.: Campus Crusade for Christ, 1975.

Merkley, Paul. "The Gospels as Historical Testimony." *Evangelical Quarterly* 58, no. 4 (1986).

Merrill, Eugene. *An Historical Survey of the Old Testament*. 2nd ed. Grand Rapids: Baker, 1991.

_____. *Deuteronomy*. New American Commentary. Vol. 4. Nashville: Broadman, 1994.

_____. *Kingdom of Priests: A History of Old Testament Israel*. Grand Rapids: Baker, 1987.

Metzger, Bruce M. *An Introduction to the Apocrypha*. New York: Oxford University Press, 1957.

_____. *The Text of the New Testament*. 3rd ed. New York: Oxford University Press, 1992.

Montgomery, James A. *A Critical and Exegetical Commentary on the Book of Daniel*. Edinbugh: T. & T. Clark, 1927.

Montgomery, John Warwick. *History and Christianity*. Downers Grove, Ill.: InterVarsity, 1965.

Moorey, P. R. S. *Ur "of the Chaldeans."* Ithaca, N.Y.: Cornell University Press, 1982.

Moreland, J. P. *The Creation Hypothesis*. Downers Grove, Ill.: InterVarsity, 1994.

Morris, Leon. *The First and Second Epistles to the Thessalonians*. Grand Rapids: Eerdmans, 1959.

_____. *The Gospel According to John*. Grand Rapids: Eerdmans, 1971.

Moseley, Ron. *Yeshua: A Guide to the Real Jesus and the Original Church*. Baltimore: Messianic Jewish Publishers, 1996.

Motyer, J. Alec. *The Prophecy of Isaiah: An Introduction and Commentary*. Downers Grove, Ill.: InterVarsity, 1993.

Mowinckel, Sigmund. *The Psalms in Israel's Worship*. 2 vols. Nashville: Abingdon, 1962.

Mounce, Robert H. *The Book of Revelation*. Grand Rapids: Eerdmans, 1977.

Mounce, William D. *Pastoral Epistles*. World Bible Commentary. Vol. 46. Nashville: Nelson, 2000.

Muller, Jac J. *The Epistles of Paul to the Philippians and to Philemon*. Grand Rapids: Eerdmans, 1955.

Murray, John. *The Epistle to the Romans*. Grand Rapids: Eerdmans, 1968.

Neev, David, and K. O. Emery. *The Destruction of Sodom, Gomorrah, and Jericho*. New York: Oxford University Press, 1995.

Neusner, Jacob. *A History of the Jews in Babylonia*. 4 vols. Leiden: E. J. Brill, 1965–69.

Newsome, James D., Jr. *The Hebrew Prophets*. Atlanta: John Knox, 1984.

Nickelsburg, George W. E. *Jewish Literature between the Bible and the Mishnah*. Philadelphia: Fortress, 1981.

Niehoff, Maren R. *Philo on Jewish Identity and Culture*. Tübingen: Mohr Siebeck, 2001.

Noth, Martin. *The Deuteronomistic History*. Sheffield, UK: Sheffield, 1981.

_____. *A History of Pentateuchal Tradition*. Atlanta: Scholars Press, 1981 reprint.

Oates, Joan. *Babylon*. London: Thames & Hudson, 1979.

Olmstead, A. T. *History of Assyria*. Chicago: University of Chicago Press, 1975.

Orelli, Han Conrad von. *The Prophecies of Jeremiah*. 1889; reprint, Minneapolis, Minn.: Klock & Klock, 1977.

Oswalt, John N. *The Book of Isaiah*. 2 vols. Grand Rapids: Eerdmans, 1986–98.

Pentecost, J. Dwight. *Things to Come*. Grand Rapids: Zondervan, 1964.

Perrin, Norman. *What Is Redaction Criticism?* Philadelphia: Fortress, 1969.

Petersen, Norman R. *Literary Criticism for New Testament Critics*. Philadelphia: Fortress, 1978.

Pettinato, Giovanni. *The Archives of Ebla*. Garden City, N.Y.: Doubleday, 1981.

Pfeiffer, Robert H. *History of New Testament Times, With an Introduction to the Apocrypha*. New York: Harper, 1949.

Philo. *The Works of Philo*. Trans. by C. D. Yonge. Rev. ed. Peabody, Mass.: Hendrickson, 1993.

Pohill, John B. *Acts*. New American Commentary. Vol. 26. Nashville: Broadman, 1993.

Porteous, Norman W. *Daniel: A Commentary*. Philadelphia: Westminster, 1965.

Price, Randall. *In Search of Temple Treasures*. Eugene, Ore.: Harvest House, 1994.

_____. *Secrets of the Dead Sea Scrolls*. Eugene, Ore.: Harvest House, 1996.

_____. *The Stones Cry Out*. Eugene, Ore.: Harvest House, 1997.

Pritchard, James B., ed. *Ancient Near Eastern Texts Relating to the Old Testament*. 3rd ed. Princeton: Princeton University Press, 1969.

Rad, Gerhard von. *Genesis: A Commentary*. Philadelphia: Westminster, 1972.

Ramsey, W. M. *The Cities of St. Paul*. 1908; reprint, Grand Rapids: Baker, 1979.

_____. *The Teaching of Paul in Terms of the Present Day*. London: Hodder & Stoughton, 1913.

Robinson, James M. *The Nag Hammadi Library in English*. 4th ed. Leiden: Brill, 1996.

Ross, Allen P. *Creation and Blessing: A Guide to the Study and Exposition of the Book of Genesis*. Grand Rapids: Baker, 1988.

Rostovtzeff, M. *Rome*. New York: Oxford University Press, 1960.

Roux, Georges. *Ancient Iraq*. 2nd ed. London: Penguin, 1980.

Rudolph, Kurt. *Gnosis*. New York: Harpter & Row, 1987.

Saldarini, Anthony J. *Pharisees, Scribes, and Sadducees in Palestinian Society*. Grand Rapids: Eerdmans, 2001.

Sanders, E. P., and Margaret Davies. *Studying the Synoptic Gospels*. London: SCM Press, 1989.

Sauborin, Leopold. *The Psalms: Their Origin and Meaning*. New York: Alba House, 1974.

Schiffman, Lawrence W. *Reclaiming the Dead Sea Scrolls*. New York: Doubleday, 1995.

Schroeder, Gerald. *The Science of God*. New York: The Free Press, 1997.

Seiss, Joseph Augustus. *The Apocalypse: Lectures on the Book of Revelation*. Grand Rapids: Zondervan, 1972 reprint.

Shapiro, Sidney. *Jews in Old China*. New York: Hippocrene Books, 1988.

Sherwin-White, A. N. *Roman Society and Roman Law in the New Testament*. Grand Rapids: Baker, 1978 reprint.

Smith, David E. *The Canonical Function of Acts*. Collegeville, Minn.: The Liturgical Press, 2002.

Soron, David, Aicha ben Abed ben Khader, and Hedi Slim. *Carthage*. New York: Simon & Schuster, 1990.

Stambaugh, John E., and David L. Balch. *The New Testament in Its Social Environment*. Philadelphia: Westminster, 1986.

Stein, Robert H. *Jesus the Messiah*. Downers Grove, Ill.: InterVarsity, 1996.

_____. *The Synoptic Problem*. Grand Rapids: Baker, 1987.

Stibbs, Alan M. *The First Epistle General of Peter*. Grand Rapids: Eerdmans, 1959.

Strickland, Wayne, ed. *The Law, the Gospel and the Modern Christian: Five Views*. Grand Rapids: Zondervan, 1993.

Stulac, George M. *James*. Downers Grove, Ill.: InterVarsity, 1993.

Swete, Henry Barclay. *Commentary on Revelation*. Grand Rapids: Kregel, 1977 reprint.

Tacitus, Publius Cornelius. *The Histories*. Trans. by Alfred John Church and William Jackson Brodribb. Great Books of the Western World. Vol. 15. Chicago: Encyclopaedia Britannica, 1952.

Tcherikover, Victor. *Hellenistic Civilization and the Jews*. New York: Atheneum, 1982.

Thiele, Edwin R. *A Chronology of the Hebrew Kings*. Grand Rapids: Zondervan, 1977.

_____. *The Mysterious Numbers of the Hebrew Kings*, 3rd ed. Grand Rapids: Zondervan, 1983.

Thiselton, Anthony C. *The First Epistle to the Corinthians: A Commentary on the Greek Text*. Grand Rapids: Eerdmans, 2000.

Thompson, John Arthur. *The Book of Jeremiah*. Grand Rapids: Eerdamans, 1980.

Toussaint, Stanley D. *Behold the King: A Study of Matthew*. Portland, Ore.: Multnomah, 1980.

Tucker, Gene M. *Form Criticism of the Old Testament*. Philadelphia: Fortress, 1971.

Tyldesley, Joyce. *Hatchepsut: The Female Pharaoh*. London: Viking, 1996.

Unger, Merrill F. *Zechariah: Prophet of Messiah's Glory*. Grand Rapids: Zondervan, 1963.

Van Dam, Cornelis. *Urim and Thummim*. Winona Lake, Ind.: Eisenbrauns, 1997.

Vaux, Roland de. *Ancient Israel*. 2 vols. New York: McGraw-Hill, 1965.

Virkler, Henry A. *Hermeneutics: Principles and Processes of Biblical Interpretation*. Grand Rapids: Baker, 1981.

Waltner, Erland and J. Daryl Charles. *1–2 Peter, Jude*. Scottdale, Pa.: Herald Press, 1999.

Walvoord, John F. *Daniel: The Key to Prophetic Revelation*. Chicago: Moody Press, 1971.

_____. *The Millennial Kingdom*. Grand Rapids: Zondervan, 1959.

_____. *The Revelation of Jesus Christ.* Chicago: Moody Press, 1966.

Warfield, Benjamin Breckenridge. *The Inspiration and Authority of the Bible.* Philadelphia: Presbyterian and Reformed, 1970.

Welhausen, Julius. *Prolegomena to the History of Ancient Israel.* Gloucester: Peter Smith, 1973.

Wells, Colin. *The Roman Empire.* 2nd ed. Cambridge, Mass.: Harvard University Press, 1992.

Wenham, Gordon J. *The Book of Leviticus.* Grand Rapids: Eerdmans, 1979.

Wenham, John. *The Easter Enigma.* Grand Rapids: Baker, 1992.

_____. *Redating Matthew, Mark and Luke.* Downers Grove, Ill.: InterVarsity, 1992.

Westcott, Brooke Foss. *The Epistle to the Hebrews.* Grand Rapids: Eerdmans, 1980 reprint.

_____. *The Epistles of John.* 1883; reprint, Grand Rapids: Eerdmans, 1966.

Westermann, Claus. *Genesis: A Commentary.* 3 vols. Minneapolis, Minn.: Augsburg, 1984–86.

Wilkens, Michael J., and J. P. Moreland, eds. *Jesus under Fire.* Grand Rapids: Zondervan, 1995.

Wilson, John A. *The Culture of Ancient Egypt.* Chicago: University of Chicago Press, 1956.

Wiseman, Donald J. *1 and 2 Kings.* Downers Grove, Ill.: InterVarsity, 1993.

Witherington, Ben III. *The Jesus Quest.* Downers Grove, Ill.: InterVarsity, 1995.

Wood, Leon. *A Survey of Israel's History.* Grand Rapids: Zondervan, 1970.

Woodmorappe, John. *Noah's Ark: A Feasibility Study.* Santee, Calif.: Institute for Creation Research, 1996.

Woudstra, Marten H. *The Book of Joshua.* Grand Rapids: Eerdmans, 1981.

Wouk, Herman. *This Is My God.* New York: Pocket Books, 1974.

Yadin, Yigael. *The Art of Warfare in Biblical Lands.* New York: McGraw-Hill, 1963.

Yamauchi, Edwin M. *Persia and the Bible.* Grand Rapids: Baker, 1996.

_____. *Pre-Christian Gnosticism.* 2nd ed. Grand Rapids: Baker, 1983.

_____. *The Stones and the Scriptures.* Grand Rapids: Baker, 1972.

CREDITS AND PERMISSIONS

MAPS

All maps except for those on pages 133 and 335 are produced by Zondervan on backgrounds prepared by Mountain High Maps® Copyright © 1993 Digital Wisdom, Inc.

The map on page 335 was created by Lawrence Dolphin.

PHOTOGRAPHS AND ILLUSTRATIONS

All photographs and illustrations not included in the list below are provided by the author and are copyright © by Michael Harbin.

Other photographs and illustrations come from the following sources and are used by permission of the copyright owners:

Bridgeman Art Library

© Bridgeman Art Library/Courtesy of Victoria Art Gallery, Bath and North East Somerset Council/Bridgeman Art Library: Page 65.

© Birmingham Museums and Art Gallery/Bridgeman Art Library: Page 321.

Art Institute of Chicago, IL, USA/Bridgeman Art Library: Page 323.

Dr. James C. Martin

© Dr. James C. Martin: Pages 35, 70, 105, 108, 185, 192, 221, 270, 374, 390, 487, 512, 546, 554.

© Dr. James C. Martin. The British Museum; photographed by permission: Page 36.

© Dr. James C. Martin. The Cairo Museum; photographed by permission: Page 38.

© Dr. James C. Martin. Amman Archaeological Museum; photographed by permission: Page 180.

© Dr. James C. Martin. The Istanbul Archaeological Museum; photographed by permission: Page 362.

© Dr. James C. Martin. The Yigal Allon Center; Kibbutz Ginosar, on the western shore of the Sea of Galilee. Photographed by permission: Page 396.

© Dr. James C. Martin. Collection of the Israel Museum, Jerusalem, and courtesy of the Israel Antiquities Authority, exhibited at the Rockefeller Museum. Photographed by permission: Page 416.

Israelimages.com

© Israelimages.com/Richard Nowitz: Page 129.

© Israelimages.com/Cathy Raff: Page 153.

© Israelimages.com/Israel Talby: Page 155.

United States Government

National Aeronautics and Space Administration (NASA), U.S Government: Page 40.

National Aeronautics and Space Administration—Jet Propulsion Laboratory (NASA–JPL): Page 45.

Courtesy of Jeff Hester and Paul Scowen (Arizona State University) and NASA: Page 58.

Image by Stöckli, Nelson, Hasler/Laboratory for Atmospheres, Goddard Space Flight Center, http://rsd.gsfc.nasa.gov.rsd: Page 62.

U.S. Government: Page 66.

U.S. Department of Energy: Page 74.

Other Sources

© The John Rylands University of Manchester, United Kingdom/Reproduced by courtesy of the Director and Librarian, the John Rylands University of Manchester: Page 50.

© The Israel Museum, Jerusalem: Page 53.

Image by Francis Leroy, Biocosmos/Science Photo Library: Page 60.

© 2004, PALEOMAP Project/www.scotese.com: Page 66.

© Hirmer Verlag, Munchen: Page 88.

© Erich Lessing/Courtesy of Art Resources, NY: Page 142.

Copyright © by Zev Radovan, Jerusalem: Page 147.

Reconstruction copyright © Dr. Leen Ritmeyer, Ritmeyer Archaeological Design, Harrogate, England: Pages 150, 154, 218.

© Direct Design: Page 210, 503.

© Associates for Biblical Research: Pages 188, 207.

© 2002 Magic Eye Inc./www.magiceye.com: Page 273 (2).

Courtesy of the Oriental Institute of the University of Chicago: Page 327.

Image courtesy of Boston University, Department of Archaeology, © Boston University: Page 341.

© Richard Rigsby: Page 528.

Neal Bierling/Zondervan Image Archives, copyright © 1995–1999 by Zondervan: Pages 35, 44, 92, 94, 97, 106, 107, 122, 123, 126, 137, 140, 148, 152, 161, 165, 168, 172, 173, 180, 185, 190, 199, 214, 217, 221, 223, 228, 234, 241, 246, 248, 251, 266, 277, 290, 297, 302, 308, 316, 317, 332, 351, 393, 404, 415, 430, 443, 444, 451, 453, 456, 458, 464, 471, 480 (2), 481, 487, 515, 522, 537, 545, 552, 554, 557, 564 (2), 579, 580, 590.

NOTES

INTRODUCTION

1. We must exercise care here, since this description does not mean that conservative scholars accept the biblical documents uncritically or without thought. Rather, they begin by taking the text at face value and then try to evaluate how all the elements fit together. This defining statement is to be taken as counter to the view that looks at the biblical documents with suspicion and only grudgingly grants acceptance when overwhelming supportive evidence appears. The problem has been that other evidence, either supportive or contradictive, has been largely lacking. What has been fascinating is that over the past century and a half, as more external evidence has appeared, it has tended to support the biblical text.

2. The issue is whether God can intervene in space-time history. *Supernatural* carries a connotation of a violation of natural law. *Supernormal* reflects only that the act transcends normal processes.

3. *Critical* is a word that is used ambiguously. It can mean finding fault, or it can mean skilled judgment. In biblical scholarship the latter perspective is normally in mind.

4. These scholars use the word *myth* in a technical sense. This sense, they argue, does not necessarily suggest a lie or falsehood, but merely refers to a story that conveys certain truths (usually of a moral nature) by means of supernatural imagery. As Otto Eissfeldt maintains, "If a narrative is concerned with the world of the gods, or if gods are to a considerable extent involved in it, we may speak of a myth" (*The Old Testament: An Introduction* [New York: Harper & Row, 1976], 33). By definition, then, the biblical material, which involves interaction with God, is "mythical." However, the term is such an emotionally loaded word that most traditional scholars avoid using it. Because the term *myth* does allow for a kernel of historicity or factuality, critical scholars suggest that the word allows us to recognize a historical background behind the text—with some embellishing. Or, as G. H. Livingston defines it, a myth is "a fanciful story that seeks to explain some practice of unknown origin, or some belief embodied in a ceremony or institution.... A myth *largely* lacks factual basis, but the community that preserves it accepts it as true" (*The Pentateuch in Its Cultural Environment* [Grand Rapids: Baker, 1974], 94; italics added).

5. Key people who contributed to this process include Benedict Spinoza (1632–77), Jean Astruc (1684–1766), Alexander Geddes (1737–1802), and Karl Heinrich Graf (1815–69), among others. For an excellent overview of the entire process, consult R. K. Harrison, *Introduction to the Old Testament* (Grand Rapids: Eerdmans, 1969), 1–82, 493–662.

6. Wellhausen's work is a very persuasive argument built on a number of presuppositions. The assumptions and conclusions of the Documentary Hypothesis are not accepted by all scholars, although modern writers sometimes give the impression that it is only the ignorant who do not hold to this position. In this light, the reader is referred to the thorough, thought-provoking, and scholarly critique of this theory by the Jewish scholar Umberto Cassuto, *The Documentary Hypothesis and the Composition of the Pentateuch* (Jerusalem: Magnes, 1961). For an excellent critique by a layperson, consult Herman Wouk, *This Is My God* (New York: Pocket Books, 1974), 272–80.

7. These four sources are J (Yahwist—the name Yahweh is spelled Jahwe in German), E (Elohist), D (the Deuteronomistic history), and P (the Priestly tradition). For a more recent interpretation of how they came together, see Bernhard W. Anderson, *Understanding the Old Testament*, 4th ed. (Englewood Cliffs, N.J.: Prentice-Hall, 1986), 449–66. R. K. Harrison gives an extended discussion of the development of these concepts and shows how quickly more and more supposed sources had to be hypothesized (*Introduction to the Old Testament*, 500–505).

8. An interesting work that clearly documents the spiritual warfare taking place behind the scenes is Greg Boyd's *God at War* (Downers Grove, Ill.: InterVarsity, 1997), although the author seems to push past the evidence in some areas.

9. See Josh McDowell, *More Evidence That Demands a Verdict* (San Bernardino, Calif.: Campus Crusade for Christ, 1975), 5–6; and John Warwick Montgomery, *History and Christianity* (Downers Grove, Ill.: InterVarsity, 1965), 16–22.

10. J. P. Moreland, *The Creation Hypothesis* (Downers Grove, Ill.: InterVarsity, 1994), 32–37.

11. In this light, the observation of William Hallo is pertinent. After discussing the difficulties involved in understanding OT numbers, he warns against resorting to assuming "scribal errors." He states, "Once such scribal errors are admitted, scholarly unanimity with respect to the proper emendation [changing of the text] becomes almost impossible to achieve" (William W. Hallo, "From Qarqar to Carchemish," in *BAReader2*, 154).

12. Alfred Hoerth (*Archaeology and the Old Testament* [Grand Rapids: Baker, 1998], 18–21) notes how archaeology primarily illuminates the Bible by giving insight into various aspects of history. It also corroborates or supports the biblical account of specific events or people, but we don't consider that "proving" them.

13. This was brought home to me again recently when I attended a session at the Society of Biblical Literature's annual

meeting. An archaeologist who was excavating Ashkelon showed a peculiar structure of buried half-pots. Similar pots had been found in other sites, but their use had puzzled archaeologists for years. He then related visiting a village in Crete where a similar setup is still used for distilling alcoholic beverages, which gave insight into this peculiar structure.

14. Matt Crenson, "Ancient Remains Get More Accurate Dating," *Dallas Morning News*, 27 October 1992, A21. The point of the article was that the radiometric dating of a given skeleton did not fit the theory of how America was originally settled. By changing an assumption, he was able to get a "more accurate date," which was defined as fitting the current theory. One wonders how the changes in the settlement theories over the past few years affect this case.

15. The assumptions of ^{14}C dating are several and somewhat debated (Seung-Hun Yang, "Radiocarbon Dating and American Evangelical Christians," *Perspectives on Science and Christian Faith* 45 [December 1993]: 229–40). We assume we know the original ratio of ^{14}C to its daughter element. We also assume the decay rate is a constant and that we know what the rate is. (After all, no one has measured the actual "half-life," which is in the range of 5,640 years. Rather, scientists have measured for a short period of time and then extrapolated the data.) However, the decay rate of ^{14}C has been corrected a number of times during the past forty years. Further, whenever an item is dated through ^{14}C, the date that is given includes a range that shows the projected margin of error, often a couple of hundred years. Consequently, while ^{14}C can give ballpark figures, it should not be used to pinpoint dates.

16. It is from the name of this early region that we get the term *Akkadian*, the name for the language. Akkadian became the first lingua franca (or international trade language) of the world.

17. Paolo Matthiae, *Ebla: An Empire Rediscovered* (Garden City, N.Y.: Doubleday, 1981); and Giovanni Pettinato, *The Archives of Ebla* (Garden City, N.Y.: Doubleday, 1981).

18. See, for example, David Ewert, *A General Introduction to the Bible* (Grand Rapids: Zondervan, 1990); Harrison, *Introduction to the Old Testament*; and Donald Guthrie, *Introduction to the New Testament* (Downers Grove, Ill.: InterVarsity Press, 1970). Many other works address specific topics.

CHAPTER 1—The Origin of the Bible

1. The Hebrew uses the word *man* here, but elsewhere it uses *manna*, and this is the form used consistently in English versions.

2. Scholars generally believe the completed book referred to in Exodus 17:14 included the contents of these three books.

3. What we might call Judaism did not develop until after the time of Ezra and Nehemiah, when the Israelites began to define what was meant by the Law. Modern Judaism developed after the NT period. Cf. Michael A. Harbin, *To Serve Other Gods: An Evangelical History of Religion* (Lanham, Md.: University Press of America, 1994), 50–58.

4. The time of "this day" is unclear. However, the phrase clearly refers to a time after the people were settled in the land,

since it reflects the status quo at the time of the editor. There is also some question regarding how extensive the editorial comments are. It is probably safest to err on the conservative side, limiting such comments to the geographical identification.

5. The transmission of the Hebrew Bible is a complex issue. Prior to the standardization of the text in the first century CE, there existed several textual "families" (reflected, e.g., in the Greek translations and in some of the Dead Sea Scrolls), though most of the differences among them were minor. By the time of the apostles, the essential form of the Hebrew Bible as we know it today (the Masoretic text) was the dominant "accepted" text (Lawrence W. Schiffman, *Reclaiming the Dead Sea Scrolls* [New York: Doubleday, 1995], 153–80).

6. The term *God-fearers* was first used to distinguish those within the nation of Israel who were truly committed to God from the larger, ethnic Israel. One of the problems throughout the history of the nation was the existence of a broad spectrum of belief, ranging from those who were very serious to those who basically rejected God (much like today). *God-fearers* was used later to denote those Gentiles who had come to appreciate and fear the God of Israel but were unwilling to take the steps to convert to Judaism, which was really still an ethnic religion. An example is Cornelius (Acts 10:2), the Roman centurion who was led by Peter to faith in Jesus as the Messiah.

7. *Septuagint* comes from the Latin word for "seventy," a round number corresponding to the seventy-two scholars (six from each Israelite tribe) who, according to tradition, translated the Pentateuch in seventy-two days (*Letter of Aristeas* 46–51 and 307; English translation in *The Old Testament Pseudepigrapha*, ed. J. H. Charlesworth, 2 vols. [New York: Doubleday, 1985], 2:16 and 33). It is also called the LXX from the Roman numeral for seventy.

8. Schiffman, *Reclaiming the Dead Sea Scrolls*, 161–69. Brevard Childs argues that this is why we must accept the traditional canon, although he does not discuss the role of inspiration (cf. *Introduction to the Old Testament as Scripture* [Philadelphia: Fortress, 1979]).

9. Generally, when an OT prophet wrote, the community was in the land and had close internal contact. After the Exile, that was not the case, and some of the exilic books may have taken longer to be accepted. Many of the NT books were sent as letters to specific geographical locations. While the individuals and groups that received them seem to have accepted certain letters immediately as a special revelation from God, it took longer for both the knowledge of the work and its acceptance to spread throughout the overall community, which was dispersed throughout the Roman Empire and beyond.

10. Randall Price, *Secrets of the Dead Sea Scrolls* (Eugene, Ore.: Harvest House, 1996), 126–28.

11. A good work on this subject is Bruce M. Metzger, *The Text of the New Testament*, 3rd ed. (New York: Oxford University Press, 1992). See also Josh McDowell, *Evidence That Demands a Verdict* (Arrowhead Springs, Calif.: Campus Crusade for Christ, 1972). Recently, several scholars have dated some fragments of Matthew to between 50 and 75 CE, which, if true, would place this copy possibly within the lifetime of the author (see Carsten Peter Thiede, "Papyrus Magdalen Greek 17 (Gregory-Aland P64)," *Tyndale Bulletin* 46 [1995]: 29–43, and the response by Peter M. Head on pp. 251–85).

CHAPTER 2—This Is the Way the World Was

1. Some scholars see the word as the plural of *Eloah*, an alternative singular form. This etymology seems preferable (*TDOT*, 1:273).

2. Some scholars have suggested that the use of the plural points to the Trinity. This is certainly feasible, but at present there is no way to know for sure.

3. U. Cassuto, *The Documentary Hypothesis* (Jerusalem: Magnes, 1961), 31–32.

4. There are a number of problems with taking this view. First, the text is not poetry but historical narrative like the majority of the book (cf. Gerhard von Rad, *Genesis: A Commentary* [Philadelphia: Westminster, 1972], 47–48). Second, while there are hints of the pagan cosmology in some of the terms, a closer examination suggests that this relationship is not as clear-cut as may be supposed (cf. Alexander Heidel, *The Babylonian Genesis* [Chicago: University of Chicago Press, 1963]). Third, this view runs headlong into the traditional views of inspiration.

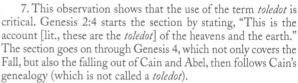

5. Another group attempts to straddle the two major views regarding the length of the days. This group argues that the word *day* should be taken literally but that it refers to the periods of time Moses used to write down the account. Thus, Genesis 1:3–5 constitutes the revelation God gave to Moses on the first day of the revelation. This argument runs into two problems. First, that is not the way the text reads, taken in a normal way. Second, this view implies that Moses could not write much at a time or that he gave a very cryptic summary of an entire day's revelation.

6. Another issue that is seldom addressed is the nature of time. Physicists are not sure what time is. Einstein's theory of relativity tells us that it is a variable depending on the observer and the physical state of the object (e.g., velocity and gravity affect time). Gerald Schroeder, an Orthodox Jew, makes a serious attempt at applying those points to a literal view of the Genesis text. He concludes that both the second and third views on Genesis 1 listed above are correct—depending on whose perspective one uses (*The Science of God* [New York: Free Press, 1997]).

7. This observation shows that the use of the term *toledot* is critical. Genesis 2:4 starts the section by stating, "This is the account [lit., these are the *toledot*] of the heavens and the earth." The section goes on through Genesis 4, which not only covers the Fall, but also the falling out of Cain and Abel, then follows Cain's genealogy (which is not called a *toledot*).

8. Genesis 1:30 states that at the original creation, all living creatures were given "every green plant for food." The issue of when carnivores developed is not addressed in the text and indeed raises many questions.

CHAPTER 3—Why the World Is Such a Mess

1. One of the more challenging scientific discoveries in the past few years possibly touches on this aspect. Scientists have discovered that at the end of the DNA strand in cells is a cap-like structure (some think of it like the tip on a shoestring) called a *telomer*. Each time the cell divides, a bit of the telomer disappears until it reaches a point that the DNA is no longer able to divide and the cell cannot reproduce. Eventually the cell dies. An enzyme called *telomerase* keeps the telomer from disappearing and thus provides for an indefinite life span. Two questions arise out of this information. Is the breakdown of the telomer a result of the Fall? Would the tree of life provide telomerase that would sustain life? This possibly would explain why Adam began dying at the point of the Fall but did not die for a number of years.

2. Some scholars have argued that the story of Cain and Abel is an archetype myth of the hunter/agrarian conflict. If that view were correct, we would expect to see one side or the other as the winner. Instead, both are losers. This outcome would suggest that what we really see here is the first tinkering with religion as Cain tried to do things "his way."

3. It is important to note that although this passage includes a genealogy, it is not introduced with the term *toledot*. Moreover, the writer quickly returns to Adam and relates the birth of Seth (Gen. 4:25), a third son who becomes the heir.

4. This issue is very complex, and the following only summarizes one key aspect. Kenneth Matthews gives a good overview of the issues in *Genesis 1–11:26*, New American Commentary (Nashville: Broadman & Holman, 1996), 322–32. Two primary arguments support the first view (the line of Seth versus the line of Cain). The first argument is that Genesis 4:26 seems to tie

the offspring of Seth to the sons of God. But chapter 5 seems to tie the daughters of men to the Seth line. Then the statement in Matthew 22:30 that the angels in heaven do not marry seems to rule out angels. The conclusion that is drawn is that angels are *unable* to have sexual relations. However, Jesus is talking about state, not ability. Since angels are spiritual beings who can manifest themselves in human form, we frankly do not know what limitations they have in that guise. Several biblical passages support the position that the sons of God were fallen angels, including Jude 6–7, 2 Peter 2, and 1 Corinthians 11 (see Michael A. Harbin, *To Serve Other Gods: An Evangelical History of Religion* [Lanham, Md.: University Press of America, 1994], 17).

5. This is the view proposed in the editions of the popular *Halley's Bible Handbook* through 1965 (but not in the greatly revised 2000 edition). Halley used the example of the excavations of Ur by C. L. Woolley as well as the excavations of Kish and Fara. One problem acknowledged in more recent years is that these deposits do not correlate in time. Rather, they suggest several different floods in different locations.

6. The evidence suggests that the Black Sea was a region below sea level that flooded when the Bosporus Straits opened, releasing the waters of the Mediterranean. While intriguing, this theory raises more questions than it answers. For example, given the rivers that flow into it, how did the basin remain dry before the deluge event?

7. This is the case whether one is talking about Mesopotamia or the Black Sea region. In both areas, there is high ground near enough that with advance notice people could escape the coming flood.

8. John Woodmorappe has done a thorough study evaluating the engineering aspects of the ark, covering everything from animal capacity to feeding and waste removal. He concludes that the ark as described would be adequate to handle representatives of all animal kinds (*Noah's Ark: A Feasibility Study* [Santee, Calif.: Institute for Creation Research, 1996]).

9. This is the amount of time from when Noah and company went into the ark until they came out. The description includes 40 days of rain, 150 days until the flood "crested," and the remainder of the period a time of subsiding. Both of the proposed local flood regions conflict with this description. In the case of Mesopotamia, it is difficult to see a river flood lasting a year. Rivers flood when excess water enters the drainage system and the streams overflow their banks. It is dissipated by the flood region moving downstream like an animal that has been swallowed by a snake moves through its digestive tract. In the case of the Black Sea, there was no receding of the waters.

10. We are not told how the narrator knew this. It is possible that it was through special revelation from God, which would correlate with some of the other data in the account. It is also possible that this reflects the draught of the ark, which did not run aground until the water started receding.

11. Witnesses who have reported seeing the ark have consistently placed it at about the 14,000-feet level.

12. The overall context of this passage needs to be noted. It does not state that God now removed the curse from the land, as has been suggested based solely on the single line, "Never again will I curse the ground" (Gen. 8:21). This is a different word for "curse" than the one used in previous passages (Gen. 3:17; 5:29). As explained in the rest of 8:21 and other passages in this section (e.g., 9:11–16), this was a promise that there would not be another *global* flood.

13. For more information on this topic, consult Arthur Custance's *The Doorway Papers*, especially volume 1, *The Three Sons of Noah* (Grand Rapids: Zondervan, 1975).

CHAPTER 4—Abraham and Son(s)

1. That God spoke to Abram in Haran seems to be the natural reading of Genesis 12:1 (literally, "And the LORD said to Abram," a statement that comes immediately after the report of Terah's death in Haran). However, Acts 7:2 states that God appeared to Abraham (Terah is not mentioned) "while he was still in Mesopotamia, before he lived in Haran" (probably for this reason, the NIV renders Gen. 12:1, "The LORD *had said* to Abram" [italics added]). It seems likely that God spoke to both Terah and Abram in Ur, and so they journeyed together. Then, after Terah's death, Abram was told to leave his family.

2. Recent geological, climatological, and archaeological studies indicate that there may have been a two-hundred-year dry spell that ended just at the time Terah and Abram were called out of Ur. During this prolonged drought, the land was abandoned (David Neev and K. O. Emery, *The Destruction of Sodom, Gomorrah, and Jericho* [New York: Oxford University Press, 1995], 59–67).

3. See William W. Hallo and William Kelly Simpson, *The Ancient Near East: A History* (New York: Harcourt Brace Jovanovich, 1971), 71–77.

4. If God wanted Terah in the land, why didn't He make him go? God seems to prefer to allow people to make choices, despite the cost. In the process, however, He manages to accomplish His objectives. This may be what Paul is referring to when he wrote, "God causes all things to work together for good" (Rom. 8:28 NASB). Regardless, we find this topic a challenging area of tension and mystery.

5. The name Abram means "exalted father." This may be a reference to the social position his father held in Ur.

6. Either Abram began as a pagan and was called by YHWH, or he had at least a degree of worship of the true God and was prevented from going after other gods by the Lord's intervention. The latter is more likely in that Joshua 24:2 is somewhat vague as to who among the Israelites' "forefathers" actually worshiped the other gods. I suggest that Abram was one of the surviving worshipers of the true God in a world that was turning increasingly pagan. See my book *To Serve Other Gods: An Evangelical History of Religion* (Lanham, Md.: University Press of America, 1994).

7. Terah may have made this decision because Haran, like Ur, was known for its worship of the moon god. Another possibility is that he had relatives there and decided to stay with them (the city has the same name as one of his sons). Whatever the reason, we may infer that this decision found disfavor with God.

8. This "barren-wife motif" appears a number of times in the OT. It almost always points to something special about the child who will eventually be born.

9. The Hebrew text of Gen. 12:3 uses two different verbs for "curse," and perhaps there is a subtle distinction in meaning. The

first verb is derived from a root that means "to be small, of no account"; the second verb usually indicates a judicial declaration.

10. Evidently the famine affected Canaan but not Egypt. The two regions have separate sources of agricultural fertility. Canaan is dependent on rain coming off the Mediterranean Sea, while Egypt is dependent on the Nile River, which flows up north from East Africa. (See also below, ch. 5, for a discussion of the famine during Joseph's time.)

11. The writer seems to indicate that this wealth was the result of Abraham's sin in Egypt. We read that Pharaoh gave him many animals and servants (Gen. 12:16), probably including Sarah's handmaiden, Hagar the Egyptian. If so, this detail suggests how one sin can lead to later failures.

12. Some scholars have argued that El Elyon is a different figure; however, Abram's response to the king of Sodom shows that he identified them as one and the same: "I have raised my hand to the LORD [YHWH], God Most High [El Elyon]" (Gen. 14:22).

13. The significance of Sarah's name change is uncertain. Hebrew lexicons suggest that the two forms are virtually interchangeable, with Sarai having an older ending. If that were the case, there would seem to be no reason to give her a new name. This is especially strange when we see how significant Abram's name change is in the same context. In any case, a change in a person's name was intended to indicate a new reality in that person's life.

14. Abraham must have felt sure that he had easily negotiated the safety of the city. Genesis 19:12 seems to indicate that Lot had a wife, two daughters who were engaged, another daughter who was married, and at least two sons who were married. Including the two fiancés, Lot's extended family thus included more than ten people, and Abraham must have considered them righteous. This was not the case; out of that entire group, only three made it to safety.

15. The location, or even the existence, of the cities of Sodom and Gomorrah has been a topic of controversy for some time. Increasing evidence points to several ruins on the southeastern littoral of the Dead Sea that show signs of having been destroyed as described in Genesis (Bryant G. Wood, "The Discovery of the Sin Cities of Sodom and Gomorrah," *Bible and Spade* 12, no. 3 [Summer 1999]: 67–80).

16. This is another passage about which critical scholars have objected, asserting that it is a different version of the same story of the lie to Pharaoh. The argument seems to be that the same person would not make the same mistake twice. However, given human nature, as well as the distinctions in the two accounts, it is at least as likely that it indeed records a separate failure on Abraham's part.

17. Abraham's offering the special "seed" God had given him is specifically designed to set the stage for the greater sacrifice of God's Son, Jesus, the ultimate "seed." This poignant event has many parallels with the crucifixion event, from the offering of an "only Son" to the location.

18. There have been reports that a young girl may have entered the cave during the 1948 war (Nancy Miller, "Patriarchal Burial Site Explored for First Time in 700 Years: 12-Year-Old Girl Lowered into the Cave of Machpelah," *BAR* 11, no. 3 [May/June 1985]: 26–43).

19. Abraham moved to the land at the age of 75 (Gen. 12:4) and rescued Lot when he had been in the land fewer than ten years (16:3), or prior to the age of 85. He was 100 when Isaac was born (21:5), and Isaac was 40 when he married Rebekah, making Abraham 140 (Gen. 25:20). Thus, at least fifty-five years had passed since his meeting with Melchizedek. We also have to remember that Melchizedek and the Jebusites seem to have been at one end of the religious and moral spectrum. Sodom and Gomorrah were at the other end.

20. According to the *Encyclopaedia Britannica*, 2003 CD-ROM, this could have been up to twenty-five gallons for each camel.

21. Apparently Nahor too had left Ur for Haran, although that event is not recorded in the earlier passage (Gen. 11:31).

CHAPTER 5—Jacob and His Tribes

1. It is not clear if his being "red" (Gen. 25:25) refers to a ruddy complexion or to his red hair. Esau later received the new name Edom, meaning "red," but that is because of the red stew he got from Jacob in exchange for his birthright (25:30).

2. The name Jacob, by popular etymology, may mean both "heel grabber" and "supplanter, deceiver." While it was given to him because he came from the womb holding on to his older brother's heel, the name also became prophetic of the way Jacob fulfilled the word given to Rebekah that the younger son would dominate his brother (Gen. 25:23; 27:36).

3. One point of discussion is how much of God's revelation Rebekah shared with either her husband or her sons. One would expect that she told Isaac about God's promise that the younger son would be preeminent. If she did, he may have either forgotten it or tried to circumvent it.

4. The text says that Leah's eyes were "weak" (Gen. 29:17). This comment is understood by many in a negative way (e.g., that she was cross-eyed); other scholars render the term "delicate, tender."

5. Laban's explanation raises the question of why he had said nothing about this custom earlier. To give him the benefit of the doubt, we might suggest that he had hoped that Leah would have been married in the interim. After all, Laban was a man of substantial means, and surely some enterprising young man would have seen Leah as an asset. Another issue is more serious from our perspective: Why does God allow Jacob to have more than one wife? As pointed out earlier (see ch. 3, above), God tolerates certain things that he does not authorize. We soon see the problems that arise when there is more than one wife (as was also evident in the case of Abraham with Sarah and Hagar). God's design, as seen in the pattern of Adam and Eve, was monogamy for life.

6. The period could have been as short as seven or eight years, but it was probably longer. The text

states that after the birth of Joseph, Jacob wanted to go to his own land. It is not clear whether his request was immediately after the completion of the second agreement to marry Rachel or later. That four women gave birth to twelve children in seven years is not impossible. However, we have to account for the time when Leah, after having six sons, was no longer bearing children. And a period of only seven or eight years leaves no room for the birth of other daughters (cf. Gen. 34:9; 37:35). Thus, it is more likely that the time involved was about ten years.

7. How Jacob acquired his portion of the livestock is problematic (Gen. 30:37–43). His scheme does point to a belief in magic. Yet later he told his wives that it was God who gave him the increase as opposed to Laban. One possibility is that while Jacob peeled the poplar and almond rods, he was doing this solely for the benefit of observers (spies for his father-in-law?). Another possibility is that he may indeed have picked up cultural ideas regarding magic and tried to use them to his own advantage. We need to remember that Jacob, at this point, had not established a solid personal faith in God. Even so, at some point it became clear to him that it was God who was working on his behalf.

8. One fascinating point is that Esau was now a rich man who had four hundred men working for him. Were Esau's riches his portion of the inheritance—perhaps even the larger portion (that is, the birthright)? He was not living with Isaac anymore. He had crossed the Jordan and was living in the area that came to be known as Edom (his nickname), while Isaac lived in the Hebron region. Jacob settled further north, first at Shechem and then at Bethel. When Jacob returned, Isaac would have been about 156, with about twenty more years of life. However, there is no record that Jacob went to visit his father prior to the death of Rachel (Gen. 35:19, 27); very likely, Jacob was not motivated to return home, since his mother had already passed away. We do note that the brothers got together to bury their father after his death. In the interim, the three lived in widely separated locations.

9. One of the ironies of history is that Leah was buried with Jacob in the family tomb at Machpelah, near Hebron (Gen. 49:29–31), whereas Rachel, who had been the favorite wife, was buried in a separate tomb and left by herself.

10. For example, Reuben is reported to have slept with one of Jacob's concubines (Gen. 35:22); Simeon and Levi killed all the men of Shechem (34:25–26); Judah later married a Canaanite woman, deceived his daughter-in-law Tamar regarding his third son, and ended up sleeping with her when she disguised herself as a temple prostitute (ch. 38). These men plainly had a wild streak.

11. A cistern is a pit carved out to hold water. A layer of fairly soft limestone underlies the Israelite countryside. Pits are carved into this stone to hold rainwater in areas where the water table is too deep for a well.

12. The phrase "did evil [or what is wicked] in the eyes of the LORD" is the phrase used in the book of Judges (2:11; 3:7; et al.) to refer to worshiping other gods. Given what we see Er's uncles doing (e.g., adultery in the case of Reuben, murder in the case of Levi and Simeon, and the selling of Joseph), we know that Er had to be especially bad for God to strike him dead.

13. God took Onan's life not because of his practice of birth control but because of his motives. He was supposed to provide a son in his brother's place. He was willing to sleep with his brother's widow, but not to get her pregnant, because the child would not be his legally. This refusal to raise progeny for his brother is the reason God struck him down.

14. I find this type of information very affirming of the historicity of the OT accounts. If these accounts were made up, as some have claimed, it is likely that a more positive lineage would have been devised.

15. Very subtly, this action seems to show that Potiphar did not really believe his wife. Given his position and the customs of the time, if Joseph had done what she claimed, it is more likely that Potiphar would have had him executed.

16. We are not told which pharaoh this is. However, if our understanding of the biblical chronology is correct (see ch. 6, below, for the arguments), the incident would have taken place about 1885 BCE, during the reign of Sesostris II (or Sen Usert II), who reigned from about 1897 to 1878 BCE If so, it would appear that he died during the years of prosperity and was succeeded by his son, Sesostris III (or Sen Usert III), who reigned from about 1878 to 1841 BCE. The latter then would have been the pharaoh whom Jacob met and who reigned during the famine. In this light, it is suggestive that archaeological evidence points to a period of flood aberrations during his reign, and these may have led to a period of famine. We have a number of records showing the flood heights throughout the Middle Kingdom period. From an agricultural perspective, an excessively high and late flood could be as devastating as an inadequate flood (Barbara Bell, "Climate and the History of Egypt: The Middle Kingdom," *American Journal of Archaeology* 79 [1975]: 223–69).

17. We are given no explanation as to why Simeon was chosen. He was the second-born son of Jacob and, at the moment, may have been the one to whom Jacob planned to give the birthright, since Reuben had offended his father by sleeping with Bilhah. However, Simeon and Levi had also offended Jacob by the attack on the men of Shechem. Perhaps Joseph's decision was arbitrary.

18. The ages of the brothers at this point are difficult to determine. We do know that several of them were already married. Reuben, for example, had two sons (Gen. 42:37). Judah, younger than Reuben, apparently was old enough to be a grandfather, since this incident would seem to have taken place after his encounter with Tamar. Joseph was 17 when he was sold into slavery (37:2) and 30 when he interpreted Pharaoh's dreams (41:46). Since the move of the family took place in the second year of the famine after the seven years of prosperity, Joseph was 39 at that point and had been in Egypt twenty-two years (Jacob was 130 that same year). This information puts Judah in his forties at least, if not in his early fifties. Since Benjamin was born after Jacob's return to the Promised Land, he would have been around 30 at this time.

19. Goshen is apparently the region in the eastern delta of the Nile, along the Wadi Tumilat. Today it would be the region between Ismailia and the main delta region. In that day, it would have been the frontier spaces behind the eastern fortifications and

the main part of Egypt. One of the factors that Pharaoh may have included in his thinking was that this group would provide a buffer along the frontier (although a "nation" of around seventy people may not have been that great of a buffer) and would not be a burden on the economy.

20. Robert L. Alden does an excellent job of summarizing these issues in his commentary, *Job* (Nashville: Broadman & Holman, 1993), 25–41.

21. As we read the Pentateuch, we see that Moses makes reference to a number of other books. Some of these he may have written and others seem to have predated him. I suggest that Job was among the latter and that the people at Mount Sinai included it within the special collection we call the canon.

22. The issue is sometimes viewed in a more general manner in a form that I call the principle of retribution. This idea is that we get out of life what we put into it: if we do good, good things will happen to us; if we do bad, bad things will happen to us. This principle seems to most people to be only just. The problem is that as we go through life we soon see that such is not the case. Even so, we tend to ask, "What did I do to deserve this?"

23. One of the teachings of the book of Job is that this figure is a free moral agent; however, he is also limited in what he can do. In other words, although Satan is currently the ruler of this world, he is a finite ruler who can be overruled by the one who rules the entire universe. He is also a "lame duck" ruler who is in the process of being deposed—but that idea is the premise of the entire Bible.

24. Not all interpreters agree that these two chapters talk about Satan. Contrast John A. Martin ("Isaiah") and Charles H. Dyer ("Ezekiel") in *BKC*. Given this extreme hyperbole, it seems more likely that Satan is in view.

CHAPTER 6—Let My People Go!

1. There were two additional but short-reigned rulers, Amenemhet IV and Queen Sobekneferu. Amenemhet III was the son of Sesostris III, who, I suggested in chapter 5, was the pharaoh of the famine period. Interestingly, Amenemhet III is considered the most prosperous ruler of the dynasty, which after his death went rapidly downhill. In this light, one must wonder how much the work of Joseph had to do with the fall of the dynasty and kingdom. In Genesis 47:20–26, we read how Joseph bought all the land of Egypt for Pharaoh during the famine. Clearly this would have been a destabilizing element, and thus it would not be surprising if the dynasty imploded as a result.

2. The form -*mose* in Egyptian is derived from the verb *msi*, meaning "to bear, give birth, form, or fashion" (Alan Gardiner, *Egyptian Grammar*, 3rd ed. [Oxford: Griffith Institute, 1957], 570). In this usage, it seems to mean "son." Thus, Kamose means "son of Ka" (an Egyptian god). As noted earlier, many of the Egyptian terms may be transliterated in a variety of ways. This term can be written as *meses, mos, mose*, and *moses*. Because of the obvious association with Moses, we will use the -*moses* form from this point on.

3. Several books have been written about her. A good recent work is Joyce Tyldesley, *Hatchepsut: The Female Pharaoh* (London: Viking, 1996).

4. According to our chronology, Moses would have been born in 1526 BCE. It would seem logical that the decree to kill all the male children was given near the end of the reign of a pharaoh, since his death would be a convenient opportunity to revoke it. We then note that the birth of Moses was about a year before Amenhotep I died. Apparently the decree was revoked by the subsequent pharaoh, perhaps at the instigation of his daughter, Hatshepsut. Aaron, the older brother of Moses, had been born three years earlier (Ex. 7:7), thus before the decree.

5. Incidentally, Thutmoses II, the husband of Hatshepsut, ruled but five years and died under somewhat suspicious circumstances. Would a dominating woman like Hatshepsut have killed her husband in order to ensure that she had power? History gives enough examples to leave that as a very real possibility.

6. Because of infant mortality, it was apparently not all that unusual for the oldest son not to follow his father (e.g., the evidence suggests that Rameses was not succeeded by his oldest son). In this case, the death of an apparently adult son (remember that Amenhotep II's father ruled forty years) and the failure to mention why he died may be suggestive.

7. If this chronology is correct, it also points toward another interesting phenomenon. The grandson of Thutmoses IV was Amenhotep IV, who is better known as Akhenaton. He is noted for his attempt to move Egyptian religion toward a monotheistic worship of Aten. Could it be that he derived the concept of monotheism from the earlier conflict between the gods of Egypt and the single God of the Israelites? Our understanding of the religions (the plural is intentional) of Egypt is still very poor. Two works that show the complexity are Jaroslav Černý, *Ancient Egyptian Religion* (London: Hutchinson's University Library, 1952), and H. Frankfort, *Ancient Egyptian Religion* (New York: Columbia University Press, 1948).

8. In my book *To Serve Other Gods: An Evangelical History of Religion* (Lanham, Md.: University Press of America, 1994), 32, I suggest that Jethro was one of a remnant of worshipers of the true God who were scattered throughout the ANE.

9. In fact, Aaron was on his way to find Moses (Ex. 4:27). This detail suggests several possibilities. Moses may have been maintaining contact with his birth family over the years through go-betweens. However, the text indicates that God had spoken to Aaron just as he was speaking with Moses. This experience may explain the later conflicts between the two, when Aaron challenged Moses, questioning whether he was the only prophet of God (Num. 12:1–2).

10. We read that on the way back to Egypt, Moses was confronted by God for failing to circumcise his son (Ex. 4:24–26). This is a very difficult passage, since it seems somewhat contradictory both to our understanding of what has happened to

this point and to our understanding of God. The best explanation seems to be that it was at the wish of his wife that Moses had disobeyed God's directive for circumcision. When Moses' life was threatened, however, she realized the wrongfulness of her position. As a result, she circumcised the boy, but she did it in anger.

11. Of course, when we look at the overall pattern of plagues, a straightforward reading leaves us wondering why the sudden hang-up on the supernormal. The reason is that those scholars who object to the supernormal either ignore the plagues or, more likely, look for a naturalistic explanation for them, such as a volcanic eruption.

12. As a technical point of Hebrew grammar, in this case the form *suph* is interpreted as the passive participle of a verb meaning "come to an end." The name *Yam Suph* could then denote a sea where there was an ending (of the enemy? of the slavery?), or it could possibly mean "the Sea of Destruction." The name may, however, be a carryover from the time in Egypt, since the Egyptians viewed the Red Sea as the "terminal sea." As a point of interest, modern Arabic has two names for the Red Sea, and the less common one could be translated "the Sea of Extermination."

13. In Exodus 14:1, God gives Moses specific geographical directions. The people are to camp in front of Pi Hahiroth, between Migdol and the sea. They are to be opposite of Baal Zephon. The problem is that these three sites are unknown today. Migdol is probably a generic fortress. The other two are place names no longer used. Joel D. McQuitty has made a persuasive argument for an Israelite camp on the west side of Suez Bay as shown in the map on page 133, although he places Pi Hahiroth on the northeastern slopes of Jebel 'Ataqa ("The Location and Nature of the Red Sea Crossing," Th.M. thesis, Capital Bible Seminary, 1986; microfiche copy produced by Theological Research Exchange Network, Portland, Ore.).

14. See Doron Nor and Nathan Paldor, "Are There Oceanographic Explanations for the Israelites' Crossing of the Red Sea?" *Bulletin of the American Meteorological Society* 73 (1992): 305–14. These oceanographers modeled the situation both mathematically and with a wind tunnel. They found that a 40–45 knot wind blowing steadily for ten hours would open up a section about a kilometer wide. When the wind stopped, the waters would return in the form of a wave in a matter of minutes.

15. There are three basic views on the nature of the exodus account. The more "liberal" scholars argue that there never was an actual exodus from Egypt; the story was developed to explain why there were twelve tribes united in one land (e.g., Martin Noth, *A History of Pentateuchal Tradition* [Atlanta: Scholars Press, 1981 reprint]). Most scholars accept some type of exodus event, but not as described in the Bible (e.g., William F. Albright, *From the Stone Age to Christianity* [New York: Doubleday, 1953]). The more "conservative" scholars accept the biblical account as the record of an actual event but disagree on the details. For example, John Bright follows a late date; in his view, the Exodus was accompanied by naturalistic events in which "Israel saw the hand of God" (*A History of Israel*, 4th ed. [Louisville: Westminster John Knox, 2000], 118–22). In contrast, Eugene Merrill follows an early date and believes that the Exodus was accompanied by

obviously supernatural events (*An Historical Survey of the Old Testament*, 2nd ed. [Grand Rapids: Baker, 1991], 97–116). While this last view is only one of several possible ways to understand the data, it is the one I think best fits the facts and explains the most details.

16. Manetho's list includes some dynasties that apparently overlapped or coexisted during the times when the country was divided. Likewise, there is some question about the names of some of the pharaohs, but there is general agreement that the list is essentially sound. Manetho's list also gives the approximate lengths of the reigns of the various pharaohs. In principle, the chronology is based on solid data, since the Egyptian calendar worked around the flooding of the Nile each year and what we call the Sothic cycle. So this is the Egyptian name for the star we call Sirius (the Dog Star). At some unknown point early in Egyptian history, it was noted that the annual rising of the Nile could be correlated to the rising of Sothis. This correlation became the basis of the Egyptian calendar. But they observed a 365-day year (12 months of 30 days each, coupled with a 5-day add-on at the end). The problem, of course, is that the solar year has an additional one-fourth day, which meant that the calendar was off by one-fourth day every year. While the Egyptians noted this discrepancy, they did nothing about it. For years the two events diverged, but after centuries passed, they came back together. In fact, every 1,460 years the two would be back in sync. The last recorded synchronization was by the Latin writer Censorinus, who observed a correlation in 139 CE. This meant that previous correlations included 1321 and 2781 BCE. In addition, we have record of a solar eclipse that took place on July 14, 568 BCE. These two celestial events give our Egyptian calendar a fairly solid foundation. Still, there is some question regarding the accuracy of some of the data. For example, John Baines and Jaromir Malek warn that their dating has a margin of error of about 150 years for dates around 3000 BCE, decreasing to about ten years for 1000 BCE (*Atlas of Ancient Egypt* [New York: Facts on File, 1980], 319).

17. Exodus is not as clear as Acts on the age of Moses, but it does note that he was eighty when he spoke to the pharaoh after his exile in Midian (Ex. 7:7). This information correlates with Acts, which states that Moses was in Midian forty years and that he was approaching forty when he struck the Egyptian.

18. There are many variations in the spelling of the various names of the pharaohs; these discrepancies do not necessarily signify different individuals. Part of the problem is that our English name of the city (Raamses) is drawn from the Hebrew, while the name of the pharaoh (Rameses or Ramses) is a direct transliteration from the Egyptian.

19. The lists we have cover the period from 892 to 648 BCE. The particular official (or *limu*) for which the year was named varied. For the first year of his reign, it was the king. Other years were determined by lot (during the earlier reigns) or by position (during the later reigns); the second method showed how the status of different positions varied. For some examples, see *ANET*, 274.

20. Jehu actually shows up several times in Assyrian inscriptions (*ANET*, 280–81).

21. Using this date for the Exodus also allows us to date the patriarchs. According to Exodus 12:40, the Exodus took place 430 years after Jacob moved to Egypt, making that date 1876 BCE. Jacob was 130 at that point (Gen. 47:9), making his birth date 2006 BCE. His father, Isaac, was 60 when he was born (Gen. 25:26), placing Isaac's birth in 2066. And finally, Abraham was 100 at the birth of Isaac (Gen. 21:5), placing his birth in 2166. Unfortunately, we can go no further back, since we are not told how old Terah was at the birth of Abraham.

22. John J. Bimson presents a detailed analysis of these data in his book *Redating the Exodus and the Conquest* (Sheffield: Almond, 1981).

CHAPTER 7 — Making a Nation Out of a Mob

1. The Amalekites were a desert tribe that preyed on some of the stragglers as the nation moved toward Sinai. This incident shows that the Israelites were not yet organized. While they were able to drive off the Amalekites, God did not allow Joshua to finish them off, since that was not the business at hand. Rather, they would be saved for a later day, which arrived when Saul was king (1 Sam. 15). The future judgment for this generation's sin presents a concept of national guilt that does not sit well in our individualistic culture. In order that the people should not forget this pending judgment on the Amalekites, God had Moses write it in a book for future reference (Ex. 17:14). Since this book was written before the material given at Mount Sinai, this portion must have been copied into what we now call Exodus.

2. A full discussion is beyond the scope of this book. An excellent work that surveys some of the most common answers to this question is *The Law, the Gospel and the Modern Christian: Five Views*, ed. Wayne Strickland (Grand Rapids: Zondervan, 1993).

3. Kenneth Kitchen, "The Patriarchal Age: Myth or History?" *BAR* 21, no. 2 (March/April 1995): 48–57, 88–90. These structures changed through time. As a result, an analysis of a particular treaty can help place its composition in a general time frame. The analysis of the treaty at Sinai places it between 1500 and 1200 BCE.

4. Some of the most striking differences include the use of the Sabbath year and the year of Jubilee, the prohibition against interest, and the restrictions on indentured servitude. A few practices, such as gleaning, seem to have been allowed in at least some other societies, although there is not much evidence from those cultures.

5. We are told in Exodus 24:1 that seventy *of* the elders went up to the mountain. This language suggests a group chosen from a larger number. In 18:21 the highest level listed is "officials over thousands." The most likely scenario is that the seventy made up an overall national council that provided advice and counsel to Moses. The assumption is that this system continued on under Joshua and then beyond. However, there is no firm data on this matter.

6. For example, the well-known Code of Hammurabi contains almost three hundred edicts, many of which dictate execution for crimes such as theft (*ANET*, 166–77, nos. 6, 22, et al.).

The same is true of other legal codes that we have recovered from the ANE.

7. This area of the law is not entirely clear, but two factors support the view presented above. The first is in the same passage we have just addressed: the husband of the woman who has given birth prematurely as a result of being struck (not miscarriage) shall pay a fine as the husband and judges decide (Ex. 21:22). The second is that in certain cases God warns that there are crimes for which the judgment *is* mandatory, and no pity is allowed. One of the most significant is leading the people after false gods (Deut. 13:8).

8. So the NIV and most versions (the NASB has "a god"); the Hebrew word is *'elohim*, which is plural in form but is commonly applied to the one true God.

9. An interesting observation is that this edition of the tablets with the commandments had been written by God himself (Ex. 32:16), while the replacement tablets were written by Moses (34:27–28). No reason is given for this change.

10. The location of worship was to be "the place the LORD your God will choose as a dwelling for his Name" (Deut. 12:11). We tend to read this statement through the lens of the temple in Jerusalem and infer that it is a reference to that establishment. Throughout the pre-temple period, however, we find that the tabernacle was located in different cities, including Gilgal (Josh. 4:19), Shiloh (Josh. 18:1), Nob (1 Sam. 7:1), Jerusalem (2 Sam. 6:17), and Gibeon (1 Kings 8:4).

11. These figures represent the approximate value of the measurements, which are given in cubits. There is some question as to whether the length of the inner tent was 30 feet, with the length of both the Holy Place and Holy of Holies 15 feet each, or whether the Holy Place was 30 feet and the Holy of Holies another 15 feet beyond this, making the tabernacle 45 feet long. Within the 150-foot-long courtyard, there would have been room for either.

12. The word *Shekinah* means "dwelling" or "royal residence." It does not occur in the Hebrew OT but is used in the targums (Aramaic translations of the OT) and other rabbinic writings. The term describes God's presence in the world. In the OT, the qualities of that presence are demonstrated in Exodus 40:34 and 1 Kings 8:10–11.

13. The sacrifices can be divided into several categories. Various writers have noted from three to five major ones and up to nine subcategories. My development here is somewhat simplified but seems to catch the essence of what was involved. It is basically derived from the work of Anson F. Rainey, "Sacrifice and Offerings," in *ZPEB*, 5:194–211.

14. The Hebrew verb usually translated "to atone" conveys the sense "to cover" and thus seems to reflect the breaking of the relationship between God and man at the Fall. Thus, these sacrifices focus on bridging that gap.

15. Rainey notes that in terms of procedure, expiatory offerings always come first. He blurs the issue by associating the shedding of blood of the consecratory offerings with the idea of atonement in the sin/guilt offerings.

16. Votive offerings were still being made by Jewish believers in the NT. For example, Paul performed votive offerings at the end of his second and third missionary journeys (see Acts 18:18; 21:23–26).

17. The term derives from the process of taking oil and pouring it on the head of the designated person. Two offices were normally associated with anointing—priest and king. The emphasis in the OT seems to be on the latter. Thus, in the minds of the Israelites, the Anointed One would be the Great King.

18. We tend to find this entire process harsh. However, two things must be kept in mind. First, from God's perspective, physical life is not the final end. What happens in terms of eternity is far more important (and in the OT we are given little information regarding that). Second, the issue at stake seems to be God's holiness. I observed through my years in the navy that there is a very human tendency to downplay safeguards. I have seen a number of sailors injured or killed because they felt they could take shortcuts. These shortcuts have also led to compromises of our national security. From an objective perspective, I need to ask, How much more should we respect God's standards?

CHAPTER 8—Just a-Lookin' for a Home

1. An example seems to be Caleb, one of the twelve "spies" who reconnoitered the land, and identified as "son of Jephunneh the Kenizzite" (Num. 32:12). The Kenizzites were one of the tribes whose land Abraham was promised (Gen. 15:19). When the Israelites entered Canaan and Caleb claimed his inheritance, he reminded Joshua it had been promised to him because of his faithfulness (Josh. 14:6–15).

2. Included in this category was sexual intercourse, after which both the man and the woman were regarded as unclean until sundown and were required to bathe.

3. Giving birth also required an additional purification period—a total of forty days for a male child and eighty days for a female. A woman during this phase was said to be "in the blood of *her* purification" (Lev. 12:4–5, literal translation). In part it may have been a healing period for the woman, but that does not explain the disparity between the births of boys and girls.

4. This passage is another one that seems strange to us today. The issue is suspected marital infidelity on the part of the woman. There seem to be two purposes for this section. For the original audience, there is a degree of protection for a woman accused of adultery in that this process allowed her to prove her innocence. The second purpose seems to be to warn husbands to refrain from false accusations.

5. If our chronology is correct, it was approximately 1876 BCE when Joseph presented himself to his brothers and urged them to come down to the land because there were five more years of famine (Gen. 45:6). It was now the summer of 1445 BCE, or 431 years later.

6. Three phases are described (Num. 11:1–6): grumbling from the people in general; judgment from God (described as God's anger burning, consuming some outskirts of the camp); and grumbling from a smaller group described as "rabble" (KJV, "the mixed multitude that was among them") who had greedy desires. Their request was for meat.

7. While some may argue that what happened here was a timely earthquake, obviously something more is intended. There were at least three fissures in different parts of the camp. That these swallowed up the rebels and their tents while leaving the rest of the nation untouched shows how discrete God's judgment could be.

8. Most atlases identify Kadesh with Kadesh Barnea, but this is problematic. According to the travel sequence given in Numbers 33, this stop came after Ezion Geber. That would put it east of the southern extension of the rift valley that stretches from the Dead Sea to the Red Sea. The next stop was Mount Hor, where Aaron died. According to Numbers 33, this was on the edge of the land of Edom. Also, Josephus identifies Mount Hor as one of the mountains surrounding Petra. Still, it is possible that the nation had backtracked after Ezion Geber.

9. It seems likely that this is a list of the more significant sites where the people stayed, places where they spent several months. However, it is noted in Numbers 9:19–23 that the cloud sometimes settled only for overnight, other times for a period of a year.

10. Today this region is very arid. Moses, however, refers to its fields and vineyards. This detail highlights a point made earlier regarding the fertility of the land in the time of Abraham and how it has been drying out since.

11. Josephus associated Mount Hor with the mountains around Petra (*Antiquities of the Jews*, 4.4.7). Islamic tradition puts Aaron's tomb on top of Jebel Neby Harun (about halfway between the Dead Sea and the Gulf of Aqaba). Many scholars believe that this site would be too centrally located in Edom. They suggest another peak called Jebel Madurah (further northwest) as a more likely identification.

12. This entire incident is very enigmatic and seemingly beyond understanding. Why would God choose to use serpents as a means of punishment? More than this, why would he direct the construction of a bronze serpent to be the means of deliverance? The best answer seems to be that he was using events in the life of the nation to anticipate theological truths that would become evident during the life of Jesus—i.e., His being lifted up on the cross and His identification with sin. This passage also seems to point to the antiquity of the account, for it seems unlikely that such a story would be accepted into the canon at a late date, when the nation was trying to purge all semblance of idolatry from their midst.

13. According to the recounting of this journey in Deuteronomy 2, the nation had previously bypassed both Moab and Ammon. God gave them specific directions not to disturb either of these nations.

14. The eradication process seen here is later called *ḥerem*. We will examine this topic in more detail in chapter 9. Interestingly, in this case, the land had formerly belonged to Moab, but the Amorites had taken it from them.

15. Although it seems to have been out of the way, the people were directed to battle Og and his people. God promised that he would give Israel victory. This appears to have been a preemptive strike that would eliminate a foe who otherwise would have proven to be excessively troublesome. Deuteronomy 3:11 notes that they were among the last of the Rephaites (Rephaim), a race of people who were very large and fierce.

16. *Baal* is a Semitic word meaning "lord" or "master." It is also the name of one of the Canaanite gods, which will be discussed in more detail in chapter 9.

17. Paul puts the number at 23,000 (1 Cor. 10:8). One possible explanation is that Paul refers only to those who died "in one day."

18. We are not told specifically why certain tribes grew and others shrank, but the numbers appear to reflect how each tribe fared under the various plagues God sent. If so, growth would then seem to reflect a prospering based on tribal faithfulness.

19. These tribes say that they will build cities (Num. 32:16), but other passages indicate that they settled into the Canaanite cities from which they had eradicated the population (see Deut. 2:33–35). It is possible that what they built were walls around the cities they had taken (or at least rebuilt them). We are not told at what point this activity occurred, but it would seem that this is one reason the nation camped on the east side of the Jordan River for an extended period of time—so that the fighting men of these tribes were able to settle their families and then return to the camp.

20. Deuteronomy 19:9 suggests that provision was given for three more cities of refuge if the nation expanded. When we look at the land that was promised to Abraham, we see that it extended much farther north than the land encompassed by the conquest under Joshua. This information indicates that there was an anticipation of possible further expansion and that these guidelines would cover that development. The conquests of David moved north, but he never really conquered the land in that area—he just held dominion over some of it.

21. The material that follows is sometimes called the "Palestinian Covenant," since it is described as being "in addition to" the covenant God had established earlier. However, since the overall context of the book is a renewal of that earlier covenant, it is likely that the covenant being referred to in Deuteronomy 29:1 is the entire renewal set forth in the book of Deuteronomy. The understanding of chapters 29–30 outlined here is within that framework.

22. There are a number of references to their descendants (e.g., "your children who follow you in later generations and foreigners who come from distant lands," Deut. 29:22), although these references occur in the context of curses that would come

if they disobeyed, and these later generations are viewed as witnesses. Even so, it is clear that the judgment would be on those later generations who were part of the covenant.

23. Here we must take note of the preceding verse (Deut. 31:9), which points out that Moses wrote "this law and gave it to the priests, the sons of Levi, who carried the ark of the covenant of the LORD, and to all the elders of Israel." This seems to indicate that there were multiple copies of the Law in addition to the large copy put on the stones at Gerizim and Ebal.

24. According to 2 Chronicles 36:21, the Exile was to last long enough (seventy years) for the land to enjoy the Sabbath years that had been overlooked, as prophesied by Jeremiah. The guidelines in 2 Chronicles would suggest a period of 490 years of failure to observe Sabbath years. Since the Exile began in 605 BCE, this figure (if it reflects an explicitly linear chronology) takes us back to about 1095. However, there were a few kings who did seem to try to obey the Law (e.g., David and Hezekiah). In those cases, they may well have observed the Sabbath years and the covenant renewals also. Possibly the seventy Sabbath years missed were combined for a cumulative total, but we are not given enough data to know that with certainty.

25. Recall our earlier discussion of blessing (see above, ch. 5). I said that the term does not necessarily relate to a hope for good things, but denotes an expectation of future outcomes. That seems to be the case here, where we have a sequel to Jacob's blessing of his twelve sons in Genesis 49. In Deuteronomy 33, however, Simeon is missing, which seems to point to a fulfillment of Jacob's blessing on Simeon by his absorption into the tribe of Judah. This change was hinted at in the two censuses, which indicate that Simeon lost about two-thirds of its population during the desert period.

CHAPTER 9—Joshua Fit the Battle of Jericho—and Hazor Too

1. While the term *ḥerem* is often viewed as reflecting total destruction, when we look at the various Semitic languages, we quickly see that this cannot be the sole meaning of the root (the English word *harem*, for example, comes from *harim*, an Arabic term derived from the same root and meaning "sacred, forbidden place"). A broader range of meaning is also very evident in the Hebrew data. For this reason, some Hebrew lexicons list two senses, one of which is "separation" or "dedication," and the other, "[complete] destruction."

2. These three cities were Jericho, Ai, and Hazor. The text specifically notes that in the northern campaign only Hazor was burned (Josh. 10:11). Clearly, then, the concept does not involve total destruction in a sense that applies to the physical city. This is very important to keep in mind when we note the reports of archaeologists.

3. This qualification is not as evident in English translations, since in a number of places where the Hebrew term is used, it is translated "totally destroy" (NIV) or "utterly destroy" (KJV, NASB, NRSV). For example, in the account of the southern campaign, we read in Joshua 10:28 that he "totally destroyed everyone in it" (NIV). The overall context here points to human life as

opposed to animal life. Moreover, as Joshua concluded the conquest, he reminded the people that they were living in cities that they did not build (Josh. 24:13).

4. It is also clear that God is more interested in the state of humanity as a whole than in the physical life of individuals. We see this principle exhibited throughout history when God sends individual witnesses forth to be martyrs in order to save groups of people. Another aspect of this problem has to do with those we call "innocents." Consider the case of Nineveh, where God chastises Jonah for not having compassion on the children (probably what is meant by the ones "who cannot tell their right hand from their left," Jonah 4:11); this shows that God has special compassion for children. Is it possible that God allows some children to die in their innocence so that they do not have the opportunity to rebel at a later age?

5. This is the term used by Eugene Merrill in *An Historical Survey of the Old Testament* (Grand Rapids: Baker, 1991), 163. For what follows, consult *ANET,* "Poems about Baal," 129–42.

6. Some other gods that we might mention include Yam, a sea god; Shapash, a sun goddess; Yarikh, a moon goddess (Jericho possibly means "[city of the] moon god"); Melqart, who was the patron god of Tyre; and Eshmun, the patron god of Sidon.

7. One indication of this is the picture of judgment against the nation of Israel as they adopted the same practices. The prophets repeatedly condemned the people for practicing the religions of the nations around them.

8. Sometimes this concept is referred to as imitative magic. The ritual was viewed as an action that the god or goddess was expected to imitate (or another way of describing it is to say that the worshiper was imitating the act expected of the god).

9. This lie is just reported. While it is not condemned, it is not praised either. What is praised is Rahab's willingness to risk herself because of her belief in the God of the Israelites.

10. The key role of this pile of rocks along the riverbank was to cause children to ask questions and thus induce parents to recount what God had done. This and other monuments served to remind later audiences that God is a God of history.

11. This event was apparently a theophany—an appearance of God in human form. The key indicator is that the figure accepted the worship of Joshua and told him to take his shoes off because he was on holy ground. These were not the acts of an angel. Many scholars suggest that this was really the preincarnate second person of the Trinity, the Son who became Jesus the Messiah.

12. There seem to have been several ways of selecting by "lots." One consisted of dividing the camp and taking half; then this half would be divided, and so on until they ended up with an individual. In the case of Ai, however, it appears to have been a process of selecting one of many, perhaps somewhat like drawing straws. The high priest and

the Urim and Thummim would have been critical for ascertaining that the results were valid.

13. While executing the entire family appears harsh, it is unlikely that he could have hidden his crime from them; they had undoubtedly tried to help cover up the crime. In today's parlance, they were accessories after the fact.

14. Interestingly, this group included not just the Gibeonites but also the cities of Kephirah, Beeroth, and Kiriath Jearim. As we look at this incident, we find more evidences of God's grace in that he not only allowed these people to live but also to serve him. Later we will see the faithfulness of the men of Kiriath Jearim when the ark of the covenant is returned from the Philistines (1 Sam. 6).

15. We will not be able to resolve this issue here. Various proposals have included trying to reinterpret the text to explain away the long day. A number of legends throughout the world talk about a long day (or night). If there was such a long day, it would fall into the class of major miracle. It must be emphasized that even with modern computer technology, no one has proven the existence of this long day, nor can it be done. If someone could document that some event such as a solar eclipse occurred prior to this incident and in a place other than where it was supposed to occur . . . but so far no one has done so.

16. Based on the names and Egyptian data, many scholars put the location further north, about 15 kilometers west of Hazor (A. F. Rainey, "Merom, Waters of," *ZPEB,* 4:192–93). While this is certainly feasible, the country there is much more rugged. It is possible that this was to be a staging area from which the campaign was to develop—but Joshua and his troops surprised them, defeating them before they were able to get under way.

17. This situation had been addressed in advance while Moses was alive. In Numbers 27 a precedent was established that women could inherit the land if there were no male descendants.

18. Caleb states in Joshua 14:10 that it had been forty-five years since Kadesh Barnea. That was a year after the arrival at Sinai.

CHAPTER 10—The Best of Times, the Worst of Times

1. It is not really clear what "iron chariots" means. Chariots were basically mobile platforms for armed warriors (e.g., archers), so they had to be stable. They also needed to be light (for speed) and maneuverable, which ruled out chariots made of iron as the primary material. Based on wall reliefs found in a multitude of places as well as an actual chariot discovered in an Egyptian tomb, the iron portions were the axle hubs (which provided strength) and some plating to provide minimal protection for the warrior within (Yigael Yadin, *The Art of Warfare in Biblical Lands* [New York: McGraw-Hill, 1963], 86–90).

2. Given its springs and its key location, Jericho would have remained a prime site for administration. Eglon, however, did not occupy the site long enough to rebuild a city. Thus, it seems likely that here we have an explanation for the Late Bronze period buildings excavated by both Garstang and Kenyon, which were

too few and small to be the city destroyed by Joshua (John J. Bimson, *Redating the Exodus and Conquest* [Sheffield: Almond, 1981], 135–36).

3. Later, in her victory song, Deborah makes reference to Shamgar in the same verse in which she mentions Jael (Judg. 5:6), who is given credit for the victory over the Canaanites out of Hazor (5:24–27). This detail would suggest that Shamgar served at about the same time as Deborah.

4. As noted earlier, the book of Judges follows in general the flow of the period (followed by two appendixes that cover significant, nondated events). The main portion of the book consists of sixteen chapters, ten of which focus on the three major judges.

5. The term used here is the feminine form of the word we translate "prophet," which, as we will see in later chapters, denoted a person who was a spokesperson for God. This designation shows not only that she was pious, but also that God was already using her.

6. Turkish rug weavers have explained to me that originally their rugs were designed to be coverings (or wall hangings), and the nap side would be down. It was only later that rugs were reversed and used on floors.

7. This event shows that religious compromise was occurring in even the best of families but that even out of a religiously compromised family a person could arise who took God seriously.

8. I find it interesting that Gideon is never condemned for these requests. This seems to suggest that God is willing to verify His word to someone who is honestly seeking and will then act on the word when it is confirmed. In this case, Gideon had already shown himself obedient by destroying the altar to Baal and calling the troops together. We soon see, however, that God had more in mind than just a military victory.

9. This was a national alarm system. After the initial blast, people hearing the trumpet (a ram's horn, or *shophar*) would then blow their own trumpets, so the alarm would pass from village to village.

10. Clearly this dream created among the Midianites a mindset of uncertainty and fear, which would dispose them toward fleeing at a critical moment. Modern armies try to do something similar with what is called psy-ops (psychological operations).

11. That the situation had been deteriorating is clear from this section, which indicates that not just the Ammonites but also the Philistines were oppressing Israel. Furthermore, earlier we had read only that the Israelites were serving the Baals and the Ashtoreths (Judg. 2:13), but now we see them worshiping, in addition, the gods of several nations (10:6). Ironically, two of the nations whose gods they were now serving were the Philistines and the Ammonites.

12. The Hebrew letter *waw*, which is prefixed to the word that begins a new sentence or clause, may be translated in a variety of ways, including "and," "or," "but," "also," "therefore" (the clause can also be made subordinate, with such renderings as "when, since, though"). The translator must look at the context to

decide how to render it in a particular case (see David Marcus, *Jephthah and His Vow* [Lubbock: Texas Tech Press, 1986], 13–27).

13. We noted in chapter 8 the criteria required for a Nazirite vow. Note how those three items are explicitly addressed in the guidelines for Manoah's son.

14. Here we are introduced to a phrase that will later be used to characterize the age. He told his parents that he should marry her since "she is right in my eyes" (Judg. 14:3, my translation). Note that the writer gives insight into God's purpose in all of this—His plan to confront the Philistines (v. 4).

15. There is debate about the time frame. The inquiry at Bethel and the mention of Phinehas as high priest suggest a relatively early date, but the depravity involved and the mention of the festival at Shiloh suggest a later time. Actually, both incidents could have happened anytime during the period.

16. Jonathan was either the son or a descendant of Gershom. Moses had a son by the name of Gershom, so if this was the same person, it points out that even descendants of spiritual giants can and do go astray.

17. We are given no explanation as to why that was the case. One possibility might be that the position of the nation as a whole was somewhat hypocritical and God was trying to drive that point home.

18. As would be the case in a small town, he had also heard of what she had done for her mother-in-law. This had impressed him, which tells us also something about his character.

19. His reason was that serving as kinsman-redeemer would jeopardize his own inheritance. This response would seem to suggest that at that point he did not have another heir, although he may have been married. If that was the case, and if he were to have a son with Ruth, that son would not only become the heir of Elimelech's property, but would inherit some of his own as well.

CHAPTER 11—Give Us a King Like the Rest of the Nations

1. The term *theocracy* may imply that God was acting as king. Technically, as we have seen, God was to be the suzerain. That is, God as the ultimate ruler gave guidelines that the people followed, making many of the decisions themselves. As we look at this situation, we wonder why there was not a mediator for the covenant appointed after Joshua. It is possible that the priesthood was designed to perform that function. In that case, it is not clear why Joshua was appointed.

2. As noted earlier, polygamy is a practice that God never desired or authorized but that He tolerated among His people. The only place the Law addresses the issue is to give guidelines regarding inheritance (Deut. 21:15–17). However, as we see from this text, multiple wives led to relational problems within the family. As we have also seen, the plight of a barren wife was often used to give special notice regarding a coming child.

3. We are not told the occasion of Hannah's time of prayer. From our discussion of the Law, we know that the people were to go up to the central sanctuary on three occasions through the year: Passover, Pentecost, and Sukkoth. The worship mentioned in this passage was likely during one of those feasts.

4. We know from a later passage that Phinehas was married (1 Sam. 4:19), and we can assume that Hophni was married as well, so they were also guilty of adultery, a capital crime.

5. The response of the Philistines when they heard that the ark had been brought to the camp (1 Sam. 4:6–8) suggests that the Israelites had not taken this step before. Likewise, we have no indication that at any time throughout the period of the judges the ark had been misused in this manner. This action would suggest that the nation still had memories of the period of the conquest when God went before the people.

6. According to 1 Chronicles 2:52–53, however, some of the leaders of the city were descended from Caleb. This detail may indicate that some of the Canaanite towns taken over and ruled by the Israelites retained much of their original population.

7. Once again we see the use of memorials to remind the people of how God had intervened on their behalf. As pointed out earlier, these monuments demonstrated the historical nature of the acts as well as the importance of passing that information on to the next generation.

8. The text also notes that he built an altar to God in Ramah, where he apparently performed sacrifices on behalf of the people. This comment is another indicator that certain sacrifices were permitted throughout the land, although clearly some of them had to be performed at the tabernacle (which was why Samuel's father went up to Shiloh each year). One unanswered question is how the priests performed the national sacrifices, especially Yom Kippur, during the twenty years or so that the ark was in Kiriath Jearim and the tabernacle remained in Shiloh.

9. One of the challenging points raised by this incident is that God had anticipated this request before the people entered the land. In Deuteronomy 17, God told the nation through Moses that the people would ask for a king and warned them both about the type of king they should choose and what a king should do.

10. We are not told what type of sacrifice was involved here. As we look at this text, however, we see the type of pattern involved in a communal sacrifice as discussed in chapter 7. Note that in this case about thirty people were invited to the sacrifice.

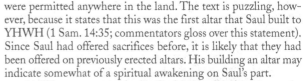

11. This detail about where Saul was hiding is one of several illustrations showing that the process of seeking God's will through lots or through Urim and Thummin must have been more complex than just drawing straws. For further information on this issue, consult Cornelis Van Dam, *Urim and Thummim* (Winona Lake, Ind.: Eisenbrauns, 1997).

12. In the patriarchal period, family leaders could offer sacrifices, but subsequent to the national organization at Sinai, the ritual was a prerogative restricted to the Levitical priesthood. Saul felt that as king he was above the Law and could do whatever he liked, should he feel the situation warranted. God would not tolerate that view of right and wrong.

13. The type of sacrifice offered would have been communal, celebrating God's victory. We noted earlier that such sacrifices were permitted anywhere in the land. The text is puzzling, however, because it states that this was the first altar that Saul built to YHWH (1 Sam. 14:35; commentators gloss over this statement). Since Saul had offered sacrifices before, it is likely that they had been offered on previously erected altars. His building an altar may indicate somewhat of a spiritual awakening on Saul's part.

14. We are never told why God held off judgment on the Amalekite people this long or why he chose this moment to carry it out. It is clear that this was to be a test for Saul—which he failed.

15. Several significant contrasts exist between the anointing of the two kings. Saul went to Samuel, while Samuel went to David (although God had made it clear to Samuel in both cases who had been chosen). Saul was anointed in secrecy even from his family, while David was anointed before his entire family. When the Spirit of the Lord came upon Saul, he prophesied, but we are told of no outward manifestations in the case of David.

16. The concept of a warrior-hero who fights a "winner-take-all" battle on behalf of his people is widespread in the ANE. The concept is also evident in and viewed as one of the foundations of "the day of the Lord." While fulfilling this role was not required of kingship, the people naturally looked to the warrior-hero as their leader. Later, Joab, David's loyal general, called his king out of the battlefield so that the honor would not go to him (1 Sam. 12:26–30). See also Roy B. Zuck, ed., *A Biblical Theology of the Old Testament* (Chicago: Moody Press, 1991), 295.

17. First Samuel 18:11 says that David escaped Saul's spear twice, but it is not clear if that is a reference to a second occasion before he was driven from Saul's home. If so, 19:10 would be a third attempt.

18. In addition to being an attempt to get David killed, this requirement was a crude joke that Saul was trying to play. It was not uncommon in the ANE for armies to cut off a certain body part, such as a right hand, from the enemy soldiers in order to provide "body counts." The Philistines were uncircumcised, and thus Saul's demand required David (perhaps along with other soldiers under his command) to perform this distasteful procedure on the bodies of his enemies.

19. In addition, there was the occasion when Jonathan interceded on behalf of his friend and Saul threw a spear at him. At that time, David was in hiding. The end of that story was the famous scene where Jonathan shot arrows and, through the instructions he gave to his chaser, told David that he was in danger and should flee (1 Sam. 20:30–42).

20. This passage records an interesting case of a prophecy that was contingent on a future event. David asked God through the priest Abiathar (who used the ephod and Urim and Thummim) whether Saul would pursue him to Keilah. God said yes. He then asked if the men of Keilah would turn him over, and the answer was yes. At this point, David left Keilah, and because David was not there, Saul did not come.

CHAPTER 12—A Kingdom United

1. These provisions consisted of 200 loaves of bread, 2 skins of wine (volume uncertain, but probably these were full skins

and thus had a capacity of about 4 to 5 gallons each), 5 dressed sheep, 5 seahs of roasted grain (about 2 bushels), 100 cakes of raisins, and 200 cakes of pressed figs. Such a large amount may have included additional provisions to compensate for her husband's insult. Still, the fact that she could gather this much on short notice suggests that they were well off.

2. David's first wife, Michal (Saul's daughter), had not been living with him since he fled; and Saul gave her to another man as a wife. Sometime later, David married Ahinoam of Jezreel, who was now living with him. As for polygamy, see ch. 11, n. 2.

3. Obviously, this description does not answer all the questions, for in every language there are various categories of poetry that follow very strict rules in terms of composition—for example, English sonnets or limericks. These, of course, are much easier to define. The broader definition helps in the less obvious cases.

4. Leopold Sabourin, *The Psalms: Their Origin and Meaning* (New York: Alba House, 1974), 25–28.

5. Scholars have identified a number of different types of parallelism that are useful for the technical analysis of the Hebrew poem. It should also be noted that in our modern English translations, a large segment of the prophetic literature is laid out in poetic form as well, though there would seem to be more question regarding the nature of this material. Both of these issues are beyond the scope of our study.

6. Laments are divided into two subcategories, depending on whether they reflect something wrong in the writer's personal life (e.g., Ps. 3), or something wrong in the life of the larger community (Ps. 80). They are called, respectively, individual and communal laments.

7. As noted before, the word *messiah* means "anointed one." Kings were anointed, but when *messiah* is used with the definite article, it usually refers to this future figure (e.g., Ps. 2:2). Thus, these poems are sometimes called *messianic psalms.*

8. Andrew E. Hill and John H. Walton, *A Survey of the Old Testament,* 2nd ed. (Grand Rapids: Zondervan, 2000), 344. See also Sigmund Mowinckel, *The Psalms in Israel's Worship* (Nashville: Abingdon, 1966), 2:26–42.

9. This topic is developed further by Paul R. House, *Old Testament Survey* (Nashville: Broadman, 1992), 202–11.

10. The material in 1 and 2 Chronicles relates another perspective on people and historical events, and we will refer to it as occasion warrants. Those books focus on the Davidic dynasty—that is, the Southern Kingdom—whereas the material in 1 and 2 Kings covers both kingdoms.

11. The nature of this contest is not clear. It could have been a form of athletic competition that got out of hand, or it could have been a modified type of the individual combat we saw earlier in the case of Goliath. If the latter was the case, it is surprising that the "generals" were not involved. But perhaps the reason is that the two kings were not present. Most likely the contest was designed to be a show of skill at arms with no limits. In any case, the men were equally matched and all fell together.

12. One of the interesting aspects of this case is that Joab was ostensibly serving as a *go'el* (kinsman-redeemer), avenging the death of his brother. However, Abner was killed in Hebron, one of the cities of refuge, showing Joab's low view of the Law. Later we will find Joab himself claiming refuge in the tabernacle. For his crimes, however, God had already declared that there could be no refuge.

13. The meaning of the Hebrew word here is somewhat obscure, but the evidence seems to suggest that they were able to enter through the water system. Today this area is called Warren's Shaft and connects this portion of Jerusalem to the Gihon Spring in the Kidron Valley. For an excellent article about how it may have worked, consult Terence Kleven, "Up the Waterspout," *BAR* 20, no. 4 (July/August 1994): 34–35.

14. One purpose of having multiple wives for ANE kings was to establish political alliances. By making the observation that he took more wives and concubines, the text indicates that David was becoming stronger politically. Unfortunately, it appears that he was using the wrong means to do so.

15. The text notes that Michal never had any children. Given the context, one has to wonder whether this was God's punishment on her for her heart attitude.

16. We noted earlier that Solomon probably became king in 971 BCE. David likely had begun his reign in Hebron forty years earlier and then moved to Jerusalem seven years later, or about 1004 BCE. And according to the early date for the Exodus adopted in this book, the tabernacle must have been built in 1446–1445. Modern Israel, having placed the capture of Jerusalem at 1000 BCE (as a round number), recently celebrated its 3000th anniversary.

17. The palace was on the heights. As was the common practice in the ANE, the roof was designed as a place to relax in the evening and enjoy the cool breezes. This put him in a position to look over the wall of Bathsheba's place.

18. The way Joab sent the message suggests that he was very much aware of what was going on. It is highly likely that gossip about the king's "indiscretion" was circulating around Jerusalem, and Joab must have heard the stories. David's reaction to Joab's message confirmed Joab's suspicions.

19. This passage is viewed by many theologians as demonstrating David's belief in life after death.

20. Amnon was David's oldest son (2 Sam. 3:2; 1 Chron. 3:1) and thus most likely the one who had been primed to follow him on the throne. Absalom was the third-oldest, with Kileab (or Daniel) in between (we are never told what became of him).

21. Mephibosheth was Jonathan's son who was disabled. David had provided special benefits for him after the death of his friend (2 Sam. 9:1–8). Ziba, his servant, used this situation to get his master's estate.

22. For example, in the life of Solomon, the writer of Chronicles refers the reader who wants more details to the records of

Nathan the prophet, to the prophecy of Ahijah the Shilonite, and to the visions of Iddo the seer, all written records (2 Chron. 9:29). Unfortunately, we do not have any of those today.

23. This event brought to fruition a prophecy made to Eli by a prophet of God in 1 Samuel 2 that his house would be lost from the priesthood. Abiathar was a descendant of Eli in the line of Aaron's son Ithamar. Zadok descended from another son of Aaron, Eleazar.

24. Second Chronicles 1:3 asserts that the tabernacle with the bronze altar was now located in Gibeon, but without the ark of the covenant, which David had brought to Jerusalem. First Kings 3:4 characterizes this altar as one of the "high places" that was used before the temple was built.

25. In addition to Proverbs, wisdom books in the OT include Ecclesiastes and Job. Several other books in extrabiblical Hebrew literature fall into this category (e.g., Ecclesiasticus and the Wisdom of Solomon in the Apocrypha).

26. Actually, Proverbs includes two others, which are subcategories of the foolish: the sluggard and the scoffer (the latter is an extreme or uncorrected fool). The distinction between wise and foolish corresponds to the distinction between righteous and unrighteous.

27. There are a number of problems with the allegorical view. The book gives no indication that it was intended as allegorical; nor does it give any hints for interpreting the supposed symbols. It appears that Solomon is the protagonist, and he would seem to be a poor symbol of a loving God, whether that love is directed toward Israel or toward the church.

28. This interpretation is well developed in Craig S. Glickman's work, *A Song for Lovers* (Downers Grove, Ill.: InterVarsity, 1976).

29. Hill and Walton give seven reasons (*A Survey of the Old Testament*, 240).

CHAPTER 13—The Failure of the North

1. This very nomenclature indicates that the biblical account reflects real events in history. From the perspective of the writers, it was the Southern Kingdom that preserved the true line of Abraham leading to the Messiah, since its kings were the heirs of David. It is then surprising that the renegade Northern Kingdom retained the national name Israel.

2. Strictly speaking, the term *dynasty* refers to a succession of rulers from the same family line; some of the "dynasties" in the north consisted of only one king.

3. At least two areas had been lost: Solomon had given a region in the northwest corner to Hiram of Tyre (1 Kings 9:10–14); and in the southeast, Edom had revolted (11:14–22). Moreover, the Arameans were causing problems in the northeast (11:23–25); and there is also some question about the southwest, since Egypt had taken at least part of Philistia (9:16, which states that Pharaoh then turned around and gave Gezer to Solomon as a wedding gift).

4. In their excavations of Dan, archaeologists have uncovered a large altar that may be that very shrine (Randall Price, *The Stones Cry Out* [Eugene, Ore: Harvest House, 1997], 228).

5. The fulfillment took place about three hundred years later, during Josiah's revival. There are several striking aspects to this prophecy. The human agent, Josiah, is not only mentioned by name, but he is also identified as "born to the house of David," therefore from the now foreign country of Judah. There was also validation by two supernormal acts, the splitting of the altar and the paralysis of Jeroboam's hand. This is an amazing prophecy because of its specificity, but critical scholars dismiss it on the grounds that the text postdates the fulfillment.

6. The old prophet stated that he had been given a new message by "an angel" (1 Kings 13:18; the Hebrew word means "messenger," but in contexts like this one, it usually refers to a spiritual being). The question here is whether he lied about the message or had actually received it. If the latter, the message must have come from a lying spirit, such as is mentioned later in the account of Ahab. In either case, the younger, unnamed prophet was guilty of accepting the word of the other prophet without verifying it from God.

7. One question that is not clear is whether Tibni was considered "king." He was a claimant to the throne and had at least as much support as Zimri. He also appears to have lasted longer, but we are not given any time frame, and he is not listed as a king by the writer.

8. This entire section focuses on the Northern Kingdom, that is, the part of Israel that had broken away and was going after other gods. If the OT was written at a late date in the south, as suggested by critical scholarship, one has to wonder how much "press" the Northern Kingdom would have gotten. Even though the kings are portrayed as evil, Elijah and Elisha clearly are people who figured strongly in the development of later Judaism after the return of the Southern Kingdom from exile. Yet they do not figure at all in the history of the Southern Kingdom. That is especially interesting, given that this period was the time that the two kingdoms were most closely related with the intermarriage of the two royal families.

9. This evaluation suggests that Ahab was the first of the northern kings who overtly served pagan gods. The fact that he worshiped Baal was very important, as will be shown in the subsequent "battle of the gods." Baal and Asherah were discussed in chapter 9 in connection with the conquest and the *herem*.

10. This situation was different from that of David and Saul: David refused to kill Saul because the latter was God's anointed king over God's people; Ben-Hadad was a pagan king fighting against God's people.

11. Returning this city was apparently part of the treaty that Ahab had signed in 1 Kings 20 when he let Ben-Hadad free. The incident would then seem to show how failure to obey God can produce ongoing problems.

12. This issue is addressed in more detail in my book *To Serve Other Gods: An Evangelical History of Religion* (Lanham, Md.: University Press of America, 1994), 222–23.

13. While most prophets were men, several women are specifically cited. When King Josiah rediscovered the Book of the Law, he consulted the prophetess Huldah (2 Kings 22:14). Likewise, when Jesus was presented in the temple, one of the observers was Anna, a prophetess (Luke 2:36).

14. While many of the pagan gods were nothing but lifeless lumps of stone, wood, or metal, some were rooted in actual demonic forces. However, while such forces had some ability to act in space-time history, that power was restricted; and they were unable to announce their intentions in advance and then carry them out (Isa. 40:13–31; 44:9–26).

15. The phrase denotes that he is asking to be designated Elijah's heir. This dialogue is somewhat puzzling, since we have seen that God had already told Elijah to anoint Elisha to replace him. It seems to have been a test to validate that selection in Elisha's mind.

16. We find this matter troubling and difficult to understand. How could God use a lying spirit? Part of the answer comes from the insight we got from the book of Job when we noted that Satan had access to God's throne. The lying spirit that Micaiah referred to would seem to be of the same ilk, and God allowed him a certain amount of leeway to follow his own disposition. Of course, this observation does not really answer all of our questions.

17. David A. Baker gives a good concise overview of the situation (*Obadiah: An Introduction and Commentary* [Downers Grove, Ill.: InterVarsity, 1988], 22–23). He points out that there

is really nothing in the book to date it and that there are several times in history that it could fit. Raymond B. Dillard and Tremper Longman III (*An Introduction to the Old Testament* [Grand Rapids: Zondervan, 1994], 386–87) are certain that the book was written late (that is, the sixth century BCE); while Eugene Merrill (*Kingdom of Priests: A History of Old Testament Israel* [Grand Rapids: Baker, 1995], 382) is just as certain that the book was written early. Gleason Archer (*A Survey of Old Testament Introduction* [Chicago: Moody Press, 1994], 333–38) gives the most thorough evaluation of the early date.

18. Because of the marriage of Athaliah (daughter of Ahab and Jezebel) to Jehoram (son of Jehoshaphat, king of the Southern Kingdom), the house of David was also the house of Jezebel. As we will see in the next chapter, the eradication of her line meant that the lineage of David was being wiped out (although likely there were some more distant relatives, such as descendants of the brothers of Jehoshaphat).

19. Jehu is mentioned in the stela known as the Black Obelisk (see above, ch. 6), where he is identified as *ben Omri*, "son of Omri." This reference illustrates that the Hebrew word *ben* can also mean "follower," although Tammi Schneider has argued that Jehu may indeed have been a descendant of Omri but from a brother of Ahab ("Did Jehu Kill His Own Family?" *BAR* 21, no. 1 [January/February 1995]: 26–33).

20. During this period, Assyria was less expansionistic, which some historians have interpreted as a time of weakness. The situation was suddenly reversed when Tiglath-Pileser III usurped the throne in 744 BCE (see William W. Hallo and William

Kelly Simpson, *The Ancient Near East: A History* [New York: Harcourt Brace Jovanovich, 1971], 131–32).

21. Later Pekah will be credited with having reigned for twenty years before he was replaced by Hoshea. Comparing the reigns of the last four kings of the Northern Kingdom with their contemporaries in the Southern Kingdom, the only way this figure fits is if Pekah reigned at the same time as Menahem and Pekahiah. When we get to the end, we find two Assyrian emperors claiming credit for the victory (Merrill, *Kingdom of Priests*, 395–98).

22. Tiglath-Pileser III claims that he placed Hoshea on the throne after the people in *Beth-Omri* (Israel) overthrew Pekah and that he received from the Israelites ten talents of gold and one thousand talents of silver (*ANET*, 284; the reading "one thousand" is uncertain).

23. The entire reign of this king is obscure. The summary above seems the best way to understand the material in 2 Kings 17:4–5, which has Hoshea in prison and then mentions the siege. It is possible that Hoshea had been released from prison when Tiglath-Pileser died in 727 BCE upon promising loyalty to the new king, Shalmaneser V. If so, his loyalty lasted about two years.

24. Because Sargon II claims credit for the conquest of Samaria (*ANET*, 284–85), some have thought that Shalmaneser may have died before the end of the siege (however, see *HBC*, 250–51).

CHAPTER 14—The Roller-Coaster South

1. Of course, the real reason for the split of the kingdom was the spiritual failure of its leadership. The divine purpose behind this division may have been to demonstrate that only God's grace would preserve the Southern Kingdom. But then we observe that the Southern Kingdom failed also. Apparently we are being shown that human instruments are inadequate—pointing to a future Messiah who would be divine.

2. One of the ironies of history is that the only tribes that remained with Rehoboam were the two leading tribes on the opposite sides during the previous civil war after the death of Saul.

3. The date would be about 875 BCE, which creates a difficulty, for there was war between him and Baasha, who apparently died about eleven years earlier. Probably the best solution is that the thirty-fifth year refers to the age of the Southern Kingdom (Eugene H. Merrill, *Kingdom of Priests: A History of Old Testament Israel* [Grand Rapids: Baker, 1995], 333–34). This then correlates well with the earlier declaration that Asa had ten years of peace (2 Chron. 14:1).

4. I suggested in chapter 13 (see n. 17) that these events tied in with the message of Obadiah. I included Obadiah in my discussion of the Northern Kingdom, but that was an arbitrary call, because the book could also fit here. As seen by Elijah's letter to Jehoram, while a given prophet would have a primary ministry with one or the other of the two kingdoms, he would actually work with both of them *as well as* with the kingdoms around them.

5. In addition to the crown, the boy had a copy of "the covenant." It is not clear if this refers to the covenant given on

Mount Sinai or the covenant the people had just made to agree to serve God and the king (2 Chron. 23:3, 16). Given the word choice and the context, it was probably the latter.

6. It is important to recall that prophetic declarations were given in anticipation of the judgment rather than as an interpretation of why bad things had happened. This pattern does not seem to be completely followed in the book of Joel, since the locust swarm is discussed in past tense. However, the focus of the book is not the locust swarm but the more fearsome things to come, that is, the day of the Lord.

7. The text says "son" (2 Chron. 24:20), but we have already seen that the Hebrew word can mean descendant. This is probably the same Zechariah that Jesus mentioned in Matthew 23:35. There he is termed the son of Berekiah, who was possibly a son of Jehoiada.

8. In chapter 13, I discussed the practice of coregency in the case of Jehoash and his son Jeroboam II. Coregency was more common in the Southern Kingdom than in the north. The text seems to suggest that in the case of Amaziah, it was an act forced on him by the people, probably because they disagreed with his spiritual defection (Merrill, *Kingdom of Priests*, 375–76).

9. The political maneuvers of this era are not clear, but it is possible that the Assyrians provided some of the impetus for putting Ahaz on the throne.

10. It has been suggested that these three years correlate with a period when the Assyrians under Tiglath-Pileser III were distracted elsewhere (William W. Hallo, "From Qarqar to Carchemish," *BAReader2*, 170–71).

11. The figure of sixty-five years is stated explicitly, while that of ten to thirteen years is an inference from the statement, "before the boy knows enough to reject the wrong and choose the right." The boy apparently refers to Shear-Jashub (Isa. 7:3), whom Isaiah had been directed to take with him to meet Ahaz. Thirteen was deemed the age of accountability for Hebrew men. Shear-Jashub was young at the time, apparently one to three years of age. In ten years from that event, the Northern Kingdom had been reduced to a small fraction of its former self and Samaria was under siege. It fell in 722 BCE, about thirteen years after Isaiah's declaration. In 670/669 BCE, Esarhaddon or Ashurbanipal restarted the process of carrying captive people into exile, leaving the Northern Kingdom nearly desolate.

12. The expression translated "sacrificed his sons in the fire" (2 Chron. 28:3) has been debated. The Hebrew phrase means literally "caused his sons to pass through the fire." Increasing evidence solidifies the understanding that it refers to infant sacrifice (see ch. 9, sidebar "Infant Sacrifice").

13. Normally Passover would have been celebrated in the first month, but at that time the people were still cleansing the temple. Drawing on legal precedent (Num. 9:10–11), they were able to move it back a month.

14. If my chronology is correct, this celebration of the Passover would have taken place about seven years after the destruction of Samaria. It is likely that some of those who ridiculed the messengers may have been aliens who had been resettled into the region by the Assyrians. Most, however, had been citizens of the former Northern Kingdom. They would have been aware of the issues and the history of both the Passover and the split of the nation.

15. The exact nature of this ailment is not clear. The writer of Chronicles essentially ignores this issue, although he hints that the cause was pride on the part of both Hezekiah and the people of Jerusalem. The cure involved a poultice of figs laid on a "boil," which we normally don't think of as a life-threatening affliction. The Hebrew word for "boil" here in essence means "an inflamed spot," perhaps indicating a major infection, which is quite possible, especially if the city was under siege at the time. When we look at the account in Kings, where more information is given, we note that the illness was very close to the time of the siege (Isaiah promised deliverance from Assyria, and Hezekiah was given fifteen more years of life and lived to 686 BCE).

16. This comment is an interesting anticipation, since at the time the invincible power was Assyria. The idea that the Babylonians would not only throw off the Assyrian yoke but also replace their masters and be just as bad probably had not crossed Hezekiah's mind.

17. Traditionally Jeremiah is viewed as the author of Kings (Donald J. Wiseman, *1 and 2 Kings* [Downers Grove, Ill.: InterVarsity, 1993], 52–58). While it is likely that Jeremiah did the final revision, it seems probable that an earlier work provided the nucleus on which he built. This nucleus was developed to encourage God's people in a time of distress. The structure of Kings allows this type of development, since each king's entry is a clear unit. There are points in the two books where the writers note a practice that has been continued until the time of writing (e.g., "To this day their children and grandchildren continue to do as their fathers did," 2 Kings 17:41). Such a comment could suggest that the writer was at the end of the entire kingdom period, but it could also reflect a practice that continued as the writer wrote, whenever that was, or it could be an editorial comment from a later writer who brought the record up to date. The key to remember is that Kings covers about a four-hundred-year period.

18. There is some question as to whether the writing mentioned in Chronicles ("the vision of the prophet Isaiah son of Amoz in the book of the kings of Judah and Israel") is the same book we call Isaiah. The wording of Chronicles seems to suggest that the writer had another book in mind, since he talks about "other events" (lit., "the remainder of the deeds"), whereas the items mentioned in our book of Isaiah are all recorded in Chronicles.

19. As argued, for example, by George Buchanan Gray in *A Critical and Exegetical Commentary on the Book of Isaiah (I–XXVII)*, International Critical Commentary (Edinburgh: T. & T. Clark, 1912), xxxi. Actually, Gray argues primarily that since the text of Deutero-Isaiah presupposes the Babylonian captivity, it necessarily was written during or after that period. That is a non sequitur, however, since one of the arguments of Isaiah is the certainty of a captivity (see Isa. 39:6). If that were the case, then Isaiah 39 would also have to be viewed as postexilic, which it is not. Therefore, viewing the last half of Isaiah as written after the exile does not eliminate the problem. J. Alec Motyer also addresses this issue in *The Prophecy of Isaiah: An Introduction and Commentary* (Downers Grove, Ill.: InterVarsity, 1993), 25.

20. Critics have argued that the Hebrew word used for the mother in Isaiah 7:14 (*'almah*) merely announces that a baby would be born to a "young woman," probably to either Ahaz's or Isaiah's wife. The word choice actually seems to reflect the opposite: a woman who had never had sexual relations (Motyer, *Prophecy of Isaiah,* 84–86). This understanding is evident also in the LXX, which renders the Hebrew term as *parthenos,* a Greek word that clearly means "virgin" (the Greek translation of Isaiah was probably produced in the second century BCE).

21. Other thought-provoking items in this section include the declaration that the Messiah would be with a rich man in his death and the idea that the Messiah would serve as a guilt offering. The latter concept suggests a human sacrifice, which was totally anathema to pious Hebrews.

22. See especially Motyer, *Prophecy of Isaiah,* 22–25. Note also Oswald T. Allis, *The Unity of Isaiah* (Phillipsburg, N.J.: Presbyterian and Reformed, 1980), and Hobart E. Freeman, *Introduction to the Old Testament Prophets* (Chicago: Moody Press, 1977).

23. Deuteronomy 30 is also the first reference to the "new covenant" that Jeremiah would talk about later. Moses writes how after the return from the exile, "The LORD your God will circumcise your hearts and the hearts of your descendants, so that you may love him with all your heart and with all your soul, and live" (Deut. 30:6).

24. One point of uncertainty is the role of the nation in that final restoration process. Isaiah presents it as involving all of Israel. At least three different views are currently held: (1) a restored national Israel will be involved in an actual final restoration; (2) it will not be a national Israel, but a spiritual Israel (i.e., the church) that will be involved in an actual final restoration; (3) the entire description of restoration is allegorical.

25. This emphasis is shown in passages such as Micah 2:1–2, where he condemned those who violated the guidelines of the covenant pertaining to personal property and the rights of others. Likewise, in 3:9–10, he condemns leaders who pervert justice and "distort all that is right" (lit., "twist all that is straight [or upright]").

26. As Matthew quotes the Jewish leaders, their citation of Micah 5:2 contains four lines. The first three lines are very close to the LXX version of Micah. However, the last line includes a phrase that does not show up in Micah 5:2, "who will be the shepherd of my people Israel." This line seems to be giving a summary paraphrase of the next several verses of Micah, which talk about the Messiah as a shepherd (cf. also 2 Sam. 5:2).

27. Although Josiah carried his reformation into these areas, that does not mean that he "annexed" the Northern Kingdom, as argued by John Bright (*A History of Israel* 4th ed. [Louisville: Westminster John Knox, 2000], 320), and others.

28. The choice of Huldah is very interesting, since at least four male prophets were active: Nahum, Habakkuk, Zephaniah, and Jeremiah. The latter specifically records his first visions as being in the thirteenth year of Josiah, six years before this discovery of the Book of the Law (Jer. 1:2).

29. We also must not assume that his actions were totally devoid of international politics (Bright, *History of Israel,* 319–22). Most likely, he took advantage of the power vacuum to follow his spiritual leanings. Given our discussion of the role of the spiritual realm has played in human affairs, it is possible that behind the scenes a spiritual battle had set the stage for his political actions, but that is conjecture.

30. Archaeologists have noted how heavy rains helped undermine the extremely massive walls of Nineveh. The archives reveal that on the night the city fell, the guards on the walls were drunk, which helped the attacking forces. All in all, it reflects a deterioration in the discipline of the Assyrian forces. For a more detailed study of this period, see A. T. Olmstead, *History of Assyria* (Chicago: University of Chicago Press, 1975 reprint), 440–52. For a condensed overview, see Merrill, *Kingdom of Priests,* 436–42.

31. Conspicuously absent is Edom. This omission might suggest that the judgment on this nation spoken earlier by Obadiah had already occurred. However, it is also possible that Edom somehow "sat this one out." We see Edomites (Idumeans), such as King Herod, involved in later historical affairs up to Roman times.

32. Interestingly, Riblah was not in Egypt, but to the north, in the same direction that Josiah had attempted to keep Neco from going. Apparently from there Jehoahaz was taken back to Egypt where he died. We hear of the man on only one other occasion. Jeremiah stated to Zedekiah that his brother Jehoahaz (called Shallum) would die in exile and not return (Jer. 22:11).

33. It is not really clear whether this declaration followed the recent Babylonian victory and anticipated the future destruction of Jerusalem or whether it anticipated both. In either case, the key concern was the upcoming destruction of Jerusalem.

34. Because of Manasseh, the certainty of judgment on the Southern Kingdom was announced (2 Kings 21:11–16). However, because of Josiah's revival, judgment was deferred until after his death (22:18–20).

35. Jeremiah clearly asserted that those false prophets were not from God. Rather, he maintained that they prophesied via Baal or other false gods (e.g., 23:13) or their own minds (e.g., 14:14).

36. Charles Dyer has prepared an excellent chart showing the general chronological flow of the book (*BKC,* 1:1126). Another problem is the fact that the LXX translation is both shorter and arranged differently than the Hebrew text. The omissions are numerous (totaling about 2,700 words), but R. K. Harrison considers that they are "rather minor" (*Introduction to the Old Testament* [Grand Rapids: Eerdmans, 1969], 817–18).

37. These dates are corroborated by both Babylonian and Israelite records. The first is the ninth day of the fourth month of the eleventh year of Zedekiah's reign (2 Kings 25:2–3), which would be the ninth of Tammuz. The second, the tenth of Ab, is recorded by Jeremiah 52:12. Rabbinic tradition suggests that the burning of the city began on the seventh of Ab, but the temple was set on fire on the ninth and finished burning on the tenth (*HBC*, 259–60).

CHAPTER 15—The Nation in Exile

1. Consider, for example, Jeremiah's confrontation with Hananiah (Jer. 28). It was about 593 BCE, and Jeremiah was wearing his yoke as an object lesson. Hananiah took the yoke off Jeremiah and proclaimed that he had revelation from God that the people would be back within two years. Jeremiah at first said that he hoped it was true, but God sent him back with a stronger message. Because Hananiah was giving false revelation, he would be dead within a year.

2. The only time the pagan names are used in the book is when these three men are addressed by the Babylonians. However, the interaction with Nebuchadnezzar in the furnace episode is so grabbing that we overlook that detail and call them by their Babylonian names.

3. Where was Daniel in this incident? We have no information on which to draw a conclusion. That Daniel is conspicuous by his absence points to a historical event. It is likely that a redactor (or editor) would have tried to account for that very serious omission if this story had been made up.

4. We are not told what his motive was in this case. It could have ranged from defiance to a semipious desire to seek divine intervention. In the latter case, his act would seem to be a somewhat magical attempt to invoke the power of the Israelite God on behalf of the nation of Babylon. Whatever the case, it clearly backfired.

5. The text indicates that the king and his advisors were unable to read the text, suggesting that it was in a script they were unfamiliar with. The NIV transliterates the text as shown. Most translations transliterate the last word as *Upharsin* (the first letter represents the conjunction "and" in both Hebrew and Aramaic).

6. This protection was not guaranteed, nor was it an absolute principle. We see Daniel and his friends exiled even though they personally had not gone the evil way of their culture. They still suffered because of the culture's failures. While Daniel and friends were preserved mightily during this time, there was and is no guarantee that others would experience similar deliverance. The lives of Isaiah and Jeremiah demonstrate that.

7. The apocalyptic material in the Gospels is found primarily in a discourse that took place during the last week of Jesus' life (Matt. 24–25; Mark 13; Luke 21). This section is sometimes called the Little Apocalypse or the Olivet Discourse, since it reports things Jesus said on the Mount of Olives about the future of the temple and the nation of Israel.

8. One of the key points of discussion is why some apocalyptic books were considered canonical and others were not. This question takes us back to the more basic issue of why *any* books were included in the canon, which we addressed earlier. The three most important criteria were authorship, subject matter, and the reaction of the believing community.

9. See *ANET* 308, for several economic texts that list rations given to Jehoiachin and his sons.

10. One of the perplexing aspects of this object lesson is the way Ezekiel had to lie on his left side (bearing the sins of the Northern Kingdom) and then on his right side (the Southern Kingdom) to represent the years of sin of the nation. Each day of lying on his side is said to correspond to one year. It is not clear what the figures represent, since we do not find two clearly demarcated periods in the history of the nation that would correlate to 390 years and 40 years.

11. God originally told Ezekiel to use dried human dung to illustrate the horrible conditions coming. Ezekiel protested because doing so would render the food unclean. God then allowed the substitution of dried cow manure instead.

12. As seen in these chapters, this vision clearly demarcates a yet-future event, since it points to a dual restoration of Judah and Ephraim (the Southern and Northern Kingdoms). The heir of David will rule. The people of both kingdoms will dwell in the land. This prophecy is characterized as a new, everlasting covenant. The events in the valley of bones also seem to indicate a physical restoration of the nation before the spiritual restoration takes place.

13. Like his predecessor Isaiah, Ezekiel seems to switch at points into judgment of spiritual forces behind the scene. In Ezekiel 28:11–19, the description of the King of Tyre assumes characteristics beyond the physical realm, leading many to see here a judgment on Satan (see Isa. 14:12–21, where Isaiah makes a similar shift while talking of the king of Babylon).

14. The timing suggests that this was more than a party, and it may well have been the planning session for the invasion of Greece that took place in 480 BCE, about a year after these initial events.

15. Since the divorce was done through the prompting of some of his advisors, it is likely that there were some political issues underlying the entire matter. Unfortunately, we have no further information.

16. Mordecai raised Esther, who was the daughter of his uncle, which made her a cousin. However, he seems to have been much older than she was. Her Hebrew name was Hadassah, which means "myrtle."

17. Esther's night with the king was in the tenth month of the seventh year of his reign (Est. 2:16), approximately four years after the Vashti incident, and the text implies that she was made queen a very short time afterward. Haman began plotting in the first month of Xerxes' twelfth year, that is, during the March-April period of 474 BCE. The number of specific dates point to historical events, since they easily could have been checked by

records of the Persian Empire, records that are now for the most part destroyed.

CHAPTER 16—Home Again

1. These observations should not be construed as a condemnation of those who did not return. There would have been many reasons why some people did not or could not make the journey. In the case of Daniel, it was clearly his age.

2. One is immediately taken by the sheer number of items involved: Ezra inventories 5,400 items. Yet not everything was taken back. As 2 Kings 25:13–15 points out, many of the larger bronze items had been broken up for shipment and were irretrievably lost. Cyrus did allow them to take the various dishes and other utensils used in the temple service. One item that is not mentioned is the ark of the covenant. This lack has caused much discussion, and no firm conclusions are forthcoming. It seems likely that the ark had been hidden prior to the destruction of Jerusalem and its location forgotten during the three-generation transition (see Randall Price, *In Search of Temple Treasures* [Eugene, Ore.: Harvest House, 1994]). This detail does serve to show that, as central as the ark had been to the nation, it was not critical to the worship of God.

3. As was noted in chapter 14, not all Israelites had been deported, although we have no idea of the numbers left in the land awaiting the return of their countrymen. Some of the people recalled Solomon's temple, which had been destroyed fifty years earlier. The text of Ezra does not make it clear whether this weeping was for joy or sorrow. Haggai suggests, however, that the weeping was from their comparison of the splendor that had been lost with the lessened splendor of the new project (Hag. 2:3).

4. It was not the intermarriage as such that created the problem, but rather the resulting apostasy from the worship of God. There also seems to be evidence that just as the worship of YHWH had been affected by the pagan cults, so also those cults tried to incorporate YHWH into their pantheons as one more god. Unfortunately, we do not have a good record of the process, especially during this period.

5. One of the confusing things about the biblical material is that Ezra 4:6–23 is out of chronological order with what precedes and follows. The passage, which traces a later opposition to the Jews, is inserted between a cause-and-effect sequence (Samaritan opposition in v. 5 and Jewish cessation of work in v. 24). But we need to remember that Ezra was writing during a later period and was putting the two sequences together to show a pattern.

6. Between Cyrus and Darius came Cambyses (530–522) and Smerdis (sometimes called Pseudo-Smerdis), apparently a pretender who seized the throne briefly in 522. According to Darius's summary in the Behistun Inscription, Cambyses had taken the throne by killing his brother Bardiya (the real Smerdis), and later a certain Gaumata (Pseudo-Smerdis) pretended to be that brother who had somehow survived (though some scholars suspect Darius invented this story to justify his own claim to the throne). Cambyses committed suicide, but Darius and six other noblemen eventually overthrew (Pseudo-)Smerdis and Darius

became the new king (Edwin M. Yamauchi, *Persia and the Bible* [Grand Rapids: Baker, 1996], 138–48).

7. See Nehemiah 12:1, 16. In his own book, Zechariah records that his father was Berekiah and his grandfather Iddo. Both Ezra and Nehemiah cite him as the heir ("son") of Iddo, suggesting that his father may have died young.

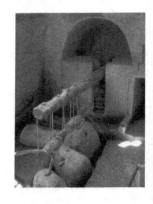

8. While the message had an immediate application to the completion of the temple, the several references to "the Branch" recall earlier prophetic announcements of the Messiah. Thus, there is a more complete fulfillment to come at a later date.

9. Matthew 21:4–5 views this declaration as a messianic prophecy fulfilled on what we know as Palm Sunday. It is important to remember that at the time Zechariah wrote, the nation had not had a king for about seventy years. It is also important to observe how this king was characterized—as "righteous and having salvation."

10. This is a very provocative passage in which God himself, speaking in the first person, says that at some point in the future the nation would "look on me, the one they have pierced." The text then switches to the third person and says that the nation would mourn for "him." At the same time, God would be pouring out "a spirit of grace," probably a reference to God's own Spirit (see NASB and the note in NIV).

11. This number is somewhat confusing. It consists of two major groups, the first of which consists of twelve smaller groups. Each of these lists one to four names plus the number of men accompanying them, totaling 18 named individuals plus 1,496 unnamed men with them. When Ezra mustered his company, he realized there were no Levites; after asking for help, 38 Levites and 220 temple servants responded, raising the total to 1,772.

12. This point is evident in Ezra 7:25, which indicates that Ezra was authorized to appoint magistrates who knew the Law and who were to teach it to the people. It is especially evident in 7:26, which warns Ezra against those who do not "obey the law of your God and the law of the king." Moreover, those who disobeyed the Law were to be severely punished.

13. We have seen a number of occasions when intermarriage was not only tolerated but was included within the lineage of the most notable people (e.g., Rahab and Ruth as ancestors of David).

14. Translators disagree on how Ezra 10:38 should be translated. Some render the first two words as "Bani" and "Binnui" (KJV, NASB). Others, such as the NIV and NRSV, have "the descendants of Binnui." If the latter is correct, the list would contain only 112 names.

15. Hanani may have been one of the returnees, in which case perhaps he had gone back to Susa to visit. Another possibility is

that he had been sent to Jerusalem on a fact-finding mission and was thus returning home. It is also possible that he too was an official who had gone to Jerusalem on government business, in which case his report to Nehemiah would have been incidental to his primary job.

16. We cannot be certain whether Ezra intended the expression "to give us a wall" (cf. KJV and other versions) in the literal sense that God intended that they should rebuild the walls of the city as well as the temple or in a figurative sense to reflect God's protection while they rebuilt the temple (cf. NIV).

17. The opposition made several attempts to stop the work, including ridicule, subterfuge, treachery, and threats of violence. Nehemiah ignored the efforts that could be ignored and pointedly contradicted the more overt attempts.

18. The last two-thirds of the book of Nehemiah are difficult to follow because the events apparently are not placed in chronological order. For example, chapter 13 seems to begin on the day of the dedication of the people, but Nehemiah then states that he was not present during those events, which occurred after his first twelve-year term as governor had expired.

19. Scholars have debated the significance of the reversal of the two holidays. The most likely explanation is that the leaders wanted to ensure that the people understood what was going on first. The wall had just been completed. They started reading the Law and discovered the Festival of Booths (Sukkoth). The national dedication was stopped while the people gathered branches for the festival. Then, during the Festival of Booths, they read the Law for the entire period (Neh. 8:18; see Deut. 31:10ff.). Now that they had a clear understanding of the Law, it was time for dedication, which actually came two days after the completion of Sukkoth.

20. This issue has convinced some scholars that the chronology of the two books is inaccurate and that Ezra came a number of years later. The argument is that the people would not have had a relapse so quickly after Ezra, so Ezra must have come later (John Bright, *A History of Israel*, 4th ed. [Louisville: Westminster John Knox, 2000], 391–402). This logic assumes that a revival would be longer lasting than the twenty to twenty-five years between the two events. Human nature and our own society suggest that is not necessarily the case.

CHAPTER 17—Bridges to the New Testament

1. The inclusion of the Apocrypha is usually thought of as a feature of the Roman Catholic Bible; however, the original King James translation included these books as well. In Catholic Bibles (also in those of Eastern Orthodox churches), the apocryphal books are integrated into the OT, whereas in the KJV and other Protestant versions, they have been brought together into a separate section after the OT. A number of books cover the content and origin of the Apocrypha. One good work is Bruce M. Metzger's *An Introduction to the Apocrypha* (New York: Oxford University Press, 1957).

2. Metzger, *Introduction to the Apocrypha*, 175–80.

3. R. K. Harrison, *An Introduction to the Old Testament* (Grand Rapids: Eerdmans, 1969), 1186.

4. Phillip Sigal, *Judaism: The Evolution of a Faith* (Grand Rapids: Eerdmans, 1988), 100–106.

5. Ron Moseley suggests that there was also a reaction in the church as it became increasingly Gentile (*Yeshua: A Guide to the Real Jesus and the Original Church* [Baltimore: Messianic Jewish Publishers, 1996], 60).

6. For example, a number of works give guidelines to the community at Qumran on how to live and worship. Instructional works have been found that give us insight into the beliefs of this Jewish group.

7. While the postexilic Judean culture was homogeneous in outward ritual, we have already seen hints of a wide spectrum of attitudes. The postexilic prophets such as Malachi were already condemning the people for following outward ritual without having a heart that focused on God.

8. A good overview of the complex issues involved in these groups is Anthony J. Saldarini, *Pharisees, Scribes and Sadducees in Palestinian Society* (Grand Rapids: Eerdmans, 2001).

9. Moseley observes that of these twenty, Josephus mentions only three: the Pharisees, the Sadducees, and the Essenes (*Yeshua*, 87).

10. Josephus, *Wars of the Jews*, 2.8.14.

11. The origin of the name is debated with Aramaic and Hebrew possibilities also suggested (R. K. Harrison, s.v. "Essenes," *ZPEB*, 2:315).

12. Alan D. Crown and Lena Cansdale, "Qumran: Was It an Essene Community?" *BAR* 20, no. 5 (September/October 1994): 25–35, 73–74.

13. Josephus, *Wars*, 2.4.1.

14. The battle of Thermopylae was technically a defeat for the Greeks, but the holding action of the three hundred Spartans who fought to the death allowed the Greeks to gather their forces. The battle of Platea in 479, although not as noted as the other three, was the final victory, after which the Persians no longer threatened the Greek mainland. For a more in-depth study of this fascinating period, see Edwin M. Yamauchi, *Persia and the Bible* (Grand Rapids: Baker, 1996).

15. Carthage had been originally settled by Phoenicians, adventurers from Tyre and Sidon. It subsequently became independent. When the founding cities were destroyed by Alexander, Carthage stood alone and prospered until it faced the growing power of Rome. See David Soron, Aicha ben Abed ben Khader, and Hedi Slim, *Carthage* (New York: Simon & Schuster, 1990).

16. While we think of the Exile as being predominantly in Mesopotamia, many Judeans had fled to Egypt to avoid the Babylonian invasion. Jeremiah was kidnapped and taken there

(Jer. 43–44). This Jewish population was still in Egypt, especially Alexandria, during the early church age.

17. Palestine fell to Syria as a result of the battle of Panium (c. 200 BCE), which also involved the Macedonians. It was during the reign of Ptolemy V that the Rosetta Stone was inscribed. This monument was discovered by the French in the early 1800s and became the key through which the modern world was able to unlock hieroglyphics (see above, ch. 6).

18. Antiochus IV took the throne after his brother, Seleucus IV, was assassinated by Heliodorus, who tried to take over. Antiochus defeated this usurper and took the throne.

19. The information we have on the Maccabean revolt comes predominately from 1 Maccabees and Josephus (*Antiquities of the Jews*, books 12–14). The following is a synopsis of that information.

20. This decision laid the foundation for the Jewish actions in the Yom Kippur War of 1973. Based on this precedence, the Jews were willing to fight even on the holiest day of the year.

21. A good overview of Roman history is Mikhail Rostotzeff, *Rome*, trans. Elias Rickerman (New York: Oxford University Press, 1960).

22. These conflicts with Carthage are called the Punic wars (from "Phoenician," the ethnic and linguistic identity of the city; see above, ch. 13, for a discussion of the relationship between the Northern Kingdom and the Phoenicians who dwelt in Tyre and Sidon). The initial cause of the war was control of the Straits of Messina between Sicily and Italy. There were three major wars, 264–261, 218–201, and 149–146 BCE. After Carthage was burned, the remaining 20 percent of the population was sold into slavery and the region became a Roman province named "Africa" (see Soron et al., *Carthage*).

CHAPTER 18—Who Is Jesus the Messiah?

1. The motivation of some Jewish leaders is evident in the report of the discussion of the Sanhedrin (the ruling council of the Jews) following the raising of Lazarus. Their consensus was, "If we let him go on like this, everyone will believe in him, and then the Romans will come and take away both our place and our nation" (John 11:48). In other words, their main concern was their personal prestige and affluence.

2. The ancestry would be a matter of record and would be kept in the genealogical archives of the temple. The birthplace would probably be less evident, since this era predated birth certificates; even so, a skilled investigator would be able to ask around and determine that a person had indeed been born in a given location. The claim of a virgin birth could only come from the testimony of the parents (by the time the gospel accounts were being written, the purported father, Joseph, was probably already deceased, so this matter depended on the testimony of the mother, Mary).

3. This is a cumulative figure for all of the verses in the four gospel accounts. The postresurrection events were included within this period, although technically they go beyond the last week. The individual books break down as follows: Matthew, 36 percent; Mark, 37 percent; Luke, 25 percent; and John, 39 per-

cent. While these numbers include sections that some modern translations omit, there is no question but that the bulk of the material of these books covers less than one tenth of one percent of the days He walked on this world. Clearly, there is a disproportionate emphasis on that last week.

4. Robert Stein, *The Synoptic Problem* (Grand Rapids: Baker, 1987), 29–44.

5. The term *synoptic* (from two Greek words that mean "with" and "view") is applied to these three gospels because they present the life of Jesus from a similar perspective that is different from that of the gospel of John.

6. The premises underlie the thinking of key individuals who developed the theories. This does not mean that everyone who accepts either of the theories necessarily accepts all of the premises. In fact, many scholars reject several of the premises but still accept the developmental processes that have been set forth as explanations for the synoptics.

7. William R. Farmer, *The Synoptic Problem* [Dillsboro, N.C.: Western North Carolina Press, 1976], 19.

8. Robert H. Stein, *Jesus the Messiah* (Downers Grove, Ill.: InterVarsity, 1996), 17–24.

9. Stein, *Synoptic Problem*, 48–52. However, it is interesting to note that while Mark has omitted many incidents, as well as many extended teaching sections that Matthew and Luke included, what he has included is much more developed. For one example, note the healing of Simon Peter's mother-in-law of a fever (Matt. 8:14–15; Mark 1:29–31; Luke 4:38–39). Matthew and Luke cover the event in two verses, Mark (the shorter gospel) takes three. Thirty Greek words are used in Matthew, forty-four in Mark, and thirty-eight in Luke. Mark includes additional information, such as that the house also belonged to Andrew, and James and John were present. When we trace the wording, I find only two words in common to all three (three if I include the word "mother-in-law," which is spelled differently in Matthew).

10. The key work on this theory was done by a German scholar named H. J. Holtzmann, who published *Die Synoptischen Evangelien* (The Synoptic Gospels) in 1863.

11. John Wenham, *Redating Matthew, Mark and Luke* (Downers Grove, Ill.: InterVarsity, 1992), 40–87.

12. According to this theory, M was a source (probably originating in Jerusalem) used by Matthew alone; thus it contained the material that is unique to him. Likewise, L is a special source (possibly from Caesarea) used by Luke and containing the material found only in his gospel. This theory was set forth by B. H. Streeter in 1924 (*The Four Gospels: A Study in Origins*). Streeter also hypothesized several revisions of Luke before the final product was reached. This proposal has received mixed reactions.

13. For example, Eta Linnemann, a German scholar trained in the critical methods, has rejected these views for a variety of reasons. She notes that she had always assumed the critical position until she started looking at the text and realized that her views were not substantiated (*Is There a Synoptic Problem?* [Grand Rapids: Baker, 1992]). Another author who has addressed the issue is John Wenham (*Redating Matthew, Mark and Luke* [Grand Rapids: Baker, 1992]).

14. Cf. Wenham, *Redating*, 1–10.

15. The term "gospel of the kingdom" was used by Matthew to describe the message that Jesus brought and passed on to His disciples. The phrase is used three times in Matthew. The first two times (4:23 and 9:35) it describes the message Jesus brought. In Matthew 24:14 it describes the future message that His disciples would bring. It is also used in Luke 16:16 in a broader sense that covers both ideas.

16. This statement probably oversimplifies the issue, since we read that during the life of Jesus, He sent His disciples out several times on preaching ministries to preach the gospel of the kingdom. Here we are looking at the first postresurrection promulgation. In Peter's sermon, we find a succinct declaration of the gospel message: "Jesus of Nazareth was a man accredited by God to you by miracles, wonders and signs, which God did among you through him, as you yourselves know. This man was handed over to you by God's set purpose and foreknowledge; and you, with the help of wicked men, put him to death by nailing him to the cross. But God raised him from the dead, freeing him from the agony of death, because it was impossible for death to keep its hold on him" (Acts 2:22–24). Peter follows this with more information substantiating his assertions and an invitation to accept those claims.

17. Most of the NT letters were directed to one church or person. When they received their letter, they kept it for rereading. It is clear that a number of other letters were written by the apostles, but only some achieved canonical status. This was both an immediate and a gradual process. It was immediate in the sense that the writer was inspired when he wrote and the recipient understood that the letter was special. It was gradual in that it took time for the churches throughout the Roman Empire to get copies of all of the letters. Some took longer than others. By the middle of the second century, the church as a whole agreed on which letters were to be considered canonical, although some churches questioned certain letters for some time yet. This is the same canon we have today.

18. One of the difficulties in correlating the four accounts derives from the assumption that each writer followed a strictly chronological sequence. However, the writers were more concerned with proving a point than with developing a chronological arrangement. As such, some items are placed in different locations in the different books. For example, the calming of the sea in Matthew (8:23–27) comes before the healing of a man with a shriveled hand on the Sabbath (12:10–13) and the parable of the sower (13:1–23), while in Mark and Luke it comes after.

19. On the surface, Mary's question seems to be the same one Zechariah asked. However, we do not have the intonation in the way they spoke, nor do we see their intent. Moreover, there is a significant difference in the two events. John was conceived in a normal manner, even though Elizabeth was postmenopausal. For this type of situation, there were OT precedents, beginning with Sarah and Abraham. But it is one thing for an older married couple to have a child. It is an entirely different thing for an unmarried woman who has never had sexual relations to conceive. There was no precedent for the latter. Clearly God was raising the standard to reflect a truly unique birth.

20. Two items of note are seen here. First, an engaged couple, while not married, were legally bound to one another. As such, had Joseph died prior to the marriage, Mary still would have been considered a widow (Mishnah, *Ketub.* 5:1). Second, in that situation, her pregnancy would be a clear indication of adultery. This is what Joseph struggled with, and when Mary told him what had happened, he probably did not believe her explanation.

21. Critical scholars have questioned Luke's statement based on extrabiblical information that Quirinius was governor at a later point and that a census was taken under him in the year 6 CE. Other data, however, corroborates Luke (see *HBC*, 302–6). Luke is very specific when he says, "This was the *first* census that took place while Quirinius was governor of Syria" (Luke 2:2, italics added); this comment can be naturally understood to mean that more than one census was taken during the administration of Quirinius. Furthermore, the early church fathers apparently were aware of the data  and even asserted that the records could still be read in Rome (e.g., Justin Martyr, *Apology*, 1.34 [see *ANF*, 1:174]; and Tertullian, *Against Marcion*, 4:7 [see *ANF*, 3:352]).

22. Anna is an interesting person. Luke declares that she was a prophetess, which means that she gave revelation from God to those who sought it. He also notes that she was from Asher, one of the tribes of the Northern Kingdom.

23. Egypt still had a large Jewish population remaining from the Exile. However, they apparently used Greek as their language, since it was in Alexandria, Egypt, that the Greek translation of the OT (the LXX) had been made. The evidence is that Joseph's family also would have likely used Greek in Galilee. The actual time in Egypt is recorded by the church fathers as about two years (see *HBC*, 297). Jesus probably would have been four to five years old when they returned.

24. This education lasted until about the age of thirteen. Apparently some young men were accepted for advanced training under leading rabbis. This training was not for the priesthood, however, which was limited to the tribe of Levi. A leading example of such an apprentice would be Paul, who was of the tribe of Benjamin.

25. This omission has led, over the years, to a number of speculations. For example, several documents included in a book by Frank Crane called *The Lost Books of the Bible* (New York: Alpha House, 1926) relate spectacular things that the young Jesus supposedly did. Contrary to the blurbs on the 1973 paperback copy, these books were neither suppressed nor lost. Rather, as Crane points out in his introduction, they clearly show the difference between what was viewed as canonical and what was rejected. They also show that while myths about Jesus did arise, the church was quick to reject them.

26. As suggested above, Jesus was born about 5 (but possibly 3) BCE. John began his ministry in 29 CE (note how carefully this event is dated in Luke 3:1). This would make Jesus between

thirty-one and thirty-three years of age when He approached John—that is, *about* thirty.

27. Harold Hoehner spells out in detail how these dates are determined in *Chronological Aspects of the Life of Christ* (Grand Rapids: Zondervan, 1978). Many scholars hold to an alternate set of dates: 26 or 27 CE for the beginning of Jesus' ministry and 30 CE for the crucifixion.

28. The gospel of John does not directly record the voice from heaven, but it does mention a later event when Jesus walked by and the Baptist gave testimony to what had happened earlier (John 1:29–34).

29. Here we have inside information that had to have been given to the writers either from Jesus or directly from God, since Jesus was alone during this period. One point of interest is that the three temptations recorded in Matthew and Luke illustrate the three areas of temptation that John sees as encompassing all temptation for all people (1 John 2:16).

30. The text states, "There they stayed for a few days." The phrase "for a few days" seems to correlate to our expression "for a while" and can be somewhat open-ended. Later events indicate that Jesus' center of operations was in Capernaum and that He actually had a house there.

31. Monetary equivalences are difficult to ascertain. The temple tax was one half-shekel per male citizen, which represented two days' wages for an average laborer; if we assume a correspondence between that income and today's minimum wage, the amount would be about $80. However, to complicate matters, the total profits for individuals and the temple mentioned above were calculated more than a century ago in England (Alfred Edersheim, *The Life and Times of Jesus the Messiah* [1896; reprint, Grand Rapids: Eerdmans, 1971], 368). The figures I have given reflect a conversion from pounds sterling using an exchange rate of $5 to £1, and adjusting for inflation. If anything, my figures are low.

32. Their reference to the forty-six years it had taken to build the temple is another time indicator. The base date was 17 BCE (*HBC*, 349), placing the conversation in 30 CE.

33. There was tremendous animosity between the Jews and the Samaritans at this time. The roots of this lay in the resettlement of the area by the Assyrians and the troubles that Ezra and Nehemiah had had following their return from exile. By this time, pious Jews would go east from Jerusalem down to Jericho, cross the Jordan, and travel north to Galilee on the other side of the river rather than pass through Samaria. In this light, the phrase "he had to go through Samaria" (John 4:4) is surprising. This is especially the case if they were already in the Jordan Valley.

34. Actually, Jesus stopped in the middle of a sentence and closed the book. The part He did not read proclaimed "the day of vengeance of our God." As He addressed His hometown audience, He now chastised them for their unwillingness to see Him beyond the hometown boy, which would not allow them to see Him as a true prophet. Enraged, the people tried to throw Him over a cliff.

35. The fact that Jesus went up to Jerusalem in conjunction with the feast points to one of the three festivals at which all males were commanded to present themselves to God: Passover, Pentecost, and Sukkoth or Tabernacles (Deut. 16:3). If this was not Passover 31 CE, then the second most likely alternative would be Sukkoth in the fall of either 30 or 31.

36. Houses in Judea tended to have flat roofs made of a variety of materials. Luke indicates that this particular roof consisted of clay tiles, which would be relatively easy to remove and then replace.

37. According to Luke 5:10, the four brothers were partners. In this passage (5:1–11), Luke seems to add a third occasion when Peter was called, or at least he adds more details to the second. According to Luke, on this occasion Jesus used Peter's boat as a pulpit after Peter and his partners had been fishing all night without success. Peter was in the boat, and at the end of the teaching session, Jesus told him to cast his nets into the water. Peter, the professional fisherman, was willing to do what the carpenter and itinerant preacher told him even though he felt that it would be useless. He was overwhelmed by the size of the catch.

38. This issue of the Sabbath was part of the overall discussion going on regarding how to keep the Law. We noted in chapter 17 that some of that discussion is recorded in the Mishnah.

39. Likewise, the Pharisees never objected to the priests working on the Sabbath—that was their job, ministering in the Lord's service. The greater issue was the motivating principle. Was the purpose of the Sabbath to enslave people or to serve them? The latter was clearly Jesus' perspective.

40. Archaeologists have found the remains of this pool in the excavation of Jerusalem, but we have no other information about the tradition of healing and no record that anyone was ever healed. Beyond this, the question Jesus asked seems ludicrous, given the circumstances, but it apparently sets the stage for Jesus' command. That is, if he really wanted to be healed, he would obey out of faith.

41. The confrontations that led to this conclusion are interesting, showing the extent to which those men went to deny the truth of what they were seeing. Jesus penetrated to the fallacy of their arguments in two ways. If what they were saying was true, then that meant Satan's realm was divided and thus doomed to failure. It also then raised a question regarding the source of power for others who also cast out demons (apparently some of the Pharisees did so).

42. Matthew places this event earlier in the sequence of his book (Matt. 8:28–34); he also speaks of two Gadarene demoniacs, whereas Mark and Luke mention only one Gerasene. The reference to swine herders is challenging: either they were Jewish, in which case they were violating the Law, or they were Gentile, in which case Jesus was branching out into Gentile population groups. The latter is the more likely.

43. Herod was enticed by the daughter of his wife, Herodias, the former wife of his brother Philip. While John was in prison he talked with Herod, who was intrigued by what he had to say but was turned off by John's condemnation of his marriage. Herodias was greatly offended by that, and on Herod's birthday, her daughter danced before her stepfather, and he promised her whatever she asked. At the instigation of her mother, she asked for John's head on a platter. Out of pride, Herod delivered.

CHAPTER 19—An Empty Tomb

1. As indicated in chapter 18, above, the feeding of the five thousand involved events that took at least two days and included the traversing of the Sea of Galilee. The exact sequence is not clear, because each witness reports only part of the various activities. It began with the report of John the Baptist's death. Jesus tried to take His disciples away to a more remote place, probably for discussion and evaluation. It didn't work; the crowds found Him anyway. After He fed the five thousand, He sent the disciples on ahead, apparently first to Bethsaida, with plans to meet in Capernaum. It would have been on the final leg of their journey that Jesus met them that night. They ended up in Gennesaret, just southwest of Capernaum. From there it would have been an easy walk into Capernaum, where the crowd caught up with them.

2. The Corban worked like a modern trust. The declarer would assert that the property was dedicated to God, and then, although he could live on it while he was alive, it could not be used for anything else, such as to take care of aging parents. The Mishnah addresses the issue of vows in tractate *Nedarim*. While this specific situation is not addressed, it is hinted at in *Nedarim* 5:6.

3. This is a difficult section. In our climate of political correctness, Jesus' statement seems very offensive. That is not necessarily the case. It is probable that He was referring to His ministry to the Jews as primary (as shown by his response in Matt. 15:24). In comparison the Gentiles were "dogs." This view suggests that He was focused on teaching the disciples, and anything else at that time distracted from His purpose. Another possibility is that He was quoting a proverb with which the woman would have been familiar. BDAG characterizes the Greek word here as referring to a house dog or lap dog; that is, it was more of an endearing term but still reflected a hierarchical distinction.

4. The image seems vague to us. However, Jesus had used the term *sign* before, when He compared Jonah's three-day stint in the belly of the fish to the Son of Man's spending three days in the grave (Matt. 12:39–40). His statement here seems harsh, but Jesus must have been exasperated, given the number of signs that He had already performed. There are some people for whom no number of "signs" will be adequate. But more important, the resurrection was to be the most significant sign validating His claim to be the Messiah. Now events were moving rapidly in that direction.

5. This question is very thought-provoking. First, there is the terminology. Matthew 16:13 has Jesus using the title "Son of Man," which He uses as a technical term for the Messiah. It is used 82 times in the Gospels (Matthew uses it 30 times; Mark, 14; Luke, 25; and John, 13). Mark and Luke, however, have Jesus asking, "Who do people [Luke: "the crowds"] say *I* am?" Because of the way the term is used, the questions are essentially synonymous (note especially Matthew's follow-on).

6. The term used in most translations, including the NIV, is "Christ" (the Greek word for the Hebrew Messiah, "Anointed One"). As is often the case, the different witnesses express the event differently. Mark 8:29 reports that Peter called Jesus simply "the Messiah," while Luke 9:20 has "the Messiah of God." It in Matthew, the gospel most scholars view as the one written to the Jews, that the fuller description is recorded. Matthew's statement would have greater shock impact on that audience. Mark is normally viewed as writing to a Roman audience, and Luke to an overall Gentile audience. Those audiences would be less surprised by a human-divine figure based on their mythology (which may be why those writers did not include the phrase "the Son of the living God").

7. Jesus uses the term "Satan" here. In the context of their Hebrew/Aramaic background, this word means "adversary," although it is also the title of God's chief adversary.

8. We are not told how they knew it was Moses and Elijah. The incident does indicate, however, that in the afterlife, we will be able to identify others, apparently even those we have never met.

9. Here the disciples asked a question that was troubling them: "Why do the teachers of the law say that Elijah must come first?" Jesus responded by saying that Elijah does come first and restores all things. In fact, he has already come and been rejected. The disciples understood this description to refer to John the Baptist. The context then points to two comings of "Elijah" the forerunner, as there would be two comings for the Messiah.

10. We need to remember that these disciples were either the remaining nine from the twelve or other disciples who were not part of the inner group. They were most likely the former, who would have been part of one of the groups sent out shortly before the feeding of the five thousand (Mark 6:7–13). Some have suggested that exorcism required having the demon divulge its name. If the victim was rendered dumb, this made the exorcism much more difficult. That would explain why Jesus said that kind of demon could be exorcised only by prayer.

11. Two points seem to derive from the incident. The first is that God would provide what was needed. The second is that Jesus was ensuring that things would come to a head only at the right time. Peripheral issues would not be allowed to interfere.

12. The healings were to be validation of the claim that the kingdom of heaven was near. This built on the expectation of the people that the Messiah would be king, although not in the way they were expecting.

13. Jesus' instruction to the rich man was not a command for all people to commit to poverty. This particular person asked a question and claimed that he was conforming to the OT law. Jesus sensed both a hunger in his heart and tension caused by his wealth. He wanted more spiritually than he had, so Jesus challenged him to follow Him directly. This directive is interesting when contrasted with His instructions to the number of other people He sent back to their homes to tell what He had done for them.

14. Bethany was a village about two miles from Jerusalem, on the east side of the Mount of Olives, on the way to Jericho. Martha's house would become a staging area for Jesus and the Twelve during His last week of ministry.

15. It helps to note the progression through this section. On four occasions, Jesus had run-ins with Jewish leaders (and we should not assume that it was the same group every time).

Shortly after the feeding of the five thousand (the previous spring), Jesus was very blunt with them (Matt. 15:1–20). Later, when they requested a sign, He was brusque and dismissed them (16:1–12). Then, when the tax collectors asked about Jesus paying taxes, He avoided giving offense (17:24–27). Now, however, it was fall, approximately six months before the crucifixion. Jesus had begun to be more confrontational, starting the sequence of events that would lead to Golgotha.

16. This summary assumes that the events in Luke preceded Sukkoth (the Feast of Booths), a weeklong feast that began on the fifteenth day of the seventh month (September-October). It would be fifteen days after "trumpets," more familiarly known as Rosh Hashanah (see Lev. 23:34–44). The time would thus be about six months after the Passover, when He fed the five thousand, and six months before the crucifixion. It would seem that those confrontations with the Pharisees fit in that time frame. The result was a plot to kill Him, but not everyone would be aware of it yet. The declarations at Sukkoth would be designed to continue that confrontational process, forcing the Jewish leaders to make a choice.

17. Scholars debate whether this story was part of the original composition, since a number of manuscripts do not include it. However, it seems likely that the passage records an actual event, and it fits this context well. If this passage were not there, then the jump from John 7:52 to 8:12 would beg for some type of transition. The latter verse seems to build on this episode (although not all scholars agree with this perspective).

18. The Jewish leaders had hoped to pose a dilemma for Jesus. If He said to let the woman go, then He was advocating breaking the OT law. If He advocated stoning her, He was breaking Roman law. What Jesus wrote is speculation, but I would suggest that He wrote out the OT law that covered this incident: "If a man is found sleeping with another man's wife, both the man who slept with her and the woman must die" (Deut. 22:22, emphasis added; see Lev. 20:10). If she was caught in adultery, then they knew who the man was. Why was he not there? As for the second time Jesus wrote on the ground, some have suggested that He started writing the names of members of the mob and their sins. I suspect it more likely that He added further OT laws, such as Exodus 23:1–2, which talks about a malicious witness, or Deuteronomy 19:18–19, which talks about false witnesses—and that they are to receive the punishment for the crime they accuse a person of having committed.

19. It is interesting that the Jews could assert that God was their Father but then be upset when Jesus claimed that God was His Father. It shows that they understood His claim to be of a different quality than theirs.

20. Their motives are not clear. They may have been attempting to vindicate Jesus by showing His power. On the other hand, they may have been using the opportunity to add more fuel to the fire.

21. In the Mishnaic discussion on the Sabbath, one of the criteria of work mentioned is that if a person makes as much clay as needed to seal a letter, then work has been performed (Shabbat 8:5). Jesus challenged this interpretation by putting clay on the man's eyes (John 9:6).

22. Here is a case of a person not realizing that he was making a prophetic declaration. Caiaphas meant that it was better that one man die than that the nation be destroyed by the Romans, but John sensed in those words a prophecy (vv. 51–52) that Jesus would die on behalf of the nation—what Isaiah saw when he stated of the Messiah, "He would render Himself as a guilt offering" (Isa. 53:10 NASB).

23. This directive is not a blanket command for all to adopt poverty. For example, Nicodemus was wealthy, as apparently was Lazarus, yet neither of them was told to sell everything. Rather, it seems that in this case the man's wealth may have been blinding him to his true spiritual condition.

24. Dropsy is a disease that causes swelling of either a body cavity or connective tissues by the accumulation of blood serum. The swelling caused by the accumulation of fluids would have been obvious. Normally, even under treatment, it would take some time for the swelling to decrease. When the observers saw the rapid, if not instantaneous, swelling reduction, such healing would have been a clear sign of Jesus' power.

25. Matthew says Jesus healed two men while leaving Jericho; Luke says He healed one while entering; Mark says Jesus healed one while leaving and calls him Bartimaeus (the son of Timaeus). These accounts can be reconciled when we recognize that in Jesus' time, there were two Jerichos—old and new (archaeology has shown that they were a short distance apart). Thus, as Jesus was leaving old Jericho and approaching the new, two men cried out, one of whom was more noticeable or perhaps known (cf. John Wenham, *Redating Matthew, Mark and Luke* [Downers Grove, Ill.: InterVarsity, 1992], 210–11).

26. HBC, 8. This dual reckoning should not be too surprising. We have already seen that the Jews had two New Years, one in the spring (Passover) and one in the fall (Rosh Hashanah).

27. Mishnah, *Pesaḥim* 4:5 gives two views of when work before Passover must stop—one is at sunset the night before, the other, sunrise the day before. This view fits well with all of the gospel accounts, as well as with early Jewish records, which record that Jesus was crucified on the eve of the Passover (Babylonian Talmud, *Sanhedrin* 43a). For a more extensive evaluation of the arguments, see Harold Hoehner, *Chronological Aspects of the Life of Christ* (Grand Rapids: Zondervan, 1977), 74–90. However, this approach does not answer all of the questions, since earlier in the ministry of Jesus, while He was at Capernaum, the people are said to have brought their sick and demon-possessed to Jesus *after sunset* at the end of Sabbath (Mark 1:32).

28. We have already noted John 2:20, where the Jews talked of the temple standing for forty-six years. The project was begun in 20/19 BCE, with the main building *(naos)* completed by 18/17 BCE, and the rest of the project *(eiron)* continuing on to about 63 CE. The passage in John refers to the *naos;* thus the event recorded took place in 29/30 (cf. HBC, 349, although many scholars still hold to a date of 30 CE for the crucifixion).

29. Matthew and Mark include this incident among events occurring later during the week. However, they do not expressly state that it took place later. Rather, they note that it happened "while Jesus was at Bethany" (Matt. 26:6; cf. Mark 14:3). Their point is that the event put Judas over the edge. As such, he began

looking for an opportunity, which must have occurred later in the week. John notes that Judas was the treasurer and was skimming money off the top (John 12:6). We will never know all the motives of the man, but it does seem clear that money was a priority for him. It may be that Judas, because of the triumphal entry, hesitated for a day or two before determining which direction events would go.

30. Mark, Luke, and John mention only the colt. Critics have seized on this difference, which they consider a contradiction. Others have gone further and ridiculed Matthew's account, wondering how Jesus could ride both animals. The text in Matthew does not require that Jesus rode straddled across the two. Common sense suggests that He rode the colt accompanied by its mother.

31. Jesus' comment about the fact that angels do not marry reflects the spiritual nature of the afterlife as opposed to our current physical life. The premise on which He based His argument is the use of the present tense as opposed to the past tense when God told Moses that He was the God of Abraham, Isaac, and Jacob (Ex. 3:6).

32. Matthew 26 and Mark 14 seem to imply that the dinner at Simon the Leper's house occurred on Wednesday. However, a closer examination suggests that Jesus' comment to His disciples about the crucifixion (Matt. 26:1–2) took place on Tuesday. In Mark the chapter division seems to fix the dinner to the plot of the Jewish leaders. As such, the dinner at Simon's seems to be a flashback, setting the stage for Judas's actions.

33. Although they are called Greeks, they must have been either Greek-speaking Jews or proselytes, since they were in Jerusalem for the Passover. The significance seems to be that word about Jesus was going beyond the borders of Judea, another sign that the hour had come.

34. Some traditions hold that the upper room was owned by the mother of John Mark. This is not certain. However, it may have been expected that the owner of the room would have provided a servant to perform the task. Apparently the basin had been provided, because Jesus was able to procure it readily. Perhaps it just had not been put out. Or it may be that, in the hubbub, the disciples merely overlooked this act. After all, they were now used to traveling and probably had spent many evenings with unwashed feet.

35. It is not really clear what this means. Was Satan prevented up to this time by God? Was there something in Jesus' response that triggered Judas's response and as such allowed Satan to enter? These are all matters we do not know.

36. This prayer (John 17) is often called the High Priestly Prayer of Jesus. First He prayed for Himself that God might glorify Him and that He might be able to grant eternal life to those who believed. He then prayed for His disciples that they might have unity and safety in the face of a hating world. Finally, He prayed for the unity of all who would come to believe that He was the Messiah and could grant eternal life.

37. This is an interesting accusation. While the Jewish law covered blasphemy, the concept dealt with acts that showed disrespect for God. In John 10:31–38, the Jews accused Jesus of claiming to be God, which He did not deny. However, claiming

to be God would be blasphemy only if proven to be wrong. Jesus told them in John 10 to look at His actions. As is often the case today, however, Jesus' claim was not really examined but dismissed without serious evaluation.

38. We know little else about Barabbas. Apparently he was a notorious thief who had robbed the very Jewish leaders standing before Pilate. As such, by asking Pilate to free Barabbas, they would be jeopardizing their own property and lives.

39. According to Mark 15:25, "It was the third hour when they crucified him." Following Jewish custom, Mark is counting three hours after dawn. In contrast, John 19:14 ("sixth hour") follows the Roman custom of counting from midnight.

40. This inscription was in three languages, Hebrew, Latin, and Greek. The point apparently was a warning against insurrection—and a not-so-subtle reminder to the Jews of who was really in control.

41. In the ancient world, clothing was a much more valuable commodity than it is today. Most people had but a change or two of clothing, which they used daily until the garments wore out.

42. Different translations handle John 19:39 differently. The Greek text states about 100 pounds (litra). However, these are Roman pounds of about 12 ounces each, totaling about 75 of our pounds.

43. We need to keep in mind that there were not many tombs in the area, and the grave of a rich man would be especially evident. Given all the data, it is unlikely that they went to the wrong tomb.

CHAPTER 20—The First Church Was Jewish

1. Mark 16:9-20 does not appear in two significant manuscripts, raising questions about its origin. If this section is not part of the original, then the ending of Mark is very abrupt.

2. Paul notes that Jesus made a special resurrection appearance to His half brother James (1 Cor. 15:7). Matthew 13:55 and Mark 6:3 list three other half brothers: Joseph (Joses), Simon, and Judas. We know little about these three, although Judas is generally accepted as the author of the letter of Jude.

3. This detail shows that the group that regularly met with Jesus was larger than the Twelve. The terminology here is also interesting: "men who have been with us the whole time the Lord Jesus went in and out among us" (Acts 1:21). This language may point to the process suggested earlier, namely, that many of the disciples were part-time followers for much of the ministry of Jesus. The troubling part of this episode is that the disciples did not ask critical questions of God. The most important question they did not ask was, "Should we select someone to take Judas's place?" Many NT indications suggest that Paul was the replacement. Rather, they presumed they knew God's will from the prophecies, moved to fulfill those predictions, and then gave God a choice between two. While God does not condemn them for this action, we see nothing that shows He endorsed it either.

4. Note that in this case, three separate things occurred as the disciples were baptized with the Holy Spirit. The first two, the appearance of the wind and fire, were the clearest indications of the work of God. The ability to speak in various languages made

it possible for them to communicate to the people from other lands, as shown in subsequent verses. One question that is not clear is whether this happened just to the Twelve or to the one hundred and twenty. The text says they were all gathered together, but it is not clear which group is in view.

5. The text implies that this address took place in the narrow streets around the house. However, given the size of the group that responded, it is more likely that the meeting had moved to the outskirts of the temple.

6. This is an interesting reaction. Clearly many, if not most, of the crowd were Jews from out of town, hence, people who had no part in the crucifixion. There would have been a number from Judea, but it is an open question as to whether they had been part of the group in front of Pilate on the day of the crucifixion. Yet even if they weren't, they too felt the guilt. Clearly, this was a work of the Holy Spirit, showing general guilt for the treatment of Jesus even if they had not had an active role.

7. The selection of deacons (Acts 6:1–6) has to be sandwiched between Pentecost (ch. 2) in 33 CE and the martyrdom of Stephen (ch. 7; Stephen was one of the deacons), which in turn took place before the conversion of Saul/Paul (ch. 9). Paul indicates that his conversion occurred fourteen years before his journey to Jerusalem referenced in Galatians 2:1, placing it in 35 CE, or a little over two years after the crucifixion (*CAA*, 200–204; some believe that this journey took place fourteen years after his three-year stay in Damascus, Gal. 1:17–18, and thus seventeen years after his conversion).

8. This practice in the early church has often been referred to as a form of communism. That is far from the case; it was rather a voluntary sharing of private property. Moreover, there were no demands on the people to sell anything. Communism argues that there is no private property but that it all belongs to the state. "Sharing" is mandatory under communism.

9. We are not told on what date this incident took place. Given the size of the crowd, it is likely that it happened during one of the three festivals when all Jewish men were supposed to go up to the central sanctuary or temple. Given the conditions of the Diaspora (the ongoing dispersion of Jews after the Exile) and the slowness of travel, Jews from other lands would make it to Jerusalem rarely. Even so, the city swelled with visitors during each of these three festivals. If so, then the first possibility would have been Sukkoth in 33 CE; another option would be Passover the following year.

10. It is likely that they had seen this man a number of times, since he was taken to the same location every day. It is even possible that Jesus had seen him. At the end of the episode we learn that the man was over forty at the time of his healing. However, before this occasion there had been no attempt on the part of Jesus or the disciples to heal the man.

11. The Greek verb translated "raised up" here refers to Jesus' resurrection (it is the same verb translated "raised from the dead" in Acts 2:24). The way Acts 3:26 is structured ("he sent him first to you") anticipates the promulgation of the gospel to the Gentiles. However, it would be several years before that occurred.

12. Barnabas was from Cyprus, but apparently the field was in Judea. Had Barnabas moved from Cyprus back to Judea? Was this a piece of land belonging to the family? It would appear from this incident that the Jews were no longer observing the stringent guidelines regarding family ownership of the land (Lev. 25:23–34).

13. The Greek word for *church* means "assembly." It may consist of a group of pagans (as used in Acts 19:32 and 39, referring to two separate groups). In theological terms, we think of a church as a local group of those who believe Jesus is the Messiah. However, many times in the NT, it refers to all who have believed throughout the ages.

14. According to Hoehner's meticulously developed chronology, the episode of Ananias and Sapphira occurred in late 34 or early 35 CE, that is, a year or so after the founding of the church (*CAA*, 381).

15. It may be that Gamaliel sensed the significance of what had happened the night before. Acts 22:3 informs us that Gamaliel had been the teacher of Saul (later to be Paul the Apostle). One wonders if the student was sitting in on this meeting.

16. Note that these are half truths. In the case of "destroying this place," this was the same argument used against Jesus when He spoke of his resurrection (Matt. 26:61; Mark 14:58; cf. John 2:19–22). The charge about changing the customs handed down by Moses probably referred to areas where Jesus disagreed with rabbinic interpretation of the law (for example, about what was permitted on the Sabbath). But  up to that point the disciples had not changed anything of the Judaism in which they had been raised. They *may* have questioned the value of expiatory offerings, but those were not regular offerings given by people (see above, ch. 7). For most Jews, the religious ritual at this point involved weekly worship in synagogues and study of the OT. Those Jews who accepted Jesus as the Messiah had a greater appreciation of some of the festivals, such as Passover. We are not given any indications as to when the sacrificial system as a whole was challenged.

17. Acts 19:1–6 has the very unique situation of a group who are characterized both as disciples and believers, but who had not yet received the Holy Spirit. The received the Holy Spirit after they were baptized in the name of Jesus, and Paul laid hands on them. The significance of this event is very obscure.

18. In Acts 1:8 Jesus told His disciples that they would be witnesses in Jerusalem, Judea and Samaria, and then the uttermost parts of the earth. Acts can be broken into three major sections, reflecting each of those three geographical areas (Jerusalem, 1:1–8:3; Judea and Samaria, 8:4–12:25; the uttermost parts of the earth, 13:1–28:31).

19. Tradition has it that Judaism was introduced into Ethiopia at the time of Solomon, after the queen of Sheba visited him (1 Kings 10:1–13). Many scholars question that claim. The current thinking is that Sheba was the region of the Sabeans, a kingdom in the southern portion of the Arabian peninsula. In any

case, by NT times there was a Jewish presence in Ethiopia, where the official was headed. The person is described as a "eunuch," but this term apparently had become a title. If he had indeed been castrated, he would not have been able to worship at the temple according to OT law.

20. Given the roughness of the terrain, this journey would have taken several days on foot.

21. Saul (or Paul) reports in Galatians 1:17 that he went to "Arabia" during his time at Damascus. This term is vague and may refer to a large area south of Damascus, as far south as Sinai. The period in Arabia could have been before he started proclaiming Jesus in the synagogues (Acts 9:20–22), or during a hiatus in that ministry. In any event, he spent about two years in Arabia before returning to Damascus.

22. One wonders if he met with Philip while in Caesarea. Paul's probable purpose in going there was to catch a ship to take him up the coast.

CHAPTER 21—Reaching Out to Gentiles

1. It does not seem to be coincidental that Peter was the initial spokesman to the three groups Jesus had mentioned in His final instructions—Jerusalem, Samaria, and the Gentile world. That and the fact that each group had similar manifestations of the Holy Spirit point to an equality of the three groups before God.

2. *CAA*, 381.

3. Even if the animals had been among those considered clean, it may be questioned whether Peter had the means to kill them in the prescribed manner. Wrong slaughtering could also render an animal unclean. This episode reminds us of Mark's observation that Jesus declared all foods clean (Mark 7:19). However, the purpose of this vision was not to address the issue of what meats Peter should eat, but to prepare his mind for the call from Cornelius. Since Cornelius was a Gentile, Peter would have viewed him as unclean like the meat.

4. Luke calls them "those of the circumcision" (Acts 11:2, literal translation). Here, both the NIV and the NASB are somewhat misleading when they translate the phrase, "circumcised believers." Up to this point, *all* believers had been circumcised. The RSV is much better when it calls them the "circumcision party."

5. We have already been using the two terms *Jew* and *Christian* not only for convenience' sake, but also because they are used in the Bible. At this point both groups were in flux and would be for several centuries as they sorted out the implications of their respective views on Jesus. As we discussed in chapter 17, modern Judaism is based on the Talmud, which would not be complete until the sixth century CE.

6. It later became evident that the answer did not satisfy everyone, but that would be a few years down the road (Acts 15).

7. It is not absolutely clear that this reaching out to the Gentiles occurred after the incident of Peter and Cornelius, but the order of Luke's narrative at least suggests a chronological sequence. Furthermore, Cornelius's conversion was about five to six years after Stephen. That would seem to be an appropriate period for the dispersion of Christians, the forming of a church in Antioch, and then for believers to come over from Cyprus and Cyrene and begin preaching to Greeks. So we may safely assume that this development followed the conversion of Cornelius.

8. This seems to be the trip that Paul refers to in Galatians 2:1–10. At that time, he discussed with the leaders of the church in Jerusalem what was happening in Antioch among the Gentiles. In Galatians, Paul points to Titus as a prime example: he was with him meeting with the apostles and they did not require him to be circumcised. As we will discuss later, the Galatian letter was probably written just after Paul's first missionary journey but before another trip to Jerusalem in connection with the Jerusalem Council (Acts 15).

9. *CAA*, 381.

10. It is very difficult for us to grasp this concept of God allowing one to die but intervening to save another, especially when someone close to us suffers. But the key to remember is that the same God who allowed James to be executed also sent His angel to release Peter. Apparently, just as Peter glorified God in being released, James glorified God in dying.

11. Actually, it is termed the house of his mother, since John Mark was at this point still a young man. Many scholars suspect that the young man mentioned in Mark 14:51–52 was John Mark. Some have also suggested that "the upper room," the location of the last Passover Jesus celebrated, was in this house.

12. Here we can only speculate about what happened and what their defense was. It would seem that from their perspective nothing untoward happened. It is possible that they had been put into a trance. It is more likely that the spiritual being (the angel) slipped Peter into the spiritual realm (see discussion on Micaiah in ch. 13 above) through which he was able to extract Peter out of the cell. What is more mystifying, however, is the fact that Peter was not missed until morning. However, Peter had been sound asleep, and the cell was probably dark until dawn. Under those conditions, it may very well be that the guards did fall asleep. Even had that been the case, there would be no way for Peter to escape under normal circumstances.

13. Josephus (*Antiquities of the Jews* 19.8.2) relates the same event, and the main point of his narrative is very similar. The date of Herod Agrippa's death in 44 CE is well attested.

14. There are twenty-seven books in the NT. Of these, there are four gospels and the history book of Acts. The book of Revelation is unique and fits more into the OT apocalyptic genre (see above, ch. 15). The remaining twenty-one NT books are letters.

15. *American College Dictionary* (New York: Random House, 1964), s.v. "epistle."

16. Moisés Silva, "How to Read a Letter," in *An Introduction to Biblical Hermeneutics*, by Walter C. Kaiser Jr. and Moisés Silva (Grand Rapids: Zondervan, 1994), 125.

17. In this respect, it differs from Paul's letters in that while Paul includes a practical section in his letters, he also approaches most of the issues in a more theological manner. Paul tends to lay a theological foundation on which he builds his application at the end, whereas James assumes that theological foundation and gets right to the practical points.

18. James picks up on the concept of faith, not to repudiate it, but to assert that faith should result in actions (James 2:20-26). Paul says the same thing in a different way. In 1 Corinthians 13, he expresses it with the concept of love. This is the way Jesus had expressed it in His story of the Good Samaritan. In 2 Corinthians 13:5, Paul tells the same audience to look at their lifestyle and see if they really are believers. In other words, both argue that true faith produces lifestyle changes (i.e., works).

19. Famine denotes a time when food prices escalate and the poor, at least, are unable to procure adequate sustenance. That is why money was an adequate aid for famine relief in Jerusalem. Usually this price increase is associated with a poor crop (supply and demand). This famine started with an excessive flood by the Nile in Egypt, causing crop failure (*CAA*, 44–49). Again, Josephus corroborates the famine (*Antiquities of the Jews* 3.15.3 and 20.5.2).

20. Because of winter storms, travel on the Mediterranean was curtailed during those months. Most travel occurred from late spring through early fall (basically between Passover and Sukkoth).

21. One is hesitant to presume that Luke's silence indicates a lack of response to their preaching. Still, there is a sharp contrast between Luke's report about Cyprus and his report about the Galatian region later in the journey. On the other hand, when Saul suggested the second journey, it was to check up on the churches, and Cyprus seems to have been on the agenda. When Barnabas and Saul split up, Luke reports that Saul went "strengthening the churches," while Barnabas "sailed for Cyprus," implying the same purpose (Acts 15:36–41).

22. This judgment is very reminiscent of Paul's own blindness on the road to Damascus. We do not know what happened to Elymas, however.

23. Jerusalem was John Mark's home, although he had been living in Antioch for about a year before the trip. We are not told why he left Paul and Barnabas. A wide variety of reasons have been suggested, from home-sickness to a bout with malaria. A more recent suggestion has been that John Mark rejected Paul's new focus on Gentiles. Whatever the reason, Paul did not feel it was adequate, as would become evident when they began to plan the follow-up journey (Acts 15:37–38).

24. Today Antioch of Pisidia is a ruin that lies several miles off the main east-west road.

25. Of course, one wonders how much discussion Paul and Barnabas were generating throughout the week. It is unlikely that they merely had this one session and then were silent for the next six days.

26. The miraculous healing may have brought to mind the story that at one time in the past the gods had visited that region; if so, it would have suggested that the coming of Paul and Barnabas was another divine visit.

27. Apparently some of the action was taking place in the Lycaonian language, which Paul and Barnabas did not understand. It is likely that they communicated in Greek, which may have added to the confusion. Here the gift of tongues would have been invaluable.

28. One may wonder whether Paul indeed died and then was resurrected. However, in his account of his persecutions in 2 Corinthians 11, he does not seem to indicate that to be the case.

CHAPTER 22—What about the Gentiles?

1. Paul had already been to Jerusalem twice (Acts 9:26; 11:30). The evidence is that he had talked to Peter on both occasions (Gal. 1:18 and 2:1–10, assuming that the latter passage refers to the second or famine visit and not to the Jerusalem Council). The apostles knew about and endorsed Peter's work with Cornelius. They also knew that Paul and Barnabas had worked with Gentiles in Antioch for several years. Thus, Paul must have discussed the implications of Gentile conversion with the rest of the apostles earlier. Now, however, they needed to resolve the question of the process of incorporating Gentiles for the rest of the church.

2. Cf. the sidebar on Galatia above, in chapter 21.

3. Galatians gives a history of Paul's ministry after his conversion. The second trip up to Jerusalem mentioned there (Gal. 2:1–10) does not really fit the Jerusalem Council trip as laid out in Acts 15. The problem is Paul's reference to fourteen years in Galatians 2:1; however, this likely refers to fourteen years after his conversion (see *CAA*, 158–90).

4. This section is hard to mesh with the events in Acts. The key is that the trip to Jerusalem mentioned in Galatians 2:1 is most likely not the same trip he took when he attended the Jerusalem Council (Acts 15). The one mentioned in Galatians was taken more covertly. There was no council decision, but personal affirmations. The results were different: according to Galatians, Paul was told to remember the poor; according to Acts 15, a written declaration of the council decision was made, and the decision itself addressed the Gentiles, not Paul. The kind of meeting described in Galatians would be expected if the letter was written prior to the Jerusalem Council.

5. This point is evident in 3:3, where Paul notes that the Galatians had been sidetracked (1:6–7). To use Paul's words, they had begun in the Spirit, but now they were working in the flesh (3:3).

6. Here noticing the audience is important. James was addressing Jewish believers. Paul was addressing Gentile believers. The greatest distinction was their backgrounds, especially with respect to their knowledge of the OT.

7. This was technically the first council held in Jerusalem. A second was held in 415, but it was relatively minor.

8. Here, the word *church* is referring to the collective body of individual groups throughout the world.

9. This statement is somewhat of an extrapolation from the data we have, but the record indicates increasing numbers of Gentiles, especially in the Antioch region. They were probably, even there, still in the minority and perhaps still viewed as some-

what of a novelty. But with increasing numbers, as soon as some elements began requiring circumcision, a dispute would (and did) arise.

10. Korah's point of truth was that God was in the midst of the entire people of Israel. His logical fault was assuming that therefore the entire people of Israel were holy and had interchangeable roles before God. Specifically, he argued that despite the direction that Moses gave, any Levite could be high priest. In his case, he wanted the position. As such, it was a power play rather than a real issue of how he could best serve God. It seems that some of the Pharisees' concern was their position. They apparently anticipated (somewhat correctly) that if circumcision was not required, then their Jewish heritage was in danger.

11. This statement echoes Paul's terminology in Galatians, where the Greek word for *faith* occurs some twenty-two times. While common to us today and in the NT, the idea of hearts being cleansed by faith was still somewhat new to Jewish believers. In this short piece, Peter also echoes Paul's characterization of the OT as a "yoke" (Gal. 5:1).

12. The citation seems to be a paraphrase of the Greek translation, the Septuagint. Given the makeup of the council, with believers from the Diaspora (on both sides of the argument), it is very possible that the meeting was conducted in Greek. Recall that Amos was one of the three prophets to the Northern Kingdom (see above, ch. 13). He condemned syncretistic religion and social injustices (which resulted from a failure to have proper relationships).

13. Some scholars tie the last two items together as one. However, if they reflect issues of worship, there would be a distinction. Strangling would refer to the process of killing the animal. Blood would allude to how the carcass was handled after death (the point of the admonition in Lev. 17).

14. Most of the OT law was directed to the Israelite community, who were in covenant relationship with God. As we have already noted (above, ch. 8), what we call "law" was really teaching on how to live out the covenant with God in relationships. Most of the actual practices applied to human relationships, but many applied to the relationship with God in worship. Outsiders were not required to participate in the worship, and in many cases were not allowed to. Some items, however, were specifically directed to sojourners. For example, Leviticus 17:13 forbids the eating of blood by the sojourner as well as the Israelite.

15. Many of us today tend to read this passage through Gentile eyes and fail to observe that the Jewish believers continued in their association with other Jews. We have already noted this in several cases. We will see it further as we continue through Acts, when even Paul continued to worship in the temple and offer certain sacrifices.

16. One point that has not been addressed is the theological spectrum of the group that the last half of the book of Acts calls "Jews." Traditionally, we have viewed it monolithically. That does not seem to be the case. Historically, we are looking at the beginning of the schism between Christianity and Judaism, which focused on the question of whether Jesus was the Messiah. It seems that there were some in the Judaism camp who had initially accepted Jesus as the Messiah but only within a Jewish

context. That is, they were looking for an immediate establishment of the messianic kingdom and all the power issues involved with that. When that did not materialize, that group dissipated. To complicate matters further, there were the Ebionites. They consisted of several different groups who viewed Jesus as the Messiah, but who still adhered to the law (although they allowed that Gentiles were not subject to the law).

17. The disagreement between Paul and Barnabas seems to be a situation where God made good out of bad. From the split, two teams went out instead of one. They also went in different directions and thus actually covered more territory.

18. According to Philo, a contemporary of Paul, a Jew (by birth) was "someone born to two Jewish parents, who had been legally married at the time of his or her birth" (Maren R. Niehoff, *Philo on Jewish Identity and Culture* [Tübingen: Mohr Siebeck, 2001], 17–23). Philo's position was a change from the earlier Jewish view that looked to the father (as seen in most OT examples, e.g., Boaz and Ruth, or Joseph and his wife). Apparently this change accommodated Roman law in Egypt. In the Mishnah, a person born of a Jewish mother but a Gentile father was considered of lower status (Kiddushin 3:12). By the time of the Talmud, he or she was viewed as a regular Jew, although the texts used to support this perspective seem to assume a Jewish father (Kiddushin 6:86).

19. How this prohibition was conveyed, we are not told. Paul and his party clearly understood that they were forbidden to travel in that direction, but we are not told whether that was by vision or by prophetic word, or whether there were some actual obstacles.

20. Strictly speaking, Mysia and Troas both were in the Roman province of Asia, but the name was often applied to the area between Mysia on the north and Caria on the south.

21. It is also possible that God had other witnesses in mind for portions of these regions. For example, when Paul ended up at Philippi, his first convert was a merchant who had come from Thyatira in Asia. It is possible that Lydia later returned to the province of Asia and served as a missionary to that region.

22. The person mentioned in this vision is not identified, nor is he mentioned again. Commentators have made a variety of speculations on his identity, and a number just dodge the issue (e.g., F. F. Bruce, *The Acts of the Apostles: The Greek Text with Introduction and Commentary,* 3rd ed. [Grand Rapids: Eerdmans, 1990] 356). Suggestions include God the Father (John B. Polhill, "Acts," *The New American Commentary,* vol. 26 [Nashville: Broadman, 1992], 289); Luke, who apparently joined Paul in Troas (W. M. Ramsey, *St. Paul the Traveller and the Roman Citizen* [New York: G. P. Putnam's Sons, 1896], 202–3); and an angel (John Wesley, *Wesley's Notes on the Bible* [Grand Rapids: Zondervan, 1987], 485). The latter seems more likely. If so, such an angelic being might correlate with the spiritual princes noted in Daniel 10:13, 20–21, who are involved in spiritual warfare. In that light,

we should note that the "Prince of Greece" noted in Daniel would really reflect the region and people of Alexander, which in Acts is called Macedonia. In that case, Paul's vision may be setting the stage for the confrontation over the demon-possessed slave girl who was freed in Philippi.

23. We tend to think of Christianity as a European religion, but it began in the Middle East (which can be described as the southwest part of Asia) and expanded first into Africa, Asia Minor, and Mesopotamia. It did not become a "European religion" until after Islam began suppressing it in those three regions, forcing "Christians" to convert.

CHAPTER 23—Moving into Europe

1. While there is no specific record showing this, it seems to be the most likely explanation for the data in this account, especially the distance of the "place of prayer" from the city (cf. John E. Stambaugh and David L. Balch, *The New Testament in Its Social Environment* [Philadelphia: Westminster, 1986], 155–56).

2. Purple fabrics were textiles dyed by a material extracted from murex shellfish. It was both beautiful and expensive. As such it became a symbol of wealth and nobility. The actual color was more like crimson, although it varied from a more bluish to a more reddish tint. In the OT, these colors were used both in the tabernacle (Ex. 26:1) and for the priestly robes (39:3).

3. We are not sure who all was in the party. We know that Silas was there, since he was thrown into prison with Paul. Luke must have been there too, since this is one of the "we passages." In addition Timothy was traveling with Paul at this point (and is referred to later on the journey). So there were at least four men involved in this missionary group, two Jewish, one half-Jewish (Timothy), and one apparently Gentile (Luke).

4. The proclamation that the girl made was true, so the question is, Why was Paul annoyed? There seem to be a couple of reasons. First, her proclamations would start drawing the attention of the authorities, and Paul and company would face persecution as Jews. Second, the source of the corroborating message (the demon) was not the type of support that Paul really desired. More importantly, acquiescence in her proclamation risked leaving her and her masters in a powerful position to influence any new believers after Paul left Philippi.

5. This assertion illustrates several points. First, it suggests that Philippi had followed the lead of Rome in persecuting Jews. The issue of being "lawful" suggests legal ramifications following the lead of Claudius. Third, it shows that Paul and Silas had been teaching within the town sufficiently that their message had gotten around.

6. To give the benefit of the doubt to the magistrates, this act seems to suggest that they recognized the charges against Paul and Silas were flimsy at best. It could be argued that they had been thrown into jail as a form of protective custody. That does not explain the beating, but even this punishment may have been ordered to placate the crowd rather than as a real retribution.

7. That Paul was a Roman citizen is mentioned elsewhere (Acts 22:25–29; 23:27), but this is the only time reference is made to Roman citizenship for Silas.

8. This important highway traversed the southern Balkans from the Adriatic on the west, in what is now Albania, to Byzantium (modern Istanbul) on the east. Like all of the Roman roads, its primary purpose was military—to allow rapid troop movements.

9. This statement seems to limit the time that Paul stayed in Thessalonica, which, based on the information presented in 1 and 2 Thessalonians, does not seem adequate for all that he taught the fledgling church. There are two points to note. First, he spent three Sabbaths in the synagogue before the riot. It is not really clear that the riot occurred immediately following the third Sabbath. It may be that after the three Sabbaths, Paul met elsewhere with a fledgling church, and the riot occurred later. Second, Paul's teaching was probably greatly concentrated as he addressed Jewish believers who really understood the OT. They in turn would teach the Gentiles about items that might be unclear. Apart from this, three weeks of concentrated teaching can convey much material.

10. We are not told exactly when Aquila and Priscilla became believers. However, since Luke does not mention their conversion, it seems likely that they already believed in the messiahship of Jesus when they arrived in Corinth. As we have noted, Jews from Rome were present at Jerusalem on the day of Pentecost and likely established a church back in Rome soon afterward. Aquila and Priscilla may have been part of that group. More likely they were converted in Rome.

11. *ZPEB*, 1:961.

12. Timothy must have returned with Silas, since they are both included in the opening of Paul's letter. He probably picked up Silas from Berea as he passed through. If so, then either the Bereans were doing fine or any letter sent to the Bereans has not been preserved. It is also possible that when Paul told the Thessalonians to read the letter to all the brothers, he had in mind those in Berea and Philippi as well.

13. Paul does not address the issue of salvation in this letter. Apparently that question had been resolved in his teaching while he was in Thessalonica. His directives point rather to several areas where there were problems regarding the implications of that step.

14. This passage addresses the issue of the resurrection from the dead, a doctrine Paul would have to deal with in greater detail later when writing to the Corinthians. A physical resurrection seems to have been a difficult concept for the Greeks to grasp.

15. Paul does not explain why they would think that to be the case. Most likely they were associating their persecution with what John would address later in the book of Revelation, that is, the tribulation associated with Jesus' second coming. An important distinction must be made between persecution and tribulation. Persecution is from satanic elements against Christians alone. Tribulation is from God against the godless. While directed against the ungodly, it is clear that any believers alive at the time would experience the consequences (like Daniel or Habakkuk).

16. Apparently some had become so convinced that the return of Jesus was imminent that they had stopped working, waiting for the return of the Lord. Others had just become "busybodies."

17. It is not clear whether this change came about after their initial return (1 Thess. 3:6) or after the two letters to the Thessalonians were delivered. It seems likely that when Timothy and Silas first arrived, they began working with Paul, while one of the two took the letters as needed.

18. This information suggests that Paul would have remained at the other churches for much longer had he been allowed to. It is difficult to understand why God provided special protection for Paul here and not elsewhere. The key seems to be strategy. Corinth was significant in terms of its location and commerce to send the good news about Jesus through the rest of the Mediterranean region. Of course, we have to recognize that God had preserved Paul's life in those other locations while he allowed him to be moved on.

19. The trial under Gallio can be dated to the summer of 51 CE. However, this incident seems to have taken place early in Paul's time in Corinth rather than late (as suggested by Jack Finegan, *HBC*, 391).

20. Sosthenes must have replaced the earlier leader, Crispus, who had become a believer. It is not clear what group attacked Sosthenes. Some have suggested that it was a Gentile crowd that turned on him. More likely it was the Jews who had gone with him to court and were humiliated by how Gallio had received them.

21. As discussed in chapter 7, the Nazirite vow was taken when a Jew made a promise to God over a specific issue. Protection for a journey would be a typical purpose. As part of the vow,  the Nazirite would not cut his hair, would avoid a dead person, and would abstain from alcohol (Num. 6). At the completion of the vow, he would cut his hair and perform a votive offering. At the end of Paul's third journey, he performed a votive offering in the temple apparently as another Nazirite vow. Here we are given no indication whether he performed that offering with the church in Cenchrea or more probably waited until he got back to Jerusalem. Bruce argues that this was not a Nazirite vow, because Paul was in a Gentile environment (F. F. Bruce, *The Acts of the Apostles* [Grand Rapids: Eerdmans, 1990], 398). However, the Mishnah passages he cites seem to support Nazirite vows in Gentile lands. At the very least, Paul was completing a Nazirite-like vow associated with his Jewish heritage.

CHAPTER 24—Tentmaker and Troubleshooter

1. According to Colossians 1:7, that church in Colosse was founded by Epaphras. He apparently also founded the churches in Laodicea and Hierapolis (Col. 4:12–13), cities that were nearby. It is generally assumed that Paul had not visited these cities prior to his letters to them (written later, during his Roman imprisonment), in which he talks about first hearing of their faith, love, and hope (Col. 1:4–5).

2. *CAA*, 383.

3. This is one of those areas where we wish that Luke had given us more information. Today there is debate as to whether the kingdom of God is solely a spiritual kingdom within the hearts and souls of people, or a yet-future physical kingdom, or possibly both. It seems likely that the Jewish believers at least still looked for a physical kingdom.

4. The term "the Way" in this verse seems to have been a Jewish expression for the believers in Jesus as the Messiah. We first encountered it in Acts 9:2, where it is said that Paul was persecuting those "who belonged to the Way." Paul will use it later when he addresses the Jews in Jerusalem (22:4) and before Felix (24:14).

5. Titus is mentioned in 2 Corinthians approximately nine times, where he seems to have been Paul's regular messenger between Corinth and Ephesus. He also is mentioned in Galatians 2:1–3 as being in Jerusalem with Paul. Scholars generally view this either as the famine visit (Acts 11) or the Jerusalem Council visit (Acts 15). In either case, it would seem that Titus had become a regular traveling companion with Paul, even though he was Greek.

6. This incident suggests two significant points. First, there have always been many opportunists who have claimed the name of Jesus for their own advantage. Second, God demands true honor for His name. While He will tolerate disrespect for some time, He will set things straight.

7. The cost of books back then was much higher than today, relatively speaking. Even so, if we assume an average wage in the range of $8–10 an hour, this would put the value of the books burned at between three to four million of today's dollars.

8. We have already discussed Paul's ministry at Corinth and how Apollos had left Ephesus to minister in Corinth just a few years earlier. We do not have record of when Peter was in Corinth, but this passage is one indicator that the other apostles were now traveling outside of Jerusalem in their own missionary journeys. It is likely that the factions Paul refers to represented different house churches, rather than individuals within the same house church. Later, Paul would address problems evident within the house churches, especially communion and the worship services.

9. Since Paul uses the term "father's wife" (literal translation) rather than "mother," most scholars suggest that it refers to the man's stepmother.

10. We have no idea what the lawsuits were about. Paul merely said that they were occurring. He used a number of arguments against this practice, one of which is not clear. He stated that the saints would judge angels (1 Cor. 6:3). Apparently that will be in the day of the Lord or when Jesus returns, but Paul does not expand the issue. One of the most thought-provoking arguments is his question whether there was not a wise person in their midst who could judge (v. 5). Throughout the letter Paul deals with an attitude among the Corinthians that they were wiser than Paul and the other apostles. Here Paul subtly points out that if that really were the case, they wouldn't be having these types of problems.

11. Paul listed here a number of lifestyle characteristics that fit into this category. People today have sometimes picked up on one or two to camp on, such as "homosexual" (1 Cor. 6:9) Paul asserted that people living in sin could not claim to be part of the

kingdom of God. He did not view homosexuality as any worse than the others he mentioned but merely listed a wide variety of things occurring in the church in Corinth. At the same time, he did not view any of those characteristics as fitting for Christians. Paul's point was that in Jesus the Messiah, these issues became past history and as such were no longer to be current lifestyles.

12. Because of the contrast with sexual immorality, most modern translations add the word "other" to every sin in the first part of v. 18. If this is understood as a slogan that some Corinthians were using, that addition is not needed.

13. These questions were: Should a person get married? What about sex within marriage? Isn't it better to stay single? If it's better to be single, then what about the person already married? What about other "already" issues (states in which one lived before becoming a believer)? Should a virgin marry? What about widows?

14. From what we can determine about the way worship was conducted in the early church, prayer and prophecy were both important functions within the worship service. Later (1 Cor. 14) Paul would lay out guidelines for worship services. In those, prophecy would be the process of giving God's revelation and guidance to the congregation. Here he assumes women would be doing this but merely places limits on how it was to be done.

15. There are several items in this passage about which Gordon Fee says "we must beg ignorance" (*The First Epistle to the Corinthians*, NICOT [Grand Rapids: Eerdmans, 1987], 521), including Paul's meaning of the phrase "because of the angels." Fee rejects out of hand the view taken here, assuming it would require a veiling of women somewhat analogous to what is seen in some radical Islamic cultures today. This does not follow, especially given Paul's comments regarding long hair (11:15). A common view of this passage ties it into the situation observed in Genesis 6, which, as we noted in chapter 3, apparently involves illicit sexual relations between fallen angels and human women. Given the fact that this is the view of Genesis 6 taken by Jewish contemporaries Philo (*The Works of Philo* [Peabody, Mass.: Hendrickson, 1993], 152) and Josephus (*Antiquities of the Jews*, 1.3.1), it would not be surprising if Paul held the same view. This would seem to fit well with his other mentions of angels in his letters. In 4:9, he notes two realms of witnesses to what was happening to the apostles, men and angels. In 13:1, he mentions two realms of beings that praise God, men and angels. Then in 6:3, he notes that believers will judge [fallen?] angels. As such, it would seem that the best understanding of this phrase would be that Paul was referring to fallen angels who were attracted in some manner to women.

16. The discussion here should include what Paul says in 1 Corinthians 14:34–36, which suggests that there was, indeed, disturbance within the church by some of the women. That ties Paul's statement in the first part of chapter 11 with his premise that worship should be orderly and be done decently. Moreover, the discussion regarding the Lord's Supper in the second part of the chapter suggests that the problem with women in the church was not the roles they were performing but abuses of them. In other words, Paul was writing to the church to stop various abuses, not to restructure a program.

17. We should note something very important here. Paul never told the Corinthians not to desire spiritual gifts, but told them to recognize three things: Not everyone has all of the gifts. Likewise, not everyone has the same gift—just as not everyone is an apostle, not everyone speaks in tongues. When we desire gifts, we should ask for the greatest, not the least. There is a better way.

18. When we read through this section, we need to keep in mind that this was a time when the only Bible the church in Corinth had was the OT. They may have had a copy of one or two of Paul's earlier letters. They may have had a copy of Matthew's gospel (if it indeed was written by then). As such, they were much more dependent on the gift of prophecy to give guidance than we are.

19. We are given no information regarding the situation, but this may be a situation like Paul found in Athens (Acts 17:32).

20. First, he pointed out that if Christ was not resurrected, then the gospel he was preaching was wrong, because he was teaching something that had not taken place. As such, their faith would be in vain. Why then were they even meeting as a church? Moreover, they would still be guilty of their sins and there would be no hope beyond this world—in which case, the Christian who gives up so much that the world seems to offer and who faces persecution for his beliefs is indeed a pitiful person. However, the inverse is true. Since it is demonstrated that Christ has been resurrected, then we can be confident we will be resurrected also. More than this, there is yet a coming reign when He will ultimately defeat all enemies, the last of which is death.

21. Given the dating of the letter, that means that the change probably happened within twenty years of the resurrection. It is important to note that this practice was also being observed in the churches in Galatia (1 Cor. 16:1). We are given no information as to why the change occurred, but it does seem to correlate with the increased Gentile element within the church.

22. This detail could be another indication that between the writing of 1 and 2 Corinthians, Paul sent the church a letter in which he mentioned he would go to Corinth first. In 1 Corinthians 16:5, Paul stated that he would go through Macedonia first and then to Corinth, whereas according to 2 Corinthians 1:15–16 he had planned to go to Corinth first (then to Macedonia and then back to Corinth). The question is whether 1 Corinthians reflects a change from his original plans or whether the change was later, between 1 and 2 Corinthians. The evidence points toward the latter: he apparently made his painful visit to Corinth between 1 and 2 Corinthians; in the aftermath of this visit, he resolved not to see them again until conditions improved. Then, when he left Ephesus, it was suddenly as a result of the riots.

23. There is debate about who was the repentant person. In some respects, Paul's comments here correlate with the situation discussed in 1 Corinthians 5. However, since the previous verse (2 Cor. 2:4) mentions an apparently lost "sorrowful letter," many scholars suggest that the passage refers to another person, specifically one who challenged Paul's authority. This argument seems more conjectural.

24. This is an area that needs careful thought. Restoration does not necessarily mean that a person is given back his or her previous position and responsibilities as if nothing has happened. There may indeed be a loss of office. However, the person should no longer be ostracized. The church has a history of going to either extreme.

25. Paul does not state what the issues were, but it would appear that they were similar to the problem we saw in Galatians: a legalistic following of the law rather than salvation through grace. There are several hints of this problem throughout the letter, especially in the section where he gives his credentials as compared to the false apostles. One hint is they all were Jewish. Another one lies in the contrast Paul made between the Mosaic covenant and the new covenant.

CHAPTER 25—The Road to Rome

1. Five times, he specifically talks about a church that is meeting in a given house. However, some have suggested that each time he used the word "greet," he was addressing another house church. If this is so, then he addressed fifteen.

2. Some scholars have suggested that Paul used what is called an "ambassadorial" style as he introduced himself (James D. G. Dunn, *Romans 1-8*, Word Bible Commentary, 38a [Dallas: Word Bible Books, 1988] lvi). This might explain some of the style differences between Romans and 2 Corinthians, which is more personal and passionate.

3. Peter would not arrive there until about 62 CE—about five years later (*CAA*, 384). There is no record that any other apostle ever visited the city, although some traditions show other apostles working in France, Spain, and Britain. Even if they went through Rome, those trips were all apparently later.

4. Although Paul talks of the Romans as being "from among the Gentiles," it is clear that his audience includes both Jews and Gentiles. This is evident from the way he addressed the Jews throughout the book. If nothing else, the list of names in Romans 16 verifies the matter.

5. Paul's directions here reiterate the same principles that he had communicated to the church in Corinth earlier. More sig-

nificantly, they reflect principles that James had addressed to the Jewish believers in his letter several years prior. It is in these areas that we see most clearly the unity of the apostles in their view of what the messiahship of Jesus meant.

6. As we will see, there are several great themes in the book, including salvation by grace and how to live a life pleasing to God. However, these are meaningless if the resurrection had not occurred. In this sense, Paul is building on what he had already laid out in 1 Corinthians 15.

7. This temporal sequence was a powerful argument against the Jews who had tried to make the Gentiles become circumcised. If Abraham was righteous before he was circumcised, then they could not force the Gentiles to be circumcised to become righteous.

8. Paul is not arguing for asceticism. The key is that we are no longer subject to our passions, but can instead live life more along the way it was intended, enjoying physical pleasure, but not being driven by it.

9. One thing that should be remembered is that when Paul wrote this, Israel was still functioning as a nation in Judea, including an operating temple with daily sacrifices. It would be more than a decade before the temple was destroyed.

10. We have seen this illustrated in the OT a number of times—e.g., the mixed company that came out of Egypt, Rahab, and Ruth. Others show up in different ways throughout the OT. Paul merely cites OT prophets (specifically Hosea and Isaiah).

11. Again, we need to recall that the corporate guidelines were designed to show how to make established relationships work best. Given that people (corporate body) were in a covenant relationship with God, some of the directives governed the God-man relationship; the rest governed relationships within the covenant community (see above, ch. 7).

12. Paul expressed it this way: "If you confess with your mouth, 'Jesus is Lord,' and believe in your heart that God raised him from the dead, you will be saved" (Rom. 10:9). We should pay careful attention to the terminology here. The belief is in the resurrection. The confession that results from this is an acknowledgment of His position as Messiah, not only in the sense that He fulfilled OT promises, but that He would ultimately reign over the entire world. The result of this faith and confession would be salvation (in the sense of deliverance from sin). We tend to think of salvation only in terms of being saved from going to hell. Paul seems to have a much richer and broader concept in mind. It seems to include not only being saved from judgment, but being saved to represent God in this world, being saved from being a slave of sin, and being saved to be part of God's ruling hierarchy when He establishes His final reign on earth (that is, the kingdom of God). It is this last part that truly reflects the concept of salvation as victory over enemies (especially national enemies).

13. When we step back and look at the overall theme of Romans, we realize that the national covenant and the new covenant had two entirely different functions. The former was designed to illustrate how God's guidelines for relationships should work within a national structure. The operative phrase was that the nation of Israel was to be a holy people, that is, a people who were Godlike. The function of the nation was to be

a nation of priests, that is, intermediaries between God and the rest of the world. Ultimately, this function would culminate in the Messiah, who not only was to be the perfect intermediary, the one who would provide constant access to God (this is the present aspect of the redemption process, or salvation), but He would also be the ultimate sovereign, thus bringing the national and new covenants together.

14. The party included Sopater son of Pyrrhus from Berea; Aristarchus and Secundus from Thessalonica; Gaius from Derbe; and Tychicus and Trophimus from the province of Asia. In addition, Timothy and Luke went with him. It is interesting that three men (Sopater, Aristarchus, and Secundus) were from Macedonia, but none were from Achaia or the Corinthian region.

15. Actually, the trip was a bit more complicated. Paul's companions boarded the ship in Troas, which then sailed around the northwest corner of Asia Minor (Turkey). Paul traveled by foot across the peninsula and met them in Assos. Luke gives no hint of why they did that or why that detail of their itinerary was included in his account. From there they sailed to Miletus after putting into the port of Mitylene and the island of Samos.

16. The Greek text says, "the Hebrew dialect" (Acts 21:40; 22:2). The Jews of the day spoke Aramaic, a Semitic language closely related to Hebrew. It is thus commonly understood that on this occasion Paul spoke in Aramaic.

17. We are not sure what the difference between the commander's and Paul's citizenship was in that culture. Clearly, being born a citizen was a higher status than being a "naturalized" citizen. So the minimum the distinction involved was a degree of ranking.

18. He probably did not recognize him because he was not wearing the robes of his office. Furthermore, it had been years since Paul had last seen the high priest. It is interesting, though, that Paul did not really apologize. What Ananias had done was wrong, and it illustrated how much he had let his hard-heartedness affect his judgment and actions. Paul's use of the OT here might have been an effort to show that he still knew and understood the OT law.

19. There were likely some questions in the minds of the Romans. Every time this man talked to the Jews, they erupted in violent argument. What was he saying to them? Was he a rabble-rouser? Of course, the Romans were aware that the Jews had a violent history since they had become part of the empire. And Paul *was* a Roman citizen. It was probably for this last reason that the Romans took care of him.

20. This action would be a form of a Nazirite vow. By fasting, they were doing two things: they were asserting that it would be quick action; and as Jews, they were invoking God's aid. By making a vow of it, they were asking for God's help to ensure that they carried out the action they promised. We are not told what happened to them when they were unable to complete their action. Most likely they had to ask the high priest to be absolved of the vow once Paul reached Caesarea.

21. We are not told any more about the nephew. The term for "young man" (Acts 23:17) could refer to a man even in his thirties (by this time, Paul was probably in his fifties, which gives some latitude for the age of a nephew). He may even have been

a member of the Sanhedrin. In any case, he was considered a competent source.

22. The name Tertullus is Latin, suggesting that he may have been a Roman lawyer. However, that is not conclusive, since many Hellenistic Jews had Latin names. In either case, he was well read and competent in Roman law.

23. Luke notes that Felix's wife, Drusilla, was Jewish (Acts 24:24), so he probably had some awareness of Judaism. Luke makes it clear that he also had some understanding of "the Way" (v. 22)

24. This was Herod Agrippa II, son of Herod Agrippa I (who had killed James, Acts 12:1) and great-grandson of Herod the Great.

25. They were past "the Fast," or Yom Kippur. In 59 CE, this holy day fell early, on October 5, but that was already late in the sailing season.

CHAPTER 26—Rome and Beyond

1. *CAA*, 384.

2. Because of the detailed account leading up to their time in Rome but virtually nothing afterward, the book must have been written during that two-year period. As already pointed out (see above, ch. 18), the gospel of Luke, which was a precursor, had to have been written earlier, most likely during Paul's imprisonment in Caesarea.

3. The significance of this is debated. Ramsey notes that by the third century, a capital crime had to be tried within eighteen months. He concludes that the first century had a similar practice (W. M. Ramsey, *The Teaching of Paul in Terms of the Present Day* [London: Hodder and Stoughton, 1913], 365–66). More recently, Bruce has disagreed with Ramsey's conclusion, although Bruce's rationale is not clear (F. F. Bruce, *The Acts of the Apostles: The Greek Text and Commentary* [Grand Rapids: Eerdmans, 1990], 541).

4. Paul requests that Philemon prepare a place for him to lodge on an upcoming visit. This detail shows that Paul was starting to anticipate his release. However, it was not as strong an anticipation as we find later in Philippians.

5. In Colossians, Paul stated that Tychicus was carrying personal news and traveling with Onesimus (Col. 4:7-9). Clearly, then, Colossians and Philemon were carried at the same time. Paul told the Ephesians that Tychicus would fill in the personal information not included in his letter (Eph. 6:21). The most likely route to Colosse was through the port of Ephesus. While it is possible that Tychicus made two trips to Asia, one trip is more likely. As such, he would have landed at Ephesus and traveled inland to Colosse, where he delivered Onesimus and the two letters. Based on the end of Colossians, it is likely that he also carried another letter to the church in Laodicea (a city between Ephesus and Colosse, about forty miles west of the latter). That letter was not included as part of the canon and has been lost.

6. He did hint to Philemon that Onesimus would be helpful to Paul if he were released (v. 11). Still, Paul did not ask for that much. It is very tempting to read into the text our modern ideas

about slavery and suggest that he sought Onesimus's release, but the hint, though strong, is there only between the lines.

7. These letters then had the same place of origin (Rome), and apparently were even carried by the same messengers, Onesimus and Tychicus (see Eph. 6:21 and Col. 4:7). Most likely, since Philemon lived in Colosse, Onesimus passed through Ephesus en route home.

8. Throughout this work, we have used the Hebrew term *Messiah* rather than the Greek term *Christ*. While originally identical, at about this time in history, the Greek term seems to have begun to accumulate theological connotations in some circles that had never been evident in the Hebrew. One was a distinction between Jesus and "the Christ." Later this would lead to the idea that "the Christ" was a spiritual being who came upon the physical Jesus. This distinction would be important in the development of Gnosticism, which will be discussed later.

9. The use of false premises, often leading to the development of cults, seems to have been one of the biggest problems for the church throughout its history. For example, Mary Baker Eddy had a premise that God would not send someone she liked to hell. Therefore, she had to rewrite the gospel—and ended up with a worldview that held that suffering is not real. False premises have led to the modern attacks on the Bible from a variety of sources. We noted in the introduction how Julius Wellhausen began with a number of false premises, including naturalism. That presupposition is one that lies behind the current controversy between historic Christianity and so-called science.

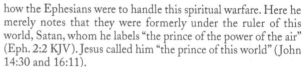

10. The concept of slavery is generally alien to our culture. Given the universality of the practice in Paul's day and the function that slaves performed in the workplace, it would not be stretching the concept to apply the principles to employer-employee relationships within our own culture.

11. Some scholars have suggested that Ephesians was the first of the three to be written, possibly a year prior to Philemon and Colossians. This would mean that Tychicus had made a round trip to Asia (Rome–Ephesus–Rome) and then later returned to the same region with the latter two letters. While this reconstruction is possible, it is more likely that they were all sent at the same time. If so, Ephesians would have been written between late 60 and late 61 CE, probably closer to the end of that period.

12. E. K. Simpson, *Commentary on the Epistle to the Ephesians* (Grand Rapids: Eerdmans, 1957), 18.

13. This is a literal translation. English Bibles usually render it "in [the] heavenly places" (e.g., KJV, NRSV, NASB); the NIV translates it "in the heavenly realms."

14. We have observed that a descriptive praise psalm praised God primarily by describing His attributes (see above, ch. 12). It could also, secondarily, note how those attributes were evidenced by the deeds He had done. Here the deeds revolve around what Jesus the Messiah has done for us.

15. An important premise of this book is that there is a spiritual realm with two opposing forces. Later Paul will address how the Ephesians were to handle this spiritual warfare. Here he merely notes that they were formerly under the ruler of this world, Satan, whom he labels "the prince of the power of the air" (Eph. 2:2 KJV). Jesus called him "the prince of this world" (John 14:30 and 16:11).

16. Paul mentions that he wrote of this briefly before (Eph. 3:3). This comment could be a reference to Colossians 1:26ff. But that would make Ephesians a later letter than Colossians, which seems unlikely. Most commentators take it as a reference to one or more earlier comments within this letter (cf. Eph. 1:9–10; 2:11–21). However, it seems unlikely that Paul would make this type of reference to something he had just said. The other possibility is a lost letter (cf. S. D. F. Salmond in *The Expositor's Greek Testament*, ed. W. R. Nicoll [London: Hodder and Stoughton, 1897–1910], 3:303). Given that it had been almost five years since his last visit, it is highly likely that he had written this church earlier to inform them of his circumstances.

17. Paul was aware of their concerns, pointing to previous correspondence after Epaphroditus had arrived. He also stated that he hoped to send Timothy in the near future. If we assume that he is referring to a separate journey and that Timothy actually went, it is likely that Paul sent a follow-up letter with him. These would be other letters of Paul's that we do not have.

18. In Philippians 2:5–11, Paul explains how Jesus modeled humility. Some scholars call verse 7 the *kenosis* passage, from the Greek word for "emptying," which expresses somewhat the work that the Son had done in the incarnation. The exact implications of the term in the case of Jesus are debated.

19. Apparently Jews had been allowed back into Philippi at about the same time they had been allowed to return to Rome (see above, chs. 23 and 25). Some of these may have come from Thessalonica, where they had driven Paul out of town during the second missionary journey.

20. As shown by Hoehner, *CAA*, 321–48.

21. This is the account of Josephus (*Antiquities of the Jews,* 20.9.1), who notes how the early reign of Nero was positive toward the Jews. When Festus died, Nero sent Albinus to be governor of Judea. In the interim, the high priest, Ananius, took advantage of the situation and assembled the Sanhedrin. Several leaders of the church, including James, "the brother of Jesus, who was called Christ," were condemned and executed by stoning.

22. The information we have is gleaned from early church sources. One of the best compilations of that data is William Steuart McBirnie's *The Search for the Twelve Apostles* (Wheaton, Ill.: Tyndale House, 1973).

23. McBirnie concludes that it is unlikely that James visited Spain. He does think it is likely that the bones of James were taken to Spain after his death (*Search*, 94–99). However, that raises a question as to why his bones would be taken so far away if he had never visited the place. In terms of history, there were Jewish settlements that he could have visited, and there would have been enough time between the two events for which we have records. McBirnie does agree that if James visited Spain, he would have gone only to Jewish settlements (*Search*, 104).

24. While the identity of "the disciple that Jesus loved" is debated, John is the most likely candidate (Donald Guthrie, *New*

Testament Introduction, 3rd ed. [Downers Grove, Ill.: InterVarsity, 1970], 245–49).

25. There is also some evidence that John journeyed to what is now northern Iran and preached to the Parthians. McBirnie cites Augustine on this, but he does not give a specific reference. If so, it would have been before going to Ephesus.

26. Eusebius, *Ecclesiastical History* 3.1.1; see *NPNF* Series 2, 1:132.

27. McBirnie also notes that the cross on which he died (known as St. Andrew's cross) was shaped like an X as opposed to the Latin T or †. The Patros tradition suggests that the reason for his martyrdom was that he converted the wife of the governor, who executed him out of revenge (*Search*, 80–81).

28. On Philip's going to Scythia, McBirnie quotes Anna Jameson, *Sacred and Legendary Art* (Boston: Houghton, Mifflin, 1957); there is no other substantiation. That he went to France is based on records from a number of places dating from the sixth century. While this suggestion is questioned, one of the issues focuses on the identity of the Gauls. Galatia (in Asia Minor) was settled by Gauls in the third century BCE. When Philip is identified as going to Gaul, some ask if that meant that he went to the Gauls in France or those in Galatia. Either is possible.

29. McBirnie, *Search*, 127. He cites a seventh-century source (Cardinal Baronius), who attributes it to John Chrysostom (347–407 CE). However, the location within the writings of Chrysostom is not clear.

30. As a point of reference, there were Jewish settlements as far south as Bombay by this period, and Roman trade centers all the way around to Madras (see also below, sidebar on Thomas).

31. McBirnie, *Search*, 133.

32. McBirnie attributes this information to Clement of Alexandria (*Search*, 175). Some argue that "Ethiopia" here may refer to an obscure region in Asia beyond Persia. McBirnie suggests that at some point he did indeed visit the Ethiopia we know by that name today (ibid, 181).

33. McBirnie, *Search*, 230.

CHAPTER 27—The End of the Apostolic Age

1. For example, Robert H. Gundry asserts that "Mesopotamian Babylon had lost almost all its inhabitants by the beginning of the Christian era" (*A Survey of the New Testament*, 4th ed. [Grand Rapids: Zondervan, 2003], 439). In reality, Babylon was recognized as a thriving entity for some time after this. In 41 CE Caligula persecuted Jews in the city of Babylon, starting a Jewish migration from the city itself to Seleucia (followed by a plague five years later). D. J. Wiseman argues that it was an active city until the second century (*ZPEB*, 1:448). Jacob Neusner seems to agree with this view (*A History of the Jews in Babylon* [Leiden: E. J. Brill, 1965], 3). Beyond this, there is some evidence that the first-century Jews interchanged Babylon and Babylonia (Josephus, *Antiquities of the Jews*, 15.2.1–3). It was in this larger region that the Babylonian Talmud was written by Jewish rabbis several centuries after Peter.

2. There is too often a tendency to look for hidden or allegorical meanings in the middle of simple and matter-of-fact sayings. Unless there is a guide indicating that the writer was using a term in an allegorical sense, it is best to take it at face value.

3. As we have already noted, the tendency is to view this persecution as the one started by Caesar Nero, but that does not have to be the case. There is solid biblical and extrabiblical evidence for a variety of persecutions against the church almost from its inception (Nero's *was* one of the most severe, and more universal). The list of addressees of the letter hints at a fairly localized problem in the northern part of Asia Minor, far from Rome. It would be expected that the apostles would have addressed the issue of persecution early in the history of the church rather than waiting until it became empire-wide.

4. First Peter had Silas (or Silvanus) as a scribe. The person who actually wrote down 2 Peter is not known.

5. Michael Green, *The Second Epistle of Peter and the Epistle of Jude*, Tyndale New Testament Commentaries (Grand Rapids: Eerdmans, 1968), 35.

6. One of the points of controversy about this book is its relationship with Jude, a matter that will be addressed in our discussion of the latter.

7. These hidden spiritual secrets were layered. An initiate could learn only a certain level of the hidden or mystical knowledge. After he showed himself worthy, he could be passed to a higher level of knowledge. The number of levels varied.

8. Greek dualism is evident in Plato, but dualism itself is evident in other cultures, such as Iranian Zoroastrianism. While the actual development is debated, it would appear that one of the key factors was the interaction of Greek philosophy and Judaism, especially after the spread of Christianity. The early church fathers pinpointed this in the region of modern Syria (Kurt Rudolph, *Gnosis* [New York: Harper & Row, 1987], 275–85; see also Edwin M. Yamauchi, *Pre-Christian Gnosticism*, 2nd ed. [Grand Rapids: Baker, 1983], 233–49).

9. As can be seen, some nuances of Gnosticism were based on the truths of Christianity. This is a characteristic of all false teaching—there is an element of truth to it. In false teaching, however, the truth is distorted to facilitate personal advancement of the teachers.

10. For example, *1 Clement* 5 states that Paul came "to the extreme limit of the west" (*ANF*, 1:6). Clement lived between 30 and 100 CE, and he may have met Paul at Philippi (so believed many church fathers, including Ignatius, *ANF*, 1:122, and Eusebius *NPNF* Series 2, 1:201). Today this identification is questioned.

11. That Paul was released from prison is indicated by his expectations in Philemon and Philippians. Stronger evidence is seen in the Pastoral Epistles, which record itineraries not found in the journeys related in Acts. The early church fathers also indicate this. In Romans 15:24, Paul notes a desire to go to Spain, a journey that the early fathers indicate he took. In both Philippians and Philemon, he notes plans to return to Philippi and Colosse. Philippians 2 gives Paul's plans to send Timothy ahead. It would then seem that Paul met Timothy in Ephesus after visiting Colosse. Paul left Timothy in Ephesus while he went to Philippi, from which he wrote 1 Timothy. Following this itinerary, he then journeyed to Spain. This would leave Crete, which

Paul visited with Titus and then left Titus there (Titus 1:5). In his letter to Titus, Paul requested Titus to meet him in Nicopolis on the west coast of Greece, where he planned to spend the winter (Titus 3:12). Apparently Paul was arrested the following summer, perhaps in Corinth (*CAA*, 321–48).

12. *CAA*, 321–32. This view is much preferable to the argument that the Pastorals were written during the two years of the Acts imprisonment. The latter theory creates unsolvable conflicts, which critical scholars take to indicate that someone else had to have written the Pastoral Epistles at a much later date—specifically, someone who didn't know what was going on.

13. Because of this purpose, Paul seems to have abandoned the practice we saw earlier of focusing on the three traits of Christian maturity: faith, hope, and love. These letters are very practical on specific issues.

14. The issue of the controversy is twofold. First, there is what Paul said. Beyond this is the question of whether it was addressed to the Ephesian church solely, or whether it expressed principles designed for all churches. While the text reads in terms of general or universal statements, they also need to be considered within the overall context of Paul's teachings. This consideration would suggest that while Paul would not restrict women totally, he did have certain ideas regarding authority and the problem of false teaching. On the other hand, it would not seem proper to emphasize these guidelines for women within a church if the men were not following very seriously what Paul had just noted as being his most important instructions.

15. We express this characteristic in a qualified manner because the degree of relational and emotive qualities varies among women. We might express it as a spectrum. The distribution of relational qualities along this spectrum within a given population of women would seem to fall into a normal distribution (or bell) curve. The same would be said for a given population of men. While the norm of the curve for men would be less relational than that for women, the curves would overlap. This would mean that some men are more relational than some women. In many ways, the tendency of men would be the inverse of the relational tendency of women. The flip side of being relational is more difficult to define. When I ask the women in my classes to use a term, very often they propose "logical." However, I am hesitant to use that term because of many negative connotations. Another nuance is being goal oriented to the detriment of relationships. Tentatively, I have chosen the term *dialectical*. While the norm for a population of men would be more dialectical and direct than the equivalent population of women, again some women would be more dialectical and direct than some men. However, Paul did not seem to address these exceptions, but rather focused on the norms or general cases.

16. Paul suggests a parallel with the situation in the Garden of Eden. Eve succumbed to the Serpent because in her relational strength she was too trusting. Adam was the discerner, and as an act of the will he ate of the fruit. Thus, because of the deliberate nature of his sin, Adam was the one who received the blame for the fall of humankind.

17. This background is important to an understanding of 1 Timothy 2:15. On the surface, this verse seems to limit the role of women to bearing children and keeping quiet (from v. 11). But Paul never seemed adverse to women leaders, either in the church or in business (e.g., Lydia, Priscilla, and Phoebe). It would appear that the false teachers in Ephesus were producing an attitude that was pushing some women to try to take control of the church by using their sexuality and to look down on having children. Paul's desire seems to be to correct that attitude, maintaining that raising children was an exalted role (William D. Mounce, *Pastoral Epistles*, Word Bible Commentary 46 [Nashville: Thomas Nelson, 2000], 103–49).

18. In this passage Paul never stated that being rich was wrong. He did note that excessive *love* of money caused all kinds of problems (1 Tim. 6:10).

19. Both discuss the role of elder or overseer. The letter to Timothy includes deacons, a topic omitted in Titus.

20. Some ancient Christian writers attribute the quotation to Epimenides, a philosopher from about 600 BCE.

21. It is generally accepted that Paul was executed by Nero. Nero died in early June 68 (*HBC*, 379). Hochner demonstrates that Paul was executed after Nero returned from Greece in January 58 but before a revolt began in April (*CAA*, 335–37).

22. This Tychicus was the same person who had carried the letters to the Ephesians, the Colossians, and Philemon.

23. The parchments are generally viewed as particular books, e.g., his copy of the OT. They may also have been legal documents, perhaps his citizenship papers (A. N. Sherwin-White, *Roman Society and Roman Law in the New Testament* [Grand Rapids: Baker, 1978 reprint], 144–62).

24. Priscilla and Aquila had apparently again left Rome. At this point they might have been back either in Ephesus or Corinth, having previously lived and ministered in both cities. Because of Paul's references to the province of Asia, they were most likely in Ephesus. From there Timothy could catch a ship to Rome.

25. Paul's execution is noted by Clement of Rome (*ANF*, 1:6) as well as by the historian Eusebius (*NPNF* Series 2, 1:129). Hochner develops the date (*CAA*, 334).

26. Hebrews was quoted heavily by Clement of Rome, who wrote in about 95 CE. The evidence is that many churches had accepted it as part of the canon within thirty years of its writing. The discussions in the early church again demonstrate that Christians were very critical of what they included in the canon. It also points out that the NT we have today developed as a result of evaluation of the data by the church as a whole.

27. Clement of Alexandria, *The Stromata* and "Fragments from *Cassiodorus*" (see *ANF*, 2:442 and 2:573). While other early writers agreed that the letter may have been written in Hebrew and translated into Greek, they disagreed on the translator. Today most commentaries suggest that it was originally written in Greek.

28. In fact, Barnabas is called an apostle in Acts 14:14, although there is some question of what this means in the context. Whether or not he was indeed an "apostle," he had a close relationship with the apostles, much as Luke (who wrote Luke/Acts) had.

29. Donald Guthrie, *New Testament Introduction*, 3rd ed. (Downers Grove, Ill.: InterVarsity, 1970), 689.

30. Zane Hodges, *BKC*, 2:777.

31. Guthrie, *New Testament Introduction*, 690.

32. Origen, *NPNF* Series 2, 1:273.

33. Since neither the book of Acts (62 CE) nor the letters of Paul (including his letters to Timothy) make mention of Timothy's being imprisoned, the letter to the Hebrews should probably be dated during the later persecutions of Nero.

34. It is interesting and perplexing that in these comparisons the writer passes over Abraham, Paul's favorite example. Even if the writer was not Paul, one would expect a prominent place given to Abraham in this part of his argument. Abraham is mentioned later, especially in ch. 11.

35. This theme seems to parallel the writings of Paul (e.g., 1 Cor. 2:6–3:2).

36. See Hodges, *BKC*, 2:795.

37. Josephus, *Jewish War*, 2.14; Tacitus, *The Histories*, 5.9–13. Tacitus also shows, however, that the Romans never really understood how the Jews were different from other peoples in their worship. One of the key points of controversy was the imposition of emperor-worship on them.

38. According to Josephus, the temple was burned on 10 Ab (July–August), the same date the first temple had been destroyed by the Babylonians (*Jewish War*, 6.4.5, where the month Lous corresponds to Ab; the Mishnah, *Ta'anit* 6:4, says both events took place on 9 Ab).

39. Jesus did prophesy the destruction of Jerusalem and tied it to the nation's rejection of Him (Matt. 23:37–39), but we do not see a prophet similar to Jeremiah clearly announcing an immediate destruction. As we will see in the next chapter, some have argued that the book of Revelation was such a pronouncement. Consequently, they would date the book prior to the destruction of Jerusalem. However, that view does not seem to fit the data as well.

40. Guthrie, *New Testament Introduction*, 824.

41. This would mean that at the time of the composition of the letter, Jude would have been in his sixties. He would have been old enough to remember the older half brother but young enough to have worked several decades after the crucifixion and resurrection.

CHAPTER 28—But What about John?

1. As we have noted, the Jews always understood salvation in two senses. One was physical deliverance; the other spiritual. Now that spiritual salvation was present, the Jewish believers, like the Gentile believers, were looking for the physical salvation of the kingdom.

2. As has been the case with most NT books, the authorship of the five books traditionally attributed to John has been challenged by critical scholars. There really are two questions. The first question is whether the same author wrote all five books. Guthrie addresses this question extensively and notes that based on early church tradition and stylistic issues, the same author most likely wrote all five (*Introduction*, 864–69, 884–90, 895, 934–49). The second question is who the author is. Traditionally, the church had viewed the author as the apostle John. The argument against this identification, especially with respect to the gospel of John, has been discussed extensively with many different hypotheses (Donald Guthrie, *New Testament Introduction*, 4th ed. [Downers Grove, Ill.: InterVarsity, 1990], 241). The argument against John the apostle is based on several concerns. The first is theological. The concern lies in the very distinct differences between the gospel of John and the Synoptic Gospels in terms of material covered, apparent contradictions in chronology, and the way John presents a much more profound understanding of the persona of Jesus. However, this is a matter of interpretation. The second concern is that Papias, as quoted by Eusebius, cites an individual he calls "the presbyter John," or John the elder (*NPNF* Series 2, 1:171). The term *elder* is also used in the introductions to 2 John and 3 John (2 John 1:1; 3 John 1:1). The argument then is that the early church confused John the apostle and John the elder. However, there is really no evidence for any other early church leader named John the elder. Further, a careful reading of the Papias quote shows that he also uses the same title, *elder*, to refer to Peter, Andrew, Philip, Thomas, Matthew, and the other "disciples of the Lord." Moreover, the early testimony of the church fathers points consistently to John the apostle (see Guthrie, *New Testament Introduction*, 258, 864–65). Thus, it seems that the best conclusion is that the apostle wrote all five books near the end of his life.

3. Proponents of this view argue that the letters act as a commentary on the gospel (e.g., I. Howard Marshall, *The Epistles of John* [Grand Rapids: Eerdmans, 1978], 2). Yet John, like other NT writers, probably shared his good news orally many times before committing it to writing. If so, then his letters would reflect the gospel whether written down before or after (e.g., Brooke Foss Westcott, *The Epistles of John*, 3rd ed. [1892, reprint Grand Rapids: Eerdmans, 1966], xxxi).

4. Robert Gundry, *A Survey of the New Testament*, 3rd ed. (Grand Rapids: Zondervan, 1994), 253–54.

5. The two miracles in common with the Synoptics are the feeding of the five thousand (John 6:1–15) and the walking on the sea (6:16–21).

6. How did John remember such specific details so long after the fact? First, the greatest amount of detail is associated with the most significant events—occasions that John would be most prone to recall. Second, even those accounts are not really detailed, but are synopses of what happened and what was said. Third, Jesus told His disciples that after His death, the Holy Spirit would help them recall what they had been taught (John 14:26).

7. Some maintain that the letter referred to was 2 John. However, the letter that 3 John mentions was apparently received or intercepted by Diotrephes. The circumstances and implied content of that letter do not seem to correlate with 2 John.

8. The book was being quoted by 150 CE, and some allusions or quotations can be dated as early as 105–10. John's authorship was generally accepted until after 250, by which time it was already well established in the canon of the Western church.

9. Clearly history shows differing degrees of conflict between Christianity and the Roman government during the first few centuries. But the general perception seems to be that there was continuous antagonism up to Constantine's "Edict of Milan" in 313, after which it abruptly stopped. However, there were significant pagan backlashes after Milan. Likewise, a careful review of the evidence points to an increasing tolerance of Christianity by the Roman government leading up to that event. What is not clear is how much the thinking of the Christians was being affected as more and more wealthy Roman citizens were becoming Christians, nor when the changes started occurring (Kenneth Scott Latourette, *A History of Christianity*, vol. 1, *Beginnings to 1500* [New York: Harper and Row, 1975], 80–81, 252–64). Clearly history shows that the background culture of a believer often affects spiritual perceptions. Some have suggested that by the third generation, the grandeur that was Rome was beginning to affect the way Roman Christians viewed God's kingdom.

10. Because of this, one of the biggest questions that must be addressed is the relationship of the two entities, Israel and the church. Specifically, the question is whether the Israel here is to be viewed primarily as the seed of Abraham in a physical sense and thus as a national entity (see John F. Walvoord, *Israel in Prophecy* [Grand Rapids: Zondervan, 1962]), or the seed of Abraham taken in a spiritual sense (see Phillip Mauro, *The Hope of Israel* [Swengel, Pa.: Reiner, n.d.]). Those who hold the former view see a major distinction between Israel and the church. Those who hold the latter view see the church as the spiritual successor to Israel.

11. Henry A. Virkler, *Hermeneutics: Principals and Processes of Biblical Interpretation* (Grand Rapids: Baker, 1981), 196.

12. Louis Berkhof, *Principles of Biblical Interpretation* (Grand Rapids: Baker, 1950), 152, italics added.

13. Steve Gregg, *Revelation: Four Views, a Parallel Commentary* (Nashville: Thomas Nelson, 1997), 277.

14. In this case, the question that is debated is the interpretation of 12:6 which tells of her fleeing to the desert or wilderness for a period of 1260 days. There seems to be a commonality of understanding up to that point.

15. Most of the "literal" interpreters and even many of the "allegorical" interpreters would agree that the figure termed here as Satan is an actual being, a fallen angel sometimes called Lucifer. Some of the *more* "allegorical" interpreters would view Satan as merely a symbol of evil.

16. John Walvoord, *The Revelation of Jesus Christ* (Chicago: Moody Press, 1966), 16.

17. Origen argued for spiritual fulfillment of prophetic declarations (*First Principles* 4.1.7.13; see *ANF*, 4:354–68), which seems to have laid a foundation for Augustine's later work.

18. Alcázar's work, *Investigation of the Hidden Sense of the Apocalypse*, was published in Antwerp in 1614, a year after his death. It actually seems to argue that Revelation was fulfilled in the first six hundred years after Christ. More recent preterists narrow that to the first century.

19. Gregg, *Revelation: Four Views*, 352–56.

20. J. Dwight Pentecost traces this topic through the church fathers (*Things to Come* [Grand Rapids: Zondervan, 1964], 373–81). Among modern writers, one of the more interesting quotes is from Daniel Whitby, considered the founder of postmillennialism. Whitby noted that futurism was the dominant view of the church for its first 250 years.

21. Two groups are mentioned. The first is the group of martyrs who died because of their belief in Jesus. The second is the group of those who believed and maintained their spiritual integrity by not serving idols.

22. This was apparently the view of the apostles, based on the focus on the kingdom in Acts 1:6 and 28:23, 31. It also seemed to be the view of the early church (Gregg, *Revelation: Four Views*, 28).

23. Robert G. Clouse, *The Meaning of the Millennium* (Downers Grove, Ill.: InterVarsity, 1977), 9.

24. Loraine Boettner, *The Millennium* (Philadelphia: Presbyterian and Reformed, 1957), 14.

25. The seven churches are identified in chapters 2 and 3. These were not all of the churches in the region (for example, the church in Colosse is not mentioned). It has been estimated that there were more than two hundred churches in the region by this time. The seven churches mentioned were chosen because of their specific characteristics.

26. The imagery in these two chapters is very similar to visions that Ezekiel and Daniel had seen several centuries earlier.

27. There are two groups in this section: one consists of 144,000 described as being from the nation of Israel, and the other one is an unnumbered group from all the nations. According to John's angelic guide, they were believers who had been martyred because of their belief.

28. This is a very interesting statement. There are two possible interpretations. First, this was the ark made by the nation of Israel at the time of Moses, which had been translated to heaven to prevent it from being stolen at the Babylonian captivity. Or, this was the spiritual model or heavenly original, of which the one in the tabernacle was a copy (Ex. 25:9 suggests that the ark made by the craftsman according to Moses' direction was a copy).

29. The identity of Babylon here is one of the more intensely discussed elements of the book. Was it literally Babylon? Rome? Jerusalem? Did it merely represent apostate religion? The least difficult seems to be the city of Babylon itself. But that still leaves many problems.

30. This seems to be a very anticlimactic end. The sword would appear to represent a spoken word. As such, the "Battle of Armageddon" would be completed by something that Jesus said. To quote Martin Luther, "One little word shall fell him" ("A

Mighty Fortress Is Our God," stanza 3). This description also illustrates the difficulty of deciding what is "clearly symbolic." In the case of the thousand-year period, interpreters differ, while here they generally agree that the sword is a symbol. The reason seems to be that while it is possible that the millennium is indeed an actual kingdom on earth that lasts for a thousand years, it is much more difficult to visualize a human figure with a sword sticking out of his mouth that kills multitudes.

INDEX

Day of Atonement. *See* Yom Kippur

Day of the Lord, 278, 290, 307, 345, 487, 488, 622n16, 626n6, 642n10

deacon, 440, 512, 535, 561, 637n7, 648n18

deaconess, 512

Dead Sea, 93, 98, 166, 172, 374, 596, 613n15, 618n8, 618n11

Dead Sea Scrolls, 54, 226, 299, 344, 352, 354, 596, 610n5

death, 44, 72, 77, 99, 105, 110, 112, 115, 124, 126, 128, 159, 162, 163, 164, 166, 167, 170, 174, 191, 192, 205, 207, 208, 209, 216, 223, 224, 229, 234, 238, 239, 240, 243, 245, 246, 247, 269, 272, 289, 293, 300, 302, 304, 306, 319, 362, 370, 376, 388, 396, 401, 403, 404, 409, 410–11, 413, 418, 420, 423, 430, 443, 448, 451, 464, 486–87, 503, 515, 517, 520, 525, 543, 545, 546, 547, 553, 554, 556, 569, 580, 597, 614n8, 615n1, 623n12, 623n21, 625n2, 627n21, 627n34, 632n16, 634n1, 638n13, 643n20, 646n23, 649n6, 650n18

Debir, 189, 198

Deborah, 197, 198, 199–200, 202, 237, 621n3

deism, 31

Delilah, 206

Delphi, 479

Demetrius (silversmith), 497, 505, 540

Demetrius (traveling teacher), 578–79

Demiurge, 556

demon, 109, 224, 357, 393, 396, 404, 409, 479, 480, 495, 625n14, 633n41, 633n42, 634n10, 636n27, 640n22, 641n4

Derbe, 458, 459, 460, 472, 645n14

determinism, 484

Deuteronomy, 46, 49, 152, 170–74, 304, 518

Deutero-Isaiah, 299, 627n19. *See also* Isaiah

de Vaux, Roland, 240

dialectica, 648n15l. *See also* relational

Diana, 496

Diaspora, 47, 92, 328, 350, 351, 357, 364, 437, 439, 440, 441, 596, 637n9, 640n12

Dillard, Raymond B., 625n17

Dinah, 109

Dionysisus, 384

Diotrephes, 578–79, 649n7

disciples, 381, 387, 389, 391, 393–97, 400, 402, 403, 404, 406, 407, 409, 410, 414–21, 424, 425, 426, 430, 431, 432, 433, 435, 437, 439, 443, 448, 449, 454, 459, 460, 469, 494, 495, 575, 576, 580, 632n15, 632n16, 634n1, 634n3, 634n9, 634n10, 636n34, 636n36, 637n3, 636n4, 637n16, 637n17, 637n18, 646n24, 649n2, 649n6

divorce, 280, 340, 341, 384, 405, 406, 628n15

docetism, 454, 577, 596

documentary hypothesis, 30–31, 60, 378, 596, 609n6. *See also* JEDP theory

Domitian, 579, 583

donkey, 167, 202, 206, 208, 220, 233, 339, 415, 636n30

Dorcas, 449

Dorman, Ted, 468

dragon, 583

dream, 100, 111, 112, 113, 203, 318, 319, 320, 583, 621n10

Dream Stele, 124

drink offering, 149

dropsy, 635n24

Drumwright, Huber L., 575

drunk/drunkenness, 124, 233, 263, 320, 326, 435, 484, 503, 627n30

Drusilla, 645n23

dualism, 556, 647n8

Dunn, James D. G., 644n2

Dyer, Charles H., 324, 627n36

Easter, 130, 425

Eastern church, 130, 425. *See also* church

Eastern Gate, 415, 591

Eastern Orthodox, 630n1

Ebal, 172, 173, 188, 335, 619n23

Ebenezer, 216, 219

Ebionites, 640n16

Ebla, 38, 94

Ecbatana, 336

Ecclesiastes, 249, 624n25

Ecclesiasticus, 352, 624n25

eclipse, 36, 137, 423, 616n16

Eddy, Mary Baker, 646n9

Eden, garden of, 64–66, 71, 75, 77, 438, 648n16

Edersheim, Alfred, 633n31

Edict of Milan, 584, 585, 588, 650n9

Edrei, 167

Edom, 110, 132, 165, 166, 223, 260, 273–74, 287, 288, 291, 325, 366, 367, 368, 374, 385, 613n1, 614n8, 618n8, 618n11, 624n3, 627n31

Edwards, Jonathan, 536

Eglon, 189, 620n2

Egnatian Way, 480, 482, 641n8

Egypt, 34, 37–38, 44, 45, 78, 85, 90, 91, 92, 93, 96, 100, 104, 108, 111, 112, 113, 114, 115, 116, 118, 122–24, 127, 128, 132, 133, 140, 143, 147, 154, 159, 161, 162, 165, 166, 169, 174, 182, 185, 186, 191, 192, 196, 197,

Jordan River, 45, 47, 129, 141, 165, 167, 169, 170, 171, 178, 183, 184–85, 187, 188, 190, 221, 271, 386, 387, 388, 402, 410, 412, 614n8, 619n19, 633n33

Joseph (half brother of Jesus), 636n2

Joseph (husband of Mary), 353, 370, 375, 384, 385, 455, 631n2, 632n20, 632n23

Joseph (son of Jacob), 110–15, 116, 118, 122, 319, 583, 613n10, 614n6, 614n12, 614n15, 614n17, 614n18, 615n1, 618n5, 640n18

Joseph Barsabbas, 434

Joseph of Arimathea, 423, 549

Josephus, 220, 354, 358, 359, 383, 568, 618n8, 618n11, 630n9, 630n10, 630n13, 631n19, 638n13, 639n19, 643n15, 646n21, 647n1, 649n37, 649n38

Joshua (general), 49, 140, 162, 168, 169, 172, 174, 178, 179, 182, 183, 184, 187, 188, 189, 190, 191, 192, 193, 196, 197, 223, 241, 566, 617n1, 617n5, 618n1, 619n20, 620n3, 620n11, 620n16, 621n2, 621n1

Joshua (priest), 333, 334, 336, 337

Joshua, book of 28, 30, 49, 174, 182–93, 196

Josiah, 30, 172, 259, 261, 288, 295, 303, 304–6, 307, 310, 624n5, 624n13, 627n27, 627n28, 627n32, 627n34

Jotham, 261, 279, 293, 298

Jozabed, 291

Jubilee, year of, 144, 155, 211, 617n4

Judah, 105, 110, 111–12, 113, 115, 187, 191, 196, 198, 206, 218, 232, 233, 237, 239, 240, 245, 256, 258, 259, 261, 278, 284, 291, 323, 326, 332, 333, 334, 338, 340, 341, 343, 344, 350, 374, 549, 590, 614n10, 614n18, 619n25, 624n5, 626n18, 628n12

Judaism, 46, 48, 49, 153, 353, 355, 359, 366, 368, 440, 443, 448, 449, 450, 479, 526, 552, 556, 565, 566, 568, 585, 596, 599, 610n3, 624n8, 637n16, 637n19, 638n5, 640n16, 645n23, 647n8

Judaizers, 543

Judas (half brother of Jesus). See Jude

Judas Barsabbas, 470, 471

Judas Iscariot, 415, 417, 418, 419, 420, 434, 549, 635n29, 636n32, 636n35, 637n2

Judas Maccabeus, 366, 598

Judas Thaddaeus, 548, 549

Jude, 552, 569, 577, 636n2, 649n41

Jude, letter of, 569–70, 636n2, 647n6, 649n41

Judea, 249, 257, 322, 333, 337, 338, 343, 344, 350, 351, 359, 362, 363, 364, 366, 367, 368, 369, 370, 374, 381, 385, 388, 397, 406, 407, 410, 413, 414, 421, 435, 436, 440, 441, 442, 445, 448, 449, 464, 507, 520, 522, 545,

549, 566, 568, 576, 598, 630n7, 630n16, 633n36, 636n33, 637n6, 637n12, 637n17, 644n9, 646n21

judge, 145, 180, 190, 196, 197, 198, 199, 201, 204, 214, 219, 221, 251, 258, 264, 267, 275, 277, 298, 341, 407, 488, 500, 514, 621n4, 622n5

Judges, book of, 47, 138, 145, 193, 196–209, 211, 216, 219, 614n12, 621n4

judgment, 76, 81, 83, 84, 91, 96, 144, 162, 179, 182, 211, 243, 252, 265, 269, 270, 271, 274, 277, 278, 280, 281, 285, 288, 290, 297–98, 300, 301, 303, 304, 305, 307, 309, 310, 325, 338, 339, 401, 416, 418, 438, 457, 500, 507, 514, 518, 526, 568, 583, 586, 587, 590, 591, 592, 595, 617n1, 618n6, 618n7, 619n22, 620n7, 622n14, 626n6, 627n34, 628n13, 645n12, 645n18

Julius Caesar, 364, 369, 370

Julius the Centurion, 527, 528, 529

justice, 146, 278, 597, 627n25, 640n12

justification, 466, 516, 597

Justin Martyr, 632n21

Kadesh Barnea, 141, 164, 165, 170, 173, 174, 184, 189, 190, 618n8, 620n18

Kadmonites, 89

Kamoses, 123, 615n2

Katzenstein, H. Jacob, 263

Kebar River, 324

Kedor-laomer, 93

Keil, C. F., 339

Keilah, 228, 622n20

Keliab, 623n20

Kenite, 89, 200

Kenizzites, 89, 618n1

kenosis, 646n18

Kenyon, Kathleen, 186, 620n2

Kephirah, 620n14

Ketib, 54

Keturah, 98

Khader, Aicha ben Abed ben, 183, 631n15

Kidner, Derek, 340

Kidron Valley, 244, 246, 419, 623n13

king, 93, 137, 166, 167, 189, 196, 199, 203, 209, 219–21, 224–25, 226, 232, 233, 237, 238–39, 240, 245, 246, 249, 258, 259, 260–61, 263, 266, 267, 272, 274, 275, 276, 281, 287, 289, 290, 291, 292, 293, 294, 295, 297, 298, 301, 303, 304, 307, 310, 317, 318, 319, 320, 322, 323, 326, 332, 333, 339, 340, 362, 363, 369, 374, 385, 392, 397, 400, 404, 407, 412, 422, 457, 478, 482, 514, 560, 596, 599, 617n1, 618n17, 619n24, 622n9, 622n12,

Sennacherib, 296, 297, 298, 302, 305

Septuagint, 48, 115, 226, 352, 363, 364, 386, 584, 599, 610n7, 627n20, 627n26, 627n36, 632n23, 640n12

Sergius Paulus, 456–57

Sermon on the Mount, 389, 390, 395, 406

serpent, 73, 76–77, 166, 618n12, 648n16. *See also* snake

Servant Songs, 300

Sesostris II, 614n16

Sesostris III, 614n16, 615n1

Seth, 78, 80, 81, 611n3, 611n4

Seurat, Georges, 323

sex, 71, 84, 182, 209, 250, 300, 384, 470, 486, 500, 501, 538, 559, 611n4, 618n2, 627n20, 632n19, 643n12, 643n13, 643n15, 648n17

Shadrach, 317

Shakespeare, 362

Shallum. *See* Jehoahaz

Shalmaneser III, 137, 265, 275

Shalmanezer V, 281, 294, 625n23, 625n24

shalom, 150, 244

Shallum, 261, 278, 279

Shamgur, 198, 199, 204, 620n3

Shapash, 620n5

Shapiro, Sidney, 357

Shealtiel, 334

Shear-Jashub, 626n11

Sheba, 245, 637n19

Shecaniah ben Jehiel, 341

Shechem, 91, 109, 204, 257, 258, 284, 614n8, 614n17

sheep, 202, 272

shekel, 111, 159, 339, 343, 633n31

Shekinah, 148, 160, 251, 599, 617n12

Shelah, 80

Shem, 80, 84, 85

Shemaiah, 284

Shephelah, 192

Shepherd of Hermas, 52

Sherwin-White, A. N., 648n23

Sheshbazzar, 336

Shiloh, 209, 215, 216, 617n10, 621n15, 622n8

Shimei, 244, 246

Shinar. *See* Mesopotamia

Shishak, 285

shophar, 621n9

Shunammite woman, 271

Sicily, 529, 530, 631n22

Sidon, 183, 190, 260, 263, 266, 270, 362, 401, 620n6, 631n22

Sihon, 166–67, 179, 198, 629n15

Sigal, Phillip, 364, 630n4

sign, 44, 79, 95, 99–100, 127, 128, 135, 221, 222, 232, 258, 269, 270, 293, 294, 380, 390, 393, 395, 397, 400, 401, 403, 407, 417, 435, 436, 438, 442, 469, 488, 495, 576, 613n15, 624n5, 632n16, 634n4, 634n15, 635n24, 636n33

Silas, 470, 471, 472, 473, 474, 478, 479, 480, 481, 482, 483, 485, 488, 489, 490, 565, 641n3, 641n5, 641n6, 641n7, 641n12, 642n17, 647n4

Siloam, pool of, 296

Silva, Moisés, 638n16

Silvanus, 554, 647n4. *See also* Silas

silver, 111, 113, 130, 204, 207, 250, 252, 339, 497, 500

Simeon, 109, 113, 114, 169, 191, 196, 284, 286, 304, 345, 385, 614n10, 614n12, 614n17, 619n25

Simeon Niger, 456

Simon (half brother of Jesus), 636n2

Simon Hasmonean, 366, 367

Simon of Cyrene, 421

Simon Peter. *See* Peter

Simon the Leper, 406, 636n32

Simon the Magician, 442

Simon the Pharisee, 406

Simon the Tanner, 449

Simon the Zealot, 549

Simpson, E. K., 646n12

Simpson, William Kelly, 612n3, 625n20

sin, 70–77, 91, 118, 149, 151, 154–55, 159–60, 164, 218, 222, 223, 243, 269, 300, 301, 340, 390, 408, 409, 410, 418, 438, 500, 501, 504, 506, 514, 515–16, 517, 541, 558, 568, 596, 597, 599, 613n11, 617n1, 618n12, 628n10, 642n11, 643n12, 644n12, 648n16

Sin, 90

Sinai, 44–45, 46, 52, 58, 63, 78, 83, 85, 88, 90, 91, 96, 98, 110, 114, 116, 125, 126, 127, 133, 140, 145, 148, 158, 159, 161, 170, 171, 174, 258, 311, 356, 598, 615n21, 617n1, 617n3, 620n18, 622n12, 625n5, 638n21

sin offering, 149, 154–55, 618n15

Sisera, 198, 199, 200, 201

slaves/slavery, 45, 76, 84, 92, 111, 116, 127, 131, 143, 145, 269, 409, 479, 517, 535, 536, 539, 542, 555, 561, 617n4, 645n12, 645n6, 646n10

Slim, Hedi, 183, 631n15

sluggard, 624n26

Smerdis, 629n6

Smyrna, 588, 589